Spätmittelalter, Humanismus, Reformation

Studies in the Late Middle Ages,
Humanism, and the Reformation

herausgegeben von Volker Leppin (Tübingen)

in Verbindung mit

Amy Nelson Burnett (Lincoln, NE), Johannes Helmrath (Berlin)
Matthias Pohlig (Berlin), Eva Schlotheuber (Düsseldorf)

108

Andrew J. Niggemann

Martin Luther's Hebrew in Mid-Career

The Minor Prophets Translation

Mohr Siebeck

Andrew J. Niggemann, 1995 BA in Psychology and BBA in Marketing, University of Wisconsin, Milwaukee (USA); 2000 BBA in Management Information Systems, University of Wisconsin, Milwaukee (USA); 2014 MA in Judaism and Christianity in Antiquity, Marquette University (USA); and 2018 PhD in History, Theology, and Religious Studies, University of Cambridge (UK).

ISBN 978-3-16-157001-8 / eISBN 978-3-16-157002-5
DOI 10.1628/978-3-16-157002-5

ISSN 1865-2840 / eISSN 2569-4391 (Spätmittelalter, Humanismus, Reformation)

The Deutsche Nationalbibliothek lists this publication in the Deutsche Nationalbibliographie; detailed bibliographic data are available at *http://dnb.dnb.de*.

© 2019 Mohr Siebeck Tübingen. www.mohrsiebeck.com

This book may not be reproduced, in whole or in part, in any form (beyond that permitted by copyright law) without the publisher's written permission. This applies particularly to reproductions, translations and storage and processing in electronic systems.

The book was typeset by epline in Böblingen using Times typeface, printed by Gulde Druck in Tübingen on non-aging paper, and bound by Buchbinderei Spinner in Ottersweier.

Printed in Germany.

Preface

This study provides a comprehensive account of Martin Luther's Hebrew translation in his academic mid-career. Apart from the Psalms, no book of the Hebrew Bible has yet been examined in any comprehensive manner in terms of Luther's Hebrew translation. Moreover, research to date has predominantly focused on either ascertaining Luther's personal Hebrew skills, or on identifying his sources for Hebrew knowledge. This study furthers the scholarly understanding of Luther's Hebrew by examining his Minor Prophets translation, one of the final pieces of his first complete translation of the Hebrew Bible. As part of the analysis, it investigates the relationship between philology and theology in his Hebrew translation, focusing specifically on one of the themes that dominated his interpretation of the Prophets: his concept of *Anfechtung*.

Chapter 1 establishes the context of Luther's academic mid-career Hebrew, providing a brief sketch of the history of his Minor Prophets translation, followed by an overview of the Hebrew resources in and around Wittenberg which he had to draw upon. Chapter 2 examines the role of the obscurity of the Hebrew text in his translation, and how this obscurity led to various types of contradictions and vacillations in his interpretations. Chapter 3 investigates the role that Luther's sense of the semantic intensity of the Hebrew language played in his translation. Chapter 4 examines Luther's use of "inner-biblical interpretation" – i.e. biblical quotations and references – to support, and moreover, to build his translations of the Hebrew texts. Finally, Chapter 5 examines the influence of Hebrew on Luther's exploitation of the mystical tradition in his translation of the Minor Prophets.

This study, in short, shows that by mid-career, the impact of Hebrew on Luther's Bible translation was immense and very diverse, more so than has been appreciated. It expands the frame of reference with which scholars can understand Luther's Hebrew. It provides detailed analyses of many examples of his Hebrew translation which have never before been discussed or examined in any depth, and it provides hundreds of examples of his methodological handling of Hebrew translation issues. And it includes one of the most exhaustive analyses to date of three key philological challenges that confronted him in translating the Bible: Hebrew figures of speech, the Hebrew trope of repetition, and Hebrew transliteration. This study also includes as an Appendix a substantial body of refined data from Luther's Hebrew translation, which further illuminates the examples in this study, and facilitates additional analysis for future research.

This book originated as my doctoral thesis at the University of Cambridge. That thesis was awarded the 2018 Coventry Prize for the PhD dissertation in Theology with the highest mark and recommendation, University of Cambridge, St. Edmund's College. The list of individuals who have made this research possible is long, and I undoubtedly will unintentionally omit names and for this I ask forgiveness. The first thanks is to God for the hand he has always had on my life and for orchestrating this opportunity to work and study at Cambridge, to complete this study, and to see it published as a monograph. My parents' love and support has made this and every opportunity in my life possible. I would like to thank Prof. Dr. Richard Rex and Dr. Katharine Dell for taking a chance on the dissertation, for their diligent support of this research, their generous advice and unfaltering sense of humor, and their guidance throughout this process. I would also like to thank Prof. Dr. Volker Leppin and Dr. Jim Aitken for their feedback and advice concerning this research and the book project. Thank you also to Prof. Dr. Stephen Burnett, who generously offered much guidance during the writing of the thesis and the book. And thank you to everyone at Mohr Siebeck for accepting the manuscript for publication in the *Spätmittelalter, Humanismus, Reformation* series, and for all of the support during the review and editing process.

The language instructors I have had over the years are many, and all were integral to the success of this project (and incidentally, tacitly to blame for any errors I have made): Yael Gal Ben-Yitschak, Brian Boeckeler, Shlomit Chazani, Dr. Barak Dan, Dr. Deirdre Dempsey, Fr. Reggie Foster, Michel Gottlieb, Ehud Har Even, Paul Hoegger, Dr. Julian Hills, Raz Kehat, Idit Levinger, Tamar Perles, Etan Pinsky, Fabio Redak, Martina Senfle, Dr. Jeanne Schueller, Dr. Neal Wright, and Irit Zilbershatz.

In addition, numerous individuals inside and outside of the University of Cambridge have supported this research in various ways: Oz Aloni, Dr. Tali Artman, Dr. Matthias Becker, Dr. Theodore Dunkelgrün, Dr. Peta Dunstan, Dr. Efraim Feinstein, Dr. Julian Hills, Dr. Howard Jones, Dr. Edward Kessler, Rev. Dr. John Kleinig, Prof. Dr. Henrike Lähnemann, R. Reuven Leigh, Dr. Nathan MacDonald, Prof. Dr. Mickey Mattox, Rev. Dr. Benjamin Mayes, Dr. Onesimus Ngundu, Prof. Dr. Sharon Pace, Dr. James Nicholas Carleton Paget, Dr. Kim Phillips, Dr. Jim Prothro, Lea Reiff, Rev. Dr. Harold Senkbeil, Dr. Bruria Shachar-Hill, R. Shloime Shagalow, Rev. Prof. Dr. Andrew Steinmann, Dr. Chris Thomson, Dr. Stephen Tong, Dr. Damian Valdez, Dr. Giles Waller, Dr. Sheila Watts, Dr. Daniel Weiss, Dr. Andreas Zecherle, and many other academic colleagues whose conversations and insight have sharpened this research. I owe a special thank you to Dr. Andrew McGuire and everyone at Milton Road, and to Rev. Dr. Bruno Clifton O.P. and everyone at the Castle Inn. I also owe a debt of gratitude to many of my German friends whom I incessantly harassed over the past several years with petitions of "But have you ever heard of *this* phrase…," and my Israeli friends with "I've never seen *this* before…" I hope that we can still be friends.

I have utilized many library facilities and resources for this research, including those of: the University of Cambridge, University of Oxford, Hebrew University of Jerusalem, National Library of Israel, British Library, Marquette University, University of Wisconsin Milwaukee, Ludwig-Maximilians-Universität München, Humboldt-Universität zu Berlin, and Leucorea (Martin-Luther-Universität Halle-Wittenberg). Thank you to the University of Cambridge, Staatsbibliothek zu Berlin, Sächsische Landesbibliothek – Staats- und Universitätsbibliothek Dresden (SLUB)/Deutsche Fotothek, and Presbyterian Historical Society (Philadelphia, PA) for images; and to the Stiftung Luthergedenkstätten in Sachsen-Anhalt, and Leucorea – Stiftung des öffentlichen Rechts an der Martin-Luther-Universität Halle-Wittenberg, for photograph permissions.

Finally, I owe a special thank you to the numerous individuals and organizations who have supported me financially for this research: Aschenbach Grant, Bethune Baker Fund, Hebrew University of Jerusalem Rothberg Endowment, Kelly Grant, Dr. Joseph and Mrs. Robin Lasnoski Scholarship, Marquette University Department of Theology, Ruth N. Martens Grant, Pallottines Societas Apostolatus Catholici, St. Edmund's College (University of Cambridge), St. Luke's College Foundation, William & Irene Schumer Scholarship Endowment Fund, Spalding Trust, University of Cambridge Faculty of Divinity, University of Cambridge Graduate Language Scholarship, and University of Cambridge Theological Studies Trust.

Cambridge, 2018   Andrew J. Niggemann

Table of Contents

Preface V
Abbreviations XI

Chapter One
Luther's Academic Mid-Career Hebrew in Context 1

Chapter Two
"The Obscure Hebrew" 47

Chapter Three
Hebrew Semantic Intensity 99

Chapter Four
Inner-Biblical Interpretation in Luther's Hebrew Translation 131

Chapter Five
Hebrew and Luther's Exploitation of the Mystical Tradition 165

Chapter Six
Conclusion 217

Appendix 225

Table A.1: Luther's General Interpretative Variances 226
Table A.2: Luther's Translation of Hebrew Figures of Speech 234
Table A.3: Luther's Translation of the Hebrew Trope of Repetition 304
Table A.4: Luther's Use of Hebrew Transliteration 316
Table A.5: Luther's Use of the "Reduced To" Idiom 336

Bibliography 345

Index of Scriptural, Ancient, and Medieval Sources 365
Index of Hebrew, German, Latin, and Greek Terms 379
Index of Subjects 403

Abbreviations

Aland	Aland, Kurt, Ernst Otto Reichert, and Gerhard Jordan. Hilfsbuch zum Lutherstudium. 3rd rev. ed. Witten: Luther-Verlag, 1970.
BDB	Brown, Francis, S. R. Driver, and Charles A. Briggs, eds. *A Hebrew and English Lexicon of the Old Testament: With an Appendix Containing the Biblical Aramaic. Based on the Lexicon of William Gesenius as Translated by Edward Robinson*. Rev. ed. Oxford: Clarendon Press, [1959].
CCSL	*Corpus Christianorum. Series Latina*. 212 vols. Turnhout: Brepols, 1953–.
DCH	Clines, David J. A., ed. *The Dictionary of Classical Hebrew*. 9 vols. Vols. 1–5: Sheffield: Sheffield Academic Press, 1993–2001. Vols. 6–9: Sheffield: Phoenix Press, 2007–16.
DDU	Dudenredaktion. *Duden Deutsches Universalwörterbuch*. 5th ed. Mannheim: Dudenverlag, 2003.
DWB	Grimm, Jacob, and Wilhelm Grimm. *Deutsches Wörterbuch von Jacob und Wilhelm Grimm*. 16 vols. Leipzig: S. Hirzel, 1854–1961.
HALOT	Koehler, Ludwig, and Walter Baumgartner. *The Hebrew and Aramaic Lexicon of the Old Testament*. 5 vols. Subsequently revised by Walter Baumgartner and Johann Jakob Stamm, with assistance from Benedikt Hartmann, Ze'ev Ben-Hayyim, Eduard Yechezkel Kutscher, and Philippe Reymond. Translated and edited under the supervision of M. E. J. Richardson. Leiden: E. J. Brill, 1994–2000.
HCLOT	Fuerst, Julius. *A Hebrew & Chaldee Lexicon to the Old Testament. With an Introduction Giving a Short History of Hebrew Lexicography*. Translated by Samuel Davidson. 3rd ed. Leipzig: Bernhard Tauchnitz; London: Williams & Norgate, 1867.
KB	Koehler, Ludwig, and Walter Baumgartner, eds. *Lexicon in Veteris Testamenti Libros*. Leiden: Brill, 1953.
KLE	Klein, Ernest. *A Comprehensive Etymological Dictionary of the Hebrew Language for Readers of English*. Jerusalem: Carta Jerusalem; Haifa: University of Haifa, 1987.
LDH	Georges, Karl Ernst. Ausführliches lateinisch-deutsches Handwörterbuch. 2 vols. 8th rev. ed. by Heinrich Georges. Hannover: Hahn, 1913–18.
LS	Lewis, Charlton T., and Charles Short, eds. *A Latin Dictionary Founded on Andrews' Edition of Freund's Latin Dictionary. Revised, Enlarged, and in Great Part Rewritten by Charlton T. Lewis*. Oxford: Clarendon Press, 1987.
LSJ	Liddell, Henry George, Robert Scott, and Henry Stuart Jones, eds. *A Greek-English Lexicon*. 9th ed. with rev. supplement. Oxford: Clarendon Press, 1996.

Abbreviations

LW   *Luther's Works.* 75 vols. Edited by Jaroslav Pelikan, Helmut T. Lehmann, and Christopher Boyd Brown. Philadelphia: Fortress Press; St. Louis: Concordia Publishing House, 1955–.

LXX   Septuagint.

MERZ   Merzdorf, J. F. L. Theodor. *Die deutschen Historienbibeln des Mittelalters. Nach vierzig Handschriften.* 2 vols. Tübingen: L. F. Fues, 1870 [for Stuttgart: Litterarischer Verein].

MG   *Mikra'ot Gedolot Haketer* [*Miḳra'ot gedolot ha-Keter*] [מקראות גדולות הכתר]. *A Revised and Augmented Scientific Edition of "Mikra'ot Gedolot." Based on the Aleppo Codex and Early Medieval MSS.* 13 vols. Edited by Menachem Cohen. Ramat-Gan: Bar-Ilan University, 1992–.

OXDUD   Dudenredaktion and the German Section of the Oxford University Press Dictionary Department, eds. Oxford Duden German Dictionary. 3rd ed. Oxford: Oxford University Press, 2005.

OXLAT   Glare, P. G. W. Oxford Latin Dictionary. 2 vols. 2nd ed. Oxford: Oxford University Press, 2012.

Rudimenta   Reuchlin, Johann. *De rudimentis Hebraicis.* Pforzheim: Thomas Anselm, 1506.

SING   Singer, Samuel. *Sprichwörter des Mittelalters.* 3 vols. Bern: Herbert Lang, 1944–47.

SMY   Smyth, Herbert Weir. *Greek Grammar.* Rev. ed. Cambridge, MA: Harvard University Press, 1956.

SPAL   Spalding, Keith. *An Historical Dictionary of German Figurative Usage.* 60 Fascicles. Oxford: Basil Blackwell, 1959–2000. [Fascicles 1–40 with the assistance of Kenneth Brooke; Fascicles 51–60 with the assistance of Gerhard Müller-Schwefe.]

StL   *Dr. Martin Luthers Sämmtliche Schriften.* 23 vols. Edited by Johann Georg Walch. St. Louis: Concordia Publishing House, 1880–1910.

STR   Strong, James. The Exhaustive Concordance of the Bible. London: Hodder and Stoughton, 1894.

TDOT   Botterweck, G. Johannes, Helmer Ringgren, eds. *Theological Dictionary of the Old Testament.* Translated by John T. Willis. 15 vols. Vols. 1 and 2: rev. ed., 1977. Vols. 4–7: translated by David E. Green. Vol. 8: translated by Douglas W. Stott. Vols. 7, 8, and 14: edited by Heinz-Josef Fabry. Grand Rapids, MI: Eerdmans, 1974–2006. [Originally published in German as Botterweck, G., Helmer Ringgren, and Heinz-Josef Fabry, eds. *Theologisches Wörterbuch zum Alten Testament.* 8 vols. Stuttgart: W. Kohlhammer, 1970–2000.]

WA   *D. Martin Luthers Werke. Kritische Gesamtausgabe.* 73 vols. Weimar: Böhlau, 1883–2009.

WA Ar   *Archiv zur Weimarer Ausgabe der Werke Martin Luthers. Texte und Untersuchungen.* 10 vols. Weimar: Böhlau, 1981–2017.

WA BR   *D. Martin Luthers Werke. Kritische Gesamtausgabe. Briefwechsel.* 18 vols. Weimar: Böhlau, 1930–85.

WA DB   *D. Martin Luthers Werke. Kritische Gesamtausgabe. Die Deutsche Bibel.* 12 vols. Weimar: Böhlau, 1906–61.

WA TR   *D. Martin Luthers Werke. Kritische Gesamtausgabe. Tischreden.* 6 vols. Weimar: Böhlau, 1912–21.

WAN	Wander, Karl Friedrich Wilhelm, ed. *Deutsches Sprichwörter-Lexikon: Ein Hausschatz für das deutsche Volk*. 5 vols. Leipzig: Brockhaus, 1867–80.
WDS	Sanders, Daniel. *Wörterbuch der deutschen Sprache*. 2 vols. Leipzig: Otto Wigand, 1860–65.

Porträt Martin Luther [ca. 1810; Ludwig Emil Grimm after Lucas Cranach der Jüngere, ca. 1560] (*source:* Dresden, Sächsische Landesbibliothek – Staats- und Universitätsbibliothek Dresden (SLUB) / Deutsche Fotothek, Signatur/Inventar-Nr.: 23.8.4939).

Chapter One

Luther's Academic Mid-Career Hebrew in Context

On the evening of March 3, 1522, two men walked into the Schwarzer Bär Inn in Jena, Germany and encountered a dark-bearded knight, sword at his side, sitting alone at a table in the hotel parlor, the Hebrew Psalter propped up in front of him.[1] He invited them to sit with him. As they began to talk, the knight was immediately struck by the men's language. He asked where they came from. But he didn't wait for an answer. "You are Swiss," he said.[2] They engaged in conversation for a time, which eventually turned to theology. As it turned out, the men were students on their way to enroll at Wittenberg University to study scripture. At first suspicious, the two were nevertheless impressed by the knight's knowledge. The occasional Latin word that he let slip struck the two men as curious, not to mention the Hebrew book that he was reading – "a very uncommon knight," as one of the men recounted.[3] As the conversation continued, they pressed him for advice on how to understand scripture. The knight responded that if they wanted to truly understand scripture, they needed to learn the biblical languages. The cavalier candidness of the gentleman, not to mention his open reading of the Hebrew Bible, would never have suggested to these two that he was a wanted man, traveling through what for him was dangerous territory.[4] The next morning, after a brief conversation with the knight, the two

---

[1] For the complete account, see Johannes Kessler, *Johannes Kesslers Sabbata mit kleineren Schriften und Briefen. Unter Mitwirkung von Prof. Dr. Emil Egli und Prof. Dr. Rudolf Schoch in Zürich* [1519–39], ed. Historischer Verein des Kantons St. Gallen (St. Gallen: Fehr, 1902), 76–80. This story is cited and recounted by many scholars. See: M. Michelet, *The Life of Luther. Written by Himself*, trans. William Hazlitt (London: David Bogue, 1846), 116–8; Preserved Smith, *The Life and Letters of Martin Luther*, ed. Robert Backhouse (London: Hodder & Stoughton, 1993) [First published by John Murray (London, 1911)], 130–3; E. G. Rupp and Benjamin Drewery, eds., *Martin Luther* (London: Edward Arnold, 1970), 82–86; Thomas M. Lindsay, *Luther and the German Reformation* (Edinburgh: T. & T. Clark, 1900), 147–9; and Stephen G. Burnett, "Luthers hebräische Bibel (Brescia, 1494) – Ihre Bedeutung für die Reformation," in *Meilensteine der Reformation: Schlüsseldokumente der frühen Wirksamkeit Martin Luthers*, ed. Irene Dingel and Henning P. Jürgens (Gütersloh: Gütersloher Verlaghaus, 2014), 62.

[2] "Ir sind Schwitzer." Kessler, *Sabbata*, 77. Unless otherwise noted, all English translations in this study are my own. Where I provide the LW references, I generally make critical adjustments as necessary in order to align with the WA.

[3] "Er were ain ander person dann ain gemainer rüter." Kessler, *Sabbata*, 78.

[4] Burnett notes that the ban on Luther had been lifted prior to this journey, often cited by scholars as in February, 1522; Burnett, "Luthers hebräische Bibel," 62. Nevertheless, Luther's letter to Frederick the Wise on March 5, 1522, with numerous mentions of Duke George, sug-

men went on their way. It was revealed later that the knight was none other than Martin Luther, donning a disguise on a secret trip from the Wartburg Castle – his "Patmos" as he called it – to Wittenberg.[5]

Luther's private moments, cordially interrupted by the two men, were being spent reading Hebrew. He was at least to some extent at death's door. If he were caught, his life would surely have been in danger, and he would have been seized by the men of Duke George of Saxony as he went on to pass through his territory on his way to Wittenberg.[6] But his focus in this precarious time was a tranquil inquiry into language. The entire encounter between him and the two men was, in fact, premised on language. It was the dialect that gave away that the two men were Swiss. It was the erudite use of Latin which tipped them off that this was someone a little different from an ordinary knight. It was the discussion of scriptural languages which bonded the new acquaintances in conversation. Most importantly, Luther's advice for their ambition – the mechanism by which they could understand scripture, which they were traveling to Wittenberg to find – was not more books, better theology, or a recommendation to follow this man or that man. It was simply the language. Of all the things he could have told them, it was the language that was the doorway to the place they wanted to go.

This study is an investigation of Luther and language. Understanding his language, as with any other person of another time, opens a door into his world in a way that not many other facets of his work can. If you have ever been in a social setting with a group completely comprised of another nationality, where they speak your language, they will carry on the conversation in your language so that you understand. And it works fine. Everyone can understand. But there is always a figurative wall, even if it goes at first unnoticed. That wall sheds its disguise when the other members of the group turn to speak to each other in their own tongue. Here, the conversation takes a different turn. The eyes light up. The emotion of the conversation changes. The laughter is a little harder. The connections run deeper, even if just for a sentence or two as they move away

---

gests that he still was very much in danger; WA BR 2:453–7 [§ 455]. See also: Julius Köstlin and D. Gustav Kawerau, *Martin Luther: Sein Leben und seine Schriften*, vol. 1, 5th rev. ed. (Berlin: Alexander Duncker, 1903), 494–5; Lindsay, *Luther and the German Reformation*, 146–7; and Heinrich Bornkamm, *Luther in Mid-Career 1521–1530*, ed. Karin Bornkamm, trans. E. Theodore Bachmann (London: Darton, Longman & Todd, 1983), 64–68.

[5] Luther signed a number of letters with some variant of "from the Greek Island of Patmos." For example, he wrote in a June 1, 1521 letter to Francis Von Sickingen, "Geben ynn meyner Pathmoß ('Given [Written] on my Patmos')"; WA 8:140.6; LW 48:247. He signed a June 10, 1521 letter to Spalatin, "Ex insula pathmos ('From the Isle of Patmos')"; WA BR 2:355.37–38 [§ 417]; LW 48:256. He also noted "ex Pathmo mea ('from my Patmos')" in his *Rationis Latomianae confutation* (1521); WA 8:128.29. Cf. WA 8:44.2; WA 8:139.22. See also Roland H. Bainton, *Here I Stand: A Life of Martin Luther* (London: Hodder and Stoughton, 1951), 191–204.

[6] Thomas M. Lindsay, *Luther and the German Reformation*, 147.

from your language. You stand on the outside, an observer. But if you can speak their language, you experience an entirely different encounter. The figurative wall fades away. You enter a world that never would have been available, and discover things you never would have known existed. The language opens a door that never would have been open without it. This study looks to draw down a piece of the wall that divides our world and Martin Luther's world and learn more about him through his use of language.

Given that one of Luther's most powerful and lasting influences on the world is his Bible translation, it is a paradox that there is a large remaining lacuna – or frontier, if you will – in Luther scholarship concerning his use of language. This is particularly so for Hebrew. Far and away the books of the Bible which he most often talked about, lectured on, and spent time translating were those of the Hebrew Bible. He began his study of the Hebrew language before Greek, and long before he translated his first piece of either the Old or New Testament.[7] His very first lectures as Professor at Wittenberg were on the Old Testament, as were his very last. But despite this, not one book in the Hebrew Bible outside of the Psalms has been comprehensively examined in terms of Luther's Hebrew translation. Every major study on Luther's Hebrew translation to date has, in fact, exclusively focused on his translation of the Psalms.[8] Luther's translation of, exploitation of, and relationship with the Hebrew language thus remains in many ways a wide open frontier – perhaps one of the last, great frontiers in Luther scholarship.

This study investigates the role of Hebrew in Luther's translation of the Minor Prophets. This period, essentially Luther's academic mid-career, was a tumultuous time.[9] His health was poor. His battles – religious and political – were in full swing. He acquired a new family. And his spiritual attacks, which plagued him in his early years, were about to come back.[10] A competing German translation of the prophetic books of the Hebrew Bible, the *Wormser Pro-*

---

[7] Karl August Meissinger, *Luthers Exegese in der Frühzeit* (Leipzig: M. Heinsius Nachfolger, 1911), 55–56. M. Reu, *Luther's German Bible: An Historical Presentation, Together with a Collection of Sources* (St. Louis: Concordia Publishing House, 1984 [Concordia Heritage Series]. Reprint of Columbus, OH: The Lutheran Book of Concern, 1934), 118. Heiko A. Oberman, *Luther: Mensch zwischen Gott und Teufel* (Berlin: Severin und Siedler, 1982), 131. Oberman says that Luther learned to write his first Greek letters of the alphabet from Melanchthon in 1519.

[8] Of course, these studies make ancillary references of other books to support the broader study on the Psalms, but these references are sporadic and not the primary focus. Studies on Luther's exegesis and general examinations of his Bible translation lack any comprehensive examination of the Hebrew.

[9] Luther entered the monastery in 1505, and died in 1546. Thus, I consider this period (roughly the mid-1520s to the early 1530s) to be his academic mid-career. For more on Luther's life, see Bornkamm's biography, which identifies 1521–30 as Luther's mid-career: Bornkamm, *Luther in Mid-Career*.

[10] 1527–28. Gerhard Ebeling goes into great detail about Luther's *Anfechtungen* during this time. See Ebeling, *Luthers Seelsorge: Theologie in der Vielfalt der Lebenssituationen an*

pheten, while begun after he had started his translation, was about to be published before his because of the delays which his own project suffered. He was under enormous pressure to get that and his full German Bible completed, and at the same time to hold his Wittenberg team together, which was under constant religious, political, and ideological threat. It was during this time that he made great strides with the Hebrew language, which this study will show ultimately defined his German Bible much more than has been appreciated to date.

History of Luther's Minor Prophets Translation

Luther originally wanted to issue his translation of the Old Testament in three sequential parts: the Pentateuch; the historical books; and finally the prophets and poetic books.[11] He completed and issued the first part in 1523 under the title *Das Alte Testament deutsch*.[12] In 1524, he issued the second portion, containing Joshua-Esther, under the title *Das Ander teyl des alten testaments*.[13] This followed with a third issuing in 1524, *Das Dritte teyl des alten Testaments*, which included Psalms, Proverbs, Job, and Ecclesiastes, but not the Prophets as he had originally envisioned.[14] There were a number of reasons for this. He explained in a Feb. 23, 1524 letter to Georg Spalatin that the complicated Hebrew in Job was delaying the translation.[15] But a long list of additional difficulties and distractions most certainly extended the delay, including: the Peasants Revolt in 1524–25; the death of Friedrich III on May 5, 1525; his marriage to Katharina von Bora on June 13, 1525; the births of his first three children; the death of his daughter; the controversy with Erasmus; his struggles with the "fanatics" and conflicts about the Sacrament of the Altar; the Visitations; the Diet of Augsburg; and numerous health issues.[16] It was during this period that he was lecturing on the Minor Prophets (1524–26). These lectures laid the groundwork for what would be his *Deutsche Bibel* translation of the books.

A Latin commentary on Hosea was published on behalf of Luther in 1526.[17] It was not penned by him, but was based on his students' lectures notes. From

---

seinen Briefen dargestellt (Tübingen: J. C. B. Mohr (Paul Siebeck), 1997), 364–446, and especially pp. 364–76.

[11] WA BR 2:613–4 [§ 546]. Reu cites this in *Luther's German Bible*, 187. See also Siegfried Raeder, "The Exegetical and Hermeneutical Work of Martin Luther," in *Hebrew Bible/Old Testament: The History of Its Interpretation. Vol. 2: From the Renaissance to the Enlightenment*, ed. Magne Sæbo (Göttingen: Vandenhoeck & Ruprecht, 2008), 397.

[12] WA DB 2:217. Reu, *Luther's German Bible*, 187–8.

[13] WA DB 2:272. Reu, *Luther's German Bible*, 195.

[14] WA DB 2:276. The register of contents on the reverse of the title pages listed the prophets, even though they were not included. See Reu, *Luther's German Bible*, 200, 225.

[15] WA BR 3:248–9 [§ 714]. Reu cites this in *Luther's German Bible*, 197.

[16] Reu, *Luther's German Bible*, 204–5.

[17] Martin Luther, *In Oseam prophetam annotationes* (Basel: Thomas Wolffius, 1526).

his own hand, he issued German commentaries on Jonah in March, 1526; on Habakkuk in June, 1526; and on Zechariah in December, 1527.[18] He was also working on numerous other projects at this time, including university lectures, publishing his translations of other books of the Bible, sermons, and letters.[19] Because of the delays, two competing German translations of the Prophets – Hätzer and Denck's *Alle Propheten nach Hebräischer sprach verteutscht* (1527), commonly called the *Wormser Propheten*; and the *Prophetenbibel* (1529), also called the Zürich translation – beat Luther to print.[20] These translations included not only the Minor Prophets, but all of the prophetic books of the Old Testament. Luther finished his translation of the prophetic books during his stay at the Coburg Castle, between April and October, 1530, though he lingered over the final revision.[21] In an Oct. 10, 1531 letter to Spalatin, he wrote of the final stages: "'Every day I spend two hours revising the prophets.'"[22] Luther's German translation of the entire set of prophetic books of the Hebrew

---

This is in the catalog of the Universitätsbibliothek Basel, Rf 299, Bibliographical reference: VD16 B 3846. 23, [1] Bl.; 8°. The critical edition to the lecture notes appears at WA 13:1–66; LW 18:2–76; this excludes Luther's 1545 additions to Hosea 13. Veit Dietrich published Luther's "commentaries" on Joel, Amos, and Obadiah in 1536; Micah in 1542; and Hosea in 1545. See Martin Brecht, *Martin Luther: Shaping and Defining the Reformation 1521–1532*, trans. James L. Schaaf (Minneapolis: Fortress Press, 1990), 246. See also Mary Jane Haemig, "Martin Luther on Hosea," *Word & World* 28 (2008): 170.

[18] The Jonah commentary appears at WA 19:169–251; LW 19:33–104. The Habakkuk commentary appears at WA 19:337–435; LW 19:149–237. The Zechariah commentary appears at StL 14:1768–1975. For more on these, see: Brecht, *Martin Luther 1521–1532*, 246; Aland, 154, 658; and Gerhard Krause, *Studien zu Luthers Auslegung der Kleinen Propheten* (Tübingen: J. C. B. Mohr (Paul Siebeck), 1962), 2. His commentary on Zechariah was published in Dec., 1527, but had a date of 1528. See Aland, 154, 658; Reu, *Luther's German Bible*, 205; Dominique Barthélemy, *Studies in the Text of the Old Testament: An Introduction to the Hebrew Old Testament Text Project. Textual Criticism and the Translator*, vol. 3, trans. Sarah Lind (Winona Lake, IN: Eisenbrauns, 2012), 162; and Brecht, *Martin Luther 1521–1532*, 247.

[19] See Aland, especially pp. 649–69 for a chronological listing of Luther's writings. See also Krause, *Studien*, 11–14 for the 1524–34 period.

[20] The *Wormser Bibel* ("The Combined Bible"), a complete Bible translation which combined various translations, including part of Luther's Old Testament translation, and included the *Wormser Propheten*, also followed in 1529. The *Zürcher Bibel* followed in 1531, which included the Zürich prophets translation. For more on these Bibles, translations, and their complicated printing history, see: Reu, *Luther's German Bible*, 206–7; G. Baring "Die 'Wormser Propheten,' eine vorlutherische evangelische Prophetenübersetzung aus dem Jahre 1527," *Archiv für Reformationsgeschichte* 31 (1934): 23–41; and Bruce Gordon, *The Swiss Reformation* (Manchester: Manchester University Press, 2002), 239–44. See also Krause, *Studien*, 15–19 for a discussion of the *Wormser Propheten* and Zürich's *Prophetenbibel* (which Krause calls simply the Zürcher Bibel of 1529), and 19–60 for his broader analysis of the *Wormser Propheten* translation.

[21] Hans Volz, "German Versions," in *The Cambridge History of the Bible. Vol. 3: The West from the Reformation to the Present Day*, ed. S. L. Greenslade (Cambridge: Cambridge University Press, 1963), 96.

[22] "Duas horas singulis diebus impendo prophetis corrigendis." WA BR 6:203.14 [§ 1872]. See Reu, *Luther's German Bible*, 208.

Bible, including the Minor Prophets, finally appeared in 1532 as *Die Propheten alle Deudsch*.[23]

Figure 1.1: Die Propheten alle Deudsch, Martin Luther [Wittenberg: Hans Lufft, 1532] (*source:* British and Foreign Bible Society (BFBS), Cambridge University Library, Classmark BSS.228.B32).[24]

---

[23] WA DB 2:512.

[24] The sequential numbering of Figures and Tables in the study are kept separate at the advice of Oxford University Press. The differentiation between "Figure" and "Table" is also made according to OUP standards. On the BFBS copy, see also T. H. Darlow and H. F. Moule, *Historical Catalogue of the Printed Editions of Holy Scripture in the Library of the British and Foreign Bible Society. Vol. 2: Polyglots and Languages other than English* (London: Bible House, 1911), 491 [§ 4197].

The same translation appeared in his complete 1534 *Deutsche Bibel*, not under the subtitle of the "official" third part of his Old Testament translation as originally planned, but rather as its own independent section with a distinct title page.[25] Luther made numerous subsequent revisions to his Minor Prophets translation. Records of his deliberations over those revisions appear in Georg Rörer's notes from Luther's 1539–41 revision meetings, as well as in Luther's notes in his own 1538/39 edition of the Old Testament.[26] His complete lectures on the twelve books were not published until 1552 and 1554, with subsequent publications in various editions of Luther's works.[27] These were, like the Hosea commentary, edited compilations of student notes.

Value of the Minor Prophets as an Area of Focus

The Minor Prophets are a natural place to examine Luther's Hebrew translation in mid-career. Thanks to numerous extant and previously identified manuscript texts of Luther's lectures on all twelve Minor Prophets, as well as his German commentaries on Jonah, Habakkuk, and Zechariah, a thorough view into the thinking that lay behind his translation of these books is readily available. Together with his *Deutsche Bibel* translations, glosses, and revision notes, there is a wealth of information available concerning his Hebrew translation at this point in his academic life. From a pragmatic standpoint, there are several hundred references to Hebrew in Luther's lectures and commentaries on the Minor Prophets. Thus, in contrast to his earlier Psalms lectures, where studies to date have largely speculated about the extent of his use of Hebrew, here it is unnecessary. It was massive. Because of the large number of examples of his engage-

---

[25] Reu, *Luther's German Bible*, 208–11. The Apocrypha also appeared in the 1534 *Deutsche Bibel*. Luther completed Wisdom of Solomon in 1529, and Ecclesiasticus and Maccabees in 1533. The remainder appeared in full in the 1534 *Deutsche Bibel*. See Reu, *Luther's German Bible*, 211.

[26] The full 1539–41 protocols and Luther's entries in his 1538/39 edition of the Old Testament appear in WA DB 4:1–278. Rörer's protocols and Luther's Old Testament are both located at Jena. See Barthélemy, *Studies*, 168–9. Reu provides a detailed summary of Luther's revisions, beginning in 1534; in Reu, *Luther's German Bible*, 233–56. See also Otto Reichert, *Die Wittenberger Bibelrevisionskommissionen von 1531–1541 und ihr Ertrag fuer die deutsche Lutherbibel* (Leignitz: Sehffarth, 1905). The Pentateuch in Luther's 1538/39 Old Testament is dated 1539; Joshua – Malachi are dated 1538. Thus, this is noted as 1538/39. See WA DB 4:xxxi–xxxii.

[27] For the complex history of the Latin texts of Luther's lectures on the Minor Prophets, see WA 13:iii–xxxvi and LW 18:ix–xii. For more information, see also Aland (entire volume); Eike Wolgast, *Die Wittenberger Luther-Ausgabe. Zur Überlieferungsgeschichte der Werke Luthers im 16. Jahrhundert* (Niewkoop: De Graaf, 1971); and Josef Benzing and Helmut Claus, *Lutherbibliographie. Verzeichnis der gedruckten Schriften Martin Luthers bis zu dessen Tod*, 2 vols. (Baden-Baden: Librairie Heitz, 1966 (vol. 1). Baden-Baden: Valentin Koerner, 1994 (vol. 2)).

ment with Hebrew, patterns in his translation can be established which facilitate a more broad analysis, rather than simple one-off observations of independent phenomena.

An exceptional abundance of certain Hebrew philological phenomena is also found in the Minor Prophets, in comparison to other books of the Bible. These texts are laden with supernatural imagery and prophetic theological discourse, which the authors articulate through semantically intense terminology, repetitive language, and a massive number of figures of speech. Consequently, many aspects of Luther's translation method can be thoroughly examined, which would not be possible with other books of the Hebrew Bible. These are also the books of the Bible, together with Job, to which Luther explicitly called attention as especially difficult for him because of such language, and moreover those which delayed the publication of his Bible because of the complexity. Consequently, they also elucidate especially well how he handled difficult Hebrew.

The Minor Prophets also represent a decisive period in Luther's Bible translation. Given that the prophets were the final segment of his Old Testament translation, these books show a more mature, developed use of Hebrew than his initial Psalms translations. He was well-advanced in the language at this point, and his skills were vastly improved from his early years – a drastically different place than he was at with his initial Psalms translations, particularly during his first and second Psalms lectures. Nevertheless, his struggles with the language were far from over. It is thus a distinctive time to get a glimpse into his exploitation of Hebrew. This was a particularly crucial juncture in his Bible translation. It is also the period when he wrote the two most considered accounts of his translation methodology: *Sendbrief vom Dolmetschen* (1530); and *Summarien über die Psalmen und Ursachen des Dolmetschens* (1531–33).[28] His most insightful and most current self-reflection concerning his translation methodology comes from this time of his Bible translation history.

Finally, the Minor Prophets are a valuable place to examine the relationship between theology and philology in Luther's Hebrew translation. One concept in particular dominated his reading of the Minor Prophets: his theology of *Anfechtung*.[29] The word *Anfechtung* itself is a linguistic puzzle. Luther never ex-

---

[28] *Summarien über die Psalmen und Ursachen des Dolmetschens* (1531–33) appears in WA 38:1–69. *Sendbrief vom Dolmetschen* (1530) appears in WA 30.2:632–46.

[29] A great number of scholars have examined Luther's concept of *Anfechtung*. The most important are: Erich Vogelsang, *Der angefochtene Christus bei Luther* (Berlin: Walter de Gruyter, 1932); Paul Bühler, *Die Anfechtung bei Martin Luther* (Zürich: Zwingli-Verlag, 1942); Clarence Warren Hovland, "An Examination of Luther's Treatment of *Anfechtung* in his Biblical Exegesis from the Time of the Evangelical Experience to 1545" (PhD diss., Yale University, 1950); and Horst Beintker, *Die Überwindung der Anfechtung bei Luther: Eine Studie zu seiner Theologie nach den Operationes in Psalmos 1519–21* (Berlin: Evangelische Verlagsanstalt, 1954). Other important studies that address *Anfechtung* include: Theod. Harnack, *Luthers Theologie: mit besonderer Beziehung auf seine Versöhnungs- und Erlösungs-*

plicitly defined it, and he was never able to compose a formal work explaining it. Consequently, scholarship can only extrapolate its meaning through analysis of its use in his texts. In short, *Anfechtung* is a struggle with God, often framed as an encounter with God's wrath in a type of spiritual battle, sometimes also described in terms of a struggling conscience or a trial of faith. Luther identified these spiritual struggles in German as *Anfechtungen*, but in Latin he used a number of synonyms and related terms, most frequently *tentatio*.[30] These battles plagued Luther for much of his life, causing profound mental and physical distress. These were no ordinary conflicts. He saw them as death struggles between himself and God – experiences of terror and wrath which took him to the perimeter of both spiritual and physical death. He described *Anfechtung* as an assault on the soul, a cosmic struggle between God and the devil, and a spiritual attack in its darkest form.[31] He explained in a 1524 sermon, "If he [the person] still stands alive, he [God] does not grab him by the skin, but rather on the inside, so that the marrow wastes away from hunger and thirst and the bones become as tender as flesh."[32] He identified the *Anfechtung* of the prophets as a unique strain, where the prophets both experienced and dispensed *Anfechtung* – as they themselves saw the visions in their confrontation with God, and also as they delivered the messages of those visions to the people.[33]

Luther asserted that *Anfechtung* was indispensable for a proper understanding of scripture. He said during a 1530 gathering at his home in the Black

---

lehre. Vol. 1: Luthers theologische Grundanschauungen (Erlangen: Theodor Blaesing, 1862), especially pp. 411–29; Karl Holl, "Was verstand Luther unter Religion?" in *Gesammelte Aufsätze zur Kirchengeschichte. Vol. 1: Luther*, 6th rev. ed. [compiled volume by Holl] (Tübingen: J. C. B. Mohr (Paul Siebeck), 1932), 1–110; Egil Grislis, "Luther's Understanding of the Wrath of God," *The Journal of Religion* 41 (1961): 277–92; Walther Von Loewenich, *Luthers Theologia Crucis* (Witten: Luther-Verlag, 1967); Egil Grislis, "The Experience of the *Anfechtungen* and the Formulation of Pure Doctrine in Martin Luther's *Commentary on Genesis*," *Consensus* 8 (1982): 19–31; David P. Scaer, "The Concept of *Anfechtung* in Luther's Thought," *Concordia Theological Quarterly* 47 (1983): 15–30; Ebeling, *Luthers Seelsorge*; Thorsten Dietz, *Der Begriff der Furcht bei Luther* (Tübingen: Mohr Siebeck, 2009); Alister E. McGrath, *Luther's Theology of the Cross: Martin Luther's Theological Breakthrough*, 2nd ed. (Oxford: Wiley-Blackwell, 2011); and Simon D. Podmore, *Struggling with God: Kierkegaard and the Temptation of Spiritual Trial* (Cambridge: James Clarke, 2013).

[30] Every comprehensive study of Luther's theology of *Anfechtung* to date has identified *tentatio* as a synonym of *Anfechtung* in Luther's texts, including those by Bühler, Beintker, Hovland, Harnack, and Holl. Concerning Luther's explicit identification of *Anfechtung* as *tentatio*, see WA 50:660.1–4; LW 34:286–7. See also Ch. 3 of this study for more on the various terminology that Luther employed in his discussions of *Anfechtung*.

[31] See WA 1:557.33–WA 1:558.18 and LW 31:129–30 [*Resolutiones disputationum de indulgentiarum virtute* (1518)], and note the reference to Ps. 31:23, which this study addresses in Ch. 5.

[32] "Wenn er nach dem leben stehet, greiffet er nicht nach der haut, sondern hynein, das das marck verschmacht und die beyn so muerb werden wie das fleisch." WA 24:577.31–33. Many scholars cite this.

[33] See StL 14:1796.67; LW 20:178–9. Cf. WA 19:378.29–30; LW 19:180.

Cloister monastery in Wittenberg, "If I should live a little while longer, I would like to write a book about *Anfechtungen*, without which man can neither understand Holy Scripture, nor recognize the fear and love of God. Yes, he cannot know what spirit is."[34] This mirrors similar statements that he made about Hebrew that same year:

> If I were younger I would want to study this language, because without it one can never properly understand Holy Scripture ... Thus they have correctly said: 'The Hebrews drink out of the original spring; the Greeks out of the streams that flow from the source; the Latins out of the puddles.'[35]

A trove of opportunities to examine Hebrew and *Anfechtung* together in Luther's arguments is found in his consideration of the Minor Prophets. This study explores, as a secondary line of investigation, the role of Hebrew in Luther's interpretation of *Anfechtung* in the Minor Prophets.

Luther's Context:
Human Hebrew Resources In and Around Wittenberg[36]

The main context of Luther's Hebrew training, development, and translation activities was where he completed his theological studies and spent his academic career – at the University of Wittenberg, initially named Leucorea. The institution was approved by Maximilian I and founded by Friedrich III (Frederick the Wise), Elector of Saxony, in 1502.

The history of Hebrew studies at the University of Wittenberg is rich, though it had modest beginnings. While Wittenberg was the first German university to hire a permanent Hebrew professor, this did not happen until 1518 with the appointment of Johannes Böschenstein, followed by Matthäus Adrianus in 1520.[37] Its first Hebrew chair appointment followed in 1521 with Matthäus Au-

---

[34] "Wenn ich noch ein Weile leben sollt, wollt ich ein Buch von Anfechtungen schreiben, ohne welche kein Mensch weder die heilige Schrift verstehen, noch Gottesfurcht und Liebe erkennen kann; ja, er kann nicht wissen, was Geist ist." WA TR 4:491.40–42 [§ 4777]. Many scholars cite this.

[35] "Wenn ich jünger wäre, so wollte ich diese Sprache lernen, denn ohne sie kann man die h. Schrift nimmermehr recht verstehen ... Darum haben sie recht gesagt: Die Ebräer trinken aus der Bornquelle; die Griechen aber aus den Wässerlin, die aus der Quelle fließen; die Lateinischen aber aus der Pfützen." WA TR 1:525.15–17, 18–20 [§ 1040]. Many scholars cite this.

[36] Much Hebrew tradition preceded Luther, and significantly influenced him and the Wittenberg circle. This includes Jewish translators and rabbinic exegesis, the Christian Church Fathers, and monastics. For reasons of space, these are not addressed in detain in this study. Nevertheless, they form an important part of the background of late medieval and early modern Christian Hebraism. For more on this, see Stephen G. Burnett, *Christian Hebraism in the Reformation Era (1500–1660). Authors, Books, and the Transmission of Jewish Learning* (Leiden: Brill, 2012), Ch. 1, especially pp. 11–14.

[37] Concerning Böschenstein, see Burnett, *Christian Hebraism in the Reformation Era*, 29.

Figure 1.2: Present day Leucorea, original site of the University of Wittenberg (*source*: photograph is mine; *permission*: Leucorea – Stiftung des öffentlichen Rechts an der Martin-Luther-Universität Halle-Wittenberg).

rogallus, who remained until his death in 1543.[38] But the connection with Hebrew and the university began long before. Since 1502 there were Hebraists in Wittenberg. Among the first was Nikolaus Marschalk, though his Hebrew was limited.[39] Andreas Bodenstein (Andreas Karlstadt), who went on to be profes-

---

Concerning Adrianus, see Walter G. Tillmanns, *The World and Men Around Luther* (Minneapolis: Augsburg, 1959), 134. For more on Luther's discussions with Spalatin about bringing Hebraists to Wittenberg, see Jerome Friedman, *Most Ancient Testimony: Sixteenth-Century Christian-Hebraica in the Age of Renaissance Nostalgia* (Athens, OH: Ohio University Press, 1983), 33–35. Luther and Melanchthon also mentioned the Hebraist John Keller being at Wittenberg; in Friedman as noted; and also WA BR 1:404.8–11 [§ 179] and Note 2.

[38] His birth name was Matthäus Goldhahn. Burnett, *Christian Hebraism in the Reformation Era*, 58.

[39] For more on the history of Hebraists in Wittenberg, see Gustav Bauch, "Die Einführung des Hebräischen in Wittenberg. Mit Berücksichtigung der Vorgeschichte des Studiums der Sprache in Deutschland," *Monatsschrift für Geschichte und Wissenschaft des Judentums* 48 (1904): 22–32; 77–86; 145–60; 214–23; 283–99; 328–40; 461–90; especially pp. 145–60; the 1502 reference is on p. 145. See also WA Ar 1:1.92–106; Siegfried Raeder, *Die Benutzung des masoretischen Textes bei Luther in der Zeit zwischen der ersten und zweiten Psalmenvorlesung (1515–1518)* (Tübingen: J. C. B. Mohr (Paul Siebeck), 1967), 5; and Hans-Jürgen Zobel, "Die Hebraisten an der Universität zu Wittenberg (1502–1817)," in *Altes Testament – Literatursammlung und Heilige Schrift. Gesammelte Aufsätze zur Entstehung, Geschichte und Aus-*

sor of Hebrew at Basel, was in Wittenberg since 1504.[40] Private Hebrew tutoring at the university began as early as 1513 with Tilman Conradi, whom Franz Posset calls "the first instructor who demonstrably taught Hebrew at Wittenberg."[41] As the years went on, the circle of Hebraists grew and took on a more formal structure with the hiring of Philip Melanchthon and the subsequent arrival of Böschenstein, Adrianus, and Aurogallus. It was in this group that Luther found himself increasingly immersed from the time that he arrived at the university in 1508, and especially from 1511, after he had left Erfurt for good and made Wittenberg his permanent home.

By all indications, Luther's private Hebrew studies began early in his academic career, not long after the appearance of Johannes Reuchlin's monumental Hebrew grammar guide and lexicon, *De rudimentis Hebraicis* (Pforzheim, 1506), called the *Rudimenta* for short.[42] Karl Meissinger argues that Luther began his engagement with the *Rudimenta* as early as 1506, and at the latest 1509.[43] G. Lloyd Jones believes that Luther acquired it around 1507.[44] Raeder advises sometime prior to 1509.[45] According to Michael Reu, the first definitive

---

legung des Alten Testaments, ed. Julia Männchen and Ernst-Joachim Waschke (Berlin: Walter de Gruyter, 1993), 201–28. Prior to arriving in Wittenberg, Marschalk published *Introductio ad litteras hebraicas utilissima* (1501), followed *by Introductio perbrevis ad hebraicam linguam* (ca. 1502), included earlier in Constantine Lascaris's *De octo partibus orationis liber primus* (Venice, 1500). See Gianfranco Miletto and Giuseppe Veltri, "Hebrew Studies in Wittenberg (1502–1813): From Lingua Sacra to Semitic Studies," *European Journal of Jewish Studies* 6 (2012): 3–4. Miletto and Veltri also advise that from its very beginnings, lecturers at the university assembled circles of individuals who had similar interests in studying humanist disciplines, among them, languages including Hebrew. Miletto and Veltri, "Hebrew Studies in Wittenberg," 1–4. For more on humanism and Hebrew studies in Wittenberg, see Helmar Junghans, *Der junge Luther und die Humanisten* (Weimar: Böhlau, 1984); Lewis Spitz, *Luther and German Humanism* (Aldershot: Variorum, 1996); and Arjo Vanderjagt, *"Ad fontes!* The Early Humanist Concern for the Hebraica veritas," in *Hebrew Bible/Old Testament: The History of Its Interpretation. Vol. 2: From the Renaissance to the Enlightenment*, ed. Magne Sæbø (Göttingen: Vandenhoeck & Ruprecht, 2008), 154–89.

[40] Karlstadt's *Distinctiones Thomistarum* (1507) was the first text printed in Wittenberg which included Hebrew typeset. Miletto and Veltri, "Hebrew Studies in Wittenberg," 5. See also Raeder, *Die Benutzung*, 5; and Alister E. McGrath, *The Intellectual Origins of the European Reformation*, 2nd ed. (Oxford: Blackwell Publishing, 2004), 128.

[41] He was also known as Thiloninus Philymnus Syasticanus. Franz Posset, *Renaissance Monks: Monastic Humanism in Six Biographical Sketches* (Leiden: Brill, 2005), 159.

[42] Johannes Reuchlin, *De rudimentis Hebraicis* (Pforzheim: Thomas Anselm, 1506); also called *Rudimenta Hebraica*. The *Rudimenta* contained a Hebrew lexicon and a Hebrew grammar. It is more thoroughly addressed later in this chapter. Also, I call this Luther's "early academic career," understanding that he was still attending university between 1506 and 1509.

[43] Meissinger, *Luthers Exegese in der Frühzeit*, 55.

[44] G. Lloyd Jones, *The Discovery of Hebrew in Tudor England: A Third Language* (Manchester: Manchester University Press, 1983), 57.

[45] Raeder, "The Exegetical," 397. Burnett follows Raeder. See Burnett, "Luthers hebräische Bibel," 63; and Stephen G. Burnett, "Martin Luther and Christian Hebraism," in *Oxford Research Encyclopedia of Religion* (Oxford: Oxford University Press, 2016), DOI: 10.1093/acrefore/9780199340378.013.274.

evidence of Luther's study of Hebrew appears in his 1510–11 marginal notes on Peter Lombard's *Libri Quattuor Sententiarum*.[46] His comprehensive engagement with Hebrew began, following receipt of his doctorate in theology in 1512, with his first lectures as a professor at Wittenberg on the Psalms, collected from student notes as *Dictata super Psalterium* (1513–15).[47] From that point on, his systematic study and working use of Hebrew becomes more and more apparent in his subsequent lectures, which he called *Operationes in Psalmos* (1519–21), where he increasingly referenced Hebrew terminology and drew upon various secondary sources for support in understanding the Hebrew.[48] It was these lectures, and the translation and exegetical work which fed them, which would serve as the base for his subsequent *Deutsche Bibel* translation. This was so not only for the Psalms, but for all of the books of the Hebrew Bible on which he subsequently lectured, for some of which he also wrote commentaries.[49]

As Luther worked through his Bible translation and revisions over the years, he assembled a team of Wittenberg colleagues to support him. By the time of the later 1539–41 Bible revision meetings, he had affectionately dubbed this translation committee his "Sanhedrin," as the oft-quoted thirteenth sermon of Johannes Mathesius shows:

Dr. M. Luther at once gathered his own Sanhedrim of the best persons available, which assembled weekly, several hours before supper in the doctor's cloister ... Dr. M. Luther came into the *Consistorium* with his Old Latin and new German Bible, and he also always had the Hebrew text with him. Herr Philip brought the Greek text, and Dr. Cruciger both the Hebrew Bible and the Chaldaean Bible [the Aramaic Targums]. The professors all brought their rabbis.[50]

---

[46] Reu, *Luther's German Bible*, 114. In Luther's *Zu den Sentenzen des Petrus Lombardus. 1510/11*, he made multiple notations of "In hebreo habetur ..." [WA 9:32.9–29]. He also explicitly mentioned Reuchlin [WA 9:32.26]; discussed the transliterated name *sathan* [WA 9:63.28]; and noted "in Hebraeo ..." [WA 9:67.30]. All of these are cited by Reu. Reu also notes that Luther made handwritten entries in his copy of the *Rudimenta*, and referenced the *Rudimenta* in his copy of the Vulgate. Reu, *Luther's German Bible*, 114–5. Reu also mentions a 1522 letter to Johann Lang [WA BR 2:547–8, (§ 501)], though this is insignificant, since Raeder has shown in his investigations that Luther was using Hebrew quite a bit by then.

[47] WA 3; WA 4:1–462.

[48] WA 5.

[49] Luther only lectured on some of the Hebrew Bible, not all of the books.

[50] "Verordnet D. M. Luther gleich ein eygen Sanhedrim von den besten leuten, so deßmals verhanden, welche wöchlich etliche stunden vor dem Abendessen in Doctors Kloster zusammen kamen ... Kam D. Martin Luther inn das Consistorium mit seiner alten Lateinischen und newen Deutschen Biblien; darbey er auch stettigs den Hebreischen Text hatte. Herr Philippus bracht mit sich den Greckischen Text, D. Creutziger neben dem Hebreischen die Chaldeische Bibel, Die Professores hatten bey sich ihre Rabinen." WA DB 3:xv. The WA DB quotes this from Johannes Mathesius, *Historien, Von des Ehrwirdigen in Gott seligen theuren Manns Gottes, D. Martin Luthers, Anfang, Lere, Leben, Standhafft bekentnuß seines Glaubens, unnd Sterben, Ordenlich der Jarzal nach, wie sich solches alles habe zugetragen, Beschriben Durch Herrn M. Johann Mathesium den Eltern* (Nürnberg: Katharinam Gerlachin, und Johanns vom Berg Erben, 1580) [Originally published in 1566, Nürnberg], 151. Many scholars

Mathesius identified the Sanhedrin as: (1) Martin Luther; (2) Johannes Bugenhagen ("Dr. Pommer" or "Pommeranus"), Luther's pastor and professor of Old Testament at Wittenberg; (3) Justus Jonas (Jodocus Koch), professor of theology at Wittenberg; (4) Caspar Cruciger, professor of theology at Wittenberg, and the youngest in Luther's inner circle (Luther called Cruciger his "Elisha"); (5) Philip Melanchthon, Reuchlin's great-nephew by marriage, and essentially Luther's right hand man for his translation work;[51] (6) Matthäus Aurogallus, whom Posset calls the "first permanent professorship of Hebrew at Wittenberg," whom Burnett calls "the true founder of Hebrew studies at Wittenberg," and whom Tillmanns calls "the greatest Hebrew scholar at the university";[52] and (7) Georg Rörer ("The Corrector"), Luther's secretary, who recorded notes from the revision meetings and was responsible for editing the Sanhedrin's work.[53]

To what degree that group was in place when Luther began translating the books of the Hebrew Bible, or if it was assembled later specifically for the revisions meetings, is not clear. What is clear is that he increasingly had access to numerous Hebrew scholars of varying degrees of skill, both inside and outside of the University of Wittenberg.[54] Moreover, whatever the state of Hebrew

---

cite this. See Reu, *Luther's German Bible*, 212–3, 359–60; Stephen G. Burnett, "Reassessing the 'Basel-Wittenberg Conflict': Dimensions of the Reformation-Era Discussion of Hebrew Scholarship," in *Hebraica Veritas? Christian Hebraists and the Study of Judaism in Early Modern Europe*, ed. Allison P. Coudert and Jeffrey S. Shoulson (Philadelphia: University of Pennsylvania Press, 2004), 194; and Robert Kolb, *Martin Luther and the Enduring Word of God: The Wittenberg School and Its Scripture-Centered Proclamation* (Grand Rapids, MI: Baker Academic, 2016), 210.

[51] Melanchthon lectured at Wittenberg on Greek, on the Bible, and filled in for Hebrew, especially before the university hired a permanent, full-time Hebrew professor.

[52] Aurogallus was the only member of Luther's inner circle to publish a Hebrew grammar. He authored several, one of which included a list of common Hebrew abbreviations found in Rabbinic Bible commentaries which significantly aided those at Wittenberg who wanted to consult the commentaries.

[53] WA DB 3:xv. For Bugenhagen, Jonas, Cruciger, Melanchthon, Aurogallus, and Rörer, see Tillmans, *The World and Men Around Luther*, 90–113, 137. For Aurogallus, see also Burnett, *Christian Hebraism in the Reformation Era*, 58; Burnett, "Reassessing," 198; Burnett, "Martin Luther and Christian Hebraism"; Posset, *Renaissance Monks*, 160; Jones, *The Discovery of Hebrew*, 59; and Miletto and Veltri, "Hebrew Studies in Wittenberg," 12–13. Concerning Luther's translation team, see also Hans Volz, *Martin Luthers deutsche Bibel: Entstehung und Geschichte der Lutherbibel*, ed. Henning Wendland (Hamburg: Friedrich Wittig, 1978), 81–93.

[54] See Luther's letter from the Wartburg Castle to Amsdorf on Jan 13, 1522, lamenting that he would not be able to touch the Old Testament without his help; WA BR 2:423.50–51 [§ 449]. Reu cites this, in *Luther's German Bible*, 148. See also discussions of Luther's work with Aurogallus and Melanchthon to translate Job; WA 30.2:636.16–20. Reu also cites this, in *Luther's German Bible*, 270. Nevertheless, by the time of the 1539–41 revision meetings, which appear in Rörer's protocol records, it was obviously quite systematic and formal. Those records indicate that between 60 and 70 meetings took place between July 17, 1539 and Feb. 8, 1541, which specifically examined the Old Testament translations. Reu, *Luther's German Bible*, 234. And other meetings took place. For more on this, see Reu, *Luther's German Bible*, 211–22, 233–56; and Burnett, "Reassessing," 199.

Figure 1.3: Lutherstube. Luther's living room at the Augustinian monastery in Wittenberg, where he likely met with his team on many occasions to discuss translations (*source*: photograph is mine; *permission*: Stiftung Luthergedenkstätten in Sachsen-Anhalt).

scholarship in Wittenberg at the time of his early career, specifically his initial lectures on the Psalms from 1513–15, by mid- and late-career, he had all the more resources upon which to draw.

That Luther regularly brought in people from the outside, even for his "official" Wittenberg Sanhedrin sessions, is corroborated in Mathesius's sermon: "Often outside doctors and academics came for this great task, such as Dr. Bernhard Ziegler [professor of Hebrew and renowned Hebraist at the University of Leipzig] and Dr. Förster [student of Reuchlin and later, professor of Hebrew at the University of Wittenberg (1549–58)]."[55] Whatever the pool of available "experts" in and around Wittenberg was, it was relatively modest in number. Burnett assesses the German Hebraists at the time of Luther's mid-career to be a "surprisingly small group of scholars." He has come up with a count of twenty-five, which he limits to those whose careers began before 1535; who taught

---

[55] "Offtmals kamen frembde Doktorn unnd Gelerte zu disem hohen Werck, als D. Bernhard Ziegler, D. Forstemius." WA DB 3:xv. The WA DB quotes this from Johannes Mathesius, *Historien*, 151. Many scholars cite this. Ziegler and Förster information per Jones, *The Discovery of Hebrew*, 59. See also Burnett, *Christian Hebraism in the Reformation Era*, 58.

at a German university or Louvain University; and who wrote or edited Christian Hebrew grammars, dictionaries, portions of the Bible, and biblical introductions.[56] That list includes, in addition to the Sanhedrin, some of the more renowned scholars of the region: Reuchlin, Adrianus, Capito, Campensis, Pellikan, and Münster. That said, if one takes into account the full breadth of resources upon which Luther drew, beyond those whom Burnett deems the "community of the competent" – i. e. the Hebraists who he says "set the trends in Hebrew study that would endure through midcentury, both through the books they authored and edited and through their often critical reception of these works" – that list could certainly be broadened to include: Johannes Lang (Erfurt), who instructed Luther in Hebrew and Greek; Andreas Osiander (Nürnberg); Nikolaus von Amsdorf (Wittenberg); Georg Spalatin (Wittenberg); Wenzeslaus Linck (Nürnberg), whom Luther specifically mentioned in a 1528 letter about their struggles to translate the Prophets in the Hebrew Bible; Tilman Conradi (Wittenberg); Veit Dietrich (Wittenberg, Nürnberg); Andreas Bodenstein (Wittenberg); and Matthias Flacius Illyricus (Wittenberg), in the latter years of Luther's life.[57]

From further afield, Italian and English humanists indirectly supported Luther's Hebrew translation both through their texts and sometimes through personal interactions with members of his fraternity. Lewis Spitz claims that Italian humanists "spent much time in Wittenberg."[58] Morimichi Watanabe says that Luther was "definitely familiar with" Italian humanists such as Lorenzo Valla, Giovanni Pico della Mirandola, and even the popular Italian humanist poet Baptisma Mantuanus – all who had a connection with Hebrew in one

---

[56] Burnett, "Reassessing," 182–3.

[57] Burnett, "Reassessing," 182. For Lang, Veit Dietrich, Linck, and Amsdorf, see Tillmans, *The World and Men Around Luther*, 86–90, 135–6, 142–4. For Linck, see also WA BR 4:484.14–19 [§ 1285] [The Chadwyck-Healey (ProQuest) electronic edition of the *Weimarer Ausgabe* shows this as lines 19–23; it is clearly at 14–19 in the printed edition]; and WA DB 11.2:xii. For Osiander, see Burnett, "Martin Luther and Christian Hebraism." For Conradi, see Posset, *Renaissance Monks*, 159. For Bodenstein, see Raeder, *Die Benutzung*, 5. For Flacius, see Burnett, *Christian Hebraism in the Reformation Era*, 58. Luther would often call Amsdorf to assist with translating idiomatic expressions. See Reu, *Luther's German Bible*, 186. Spalatin assisted Luther with the Genesis translation, including the names of birds and other animals. See WA BR 2:625 [§ 553], noted in the preliminary remarks; and WA BR 2:630–1 [§ 556], noted both in the preliminary remarks and in the main text. Kolb cites this in *Martin Luther and the Enduring*, 210. See also Reu, *Luther's German Bible*, 187. Johannes Drach (Draconites) was also at Wittenberg, but only a doctoral student at this point in the 1520s, and his works were published later, so he is probably inconsequential for Luther. Nevertheless for more on Drach, see Hans-Martin Kirn, "Traces of Targum Reception in the Work of Martin Luther," in *A Jewish Targum in a Christian World*, ed. Alberdina Houtman, Eveline van Staalduine-Sulman, and Hans-Martin Kirn (Leiden: Brill, 2014), 271–2; and Stephen G. Burnett, "Christian Aramaism in Reformation-Era Europe," in *Seeking Out the Wisdom of the Ancients: Essays Offered to Michael V. Fox on the Occasion of His Sixty-Fifth Birthday*, ed. Ronald L. Troxel, Kelvin G. Friebel, and Dennis R. Magary (Winona Lake, IN: Eisenbrauns, 2005), 429.

[58] Spitz, *Luther and German Humanism*, VIII.76.

way or another.[59] Erasmus had connections to the extended Wittenberg circle through Reuchlin, and through Oecolampadius, the German Hebraist who assisted him with Hebrew explanations for his Greek translation.[60] Robert Wakefield of Cambridge also had contacts with the German Hebraists, most notably Reuchlin, whose seat he took at the University of Tübingen following his death.[61] It was thus a broad pool of resources upon which Luther and his associates drew, directly and indirectly, for their Hebrew translation knowledge.[62]

Arguably the most valuable resources for late medieval and early modern Christian Hebraists were Jewish teachers who knew the language. They were also the most difficult to come by, at least in comparison to literary Hebrew resources.[63] Nevertheless, there were a number of prominent Jewish teachers

---

[59] Morimichi Watanabe, "Martin Luther's Relations with Italian Humanists. With Special Reference to Ioannes Baptista Mantuanus," *Lutherjahrbuch* 54 (1987): 37–47.

[60] During his 1528–30 lectures on Isaiah, Luther used Oecolampadius's 1528 Isaiah commentary (a printing of his lectures). He was still translating the Minor Prophets during this time. See Dietrich Thyen, "Luthers Jesajavorlesung" (PhD diss., Universität Heidelberg, 1964), 105–9; Burnett, "Reassessing," 189; and Peter Opitz, "The Exegetical and Hermeneutical Work of John Oecolampadius, Huldrych Zwingli and John Calvin," in *Hebrew Bible/Old Testament: The History of Its Interpretation. Vol 2: From the Renaissance to the Enlightenment*, ed. Magne Sæbo (Göttingen: Vandenhoeck & Ruprecht, 2008), 407–13. Also, Luther certainly drew upon Erasmus's Hebrew references in his annotations to the New Testament. Erasmus's annotations are discussed later in this chapter, under the heading "Luther's Context: Literary Hebrew Resources in and Around Wittenberg." For more on Erasmus and Reuchlin, see Richard Rex, *The Theology of John Fisher* (Cambridge: Cambridge University Press, 1991), 57–9. See also Franz Posset, *Johann Reuchlin (1455–1522): A Theological Biography* (Berlin: De Gruyter, 2015), where he discusses many written correspondences between Erasmus and Reuchlin, especially in Ch. 11.

[61] See Robert Wakefield's inaugural 1524 lecture at the University of Cambridge, discussing the importance of Arabic, Aramaic, and Hebrew: Robert Wakefield, *Oratio de laudibus & utilitate trium linguarum Arabicae Chaldaicae & Hebraicae, atque idiomatibus hebraicis quae in utroque testamento inveniuntur* (London: Winandum de Vorde, [1524]). The English translation is: Robert Wakefield, *On The Three Languages*, ed. and trans. G. Lloyd Jones, (Binghamton, NY: Medieval & Renaissance Texts & Studies in conjunction with the Renaissance Society of America, 1989).

[62] For more on the relationship between English and German Hebraists and humanists, see Richard Rex, "Humanism and Reformation in England and Scotland," in in *Hebrew Bible/Old Testament: The History of Its Interpretation. Vol. 2: From the Renaissance to the Enlightenment*, ed. Magne Sæbo (Göttingen: Vandenhoeck & Ruprecht, 2008), 512–35, especially pp. 520–2 concerning Hebrew and Wakefield. See also Rex, *The Theology of John Fisher*, 50–64, especially pp. 57–60; and Posset, *Johann Reuchlin*, 854–5. For a general overview of the study of Hebrew in Germany during this period, see Ludwig Geiger, *Das Studium der hebräischen Sprache in Deutschland vom Ende des XV. bis zur Mitte des XVI. Jahrhunderts* (Breslau: Schletter, 1870).

[63] On this difficulty, see Stephen G. Burnett, "Philosemitism and Christian Hebraism in the Reformation Era (1500–1620)," in *Geliebter Feind – gehasster Freund: Antisemitismus und Philosemitismus in Geschichte und Gegenwart*, ed. Irene A. Diekmann and Elke-Vera Kotowski (Berlin: Verlag für Berlin-Brandenburg, 2009), 136–7. Also see David H. Price, *Johannes Reuchlin and the Campaign to Destroy Jewish Books* (Oxford: Oxford University Press, 2011), 72.

who were ready and willing to help. Giovanni Pico della Mirandola, the Italian Hebraist and kabbalist who especially inspired Reuchlin, learned from Jewish teachers, among them, Elia del Medigo, Yohanan Alemanno, and Flavius Mithridates.[64] Reuchlin himself studied with a number of Jewish teachers: a scribe named Calman; Jacob b. Yehiel Loans, Kaiser Friedrich III's physician; and Obadiah Sforno, a respected Jewish biblical commentator in Rome.[65] Böschenstein learned from R. Moshe Moellin of Weissenburg.[66] And Elijah b. Asher ha-Levi (Elijah Levita) taught Christians, including Johannes Eck, Paulus Fagius (Paul Büchelin), and Cardinal Egidio da Viterbo (Giles of Viterbo).[67] In addition to working with Jewish teachers, a number of Christian Hebraists studied with other Christian Hebraists who were Jewish converts to Christianity. Pellikan, for example, studied with Matthäus Adrianus and Michael Adam, both Jewish converts.[68] And Ziegler was a student of Anton Margaritha, a convert who Kirn says influenced Luther.[69] Whether Luther actually studied directly with Jews is uncertain, though not likely. Thomas Kaufmann advises that "very few instances of personal contact between Luther and Jews can be reconstructed with any certainty."[70]

---

[64] Posset, *Johann Reuchlin*, 625. Price, *Johannes Reuchlin*, 63–4.

[65] Burnett, "Reassessing," 184. Burnett, "Philosemitism," 137. Burnett, "Martin Luther and Christian Hebraism." Price, *Johannes Reuchlin*, 62–68.

[66] Burnett, "Reassessing," 184. Burnett, *Christian Hebraism in the Reformation Era*, 23.

[67] Burnett, "Philosemitism," 137–8. Burnett, "Reassessing," 184. For more on Levita and his connection with Christians, see Christoph Daxelmüller, "Zwischen Kabbala und Martin Luther – Elijah Levita Bachur, eine Jude zwischen den Religionen," in *Wechselseitige Wahrnehmung der Religionen im Spätmittelalter und in der Frühen Neuzeit. Vol. 1: Konzeptionelle Grundfragen und Fallstudien (Heiden, Barbaren, Juden)*, ed. Ludger Grenzmann, et al. (Berlin: Walter de Gruyter, 2009), 231–50. For more on Fagius, see Friedman, *Most Ancient Testimony*, 99–118, though Friedman discusses him throughout the book.

[68] Burnett, "Martin Luther and Christian Hebraism." Burnett identifies Jewish teachers in a summary list of Hebrew professors at Louvain and German universities, in "Reassessing," 183. See also Stephen G. Burnett, "Jüdische Vermittler des Hebräischen und ihre christlichen Schüler im Spätmittelalter," in *Wechselseitige Wahrnehmung der Religionen im Spätmittelalter und in der Frühen Neuzeit. Vol. 1: Konzeptionelle Grundfragen und Fallstudien (Heiden, Barbaren, Juden)*, ed. Ludger Grenzmann, et al. (Berlin: Walter de Gruyter, 2009), 173–88. Burnett notes that four professors of Hebrew were Jewish converts: Adrianus, Leonard, Margaritha, and Werner Einhorn; Burnett, "Reassessing," 184.

[69] Kirn, "Traces of Targum Reception," 277. Also significant, though not instructors, were: Paul of Burgos (Solomon ha-Levi; baptized as Paul de Santa María), a Spanish Jew who converted to Christianity; and the famous Daniel Bomberg printers Felix Praetensis and Jacob b. Ḥayyim, both Jewish converts to Christianity. Burnett, "Strange Career," 64–5.

[70] "Nur wenige persönliche Kontakte zwischen Luther und Juden lassen sich zweifelsfrei rekonstruieren." Thomas Kaufmann, *Luthers Juden* (Stuttgart: Reclam, 2014), 33, with a broader discussion on pp. 33–47. I would not change anything in this English translation, and thus have taken it from: Thomas Kaufmann, *Luther's Jews*, trans. Lesley Sharpe and Jeremy Noakes (Oxford: Oxford University Press, 2017), 26. Reinhold Lewin argues similarly, saying there is no evidence of personal meetings between Luther and Jews. See Lewin, *Luthers Stellung zu den Juden. Ein Beitrag zur Geschichte der Juden in Deutschland während des Reformationzeitalters* (Berlin: Trowitzch & Sohn, 1911), 9. This is cited by Moritz Freier, who

Luther's Context:
Literary Hebrew Resources In and Around Wittenberg

Luther and the extended Wittenberg circle drew upon a rich supply of literary Hebrew resources that were increasingly available as the sixteenth century unfolded. Chief among these was the Hebrew Bible.[71] Hebrew Bibles were widely available in manuscript form in Europe long before Luther began his translation of the Minor Prophets.[72] The advent of the printing press made them all the more accessible, particularly for Christian readers.[73] Three printed Hebrew Bibles in particular were important for the Wittenberg team.[74] The first was the third edition Soncino Bible, printed at Brescia in 1494. Luther owned a copy, which is housed today at the Staatsbibliothek zu Berlin.[75]

---

also finds accounts of Luther studying with a Jew named Jacob implausible; in Freier, *Luthers Busspsalmen und Psalter: Kritische Untersuchung nach jüdischen und lateinischen Quellen* (Leipzig: J. C. Hinrichs, 1918), 104. Nevertheless, there are evidences of written contact between Luther and Jews. See WA TR 4:620.13–15 [§ 5026]; cited by Kaufmann, above (Kaufmann cites WA TR 5, but it is WA TR 4). Thank you also to Prof. Dr. Stephen Burnett, University of Nebraska-Lincoln, who advised me that Luther studying directly with Jews is highly unlikely, and that conceivable tutoring from Adrianus, a Jewish convert, probably would have been the extent of it. See Burnett, *Christian Hebraism in the Reformation Era*, 23–27, for a further discussion on this subject.

[71] Many scholars debate to what extent Luther made direct use of the Hebrew Bible. The Psalms studies addressed later in this chapter address this. See also Krause, who argues that Luther compared the Vulgate and Hebrew Bible word for word in his translation of the Minor Prophets. Krause, *Studien*, 63. Burnett argues that it was less so. See Burnett, "Martin Luther and Christian Hebraism."

[72] Burnett, though, notes that many had accuracy issues. He cites Felix Praetensis's letter to Pope Leo X, where he lamented the errors in manuscript Bibles. Stephen G. Burnett, "The Strange Career of the *Biblia Rabbinica* among Christian Hebraists, 1517–1620," in *Shaping the Bible in the Reformation: Books, Scholars and Their Readers in the Sixteenth Century*, ed. Bruce Gordon and Matthew McLean (Leiden: Brill, 2012), 65–6. Christian Ginsburg also cites Praetensis's letter; in Ginsburg, *Introduction to the Massoretico-Critical Edition of the Hebrew Bible* (London: Trinitarian Bible Society, 1897), 945–7. Reu also says that Luther mentioned manuscripts that he consulted, though he does not specific whether they were Hebrew, Greek, etc.; in Reu, *Luther's German Bible*, 258. David Stern's *The Jewish Bible: A Material History* (Seattle: University of Washington Press, 2017) gives a thorough and excellent overview of the history of the material Hebrew Bible texts. See especially pp. 126–31 concerning late medieval Italy, and pp. 137–9 concerning the question of whether printed Bibles represented a "revolution" compared with the manuscript culture.

[73] Stern, *The Jewish Bible*, 139.

[74] Concerning a fourteenth century Ashkenazi Hebrew Bible codex that Luther and members of his team consulted [Luther and Jonas in 1545; Ziegler likely in 1545; and Melanchthon in 1547], see Jordan S. Penkower, "A 14th Century Ashkenazi Hebrew Bible Codex with Later Inscriptions in Latin and Hebrew by Luther, Melanchthon, Jonas and Ziegler," *Codices Manuscripti* 82/83 (2012): 43–60. I have not included this here as a major resource because of the late date.

[75] For more on Luther's copy, see: WA 60:240–309; Burnett, "Luthers hebräische Bibel"; Christoph Mackert, "Luthers Handexemplar der hebräischen Bibelausgabe von 1494 – Objektbezogene und besitzgeschichtliche Aspekte," in *Meilensteine der Reformation: Schlüssel-*

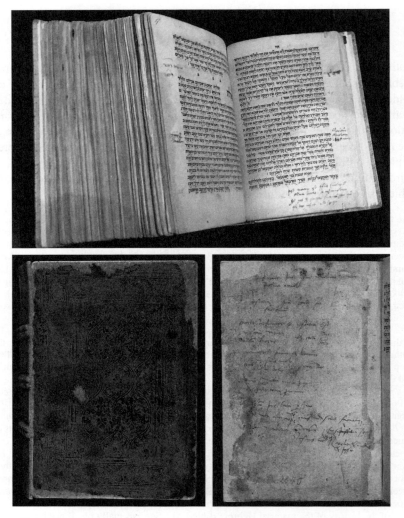

Figure 1.4: Luther's Brescia Bible (*source:* Stiftung Luthergedenkstätten in Sachsen-Anhalt and Staatsbibliothek zu Berlin – Preußischer Kulturbesitz, 8° Inc 2840, [1192], [1181]).[76]

dokumente der frühen Wirksamkeit Martin Luthers, ed. Irene Dingel and Henning P. Jürgens (Gütersloh: Gütersloher Verlaghaus, 2014), 70–78. Burnett advises that Pellikan also had a Soncino Bible; in Burnett, "Strange Career," 67.

[76] Top photograph permission per Stiftung Luthergedenkstätten in Sachsen-Anhalt; photograph is mine. Bottom photographs source: Staatsbibliothek zu Berlin: https://digital.staatsbibliothek-berlin.de/werkansicht?PPN=PPN720865522&PHYSID=PHYS_1192&DMDID= and https://digital.staatsbibliothek-berlin.de/werkansicht?PPN=PPN720865522&PHYSID=PHYS_1181&DMDID=.

Burnett estimates that Luther acquired it sometime between 1515 and 1518.[77] Christoph Mackert says 1519 at the latest.[78] Whatever the date, Luther's extensive handwritten entries in it attest to his heavy use of it.[79] Hans Volz and Johannes Schilling estimate that half of the entries are in the Pentateuch, a third of these in Genesis alone, and another third in the prophetic books, though five of the Minor Prophets have no entries.[80] Prior to Luther, it is believed to have had two previous owners – both Jewish scholars – based on handwritten entries inside it.[81]

A second Hebrew Bible that was important for the Wittenberg team and its extended network was Daniel Bomberg's Rabbinic Bible מקראות גדולות (*Mikra'ot Gedolot*, or *Biblia rabbinica*). It first appeared in a 1517 (Venice) edition, edited by Felix Praetensis.[82] A revised second edition followed in 1524–25 (Venice), edited by Jacob b. Ḥayyim. It appeared as a four volume set, and contains the Hebrew Bible text, along with the Aramaic Targum and numerous Jewish biblical commentaries, among them the commentaries of R. Solomon b. Isaac (Shlomo Yitzhaki, generally called Rashi, based on the acronym of his Hebrew initials), R. Abraham Ibn Ezra, R. David Kimhi (often called RaDaK, based on the acronym of his Hebrew initials), and Targum Onkelos.[83] The 1524–25 second edition was an improved, more accurate Bible based on additional manuscripts and "the most complete printed Masorah ever assembled," according to Burnett.[84] Bomberg also issued the Hebrew text of the 1517 Rabbinic Bible as

---

[77] Burnett, "Luthers hebräische Bibel," 62–63. See also Raeder, *Benutzung*, 85–92, cited by Burnett; and Burnett, "Martin Luther and Christian Hebraism."

[78] Christoph Mackert, "Luthers Handexemplar," 71. Presumably Mackert bases the 1519 date on WA 60:246, "terminus ante quem."

[79] WA 60:246–53.

[80] WA 60:246–53. The books that they note which have no entries are: Song of Songs, Ruth, Lamentations, Ecclesiastes, Esther, Joel, Jonah, Zephaniah, Haggai, Malachi, Ezra, and Nehemiah. Volz and Schilling caution against reading too much into the location of the entries, however, suggesting that when, and for what reason, entries were made are more likely coincidence than anything else; WA 60:246–53. They base this on, aside from the entries themselves, the belief that while the Brescia was "always on the table," Luther may have used it mainly as a convenience for certain occasions because of its small size; WA 60:253.

[81] WA 60:244–6. These two are unfortunately not identifiable, per WA 60:244; though the WA identifies one as a German Jew, WA 60:255. Christoph Mackert also notes this; Mackert, "Luthers Handexemplar," 73.

[82] Burnett, "Strange Career." Burnett argues that the 1517 edition was especially important for Reformation scholarship on the Psalms; Burnett, "Strange Career," 68. Burnett includes a list of Christian Hebraists and libraries which owned a *Biblia Rabbinica* between 1520 and 1620; in Burnett, "Strange Career," 78–79.

[83] See Burnett, "Strange Career," 65–66, 69 for a list of Jewish commentaries that were included in the 1517 and 1524–25 Bomberg Bibles; Targum Onkelos is discussed on p. 74.

[84] Burnett, "Strange Career," 68. See also Jacob ben Ḥayyim ibn Adonijah, *Jacob Ben Chajim Ibn Adonijah's Introduction to the Rabbinic Bible, Hebrew and English; with Explanatory Notes by Christian D. Ginsburg*, 2nd ed., ed. and trans. Christian D. Ginsburg (London: Longmans, Green, Reader, and Dyer, 1867).

a quarto, offering customers a smaller, less expensive option.[85] Melanchthon acquired a first edition in 1518, as did Reuchlin, Johannes Agricola, Cruciger, and likely Luther himself.[86] Numerous other Christian Hebraists had the second edition, including Martin Bucer, Sebastian Münster, and Konrad Pellikan.[87]

The third printed Hebrew Bible that was especially important for the Wittenberg team, while only relevant for Luther's later revisions given its later publishing date, was Sebastian Münster's *Hebraica Biblia* (Basel, 1534–35).[88] This Bible contained the Hebrew text, taken from the 1517 Rabbinic Bible; Münster's Latin translation; and his philological annotations following each chapter.[89] These comments were, according to Burnett, mainly annotations from the second Bomberg edition (1524–25), and other Jewish commentaries including R. Abraham Saba's *Zeror ha-Mor* (Venice, 1523) and R. Moses b. Naḥman's (also known as Naḥmanides, and RaMBaN, based on the acronym of his Hebrew initials) commentary on the Pentateuch.[90]

---

[85] Burnett, "Strange Career," 67.

[86] Barthélemy cites P. Volz and H. Ulbrich, who say that Luther possessed and utilized a folio edition of the Hebrew Bible, which Barthélemy says was likely the 1517 Bomberg. Barthélemy, *Studies*, 162, citing WA DB 11.2:xx–xxi Note 48. Raeder cites multiple sources, including a 1520 letter from Lazarus Spengler to Pirkheimer which mentioned a Hebrew Bible that Luther possessed, and suggests that Luther had a 1511 or 1518 Bomberg Bible. Raeder, *Die Benutzung*, 92–93, citing WA DB 9.1:xiii. Krause believes that Luther had a first edition since 1520, but says it is ultimately uncertain whether he used the second edition to support his Minor Prophets translation. Krause, *Studien*, 63. Melanchthon's copy was purchased for him by Spalatin. See Burnett, "Strange Career," 67–68; Burnett, "Reassessing," 187; and Burnett, "Philosemitism," 139. Hans Volz says that Melanchthon acquired two Hebrew Bibles, one with a commentary, and one without. Volz, "Melanchthons Anteil an der Lutherbibel," *Archiv für Reformationsgeschichte* 45 (1954): 202 Note 28. Raeder also cites this in *Die Benutzung*, 92. Volz says that Luther had two Hebrew Bibles: (1) the Brescia, and (2) either a first or second edition Bomberg; in Martin Luther, *Biblia, das ist die gantze heilige Schrifft: Deudsch auffs new zugericht, Wittenberg 1545. Vol. 3*, ed. Hans Volz (München: Deutsche Taschenbuch, 1974), 43* Note 32.

[87] Burnett, "Strange Career," 70.

[88] Stephen Burnett says that "Martin Luther ... assiduously read Münster's biblical annotations from 1536 until his death in 1546." Burnett, "'Spokesmen for Judaism': Medieval Jewish Polemicists and their Christian Readers in the Reformation Era," in *Reuchlin und seine Erben: Forscher, Denker, Ideologen und Spinner*, ed. Peter Schäfer and Irina Wandrey (Ostfildern: Jan Thorbecke, 2005), 49. Burnett adds that not only did Luther utilize these annotations, but Melanchthon, Aurogallus, and Cruciger likely did as well. Burnett, "Martin Luther and Christian Hebraism."

[89] Sophie Kessler Mesguich, "Early Christian Hebraists," in *Hebrew Bible/Old Testament: The History of Its Interpretation. Vol. 2: From the Renaissance to the Enlightenment*, ed. Magne Sæbø (Göttingen: Vandenhoeck & Ruprecht, 2008), 270. Burnett, "Strange Career," 67, 74.

[90] Burnett, "Strange Career," 74. See also Erwin I.J. Rosenthal, "Sebastian Münster's Knowledge of and Use of Jewish Exegesis," in *Studia Semitica. Vol. 1: Jewish Themes* [compiled volume by Rosenthal] (Cambridge: Cambridge University Press, 1971), 127–45. Rosenthal based his analysis on Münster's 1546 Bible, which has even more extensive annotations. Burnett also cites Rosenthal.

In addition to complete Hebrew Bibles, printings of individual books of the Bible – in Hebrew as well as Latin and German translations based on the Hebrew – were important resources for Luther and his team. Raeder points to several works which were integral to Luther's Psalms translations. Jerome's translation of the Hebrew Psalter was indispensable.[91] Luther also had translations of portions of the Psalms by Nicholas of Lyra and Paul of Burgos; various Psalms translations by Jacques Lefèvre d'Étaples (Jacobus Faber Stapulensis), of which the *Quintuplex Psalterium* (Paris, 1509) is especially important; and Pellikan's *Hebraicum Psalterium* (Basel, 1516).[92] Reuchlin's *In septem psalmos poenitentiales hebraicos interpretatio* (Tübingen, 1512), which was translated into German in 1517, was also very important because it included a Hebrew grammar.[93] Even for Luther's work outside of the Psalms, he frequently consulted and referenced Hebrew terminology and phrases in these books.[94] Specifically for the Minor Prophets, Hans Denck and Ludwig Hätzer's German translation *Alle Propheten nach Hebräischer Sprach verteutscht* (Worms, 1527), i. e. the *Wormser Propheten* (abbreviated to D-H based on the initials of the translators), was important for Luther's translation. He obtained a copy of it only three weeks after its release in Wittenberg.[95] Regardless of the extent to which he ultimately adopted it into his own work, it was a significant resource which he consulted.

Hebrew Bible commentaries, as well as other commentaries which incorporated Hebrew, were also essential resources for Luther and the Wittenberg team. It would be difficult to argue that many were more influential than the *Glossa Ordinaria* and Lyra's *Postillae perpetuae in vetus et novum testamentum*.[96] Paul

---

[91] Siegfried Raeder, *Das Hebräische bei Luther: untersucht bis zum Ende der ersten Psalmenvorlesung* (Tübingen: J. C. B. Mohr (Paul Siebeck), 1961), 3.

[92] Raeder, *Das Hebräische*, 3–4. Raeder, *Die Benutzung*, 1–2. Concerning Lefèvre, see Vanderjagt, "*Ad fontes!*" 174–9.

[93] Raeder, *Die Benutzung*, 2, 81; Raeder makes many other references in this book. Burnett, "Martin Luther and Christian Hebraism." Burnett, "Reassessing," 186.

[94] Ch. 4 in this study explores Luther's use of inner-biblical interpretation.

[95] Luther's 1527 letter to Spalatin [WA BR 4:196–7 (§ 1099)] and his 1527 letter to Linck [WA BR 4:197–8 (§ 1100)] both show that he acquired the D-H. He also made marginal glosses on this translation. See Krause, *Studien*, 17. Luther also mentioned it in *Sendbrief vom Dolmetschen* [WA 30.2:640.28–32]. See Barthélemy, *Studies*, 165. Scholars have differing opinions as to what extent, if any, Luther adopted that translation for his own. Volz argues that in more than fifty examples, Luther did make use of it. See WA DB 11.2:cxiii–cxxxiii; the specific claim is at WA DB 11.2:cxxxi–cxxxii. See Barthélemy, *Studies*, 165 on this also. Krause, by contrast, argues that Luther did not follow the D-H, though he certainly consulted it. This is a major focus of Krause's study, and he examines this in many places in his study. See Krause, *Studien*, especially pp. 15–60. Krause also addresses earlier German translations (Mentel, Zainer, etc.), but says that it is unlikely that Luther used earlier German translations for his *Deutsche Bibel* edition of the Minor Prophets after 1524. Krause, *Studien*, 10. For more on this, see Stefan Michel, *Die Kanonisierung der Werke Martin Luthers im 16. Jahrhundert* (Tübingen: Mohr Siebeck, 2016), 33 Note 92.

[96] The *Glossa Ordinaria* contains many explanations of Hebrew words and passages. See

of Burgos's *Additiones 1–1100 ad postillam Nicolae de Lyra, Gen.-Apoc.* (Lyon, 1490) was also important and used by Luther.[97] Jewish commentaries, most prominently those of Rashi, also had a strong influence. Lyra in particular drew heavily on Rashi, as did Paul of Burgos, Lefèvre, and many others.[98] Through his extensive use of these resources, Luther implicitly drew upon Rashi as well. Rashi's commentary also appeared in Bomberg's Rabbinic Bible, which the Wittenberg team had on hand.[99] Furthermore, Jewish Psalms commentaries were ubiquitous in the sixteenth century and were utilized by Christian Hebraists in Luther's circle. Both David Kimhi's and Ibn Ezra's Psalms commentaries were particularly important, and both appeared as part of the Bomberg.[100] Specifically for the Minor Prophets, Luther certainly utilized Jerome's commentaries.[101] It is difficult to know for certain to what extent Luther directly consulted Jewish commentaries on these books, or whether he drew upon them solely through intermediary sources.[102] But he did cite them sometimes. For

---

Hailperin, *Rashi and the Christian Scholars* (Pittsburgh: University of Pittsburgh Press, 1963), 10. On Luther's use of the *Glossa Ordinaria* and Lyra's *Postillae*, see Mickey Leland Mattox, *"Defender of the Most Holy Matriarchs": Martin Luther's Interpretation of the Women in Genesis in the Enarrationes in Genesin, 1535–1545* (Leiden: Brill, 2003), 12–13. See also Erik Herrmann, "Luther's Absorption of Medieval Biblical Interpretation and his Use of the Church Fathers," in *The Oxford Handbook of Martin Luther's Theology*, ed. Robert Kolb, Irene Dingel, and L'ubomír Batka (Oxford: Oxford University Press, 2014), 71–90. Lyra's *Postillae* was included in some editions of the *Glossa Ordinaria*. Paul of Burgos's *Additiones 1–1100 ad postillam Nicolae de Lyra, Gen.-Apoc.* (Lyon, 1490), an addendum to Lyra's *Postillae*, is also important. Both appear in the 1508 Basel Vulgate, which Luther used, per Kenneth Hagen, *A Theology of Testament in the Young Luther: The Lectures on Hebrews* (Leiden: E. J. Brill, 1974), 16.

[97] This was Paul of Burgos's addendum to Lyra's *Postillae*. Raeder, "Exegetical and Hermeneutical," 368.

[98] On Lyra, see Hailperin, *Rashi and the Christian Scholars*; Benjamin Williams, "*Glossa Ordinaria* and *Glossa Hebraica*. Midrash in Rashi and the *Gloss*," *Traditio* 71 (2016): 179–201; and Deeana Copeland Klepper, *The Insight of Unbelievers: Nicholas of Lyra and Christian Reading of Jewish Text in the Later Middle Ages* (Philadelphia: University of Pennsylvania Press, 2007). On Lefèvre, see Vanderjagt, "*Ad fontes!*" 174–9. Rashi's commentaries on the Bible and the Talmud are revered among the Jewish people, and are among the most influential in the history of biblical commentary.

[99] Burnett, "Strange Career," 65, 68–69.

[100] Burnett, "Strange Career," 65, 68–69. David Kimhi's Psalms commentary only appears in the first edition of the Bomberg. Burnett includes a chart showing the commentaries that were included in Bomberg's first and second edition.

[101] Krause, *Studien*, 64. Concerning Jerome's use of Hebrew for his commentaries on the prophets, see Jerome, *Ancient Christian Texts: Commentaries on the Twelve Prophets. Vol. 1: Jerome*, ed. Thomas P. Scheck (Downer's Grove, IL: IVP Academic, 2016), especially the general introduction.

[102] Concerning the Hebrew and Aramaic skills of Christian Hebraists, see Burnett, "Strange Career," 77. Krause cautions that it is difficult to prove Luther's unmediated use of (untranslated from Hebrew) rabbinic commentaries for his Minor Prophets translation. He believes that Luther's encounters with them were by way of Lyra, Burgos, Reuchlin's *Rudimenta*, and the Rabbinic Bible. See Krause, *Studien*, 64–65, and especially Notes 6 and 9 for more on the dif-

example, in his commentary on Zechariah, he mentioned two Jewish commentaries: "Jonatha" (R. Yonatan ben Uziel, or Jonathan ben Uzziel) and "Onkel" (Onkelos); and he also mentioned the *Babylonian Targum*.[103] Lyra also compiled a *Postilla* on the Minor Prophets, which he based on Rashi's Minor Prophets commentary.[104] And both David Kimhi's and Ibn Ezra's commentaries on the Prophets (Former and Latter) appeared in the Bomberg.[105]

Lexicons and grammatical guides were immensely important resources for Luther and the Wittenberg team. Chief among these was Reuchlin's monumental *De rudimentis hebraicis* (Pforzheim, 1506), i.e. the *Rudimenta*.[106] The *Rudimenta* was modelled on R. David Kimhi's early thirteenth-century Hebrew grammar and lexicon, מכלול (*Mikhlol*).[107] It also drew upon his brother R. Moses Kimhi's (often called ReMaK, based on the acronym of his Hebrew

---

ficulties of definitively establishing Luther's direct use of rabbinic commentaries, even in later life. Others argue that Luther did use such sources. Freier argues for Luther's use of these in his Psalms translations, both directly, and through other sources such as Lyra. Freier, *Luthers Busspsalmen und Psalter*, especially pp. 107–8, though this is the focus of his entire study.

[103] Jonathan wrote the official *Babylonian Targum* on the prophets, usually referred to as *Targum Jonathan*. "Jonatha" was spelled without the final "n" of his name in Luther's commentary. Luther mentioned these two names in his reflections on Zech. 5:10–11. StL 14:1868.34-StL 14:1869.34; LW 20:245. See also Kirn, "Traces of Targum Reception," 271 [Kirn sites the WA 23 version]. See also Krause, *Studien*, 64–65. See also Luther's 1545 additions to Hosea 13, where there is evidence of indirect influence of the Pseudo Jonathan's *Jerusalem Targum*, through Reuchlin. WA 40.3:761 Note 5, following from Note 3. Kirn cites this, and discusses it in detail; in Kirn, "Traces of Targum Reception," 274–5.

[104] Herman Hailperin, "Nicolas de Lyra and Rashi: The Minor Prophets," in *Rashi Anniversary Volume*, ed. H. L. Ginsberg (New York: Jewish Publication Society, 1941), 115–47. For Rashi's commentary, Hailperin utilized *Parschandatha* [פרשנ-דתא]: *The Commentary on the Prophets and Hagiographs. Edited on the Basis of Several Manuscripts and Editions. Part I: The Minor Prophets*, ed. I. Maarsen (Amsterdam: Menno Hertzberger, 1930); Hailperin, "Nicolas de Lyra and Rashi," 121. For more on Rashi's commentaries, see also Avraham Grossman, "The School of Literal Jewish Exegesis in Northern France," in *Hebrew Bible/Old Testament: The History of Its Interpretation. Vol. 1: From the Beginnings to the Middle Ages (Until 1300). Pt. 2: The Middle Ages*, ed. Magne Sæbo (Göttingen: Vandenhoeck & Ruprecht, 2000), 332–46. Gustav Koffmane, though, argues that Luther was becoming more and more independent from Jerome and Lyra in his Minor Prophets interpretation; WA 13:xxxiv.

[105] Burnett, "Strange Career," 65, 68–69.

[106] For more on the *Rudimenta*, see: Price, *Johannes Reuchlin*, 68–74; Mesguich, "Early Christian Hebraists," 256–64; and Posset, *Johann Reuchlin*, especially pp. 251–85. Burnett advises that this was not the earliest printed Hebrew grammar available. (Aldus) Manutius of Adrianus introduction to Hebrew *Introductio perbrevis ad hebraicum linguam* (Venice, 1500) and Pellikan's *De modo legendi et intelligendi Hebraeum* (1504) preceded it. Burnett, "Reassessing," 185–6. Concerning Aldus Manutius, see also Bauch, "Die Einführung des Hebräischen in Wittenberg," 145, 332.

[107] Freier, *Luthers Busspsalmen und Psalter*, 103–4. Burnett, "Martin Luther and Christian Hebraism." Mesguich, "Early Christian Hebraists," 259. Concerning the printing history of the *Mikhlol*, see Shimeon Brisman, *History and Guide to Judaic Dictionaries and Concordances, Vol. 3, Pt. 1 of Jewish Research Literature* (Hoboken, NJ: KTAV, 2000), 26–27. Pagninus also published a translation of Kimhi's *Mikhlol* (Lyons, 1526); Burnett, "Reassessing," 186.

PRIMVS

q̃d translatio chaldaica oñdit traducēs בְּרָם פ׳ אוּלָם ut Nũeri xiiij. ubi legitur. Viuo ego & implebit gloria dñi uniuersa terra hebraica ueritas habet. & uere uiuo ego.

אוּלָם Palatium. uestibulũ porticus. ut .iii. Re. vi. Et porticus erat ante templum. xx. cubitorum.

אָוֶן Virtus. fortitudo. iniustitia. dolor. luctus. tristis. murmurãs. ut Iob. xviij. Artabunt gressus uirtutis eius. & eiusdē. xx. Filij eius attērent egestate et manus illius reddent ei dolorē suũ. sic infra. xxi. Deus seruabit filiis illius dolorē patris. Hęc omnia simul uoluit complecti Hieronymus cum Numeri. xi. pro מִתְאֹנְנִים traduxit murmur populi dolentium prę labore. & pro murmure specialiter ponit threnorũ. iij. Quid murmurauit homo uiuens.

אָוֶן Iniquitas. vanitas. Isaię. xxxij. Et cor eius faciet iniquitatem. pro quo. lxx. uana intelliget.

אוּץ Instanter hortatus est & coegit. ut Exodi. v. Prefecti q̃q̃ operum instabāt. i. festināt cogebāt. ubi ponit אָצִים & significat אָץ festinauit. ut Iosue. x. Stetit itaq̃ sol in medio cęli et nõ festinauit. oĩa eiuscemodi significata ad festinationem. impulsionem. oppressionē. tribulationem pertinent.

אוֹר Luxit a luceo. ut Geñ. xliiij. Pro eo q̃d apud nos legit. Et orto mane dimissi sunt cum asinis suis. hebraica ueritas habet. Mane lucescebat. & uiri dimissi sunt ipsi et asini eorũ. & p̄s. cxxxix. Et dixi forsitã tenebrę cõculcabunt me & nox illuminatio mea. q̃d hebraica ueritas sic habet. Et dixi forsitã tenebrę opperiēt me et nox luxit corã me. ubi ponit אוֹר. i. luxit. quod uolēs Symmachus imitari traduxit. et nox lux circũ me sedit. potest et rectius exponi. & nox illũinauit circa me. ponit ite in imperatiuo apud Isaiã. lx. אוֹרִי surge illuminare Ierl̄m. q̃d magis grammatice diceretur surge lucesce. atq̃ dictio Ierl̄m nõ ponit ĩ hebraico. sed in iterp̄tatione chaldaica Ionethę inuēit. deide in iã dicto uersu ponit et אוֹר. i. lux uel lumē. & a superiori uerbo transitiuũ secundũ deriuamus הֵאִיר. i. fecit lucere hoc est apparere. p̄s.

42

initials) late twelfth-century Hebrew grammar, מהלך שבילי הדעת (*Mahalakh Shevilei ha-Da'at*).¹⁰⁸ Luther utilized the *Rudimenta* prolifically, especially for his Psalms translations.¹⁰⁹ He also seems to have had some direct or indirect access to the Kimhis's texts. The records of the *Tischreden* ("Table Talk") record him praising their grammars as the "purest" and "best."¹¹⁰ Reuchlin published other important works for Christian Hebraists which incorporated grammar and lexical aids, including: *In septem psalmos poenitentiales hebraicos interpretatio* (Tübingen, 1512), as mentioned earlier; and *De accentibus et orthographia linguae Hebraicae* (Hagenau, 1518).¹¹¹ Reuchlin also had a copy of David Kimhi's commentary on the Prophets (Soncino, 1485), as well as what Price calls a "spectacular manuscript of the prophets from 1105 (*Codex Reuchlinianus* 3)," and a "rare manuscript of the ancient Aramaic paraphrase of the Prophets (the Targum of Jonathan)," all of which he acquired while in Rome. These works fed Reuchlin's Hebrew grammars and other related texts, which Luther and his team in turn used to support the *Deutsche Bibel* translation.¹¹²

Some of Luther's colleagues in Wittenberg also composed lexicons and grammars of their own. Matthäus Aurogallus's Hebrew grammar, *Compendium Hebreae Grammatices* (Wittenberg, 1523), was significant – he was the only member of Luther's inner circle to publish a grammar.¹¹³ Böschenstein, though only at Wittenberg a short time, produced twelve Hebrew books between 1514 and 1524, including *Hebraicae grammaticae institutiones* (Wittenberg, 1518).¹¹⁴ Mesguich says that it was directly inspired by the *Rudimenta*, some parts copied word for word.¹¹⁵ And Adrianus, also only at Wittenberg for a short time, wrote a Hebrew grammar and published other Hebrew books.¹¹⁶

---

¹⁰⁸ Burnett, "Martin Luther and Christian Hebraism." Mesguich, "Early Christian Hebraists," 259. David Kimhi's ספר השורשים (*Sefer ha-Shorashim*) was the lexical part of the מכלול (*Mikhlol*).

¹⁰⁹ Siegfried Raeder discusses this extensively. See: Raeder, *Das Hebräische*; Raeder, *Die Benutzung*; Raeder, *Grammatica Theologica: Studien zu Luthers Operationes in Psalmos* (Tübingen: J. C. B. Mohr (Paul Siebeck), 1977); Raeder, "Exegetical and Hermeneutical," 397.

¹¹⁰ "Die reinsten und besten Grammaticos." WA TR 1:525.37–41 [§ 1040].

¹¹¹ Mesguich, "Early Christian Hebraists," 256–64.

¹¹² See Price, *Johannes Reuchlin*, 66. See also Wolfgang von Abel and Reimund Leicht, *Verzeichnis der Hebraica in der Bibliothek Johannes Reuchlins* (Ostfildern: Jan Thorbecke, 2005); Price cites 97–103, 203–6 in Abel and Leicht concerning Reuchlin's possession of these texts.

¹¹³ Burnett, "Strange Career," 71. Thank you to Prof. Dr. Stephen Burnett, University of Nebraska-Lincoln, for the guidance concerning the importance of Aurogallus's grammar for Luther, in contrast to Böschenstein's and Adrianus's.

¹¹⁴ Burnett, "Christian Hebrew Printing in the Sixteenth Century: Printers, Humanism and the Impact of the Reformation," *Helmantica: Revista de Filología Clásica y Hebrea* 51 (2000): 29.

¹¹⁵ Mesguich, "Early Christian Hebraists," 261.

¹¹⁶ He never published the grammar, though. See Vanderjagt, "*Ad fontes!*" 182–3. See also Burnett, "Reassessing," 187.

Other important Hebrew lexicons and grammars which Luther and his Wittenberg team had at their disposal include: Pellikan's *De modo legendi et intelligendi Hebraeum* (Strasbourg, 1504); W. F. Capito's Hebrew grammar *Institutiuncula in Hebraeam Linguam* (Basel, 1516), reissued as *Hebraicarum Institutionum Libri Duo* (Basel, 1518; Strasbourg, 1525); and Erasmus's *Instrumentum: Novum instrumentum omne, diligenter ab Erasmo Roterdamo recognitum ... una cum Annotationibus* (Basel, 1516), his New Testament translation with annotations that included Hebrew references.[117] Levita composed a number of very influential works: *Sefer ha-Baḥur*, which appeared in a 1517 (Rome) edition for Jews, and a 1525 (Basel) edition that included an introduction for Christians; *Pirqei Eliyahu* (Pesaro, 1520); *Sefer ha-Harkava* (Basel, 1525); and *Masoret ha-Masoret* (Venice, 1538), reprinted by Sebastian Münster (Basel, 1539).[118] Santes Pagninus's *Enchiridion expositionis vocabulorum Haruch* (Rome, 1523), his translation of David Kimhi's *Mikhlol* (Lyons, 1526), and his *Thesaurus linguae sanctae lexicon Hebraicum* (Lyons, 1529) were all important for the period.[119] And Sebastian Münster published numerous works, including his Hebrew dictionary, *ʿArukh ha-Shorashim, Dictionarium hebraicum* (Basel, 1523); his Aramaic dictionary, *Dictionarium chaldaicum* (Basel, 1527); and his *Chaldaica grammatica antehac a nemine attentata ...* (Basel, 1527) – the first Aramaic grammar written in Latin for Christians.[120]

Finally, polyglot Bibles and polyglot books of the Bible were important resources for Luther and his Wittenberg team.[121] They almost certainly used the Complutensian Polyglot (Alcalá de Henares, 1514–17), the first printed polyglot edition of the complete Bible.[122] Barthélemy suggests that to supplement

---

[117] Burnett, "Reassessing," 186. Mesguich, "Early Christian Hebraists." 265–6, 268. R. Gerald Hobbs, "Pluriformity of Early Reformation Scriptural Interpretation," in *Hebrew Bible/Old Testament: The History of Its Interpretation. Vol. 2: From the Renaissance to the Enlightenment*, ed. Magne Sæbo (Göttingen: Vandenhoeck & Ruprecht, 2008), 458. Krause, *Studien*, 65 Note 12. Raeder, *Die Benutzung*, especially pp. 6–11. Raeder based his identification of Erasmus on Hebrew citations that Erasmus utilized in his New Testament annotations, which Raeder argues influenced Luther. Raeder based his identification of Reuchlin and Pellikan on his previous study, *Das Hebräische bei Luther*.

[118] Mesguich, "Early Christian Hebraists," 272–5. Burnett, *Christian Hebraism in the Reformation Era*, 190. Brisman, *History and Guide*, 50–53.

[119] Krause, *Studien*, 65 Note 12. Stephen G. Burnett, "The Targum in Christian Scholarship to 1800," in *A Jewish Targum in a Christian World*, ed. Alberdina Houtman, Eveline van Staalduine-Sulman, and Hans-Martin Kirn (Leiden: Brill, 2014), 256–7. Burnett, "Reassessing," 186.

[120] Krause, *Studien*, 65 Note 12. Mesguich, "Early Christian Hebraists," 268–72. Burnett, "The Targum," 257. Burnett, "Christian Aramaism," 425.

[121] A polyglot is a Bible printed in multiple languages, usually arranged in columns.

[122] For more on the Complutensian, see Adrian Schenker, "From the First Printed Hebrew, Greek and Latin Bibles to the First Polyglot Bible, the Complutensian Polyglot: 1477–1517," in *Hebrew Bible/Old Testament: The History of Its Interpretation. Vol. 2: From the Renaissance to the Enlightenment*, ed. Magne Sæbo (Göttingen: Vandenhoeck & Ruprecht, 2008), 286–91. See also Burnett, "Christian Hebrew Printing."

Reuchlin's *Rudimenta*, Luther used Alphonso of Zamora's *Vocabularium hebraicum totius veteris testamenti cum aliis dictionibus chaldaicis ibi contentis*, which was included in Volume 6 of the Complutensian Polyglot.[123] Agostino Giustiniani's polyglot Psalter (Genoa, 1516), the first polyglot printed portion of the Bible, was also especially important for Christian Hebraists of the time, and likely consulted by Luther and others at Wittenberg.[124]

Short note should be made of non-Hebrew Bibles, because these clearly played a role in Luther's translation of the Minor Prophets, as he weighed the Hebrew with the Latin, Greek, and German. Luther was not the first to translate the Bible into German. The oldest preserved German translation of a part of the New Testament comes from the eighth century; and of the Old Testament, from the tenth century.[125] At least twenty-two printed German Bibles were available prior to Luther's *Deutsche Bibel*.[126] Of these, the Mentel (Strasbourg, 1466) and Zainer (Augsburg, 1475) were the most influential for the time.[127] Nevertheless,

---

[123] Barthélemy, *Studies*, 163. For more on the Zamora and the Complutenesian, see Rosa Helena Chinchilla, "The Complutensian Polyglot Bible (1520) and the Political Ramifications of Biblical Translation," in *La traducción en España: ss. XIV–XVI*, ed. Roxana Recio (León: Universidad de León, 1995), 169–90. See also Theodor Dunkelgrün, "The Hebrew Library of a Renaissance Humanist. Andreas Masius and the Bibliography to his *Iosuae Imperatoris Historia* (1574), with a Latin Edition and an Annotated English Translation," *Studia Rosenthaliana* 42–43 (2010–11): 213–4.

[124] Burnett, "Reassessing," 188. Burnett, "Luther and Christian Hebraism." See also Kirn, "Traces of Targum Reception," 266, 270.

[125] Reu, *Luther's German Bible*, 20–21. The Monsee Fragments contain parts of the book of Matthew translated into *Althochdeutsch* ("Old High German"). *Althochdeutsch* is the earliest period of the German language (approximately 700–1050). It is followed by *Mittelhochdeutsch* ("Middle High German," approximately 1050–1350); *Frühneuhochdeutsch* ("Early New High German," approximately 1350–1650); and *Neuhochdeutsch* ("New High German," approximately 1650 – present). These are rough guidelines, and opinions vary concerning specific divisions between the periods. See *The Monsee Fragments. Newly Collated Text with Introduction, Notes, Grammatical Treatise, and Exhaustive Glossary and a Photo-Lithographic Fac-Simile*, ed. George Allison Hench (Strassburg: Karl. J. Trübner, 1890), especially pp. 139–42 for a summary of Hench's analysis. Erroll F. Rhodes also mentions fragments of a Gothic version of the Bible in the fourth century. Rhodes, "Medieval Versions," in *The Oxford Companion to the Bible*, ed. Bruce M. Metzger and Michael D. Coogan (New York: Oxford University Press, 1993), 757.

[126] Andrew C. Gow, "The Contested History of a Book: The German Bible of the Later Middle Ages and Reformation in Legend, Ideology, and Scholarship," *Journal of Hebrew Scriptures* 9 (2009): 9. Reu cites "no less than" fourteen printed High German and four Low German Bibles which preceded Luther's. Reu, *Luther's German Bible*, 27. Heinz Bluhm provides the same numbers. Bluhm, *Martin Luther: Creative Translator* (St. Louis: Concordia Publishing House, 1965), 97. See also Heinz Bluhm, *Studies in Luther – Luther Studien* (Bern: Peter Lang, 1987), 110.

[127] The 1466 Mentel (Strassburg, ca. 1466) was the first printed High German Bible. Reu, *Luther's German Bible*, 27–28. Some record the Mentel as 1465 rather than 1466. See Heinz Bluhm, *Luther Translator of Paul: Studies in Romans and Galatians* (New York: Peter Lang, 1984), 31. For a thorough overview of the German Bibles which preceded Luther's, see Reu, *Luther's German Bible*, especially pp. 19–54.

the German in these Bibles was so poor that they likely had little meaningful impact on Luther.[128] Luther likely used a Vulgate similar to the 1506–08 Basel edition.[129] He certainly used the LXX, and cited it periodically in his exegesis of the Minor Prophets, though relatively infrequently compared to the Vulgate. Krause counts thirty times that Luther mentioned the LXX in his exegesis of the Minor Prophets.[130] Scholars suggest that the version Luther used was one or both of: the Greek portion of the Complutensian Polyglot (Alcalá, 1517); and the Aldine (Venice, 1518).[131]

The literary resources that Luther, his Wittenberg team, and their extended circle had access to for their Hebrew translation were far more than what has been outlined here. Nevertheless, this overview provides a good picture of those which are most frequently noted by scholars, and most likely to have been used by Luther, his team, and their extended network.[132] An indispensable reference

---

[128] Bluhm, *Creative*, 4–5, 15. Stephan Füssel, *The Book of Books: The Luther Bible of 1534. A Cultural-Historical Introduction* (Köln: Taschen, 2003), 15.

[129] Hagen, *A Theology of Testament*, 16. Reu suggests that Luther used the 1509 Basel Vulgate. Reu, *Luther's German Bible*, 149. For a fairly thorough discussion of the history of Latin Bibles and their significance for Luther's Bible, see Reu, *Luther's German Bible*, 5–19. For this study, I have consulted: *Textus biblie cu[m] Glosa ordinaria Nicolai de Lyra postilla, Mortalitatibus eiusdem, Pauli Burgensis Additio[n]ibus, Matthie Thoring Replicis Prima [-Sexta] pars*. 6 vols. (Basel: Johann Froben, Johann Petri für Johann Amerbach, 1506–08) [Cambridge University Library, classmark Sel.2.3–8], hereafter referred to as *Textus biblie* (Basel, 1506–08).

[130] Krause, *Studien*, 64. In addition, Krause emphasizes that Jerome's prophets commentary, which quotes the LXX in Latin, was also an important source for Luther's drawing upon the LXX.

[131] Krause, *Studien*, 63–64, and Note 5 (p. 63). Barthélemy, *Studies*, 164. Reu says it was probably the 1518 Venice edition. Reu, *Luther's German Bible*, 185. Samuel Prideaux Tregelles calls the Aldine (Venice, 1518) "the first text of the LXX which obtained a wide and general currency." Tregelles, *An Account of the Printed Text of the Greek New Testament: With Remarks on its Revision upon Critical Principles* (London: Samuel Bagster and Sons, 1854), 185.

[132] For more on Luther's Bible translation, the introductions to the relevant volumes in the *Weimarer Ausgabe* contain a wealth of information. Many studies in the twentieth and twenty-first centuries have examined Luther's Bible translation in depth. Some of the most excellent are: Otto Reichert, *D. Martin Luthers Deutsche Bibel* (Tübingen: J. C. B. Mohr (Paul Siebeck), 1910); Wilhelm Walther, *Luthers Deutsche Bibel: Festschrift zur Jahrhundertfeier der Reformation* (Berlin: Ernst Siegfried Mittler und Sohn, 1918); Adolf Risch, "Luthers Bibelverdeutschung," *Schriften des Vereins für Reformationsgeschichte* 40 (1922):1–82; Emanuel Hirsch, *Luthers deutsche Bibel. Ein Beitrag zur Frage ihrer Durchsicht* (München: Kaiser, 1928); Reu, *Luther's German Bible*; Bluhm, *Creative*; and Volz, *Martin Luthers deutsche Bibel*. Key studies of Luther's exegesis include: Meissinger, *Luthers Exegese in der Frühzeit*; Karl Holl, "Luthers Bedeutung für den Fortschritt der Auslegungskunst," in *Gesammelte Aufsätze zur Kirchengeschichte. Vol. 1: Luther*, 6th rev. ed. [compiled volume by Holl] (Tübingen: J. C. B. Mohr (Paul Siebeck), 1932), 544–82; Gerhard Ebeling, "Die Anfänge von Luthers Hermeneutik," *Zeitschrift für Theologie und Kirche* 48 (1951): 172–230; Jaroslav Pelikan, *Luther the Expositor: Introduction to the Reformer's Exegetical Writings* (St. Louis: Concordia Publishing House, 1959) [included as a companion volume to LW]; A. Skevington Wood, *Captive to the Word. Martin Luther: Doctor of Sacred Scripture* (Exeter: Paternoster Press,

work on this subject is Sachiko Kusukawa's 1536 catalog of the Wittenberg University library.[133] While it ultimately only provides a snapshot of the resources available at that library in 1536, nevertheless it is the most comprehensive compilation to date. The catalog includes twenty-eight Hebrew works.[134]

Current State of Scholarship Concerning Luther's Hebrew[135]

Scholarly attention to Luther's Hebrew dates back to his own day. The reflections of Johannes Mathesius, Georg Rörer, and many others in his circle are invaluable for understanding the role of the language in his *Deutsche Bibel* translation. In the nineteenth century, a number of brief analyses of Luther's Hebrew appeared as part of broader works examining his Bible translation, which paved the way for the work that followed. Heinrich Bindseil (1848–55), Christian Ginsburg (1861), Carl Siegfried (1869), and Hermann Platzhoff (1887) are among the many from this century who addressed Luther's Hebrew translation and exegesis in important, albeit circumscribed ways.[136] But it was in the early twentieth century that the greatest advancements into understanding Luther's

---

1969); and Heinrich Bornkamm, *Luther und das Alte Testament* (Tübingen: Mohr, 1948). Additional books, which focus on specialty areas [for example, Mattox's and Maxfield's studies on Luther's interpretation of Genesis], are too many to mention in this space.

[133] Sachiko Kusukawa, *A Wittenberg University Library Catalogue of 1536* (Cambridge: LP Publications, 1995). Thank you to Prof. Dr. Kusukawa, University of Cambridge, for our conversation and your insight on the Wittenberg library.

[134] Kusukawa, *Catalogue*, 1–3. This tally includes duplicate copies of some Hebrew works which were in the library. Many of the works mentioned in this chapter section appear in that 1536 list, including: Kimhi's commentaries on the Minor Prophets [Amos (1531), and Joel and Malachi (1530)]; the second edition Bomberg Bible (1525); Münster's *Dictionarium chaldaicum* (1527); Münster's *Hebraica Biblia Latina* (1534); Pagninus's *Thesaurus linguae sanctae lexicon Hebraicum* (1529); Capito's *Hebraicarum Institutionum Libri Duo* (1518); Münster's *Chaldaica grammatica* (1527); Münster's *Dictionarium hebraicum* (1539; perhaps a reprint of the 1523); and Reuchlin's *De accentibus et orthographia linguae Hebraicae* (1518).

[135] "Hebrew" and "Hebrew Bible" are often used interchangeably throughout this study. Arguments and speculation abound concerning whether, in particular cases, Luther was consulting the Hebrew Bible directly, or the Hebrew through secondary sources. These discussions are, for the most part, beyond the scope of this study and thus only addressed as relevant for particular points.

[136] Heinrich Ernst Bindseil and Hermann Agathon Niemeyer, *Dr. Martin Luthers Bibelübersetzung nach der letzten Original-Ausgabe*, 7 vols. (Halle: Druck und Verlag der Canstein'schen Bibel-Anstalt, 1848–55), cited by Freier, *Luthers Busspsalmen und Psalter*, 3. Christian D. Ginsburg, *Coheleth: Commonly Called the Book of Ecclesiastes. Translated from the Original Hebrew, with a Commentary, Historical and Critical* (London: Longman, Green, Longman, and Roberts, 1861). [Carl] Siegfried, "Raschi's Einfluss auf Nicolaus von Lira und Luther in der Auslegung der Genesis," *Archiv für wissenschaftliche Erforschung des Alten Testamentes* (1869): 428–56. Hermann Platzhoff, *Luthers erste Psalmenübersetzung sprachwissenschaftlich untersucht* (PhD diss., Universität Halle, 1887), cited by Theodor Pahl in Pahl, *Quellenstudien zu Luthers Psalmenübersetzung* (Weimar: Böhlau, 1931), vii.

Hebrew emerged. Here, a prodigious number of monographs, biographies, essays, and other theological analyses of Luther and medieval Christian and Jewish Hebraism make mention of his Hebrew translation work. The list is so long that it would likely take a volume itself to note every one.[137] But the frequent appearance of the subject creates a misleading impression of the current state of knowledge. Only a few studies have, in fact, examined Luther's Hebrew in any comprehensive manner – "comprehensive" meaning an examination which makes his Hebrew translation either the sole or a major focus, which is of substantial length and insight, and which has had a significant impact on subsequent studies by other scholars. This select body of scholarly work provides a good picture of the current state of knowledge on Luther's Hebrew.

Karl Meissinger included a section on Luther's Hebrew in his 1911 study of Luther's early biblical exegesis.[138] This work was an early standard for the field and remains a classic. Meissinger examined the relationship – both direct and through secondary sources – between Luther's Bible and the Hebrew Bible.[139] He argued for the integral role of the Hebrew language in Luther's Bible interpretation, and suggested that his private studies of Hebrew extended further than his lectures might suggest.[140] Meissinger was at times critical of Luther's Hebrew, but also argued that while he occasionally failed in the grammar, his language sense was nevertheless "ingeniously unscientific [*genial unwissenschaftliche*]."[141] While this analysis of Luther's Hebrew was an important part of his investigation into Luther's early biblical exegesis, it nevertheless was not extensive enough to make the major advances in the field of knowledge which studies that followed did. The examples that Meissinger examined were limited in number and scope, and, with minor exceptions, strictly focused on the Psalms. Thus, the lasting value today for understanding Luther's Hebrew, while still important, is limited.

Moritz Freier (1917) investigated Luther's sources for his 1517 and 1525 translations of the Hebrew Penitential Psalms, as well as his 1528 and 1531

---

[137] These works include: Johannes Ficker, *Hebräische Handpsalter Luthers* (Heidelberg: Carl Winters Universitätsbuchhandlung, 1919); and Walter Koenig, "Luther as a Student of Hebrew," *Concordia Theological Monthly* 24 (1953): 845–53. Thyen addresses Luther's Hebrew translations in various places in Thyen, "Luthers Jesajavorlesung." Volz (1957) provides a summary of Luther's Hebrew Handpsalter in "Hebräische Handpsalter Luthers," WA DB 10.2:290–349. In this summary, he says that Luther's Psalms citations in his lectures on the Book of Hebrews (1517–18) provide the first certain evidence of Luther's use of the Hebrew Bible. WA DB 10.2:292–3. Raeder also cites this in *Die Benutzung*, 1. In a more recent book, John F. Brug includes a short section with examples and discussion of Luther's Hebrew translation; Brug, *Textual Criticism of the Old Testament: Principles and Practice*, 2nd printing (Mequon, WI: Chesed VeEmet Publishing, 2014), 92–106.
[138] Meissinger, *Luthers Exegese in der Frühzeit*.
[139] Meissinger, *Luthers Exegese in der Frühzeit*, especially pp. 54–75.
[140] Meissinger, *Luthers Exegese in der Frühzeit*, 62.
[141] Meissinger, *Luthers Exegese in der Frühzeit*, 63–4.

translations of the full Hebrew Psalter.[142] He painstakingly analyzed and compared Luther's German translations, the protocol revision records, Jerome, Reuchlin, the Vulgate, Lyra, Pagninus, and various Jewish and rabbinic translations and commentaries, including the 1494 Brescia Hebrew Bible, Targums, Mishna, David Kimhi, Rashi, and Ibn Ezra. He argued that in a great number of places, Luther's translation of the Psalms can be traced back to Jewish commentaries.[143] Moreover, he argued that Luther often drew upon Jewish sources without even recognizing it, through his use of Lyra and Reuchlin.[144]

Freier's analysis was exhaustive. He used a wealth of examples to show both where Luther agreed with and disagreed with rabbinic material, and from this demonstrated where he believed Luther was using Jewish commentaries as sources. His investigation, however, is flawed insofar as it is often difficult to surmise with certainty, in the absence of explicit comment by Luther, which rabbis or other commentaries he actually consulted. Moreover, Freier was not always clear on why he chose particular rabbinic material for each case study. In the examples where he cited only Ibn Ezra, for instance, was this because he had some evidence that Luther *only* consulted Ibn Ezra for those translations, or could Luther have examined additional rabbinic sources? Freier did not say, and thus, one is left to speculate. He ultimately conceded that it is difficult to know for certain how often Luther's team consulted these sources.[145] Consequently, while Freier's analysis was groundbreaking and examined a unique facet of Luther's Hebrew translation, in and of itself it is insufficient, and additional research in this area of Luther's Hebrew is still needed.

Hans Schmidt's (1926) study of Luther's translation of Ps. 46 was also groundbreaking, albeit short.[146] Heinz Bluhm called it "the only one of its kind" because at the time, it was the only close analysis of Luther's translation of a single Psalm.[147] Schmidt elucidated how Luther considered the Hebrew text for his translation of the Psalm, comparing and contrasting his German translations (1524) and revisions (1531, 1539–41) with the Vulgate, the LXX, and the German Bible translations that preceded his – namely the 1466 Mentel and 1483 Roberger.[148] He used this information to show where Luther broke from other

---

[142] This was Moritz Freier's doctoral dissertation (1916), published as Freier, *Luthers Busspsalmen und Psalter: Kritische Untersuchung nach jüdischen und lateinischen Quellen* (Gräfenhainichen: C. Schulze and Co., 1917). I have used the subsequently published edition (Leipzig: J. C. Hinrichs, 1918). The Bußpsalmen are Ps. 6, 32, 38, 51, 102, 130, and 143, named so since Cassiodorus's sixth century commentary.
[143] Freier, *Luthers Busspsalmen und Psalter*, 119.
[144] Freier, *Luthers Busspsalmen und Psalter*, 107–8.
[145] Freier, *Luthers Busspsalmen und Psalter*, 114.
[146] Hans Schmidt, "Luthers Übersetzung des 46. Psalms," *Luther-Jahrbuch* 8 (1926): 98–119.
[147] Bluhm, *Creative*, 104.
[148] Schmidt gave special attention to Luther's copy of the Vulgate, which he printed in 1513 for his Psalms lectures, and where he sometimes made notes concerning certain words.

translations and to demonstrate the role of direct engagement with Hebrew in his translation. He also compared Luther's earlier translations of Ps. 46 (including his 1513 Vulgate glosses), where he at times interpreted against the Hebrew Bible, to later revisions where he amended his translation to agree with the Hebrew text, thus showing additional evidence of the role of Hebrew in his translation of the Psalm.

Like Meissinger, Schmidt saw limits to Luther's mastery of the Hebrew, but also praised his "truly ingenious 'Germanizing' of the difficult text [*wahrhaft genial 'Verdeutschung' des schwierigen Textes*]."[149] Schmidt overreached, however, in some places in his final assessment. For example, when he evaluated Luther's German translation against the Vulgate, LXX, and Mentel Bible, he contended that Luther *only* made allowance for the Hebrew text; and in another place, that he "fully freed himself from the Vulgate" and "gave his complete attention to the Hebrew wording."[150] Perhaps it was merely a poor choice of words; but unfortunately, this remains a common claim in discussions of Luther's Bible translation even today. No matter what Luther's "final" decision – final in quotations as he would most certainly still be revising his Bible were he alive today – his comments across the corpus of his exegetical remarks, quite clearly in the Minor Prophets, show that he always was weighing multiple translation considerations. He never translated based on consultation of the Hebrew Bible alone, even if he rejected the Vulgate as incorrect or less than ideal in a particular place. Moreover, as this study will show, he sometimes changed his mind on his assessments of the Vulgate against the Hebrew Bible. The other main shortcoming of Schmidt's study, as with those which preceded his, is its exclusive focus on the Psalms. Nevertheless, it still made strides in illuminating Luther's translation of Ps. 46, the role of the Hebrew in that translation, and thus made a unique addition to scholarship for the time.

In a 1931 study, Theodor Pahl examined Luther's translation of the Hebrew Psalter, dividing his analysis into three segments: the pre-1524 Psalms translations; the 1524 German Psalter; and the 1531 revisions. Pahl argued that Luther's Hebrew skills developed noticeably over the course of the Psalms revisions. Moreover, he contended that not only was Luther unmistakably using the Hebrew Bible rather than secondary sources in particular places; but more importantly, as his skills progressed, he would only use Jerome and the Vulgate periodically as support for particularly difficult issues.[151] Pahl argued that the

---

[149] Schmidt, "Luthers Übersetzung," 111.

[150] Schmidt, "Luthers Übersetzung," 112, 119. "Daß er wiederum nur den hebraeischen Text beruecksichtigt" (p. 112); "daß er sich von der Vulgata innerlich beim Uebersetzen voellig frei gemacht hat" (p. 119).

[151] Pahl, *Quellenstudien zu Luthers Psalmenübersetzung*, 19. Luther's comments on the Minor Prophets suggest that this is not so. He was continuously consulting and weighing various pieces of information and numerous translations for his German Bible translation of the Minor Prophets.

period between 1518 and 1521 was especially crucial for Luther's improvement.[152] He found drastic changes over the course of Luther's subsequent revisions, asserting that by 1524, he "achieved a virtuosity in the mastery of Hebrew [*eine Virtuosität in der Beherrschung des Hebräischen erreicht*]."[153] As part of his analysis, Pahl explicitly contested Freier's (1917) findings, arguing that in various Psalms translations he either saw no evidence of Luther's personal use of Jewish commentaries, or that Luther more probably used Latin sources, particularly given the challenges of the unpointed Hebrew texts from the Targum, Rashi, David Kimhi, Ibn Ezra, etc.[154] Pahl's study was thorough, and made an important challenge to Freier's work by pointing out the shortcomings in evidence and method, and thus exposing the need for further study of Luther's Hebrew translation. Moreover, his investigation provided a more robust understanding of Luther's sources for his Psalms translations, especially illuminating the relationship between his Psalter and the Hebrew Bible.[155]

One scholar stands head and shoulders above all others to date who have examined Luther's Hebrew, and this is Siegfried Raeder. The centerpiece of this work is his trilogy of studies on Luther's translation of the Hebrew Psalter (1961, 1967, and 1977).[156] All three books emanate from his Ph.D. dissertation, which was published as the first piece in the series: *Das Hebräische bei Luther: untersucht bis zum Ende der ersten Psalmenvorlesung* (1961).[157] In this first study, Raeder investigated Luther's Hebrew translation up to the end of his first lectures on the Psalms, the *Dictata super Psalterium* (1513–15).[158] He began with a general discussion of Luther's translation, followed by an analysis of various facets of Hebrew and how Luther addressed each. These included: Hebrew nouns, verbs, and prepositions, as well as various stylistic elements. Based on his analysis, Raeder argued that in 1513–15, Luther's interpretation of Hebrew was for the most part exclusively informed by secondary sources, and that only in very few cases could he discern a direct influence of the original Hebrew text (i. e., the Hebrew Bible).[159] In his view, Luther was thus dependent almost entirely on extrinsic authorities in relation to Hebrew during the time of the *Dictata*.

---

[152] Pahl, *Quellenstudien zu Luthers Psalmenübersetzung*, 127.
[153] Pahl, *Quellenstudien zu Luthers Psalmenübersetzung*, 128.
[154] Pahl, *Quellenstudien zu Luthers Psalmenübersetzung*, 128–9. Pahl tempers his criticism, though, arguing that Melanchthon, Aurogallus, and other members of Luther's circle may have been familiar with Jewish commentaries.
[155] Pahl, *Quellenstudien zu Luthers Psalmenübersetzung*, especially pp. vii–viii.
[156] See also Raeder, "Exegetical and Hermeneutical," 363–406.
[157] Raeder, *Das Hebräische*.
[158] See WA 3 [full volume]; WA 4:1–462.
[159] Raeder, *Das Hebräische*, 3. Raeder, *Die Benutzung*, 10–11. Raeder was looking back from his second book, summarizing his previous work. Raeder also suggests that Luther's Latin exegetical remarks, themselves often embedded in theological discourse, make it very difficult to say with certainty whether he used the Hebrew Bible for certain translations. Raeder, *Das Hebräische*, 217.

In Raeder's 1967 follow-up, *Die Benutzung des masoretischen Textes bei Luther in der Zeit zwischen der ersten und zweiten Psalmenvorlesung (1515–1518)*, he moved on to investigate a more specialized problem: how, in contrast to the *Dictata*, in the following years leading up to Luther's next major lectures on the Psalms, his independent use of the Hebrew Bible grew and his Hebrew skills progressed.[160] He did this by examining Luther's translations for evidence of his use of the Hebrew Bible, where secondary sources could not have been the sole authority for Luther's translations and interpretations.[161] Raeder focused on Luther's interpretation of Hebrew in: his lectures on Romans (1515–16); various work on the Psalms, specifically in 1516; the 1516–17 lectures on Galatians; his 1517 work on *Die sieben Bußpsalmen*; his 1517–18 lectures on Hebrews; the 1518 lectures on Ps. 110; and his 1517–18 sermons. He gave special attention to the following secondary sources: Reuchlin's *De rudimentis Hebraicis* (1506) and *Septem Psalmi poenitentiales Hebraici cum grammatica Latina* (1512); Pellikan's *De modo legendi et intelligendi Hebraeum* (1504); and Erasmus's *Instrumentum: Novum instrumentum omne, diligener ab Erasmo Roterdamo recognitum ... una cum Annotationibus* (1516).[162]

Raeder argued that he saw Luther using the Hebrew Bible more and more over the period between the *Dictata* and the 1519–21 Psalms lectures. He assessed that through his use of the text, Luther "gradually freed himself from the incidental limits of a knowledge that was based on extrinsic authorities."[163] This conclusion supported his supposition at the beginning of his first study that there was a noticeable gap between the *Dictata*, where the evidence suggests that Luther had used the Hebrew Bible very little, and the *Operationes*, where he found the opposite; and moreover, of what in Luther's own words was "far and wide different [*longe lateque diversa*]" from the *Dictata*.[164] This progress, Raeder argued, was made possible by Luther's systematic study of the Hebrew Bible, which could not be explained by the secondary sources.[165] Raeder also provided numerous pieces of evidence that the Hebrew Bible that Luther used

---

[160] Raeder, *Grammatica Theologica*, 4. Raeder was looking back from his third book, summarizing his previous work.

[161] Raeder, *Die Benutzung*, especially pp. 6–11.

[162] Raeder, *Die Benutzung*, especially pp. 6–11, 17–19. Raeder based his selection of Reuchlin and Pellikan on his previous study, *Das Hebräische bei Luther*. He based his selection of Erasmus on the influence that he believed certain writings of his had on Luther: Erasmus's citation of Hebrew in Ex. 33:19 in his annotations on Rom. 9:15, and Erasmus's citation of Hebrew in Is. 52:7 in his annotations on Rom. 10:15.

[163] "Befreit [er] sich allmählich von den zufälligen Grenzen eines Wissens, das sich auf fremde Autoritäten stützt." Raeder, *Grammatica Theologica*, 4. Raeder was looking back from his third book, summarizing his previous work.

[164] WA 5:22.37–38. Raeder cites this in: Raeder, *Die Benutzung*, 10 and Raeder, *Grammatica Theologica*, 303.

[165] Raeder, *Die Benutzung*, especially pp. 10, 81–93. Raeder, *Grammatica Theologica*, 303.

was the 1494 Brescia printing, including Hebrew pointing in the Brescia which did not match other sources; and various hand markings [*Tintenflecke*, "spots of ink"] in the Brescia, which he argued was evidence of someone meticulously working with the text.[166]

This insight to a large extent mirrors Pahl's conclusion. It suggests that as Luther grew in confidence – be it in his own abilities or with that of his broader translation team – he increasingly consulted the Hebrew Bible and saw less and less of a need for secondary aids. While Raeder's second study was far more circumscribed than his first, it still was an important and valuable addition, and broadened the time frame from his first book. On the other hand, this study mirrored a shortcoming in Freier's investigation. Despite all of the evidence that Raeder provided to discount Luther's use of certain secondary sources for his Hebrew translation, his use of additional secondary sources which Raeder did not make note of cannot be ruled out.

Raeder completed his threefold investigation of Luther's work in the Psalms in 1977 with *Grammatica Theologica: Studien zu Luthers Operationes in Psalmos*.[167] He took the title for this book from the heading that Luther included in his lecture notes, which introduced his exegesis of Psalm 1:2: "*Grammatica Theologica*."[168] In this final study, Raeder moved on to examine the impact of Hebrew in the next period in Luther's life: his final lectures on the Psalms, the *Operationes in Psalmos* (1519–21).[169] He divided the book into two sections: (1) an investigation of the hermeneutical function of Hebrew for Luther in the *Operationes*, in contrast to his translation work prior to the *Operationes* (i. e. the subject of Raeder's two preceding volumes); and (2) an investigation of the theological impact of Hebrew for Luther, which he further segmented as: (a) an examination of Ps. 4, 14, and 17; and (b) an examination of the influence of various Hebrew terms on Luther's understanding of three specific biblical concepts: *denken* ("to think"), *handeln* ("to act, deal with, treat [something]"), and *Kraft* ("strength, power").

Through a colossal inventory of examples, Raeder demonstrated how Luther's progress from the time of the *Dictata* to the *Operationes* was a direct result of his expanded use of the Hebrew Bible, and his improved Hebrew competency.[170] The final section of the book is an especially valuable scholarly

---

[166] Raeder, *Die Benutzung*, 86–93. Hebrew "pointing" refers to the voweling marks that appear in the Masoretic Text. Scholars generally believe that the original texts of the Hebrew Bible were unpointed.

[167] Raeder, *Grammatica Theologica*.

[168] WA 5:32.19. Luther also mentioned this idea in his interpretation of the first Psalm: "*Zuerst wollen wir auf das Grammatische achten, das ist das wahrhaft Theologische.*" WA 5:27.8. Raeder cites this in *Grammatica Theologica*, 34.

[169] Raeder, *Grammatica Theologica*, 4–5. The *Operationes* covered only Ps. 1–22. The *Dictata* covered Ps. 1–150.

[170] Raeder, *Grammatica Theologica*, 303, 308.

contribution, which differentiates it from his two preceding books. There, Raeder showed how specific nuances in different Hebrew terms influenced Luther's translation, which often bled over and had an impact on his theological interpretation of the texts where those terms appear. With this book, he thus tied the three studies together and provided a complete picture of the progression of Luther's Hebrew translation over the course of his first Psalms lectures, his second Psalms lectures, and the time in between. This third and final chapter in his investigation into Luther's Psalms translations capped off by far the most in-depth study of Luther's Hebrew to date. It is simply in its own class. Nevertheless, as strong as his analysis was, Raeder's main shortcoming is the same as his predecessors. The scope of his evaluation was limited to a single book of the Bible – the Psalms.[171]

Finally, due note should be taken of an important contribution to scholarship concerning Luther's interpretation of the Minor Prophets: Gerhard Krause's *Studien zu Luthers Auslegung der Kleinen Propheten* (1962).[172] Krause's study was not an investigation into Luther's Hebrew, although he did periodically discuss Hebrew interpretation issues, and included a short section in his book specifically addressing Luther's employment of Hebrew.[173] Nevertheless, it is the only major study to date on Luther's interpretation of the Minor Prophets, and this current study engages with it at various points. In his book, Krause noted that a comprehensive examination of Luther's Hebrew translation methodology was a remaining gap in scholarship.[174] Keeping in mind that he wrote that prior to Raeder's three studies, it nevertheless underscores the void that remains in scholarly analysis of Luther's Hebrew outside of the Psalms.

This is where the current state of scholarship on Luther's Hebrew stands. Apart from the Psalms, no book of the Hebrew Bible has yet been examined in any comprehensive manner in terms of his Hebrew translation. Moreover, research to date has predominantly focused on either ascertaining Luther's personal Hebrew skills, or on identifying his sources for Hebrew knowledge. With the exception of Raeder, scholars have yet to provide exacting studies that illuminate the relationship between philology and theology in Luther's Hebrew translation and exegesis. Raeder's *Grammatica Theologica*, while a signifi-

---

[171] In addition to these three books, see also Raeder's articles: Siegfried Raeder, "Voraussetzungen und Methode von Luthers Bibelübersetzung," in *Geist und Geschichte der Reformation. Festgabe Hanns Rückert zum 65. Geburtstag. Dargebracht von Freunden, Kollegen und Schülern*, ed. Heinz Liebing and Klaus Scholder (Berlin: Walter de Gruyter, 1966), 152–78; Siegfried Raeder, "Luther als Ausleger und Übersetzer der Heiligen Schrift," in *Leben und Werk Martin Luthers von 1526 bis 1546. Festgabe zu seinem 500. Geburtstag*, vol. 1, ed. Helmar Junghans (Göttingen: Vandenhoeck & Ruprecht, 1983), 253–78; and Raeder, "Exegetical and Hermeneutical."

[172] Krause, *Studien*.
[173] Krause, *Studien*, 61–81.
[174] Krause, *Studien*, 61.

cant step forward, left much to be done. The door that Raeder and others have opened with their examinations of Luther's work in the Psalms has thus not been followed by investigation of the role of Hebrew across the broader corpus of Luther's biblical work. Nor have these examinations been used as places from which to broaden scholars' understanding of the role of Hebrew in specific themes in Luther's theology. The present study provides this.

Moving Forward

This study furthers the scholarly understanding of Luther's Hebrew by examining his Minor Prophets translation, one of the final pieces of his first complete translation of the Hebrew Bible. It provides a detailed account of his maturing Hebrew translation in academic mid-career, and the challenges and achievements which went along with it. Furthermore, it examines the role of Hebrew in his theological interpretation of the Minor Prophets. It shows how various translation decisions collectively helped to build one of the most dominant and persistent theological themes in his interpretation of these twelve books – the *Anfechtung* of the prophets.

For this exercise, this study utilizes Luther's 1534 and 1545 *Deutsche Bibel* editions, which contain the earliest and latest translations of the Minor Prophets which appear in the critical edition of Luther's works, the *Weimarer Ausgabe*.[175] In order to maintain the accuracy of the translation dates, and moreover to align with how these translations are recorded in the *Weimarer Ausgabe*, this study refers to the "1532" *Deutsche Bibel* and the "1545" *Deutsche Bibel* throughout the main analysis, as well as in the Appendix data. While Luther's *Propheten alle Deudsch* initially appeared in 1532 and thus is recorded with this date in this critical edition, it is the same translation that appears in the 1534 Bible. In most cases, the translations in the 1534 and 1545 editions are the same, the 1545 chiefly representing a modernization of word spelling and capitalization. Nevertheless, in many instances Luther modified his translations. Including the early and later editions allows analysis of the more drastic changes

---

[175] Luther's *Deutsche Bibel* translations appear in WA DB 11.2. There were numerous editions published in between these two: 1535, 1536, 1538–9, 1540, 1540–41, 1541, 1543 (two editions), and 1545 (and also a special printing of a 1544–45 edition). A 1546 edition followed, which contained changes from Luther prior to his death; and there were even more notes in Luther's own Bible that contains entries that do not appear in the 1546 edition; these are probably the final notes that he made on his translations prior to his death, per Reu, *Luther's German Bible*, 251. The 1545 edition is the last edition of Luther's Bible which was printed under his supervision before his death in 1546. Reu, *Luther's German Bible*, 248–9. For a complete synopsis of the various editions, see Reu, *Luther's German Bible*, 233–56. See also Aland, 41–53.

in Luther's translation of the Hebrew text.[176] Moreover, it helps to illuminate Luther's thoughts and struggles at the time of the 1532 translation.

In addition to Luther's *Deutsche Bibel*, this study consults his annotations in his 1538/39 edition Old Testament; and the records from the 1539–41 revision commissions in Wittenberg, usually referred to as the "protocols," which were kept by Rörer.[177] It also consults Luther's lecture notes (1524–26) for all twelve books; and his commentaries (1526–27) on Jonah, Habakkuk, and Zechariah, the only books of the Minor Prophets for which he wrote commentaries.[178] These provide the greatest insight into Luther's translation decisions, as in his lectures and commentaries he frequently went into great detail concerning his translations, the options that he weighed, and the relevant scholarly arguments. Moreover, in these works he frequently identified the Hebrew terms and phrases at issue, thus removing any doubt as to the role of Hebrew in his translation considerations. Following the American edition of Luther's works, this study consults the Altenburg text for Luther's lectures, with the exceptions of: the Hosea lectures, which are based on the Zwickau text; and the Malachi lectures, which are based on the Wittenberg text.[179] The Michel Lotterus text is consulted for the German commentaries on Jonah and Habakkuk; and the Walch edition (St.

---

[176] I have chosen the 1545 edition because I believe that it shows the most definitive evidence of growth, where I am comparing the early and later translations. This is largely based on scholarly advice. Reu argues that the 1534–40 *Deutsche Bibel* was reprinted with only slight revisions. He argues that by contrast, the 1540–41 and 1541 editions show more important changes. Moreover, the 1545 edition catches the modifications that were made from the 1539–41 revision meetings. Reu, *Luther's German Bible*, 233–56.

[177] WA DB 4:1–278. These were not the only revision commissions. However, there is very little information about the 1534 revision meetings, and it appears that in the 1544 meetings, they only addressed the New Testament. See Reu, *Luther's German Bible*, 233, 251–6. For more background on the 1539–41 protocols and on Luther's handwritten entries in his 1538/39 edition Old Testament, see WA DB 4:xxvi–xxxviii. For more general information on the protocols, see WA DB 3:xv–xvii.

[178] There are various recensions of Luther's lectures, which appear inside and outside of the *Weimarer Ausgabe*. In general, these different recensions refer to the same lectures. Concerning the quite complex transmission and revision history of the lectures and commentaries, see LW 18:vii–xii; LW 19:vii–xi; LW 20:vii–x; WA 13:iii–xxxvi; WA 19:169–71; and WA 19:337. See also Krause, *Studien*, 5–6. Luther also addressed the Minor Prophets in three sermons. See WA 1:130–2 (1517; see the footnote in the WA concerning the date) for Mal. 3:1; WA 36:50c–63c (1532), for Mic. 5:1; and WA 49:63 (1540) for Zech. 9:9. These are minor references and bring nothing new for this study, thus they are out of scope. Krause addresses them in Krause, *Studien*, 4.

[179] These are recorded in WA 13. The LW used these manuscripts for the Hosea lectures and Malachi lectures to "complete" the set with those that appear in the Altenburg manuscript. See LW 18:xi–xii. Luther's 1545 additions to Hos. 13 appear in WA 40.3:760–75, with introductory information beginning at p. 747. These are consulted in this study as relevant. The WA editors make extensive notations with insights concerning other manuscripts as part of their records of the Zwickau, Altenburg, etc. recensions. These are taken into consideration as relevant.

Louis) for the Zechariah commentary.[180] Luther's translations of other books of the Bible are addressed as relevant for his argument in the Minor Prophets, and the *Weimarer Ausgabe* and American edition of Luther's works are consulted for these.

Finally, this study restricts its analysis to instances in which Luther explicitly addressed Hebrew in his lectures, commentaries, revisions protocols, or biblical glosses on the verse.[181] Thus, there is no speculation involved concerning his use of Hebrew on any given example in this project. If Luther did not explicitly mention Hebrew in his remarks concerning his translation, the example has no place in this study.

This study does not attempt to provide a comprehensive picture of every aspect of Luther's use of Hebrew in his translation of the Minor Prophets. No study could possibly do this, outside of a massive quantity of volumes, if at all. Rather, it analyzes four exemplary aspects of his employment of Hebrew which dominated his translation of the Minor Prophets. Each of the next four chapters of this study examines one of these.[182]

The next chapter in this study investigates the first of these aspects of Luther's employment of Hebrew: the role of the obscurity of the Hebrew text in his translation, and how this obscurity led to various types of contradictions and vacillations in his interpretations. The chapter is divided into two parts. The first section investigates interpretative contradictions in Luther's Hebrew translation. These are instances where the meaning of the Hebrew was in question, and Luther at different times made inconsistent German translations and/or exegetical interpretations of the Hebrew text. The second section examines methodological contradictions in Luther's interpretation of the Hebrew. These are instances where the meaning of Hebrew words and phrases was not in question, but rather how to properly render the Hebrew text into German. A key exam-

---

[180] Jonah: WA 19:185–251. Habakkuk: WA 19:345–435. Zechariah: StL 14:1768–1975.

[181] Given the redacted nature of the lecture notes, commentaries, and other texts which appear in the *Weimarer Ausgabe*, there is always the possibility that information concerning Luther's comments is not completely accurate. However, it is the best information that we have available at this time, and the scholars who have compiled these volumes have gone to painstaking lengths to document concerns, and to note the differences between the various manuscripts.

[182] Furthermore, this study focuses its comprehensive analysis on Luther's own remarks in his lectures, commentaries, revisions protocols, and biblical glosses; and does not comprehensively analyze the additional Hebrew literary resources summarized in this chapter, though it does engage with them in key places. This decision was made in order to provide a thorough analysis of Luther's own texts, rather than to detract from that analysis in order to make room for such a much broader study. Investigations into the role of each of these resources for Luther's Hebrew translation could easily be – and I believe should be – comprehensive studies in their own right. This latter approach will provide a far more thorough understanding of Luther's Hebrew and late medieval/early modern Christian Hebraism through the complementary and aggregate contribution of such studies, in comparison to an overly broad and thus more shallow summary work.

ple of this is his methodology for translating Hebrew figures of speech. While he often lamented the difficulty that German readers would have understanding them, he did not always render them into "understandable" German, but instead made literal translations. And while he proposed certain "rules" for such cases, the nature of and pervasiveness of such contradictions in his methodology demonstrate that these principles of translation, which he most elaborately outlined in *Sendbrief vom Dolmetschen* (1530) and *Summarien über die Psalmen und Ursachen des Dolmetschens* (1531–33), fail to fully explain the contradictions. Moreover, these rules were not nearly as reliable as Luther himself made them out to be, and scholars have been all too ready to take him at his word concerning them. This chapter shows that while scholars have long noted Luther's struggles with Hebrew, they were far more significant than has been appreciated, even in his academic mid-career and mature Bible translation.

The third chapter investigates the role that Luther's sense of the semantic intensity of the Hebrew language played in his translation of the Minor Prophets. It addresses his Hebrew translation from a particularly linguistics-based perspective, drawing on the work of linguists Birgit Stolt and Anna Wierzbicka concerning emotion and semantic intensity in language; as well as on Friedrich Schleiermacher and his notion of *Verfremdung* and *Entfremdung* in Bible translation. It further engages with the Buber-Rosenzweig Bible translation, a twentieth-century German-Jewish update to Luther's Bible, and examines how this work illuminates Luther's emphasis on features of the Hebrew language related to intensity, powerfulness of expression, and auditory elements of the text. It demonstrates that his determination to reproduce the semantic intensity of the Hebrew was one of the definitive imprints of the language in his Bible, and one of the ways he sought to differentiate it from the Vulgate. Furthermore, it shows how this intensity fed many of his theological interpretations of *Anfechtung* in the texts. This chapter expands the scholarly understanding of this facet of Luther's *Anfechtung*, particularly illuminating the Latin and German terminology that he linked to the Hebrew in his theological interpretations of the Minor Prophets. Moreover, this chapter shows how certain translations that he made, based on the influence of Hebrew, remain in the German Bible and the German language to this day.

The fourth chapter examines Luther's use of "inner-biblical interpretation" – i.e. biblical quotations and references – to support, and moreover, to build his translations of the Hebrew texts. It shows how he frequently drew upon not just a single Hebrew term, but rather multiple Hebrew terms from other books of the Bible, interweaving the meanings together to arrive at the translation of a single term in the Minor Prophets. The case studies in this chapter focus on a single theme around which he often employed inner-biblical interpretation in the Minor Prophets: the ritual language of cultic purification, mainly in Leviticus and Numbers. This helps to elucidate how he built theological interpretations into his translations of texts. These case studies further demonstrate how these interwoven interpretations specifically played a role in his interpretation of *Anfechtung* in the texts. This chapter takes a step forward in filling the gap in scholarship addressing Luther's use of biblical quotations, which has been identified by numerous scholars, including Meissinger and Bluhm, as a key lacuna.

The fifth chapter examines the influence of Hebrew on Luther's exploitation of the mystical tradition in his translation of the Minor Prophets. The analysis is divided into two parts. The first segment examines Luther's translation of the Book of Jonah as a case study. It shows how Luther appropriated key concepts from the mystical tradition in his translation and interpretation of Jonah: *conscientia* and ascent; *gemitus*; *affectus*; *excessus mentis*; and *humilitas*. It demonstrates how Hebrew terminology not only played a role in Luther's use of the mystical tradition for his exegetical interpretation, but also how it ultimately influenced his final German translations in many places in the *Deutsche Bibel*. The second part of the chapter examines Luther's exploitation of the mystical tradition behind the concept of "silence" in his translation and interpretation of the Minor Prophets. It pays special attention to his use of what this study calls the "reduced to" idiom, a reappropriation by Luther of Jerome's *redigatur ad nihilum* and similar conceptions which appear in the mystical writings of Tauler, Meister Eckhart, and Jewish mysticism. This chapter represents the first comprehensive examination of the influence of Hebrew on Luther's exploitation of the mystical tradition in his Bible translation to date, illuminating the important role that this held in his *Deutsche Bibel*. Moreover, it shows that his use of the mystical tradition was not limited to his early years, but continued to play a major role in his writings and translation work into his academic mid-career. It also elucidates how the influence of Hebrew on his exploitation of the mystical tradition in his translation of the Minor Prophets consequentially permeated into his interpretation of *Anfechtung* at various points in the texts.

In sum, this study provides a comprehensive account of Martin Luther's Hebrew translation as he moved into his academic mid-career. It provides greater insight into the ongoing struggles that he had with his translations, long beyond his early years of translation; but also shows how he was able to make deeply insightful observations concerning Hebrew, which he incorporated into his German translation. It opens a new window into one of the darker corners of Luther scholarship, moves its comprehensive knowledge of his Hebrew beyond the Psalms, and uncovers many insights into a previously unexamined area of his employment of the Hebrew language for his Bible translation. It also illuminates the role of Hebrew in many areas of his translation which have not been explored in detail to date, particularly for this period of his life: his regular attempts to incorporate the semantic intensity of the Hebrew language in his German renderings; his incessant use of inner-biblical interpretation; and his exploitation of the mystical tradition for his Bible. It challenges overly fawn-

Figure 1.6: Luther's ink set (*source*: photograph is mine; *permission*: Stiftung Luthergedenkstätten in Sachsen-Anhalt).

Figure 1.7: Luther's writing box (*source*: photograph is mine; *permission*: Stiftung Luthergedenkstätten in Sachsen-Anhalt).

Figure 1.8: Outside Luther's house at the Augustinian monastery, present day. Luther's study is believed to have been near this site. At the south wall is a latrine, where Luther frequently mentioned that his study was near to (*source*: photograph is mine; *permission*: Stiftung Luthergedenkstätten in Sachsen-Anhalt).

ing assessments of Luther's Hebrew, as well as those which unduly depreciate it. And it uncovers numerous examples of the influence of Hebrew on specific German translations that he made, many of which remain in the German Bible and the modern German language. Finally, it maps out numerous translation decisions of Luther's to demonstrate the impact of Hebrew on a key theological theme which dominated his interpretations of the texts: his conception of *Anfechtung*. This study also includes as an Appendix a substantial body of refined data from Luther's Hebrew translation, which further illuminates the examples in this study, and facilitates additional analysis for future research. This research, in short, shows that by mid-career, the impact of Hebrew on Luther's Bible translation was immense and very diverse. As German as Luther's Bible was, it was also very Hebrew, and the fingerprints of Hebrew in it are prominent.

Chapter Two

"The Obscure Hebrew"

"The text is obscure here. That is to say, it is very Hebrew."[1]
Martin Luther, June, 1526

One of the most frequently recurring frustrations which Luther expressed concerning the Hebrew of the Minor Prophets was its obscurity.[2] He lamented the obstacles that the cryptic texts posed for him, for the many translators who had faced these texts before him, and especially for the German reader who would ultimately receive his translation. How he handled the obscurities of the Hebrew language had a major impact on his German Bible. These struggles stemmed, in part, from the uniqueness of the Hebrew Bible. Unlike other scriptural languages such as Greek or Latin, it is essentially a complete literary corpus in and of itself, with little outside literature to substantiate or illuminate its texts. Numerous philological questions face the translator of the Hebrew Bible: roughly 300,000 words, 7,000–8,000 of which are distinct vocabulary units or terms; between 1,500 and 2,440 *hapax legomena* (words that only appear once in the entire Hebrew Bible), with a further 500–600 which only occur twice; grammatical uncertainties; corruption of the text because of transmission issues; and the perennial questions concerning the pointed text in contrast to the unpointed text – the קְרֵי (*qərê*, "[what is] read") in contrast to the כְּתִיב (*kəṯîḇ*, "[what is] written").[3] Theological problems further exacerbate these challenges.

---

[1] "Der text ist hie finster, das ist seer Ebreisch." WA 19:426.3–4; LW 19:228. These are Luther's remarks concerning Hab. 3:2 in his commentary on Habakkuk. There are frequently verse numbering differences between the Hebrew Bible, Vulgate, LXX, NASB, *Deutsche Bibel*, and Luther's lectures and commentaries. *In order to simplify the discussions of the texts, all Bible citations in this study are provided according to the Hebrew Bible numbering.* The volumes and pages referenced in the *Weimarer Ausgabe*, are, nevertheless, always provided "as is." Thus, the reader will be able to easily find and access the information concerning Luther's comments and his translations.

[2] Among other terminology that he used, Luther expressed this through variants of *obscuritas* in his Latin lectures and *Finsternis* in the German commentary. See, for example: WA 13:30.9; WA 13:275.13–14; WA 13:444.13–15; WA 13:690 Note 7 H; and WA 19:427.27–28.

[3] William McKane, *Selected Christian Hebraists* (Cambridge: Cambridge University Press, 1989), 142–3. These figures, of course, vary depending on the method of measurement. In general, Latin definitions provided in this study come from LS and OXLAT; Hebrew definitions come from BDB and KB; and German definitions come from DWB, DDU, and OXDUD. Definitions are only noted in the footnotes for outstanding instances. Other lexicon information, as consulted, appears in the Bibliography of this study. Transliteration is provid-

Whether interpreters were ignorant of the traditional Jewish or Christian interpretation of a particular textual issue, whether they rejected that resolution, or whether there was simply a void in tradition addressing the question, this all had to be taken into account along with the philological questions.

This chapter examines the role of "Hebrew obscurity" – *Ebreische finsternis* as Luther called it – in his Bible translation and exegesis.[4] It will show that his struggles with the obscurities of the Hebrew Bible profoundly influenced his translation – both his *interpretation* of the Hebrew and his *method*, that is, his decisions about the most appropriate manner in which to render the meaning into the German. This influence was manifested primarily through an extraordinary prevalence of contradictions and inconsistencies in his translation of the Hebrew. The prevailing arguments by scholars concerning his Hebrew translation have not fully taken into account these discrepancies.

This chapter identifies the discrepancies and analyzes them in two categories: (1) *interpretative variances* – i.e. inconsistencies in Luther's lectures, commentaries, and *Deutsche Bibel* translations and revisions, where the philological and theological meaning of the Hebrew was in question; and (2) *methodological variances* – inconsistencies where the issue at hand was not the meaning of the Hebrew, but rather how to best render it into German.[5] The segment concerning methodological variances focuses specifically on three philological questions: Hebrew figures of speech, the Hebrew trope of repetition, and Hebrew transliteration.

Part I: Interpretative Variances

Of all the inconsistences in Luther's translation of the Hebrew language, the interpretative variances between his lectures, commentaries, and *Deutsche Bibel* are perhaps the most jarring, as they testify not merely to a maturation in his grasp of Hebrew – or a refinement, as many scholars and Luther himself often portray them.[6] More than this, they show a sometimes radically changing trans-

---

ed for all Hebrew in this study, with the exception of book titles, tables, and figures. SBL style is used for all transliteration, with the support of Dr. Efraim Feinstein and the Open Siddur Project (http://www.opensiddur.org).

[4] WA 19:427.27–28; LW 19:230.

[5] These categories are not exclusive. Figure of speech challenges and other methodological questions do appear in the first segment also, but these appear within a context where Luther expresses uncertainty about the meanings. Likewise, items under consideration may fall under multiple sub-categories – for example, where Luther took issue with Hebrew repetition, but also identified it as a figure of speech. These are noted accordingly.

[6] See Luther's comments in WA DB 10.1:590.38–48. Bluhm cites this in *Creative*, 119, though he points out Luther's struggle in some translations; see, for example, pp. 49–50. Birgit Stolt also cites this, and simply accepts his statement; in Stolt, *Martin Luthers Rhetorik des Herzens* (Tübingen: Mohr Siebeck, 2000), 95. See also Philip Schaff, *History of the Christian*

lation, telling the story of an amateur Hebrew linguist who frequently made acute reconsiderations of his translations as he prepared them for print. The examples of interpretative variances which follow are divided into three groups: variances between Luther's exegesis and his *Deutsche Bibel*; variances between his lectures and commentaries; and variances between his *Deutsche Bibel* revisions. These examples appear along with additional illustrations in Table A.1 in the Appendix.[7]

The Exegesis in Contrast to the *Deutsche Bibel*

Inconsistencies between Luther's exegesis and his Bible translation offer an especially critical glimpse into his translation work. Where he argued against the Vulgate, citing the Hebrew Bible as the basis for his argument, for example, it is not unreasonable to expect that one would find his *Deutsche Bibel* translation in agreement with the Hebrew Bible. Many times, however, his Bible translation shows precisely the opposite – directly contradicting the argument he made in the exegesis. The examples which follow show key contradictions between his exegesis and the *Deutsche Bibel*, and demonstrate how these contradictions illuminate the impact of his struggles with Hebrew obscurities on his translations of the texts. They appear, along with further select examples of such contradictions, in Table A.1 in the Appendix. Table A.1 divides these examples into four categories, each showing a different pattern of how his exegesis and Bible translation agreed or disagreed with the Hebrew Bible and the Vulgate. One from each category is examined in detail below.

Table 2.1 shows the parallel Hebrew, Latin, and German translations for Nah. 2:11, Joel 2:6, Mic. 6:9, Nah. 3:2, and Joel 3:3.[8]

Church. *Modern Christianity: The German Reformation A. D. 1517–1530*, Pt. 2 (Edinburgh: T. & T. Clark, 1888), 348. Cf. Raeder, *Das Hebräische*, 3. Cf. Raeder, *Grammatica Theologica*, 4. Luther's methodological variances alone demonstrate this. Comparing many of his 1532 translations with his 1545 revisions elucidates this as well. See Table A.2 in the Appendix. It is therefore clear that Luther was not always moving closer and closer to the German with his later revisions.

[7] This table represents only a sample of such contradictions which appear in Luther's interpretation of the Minor Prophets.

[8] Throughout this study, English Bible references come from the NASB; Vulgate references come from the German Bible Society; LXX references come from the German Bible Society; and Hebrew Bible references come from *Biblia Hebraica Stuttgartensia* (BHS; German Bible Society). All appear in the Bibliography. Medieval Vulgate translations vary amongst themselves, sometimes greatly, and sometimes they differ from the German Bible Society translation. This is particularly so for the Psalms. Where Luther's remarks suggest a key divergence from the German Bible Society translation, I include the *Textus biblie* (Basel, 1506–08) and/or Lefèvre's *Quincuplex Psalter* [Jacques Lefèvre d'Étaples, *Qvincvplex Psalterium: Gallicum. Romanum. Hebraicum. Vetus. Conciliatu[m]* (Paris: Henri Estienne, 1509)] as ref-

Table 2.1: Parallel bible references: Nah. 2:11, Joel 2:6, Mic. 6:9, Nah. 3:2, and Joel 3:3.

Verse	NASB	Hebrew Bible	Vulgate	*Deutsche Bibel*
Nah. 2:11	She is emptied! Yes, she is desolate and waste! Hearts are melting and knees knocking! Also anguish is in the whole body And all their faces are grown pale!	בּוּקָה וּמְבוּקָה וּמְבֻלָּקָה וָלֵב נָמֵס וּפִק בִּרְכַּיִם וְחַלְחָלָה בְּכָל-מָתְנַיִם וּפְנֵי כֻלָּם **קִבְּצוּ פָארוּר**	dissipata et scissa et dilacerata et cor tabescens et dissolutio geniculorum et defectio in cunctis renibus et facies omnium **sicut nigredo ollae**	Aber nu mus sie rein abgelesen vnd geplundert werden, das jr hertz mus verzagen, die knie schlottern, alle lenden zittern, vnd aller angesicht **bleich sehen, wie ein toepffen**. (1532) WA DB 11.2:292.11.
Joel 2:6	Before them the people are in anguish; All faces turn pale.	מִפָּנָיו יָחִילוּ עַמִּים כָּל-פָּנִים **קִבְּצוּ פָארוּר**	a facie eius cruciabuntur populi omnes vultus **redigentur in ollam**	Die voelcker werden sich fur jm entsetzen, Aller angesicht **sind so bleich, wie die toepffen**. (1532) WA DB 11.2:218.6.
Mic. 6:9	The voice of the Lord will call to the city – And it is sound wisdom to fear Your name: "Hear, O tribe. Who has appointed its time?"	קוֹל יְהוָה לָעִיר יִקְרָא וְתוּשִׁיָּה יִרְאֶה שְׁמֶךָ שִׁמְעוּ מַטֶּה **וּמִי יְעָדָהּ**	vox Domini ad civitatem clamat et salus erit timentibus nomen tuum audite tribus **et quis adprobabit illud**	Es wird des HERRN stim vber die stad ruffen, Aber, wer deinen namen furcht, dem wird gelingen. Hoeret jr Stemme, **was gepredigt wird**. (1532) WA DB 11.2:282.9.
Nah. 3:2	The noise of the whip, The noise of the rattling of the wheel, Galloping horses And bounding chariots!	קוֹל שׁוֹט וְקוֹל רַעַשׁ אוֹפָן וְסוּס דֹּהֵר וּמֶרְכָּבָה מְרַקֵּדָה	vox flagelli et vox impetus rotae et equi frementis et quadrigae ferventis equitis ascendentis	**Denn da wird man hoeren** die geisseln klappen, vnd die reder rasseln, die rosse schreien, vnd die wagen rollen. (1532) WA DB 11.2:294.2.
Joel 3:3	I will display wonders in the sky and on the earth, Blood, fire and columns of smoke.	וְנָתַתִּי מוֹפְתִים בַּשָּׁמַיִם וּבָאָרֶץ **דָּם** וָאֵשׁ וְתִימֲרוֹת עָשָׁן	et dabo prodigia in caelo et in terra **sanguinem** et ignem et vaporem fumi	Vnd wil wunderzeichen geben im himel vnd auff erden, nemlich, **blut**, feur vnd rauch dampff. (1532) WA DB 11.2:222.3.

erence. It is difficult to choose one translation because Luther's references to the Vulgate in the Minor Prophets show that he was not just using one Latin text.

Nahum 2:11 and Joel 2:6

Luther wrestled with the phrase קִבְּצוּ פָארוּר (*qibbəṣû pārûr*, "gathered blackness, a glow"), which appears in both Nah. 2:11 and Joel 2:6. In his lectures on Nahum, he argued that the Vulgate's translation of קִבְּצוּ פָארוּר (*qibbəṣû pārûr*) in Nah. 2:11 as *sicut nigredo ollae* ("like the blackness of a pot") would be better translated as *congregentur in ollam* ("let them be gathered in a pot"), while conceding that he did not fully understand the text in the Hebrew Bible:

> *And all faces are like* [*sicut*] *a black pot.* We have also had a similar passage earlier in Joel [2:6], where the translator renders it this way: 'All their faces will be reduced to a pot [*facies eorum redigentur in ollam*].' Here he translates it '**like** a black pot [***sicut nigredo ollae***].' Since there clearly is no agreement in these translations, I translate it this way: '**Let them be gathered together** in a pot [***congregentur in ollam***].' However, what the prophet intends with this Hebrew figure of speech I do not know. Generally this is the interpretation: 'So great is their grief and sadness that they have become strained and pale, so that they appear similar to [*similes esse videantur*] black pots.' The metaphor is completely absurd. I do not believe the prophet intended this. The following pleases me more, but still I would not dare declare it a certainty that the prophet intended this: 'They are going to be consumed and destroyed the way the chunks of meat thrown into the pot for cooking are generally eaten.'[9]

But in the *Deutsche Bibel*, he translated קִבְּצוּ פָארוּר (***qibbəṣû** pārûr*) almost exactly as the Vulgate, and precisely what he argued against: *bleich sehen, **wie** ein toepffen* ("[they] look pale, **like** a pot").[10] He made the same about face in his interpretation of קִבְּצוּ פָארוּר (*qibbəṣû pārûr*) in Joel 2:6. He said in the lectures on Joel:

> *All faces are made as black as a pot* [*redigentur in ollam*]. It is not completely clear to me what this means. Almost the same figure of speech is used in the prophet Nahum, Ch. 2: 'The faces of all of them are **like** a black pot [*sicut nigredo ollae*].' The meaning of the person who translated it in this way is this, that people became so sad and worn out with grief that they went about gloomy and worn with grief, just as dark clothes are usually an indication of mourning. However, I do not approve of this idea because the Hebrew does not read that way. You see, the Hebrew reads as follows: 'All faces **will be gathered together** in a pot [*omnes vultus **congregabuntur** olla*]' ... they will be hacked to pieces,

---

[9] "Et facies omnium sicut nigredo ollae[.] Similis locus supra est [Joel 2, 6.] etiam in Iohele, ubi interpres sic vertit: facies eorum redigentur in ollam. Hic vertit: sicut nigredo ollae. Cum prorsus nulla sit harum translationum convenientia, ego sic verto: congregentur in ollam. Sed quid sibi velit propheta figura ista hebraica, ignoro. Vulgo sic solent interpretari: tantus est eorum moeror et luctus, ut prae pavore inquinati sint et pallidi, ut nigris ollis similes esse videantur. Absurda prorsus est metaphora nec puto ego hoc voluisse prophetam. Mihi hoc magis placet sed tamen nihil ausim asserere, quod voluerit propheta: sic consumendos et annihilandos esse, ut frusta carnis consumi solent, quae in ollam coniiciuntur coquenda." WA 13:386.30–WA 13:387.5. LW 18:304–5.

[10] WA DB 11.2:292.11. Unless otherwise noted, the *Deutsche Bibel* references in this study are the 1532 edition.

as meat is generally cut into pieces and thrown into a pot. They will be chopped up as in a kettle, as Micah [Mic. 3:3] says, that is, they will be unable to escape the might of their foe. You see, it is absolutely certain that the word 'gather together [*congregandi*]' is used in the Hebrew here.[11]

Yet he translated קִבְּצוּ פָארוּר (*qibbəṣû pārûr*) in the *Deutsche Bibel* as *sind so bleich, wie die toepffen* ("[they] are so pale, **like** the pots"), almost exactly as in Nah. 2:11, and as he did there, in direct opposition to his argument in the lectures and the Hebrew on which he based his argument.[12] The discrepancy in Joel 2:6 is particularly striking, given that he translated against what he said he was "absolutely certain" that the Hebrew meant.[13]

The contradictions between Luther's arguments in the lectures on Nahum and Joel and his later Bible translations underscore how his uncertainty concerning the Hebrew manifested itself in the struggle with its translation. Moreover, it shows how the obscurity of the Hebrew fueled his conflicting interpretations.

Micah 6:9

Luther expressed uncertainty concerning the meaning of וּמִי יְעָדָהּ (*ûmî yəʿādāh*, "and who appointed it") in Mic. 6:9. He said in the lectures,

And who will favor [approbabit] it? They translate the Hebrew here in different ways. The Septuagint translators rendered it 'who will adorn [*ornabit*]'; Jerome, 'who will favor [*approbabit*]'; and others in other ways. I do not at all understand what the prophet wants to say, and I am afraid that we are still ignorant of some of the Hebrew language, especially when special words of any kind, such as this is, occur in scripture. Lest we

---

[11] "Omnes vultus redigentur in ollam[.] Hoc quid sit, mihi non satis constat. Eadem autem figura loquendi est fere in propheta Naum cap. II: facies omnium sicut nigredo ollae. Eius qui sic est interpretatus haec fuit sententia, ut fierent homines tam tristes et moerore confecti, ut pro tristitia atri et confecti incederent sicut pullae vestes luctus indicia esse solent. Sed haec sententia, quia in hebraeo aliter legitur mihi non probatur. Sic enim est in hebraeo: omnes vultus congregabuntur olla … ßie werden zuschlagen ßein sicut carnes in frusta concidi et in ollam coniici solent, concidentur sicut in lebete, ut inquit Micheas [3] hoc est: non poterunt effugere adversarii vim. Id enim omnino certum est verbum congregandi hic esse in hebraeo." WA 13:97.20–26, 31–34. LW 18:93. Luther's team explained in the 1539–41 protocols that a person is *bleich* ("pale") or *schwartz* ("black") when terrified, what he calls the *Todfarbe* ("color of death"). WA DB 4:229a.29–31. References for the 1538/39 handwritten entries in Luther's Old Testament and for the 1539–41 protocol records are often included in the Appendix tables where a verse is addressed, even if the exact issue is not noted there, because they sometimes still help to illuminate particular points. The objective is to provide the reader with as much information as possible.

[12] WA DB 11.2:218.6. The Vulgate translated קִבְּצוּ פָארוּר (*qibbəṣû pārûr*) in Joel 2:6 as *redigentur in ollam* ("[they will be] collected in a pot, reduced to a pot"), precisely what Luther argued for in the lectures, but failed to translate it as in the *Deutsche Bibel*. This Vulgate rendering was obviously a deviation from its translation of Nah. 2:11.

[13] WA 13:97.33–34: *omnino certum est* ("[it is] absolutely certain").

completely bypass this passage, we will still say and translate it with others this way: 'who will transfer [*transferet*], or go away [*abibit*],' so that the meaning is. 'He has been sent by God to the ministry of the Word; he has received a divine command to preach; therefore there is no reason why he can desert the responsibility assigned.'[14]

Rather than choosing a German equivalent to *transferet* or *abibit*, as he argued for in the lectures, he translated וּמִי יְעָדָהּ (*ûmî yəʿāḏāh*) in the *Deutsche Bibel* as *was gepredigt wird* ("what will be preached [or, what is preached]").[15] By contrast, the Vulgate translated וּמִי יְעָדָהּ (*ûmî yəʿāḏāh*) as *et quis adprobabit illud* ("and who will approve, favor it"), a more close rendering of the literal Hebrew.[16] Luther's translation was thus a marked departure not only from what he identified as his translation choice in the lectures, but also from both the Hebrew Bible and the Vulgate.

Nahum 3:2

Luther was inconsistent in his rendering of the Hebrew syntax in Nah. 3:2. He argued in the lectures, in agreement with the Vulgate, that the entire verse should be read in the nominative case:

I read all these things according to the Hebrew in the nominative [*in nominativo*] as follows: '[The crack of whip] and rumble of wheel, galloping horse and bounding chariot! Horseman charging and flashing sword and glittering spear, etc.' With all these, like a painter on canvas, he depicts and sets before their eyes ... It is as if he were saying: 'With great violence and enthusiasm, the charioteers urge on their horses and chariots.

---

[14] "Et quis approbabit illud[?] Varie verterunt verbum hebraeum. Septuaginta interpretes verterunt: ornabit, Hieronymus: approbabit, alii aliter. Ego quid sibi velit, non prorsus intelligo et vereor nos adhuc ignorare quaedam hebraeae linguae, maxime siquando incidunt in scriptura huiusmodi insignia verba, quale hoc est. Ne prorsus transeamus locum, dicimus tamen et sic vertimus cum aliis: quis transferet vel abibit, ut sit sententia: missum se esse a deo ad ministerium verbi, mandatum accepisse divinitus, ut praedicet, ideo non esse, cur possit susceptam provinciam deserere etc." WA 13:335.4–11. LW 18:264. The Septuagint translation for the phrase in question is καὶ τίς κοσμήσει πόλιν ("and who will adorn [or arrange] the city").

[15] WA DB 11.2:282.9. Despite his statement that he would translate the Hebrew with *transferet* or *abibit*, his *Deutsche Bibel* translation still reflected his expanded interpretation in the lectures concerning preaching.

[16] The characterization "literal" in this study is employed specifically to indicate a translation according to the letter of the Hebrew, i. e. according to the lexical definition. This should be differentiated from the similarly called "literal sense," which is often used in a much different meaning. W. Schwarz, for example, argues that Luther understood the literal sense of scripture to be the spiritual interpretation (i. e. of the Holy Spirit), based on Lefèvre. Schwarz, *Principles and Problems of Biblical Translation. Some Reformation Controversies and their Background* (Cambridge: Cambridge University Press, 1955), 172–4. Meissinger also argued that Luther understood the literal sense as the prophetic sense. Meissinger, *Luthers Exegese in der Frühzeit*, 51. Furthermore, while the characterization "literal" is avoided by linguists today because it is seen as too problematic and imprecise, the main audience for this book is historians. It is therefore used throughout, in order not to confuse the non-technical, non-linguist reader.

54   Chapter Two

That is their noisy rumble. They are driven nearly headlong and rumble with their speed. The horsemen charge quickly on their horses, and their spears flash like lightning, etc.'[17]

In his Bible translation, however, he contradicted those remarks and translated the verse as a grammatically complete sentence. He rendered קוֹל שׁוֹט וְקוֹל רַעַשׁ אוֹפָן וְסוּס דֹּהֵר וּמֶרְכָּבָה מְרַקֵּדָה (*qôl šôṭ wəqôl raʿaš ʾôpān wəsûs dōhēr ûmerkāḇâ məraqqēḏâ*, "Sound of whip and sound of rattling of wheel and galloping horse and dancing chariot") as *Denn da wird man hoeren die geisseln klappen, vnd die reder rasseln, die rosse schreien, vnd die wagen rollen* ("For there one will hear the whips clapping, and the wheels rattling, the horses screaming, and the wagons rolling").[18] The Vulgate, by contrast, translated the verse in the nominative, in accord with the Hebrew: *vox flagelli et vox impetus rotae et equi frementis et quadrigae ferventis equitis ascendentis* ("The sound of the whip, and the sound of the rushing of the wheels and of the roar of the horse and the burning of the chariot of the ascending horseman").[19] Thus, as in his translation of Mic. 6:9, while he argued for the Hebrew as the barometer for his interpretation, Luther ultimately went against that argument in his *Deutsche Bibel* translation.

Luther's deviation from the Hebrew structure in this verse is particularly significant, as it seems to attenuate the intensity that he contended for through the use of the nominative case. That decision is atypical of his hermeneutic. He regularly rendered his German translation in a way that would replicate the more forceful or emotive expression that he saw in the Hebrew Bible in contrast to the Vulgate.[20]

Joel 3:3

Luther admitted uncertainty concerning the appropriate translation of דָּם (*dām*, "blood") in Joel 3:3. He explained in the lectures,

> Blood [*Sanguinem*]. I do not know if he is speaking in this way and is taking 'blood [*sanguinem*]' here the way he takes it in the following verse, for I would gladly [*libenter*] interpret 'blood [*sanguinem*]' here as 'redness [*rubore*].' The Hebrew word allows this. That is what we have in Gen. 49[:11]: 'He washes ... his vesture in the blood of grapes

---

[17] "Ego autem ex hebraeo omnia lego in nominativo sic: et vox impetus rotae et equus ferox et currus saltans et eques sedens et flamma gladii et fulgor hastae etc. Quibus omnibus quasi pictor in tabula depingit atque ob oculos point ... idem fecit, q. d. magna vehementia, magno ardore aurigae urgent equos et currus, quorum est impetus et vox, praecipites fere agitantur, crepant prae vehementia et equites prompte sedent in equis, hastae tanquam fulgura coruscant etc." WA 13:388.13–17, 18–21. LW 18:307.

[18] WA DB 11.2:294.2. The modern spelling of *reder* is *Räder* (wheels). Grimm defines *Geisel* as *flagellum*, DWB 5:2615.

[19] Luther's reading, translating the series of singulars into plurals, also reflected an amplified intensity. The use of the plural is one of many ways that the Hebrew language expresses intensification. Ch. 3 addresses Hebrew intensity.

[20] See Ch. 3 of this study.

[*in sanguine uvae*]'; and in Deut. 32[:14]: 'They were drinking of the most pure blood of grapes [*sanguinem uvae biberent meracissimum*],' i. e. the redness of the most choice grapes [*rubellum de electissimis uvis*]. I think he means this here too (although I am not completely sure). After all, it seems to me to be too bold, too distorted, that we should want to establish that this sign indicates the blood of Christ and of the martyrs shed on the ground – as some people do.[21]

But instead of interpreting דָּם (*dām*) as *rubore*, as he argued in the lectures that he "would gladly [*libenter*]" do, he translated it in the *Deutsche Bibel* as *blut* ("blood"), mirroring the Vulgate's *sanguinem*, and thus following the more literal Hebrew.[22] His varying interpretation of דָּם (*dām*) in Joel 3:3 is further evidence of the struggles that he faced as he decided whether to translate according to the literal Hebrew, or to mirror the Hebrew figure of speech and therefore express a different undertone within the term. Moreover, it shows Luther's restrained use of his Christological axiom for the interpretation of the Old Testament.[23] While that rule was obviously an integral part of his hermeneutic, he did not necessarily force a Christological reading into a particular text in which he did not believe it was explicitly present.

The Lectures in Contrast to the Commentaries

Inconsistencies between Luther's argument in the lectures and his commentaries also demonstrate the role that the obscurity of Hebrew played in his translation and exegesis. This category is limited to the three books of the Minor Prophets for which he provided commentaries: Jonah, Habakkuk, and Zechariah.

Table 2.2 shows the parallel Hebrew, Latin, and German translations for Hab. 1:8 and Zech. 11:7.

---

[21] "Sanguinem[.] Nescio an eo modo loquatur et accipiat sanguinem sicut accipit in sequenti versu. Ego enim libenter hic interpretarer sanguinem pro rubore, id quod hebraica vox patitur. Sicut est Genes. 49: in sanguine uvae pallium suum. Et Deuteron. 32: sanguinem uvae biberent meracissimum i. e. rubellum de electissimis uvis. Ita hic quoque significare puto (quamvis non satis certus sim). Nam quod pro signo isto statuere volumus sanguinem Christi et martyrum effusum in terram, ut quidam faciunt, nimium audax et detortum mihi videtur." WA 13:112.20–27. LW 18:110.

[22] WA DB 11.2:222.3.

[23] One of Luther's key "rules" of translation was to interpret the Old Testament in light of the New Testament (also referred to as a "Christological axiom"). See Birgit Stolt, "Luther's Translation of the Bible," *Lutheran Quarterly* 28 (2014): 379. Frederic W. Farrar cites "the reference of all Scripture to Christ," in Farrar, *History of Interpretation: Eight Lectures Preached before the University of Oxford in the Year MDCCCLXXXV. On the Foundation of the Late Rev. John Bampton* (London: Macmillan, 1886), 332. He nuances this, though, in the pages that follow.

Table 2.2: Parallel Bible references: Hab. 1:8 and Zech. 11:7.

Verse	NASB	Hebrew Bible	Vulgate	*Deutsche Bibel*
Hab. 1:8	Their horses are swifter than leopards And keener than wolves in the evening. Their horsemen come galloping, Their horsemen come from afar; They fly like an eagle swooping down to devour.	וְקַלּוּ מִנְּמֵרִים סוּסָיו וְחַדּוּ מִזְּאֵבֵי עֶרֶב וּפָשׁוּ פָּרָשָׁיו וּפָרָשָׁיו מֵרָחוֹק יָבֹאוּ יָעֻפוּ כְּנֶשֶׁר חָשׁ לֶאֱכוֹל	leviores pardis equi eius et velociores **lupis vespertinis** et diffundentur equites eius equites namque eius de longe venient volabunt quasi aquila festinans ad comedendum	Jre rosse sind schneller, denn die Parden, so sind sie auch beissiger, denn die **wolffe des abends**, Jre reuter zihen mit grossem hauffen von fernen daher, als floegen sie, wie die Adeler eilen zum ass. (1532) WA DB 11.2:302.8.
Zech. 11:7	So I pastured the flock doomed to slaughter, hence the afflicted of the flock. And I took for myself two staffs: the one I called Favor and the other I called Union; so I pastured the flock.	וָאֶרְעֶה אֶת-צֹאן הַהֲרֵגָה לָכֵן עֲנִיֵּי הַצֹּאן וָאֶקַּח-לִי שְׁנֵי מַקְלוֹת לְאַחַד קָרָאתִי נֹעַם וּלְאַחַד קָרָאתִי חֹבְלִים וָאֶרְעֶה אֶת-הַצֹּאן	et pascam pecus occisionis propter hoc o pauperes gregis et adsumpsi mihi duas virgas unam vocavi **Decorem** et alteram vocavi **Funiculos** et pavi gregem	Vnd ich huetet der schlachtschaffe, vmb der elenden schaffe willen, Vnd nam zu mir zween stebe, Einen hies ich **Sanfft**, den andern hies ich **Wehe**, vnd huetet der schaf. (1532) WA DB 11.2:352.7.

Habakkuk 1:8

As with discrepancies between Luther's *Deutsche Bibel* and his exegetical arguments, the fluctuation in his argumentation between his lectures and subsequent commentaries often shows his uncertainty concerning the meaning of the Hebrew and how to render it into German. That uncertainty was fueled by the obscurity of the Hebrew which he faced as a non-indigenous, non-expert user of the language. Such is the case with Hab. 1:8. Luther explained in his 1525 lectures on Habakkuk that despite the dispute among translators concerning the meaning of זְאֵבֵי עֶרֶב (*zəʾēḇê ʿereḇ*, "wolves of evening"), he favored the translation *lupi deserti* ("desert wolves"):

But the meaning of the word translated 'evening' is uncertain, and there is a difference of opinion among the linguists whether it ought to be translated 'evening wolves [*lupi vespertini*]' or 'wolves of the desert [*lupi deserti*].' Jerome translated 'evening wolves [*lupi vespertini*],' influenced by this line of reasoning: Since evening wolves have suffered hunger throughout the day, they attack a flock more viciously than other wolves do, and they do not leave until they have filled themselves. Who does not see that such an interpretation is weak? Therefore I prefer to adopt the other interpretation, so I translate 'wolves of the desert [*lupi deserti*],' that is, wolves that are fierce and untamed. The Germans also have this way of speaking: 'May savage wolves tear you apart [*Das dich die wilde wolff zureissen*]!'[24]

In the subsequent 1526 commentary, however, he reversed his position:

> Some people translate 'evening wolves [*Abends wolffe*]' as 'wolves from the desert [*wolffe aus der wuesten*].' The Hebrew letters admit either one. However, I believe that these are evening wolves [*abends wolffe*]. I think that this means to say that wolves, which are rapacious, ravenous, murderous beasts by nature, are far more so in the evening because they have not roamed about during the day and their hunger looks to the evening. Therefore the term 'evening wolves [*Abends wolffe*]' is practically synonymous with 'hungry wolves [*hungerige wolffe*]' who have not eaten for a long time.[25]

In the end, he followed this interpretation in his *Deutsche Bibel*, rendering זְאֵבֵי עֶרֶב (*zəʾēḇê ʿereḇ*) as *wolffe des abends* ("wolves of the evening").[26] When he said "the Hebrew letters admit either one," presumably he meant that pointed differently, עֲרָב (*ʿărāḇ*) would indicate Arabia, hence "desert."[27] Thus, the obscurity of the Hebrew in this instance likely stemmed from the multiple pointing options for ערב (*ʿrḇ*), and therefore the multiple readings that could be made based on those variants. Ultimately, despite his initial criticism of Jerome's rendering, his change of heart was based on an adjustment to how he interpreted the Hebrew letters and resolved the obscurity.[28]

---

[24] "Est autem vox ambigua et contentio est inter grammaticos, an sit vertendum: lupi vespertini an lupi deserti. Hieronymus transtulit lupi vespertini hac scil. ratione ductus, quod lupi vespertini famelici tota die famem passi magis grassentur in gregem, in quam incidunt quam alii et non discedant nisi exsaturati. Id frigidum esse quis non videt. Ideo ego alteram malo sententiam amplecti, ut vertam: lupi deserti, hoc est, saevi et non cicurati. Sic enim solent et Germani dicere: Das dich die wilde wolff zureissen[!]" WA 13:427.27–34. LW 19:112–3.

[25] "'Abends wolffe', wilchs etliche verdolmetzen 'wolffe aus der wuesten', denn es beydes ym Ebreischen mag aus den buchstaben genomen werden. Doch ich halts, das 'abends wolffe' seyen, das die meynunge sey: Der wolff, wilchs von natur eyn reyssend, raubisch, mordisch thier ist, Aber am abend viel reubischer ist, weyl er den tag uber nit gelauffen und also auff den abend hungerig ist, das gleich so viel gesagt sey 'Abends wolffe' als hungerige wolffe." WA 19:368.26–WA 19:369.5. LW 19:170. The protocol records show that his team had likely made their decision by 1539–41. These records show Luther's same reasoning about wolves being hungry in the evening: "[v. 8.] bissig, wens [wens] den gantzen tag nichts gessen haben." WA DB 4:258a.20–21. The 1538/39 handwritten entries in his copy of the Old Testament do not record any comments concerning this verse.

[26] WA DB 11.2:302.8. I omitted the מִ (*mi*, "than") for the sake of clarity.

[27] See also LW 19:112 Note 4.

[28] This same construction זְאֵבֵי עֶרֶב (*zəʾēḇê ʿereḇ*) appears in Zeph. 3:3. Luther expressed similar uncertainty in the lectures on Zephaniah, and cited Hab. 1:8 there. WA 13:500.11–23. LW 18:350–1. He translated זְאֵבֵי עֶרֶב (*zəʾēḇê ʿereḇ*) in Zeph. 3:3 as *wolffe am abend*. WA DB 11.2:316.3. See Krause, *Studien*, 27, Note 14; *Rudimenta*, 406–7; and the LXX rendering for more on this.

Zechariah 11:7

Luther's interpretation of Zech. 11:7 presents a different scenario. It shows the interaction between the philological obscurity – his uncertainty concerning the lexical meaning – and a theological problem based on that philological point – the question of whether to definitively accept any of the interpretations which others in the preceding theological tradition had made and apply them to resolve the lexical quandary. His struggle appears in his wavering translation from the time of the lectures to that of the commentary, when he ultimately decided to translate against the literal Hebrew as he saw it.

In the lectures on Zechariah, he addressed two Hebrew terms, expressing confidence as to the meaning of one and uncertainty concerning the other:

> I would prefer to have kept the Hebrew words with which he names the two staffs and not to have translated them. The first staff he calls *Noam* [נֹעַם, *nōʿam*]; the other, *Choblim* [חֹבְלִים, *ḥōbəlîm*]. There is no doubt that *Noam* [נֹעַם, *nōʿam*] means 'delight [*iucundum*]' – in German, *Lust*. But what חֹבְלִים [*ḥōbəlîm*] is I do not understand as yet. I am uncertain as to its proper meaning. Some translate it as 'a thin cord [*funiculum*],' others as 'a chief [*ducem*],' still others as 'a sailor [*nautam*].' Everyone may follow the translation he wants. Were I allowed to follow my own thoughts, I believe it means those who mourn [*dolentes*], as that he intended different staffs to be understood; the first a delightful one [*iucundum*] which does no harm to the sheep, which does not scatter but only gathers and brings them together to their feed, the other a threatening one [*asperum*] with which he can protect the sheep and drive off the wolves, as if he wished to signify a club [*clavam*]. But because we can come to no certain conclusion here, we shall not depart from the interpretation of the Septuagint and of Jerome. These translate it as a slender cord [*funiculum*]. Therefore, we take the first staff to mean *ein fein Rütlein* – a pleasant, soft wand [*iucundum et molle virgultum*]; and the second, a staff [*baculum*] to be used instead of a whip [*flagelli*] or as a whip [*flagellum*] itself. This is the grammatical rationale.[29]

He explained later in his comments on v. 10 that there was no theological consensus about the meaning of the two staffs; nevertheless, he made his judgment: "There is disagreement among the interpreters as to what these two staffs mean. I have thought of various ideas, but I see no better meaning than that which the text suggests ... Those two staffs mean the two proclamations, Gospel and

---

[29] "Mallem autem mansisse vocabula hebraea, quibusque utrumque baculum nominat et non esse translata. Primum baculum vocat Noam, alterum Choblim. Non dubium est, quin Noam significet iucundum, germanice Lust, חֹבְלִים vero quid sit, nondum intelligo, incertus sum, quid proprie significet, alii vertunt funiculum, alii ducem, alii nautam. Sequatur quisque, quod volet. Ego si mihi liceret sequi meas cogitationes, puto significare dolentes, ut diversos baculos voluerit intelligi: primum iucundum, qui non laedit oves, non dispergit sed congregat tantum et colligit ad pascua, alterum asperum, quo tueri potest oves et lupos arcere, tanquam si clavam velit significare. Sed quia nihil certi possumus hic statuere, non variabimus ab interpretatione septuaginta et Hieronymi, qui funiculum verterunt, ut scil. primum baculum intelligamus eyn feyn ruthleyn, iucundum et molle virgultum, alterum autem baculum, qui sit vice flagelli vel ipsum flagellum. Atque haec est ratio grammatical." WA 13:647.12–25. LW 20:120–1.

Law."³⁰ But at the time of the lectures, as his earlier comments concerning v. 7 show, he still was not ready to apply that interpretation and resolve his uncertainty concerning the proper lexical meaning of חֹבְלִים (ḥōḇəlîm).

But the indecisiveness did not last. By the time he wrote the commentary on Zechariah, he had made up his mind. However, in that commentary, he argued for a different translation of both נֹעַם (nōʿam) and חֹבְלִים (ḥōḇəlîm). Moreover, he explained his theologically-driven decision for deviating from what he saw as the literal Hebrew, in what would end up being his *Deutsche Bibel* translation:

> The first staff, then, is the Holy Gospel, which is a delightful [*liebliche*], merry [*lustige*] sermon of grace. He therefore calls it *Noam* [נֹעַם, nōʿam] here, that is, 'merry and pleasant [*lustig und fein*].' We have Germanized it as 'Gentle [*sanft*],' so that it might agree all the better with the second word. For 'Gentle [*sanft*]' and 'Painful [*wehe*]' go well together as opposites. The second staff, however, is the Law, which is a hard, bitter, and difficult [*harte, saure und schwere*] sermon for the old man.³¹

He translated נֹעַם (nōʿam, "pleasantness") as *Sanfft* ("gentleness") and חֹבְלִים (ḥōḇəlîm, "ropes, cords") as *Wehe* ("pain") in the *Deutsche Bibel*.³² The Vulgate translated them as *Decorum* ("seemliness, grace, elegance") and *Funiculos* ("ropes, cords") respectively. Luther deviated, albeit slightly, from the Vulgate's translation of נֹעַם (nōʿam), not because he thought it was incorrect, but in order to amplify the contrast between נֹעַם (nōʿam, *Sanfft*) and חֹבְלִים (ḥōḇəlîm, *Wehe*). Nevertheless, it was an important departure from his argument in the lectures that there was "no doubt" the Hebrew נֹעַם (nōʿam) should be translated as *Lust* ("desire, delight").

Zech. 11:7 is thus another example of a contradiction between Luther's argument in the lectures and commentary which reveals the role of Hebrew obscurity in his translation. In this verse, it shows the impact of his struggle with both a philological obscurity and a theological question stemming from that obscurity. Moreover, it shows his resolution of that Hebrew obscurity through a theologically-motivated reading that ultimately led him to go against what he saw as the literal Hebrew.

---

³⁰ "Varie controvertitur apud interpretes, quid significent duo isti baculi. Ego quoque varia cogitavi sed non video sententiam meliorem quam illam, quam ipse textus secum affert ... Significant autem duo isti baculi duas praedicationes, euangelium et legem." WA 13:648.24–26, 29. LW 20:122.

³¹ "So ist nun der eine Stab das heilige Evangelium, welches ist eine liebliche, lustige Predigt der Gnaden. Darum heißt er sie auch hier Noam [נֹעַם], das ist, lustig und fein. Wir haben's verdeutscht 'sanft', auf daß sich's auf das andere Wort desto baß reime. Denn 'sanft' und 'wehe' lauten wohl wider einander. Der andere Stab ist das Gesetz, welches ist eine harte, saure und schwere Predigt dem alten Menschen." StL 14:1941.17-StL 14:1942.17. LW 20:315.

³² WA DB 11.2:352.7.

The *Deutsche Bibel* Revisions

Numerous editions of the Minor Prophets as part of Luther's *Deutsche Bibel* appeared between 1532 and 1545. He made various revisions during this time, many of which appear in the 1538/39 handwritten entries in his Old Testament copy and in the 1539–41 protocol records. The following section focuses strictly on differences between the 1532 and 1545 publications in order to highlight the ongoing, long-term role that the obscurity of the Hebrew text played in his German Bible. These differences show that while many of his revisions represent simple growth and development in his Hebrew translation skills and understanding of the language, in some cases much more lies beneath the surface. Jon. 2:9 is a prime example of the value in examining these discrepancies, and what such investigations can reveal concerning how Luther's struggles with the obscurities of the Hebrew language influenced his German Bible translation and exegesis. Table 2.3 shows the parallel Hebrew, Latin, and German translations for Jon. 2:9.

Table 2.3: Parallel Bible references: Jon. 2:9.

Verse	NASB	Hebrew Bible	Vulgate	*Deutsche Bibel*
Jon. 2:9	Those who regard vain idols Forsake their faithfulness	מְשַׁמְּרִים הַבְלֵי־שָׁוְא חַסְדָּם יַעֲזֹבוּ	qui custodiunt vanitates frustra **misericordiam suam** derelinquunt	Aber die sich verlassen auff jre werck, die doch nichts sind, achten **der gnade** nicht. (1532) WA DB 11.2:264.9.
				DJe da halten vber dem Nichtigen, Verlassen **jre gnade**. (1545) WA DB 11.2:265.9.

Jonah 2:9

Luther made a major change against the Hebrew Bible in his translation of Jon. 2:9. In the commentary on Jonah, he explained that he intentionally translated against the Hebrew, in order to avoid an interpretation by the German reader which would contradict his theological understanding of *Barmherzigkeit* ("mercy, lovingkindness") and *Gnade* ("grace"). He focused on the term חַסְדָּם (*ḥasdām*, "their lovingkindness"):

> They who observe lying vanities forsake mercy [*barmhertzikeit*]. The Hebrew text reads: 'They forsake their own mercy [*yhre barmhertzickeit*].' However, since this lends the impression in German that Jonah is referring to mercy which is man's own, mercy that he

himself shows, I have omitted the word 'their own [*yhre*]' and for the sake of clarity have used only the word 'mercy [*barmhertzickeit*].'[33]

Later in the same commentary, he reiterated the theological grounds for his omission of םָ◌- (*-ām*, "their") in the German: "For with this verse, Jonah chastens the ignorant work-righteous and hypocrites who trust not in God's grace alone, but instead in their own works."[34] His 1532 *Deutsche Bibel* translation was consistent with that argument in the commentary. He translated חַסְדָּם (*ḥasdām*) there as *der gnade* ("the grace"), omitting the suffix *ihr* ("their"), the equivalent of which appears in the Hebrew Bible as םָ◌- (*-ām*).[35]

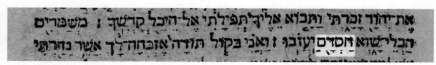

Figure 2.1: Jonah 2:9, 1494 Brescia Hebrew Bible (*source:* Staatsbibliothek zu Berlin – Preußischer Kulturbesitz, 8° Inc 2840, fol. 423r [857]).[36]

But in the 1545 *Deutsche Bibel*, he reversed that interpretation, translating חַסְדָּם (*ḥasdām*) as *jre gnade* ("their grace") and including the suffix.[37] With that modification, he now followed the literal Hebrew, but he also directly contradicted

---

[33] "Wilche aber sich verlassen auff eytelkeit vergeblich, Die lassen barmhertzikeit faren. Im Ebreischen steht: 'Die lassen yhre barmhertzickeit faren'. Aber weil das ym Deutschen laut, als rede er von der menschen barmhertzickeit, die sie beweysen sollen, habe ich das wortlin 'yhre' ausgelassen und schlecht 'barmhertzickeit' gesetzt, das es deste deutlicher were." WA 19:230.21–26. LW 19:80. Luther made a similar argument in the lectures on Jon. 2:9, though he did not explicitly describe his translation omission in detail as he did in the commentary. Notably, he also linked that interpretation to *Anfechtung* in the lectures through multiple references to *tentatio*. See WA 13:251.32–WA 13:252.6.

[34] "Denn Jona strafft mit disem vers die unverstendigen werckheyligen und heuchler, die nicht auff gottes gnade alleine, sondern auff yhr eigen werck trawen." WA 19:230.32–34. LW 19:80. Cf. Luther's interpretation of Hos. 9:11, where he argued that םָ◌ (*-ām*) is superfluous, which seems to have been on strictly philological rather than theological grounds. WA 13:45.16–26. LW 18:51.

[35] WA DB 11.2:264.9. Luther began the Jonah commentary with a complete German translation of the Book, after which he followed with the actual commentary. He translated Jon. 2:9 in that header as: *Aber wilche sich verlassen auff eytelkeyt vergeblich, Die lassen barmhertzickeyt faren*, also omitting *ihr*. WA 19:189.24–25. Luther used both *Barmherzigkeit* and *Gnade* [and *gnädig* and *barmhertzig*] in his discussions of חַסְדָּם (*ḥasdām*) in the commentary [with variant spellings, indicative of his time period].

[36] Staatsbibliothek zu Berlin: https://digital.staatsbibliothek-berlin.de/werkansicht?PPN=PPN720865522&PHYSID=PHYS_0857&DMDID=.

[37] WA DB 11.2:265.9. Luther added in the gloss: "Auff Deudsch, Werckheiligen vnd Heuchler verlassen jren Gott vnd Christum, vmb jres nichtigen Gottesdiensts willen ('In German, "works saints" and hypocrites abandon their God and Christ, for the sake of their vain worship')."

the 1532 Bible translation and his argument in the 1526 commentary.[38] Ultimately, he decided that it was more important to adhere to the literal Hebrew text, and retain the suffix, than to force the theological interpretation through. Nevertheless, the disparity between his 1532 and 1545 translations shows the struggle concerning the proper way to express the Hebrew that he deemed theologically obscure – whether one accepts that as correct or incorrect based on the text – for his German audience.

Luther's initial censure of the Hebrew text, predicated on his contention that חַסְדָּם (ḥasdām) was "not ours ... but God's alone," has eerie similarities to his notorious translation of πίστει ("by means of faith") in Rom. 3:28 as *alleyn durch den glawben* ("alone through [the] faith").[39] His argument in Jonah is particularly significant, as it is decidedly more tendentious than that of Romans. In his explanation of the translation of Rom. 3:28 which appears in *Sendbrief vom Dolmetschen*, his contention was that the issue was not only theological – in fact, in some ways, not at all – but instead was predicated upon a specific philological construction innate to the German language – *nicht* ("not") / *kein* ("no/none") and *allein* ("alone").[40] In Jon. 2:9, by contrast, his argument concerning the Hebrew obscurity was strictly theological and had no philological basis in the original biblical text.

Summary

Table A.1 in the Appendix provides an overview of numerous additional interpretative variances in Luther's translation and exegesis of the Minor Prophets across all three preceding categories. These interpretative variances demonstrate that the obscurity of the Hebrew language had a profound and persisting influence on his translation. Many of the foregoing examples have a key element in common: the Hebrew figure of speech. While not every interpretative variance was connected to a Hebrew figure of speech, that element of the language nevertheless was a key locus of his frustration. Moreover, it was the place where one often finds much of the hermeneutical and linguistic genius for which scholars praise his German Bible. The next section in this chapter examines this facet of Luther's translation.

---

[38] The Vulgate translated חַסְדָּם (ḥasdām) in Jon. 2:9 as *misericordiam suam* ("their mercy"), following the Hebrew Bible. The 1538/39 handwritten entries in Luther's Old Testament also cite חַסְדָּם (ḥasdām) as *ihre gnade* ("their mercy"), thus his decision to reverse the 1532 translation ostensibly began long before 1545. WA DB 4:244b.19–WA DB 4:245b.6. Nevertheless, the protocols record the discussion concerning the first part of the verse, without explicit attention to the issue with חַסְדָּם (ḥasdām). WA DB 4:244a.19–WA DB 4:245a.13. Luther also included a gloss in the 1545 Bible, but it focused on the first part of the verse. WA DB 11.2:265.9.

[39] See WA 7:39.28, WA 30.2:632–46, and LW 35:177–203.

[40] Cf. his comments in WA 30.2:632–46 to those in WA 19:230.29–30.

Part II: Methodological Variances
Concerning Specific Philological Challenges

To say that Luther's focus on the Hebrew language for his Bible translation was particularly philological is an important discriminating point. He was not just interested in understanding the strict grammar of the Hebrew, but rather how the language fit into the cultural context of the Hebrew world, and thus how he could transfer that over to another cultural context in Germany. It was this discrimination that would, in large part, differentiate his German Bible from German Bibles which preceded his. With this in mind, philological elements are an appropriate place to begin a further inquiry into the role of the Hebrew language in his German translation.

One of the most conspicuous observations concerning the role of Hebrew philology in Luther's Bible translation is the inconsistency of his methodology in addressing certain linguistic issues in the Hebrew Bible. Even though he himself laid down various "rules" of translation, on which many scholars base their appraisals of his method, the inconsistencies across his translation and argumentation suggest that those hermeneutical axioms were not as fast and firm as his remarks might suggest. Even semi-systematic assessments of Luther's Bible translation methodology, though they are based on his own remarks, create a deeply flawed and limiting view of his Hebrew translation.[41]

Luther called special attention to three particular philological challenges in his writings and deliberations on the Minor Prophets: (1) Hebrew figures of speech; (2) the Hebrew trope of repetition; and (3) the question of Hebrew transliteration. The remainder of this chapter will examine these three issues and demonstrate how Luther's response to each reveals the distinct role that his struggle with the obscurities of the Hebrew language played in his *Deutsche Bibel* translation. In contrast to the first section in this chapter, which focuses on issues where he specifically addressed the *meaning* of the Hebrew term(s), this second section focuses on issues where he specifically addressed the *method* of transmitting the meaning to the German reader.

---

[41] Many scholars attempt to make such systematic appraisals of Luther's translation method. See, for example: Bluhm, *Creative*, 130–1; Kolb, *Martin Luther and the Enduring*, 213–4, citing Stolt, *Rhetorik*, 90; Schwarz, *Biblical Translation*, 211; Bainton, *Here I Stand*, 327; Meissinger, *Luthers Exegese in der Frühzeit*, 39–40; and Wood, *Captive to the Word*, 166–7.

Hebrew Figures of Speech

"So great is the difficulty of this passage that in nearly every word the prophet has used Hebrew tropes or figures of speech. It makes me think that almost every figure of speech of the Hebrew language has been gathered together here. We are absolutely insane, then, when we undertake the interpretation of the prophets without a very great skill in and understanding of the Hebrew language."[42]
Martin Luther, March/April, 1525

One of the most intriguing aspects of Luther's translation of the Hebrew Bible is the varied way in which he dealt with Hebrew figures of speech. Moreover, figures of speech were one of the most crucial challenges which he faced in his translation of the Minor Prophets, which, among all the books of the Hebrew Bible, he called special attention to because of their prolific use of Hebraisms and obscure language.[43] Over and over again, he cited the "Hebrew way of speaking." He lamented the difficulties that Hebrew figures of speech presented, and warned of the special skills that the translator needed in order to untangle them. He contended that the solution lay in rendering Hebrew figures of speech into colloquial German. He explained in the *Tischreden* (1532),

> It is not possible to reproduce a foreign idiom in one's native tongue. The proper method of translation is to seek a vocabulary neither too free nor too literal, but to select the most fitting terms according to the usage of the language adopted. To translate properly is to render the spirit of a foreign language into our own idiom ... I try to speak as men do in the market place ... ***In rendering Moses, I make him so German that no one would suspect he was a Jew.***[44]

But was this really so? While scholar after scholar praises Luther's creation of a truly *German* Bible for the German people, upon close inspection of his translations of the Hebrew figures of speech in the Minor Prophets, it is not so

---

[42] "Tanta est huius loci difficultas, ut fere in singulis verbis usus sit propheta hebraicis figuris et tropis, ut putem in hunc locum fere congestum esse, quicquid est figurarum hebraeae linguae. Itaque insigniter insanimus, cum suscipimus interpretandos prophetas sine peritia et penitissima hebraeae linguae cognitione." WA 13:304.17–21; LW 18:214; from Luther's remarks concerning Mic. 1:8 in his lectures on Micah.

[43] See his comments concerning the prevalence of this language in the Minor Prophets: WA 13:161.30–31; LW 18:131.

[44] Smith, *Life and Letters*, 213, *roughly* following WA TR 2:648.3–6, 11, 13–15, 16–17 [§ 2771a (§ 976, § 978, and § 979 from the notes of Cordatus)]: "Es ist nicht moglich, das einer sein geborn sprach eigentlich rede mit einer andern zungen, vnd modus vertendi ist, das man das vocabulum nicht zu nahe suche noch zuweit, sed propriissime neme secundum quamlibet linguam ... Vere transferre est per aliam linguam dictum applicare suae linguae ... Man mus alßo reden, wie man auff dem marckt redt ... Si nunc a me Moses transferendus esset, wolt ich yhn wol deutsch machen, quia vellem ei exuere Hebraismos, et ita, ut nemo diceret Haebreum esse Mosen." Emphasis mine. See also Conrad Cordatus, *Tagebuch über Dr. Martin Luther. Geführt von Dr. Conrad Cordatus 1537*, ed. H. Wrampelmeyer (Halle: Max Niemeyer, 1885), 250. Thank you to Henry Zecher for pointing me to this.

clear-cut.[45] In fact, his methodology in translating Hebrew figures of speech is plagued by inconsistency.

The Data in the Minor Prophets

Table A.2 in the Appendix lists 217 instances in the Minor Prophets where Luther explicitly identified Hebrew words and phrases as some sort of figure of speech: Hebrew idiom, metaphor, synecdoche, Hebraism, etc.[46] Furthermore, every example represents a verse where he explicitly mentioned the Hebrew as part of his argument. Thus, the role of Hebrew in his translation decision for each is beyond dispute. Each example is assigned to one of five categories: where (1) he made a literal translation of the Hebrew figure of speech, neglecting to explain it in the German [127 instances]; (2) he interpreted the meaning of the Hebrew figure of speech in the German so that it would be clear for the German reader [fifty-two instances];[47] (3) he translated the Hebrew figure of speech by using all or some part of an existing German idiom, or German idiomatic language [thirteen instances];[48] (4) he used a mixed methodology [sev-

---

[45] For example, James Anthony Froude writes, "In that compelled retreat he bestowed on Germany the greatest of all the gifts which he was able to offer ... the Bible into clear vernacular German." Froude, *Luther: A Short Biography* (London: Longmans, Green, and Co., 1883 [Reprinted from the Contemporary Review]), 29.

[46] There are an enormous number of additional figures of speech which Luther identified beyond those which appear in Table A.2. The criteria (1) Luther specifically mentioning Hebrew in his argument, and (2) Luther specifically identifying the text as some variant of a figure of speech, limited the data to what appears here. It speaks to the incredible frequency with which he used figures of speech in his translation and exegesis. He sometimes explained figures of speech in his *Deutsche Bibel* glosses. Table A.2 contains the references for the *Deutsche Bibel*, where these glosses can be found (though it does not call out special attention to these). See Krause, *Studien*, 196–7 concerning Luther's sometimes errant use of terminology in identifying certain figures of speech. Junghans also cites this, although he adds that Luther did not do so unknowingly, but rather because he was following a particular tradition, as also taken up by Melanchthon in *Elementa rhetorices*. Helmar Junghans, *Martin Luther und die Rhetorik* (Stuttgart/Leipzig: Verlag der Sächsischen Akademie der Wissenschaften zu Leipzig: In Kommission bei S. Hirzel, 1998), 8–9 and Note 19. For more on Hebrew figures of speech in the Minor Prophets, see Krause, *Studien*, 68–72, 181–213. As a point of comparison, on Isaiah, see Thyen, "Luthers Jesajavorlesung," 109, 170–86.

[47] Luther, though, did not always fully clarify the figure of speech for the German reader. Many times, he made interpretative readings of only part of the idioms. The lines between these categories, therefore, are inevitably often blurred.

[48] The objective of the "German idiom" assignment is to differentiate Luther's use of existing German idiomatic language from his literal rendering of Hebrew into German. "German idiom" is used broadly to represent either a formal German proverb or a more general German figure of speech which Luther's contemporary Germans would understand. The criterion employed for this is that scholarly evidence shows the existence of a certain German idiom or idiomatic language during and/or prior to Luther's time, and thus it is likely that Luther was drawing upon that idiom. Given the time gap between the sixteenth century and now, it is very difficult to argue with certainty that this is so. To limit the scope and gain a reliable picture from some of the main sources used by linguistic scholars for the late medieval period, I have

enteen instances];[49] or (5) his methodology changed from his 1532 Bible to the 1545 revision [eight instances].[50] This assignment is based solely on his *Deutsche Bibel* translation, irrespective of any interpretation made in the exegetical lectures or commentaries.[51]

Figure 2.2 below summarizes this data. The full data set, showing Luther's translations in comparison with the Hebrew Bible and Vulgate for each example, appears in Table A.2. The numbers should not be interpreted as statistically significant or as an absolute delineation of his weighted use of a particular method in the Minor Prophets – they are neither. The sample is not randomized, and the examples which comprise it were identified utilizing a subjective methodology, based on Luther's own identifications of the Hebrew as different types of figures of speech.

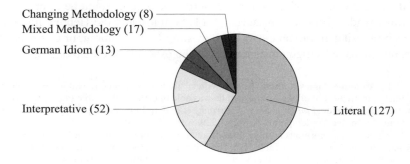

Figure 2.2: Luther's translation of Hebrew figures of speech in the Minor Prophets.

---

used the following for identifying evidence of usage during and/or prior to Luther's time: (1) Luther's personal collection of German proverbs [*Luthers Sprichwörtersammlung*], in WA 51:634–726; (2) James C. Cornette, Jr., *Proverbs and Proverbial Expressions in the German Works of Martin Luther*, ed. Wolfgang Mieder and Dorothee Racette (Bern: Peter Lang, 1997); (3) WAN; (4) DWB; (5) MERZ; (6) SPAL; and (7) SING. Thank you to Prof. Dr. Henrike Lähnemann (Oxford University), Dr. Sheila Watts (Cambridge University), and Rev. Dr. Benjamin Mayes (Concordia Theological Seminary) for the guidance on this. The footnotes in the main text and especially in Table A.2 list the relevant evidence of these idioms in Luther's time and prior. German *Lehnsprichwörter* ("loan proverbs"), which are in all likelihood derived from biblical language (based on their equivalence with the literal Hebrew text) are assigned as "literal translations," rather than "German idioms." German idiomatic language also appears in some instances as part of "Mixed" translations: Hos. 7:10; Joel 2:6; Amos 2:13, 3:3, 5:9; Nah. 2:2, 2:3, 2:11; Hab. 1:8; and Mal. 3:8. It also appears in one of the changing translations between 1532 and 1545: Hab. 1:4. These appear in Table A.2.

[49] Examples of a mixed method also sometimes appear in examples from the 1532 *Deutsche Bibel* or the 1545 revision, which are categorized as "Changing Methodology" (see Nah. 2:3 and 2:5). These appear in Table A.2.

[50] In categories 1–4, Luther's methodology was the same in 1532 and 1545.

[51] His exegesis, nevertheless, is extremely helpful for understanding how he identified Hebrew terms and phrases as figures of speech, and thus also for understanding his translation decisions.

General Variation in Luther's Hermeneutic and Key Tendencies

In general, Luther's method for translating Hebrew figures of speech was uneven. Figure 2.2 shows this quite clearly. Nevertheless, his hermeneutic has certain identifiable patterns. For instance, he tended to make literal translations of Hebrew idioms associated with cultural- and/or ethno-specific customs and practices of the ancient Israelite authors of the Hebrew Bible texts. But even this pattern in his method showed inconsistencies. For example, he translated the expression וַיִּלְבְּשׁוּ שַׂקִּים (*wayyilbəšû śaqqîm*, "and put on sacks, sackcloth") in Jon. 3:5 as *Vnd zogen secke an* ("and put on sacks").[52] He rendered וְהַעֲלֵיתִי עַל־כָּל־מָתְנַיִם שָׂק (*wəhaʿălêtî ʿal-kol-motnayim śāq*, "and I will bring up sackcloth upon all loins") in Amos 8:10 as *Jch wil vber alle lenden, den sack bringen* ("I will bring the sack over all loins").[53] And in Jon. 3:6, he translated וַיֵּשֶׁב עַל־הָאֵפֶר (*wayyēšeḇ ʿal-hāʾēper*, "and sat upon the ashes") as *vnd setzt sich jnn die asschen* ("and sat in the ashes").[54] All are essentially literal renderings of the Hebrew. By contrast, in Mic. 1:10 he rendered בְּבֵית לְעַפְרָה (*bəḇêṯ ləʿaprâ*, "at Beth-le-aphrah [in the house of ashes, dust]") as [*Sondern gehet*] *jnn die traurkamer* ("[But go] into the mourning chamber") – an interpretative translation for the German reader.[55] Moreover, while בְּבֵית לְעַפְרָה (*bəḇêṯ ləʿaprâ*) in Mic. 1:10 clearly parallels וַיֵּשֶׁב עַל־הָאֵפֶר (*wayyēšeḇ ʿal-hāʾēper*) in Jon. 3:6, and both are Hebrew figures of speech indicating mourning, his translation methodology drastically differed between the two. His tendency to make literal translations of Hebrew idioms associated with these cultural- and/or ethno-specific customs and practices was ultimately unstable.

Luther also tended to make literal translations of Hebrew idioms connected to ancient Israelite religious ritual. This also showed inconsistency, and irregularities sometimes appear within his argumentation. For example, in Zech. 9:15, he identified three metaphors, two of which he argued would be quite easily understood by non-Hebrews, and one of which he argued would be quite difficult because it was linked to ritual sacrifice:

> The prophet uses many different metaphors. In our language these are quite difficult; in Hebrew, however, they are most appropriate. Indeed, because the Jewish people regularly used sacrifices, they could easily accept metaphors therefrom – something we cannot do. Yet, the metaphors related to eating and drinking which he mentioned here are frequent even among other nations.[56]

---

[52] WA DB 11.2:266.5.
[53] WA DB 11.2:246.10.
[54] WA DB 11.2:266.6.
[55] WA DB 11.2:272.10. This is sometimes also transliterated in the English as "in Beth-le-aphrah" (in the RSV, NRSV, NIV, ESV, and NASB) or similar ("house of Aphrah" in the KJV). Cf. his translation of עָפָר הִתְפַּלָּשִׁי (*ʿāpār hiṯpallāšî*) at the end of the verse as *vnd sitzt jnn die asschen*. While he did not identify that as a figure of speech in this verse, it is almost the exact same phrase that he used to translate וַיֵּשֶׁב עַל־הָאֵפֶר (*wayyēšeḇ ʿal-hāʾēper*) in Jon. 3:6.
[56] "Utitur propheta multis et variis metaphoris, quae in nostra lingua satis durae sunt sed

Yet he translated all three into the German literally: וְאָכְלוּ (wəʾāḵəlû, "and they will devour") as *das sie fressen* ("that they may eat"); וְשָׁתוּ הָמוּ כְּמוֹ־יָיִן (wəšātû hāmû kəmô-yāyin, "and will drink, make a noise like wine") as *das sie trincken vnd rumorn als vom wein* ("that they may drink and make noise as from wine"); and וּמָלְאוּ כַּמִּזְרָק כְּזָוִיּוֹת מִזְבֵּחַ (ûmāləʾû kammizrāq kəzāwîyyôṯ mizbēaḥ, "and they will be full like the basin, like corners of an altar") as *vnd vol werden als das becken, vnd wie die ecken des altars* ("and may become full as the basin, and as the corners of the altar").[57] Despite his argument that the Germans could not easily grasp metaphors from ritual sacrifice, he treated that metaphor exactly as he did those which he said the Germans would easily understand. This underscores one of the major discrepancies between his argument in the *Tischreden* that he was making Moses unrecognizable as a Jew in his German Bible translation, and the reality of his Bible which, in fact, utilized many literal Hebraisms which most contemporary German readers would not have been able to comprehend without some explanation.

In his translation of Zeph. 3:19, Luther employed a different method. In the lectures, he identified עֹשֶׂה (ʿōśeh) as a term specifically linked to cultic purification ritual. And while it literally means "[he] does" or "[he] makes," he argued that it is "a Mosaic word" specifically used in connection with making burnt offerings for sin, and therefore should be understood as *offeret* ("he will offer") or *occidet* ("he will slay, kill").[58] He adhered to this in the *Deutsche Bibel*, translating עֹשֶׂה (ʿōśeh) as *ich wils ... aus machen* ("I will ... extinguish it"), thus offering a descriptive rendering of the Hebrew for the German reader through German idiomatic language rather than simply following the literal Hebrew.[59]

The variation in Luther's method for translating Hebrew cultural- and/or ethno-specific customs and religious ritual practices shows that while a literal translation was the norm, that method nevertheless exhibited the same perennial struggle that defined his overall translation of the Minor Prophets, a persistent vacillation over how he wanted to render unique Hebraisms to the German reader. Tables 2.4 and 2.5 below list these and other examples of Luther's translation of Hebrew idioms associated with cultural- and/or ethno-specific customs and practices, and religious ritual practice, in the Minor Prophets.

---

in lingua hebraea propriissimae, siquidem usum sacrificiorum habebat Iudaicus populus et ideo facili opera poterant inde metaphoras sumere, id quod nos non possumus. Attamen metaphorae de devorando et bibendo, quarum hic meminit crebrae sunt etiam apud alias gentes." WA 13:633.14–19. LW 20:101–2.

[57] WA DB 11.2:348.15.

[58] "Mosaicum est verbum." See WA 13:478.34–WA 13:479.5; WA 13:509.12–18; and LW 18:363–4.

[59] WA DB 11.2:318.19. *Ausmachen* can also be used to mean "to arrange" or "to account for"; but given the reference to burnt offering, "extinguish" seems the most fitting. See Table A.2 for the scholarly information concerning the idiomatic history of this term.

"The Obscure Hebrew" 69

Table 2.4: Luther's literal translation of cultural-specific Hebrew figures of speech.

Verse	Hebrew Bible	*Deutsche Bibel*	Bible References	Exegetical References
Joel 1:14	קַדְּשׁוּ־צוֹם ("Consecrate, sanctify a fast")	Heiliget eine Fasten ("Sanctify a fast")	WA DB 11.2:216.14; WA DB 11.2:217.14	WA 13:70.20–21; WA 13:92.28; LW 18:85
Amos 8:10	וְהַעֲלֵיתִי עַל־כָּל־מָתְנַיִם שָׂק ("and I will bring up sackcloth upon all loins")	Jch wil vber alle lenden, den sack bringen ("I will bring the sack over all loins")	WA DB 11.2:246.10; WA DB 11.2:247.10	WA 13:152.24– WA 13:153.2; WA 13:199.10–15; LW 18:182
Jon. 3:5	וַיִּלְבְּשׁוּ שַׂקִּים ("and wore sackcloth")	Vnd zogen secke an ("and put on sackcloth")	WA DB 11.2:266.5; WA DB 11.2:267.5	WA 13:236.3–25; WA 13:253.31–39; LW 19:24; LW 19:85–88
Jon. 3:6	וַיֵּשֶׁב עַל־הָאֵפֶר ("and sat upon the ashes")	vnd setzt sich jnn die asschen ("and sat in the ashes")	WA DB 11.2:266.6; WA DB 11.2:267.6	WA 13:236.26–33; WA 13:254.4–6; LW 19:24; LW 19:85–88
Nah. 2:1	עַל־הֶהָרִים ("on the mountains")	auff den bergen ("on the mountains")	WA DB 11.2:292.1; WA DB 11.2:293.1	WA 13:354.22– WA 13:355.8; WA 13:380.35– WA 13:381.28; LW 18:296
Zech. 2:11	בַּת־בָּבֶל ("[with] the daughter of Babylon")	bey der tochter Babel ("with the daughter of Babylon")	WA DB 11.2:334.7; WA DB 11.2:335.7	StL 14:1808.23– StL 14:1810.27; LW 20:189–91
Zech. 4:14	בְנֵי־הַיִּצְהָר ("the [two] sons of oil"; figuratively: "the two anointed ones")	die ... oele kinder ("the [two] oil-children")	WA DB 11.2:338.14; WA DB 11.2:339.14	WA 13:594.25– WA 13:595.17; StL 14:1852.20– StL 14:1855.24; LW 20:52; LW 20:229–32
Zech. 9:15	וְאָכְלוּ ("and they will devour")	das sie fressen ("that they may eat")	WA DB 11.2:348.15; WA DB 11.2:349.15	WA 13:632.10– WA 13:634.35; StL 14:1920.35– StL 14:1923.43; LW 20:100–3; LW 20:294–7

Verse	Hebrew Bible	*Deutsche Bibel*	Bible References	Exegetical References
Zech. 9:15	וְשָׁתוּ הָמוּ כְּמוֹ-יָיִן ("and will drink, make a noise like wine")	das sie trincken vnd rumorn als vom wein ("that they may drink and make noise as from wine")	WA DB 11.2:348.15; WA DB 11.2:349.15	WA 13:632.10– WA 13:634.35; StL 14:1920.35– StL 14:1923.43; LW 20:100–3; LW 20:294–7
Zech. 9:15	וּמָלְאוּ כַּמִּזְרָק כְּזָוִיּוֹת מִזְבֵּחַ ("and they will be full like the bowl, like corners of an altar")	vnd vol werden als das becken, vnd wie die ecken des altars ("and may become full as the bowl, and as the corners of the altar")	WA DB 11.2:348.15; WA DB 11.2:349.15	WA 13:632.10– WA 13:634.35; StL 14:1920.35– StL 14:1923.43; LW 20:100–3; LW 20:294–7
Zech. 11:3	הַיַּרְדֵּן ("of Yarden [Jordan]")	des Jordans ("of Jordan")	WA DB 11.2:352.3; WA DB 11.2:353.3	WA 13:645.12–22; StL 14:1937.7; LW 20:117–8; LW 20:311

Table 2.5: Luther's explanation of cultural-specific Hebrew figures of speech for the German reader.[60]

Verse	Hebrew Bible	*Deutsche Bibel*	Bible References	Exegetical References
Mic. 1:10	בְּבֵית לְעַפְרָה ("in Beth-le-aphrah/at the house of Aphara/in a house of ashes, dust")	jnn die traurkamer ("in the mourning chamber")	WA DB 11.2:272.10; WA DB 11.2:273.10	WA 13:264.20–33; WA 13:305.30–36; LW 18:216–7
Zeph. 2:5	יֹשְׁבֵי חֶבֶל הַיָּם ("residents of the cord [coast] of the sea")	denen, so am meer hinab wonen ("those who live by the sea")	WA DB 11.2:314.5; WA DB 11.2:315.5	WA 13:463.22–28; WA 13:494.16–21; LW 18:340–1
Zeph. 3:19	עֹשֶׂה ("I will deal with")	ich wils ... aus machen ("I will extinguish")	WA DB 11.2:318.19; WA DB 11.2:319.19	WA 13:478.34– WA 13:479.5; WA 13:509.12–18; LW 18:363–4

---

[60] Mic. 1:10 and Zeph. 2:5 represent interpretative renderings by Luther; Zeph. 3:19 shows him using German idiomatic language.

Inconsistencies across Different Verses

At times, Luther even used different methods to translate the same Hebrew idiom in different places. For instance, he translated עִיר דָּמִים (*'îr dāmîm*, "city of blood") in Nah. 3:1 as *der moerdischen stad* ("the murderous city"), elucidating the metaphorical use of דָּם (*dām*, "blood") for the reader.[61] By contrast, he translated בֹּנֶה צִיּוֹן בְּדָמִים (*bōneh ṣiyyôn bədāmîm*, "[Who] builds Zion with blood") in Mic. 3:10 as *die jr Zion mit blut bawet* ("Who builds its Zion with blood") – a literal rendering of the Hebrew.[62] But in the lectures on Nahum and Micah, he explicitly identified דָּם (*dām*) as the same Hebrew figure of speech, with the same contextual connotation – i. e. linked to murder and oppression.[63] That decision to translate the same figure literally in one place and interpretatively in another was not the only example of such inconsistency.

The same phenomenon appears when comparing his translation of Amos. 2:14 with that of Ps. 142:5, which he directly cited in the Amos lectures to support his interpretation. He rendered וְאָבַד מָנוֹס מִקָּל (*wə'ābad mānôs miqqāl*, "And flight will be lost from one who is swift") in Amos 2:14 as *Das der, so schnell ist, sol nicht entfliehen* ("That he who is so swift should not escape"), interpreting the Hebrew so that the German reader could more clearly understand the figure of speech.[64] By contrast, he translated אָבַד מָנוֹס מִמֶּנִּי (*'ābad mānôs mimmennî*, "flight is lost from me") in Ps. 142:5 in 1524 as *Denn mein fliehen ist verlorn* ("For my flight is lost") – a literal translation.[65] But he reversed that decision in his 1531 and 1545 Bible revisions, changing his translation of Ps. 142:5 to *Jch kan nicht entfliehen* ("I cannot escape") – now an interpretative translation that mirrored his method in Amos 2:14.[66] The contradiction in method between his 1524 explanatory rendering of the Hebraism in Amos 2:14 and his literal translation of the identical figure of speech in Ps. 142:5, not to mention his 1545 revision of that Psalm, shows the persistence of the struggle that he faced to find suitable renderings of Hebraisms in German. This struggle was a hallmark of his German Bible creation.

Mixed Methodology[67]

In some instances, Luther utilized a hybrid methodology in translating Hebrew figures of speech. For example, he translated כַּבְּרָקִים יְרוֹצֵצוּ (*kabbərāqîm*

---

[61] WA DB 11.2:294.1.
[62] WA DB 11.2:276.10.
[63] Nah. 3:1: WA 13:387.29–30; LW 18:233. Mic. 3:10: WA 13:316.1–5; LW 18:306.
[64] WA DB 11.2:234.14.
[65] WA DB 10.1:566.5. I am intentionally making a rigidly literal English translation of the Hebrew Bible in this chapter for the purposes of comparison with the other languages in scope.
[66] WA DB 10.1:567a.5 (1531); WA DB 10.1:567b.5 (1545). See also the 1531 revision protocol at WA DB 3:162.29–30.
[67] See also Luther's 1545 translation of מַרְאֵיהֶן כַּלַּפִּידִים (*mar'êhen kallappîḏîm*) in Nah. 2:5 in 1545, where he used a mixed method. This appears in Table A.2 in the Appendix.

yərôṣēṣû, "[they] will rush like the lightnings") in Nah. 2:5 as *vnd faren vnter einander her, wie die blitze* ("and drive among one another, like the lightnings").[68] While *wie die blitze* is a literal rendering of the Hebrew, *vnter einander her* is an interpretative rendering. The German powerfully conveys the randomness of the movement that he read from יְרוֹצֵצוּ (*yərôṣēṣû*), which he explained in his lectures:

> These are clearly Hebrew expressions with which he is indicating that there is no order or formation among the chariots as the Chaldeans move against the Assyrian. It is as if he were saying: 'They drive by in such hordes that no one knows which is last and which is first.'[69]

Similarly, he translated הִתְכַּבֵּד כַּיֶּלֶק (*hitkabbēḏ kayyeleq*, "make yourself heavy like the caterpillar") in Nah. 3:15 as *Es wird dich vberfallen, wie kefer* ("it will assail [attack] you, like a beetle").[70] While *Es wird dich vberfallen* explains the Hebrew for the German reader, *wie kefer*, by contrast, is strictly literal.[71] Later in the same verse, he again used a mixed method, rendering הִתְכַּבְּדִי כָאַרְבֶּה (*hitkabbəḏî kā'arbeh*, "make yourself heavy like the locust") as *Es wird dich vberfallen, wie hewschrecken* ("it will assail [attack] you, like locusts").[72] As with the first Hebrew simile, his translation of *Es wird dich vberfallen* was an interpretative rendering, while *wie hewschrecken* closely reflected the letter of the Hebrew.[73] By contrast, and showing even further variation in method within the same verse, he made an entirely literal translation of a third Hebraism: תֹּאכְלֵךְ כַּיָּלֶק (*tōḵəlēḵ kayyāleq*, "will devour you, like the caterpillar") as *Es wird dich abfressen, wie die kefer* ("it will eat away at you, like the beetle").[74]

---

[68] WA DB 11.2:292.5.

[69] "Plane autem hebraicae sunt phrases, quibus indicat nullo ordine et agminatim incedere in curribus Chaldaeos contra Assyrium q. d. Sie farn mit hauffen do her, es weiß niemant, wer der hinterst ist oder der furderst." WA 13:384.11–14. LW 18:301.

[70] WA DB 11.2:294.15–WA DB 11.2:296.15.

[71] One might, however, challenge the correctness of Luther's translation of *kefer*. Hebrew lexicons suggest that "young locust" or "caterpillar" would be the correct translation of יֶלֶק (*yeleq*). BDB, 410. KB, 383. I translate "beetle" for the German in accordance with Grimm [the modern German spelling is *käfer*]. DWB 11:18–19.

[72] WA DB 11.2:294.15–WA DB 11.2:296.15.

[73] The Vulgate was also inconsistent in this verse, although with a different term than יֶלֶק (*yeleq*). It rendered הִתְכַּבֵּד (*hitkabbēḏ*) as *congregare* and הִתְכַּבְּדִי (*hitkabbəḏî*) as *multiplicare*.

[74] WA DB 11.2:294.15–WA DB 11.2:296.15. The earlier note concerning *kefer* applies here as well. See additional evidence of mixed methodology in Table A.2, for example: Hos. 7:10; Joel 1:10, 2:6; Amos 1:6, 2:13, 3:3, 5:9; Nah. 1:14, 2:2, 2:7, 2:11; Hab. 1:8; Zeph. 1:2; and Mal. 3:8. Additional examples of this also appear in the "Changing Methodology" category, in either the 1532 or the 1545 translation.

Changing Methodology between the 1532 and 1545 Deutsche Bibel

Luther also sometimes used a different method to translate the same figure of speech in his 1532 Bible than in the 1545 revision.[75] For example, in 1532 he made an interpretative rendering of כִּי-נָתַן לָכֶם אֶת-הַמּוֹרֶה לִצְדָקָה (*kî-nātan lākem 'et-hammôreh liṣdāqâ*, "for he gives you the teacher [or, early rain] for righteousness") in Joel 2:23 as *der euch gnedigen regen gibt* ("who gives you merciful rain") – *gnedigen* expressing a nuance not in the literal Hebrew.[76] But in the 1545 Bible, he changed his translation to *der euch Lerer zur gerechtigkeit gibt* ("who gives you a teacher for righteousness") – a literal rendering of the Hebrew text.[77] Similarly, in 1532 he translated מַשְׁמִיעַ שָׁלוֹם (*mašmîaʿ šālôm*, "[of him] who proclaims peace") in Nah. 2:1 as *der gute mehre bringet* ("[of him] who brings good tidings") – an interpretative rendering.[78] But he changed that in 1545 to an essentially literal rendering: *der da Frieden predigt* ("[of him] who preaches peace [there/here]").[79] And in 1532, he translated וְלֹא-יֵצֵא לָנֶצַח מִשְׁפָּט (*wəlōʾ-yēṣēʾ lāneṣaḥ mišpāṭ*, "and justice [or, a judgment] never goes forth") in Hab. 1:4 literally as: *vnd kan kein recht zum ende komen* ("and no justice can come to an end").[80] But in 1545 he changed that to *vnd kan kein rechte sach gewinnen* ("and no justice can gain an advantage"), using the German idiom *sach gewinnen*.[81]

The Exceptional Use of the German Idiom

The prevalence of German idioms in Luther's translation and exegesis of the Minor Prophets cannot be overstated. It was simply immense. This should come as no great surprise. Nowhere should Luther's German Bible betray its Germanness and the masterly command of the language in the street more than through his use of German idiomatic speech. Yet his use of German idioms was

---

[75] Again, it is important to differentiate between the examples in this section, and those examples which appear in Part I of this chapter. The examples in Part I focus on changes in Luther's interpretation of the *meaning* of the Hebrew terms. The examples in Part II focus strictly on changes in the *method* for translating the Hebrew terms.

[76] WA DB 11.2:220.23. I have rendered this Hebrew in present tense, though it is often translated as past tense. Both readings are possible.

[77] WA DB 11.2:221.23. In the 1538/39 handwritten entries in his Old Testament, Luther had already made note of "der euch lerer zur gerechtigkeit gibt." WA DB 4:231b.4–WA DB 4:232b.19. Cf. the 1539–41 protocols, where Luther's team was still discussing *gnedig regen*. WA DB 4:231a.4–14.

[78] WA DB 11.2:292.1. The modern German spelling of *mehre* here is *Märe*.

[79] WA DB 11.2:293.1.

[80] WA DB 11.2:302.4. *Zum Ende komen* could certainly be considered idiomatic German, but (1) those which appear in the sources I have consulted are later than Luther; and, more importantly, (2) it is following the Hebrew so closely in its meaning that I found it difficult to classify it as a German idiom in this instance.

[81] WA DB 11.2:303.4. See additional evidence of Luther's changing method between 1532 and 1545 in Table A.2: e. g. Joel 4:14; Amos 5:5; Mic. 1:11; and Nah. 2:3, 5.

predominantly limited to his exegesis; it played only a limited role in the *Deutsche Bibel*.[82]

Luther's interpretation of Zech. 11:1 is one of many illustrations of this. In the commentary on Zechariah, he argued that לְבָנוֹן (ləḇānôn, "Lebanon") is Hebrew synecdoche, signifying the temple in Jerusalem as its building materials came from that region. He used several analogous Germanisms to illustrate his point:

> Here he calls the newly built temple Lebanon, because it was built of the cedars of Lebanon – as the grammarians teach that a part is called by the name of the whole, by synecdoche. It is as if I should say, 'The men of Wittenberg drink Faulbach and Frischbach,' that is: 'Wittenberg beer'; 'The Thuringian Forest yields many warm rooms,' that is: 'the wood from the Thuringian Forest, etc.'; 'The Rhine flows through the whole German land,' that is: 'the Rhine wine, etc.'[83]

Yet in the *Deutsche Bibel*, he translated לְבָנוֹן (ləḇānôn) simply as *Libanon* ("Lebanon"), giving no indication to the German reader that he or she should interpret it to mean the Jerusalem temple.[84]

Table 2.6 below shows further examples where Luther used German idioms in his exegesis of the Minor Prophets but not in the corresponding verse in the *Deutsche Bibel*. By contrast, Table 2.7 shows instances where he did use idiomatic German directly in his Bible translation.[85]

Table 2.6: Luther's use of German idioms in the exegesis, where they do not appear in the *Deutsche Bibel*.

Verse	Hebrew Bible	German Idiom in the Exegesis	Exegetical References
Jon. 4:11	לֹא־יָדַע בֵּין־יְמִינוֹ לִשְׂמֹאלוֹ ("does not know between his right hand and his left hand")	was weyß, was schwartz ist ("what [is] white, what is black") sie wissen nicht, was weys oder schwartz ist ("they do not know what is white or black")	WA 13:240.8–11 WA 13:257.32–39; LW 19:30–31

---

[82] Bluhm discusses Luther's paraphrasing of scripture in his writings, in contrast to the language that he used in his *Deutsche Bibel*. Bluhm, *Creative*, x, 3–36. Also see Stolt, *Rhetorik*, 112–21, 126; and Stolt, "Luther's Translation of the Bible," 393–8 concerning Luther's use of "sacred style" language in contrast to the "language on the street."

[83] "Er nennt hier den neugebauten Tempel 'Libanon', darum, dass er von den Cedern Libani gebauet war, wie die Grammatici lehren, dass ein Stück auch mit dem Namen des Ganzen genannt wird per synechdochen, als wenn ich spreche: Die Wittenberger trinken den Faulbach und Frischbach, das ist, Wittenbergisch Bier: Der Thüringer Wald gibt viel warmer Stuben, das ist, Holz aus dem Thüringer Wald etc. Der Rhein fleußt durch ganz Deutschland, das ist, der rheinische Wein etc." StL 14:1936.1–2. LW 20:310.

[84] WA DB 11.2:352.1. While this is true for the main German Bible text, which is the focus here, Luther did, nevertheless, include a gloss in this verse, pointing to Jerusalem.

[85] These are random instances, simply for the purpose of illustration.

"The Obscure Hebrew" 75

Verse	Hebrew Bible	German Idiom in the Exegesis	Exegetical References
Nah. 1:8	וּבְשֶׁטֶף עֹבֵר ("And with an overrunning flood")	es ist nuhr eyn wbergang ("it is a mere transition")	WA 13:376.28–29; LW 18:289
Hab. 2:5	וְאַף כִּי-הַיַּיִן בֹּגֵד ("And furthermore, for the wine betrays")	Ein truncken haus speyet den wyrt aus. ("A drunk house spews out its owner")	WA 19:398.17; LW 19:201
Hab. 3:16	יָבוֹא רָקָב בַּעֲצָמַי ("and decay enters into my bones")	ich frass mich drumb ("I ate my heart out") Ich saß und fras mich drumb ("I sat and ate my heart out")	WA 13:421.33 WA 13:448.2; LW 19:146
Zech. 11:8	וַתִּקְצַר נַפְשִׁי בָּהֶם ("and my soul became short in them")	Er ist kurtz angebunden ("He is shortly tethered [i. e. he has a short rope; he is impatient]")	WA 13:648.1–7; LW 20:121

Table 2.7: Luther's use of German idioms in the *Deutsche Bibel*.

Verse	Hebrew Bible	German Idiom in the *Deutsche Bibel*	Bible References
Mic. 2:11	לוּ-אִישׁ הֹלֵךְ רוּחַ ("If a man walks [in/after] wind/spirit")	Were ich ein loser schwetzer (1532) ("If I were a loose talker, babbler") WEnn ich ein Jrregeist were (1545) ("If I were an aimless spirit, fanatic, madman")	WA DB 11.2:274.11 WA DB 11.2:275.11
Mic. 4:11	וְתַחַז בְּצִיּוֹן עֵינֵינוּ ("and let our eyes gaze on Zion")	wir wollen vnser lust an Zion sehen ("we would like to see our desire/delight at Zion")	WA DB 11.2:278.11
Nah. 3:3	[וְ]כֹבֶד ("[and] a mass")	[vnd] grosse hauffen ("[and] great heaps")	WA DB 11.2:294.3
Zeph. 1:11	נִדְמָה ("is silenced, cut off")	ist dahin ("is dead, done for")	WA DB 11.2:312.11
Zech. 4:7	תְּשֻׁאוֹת חֵן חֵן לָהּ ("shoutings of 'grace, grace to it'")	das man ruffen wird, glueck zu, glueck zu ("that one will call out, 'good luck, good luck'")	WA DB 11.2:338.7

The Hebrew Trope of Repetition

Luther frequently called attention to the Hebrew trope of repetition in his lectures and commentaries on the Minor Prophets, identifying it as a distinctive trait of the Hebrew language. But as with his interpretation of Hebrew figures of speech, his method of translating this trope was inconsistent. It is thus another example of how his struggle with the obscurities of the Hebrew language influenced his German Bible.

Syntactical Forms and Functions of Hebrew Repetition

While repetition comes in many forms in the Hebrew Bible, five kinds in particular are prominent in Luther's exegesis of the Minor Prophets: *apposition of terminology* – the repetition of the same word, either immediately after the other or in close proximity; *apposition of subject matter* – the repetition of subject matter, either immediately after the other or in close proximity; *paronomastic infinitive* – a special instance of apposition, where the infinite absolute appears immediately before or after a finite form of the same verb; *cognate accusative* – another special instance of apposition, where a noun follows a verb of the same root; and *distributive* – where the repetition expresses either (a) an extension of time, or (b) distinctness (a part) relative to entirety (the whole). Repetition in the Hebrew language serves various purposes: for emphasis; to indicate an increased intensity or affection; to indicate certainty; to express a repeated series of actions or habitual behavior; to express indeterminateness; or, as appears in the distributive form, to express some type of distributive meaning.[86]

---

[86] Many other syntactical forms of repetition appear in the Hebrew language: elements connected to numbers; the use of the plural to express a repeated series of actions or habitual behavior; general paronomasia [aside from the paronomastic infinitive] – repetition of a word in a main clause and a relative clause – to express indeterminateness; repetitive apposition used distributively; repetition of pronouns; repetition of a verb in multiple *binyans* [Hebrew verb structures], etc. See Bruce K. Waltke and M. O'Connor, *An Introduction to Biblical Hebrew Syntax* (Winona Lake, IN: Eisenbrauns, 1990), especially pp. 115–6, 232–4, and 584–88. Waltke and O'Connor cite Hebrew distributive repetition as a tool to express constructions such as "each," "every," "all," "xxx by xxx," and "xxx after xxx"; to express diversity; and for emphasis; in Waltke and O'Connor, *An Introduction to Biblical Hebrew Syntax*, 115–6. See also Bornkamm, *Luther und das alte Testament*, 33–34; and Junghans, *Martin Luther und die Rhetorik*, 9–11. Cf. Raeder, *Das Hebräische*, 26–27, 281–9 concerning Luther's recognition and handling of this trope in the Psalms. Luther, ostensibly following the Vulgate, interpreted the paronomastic infinitive as "with"; see his exegesis of Zech. 1:2; WA 13:548.20–WA 13:549.9; LW 20:6–7. Aside from formal syntactical distinctions of Hebrew repetition, Luther also frequently called attention to the Hebrew repetition of narrative between different verses and/or books of the Bible; for example, Joel 1:13, Nah. 1:3, and Hag. 2:18; and in connection to Hag 2:18: Hag. 1:5, 1:7, and 2:15. Narrative repetition is not addressed here, given that Luther did not edit out narrative material, nor would one expect a Bible translator to do so except in extraordinary circumstances.

The Data in the Minor Prophets

Table A.3 in the Appendix lists thirty-four instances in the Minor Prophets where Luther explicitly called attention to Hebrew repetition.[87] For each, it shows the syntactical form of that repetition and provides Luther's corresponding translation.[88] Each example is assigned to one of four categories: (1) where he retained the Hebrew repetition by means of a literal translation of the repeated elements in the *Deutsche Bibel* [eleven instances]; (2) where he retained the Hebrew repetition through an interpretative, but not literal, rendering of the repetition in the *Deutsche Bibel* [twelve instances]; (3) where he eliminated the Hebrew repetition in the *Deutsche Bibel* [ten instances]; and (4) where his method changed from his 1532 Bible to the 1545 revision [one instance].[89] Figure 2.3 below summarizes this data. Given that the examples in Table A.3 are a narrow sample, restricted to Luther's overt observations of Hebrew repetition (many more instances of Hebrew repetition can be found in the Minor Prophets), the totals should not be seen as indicative of reliable percentages of tendencies. The purpose of the data is simply to highlight Luther's varied approach to the problem.

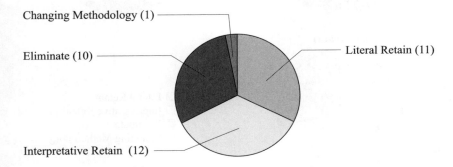

Figure 2.3: Luther's translation of the Hebrew trope of repetition in the Minor Prophets.

Figure 2.4 below further analyzes the data in terms of the syntactical form of repetition.[90] This helps to further show the fluctuation in his translation method within each particular category of Hebrew repetition.

---

[87] Table A.3 generally does not call special attention to glosses and other notes, which can be found at the main reference location.

[88] There are many additional examples of Hebrew repetition in the Minor Prophets. It is a limited sample which appears in Table A.3.

[89] As with the figures of speech, this assignment is based solely on Luther's *Deutsche Bibel* translation. How Luther argued in the exegesis is irrelevant for the categorization.

[90] These categories are not exclusive. Sometimes Luther showed uncertainty and/or ambiguity concerning the function of the Hebrew in a particular instance. For example, in Hab. 1:5,

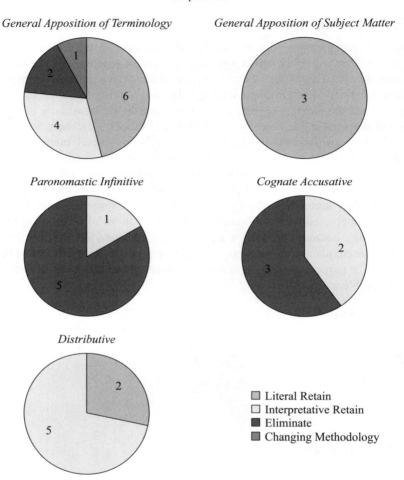

Figure 2.4: Luther's translation of the Hebrew trope of repetition in the Minor Prophets: by syntactical form of repetition.

General Inconsistency in Luther's Hermeneutic

Luther's translation methodology for the Hebrew trope of repetition was, needless so say, quite variable. Many times he followed the Hebrew Bible with a literal rendering of the repetition. For example, he translated אֲנִי אֲנִי (*'ănî 'ănî*, "I, I") in Hos. 5:14 as *Jch, Jch* ("I, I"); וּפִתְאֹם יָבוֹא ... הִנֵּה־בָא (*ûpit'ōm yāḇô' ... hinnēh-ḇā'*, "and [the Lord] suddenly will come ... behold, [he] comes") in Mal.

---

he argued that the Hebrew repetition was "for emphasis or distribution [*vel emphasis vel distributionis causa*]." See WA 13:398.3–7; WA 13:426.16–22; and LW 19:110–1.

3:1 as *Vnd bald wird komen ... Sihe, Er kompt* ("And soon will come ... Behold, he comes"); and the three instances of יְהוָה צְבָאוֹת (*'ăḏōnāy ṣəḇā'ōṯ*, "The Lord of Sabaoth [or, Hosts]") in Zech. 1:3 as *der HERR Zebaoth* ("The Lord of Sabaoth").[91]

Other times, however, he broke away from the literal Hebrew and made an interpretative rendering. For example, he translated the three instances of וְאֵרַשְׂתִּיךְ לִי (*wə'ēraśtîḵ lî*, "and I will betroth you to me") in Hos. 2:21–22 as (1) *wil ich mich mit dir verloben* ("I will betroth you"); (2) *Jch wil mich mit dir vertrawen* ("I will know you [become familiar with you], place my trust in you"); and (3) *Ja ... wil ich mich mit dir verloben* ("Yes, indeed, I will betroth you") – *Ja* ("Yes, indeed") breaking away from the Hebrew letter, yet expressing the certainty that he interpreted in the Hebrew repetition.[92] In another example, he translated וַיֵּרַע אֶל־יוֹנָה רָעָה גְדוֹלָה (*wayyēra' 'el-yônâ rā'â gəḏōlâ*, "and it displeased Jonah greatly [literally: and it was evil to Jonah a great evil or calamity]") in Jon. 4:1 as *Das verdros Jona fast seer* ("That irritated Jonah greatly") – *seer* ("very") expressing the amplified intensity expressed by the Hebrew repetition of וַיֵּרַע (*wayyēra'*) and רָעָה (*rā'â*).[93] In Mic. 7:12, he translated וְיָם מִיָּם (*wəyām mîyyām*, "and from sea to sea") with the German idiomatic expression *von einem meer zum andern* ("from one sea to the other"); and וְהַר הָהָר (*wəhar hāhār*, "and mountain to mountain") in the same verse as *von einem gebirge zum andern* ("from one mountain to the other"), both deviating from the literal Hebrew.[94] And in Hab. 1:8, he translated וּפָשׁוּ פָּרָשָׁיו וּפָרָשָׁיו מֵרָחוֹק יָבֹאוּ (*ûp̄āšû pārāšāyw ûp̄ārāšāyw mērāḥōq yāḇō'û*, "And their horsemen will spread out, their horsemen will come from afar") as *Jre reuter zihen mit grossem hauffen von fernen daher* ("Their horsemen stretch in great clusters from afar") – *mit grossem hauffen* expressing the distributive exaggeration that he interpreted in the repeated פרשׁ (*prš*).[95]

Still other times, he eliminated the repetition completely. For example, he translated וְנָהָה נְהִי (*wənāhâ nəhî*, "and lament profoundly [and lament a lamentation]") in Mic. 2:4 as *vnd klagen* ("and lament"); פָּתוֹחַ נִפְתְּחוּ (*pāṯôaḥ nip̄təḥû*, "are wide open") in Nah. 3:13 as *sollen ... geoeffent werden* ("will be opened");

---

[91] Hos. 5:14: WA DB 11.2:192.14–WA DB 11.2:194.14. Mal. 3:1: WA DB 11.2:370.1. Zech. 1:3: WA DB 11.2:332.3.
[92] WA DB 11.2:188.19–20.
[93] WA DB 11.2:266.1. *Sehr* is the modern German spelling of *seer*. Concerning רָעָה (*rā'â*) appearing as an adjective or noun, see BDB, 947–99; KB, 896–8. רעע (*r''*) is the Hebrew root, from which both Hebrew terms וַיֵּרַע (*wayyēra'*) and רָעָה (*rā'â*) are derived. The two are essentially two iterations, though different forms, of the same word. At various points, this study refers to the root when addressing multiple words that share the same root, for the sake of clarity.
[94] WA DB 11.2:284.12.
[95] WA DB 11.2:302.8. This example also appears in Table A.2. The context of the verse suggests the pronoun "their" and not "his" or "its."

and קָצַף קָצַף יְהוָה עַל־אֲבוֹתֵיכֶם (qāṣap 'ădōnāy 'al-'ăḇōṯêḵem qāṣep̄, "The Lord was very angry with your fathers [literally: The Lord angered over your fathers an anger]") in Zech. 1:2 as *Der HERR **ist zornig gewest** vber ewre Veter* ("The Lord was [or, became] angry with your fathers").[96] The instances where he eliminated the repetition are particularly noteworthy, given that he typically argued for the more intense translation when he came upon a difference between the Hebrew Bible and the Vulgate. Chapter 3 will investigate this further.

Inconsistencies in Luther's Hermeneutic within Each Syntactical Form of Repetition

Luther's hermeneutic was inconsistent even within each individual syntactical form of Hebrew repetition. This is so for every category which appears in Figure 2.4 and Table A.3 in the Appendix, with the exception of "General Apposition of Subject Matter," which includes only three instances. For example, on one hand he retained the general apposition of terminology in עַל־הַגְלוֹתָם גָּלוּת שְׁלֵמָה ('al-haglôṯām gālûṯ šəlēmâ, "because they exiled an entire exile [i. e. an exiled group of people]") in Amos 1:6 with his translation *Darumb, das sie die **gefangenen**, weiter **gefangen*** ("For this reason, that the captured were again [or, further] captured").[97] On the other hand, he eliminated the general apposition in וְהִתַּמְּהוּ תְמָהוּ (wəhittamməhû təmāhû, "and be greatly amazed") in Hab. 1:5 with his translation *vnd verwundert euch* ("and be amazed").[98] Likewise, he retained the paronomastic infinitive in כִּי־בֹא יָבֹא (kî-ḇō' yāḇō', "for it will surely come"; [literally, "for coming, it will come"]) in Hab. 2:3 with his translation *sie wird gewislich komen* ("it will certainly come") – *gewislich* ("certainly") breaking away from the Hebrew letter, yet expressing the certainty that he interpreted in the Hebrew repetition.[99] But he eliminated the paronomastic infinitive in אָסֹף אָסֵף ('āsōp̄ 'āsēp̄, "I will completely take away") in Zeph. 1:2 with his translation *Jch wil ... weg nemen* ("I will ... take away").[100] Luther's variable method for handling Hebrew repetition, therefore, does not appear to be based on any particular form(s) of the trope which he found especially obscure in comparison to the others.[101]

---

[96] Mic. 2:4: WA DB 11.2:274.4. Nah. 3:13: WA DB 11.2:294.13. Zech. 1:2: WA DB 11.2:332.2.
[97] WA DB 11.2:230.6.
[98] WA DB 11.2:302.5.
[99] WA DB 11.2:304.3.
[100] WA DB 11.2:312.2.
[101] See additional evidence of this in Table A.3.

Changing Methodology between the 1532 and 1545 Deutsche Bibel

Within the examples that appear in Table A.3 in the Appendix, Luther varied his methodology for translating Hebrew repetition between 1532 and 1545 in only one instance. In 1532, he translated כִּי בְקָקוּם בֹּקְקִים (*kî ḇəqāqûm bōqəqîm*, "because the emptiers have emptied them") in Nah. 2:3 as *Man wird dich doch rein ablesen* ("One [a person] will certainly glean you clean"), *doch* emphasizing the certainty and *rein* expressing the completeness or fullness of the action of the repeated Hebrew verb.[102] But in 1545, he amended that to *Denn die Ableser werden sie ablesen* ("Because the gleaners will glean them"), a more literal translation of the repetition which included both occurrences of בקק (*ḇqq*).[103]

Hebrew Transliteration

The question whether to transliterate certain Hebrew terms and phrases was one that Luther faced in many places of the Hebrew Bible. To address the issue, he established a clear rule of thumb. His principle, which he stated many times throughout his reflections on the Minor Prophets, was that proper nouns should be transliterated, and common nouns translated.[104] By proper nouns, he meant names of clans, groups, individuals, cities, countries, etc. But he struggled at times with that principle, and his fluctuation shows another manner in which the obscurity of the Hebrew played a significant role in his German translation.

The Data in the Minor Prophets

Table A.4 in the Appendix lists seventy-five instances where Luther explicitly addressed Hebrew transliteration issues in his lectures and commentaries on the Minor Prophets.[105] Each example is assigned to one of four categories: (1) where he transliterated the Hebrew [thirty-eight instances]; (2) where he interpreted the Hebrew for the German reader [twenty-five instances]; (3) where he used a mixed methodology [three instances]; and (4) where the methodology changed between his 1532 and 1545 *Deutsche Bibel* editions [nine in-

---

[102] WA DB 11.2:292.3. Grimm provides *aflezen* ("to glean [a field] or pick"; the modern spelling is *auflesen*) and *colligere* ("to gather") as definitions of *ablesen*. DWB 1:73. I take some liberty with *doch*, as is necessary when rendering it into English, as there is no true equivalent in English.

[103] WA DB 11.2:293.3. Cf. Hos. 10:1, where the same term בקק (*ḇqq*) appears. That example appears earlier in this chapter as an example of an interpretative variance between Luther's exegesis and *Deutsche Bibel*. Also note, only one example falls under the "Mixed" category, Joel 1:3. This example appears in Table A.3.

[104] For example, see WA 13:306.4–7. LW 18:217.

[105] Table A.4 generally does not call special attention to glosses and other notes, which can be found at the main reference location.

stances].[106] Figure 2.5 below illustrates the breakdown. As with the data for Hebrew figures of speech and Hebrew repetition, these examples are restricted to Luther's explicit discussions of Hebrew transliteration issues. Many more instances of Hebrew transliteration are found in his translation of the Minor Prophets than appear in this data.[107] Like the data for Hebrew figures of speech and Hebrew repetition, these totals should not be seen as indicative of reliable percentages of tendencies. The purpose of the data is strictly to expose, and to facilitate a more thorough examination of, Luther's inconsistent method.

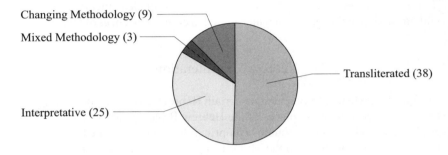

Figure 2.5: Luther's Hebrew transliteration in the Minor Prophets.

Figure 2.6 below further segments the data according to four categories of transliteration: (1) geographical regions, as well as nations, tribes, and groups associated with geographical regions; (2) names of individuals; (3) cultural- and/or ethno-specific customs, practices, and rituals of the ancient Israelites of the Hebrew Bible; and (4) technical biblical language. This helps to further show the variation of his translation method within each particular form of Hebrew transliteration. The exception is technical biblical language, which only has two instances and shows no variation.

General Variation in Luther's Hermeneutic and Key Tendencies

As a rule of thumb, Luther transliterated geographical names, as well as names of nations, groups, and tribes associated with particular geographical regions. For example, he translated גִּלְעָד (*gil'ād*, "Gilead") in Hos. 6:8 as *Gilead*; עַזָּה

---

[106] As with Hebrew figures of speech and Hebrew repetition, this assignment is based solely on Luther's *Deutsche Bibel* translation.

[107] There are an enormous number of additional transliteration issues which Luther identified beyond those in Table A.4. The criteria of (1) Luther specifically mentioning Hebrew in his argument, and (2) identifying some type of transliteration issue or making some reference to his exegesis of it in another verse where he does so, were applied to limit the data to what appears here. That said, given the quantity of names, etc. which appear in the Hebrew Bible, any methodology on this point is necessarily subjective.

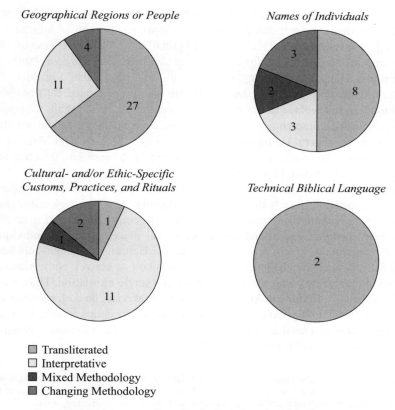

- ☐ Transliterated
- ☐ Interpretative
- ■ Mixed Methodology
- ■ Changing Methodology

Figure 2.6: Hebrew transliteration in the Minor Prophets: by category.

(ʿazzâ, "Azzah [Gaza]") in Zeph. 2:4 as *Gasa*; and גִּלְעָד וּלְבָנוֹן (gilʿād ûləbānôn, "Gilead and Lebanon") in Zech. 10:10 as *Gilead vnd Libanon*.[108] This practice followed his principle that proper nouns should be transliterated and common nouns interpreted. Periodically, however, he went against that principle and opted to interpret geographical names in his Bible translation. For example, he translated הַנֶּגֶב (hannegeḇ, "of the Negev") in Obad. 1:19 and 20 as *gegen mittage* ("toward the south [from the south]"); יֹשְׁבֵי הַמַּכְתֵּשׁ (yōšəḇê hammakṯēš, "the inhabitants of [the] Maktesh") in Zeph. 1:11 as *die jr jnn der Muele wonet* ("those who live in the mill"); and כְּרֵתִים (kərēṯîm, "of the Cherethites") in Zeph. 2:5 as *den kriegern* ("to the warriors").[109]

---

[108] Hos. 6:8: WA DB 11.2:194.8. Zeph. 2:4: WA DB 11.2:314.4. Zech. 10:10: WA DB 11.2:350.10.

[109] Obad. 1:19–20: WA DB 11.2:256.19–20. Zeph. 1:11: WA DB 11.2:312.11. Zeph. 2:5:

Similarly, Luther predominantly transliterated the names of prophets and other individuals. He translated בֶּן־אֲמִתַּי (ben-'ămittay, "the son of Amittai") in Jon. 1:1 as *dem son Amithai* ("the son [of] Amittai"); בְּיַד־חַגַּי (bəyad-ḥaggay, "by [the hand of] Haggai") in Hag. 1:1 as *durch den Propheten Haggai* ("through the Prophet Haggai"); and וְהַשָּׂטָן (wəhaśśāṭān, "and [the] Satan") in Zech. 3:1 as *Vnd der Satan* ("And [the] Satan").[110] He also transliterated נַחוּם (naḥûm, "Nahum") in his preface to the Book in his lectures, as he did with יוֹנָה (yônâ, "Jonah") in the commentary.[111] Nevertheless, even on this point he was not completely consistent. He translated מַלְאָכִי (mal'āḵî, "Malachi") in Mal. 3:1 as *meinen Engel* ("my angel").[112] And he translated מַלְכָּם (malkām, "Malcam [or, their king]") in Amos 1:15 as *jr Koenig* ("their king").[113]

The discrepancies illuminate a general dilemma with Hebrew proper nouns. Despite a particular term's function as the identifier of a geographical region, group, or individual, that name often has an ambiguous meaning – i. e. an etymological meaning underlying the geographical place, group, or individual which it represents, of which the ancient Israelite Hebrew audience would have been fully aware. The challenge for Luther was how to convey both meanings to the German reader, which was impossible in a single translation. Thus, when he did translate a Hebrew proper name as a common noun, he both transgressed one of his translation principles – i. e. names, as proper nouns, should be transliterated – and also used an inconsistent method in contrast to those occasions when he transliterated the name.[114]

WA DB 11.2:314.5. These Hebrew terms can be interpreted as common nouns also: נֶגֶב (negeḇ) as "south"; מַכְתֵּשׁ (maḵtēš) as "mortar," which Jerome argued referred to Jerusalem, and for which Luther criticized him; and כְּרֵתִים (kərētîm) as "executioners, mercenary soldiers."

[110] Jon. 1:1: WA DB 11.2:262.1. Hag. 1:1: WA DB 11.2:322.1. Zech. 3:1: WA DB 11.2:336.1.

[111] Nahum: WA 13:345.3–4; WA 13:371.2–5; LW 18:281. Jonah: WA 19:245.2–10; LW 19:97.

[112] WA DB 11.2:370.1. The Vulgate did likewise. See WA 13:538.17–18 and LW 18:377, where Luther explained that the Greek ἄγγελος ("angel, messenger") also influenced his interpretation of מַלְאָךְ (mal'aḵ, "angel, messenger") in Hag. 1:13, citing Mal. 3:1.

[113] WA DB 11.2:232.15. Translators sometimes render מַלְכָּם (malkām) as "their king," and other times transliterate it as the name of a god. See KB, 532; BDB, 575–6; and DCH 5:327. Cf. Jer 49:1 and 3, where Luther transliterated מַלְכָּם (malkām) as *Malchom* [Luther added a gloss at Jer. 49:1, however, explaining this as: "Malchom ist jr Abgott."]. WA DB 11.1:350.1, 3. Cf. Zeph. 1:5, where he translated בְּמַלְכָּם (bəmalkām, "by Malcam [or, by their king]") as *bey Malchom* ("by Malchom"). WA DB 11.2:312.5. In the lectures on Zephaniah, he admitted uncertainty concerning which reading was correct, and advised that both could stand. WA 13:453.1–20. WA 13:483.6–WA 13:484.4. LW 18:324–5. Cf. Amos 5:26.

[114] Luther would also frequently use the transliterated name in the lectures and commentaries as he discussed the meaning of the term(s), but then use the interpretative rendering in his Bible, rather than the transliteration. Cf. his discussion of *Nineveh* in Zeph. 2:13, where he argued that it could be a common noun or a proper noun depending on the context in which it appears in scripture. WA 13:497.7–9; LW 18:345, with a note pointing to LW 19:97. Many additional examples of this appear in Table A.4 in the Appendix. See also Kolb, *Martin Luther*

Moving on from proper names, Luther was just as inconsistent in his transliteration of language connected to cultural- and/or ethno-specific customs, practices, and rituals. For example, he transliterated the Hebrew unit of measurement חֹמֶר (*hōmer*, "homer, a dry measure") in Hos. 3:2 as *Homer*.[115] By contrast, he translated אֵפוֹד (*'ēpôd*, "ephod [a priestly garment]") in Hos. 3:4 as *Leibroeck* ("body skirt"); וּתְרָפִים (*ûṯərāpîm*, "and teraphim [house idols]") in Hos. 3:4 as *vnd ... Gottes dienst* ("and ... God's service") in 1532 and *vnd ... Heiligthum* ("and ... sanctuary") in 1545; and בְּבֵית לְעַפְרָה (*bəḇêṯ lə'aprâ*, "at Beth-leaphrah [in the house of ashes, dust]") in Mic. 1:10 as *jnn die traurkamer* ("into the mourning chamber").[116]

He also showed variability in his transliteration of special biblical words and technical terms in the Bible.[117] For example, he transliterated סֶלָה (*selâ*, "Selah [a technical musical term, meaning uncertain]") in both Hab. 3:3 and 3:9 as *Sela*.[118] As a point of comparison, in the *Operationes in Psalmos*, he transliterated מִכְתָּם (*miḵtām*, "Michtam [a technical term found in psalm titles, meaning uncertain]") in the title of Ps. 16:1 as *MICHTHAM*.[119] But in the *Deutsche Bibel*, he translated the entire phrase מִכְתָּם לְדָוִד (*miḵtām ləḏāwiḏ*, "Michtam of David") as *Eyn gulden kleynod Dauids* ("A golden treasure of David").[120]

The examples in each of the categories which follow help to more distinctly show the inconsistency in Luther's transliteration methodology, and thus his struggle with the obscurities of the Hebrew language.

Contradictions between Luther's Exegesis and Deutsche Bibel

The first part of this chapter showed examples where Luther's interpretation argument in the exegesis contradicted his *Deutsche Bibel* translation. These ex-

---

and the Enduring, 284, addressing the Psalms. See also Raeder, *Das Hebräische*, 184–215 concerning Luther's interpretation of Hebrew names in the Psalms. Raeder cites Augustine, Jerome, Reuchlin, Cassiodorus, Lyra, Faber, and the Vulgate as sources for Luther's interpretation of names in the Hebrew Bible.

[115] WA DB 11.2:188.2. Cf. Schaff's assessment of Luther Germanizing these types of Hebrew words. Schaff, *History of the Christian Church*, 358–9.

[116] Hos. 3:4: WA DB 11.2:188.4 (1532); WA DB 11.2:189.4 (1545). Mic. 1:10: WA DB 11.2:272.10.

[117] For more on Luther's use of technical biblical language, and the general challenges that it poses for Bible translators, see Birgit Stolt's discussion of biblical sacred language and "signals," in Stolt, "Luther's Translation of the Bible," 393–8; and Stolt, *"Laßt uns fröhlich springen!" Gefühlswelt und Gefühlsnavigierung in Luthers Reformationsarbeit. Eine kognitive Emotionalitätsanalyse auf philologischer Basis* (Berlin: Weidler, 2012), 179–80, 182–5, 211–28, and 239–41.

[118] Hab. 3:3: WA DB 11.2:306.3; Hab. 3:9: WA DB 11.2:308.9. Cf. the very similarly spelled term סֶלַע (*sela'*), which means "rock" [e. g. Obad. 1:3].

[119] WA 5:443.8. For more on this term in the Psalms, see Raeder, *Grammatica Theologica*, 17 and Raeder, *Das Hebräische*, 76–78, especially p. 78. BDB indicates that מִכְתָּם (*miḵtām*) is a technical term found in Psalm titles, which has an uncertain meaning. BDB, 508.

[120] WA DB 10.1:140.1 (1524).

amples specifically addressed *interpretative variances* – i. e. issues where the meaning of a Hebrew term was in question. The same scenario, however, also presents itself for his *methodological variances* – where his argument focused not so much on the meaning of the Hebrew, but rather on the best method of translating it into German – transliteration being one of the philological tools at his disposal. In the case of transliteration, there are instances where he explicitly argued for or against transliteration in the lectures and commentaries, but then went against that argument in the *Deutsche Bibel*.

For example, in the lectures on Amos 2:2, Luther argued that קְרִיּוֹת (*qərîyyôṯ*, "Kerioth") should not be transliterated, but rendered as the common noun *civitas* ("city").[121] Yet, he transliterated הַקְּרִיּוֹת (*haqqərîyyôṯ*, "of Kerioth") in the *Deutsche Bibel* as *zu Kirioth* ("of Kerioth"), directly contradicting his earlier argument.[122] In another example, he criticized Jerome's transliteration decision in Mic. 1:11, only to follow Jerome's example in his *Deutsche Bibel*. He argued in the lectures:

It is Jerome's custom in his translation of the Bible always to render proper nouns with common nouns; in his commentaries, on the other hand, he always translates the common nouns with proper nouns. So here, what he translates 'which dwells in the way out [*quae habitat in exitu*],' should absolutely have been translated with a proper noun.[123]

But in his 1532 Bible, he translated יוֹשֶׁבֶת צַאֲנָן (*yôšeḇeṯ ṣaʾănān*, "inhabitant of Zaanan") as *Die stoltze* ("The proud one"), exactly what he argued "should absolutely have been translated" as a proper noun.[124] That was not his only inconsistency. He amended the translation in his 1545 Bible revision to *Die Einwonerin Zaenan* ("The resident of Zaenan"), reversing the 1532 decision and finally settling in accord with his earlier transliteration judgment.[125] The vacillation is a lucid example of Luther's struggle with the obscurities of the Hebrew language and how to best render them into German.[126]

---

[121] WA 13:129.21. WA 13:166.34. LW 18:138. I have translated this as the proper noun, but there is a legitimate ambiguity in the Hebrew. While קְרִיּוֹת (*qərîyyôṯ*) may be translated as the name of a particular city [one in Judah, and another in Moab], it also may be translated as "towns." See BDB, 900; KB, 855–6.

[122] WA DB 11.2:232.2.

[123] "Hic mos est Hieronymo, ut semper nomina propria in translatione sua bibliorum vertat nominibus appellativis, econtra in commentariis suis appellativa propriis. Ita in hoc loco, quando vertit: quae habitat in exitu, omnino nomine proprio erat vertendum." WA 13:306.4–7. LW 18:217.

[124] WA DB 11.2:272.11.

[125] WA DB 11.2:273.11. The 1538/39 handwritten entries in Luther's Old Testament include a note [from his hand] indicating *zaenan/Zaenan*. Thus, that revision decision actually began earlier than 1545. WA DB 4:246b.14–WA DB 4:247b.4 and p. 246b Note 5. Cf. the notes in the 1539–41 protocols: WA DB 4:246a.14–WA DB 4:247a.2. This example fits into more than one category, as do many examples in this study. Here, there is (1) a contradiction between Luther's exegesis and his Bible translation; but also (2) a change in Luther's method between 1532 and 1545.

[126] See additional evidence of this in Table A.4; for example, Hos. 3:4; Hos. 3:14;

Inconsistency in Luther's Transliteration Decision for the Same Term in Different Verses

Sometimes, Luther's transliteration decision in one verse contradicted his decision for the same term in another verse. For example, he argued in his lectures that כְּנַעַן (kəna'an, "Canaan") in Hos. 12:8 should be interpreted as a common noun, and translated it accordingly in the Bible as *Kauffman* ("buyer, merchant").[127] Likewise, he translated כָּל-עַם כְּנַעַן (kol-'am kəna'an, "all the people of Canaan") in Zeph. 1:11 as *das gantze kremer volck* ("the entire merchant people").[128] By contrast, he transliterated כְּנַעֲנִים (kəna'ănîm, "[the] Canaanites") in Obad. 1:20 as *den Chananitern*; כְּנַעַן (kəna'an, "Canaan") in Zeph. 2:5 as *Canaan*; and כְּנַעֲנִי (kəna'ănî, "[a] Canaanite") in Zech. 14:21 as *Cananiter*.[129] Similarly, he translated מִתֵּימָן (mittêmān, "from Teman") in Hab. 3:3 in the Bible as *von mittage* ("from mid-day"), even though he argued in the lectures and commentary that תֵּימָן (têmān, "Teman") referred to Egypt.[130] By contrast, he transliterated תֵּימָן (têmān) in both Amos 1:12 and Obad. 1:9 as *Theman*.[131]

Luther's transliteration decisions for the term אָוֶן ('āwen, "Aven [or, trouble, sorrow, wickedness, etc.]") varied especially widely. In many places, he transliterated it: בֵּית אָוֶן (bêṯ 'āwen) in Hos. 4:15 as *BethAuen*; בֵּית אָוֶן (bêṯ 'āwen) in Hos. 10:5 as *BethAuen*; אָוֶן ('āwen) in Amos 1:5 as *Auen*; and לְאָוֶן (lə'āwen, "to Aven") in Amos 5:5 (1545) as *wird BethAuen werden* ("will become Beth-Auen").[132] By contrast, he translated אָוֶן ('āwen) in Hos. 12:12 as *abgoette-*

Amos 1:5; Zeph. 1:11 (given Luther's argument for ambiguity); and Hab. 2:13 and Zech. 1:3 (given that Luther argues it is a name of God, by his rule it should be entirely transliterated; on the other hand, if one argues that צְבָאוֹת (ṣəḇā'ôṯ) should be interpreted as "hosts," there is still a mild contradiction between the exegesis and the *Deutsche Bibel*).

[127] WA 13:58.22–WA 13:59.7; LW 18:66–67. WA DB 11.2:206.8.

[128] *Krämer* also means "trader", "grocer," or "shopkeeper." WA DB 11.2:312.11. His lecture comments on Zeph. 1:11 reveal that his translation team was ultimately uncertain whether כְּנַעַן (kəna'an) was a common or proper noun, which elucidates the wavering transliteration decision. Moreover, those comments also show that he changed his mind from the time of the lectures to the time of his Bible translation. See WA 13:457.17–24; WA 13:487.23–WA 13:488.2; LW 18:330–1. Modern translations vary as well; some Hebrew translations also render this "all the merchant people."

[129] Obad. 1:20: WA DB 11.2:256.20. Zeph. 2:5: WA DB 11.2:314.5. Zech. 14:21: WA DB 11.2:360.21. These three do not appear in Table A.4 because Luther did not address the transliteration issue explicitly in his exegesis. Nevertheless, they are included here for the sake of comparison.

[130] WA DB 11.2:306.3. Cf. WA 13:414.10–11; WA 13:442.11–23; WA 19:427.10–22; LW 19:137; and LW 19:229–30.

[131] Amos 1:12: WA DB 11.2:230.12. Obad. 1:9: WA DB 11.2:254.9.

[132] Hos. 4:15: WA DB 11.2:190.15. Hos. 10:5: WA DB 11.2:202.5. Amos 1:5: WA DB 11.2:230.5. Amos 5:5 (1545): WA DB 11.2:239.5. Amos 5:5 is an especially important example because of his deviation from the literal Hebrew. It is examined in greater detail in Ch. 3 of this study. Cf. Amos 5:5 (1532), where he translated לְאָוֶן (lə'āwen, "to Aven") as *jnn jamer* ("into misery, calamity, affliction, distress"). WA DB 11.2:238.5. Hos. 10:5 does not appear in

rey ("idolatry"); in Mic. 2:1 as *schaden* ("damage, harm, injury"); and in both Hab. 1:3 and 3:7 as *muehe* ("toil, trouble, effort, labor, pain").[133]

Mixed Methodology

Sometimes Luther utilized a mixed methodology for his Hebrew transliteration. His translation of Zech. 14:5 is an exceptional example of this. In this verse, he translated אֶל־אָצַל (*'el-'āṣal*, "to Azal") as *nahe hinan* ("very near to [or, right up to]") in 1532, but changed his translation in 1545 to *nahe hinan ... an Azal* ("very near to Azal [or, right up to Azal]") – now, a combination of colloquial German and transliteration of the Hebrew.[134] His commentary shows that he was not certain whether *Azal* was a preposition or a proper name: "But what the Azal is, I do not know. In German it means 'close by,' though elsewhere it is the name of a city."[135] Presumably he was interpreting אצל (*ṣl*) pointed as אֵצֶל (*'ēṣel*), where it would mean "close to, near, at, or in the possession of." Thus, he read the repetition of אֶל (*'el*, "to") and אָצַל (*'āṣal*) as "*very* close to," or "up to [the location] nearby." This reading parallels the Vulgate's *ad proximum* ("to the vicinity, to the nearest place"). By the time of his 1538/39 handwritten entries in his Old Testament copy, however, he had resolved to amend the interpretation of אצל (*ṣl*) to a city name in the form of a transliteration.[136] Nevertheless, he still retained the sense of the original interpretation of the two repetitive Hebrew elements אֶל (*'el*) and אָצַל (*'āṣal*), expressing a magnification of, or emphasis on, the closeness. Thus, he did not translate the phrase simply as *nahe hinan Azal* or *nahe Azal*, but *nahe hinan ... an Azal*.[137]

He used a similar blended method in his translations of names and epithets for God. For example, in Hab. 2:13, he translated יְהוָה צְבָאוֹת (*'ăḏōnāy ṣəḇā'ôṯ*,

---

Table A.4 because Luther did not address the issue specifically in his exegesis. Nevertheless, it is included here for the sake of comparison.

[133] Hos. 12:12: WA DB 11.2:206.12. Mic. 2:1: WA DB 11.2:274.1. Hab. 1:3: WA DB 11.2:302.3. Hab. 3:7: WA DB 11.2:308.7. Hos. 12:12, Hab. 1:3, and Hab. 3:7 do not appear in Table A.4 because Luther did not address the issues specifically in his exegesis. Nevertheless, they are included here for the sake of comparison. See additional evidence of this in Table A.4: e. g. Amos 1:15 in contrast to Zeph. 1:5; and Hab. 2:13 in contrast to Zech. 1:3.

[134] WA DB 11.2:358.5 (1532); WA DB 11.2:359.5 (1545). See also WA DB 4:274b.28–33.

[135] "Was aber das Azal sei, weiß ich nicht; im Deutschen heißt es: nahe bei, wiewohl es sonst einer Stadt Name ist." StL 14:1966.7. LW 20:339. The notes for the Zechariah lectures in the *Weimarer Ausgabe* end at Ch. 13, while the commentary extends to Ch. 14. See LW 18:ix–xii for more on the various manuscripts, and LW 20:ix–x concerning Zechariah specifically.

[136] The 1538/39 handwritten entries in his Old Testament record the change. WA DB 4:274b.28–33, with the additional note "Neuer Text = Hebr."

[137] BDB provides entries for אֵצֶל (*'ēṣel*) as a substantive, indicating proximity; as a preposition; and as the name of an uncertain city near Jerusalem. BDB, 69. The Hebrew term very well may have carried the ambiguous meaning for the ancient reader, even when used as a proper name, as shown earlier concerning Hebrew names for individuals, geographical regions, and names of groups associated with those regions.

"the Lord of Hosts") as *HERRN Zebaoth* ("[the] Lord of Sabaoth"); and יְהוָה צְבָאוֹת (*ădōnāy ṣəḇā'ōṯ*, "the Lord of Hosts") in Zech. 1:3 as *der HERR Zebaoth* ("the Lord of Sabaoth").[138] And in Hos. 2:18, he translated בַּעְלִי (*ba'lî*, "Baali [or, my lord]") as *Mein Baal* ("My *Baal*") – *Baal* the transliteration, and *Mein* ("my") the interpretative element.[139]

Changing Methodology between the 1532 and 1545 Deutsche Bibel

In certain instances, Luther's transliteration methodology changed between his 1532 *Deutsche Bibel* and the 1545 revision.[140] For example, in 1532 he translated אֵת סִכּוּת (*'ēṯ sikkûṯ*, "Siccuth [or, the Tabernacle; or the tent]") in Amos 5:26 as *die huetten* ("the huts"), only to change it in 1545 to the transliteration *den Sicchuth*; in 1532 he transliterated מַלְכְּכֶם (*malkəḵem*, "your king") in the same verse as *ewrs Molochs*, but modified it in 1545 to the interpretation *ewrn Koenig* ("your king"); and in 1532 he translated וְאֵת כִּיּוּן (*wə'ēṯ kîyyûn*, "and Chiun") in the same verse as *vnd die goetzen* ("and the idols, false gods"), then changed it in 1545 to the transliteration *vnd Chiun*.[141] Similarly, in 1545 he transliterated וְאֵיפַת (*wə'êpaṯ*, "and an epha [of]") in Mic. 6:10 as *vnd ... der Epha* ("and ... the epha").[142] However, earlier in the 1532 *Deutsche Bibel*, he translated it as

---

[138] Hab. 2:13: WA DB 11.2:306.13. Zech. 1:3: WA DB 11.2:332.3. By contrast, the Vulgate translated יְהוָה צְבָאוֹת (*ădōnāy ṣəḇā'ōṯ*) in Hab. 2:13 as *Domino ... exercituum* ("[from the] Lord ... of hosts") and יְהוָה צְבָאוֹת (*ădōnāy ṣəḇā'ōṯ*) in Zech. 1:3 as *Dominus exercituum* ("Lord ... of hosts"). Luther deviated from the Vulgate in his transliteration of צְבָאוֹת (*ṣəḇā'ōṯ*) as part of the proper name. [יְהוָה (*ădōnāy*) is often called the ineffable name of God because, among other issues, the pointing and the role of the ו (*w*) as a vowel or consonant are uncertain. Readers consequently often pronounce and render it with other addresses for God, such as Adonai, Lord, God, etc.] Cf. Amos 6:10, where Luther translated יְהוָה (*ădōnāy*) as *HERRN* ("of the Lord"), mirroring the Vulgate's *Domini* ("of the Lord"); WA DB 11.2:242.10. Cf. also Amos 7:7, where he translated אֲדֹנָי (*ădōnāy*) as *HERR*, mirroring the Vulgate's *Dominus* ("the Lord"); WA DB 11.2:244.7. Both were interpretative translations of the Hebrew, rather than transliteration. Neither appears in Table A.4 in the Appendix because Luther did not address the issue specifically in his exegesis. One might further argue that Luther's transliteration methodology for names and epithets for God is inconsistent in and of itself. While he translated certain titles for God into the German as common nouns, others he transliterated. For example, he translated וְקָדוֹשׁ (*wəqāḏōš*, "and [the] Holy One") in Hab. 3:3 as *vnd der Heilige* ("and the Holy One"); WA DB 11.2:306.3. By contrast, he translated צֶמַח (*ṣemaḥ*, "[the] Sprout, Growth, Branch") in both Zech. 3:8 [WA DB 11.2:336.8] and 6:12 [WA DB 11.2:342.12] as *Zemah*. Also see his discussion of the Tetragrammaton in Mic. 2:13; WA 13:273.24–27.

[139] WA DB 11.2:186.16. See additional evidence of this in Table A.4: e. g. Zech. 1:3.

[140] Again, it is important to differentiate between the examples in this section, and those examples which appear in Part I of this chapter. The examples in Part I focus on changes in Luther's interpretation of the *meaning* of the Hebrew terms. The examples in Part II focus strictly on changes in the *method* for translating the Hebrew terms.

[141] WA DB 11.2:240.26 (1532); WA DB 11.2:241.26 (1545). This is only addressed in the Zwickau lectures, the protocols, and the gloss; not in the Altenburg lectures or the LW. See Table A.4 in the Appendix and cf. Amos 1:15 and Zeph. 1:5.

[142] WA DB 11.2:283.10. *Epha* is a unit of measure in ancient Israel.

vnd ... das mas ("and ... the measure") – a common noun.[143] Finally, in 1532 he translated הַכְּמָרִים (*hakkəmārîm*, "the idolatrous priests") in Zeph. 1:4 as *der Muenche* ("the monks"), but modified it in 1545 to the transliteration *Camarim*.[144] The profound role that the obscurities of the Hebrew language played in Luther's transliteration methodology, even when the meanings of the Hebrew terms were not in question, is unmistakable.[145]

Implications: Luther's Translation Principles

The inconsistencies in Luther's translations in the Minor Prophets – both interpretative and methodological – help to shed light on his general Bible translation. In various writings he outlined certain principles or "rules" of his Bible translation. Scholars primarily cite those which appear in: (1) *Sendbrief vom Dolmetschen* (1530); and (2) *Summarien über die Psalmen und Ursachen des Dolmetschens* (1531–33), where he went into some detail concerning these rules of thumb.[146] Additional guidelines addressing Hebrew appear in: (3) *Von den letzten Worten Davids* (1543), mainly an argument for reading the Old Testament in light of the New Testament and Christological issues; (4) Luther's preface to the Old Testament, where he went into great detail about the difficulties of translating Hebrew; (5) the *Tischreden*, where he made various comments about his translations; and (6) the *Briefwechsel*, letters to various individuals in which he mentioned his translation work.[147] But the many inconsistencies in his Hebrew translation in the Minor Prophets suggest that these "rules" were never really rules. On the contrary, they prove to be at most idealized guidelines, and certainly not the fixed principles that his comments might lead one to believe and which some scholars frame them as. The inconsistencies and contradictions in Luther's Hebrew translation and exegesis in the Minor Prophets suggest that

---

[143] WA DB 11.2:282.10. The modern German spelling is *Maß*.

[144] WA DB 11.2:312.4; WA DB 11.2:313.4. Both the 1532 and 1545 *Deutsche Bibel* include glosses addressing *Camarim*. The notes in Luther's 1538/39 Old Testament show a modification from "Muenche und Pfaffen" to "Camarim und priester," with *Muenche* (which appears in the gloss) struck, and a note that the 1541 Bible shows the new keyword *Camarim*. A further note indicates that this is from Luther's hand. See WA DB 4:260b.21–29. The 1539–41 protocols also record his translation team addressing the issue. See WA DB 4:260a.23.

[145] See additional evidence of this in Table A.4: e. g. Amos 5:5; Mic. 1:11; and Zech. 14:5.

[146] *Summarien über die Psalmen und Ursachen des Dolmetschens* (1531–33): WA 38:1–69. *Sendbrief vom Dolmetschen* (1530): WA 30.2:632–46.

[147] *Von den letzten Worten Davids* (1543): WA 54:16–100; LW 15:265–352. Luther's preface to the Old Testament: WA DB 8:10–32. Also see his preface to the prophets, *Die Propheten alle deutsch* (1532 and 1545): WA DB 11.1:2–15; and prefaces to the individual books in the WA DB. The *Tischreden* appear in WA TR 1–6. The *Briefwechsel* appear in WA BR 1–18. Reu created a limited list of various principles which Luther mentioned, in *Luther's German Bible*, 263–77.

two particular translation principles of his should be nuanced for a more complete understanding of his Hebrew translation.

1. Lieber, wie redet der Deudsche man jnn solchem fall?
("My dear, how does the German person speak in such a situation?")[148]

One of Luther's most widely cited Bible translation principles is that the original biblical language should be translated into colloquial, contemporary German, rather than retain its indigenous characteristics that would be foreign to the German reader. He wrote in *Sendbrief vom Dolmetschen*,

> For one must not inquire of the literal Latin language for how one should speak German, as these asses do. Instead, one must ask the mother in the home, the children in the street, the common man in the market, and look at their mouths, how they speak, and then translate accordingly so that they understand it and realize that one is speaking German to them.[149]

This mirrors similar comments in *Summarien über die Psalmen und Ursachen des Dolmetschens*, where he specifically addressed the Hebrew:

> Whoever wants to speak German must not follow the Hebrew manner of expression. Instead, when he understands the Hebrew person, then he must see that he grasps the meaning and thinks, 'My dear, how does the German person speak in such a situation?' Once he has the German words to serve the purpose, let him drop the Hebrew words and express the meaning freely in the best German he can.[150]

The predominant tendency among scholars is to call attention to his inveterate insistence on colloquial German in order to make the Bible accessible to the German reader. Krause, for example, cites W. Walther's observation concerning Luther's guiding axiom: "'daß eine Bibelübersetzung echtes Deutsch reden muß ("that a Bible translation must speak real German").'"[151] Krause is not

---

[148] This is from *Summarien über die Psalmen und Ursachen des Dolmetschens* (1531–33): WA 38:11.29–30.

[149] "Den man mus nicht die buchstaben inn der lateinischen sprachen fragen, wie man sol Deutsch reden, wie diese esel thun, sondern, man mus die mutter jhm hause, die kinder auff der gassen, den gemeinen man auff dem marckt drumb fragen, und den selbigen auff das maul sehen, wie sie reden, und darnach dolmetzschen, so verstehen sie es den und mercken, das man Deutsch mit jn redet." WA 30.2:637.17–22. I made adjustments to Stolt's translation in "Luther's Translation of the Bible," 378.

[150] "Wer Deudsch reden wil, der mus nicht der Ebreischen wort weise fueren, Sondern mus darauff sehen, wenn er den Ebreischen man verstehet, das er den sinn fasse und dencke also: Lieber, wie redet der Deudsche man jnn solchem fall? Wenn er nu die Deutsche wort hat, die hiezu dienen, so lasse er die Ebreischen wort faren und sprech frey den sinn eraus auffs beste Deudsch, so er kan." WA 38:11.27–32. I made adjustments to Stolt's translation in "Luther's Translation of the Bible," 380; and LW 35:213–4. See also Reu, *Luther's German Bible*, 274.

[151] Krause, *Studien*, 19; also see p. 70, and p. 39 where Krause, citing Baring, judges Luther's efforts in translating the Minor Prophets to be a success: "Mit 'Schweiß' … [Luther]

alone. Schaff, Skevington, Beutel, Bluhm, and Ebeling assert the same, as do countless others.[152] And who could blame them? Luther himself stressed over and over again his goal of translating scripture into the language of the people on the street.[153] Yet an assiduous scrutiny of his translations in the Minor Prophets shows that this rule was anything but consistent. The profusion of inconsistencies in his translation and exegesis of the Hebrew show that he labored over the decisions again and again. Many times, in fact, he reversed his decision in later exegesis and/or Bible revisions. Thus, his principle of translating into colloquial German was neither firm nor foolproof. Moreover, the enormous number of Hebraisms which he incorporated into his *Deutsche Bibel* through literal translations demonstrate that the "rule" of idiomatic German is simply inadequate as a defining axiom for his Bible, and leads to an erroneous assessment of the *Deutsche Bibel* as being unadulteratedly *deutsch*.

Many scholars do, in fact, acknowledge the tension between the Hebrew and the German in Luther's Bible. There are two main ways that they typically handle this: either by trying to minimize it, or by calling attention to a second rule that Luther articulated. There are numerous examples of the first. Kolb, for instance, cites Stolt's observation that

Despite this translator's use of 'colloquial, day-to-day German' and 'the oft-praised freedom of Luther's translation,' it is 'truly remarkable' that he adhered closely to Greek and Hebrew expressions at times.[154]

The "at times" qualifier, in the context of "remarkable," is the problem. Raeder does the same concerning Luther's translation of the Psalms, adding the disclaimer concerning Luther's retaining of Hebrew features of the text "whenever he considers it necessary."[155] Reu argues that "the translation did not dare to be too literal."[156] And Bluhm goes so far as to argue that "It did not happen too often."[157] These scholars are simply repeating what Luther himself asserts: *zu*

---

selbst sich erfolgreich bemüht, 'die hebräischen Schriftsteller zu zwingen, deutsch zu reden.'" English translation: "[Luther] successfully strove, with sweat, to force the Hebrew authors to speak German." The Baring portion of the citation comes from: Baring "Die 'Wormser Propheten,'" 4. Baring was specifically addressing Luther's translation of Habakkuk.

[152] Schaff, *History of the Christian Church*, 345. Blum, *Creative*, 6. Stolt, "Luther's Translation of the Bible," 380. Albrecht Beutel, "Erfahrene Bibel: Verständnis und Gebrauch des verbum dei scriptum bei Luther," *Zeitschrift für Theologie und Kirche* 89 (1992): 327.

[153] WA 30.2:637.17–22.

[154] Kolb, *Martin Luther and the Enduring*, 214. He adds that Luther "wanted to avoid Hebraisms in German," citing additional statements by Luther. See Stolt, "Luther's Translation of the Bible," 397–8. Cf. Stolt, "Luther's Faith of 'the Heart': Experience, Emotion, and Reason," in *The Global Luther: A Theologian for Modern Times*, ed. Christine Helmer (Minneapolis: Fortress Press, 2009), 133, where she argues that "Luther translated the Bible so that everyone would be able to understand it."

[155] Raeder, "The Exegetical," 401–2.

[156] Reu, *Luther's German Bible*, 261.

[157] Bluhm is specifically addressing instances where Luther had to choose between theol-

weilen ("sometimes, occasionally"), that he would make literal translations of the Hebrew.[158]

The issue extends beyond the Hebrew Bible. For example, Bluhm addresses Luther's oft-cited argument that the Vulgate's rendering of κεχαριτωμένη ("having been given grace") in Luke 1:28 [the *Ave Maria*] as *gratia plena* ("full of grace") would be translated into German into *das beste deutsch* ("the best German") as *liebe* ("dear").[159] But, as he and many others point out, Luther never used that "ideal" rendering in his *Deutsche Bibel*.[160] He rendered it *holdselige* ("beloved"), albeit still a Germanization, but not the one that he contended the German would most immediately or straightforwardly identify with. Moreover, as Bluhm shows, Luther also used the more literal rendering of the Latin as *voll gnaden* ("full of grace") in two places outside of the *Deutsche Bibel* as part of his citation of the verse.[161] Bluhm simply says of the conundrum, it is "difficult to explain."[162] The many inconsistencies in the Minor Prophets show that this was not an anomaly for Luther.

The modifiers that scholars use to describe the phenomenon of literal Hebrew translations – "at times," "it didn't happen too often," "whenever he considers it necessary" – give the erroneous impression that Luther's use of Hebraisms and literal Hebrew translation was a rarity, or at least the great exception in his Bible translation.[163] It is not that scholars are absolutely incorrect, but rather that they neglect to call attention to just how often he indeed went with the literal Hebrew. Just from the sample of his translation in the Minor Prophets, it is clear that this made up a significant, if not the dominant, portion of his translation methodology for certain philological elements, most prominently for Hebrew figures of speech.[164] His German Bible was very, very Hebrew, and in it, Moses was not nearly as hidden and unrecognizable as Luther boasted.

---

ogy – his "ultimate standard" for translation, as Bluhm calls it – and a preferred German rendering. Bluhm, *Creative*, 123. He goes on to argue that most of the time Luther did not have to sacrifice his principle that the Bible should be rendered into idiomatic German, lauding Luther's Bible as "so thoroughly German in language and expressions."

[158] See Bluhm, *Creative*, 122. He quotes Luther in the *Summarien*, WA 38:17.7–8.

[159] Bluhm, *Creative*, 151–66. Stolt also addresses this in "Luther's Translation of the Bible," 383, as does Reu in *Luther's German Bible*, 271–2.

[160] See WA 30.2:638.13–26. Bluhm cites this in *Studies in Luther – Luther Studien* (Bern: Peter Lang, 1987), 77; as do many other scholars.

[161] Bluhm, *Creative*, 154–5. Luther translated it *voll gnaden* in the 1522 *Betbüchlein* [WA 10.2:408.1], and *voller gnaden* in a March, 1523 sermon [WA 12:456.24]. The second of these occurred after the publishing of his *Septembertestament* (NT translation), thus showing even more inconsistency. He translated it as *holdselige* both in the 1522 *Septembertestament* [WA DB 6:210.28] and in the 1546 *Deutsche Bibel* [WA DB 6:211.28].

[162] Bluhm, *Creative*, 155.

[163] See Rosenzweig's contention that this is "the exception [*die Ausnahme*]"; in Martin Buber and Franz Rosenzweig, *Die Schrift und ihre Verdeutschung* (Berlin: Schocken, 1936), 93.

[164] Again, while the data in this study is not statistically significant and thus should not be

2. Wo etwa an einem ort gelegenn ist, hab ichs nach den buchstaben behalten, und ... bin nicht so frey davon gangen ("Where something it is situated in a single place, I have left it according to the letter and ... not so freely deviated from it.")[165]

The other primary manner in which scholars generally manage the tension between the Hebrew and the German in Luther's Bible is by calling attention to a second rule articulated in *Sendbrief vom Dolmetschen*, which, not coincidentally, actually addresses the first rule.[166] Luther contended that where something was located in one place – which some read as meaning particularly critical, or theologically important – he would stick to the literal Hebrew:

But I have, on the other hand, not let go of the letters too freely. Instead, with great care, together with my helpers, I have seen to it that where something it is situated in a single place [*wo etwa an einem ort gelegenn ist*], I have left it according to the letter and not so freely deviated from it.[167]

The problem is understanding precisely what Luther meant by *wo etwa an einem ort gelegenn ist*. If it meant that he deemed a particular Hebrew text as especially critical or theologically crucial, it is strange that he did not meticulously call attention to this in the lectures and commentaries for those translations where he used Hebraisms and/or literal translations of the Hebrew.[168] And while he did for some, this does not account for any significant share of the examples in the Minor Prophets where he breaches the first principle, *translate into the best idiomatic German possible*. On the other hand, if he meant that the Hebrew term or phrase only appears in one place – i. e. an anomalous concept, word, phrase, or *hapax legomenon* – that would be extremely difficult to

---

interpreted as showing a perfect distribution of his tendency to use of literal translations in relation to his use of idiomatic German renderings, it does show, by means of the mere quantity of Luther's literal translation of Hebraisms, that this was a significant part of his hermeneutic, at least in the Minor Prophets.

[165] This is from *Sendbrief vom Dolmetschen* (1530): WA 30.2:640.20–22.

[166] Stolt, "Luther's Translation of the Bible," 379–80. Reu, *Luther's German Bible*, 272–3.

[167] "Doch hab ich widerumb nicht allzu frey die buchstaben lassen faren, Sondern mit grossen sorgen sampt meinen gehülffen drauff gesehen, das, wo etwa an einem ort gelegenn ist, hab ichs nach den buchstaben behalten, und bin nicht so frey davon gangen." WA 30.2:640.19–22.

[168] Moreover, without him explicitly saying so, it is difficult to discern what Luther meant by "in one place – *wo etwa an einem ort gelegenn ist*." Stolt frames this as meaning an important theological or critical point. Stolt, "Luther's Translation of the Bible," 379. Bluhm made a similar assessment of the *Ave Maria* question, concluding that there were both theological and artistic grounds for his objection to *voll gnaden*. Bluhm, *Creative*, 165. Clearly there were times where Luther identified *hapax legomena*, such as חַדְרָךְ (*ḥadrāk*, "Hadrach [a geographical region near Damascus and Hamath]") in Zech. 9:1, which he ultimately transliterated. See WA 13:623.13–24; StL 14:1907.3-StL 14:1908.3; LW 20:90; LW 20:283; and WA DB 11.2:346.1–WA DB 11.2:348.1. Stolt and Bluhm's interpretation of Luther's use of "one place" to mean important or theological thus does not solve the problem.

reconcile with what one finds in the Minor Prophets, where he incessantly cited other verses in support of his translations.¹⁶⁹

Another problem with applying this axiom to many instances of Luther's translation of the Minor Prophets is the inconsistency in his methodology for addressing identical or similar Hebrew figures of speech which appear in more than one verse. In order for the principle to be credible in these circumstances, the Hebraism which appears in multiple locations would need to carry a unique, special theological, or otherwise critical meaning in only a subset of the verses for which Luther made literal translations. One can find, however, numerous examples where his exegetical arguments in the lectures make it clear that he interpreted the Hebraism the same in all of these instances, despite the inconsistency in his translation methodology. His interpretative translation of עִיר דָּמִים (*'îr dāmîm*) in Nah. 3:1 in contrast to his literal translation of בְּדָמִים (*bədāmîm*) in Mic. 3:10 show this, as do his interpretative translation of וְאָבַד מָנוֹס מִקָּל (*wə'ābad mānôs miqqāl*) in Amos 2:14 in contrast to his literal translation of אָבַד מָנוֹס מִמֶּנִּי (*'ābad mānôs mimmennî*) in Ps. 142:5, as shown above. Moreover the very presence of the Hebraism in more than one location in the Minor Prophets, not to mention his citations of other verses for support, as mentioned earlier, casts significant doubt on the reliability of the "rule."

A final complication with this axiom is the suggestion that Luther's theology resolves the issues in its application. Stolt asserts that "It is Luther the theologian, based upon his Christological understanding, who determines 'what is important.'"¹⁷⁰ How, we don't know, and Luther often does not say. W. Schwarz makes a similar point. He argues that if Luther can find a German expression to render the meaning, he does; but "if, however, the meaning of the original language cannot be rendered into a foreign idiom without a change of its theological meaning, a word-for-word translation can be made."¹⁷¹ He cites this theological grounding of Luther's hermeneutic more than once, and uses it to dispel the contradictions: "This, his theological view, is the basis of his translation. If this is kept in mind apparently contradictory statements on translation can be

---

¹⁶⁹ The instances where Luther did cite other verses to support his translation in a specific place are clear in his lectures and commentaries, and are too many to note here. But see, for example, in Table A.2 in the Appendix: Hos. 2:17, 4:7, 6:9; Joel. 1:3, 1:14, 2:23, 2:26, 3:4, 4:14; Amos 1:3, 5:1, 5:4, 5:5, 5:26, 6:1, 6:10, 8:9, 8:10, 9:9; Jon. 1:9, 3:5; Mic. 2:1, 4:13, 5:2; Nah. 1:1, 1:8, 1:11, 2:1, 2:3, 3:15; Hab. 1:8, 1:9, 2:2, 2:15, 3:4, 3:10, 3:13; Zeph. 1:2, 1:4, 1:9, 1:17; Hag. 1:9; Zech. 2:11, 4:10, 4:14, 6:1–3, 6:8, 9:12, 9:15, 9:16, 10:1, 10:2, 10:3, 10:4, 10:8, and 11:3. Ch. 4 examines the role of scriptural citations in Luther's Hebrew translation.

¹⁷⁰ Stolt, "Luther's Translation of the Bible," 379. See also Beutel's argument concerning Luther's Christological hermeneutic in Beutel "Erfahrene Bibel," 327. This is also the focus of Beutel's entire book: Albrecht Beutel, *In dem Anfang war das Wort: Studien zu Luthers Sprachverständnis* (Tübingen: J. C. B. Mohr (Paul Siebeck), 1991).

¹⁷¹ Schwarz, *Biblical Translation*, 207.

seen as coherent and supporting one another."[172] Schwarz, like Stolt and others, is doing everything he can to argue for a continuous overriding "rule" that governs Luther's method, rather than conceding the inconsistency and the constant struggle and wavering in Luther's methodology which this demonstrates.[173] Thus he can, even while arguing that "Luther does not even adhere to a specific method," still apply a guiding rule to Luther's translation.[174]

As stated earlier, there are many more translation principles which Luther articulated in his writings. Many of the thoughts and concerns expressed here can be applied to those. These principles notwithstanding, the inconsistencies in his Hebrew translation call into question the comprehensiveness with which they can explain his Hebrew hermeneutic in many instances in the Minor Prophets. The more reliable observation about his Hebrew translation methodology seems to be its fluctuation and multiformity.

Summary and Conclusion

Luther's struggles with the obscurities of the Hebrew Bible profoundly influenced his translation – both his *interpretation* of Hebrew, and his *method* – that is, his decisions on the most appropriate manner in which to render the meaning into German. The primary way in which this influence manifested itself was through the extraordinary prevalence of contradictions and inconsistencies in his translation of Hebrew. The prevailing arguments by scholars, and Luther himself, concerning his Hebrew translation have not fully taken into account these discrepancies. Scholars notice them at times, but they fail to appreciate (1) just how much literal translation of Hebrew appears in his Bible, and (2) just how often this tension between the German and the Hebrew manifested itself as contradictions and inconsistencies in his translation. The inconsistencies and contradictions show that the struggles over which he so often lamented never really ended, but on the contrary, actually are a defining mark of his Bible translation. Moreover, while he designated his Bible the "German Bible" and many hail it as "Luther's Bible," the reality of his *Deutsche Bibel* was something in many ways different. The enormous quantity of literal translations of Hebrew, unexplained to the German reader, played a significant – if

---

[172] Schwarz, *Biblical Translation*, 206. Especially on pp. 205–12, Schwarz acknowledges the issue, but repeatedly cites various rules of thumb.

[173] Schwarz also says, "Yet however much he tried to find the right expression, the ultimate intention was to make clear his theological interpretation of the text, an interpretation based on inspiration." Schwarz, *Biblical Translation*, 208. Concerning Luther's admission of uncertainty or outright confusion, for example, see Nah. 3:8; Zeph. 1:5, 1:11, 2:14; Zech. 9:1, and 14:5. Moreover, scholarly assessments portray Luther as using one method, dependent upon each unique scenario; see Stolt, *Rhetorik*, 87–88. But these scholars do not fully account for the contradictions.

[174] Schwarz, *Biblical Translation*, 207.

not *the* identifying role – in his translation of Hebrew figures of speech and his transliteration methodology. Luther wrote in a 1528 letter to Wenzeslaus Linck:

> We are now sweating over a vernacular translation of the Prophets. Oh God, what a great and difficult task it is to force the Hebrew writers, against their wills, to speak German. They resist and do not want to give up their native Hebrew and to imitate the barbaric German. It is as though the nightingale, having given up its own elegant melody, was forced to imitate the cuckoo for a monotonous song he must certainly hate.[175]

His translation of the Minor Prophets shows that in so many instances and in so many ways the Prophets ultimately never did speak the barbaric German in his German Bible, but on the contrary, it was their native Hebrew which they never gave up.

---

[175] I. e. "Making the prophets speak the barbaric German" (my paraphrase). "Nos iam in prophetis vernacule donandis sudamus. Deus, quantum et quam molestum opus, Hebraicos scriptores cogere Germanice loqui, qui resistunt, quam suam Hebraicitatem relinquere nolunt, et barbariem Germanicam imitari, tanquam si philomela cuculum cogatur, deserta elegantissima melodia, unisonam illius vocem detestans, imitari." This comes from Luther's June 14, 1528 letter to Wenzeslaus Linck in Nürnberg: WA BR 4:484.14–19 [§ 1285] [The Chadwyck-Healey (ProQuest) electronic edition of the *Weimarer Ausgabe* shows this as lines 19–23; it is clearly at 14–19 in the printed edition]. Cf. WA DB 11.2:xii. This translation is also based on the German in StL 16:424.5-StL 16:425.5, as cited by Schaff, *History of the Christian Church*, 355: "Wir arbeiten jetzt in den Propheten, sie zu verdeutschen. Ach GOtt, wie ein gross und verdrießlich Werk ist es, die hebräischen Schreiber zu zwingen, deutsch zu reden; wie sträuben sie sich, und ihre hebräische Art gar nicht verlassen wollen, und dem groben Deutschen nachfolgen. Gleich als wenn eine Nachtigall, so ihr der übereinlautende Kuckucksgesang ganz entgegen, gleichwohl sollte ihre liebliche Melodei verlassen, und dem Kuckuck nachsingen."

Chapter Three

Hebrew Semantic Intensity

"In Hebrew these are extraordinary words. Because we do not
have a complete comprehension of this language, we cannot
translate them with words that are appropriate or expressive enough."
Martin Luther, Late 1525/Early 1526[1]

Background to the Linguistic Research and Debates
Concerning Luther's Hebrew

For Luther, the Hebrew language in general and the texts of the Hebrew Bible in particular were characterized by a special inherent intensity of expression.[2] He called attention to the peculiar energy, expressiveness, and potency of Hebrew in contrast to Latin and German over and over again in his reflections upon the books of the Hebrew Bible, and especially upon the Minor Prophets. For him, though, this semantic intensity was more than an aesthetic feature of Hebrew. It was an essential part of the meaning of the words. His determination to reproduce the semantic intensity of the Hebrew was ultimately one of the definitive imprints of the Hebrew Bible in his *Deutsche Bibel*, as he sought to differenti-

---

[1] "Insignia sunt haec vocabula in hebraea lingua, quae nos ob eius linguae non absolutam cognitionem non satis adpositis verbis et significantibus reddere possumus." WA 13:608.15–17. LW 20:69–70. Luther was addressing Zech. 6:13.

[2] Bowers defines language intensity as "the quality of language which indicates the degree to which the speaker's attitude toward a concept deviates from neutrality ... High intensity, thus, is characterized by emotionalism and extremity." John Waite Bowers, "Language Intensity, Social Introversion, and Attitude Change," *Speech Monographs* 30 (1963): 345. Bradac, Bowers, and Courtright advise that most linguistic researchers accept Bowers's definition. James J. Bradac, John Waite Bowers, and John A. Courtright, "Three Language Variables in Communication Research: Intensity, Immediacy, and Diversity," *Human Communication Research* 5 (1979): 258. On the specific use of "semantic intensity" in the field of linguistics, see: Karl Sorning, "Some Remarks on Linguistic Strategies of Persuasion," in *Language, Power and Ideology: Studies in Political Discourse*, ed. Ruth Wodak (Philadelphia: John Benjamins, 1989), 97–98; Chaitanya Shivade, et al., "Corpus-Based Discovery of Semantic Intensity Scales," in *Proceedings of the North American Association of Computational Linguistics Annual Meeting (NAACL)* (Denver: Association for Computational Linguistics, 2015), 483–93; and Joo-Kyung Kim, Marie-Catherine de Marneffe, and Eric Fosler-Lussier, "Adjusting Word Embeddings with Semantic Intensity Orders," in *Proceedings of the 1st Workshop on Representation Learning for NLP* (Berlin: Association for Computational Linguistics, 2016), 62–69.

ate his version from the Vulgate. Language experts make mixed appraisals of "extreme" or extraordinary language and its role in Bible translation. Some linguists situate this type of language as part of the question of literal translation methodology versus functional equivalence. They argue that peculiarities and extremities of the Hebrew language, often appearing as part of Hebraisms, biblical tone, or biblical signals, create a distancing effect – also dubbed "alienation effect" or "estrangement effect" – pulling non-native readers away from the text rather than drawing them into it.[3] Others see this distancing effect as a rhetorical tool which creates the opposite effect – forcing readers to detach themselves from the text emotionally in order to contemplate it more deeply on an intellectual level.[4] These modern discussions concerning culture-based language extremity are ultimately in one way or another predicated on Friedrich Schleiermacher's notions of *Verfremdung* and *Entfremdung* in Bible translation – intentionally distancing the reader from the culture of the biblical author, in contrast to modifying the text in a manner that removes the "foreignness," so that the reader feels one and the same in the cultural context of the text.[5] Luther's general tendency to replicate Hebrew intensity seems to often place him in the *Verfremdung*, or distancing effect, camp.

A key voice against criticisms of idiosyncratically intense Hebrew language being replicated in Bible translations, and perhaps the most in-depth researcher to date on the role of emotion and linguistics in Luther's German translation, is Birgit Stolt. Stolt argues that this distancing effect has been undervalued. She contends that, on the contrary, revisions of Luther's German Bible which have eliminated or reduced these peculiarities have weakened the language and stripped it of its poetic and emotive virtue.[6] Other scholars, including Karl-Heinz zur Mühlen and Helmar Junghans, put forward similar arguments, citing the integral value of rhetorical tools going back to figures such as Augustine,

---

[3] Stolt, "Luther's Translation of the Bible," 385–6, 388. Stolt, *Rhetorik*, 97, 100. Stolt, *Laßt uns fröhlich springen*, 189–90. Functional equivalence is also known as "dynamic" equivalence. For more on this, see Maria Sidiropoulo, *Linguistic Identities through Translation* (New York: Rodopi, 2004), especially pp. 4–5.

[4] Stolt, "Luther's Translation of the Bible," 386.

[5] I. e. "bring the reader to the text," compared to "bring the text to the reader." See Friedrich Schleiermacher, "Über die verschiedenen Methoden des Übersetzens," in *Kritische Gesamtausgabe. Part 1: Schriften und Entwürfe. Vol. 11: Akademievorträge*, ed. Martin Rößler and Lars Emersleben (Berlin: Walter de Gruyter, 2002), 65–94. Also see Birgit Stolt, "Luther's Translation of the Bible," 377; John Ellington, "Schleiermacher Was Wrong: The False Dilemma of Foreignization and Domestication," *Technical Papers for the Bible Translator* 54 (2003): 301–17, especially pp. 304, 310; Buber and Rosenzweig, *Die Schrift und ihre Verdeutschung*, 90–95; and Anne Schjoldager, *Understanding Translation* (Aarhus: Academica, 2014), 141–2, compared to Holger Siever, "Schleiermacher über Methoden, Zweck und Divination," in *Friedrich Schleiermacher and the Question of Translation*, ed. Larisa Cercel and Adriana Şerban (Berlin: De Gruyter, 2015), 160. Instead of *Entfremdung*, some sources read *Einbürgerung*.

[6] Stolt, *Laßt uns fröhlich springen*, 189–90.

Bonaventure, and Thomas Aquinas, which ultimately influenced late medieval and early modern humanism.[7]

Stolt and zur Mühlen argue that an *Affektenlehre* ("doctrine of affections") of the Middle Ages and early modern period governed Luther's Bible translation and interpretation, and that this *Affektenlehre* has an important role in linguistic analyses of Bible translation and language intensity.[8] They discuss the *Affektenlehre* in association with several important questions which it poses for the translator. One of these is the role of *intellectus* relative to *affectus*, often positioned against one another as exclusive alternatives – in parallel to Schleiermacher's *Entfremdung* and *Verfremdung*.[9] Arguments that the two operate largely independently of one another suggest that in the places where Luther mirrored idiosyncratic, particularly intensive Hebrew language in his German translation, he consequently separated the *intellectus* and *affectus*. Stolt is critical of this view, arguing that the two are inextricably connected in Luther's translation methodology. To demonstrate this, she draws upon various linguistic studies, which suggest that the role of emotion and intensive language as part of translation method should not be reduced to a sort of secondary status, but that on the contrary, both emotional and intellectual data are integral pieces of information which influence one another in the transmission of messages through language.[10]

German translation work which followed Luther's especially supports Stolt's view. One of the most prominent is the Buber-Rosenzweig Bible, an attempt to

---

[7] Karl-Heinz Zur Mühlen, "Die Affektenlehre im Spätmittelalter und in der Reformationszeit," *Archiv für Begriffsgeschichte* 35 (1992): 93–114. Junghans, *Martin Luther und die Rhetorik*, especially pp. 5–7 concerning humanism. See also Spitz, *Luther and German Humanism*, especially pp. VIII-69–94.

[8] Stolt, *Laßt uns fröhlich springen*, 145. Zur Mühlen, "Die Affektenlehre," 93–114. See also Daniel M. Gross, "Introduction: Being-Moved: The Pathos of Heidegger's Rhetorical Ontology," in *Heidegger and Rhetoric*, ed. Daniel M. Gross and Ansgar Kemmann (Albany, NY: State University of New York Press, 2005), 33–34.

[9] Stolt, "Luther's Translation of the Bible," 374–8, 386–9. Zur Mühlen, "Die Affektenlehre," 101–4. Beutel frames the contrast between Luther's view of Hebrew and Greek as parallel to *Affekt* and *Intellekt*, and also *Frömmigkeit* and *Weisheit*. Beutel, *In dem Anfang war das Wort*, 192.

[10] Stolt, *Laßt uns fröhlich springen*, 34–35. Stolt, "Luther's Translation of the Bible," 373–4, 389. Cf. Stolt's view (basing much of her evidence on linguistic science to supplement Luther's texts) with others such as Simeon Zahl, who argues for a separation between the two in Luther, based solely on Luther's writings. Zahl criticizes Stolt's pairing of the two as being flawed insofar as she pairs early and later texts from Luther to make the link; and he also argues that the phrase *intellectus et affectus* "disappears rapidly after the *Dictata*." See Simeon Zahl, "The Bondage of the Affections: Willing, Feeling, and Desiring in Luther's Theology, 1513–1525," in *The Spirit, the Affections, and the Christian Tradition*, ed. Dale M. Coulter and Amos Yong (Notre Dame, IN: University of Notre Dame Press, 2016), 201–2 Note 16. Zur Mühlen argues for an interaction between the two in Luther's theological thought, and moreover, in his understanding of the relationship between God and the human being. In zur Mühlen, "Die Affektenlehre," 101–2.

update and improve upon Luther's sixteenth century *Deutsche Bibel* through a rendering that was even more true to the literal Hebrew.[11] It began in 1925 as a joint venture between Martin Buber and Franz Rosenzweig, but following Rosenzweig's death in 1929, it was completed by Buber in 1961. Their attempts at mimicking Hebrew in German were overwhelmingly focused on features of the language related to intensity, expressive power, and auditory elements of the text.[12] Two particular innovations stand out: their use of (1) *Leitworte* – repeated words or word roots within texts, or a set of texts – an attempt to replicate the Hebrew root system, which they argued had a "dynamic" effect akin to feeling "the waves beating back and forth"; and (2) *Kolomotrie* – "the division of prose into units of length of a breath," which Rosenzweig argued had a "striking" effect, both in appearance on the written page, and linguistically, as he termed it, mirroring "the movements and arousals of the soul."[13] Whatever one makes of the success or failure of their attempt, their focus on intensity through word choice, structure, and phonetics dominated the entire project. Though they were trying to improve upon Luther, they ultimately mirrored the same major focus of his translation of Hebrew into German. The overwhelming concentration of their effort on language and syntactical features associated with the semantic intensity of Hebrew is all the more evident in one of the many critiques of their

---

[11] This chapter briefly discusses Buber and Rosenzweig in order to illuminate certain aspects of Luther's Hebrew hermeneutic. The Buber and Rosenzweig Bible is not meant to demonstrate any kind of historical background for Luther, but rather to serve as a brief point of comparison to show the significance of what Luther was doing with the Hebrew in certain places.

[12] Buber and Rosenzweig, *Die Schrift und ihre Verdeutschung*, particularly 136–43 on this point. Cf. their comments concerning how they strove for "the exactest rendering possible ... of scripture itself; of its discourse; of the sound, history, and meaning of the words; of the cadence, structure, and content of the verbal sequences [*genaueste Wiedergabe ... aus der Schrift selber, aus ihrer Rede, aus Laut, Herkunft und Bedeutung der Wörter, aus Tonfall, Bau und Gehalt der Wortfügungen*]"; in Buber and Rosenzweig, *Die Schrift und ihre Verdeutschung*, 297–8. Ellington cites this also in "Schleiermacher Was Wrong," 302.

[13] Concerning *Leitworte* and the characterizations of "Dynamisch" and "die Wellen hinüber und herüber schlagen," see Buber and Rosenzweig, *Die Schrift und ihre Verdeutschung*, 211. Mara H. Benjamin cites and discusses this in *Rosenzweig's Bible: Reinventing Scripture for Jewish Modernity* (Cambridge: Cambridge University Press, 2009), 147. Concerning *Kolomotrie*: and the characterizations of "am eindrücklichsten" and "die Bewegungen und Errengungen der Seele," see Buber and Rosenzweig, *Die Schrift und ihre Verdeutschung*, 81–87. Benjamin cites and discusses this in *Rosenzweig's Bible*, 155. See also Buber and Rosenzweig, *Die Schrift und ihre Verdeutschung*, 169 concerning the "intensity [*Intensität*]" of their translation of the Hebrew Bible (as a whole), a consequence of "linguistic identity, resemblance, or kinship [*sprachidentischen, sprachnahen oder sprachverwandten (Stelle)*]." See also Lawrence Rosenwald's introduction to Buber and Rosenzweig, *Scripture and Translation*, where he identifies a *Leitwort* as "a thematic word or word-complex"; in Martin Buber and Franz Rosenzweig, *Scripture and Translation*, trans. Lawrence Rosenwald and Everett Fox (Bloomington, IN: Indiana University Press, 1994), xxxix. Many scholars also refer to *Kolomotrie* as the *cola*.

efforts to update Luther's *Deutsche Bibel*. Gershom Scholem wrote in a letter to Buber on April 27, 1926:

> *What fills me with doubt* is the excessive *tonality* of this prose, which leaps out almost uncannily from the particular wording (this word is wrong; I mean the *niggun* of your translation) ... If I search in the original for what your translation gives, I can succeed only by *singing* – i. e., 'reciting' – it; the mere text without music does not yield it.[14]

Buber and Rosenzweig's translation ultimately evokes the same *Affektenlehre* that Stolt and zur Mühlen argue was integral to Luther's. Of course, Hebrew translation has special challenges in this area, given the unpointed nature of the original texts. Nevertheless, the Masoretic vowel pointing, accenting, and cantillation signs demonstrate the scribes' profound emphasis on intonation patterns and other elements related to vocalization of the text.[15] The Hebrew letters were there for the page, but the proper vocalization was essential to their correct meaning, not to mention liturgical and other religious use by the ancient Israelites and later Jewish users of the text. Buber and Rosenzweig's Bible, even if it overreached and Scholem's criticisms are justified, still helps to elucidate Stolt's and zur Mühlen's conviction that *affectus* and *intellectus* are irrevocably linked in Luther's conception of proper translation. These features of the Hebrew language – the root system, text division, etc. – on which they focused with the *Leitworte* and *Kolomotrie*, are integral elements of the meaning of the words and syntax, not simply auxiliary features. It was these same types of features of the Hebrew text on which Luther focused in his German translation, some directly linked to lexical choices, others to syntactical elements, and which he thus used to differentiate his German Bible from the Vulgate.

Despite considerable attention that scholars have given to the role of emotion and semantic intensity in Luther's Bible translation, there is much more to do, especially in terms of his Hebrew translation, and even more so, outside of the Psalms. Many elements of Luther's Hebrew have yet to be thoroughly

---

[14] *Gerhard (Gershom) Scholem an Martin Buber*, Jerusalem, 27. 4. 1926: "*Was mich mit Zweifel erfüllt*, ist die, aus der besonderen Wörtlichkeit fast unheimlich herausspringende, übermäßige *Tonhöhe* (das Wort ist falsch, ich meine den *niggun* Ihrer Übersetzung) dieser *Prosa* ... Ich kann mir, wenn ich das, was Ihre Übersetzung gibt, im Original suche, es nur *gesungen*, d. h. 'rezitiert' erreichen, der eine, nackte, musiklose Text gibt es nicht." Martin Buber, *Briefwechsel aus sieben Jahrzehnten*, vol. 2, ed. Grete Schaeder (Heidelberg: Lambert Schneider, 1973), 251–3 [§ 212]; this citation comes from p. 252. I would not change anything in this English translation, and thus have taken it from: Martin Buber, *The Letters of Martin Buber: A Life of Dialogue*, ed. Nahum N. Glatzer and Paul Mendes-Flohr, trans. Richard and Clara Winston and Harry Zohn (New York: Schocken Books, 1991), 338–9 [§ 343]. Kathleen Garner also cites this in "Rewriting Scripture for the Twentieth Century: The Buber-Rosenzweig Bible Translation and the National Politics of Language" (Thesis, University of Michigan, 2014), 9. *Niggun*: נִגּוּן (*niggûn*, "[music] playing, tune, melody").

[15] It is beyond the scope here to discuss the original texts of Hebrew Bible as unpointed (i. e. the "autographs"). Nevertheless, pointing was well established since the Masoretes.

explored, and among these are the specific elements of the Hebrew language particularly associated with intensity and how they had an impact on his translation. While Stolt and others have made modest advancements in this area, the vast majority of research which addresses it consists of recycled examples and quotations from Luther.[16] Luther's Hebrew translation thus remains largely unexamined in this regard. This chapter will expand upon the research to date and examine this facet of Luther's Hebrew translation in the Minor Prophets. It will show, with detailed attention to the Hebrew, how very specific features of the Hebrew language and the intensity associated with these features were often responsible for Luther's German renderings and hermeneutical decisions. In these examples, Luther's translation decisions were not principally predicated on a particular rhetorical tool that he was looking to apply; rather, they were sparked by things that he saw as innate to the Hebrew text. It was thus the specific elements in the language with which he worked which significantly steered his decisions.

The examples analyzed in this chapter are divided into two categories: those where a general determination to replicate the semantic intensity of Hebrew words, phrases, and sentences appears in Luther's *Deutsche Bibel* translation; and those where this effort shows a further connection with his theology of *Anfechtung*. The places where Luther either explicitly mentioned *Anfechtung* or otherwise linked his translation to it are among the most lucid examples of how Hebrew semantic intensity played a central role in his interpretation of Hebrew and in his German renderings. Moreover, they cogently show how that intensity informed his theological interpretations of the texts, thus illuminating the relationship between theology and philology in his Hebrew translation.

Part I: General Examples of Luther's Attempt to Replicate Hebrew Semantic Intensity

The examples in Part I show various translations where Luther recognized some type of semantic intensity of the Hebrew text, which differentiated it from the Vulgate, and which he furthermore sought to emulate in his German rendering. Table 3.1 provides the full Hebrew Bible, Vulgate, and *Deutsche Bibel* verse for each example in this section.

---

[16] For example, scholars often cite Luther's translation of שָׁבִיתָ שֶּׁבִי (*šābîtā šebî*, "You have taken captivity captive") in Ps. 68:19 with *Du hast das Gefängnis gefangen* ("You have imprisoned prison"). See Stolt, "Luther's Translation of the Bible," 385 and Reu, *Luther's German Bible*, 274–5. Likewise concerning Luther's Greek translation, scholars often cite his translation of the *Ave Maria* in Luke 1:28, discussed earlier in Ch. 2 of this study. See Bluhm, *Creative*, 151–66; and Stolt, "Luther's Translation of the Bible," 382–4.

Table 3.1: General examples of Luther's attempt to replicate Hebrew semantic intensity in his Bible: Mic. 2:13, Amos 1:11, Nah. 3:3, Nah. 3:15, Nah. 2:8, and Zeph. 1:15.

Verse	NASB	Hebrew Bible	Vulgate	*Deutsche Bibel*
Mic. 2:13	The breaker goes up before them; They break out, pass through the gate and go out by it. So their king goes on before them, And the Lord at their head.	עָלָה הַפֹּרֵץ לִפְנֵיהֶם פָּרְצוּ וַיַּעֲבֹרוּ שַׁעַר וַיֵּצְאוּ בוֹ וַיַּעֲבֹר מַלְכָּם לִפְנֵיהֶם וַיהוָה בְּרֹאשָׁם	ascendet enim pandens iter ante eos dividunt et transibunt portam et egredientur per eam et transibit rex eorum coram eis et Dominus in capite eorum	**Der Helt wird fur jn her durch brechen,** Sie werden durch brechen, vnd zum thor aus vnd ein zihen, Vnd jr Koenig wird fur jn her gehen, vnd der HERR fornen an. (1532) WA DB 11.2:276.13. **Es wird ein Durchbrecher fur jnen her auff faren,** Sie werden durch brechen, vnd zum Thor aus vnd ein ziehen, Vnd jr Koenig wird fur jnen her gehen, vnd der HERR fornen an. (1545) WA DB 11.2:277.13.
Amos 1:11	Thus says the Lord, "For three transgressions of Edom and for four I will not revoke its punishment, Because he pursued his brother with the sword, While he stifled his compassion; His anger also tore continually, And he maintained his fury forever.	כֹּה אָמַר יְהוָה עַל-שְׁלֹשָׁה פִּשְׁעֵי אֱדוֹם וְעַל-אַרְבָּעָה לֹא אֲשִׁיבֶנּוּ עַל-רָדְפוֹ בַחֶרֶב אָחִיו וְשִׁחֵת רַחֲמָיו וַיִּטְרֹף לָעַד אַפּוֹ וְעֶבְרָתוֹ שְׁמָרָה נֶצַח	haec dicit Dominus super tribus sceleribus Edom et super quattuor non convertam eum eo quod persecutus sit in gladio fratrem suum et violaverit misericordiam eius et tenuerit ultra furorem suum et indignationem suam servaverit usque in finem	So spricht der HERR, Vmb drey vnd vier laster willen Edom, wil ich sein nicht schonen, Darumb, das er seine brueder mit dem schwert verfolget hat, **vnd jm seine kinder vmb bracht**, vnd jmer zurissen jnn seinem zorn, vnd seinen grim stets treibt. (1532) WA DB 11.2:230.11. So spricht der HERR, Vmb drey vnd vier Laster willen Edom, wil ich sein nicht schonen, Darumb, das er seinen Bruder mit dem schwert verfolget hat, **vnd das er jre Schwangere vmbbracht**, vnd jmer zurissen in seinem zorn, vnd seinen grim ewig helt. (1545) WA DB 11.2:231.11.

Verse	NASB	Hebrew Bible	Vulgate	Deutsche Bibel
Nah. 3:3	Horsemen charging, Swords flashing, spears gleaming, Many slain, a mass of corpses, And countless dead bodies – They stumble over the dead bodies!	פָּרָשׁ מַעֲלֶה וְלַהַב חֶרֶב וּבְרַק חֲנִית וְרֹב חָלָל **וְכֹבֶד פֶּגֶר** וְאֵין קֵצֶה לַגְּוִיָּה וְכָשְׁלוּ בִּגְוִיָּתָם	et micantis gladii et fulgurantis hastae et multitudinis interfectae **et gravis ruinae** nec est finis cadaverum et corruent in corporibus suis	Er bringt reuter erauff, mit glentzenden schwertern, vnd mit blitzenden spiessen, Da ligen viel erschlagene **vnd grosse hauffen leichnam**, das der selbigen kein zal ist, vnd man vber jre leichnam fallen mus. (1532) WA DB 11.2:294.3.
Nah. 3:15	There fire will consume you, The sword will cut you down; It will consume you as the locust does. Multiply yourself like the creeping locust, Multiply yourself like the swarming locust.	שָׁם תֹּאכְלֵךְ אֵשׁ תַּכְרִיתֵךְ חֶרֶב תֹּאכְלֵךְ **כַּיָּלֶק הִתְכַּבֵּד כַּיָּלֶק הִתְכַּבְּדִי** כָּאַרְבֶּה	ibi comedet te ignis peribis gladio devorabit te ut bruchus **congregare** ut bruchus **multiplicare** ut lucusta	Aber das feur wird dich fressen, vnd das schwerd toedten, Es wird dich abfressen, wie die kefer, **Es wird dich vberfallen**, wie kefer, **Es wird dich vberfallen**, wie hewschrecken. (1532) WA DB 11.2:294.15–WA DB 11.2:296.15.
Nah. 2:8	It is fixed: She is stripped, she is carried away, And her handmaids are moaning like the sound of doves, Beating on their breasts.	וְהֻצַּב גֻּלְּתָה הֹעֲלָתָה וְאַמְהֹתֶיהָ מְנַהֲגוֹת כְּקוֹל יוֹנִים **מְתֹפְפֹת עַל־לִבְבֵהֶן**	et miles captivus abductus est et ancillae eius minabantur gementes ut columbae **murmurantes in cordibus suis**	Die Koenigin wird gefangen weg gefueret werden, vnd jre jungfrawen werden seufftzen, wie die tauben, **vnd an jre brust schlahen**. (1532) WA DB 11.2:292.8.
Zeph. 1:15	A day of wrath is that day, A day of trouble and distress, A day of destruction and desolation, A day of darkness and gloom, A day of clouds and thick darkness	יוֹם עֶבְרָה הַיּוֹם הַהוּא יוֹם צָרָה וּמְצוּקָה **יוֹם שֹׁאָה וּמְשׁוֹאָה** יוֹם חֹשֶׁךְ וַאֲפֵלָה יוֹם עָנָן וַעֲרָפֶל	dies irae dies illa dies tribulationis et angustiae **dies calamitatis et miseriae** dies tenebrarum et caliginis dies nebulae et turbinis	Denn dieser tag ist ein tag des grimmes, ein tag der truebsal vnd angst, **ein tag des wetters vnd vngestuems**, ein tag der finsternis vnd tunckels, ein tag der wolcken vnd nebel. (1532) WA DB 11.2:314.15.

Micah 2:13

Luther argued in his lectures that the Vulgate's rendering of הַפֹּרֵץ (*happōrēṣ*, "the one who breaches, penetrates, breaks out") in Mic. 2:13 as *pandens* ("the one who opens") was an overly soft reading of the Hebrew:

> For he who opens [*pandens*] the way will go up before them. What we have here, 'who opens the way [*pandens*],' is quite gentle [*Mollius*]. In the Hebrew the meaning is this: 'He who breaks through [*diruptor*] will go up before them. Therefore, they will break through [*dirumpent*] and pass through the gate.' In a marvelous way this is an elegant passage, filled with comfort.[17]

In contrast to what he saw as a subdued Latin reading of *pandens*, Luther translated עָלָה הַפֹּרֵץ לִפְנֵיהֶם (*'ālâ happōrēṣ lipnêhem*, "the one who breaches has gone up before them") in the *Deutsche Bibel* as *Der Helt wird fur jn her durch brechen* ("The hero will break forth before them") in 1532, emending this in 1545 to *Es wird ein Durchbrecher fur jnen her auff faren* ("One who breaks through will advance before them").[18] His German translation thus reflected his exegetical argument, and followed the more forceful connotations of breaking out and breaching, which he saw as a more accurate reading of the Hebrew.

Amos 1:11

Luther made a scathing criticism of Jerome's translation of וְשִׁחֵת רַחֲמָיו (*wašiḥēṯ raḥămāyw*, "and ruined, corrupted his mercy") in Amos 1:11. He said in the lectures,

> Dr. Jerome again is snoring as he translates this passage – and no wonder. After all, he was the only fellow who was not equal to the great arduous task of translating, for what he translates here as 'and he violated his mercy [*et violaverit misericordiam eius*]' has been translated with patent absurdity. It ought to be translated this way: 'And he destroyed his heart, his innermost part [*et perdidit viscera sua*].' It is as if he were saying: 'They should have embraced each other eagerly and very warmly, as brothers. They ought to have had a great and necessary union between them. However, they destroyed each other.' In German we cannot translate the word *viscera* suitably. It has a very specific meaning in Hebrew. This specific meaning we express approximately in the Latin word *viscera*.[19]

---

[17] "Ascendet enim pandens iter ante eos. Mollius est id, quod nos habemus: pandens iter, in hebraeo sic est: ascendet coram eis diruptor, ideo dirumpent et transibunt portam etc. Mirum in modum elegans est hic locus et consolationis plenissimus." WA 13:313.24–27. LW 18:229.

[18] WA DB 11.2:276.13; WA DB 11.2:277.13. Cf. WA DB 4:249a.18–26; WA DB 4:249b.18–25. I am reading *vor* for Luther's *fur* based on their phonetic similarity, as *für* does not seem to fit as the preposition here. The 1912 Luther Bible makes this adjustment.

[19] "In hoc loco transferendo iterum stertit D. Hieronymus. Nec mirum: solus enim homo impar fuit tam arduo et immenso transferendi labori. Nam quod hic vertit: et violaverit misericordiam eius, plane absurde redditum est. Sic autem oportebat reddi: et perdidit viscera sua q. d. impense et ardentissime debuissent se mutuo complecti utpote fratres, summa inter eos coniunctio et necessitudo debuisset intercedere. sed perdiderunt se mutuo. Nos in germana lingua hoc vocabulum viscera prorsus non possumus apte reddere. In hebraeo est propriissime

Yet in the 1532 *Deutsche Bibel*, he went even further, making a glaringly disparate interpretation in contrast to the Latin. He translated וְשִׁחֵת רַחֲמָיו (*wəšiḥēt raḥămāyw*) as *vnd jm seine kinder vmb bracht* ("and he murdered his own children") in 1532, with an emendation to *vnd das er jre Schwangere vmbbracht* ("and that he murdered their pregnant women") in 1545.[20] His Bible translation is barbaric and intensely personal in comparison to the Vulgate. While his exegetical argument was predicated on the lexical accuracy of the Hebrew, his Bible translation demonstrates his willingness to go far beyond the literal Hebrew in order to express the intensity that he saw in the text.

Nahum 3:3

Luther argued in his lectures against the Vulgate's translation of וְכֹבֶד פָּגֶר (*wəkōbed pāger*, "and a mass of corpses") in Nah. 3:3 as *et gravis ruinae* ("and of severe destruction"):

> By the way, the Hebrew word which our translator here renders 'severe [*gravis*]' occurs often in scripture and is always translated this way, as in Genesis [Gen. 13:2]: 'Abraham was very rich [*gravis*] in gold and silver.' Also [Gen. 12:10]: 'For the famine was severe [*gravis*] in the land,' that is, a great or extensive [*magna, multa*] famine. So also here. We have 'severe destruction [*gravis ruina*],' that is, a mass and heap of dead bodies [*multitudo et magnitudo corporum occisorum*]. You see, what we here read as 'destruction [*ruinae*]' is poorly translated. The same thing we also have in the Psalm [Ps. 110:6]: 'He will bring judgment upon the nations. He will complete the destruction.' There we ought to translate it: 'He will fill them with corpses [*implebit cadaveribus*].' That's the way we must render it here.[21]

Luther translated וְכֹבֶד פָּגֶר (*wəkōbed pāger*) in the *Deutsche Bibel* as *vnd grosse hauffen leichnam* ("and a great heap of corpses").[22] His emphasis on death and cadavers was a more literal translation of the Hebrew, but more importantly a far more emotionally intense translation than he saw in the Vulgate's rendering.

---

dictum, quam proprietatem Latini verbo illo: viscera utcunque referimus." WA 13:164.31–WA 13:165.6. LW 18:135.

[20] WA DB 11.2:230.11; WA DB 11.2:231.11. "*jm*" is not entirely clear in this context; I have interpreted it as "his own," as some variant of the dative case in its use here (i. e. "to him," or "for him"). See the 1539–41 protocols, which include the note "matres [matrices] ('mothers [wombs]')," as well as a reference to Jer. 20:17; WA DB 4:234a.3–11. See also the notes in Luther's 1538/39 Old Testament, which suggest that he may have linked his translation for this verse to *Mutterleib* ("womb") by way of μητέρα ("mother") in the LXX [those notes, though, are not from Luther's hand]; WA DB 4:234b.3–9, and Note 1.

[21] "Ceterum verbum hebraeum, quod hic noster interpres vertit gravis, frequens est in scriptura et semper etiam sic versum est, ut in Genesi: erat Abraham auro gravis et argento. Item: erat gravis fames in terra, hoc est, magna, multa. Ita hic quoque est: gravis ruina i. e. multitudo et magnitudo corporum occisorum. Nam quod nos hic legimus ruinae, male versum est, sicut et in psalmo: iudicabit in nationibus, implebit ruinas, ubi sic verti debet: implebit cadaveribus. Ita hic quoque est vertendum." WA 13:388.25–32. LW 18:307.

[22] WA DB 11.2:294.3.

Nahum 3:15

Luther referenced Nah. 3:3 in his argument concerning Nah. 3:15, and focused on a term with the same root כבד (*kbd*) as he did there. He contended that the Vulgate's translations of הִתְכַּבֵּד (*hiṯkabbēḏ*, "make yourself heavy, burdensome, grievous, numerous") in Nah. 3:15 as *congregare* ("be gathered") and הִתְכַּבְּדִי (*hiṯkabbəḏî*, "make yourself heavy, burdensome, grievous, numerous") as *multiplicare* ("be multiplied") were less than ideal:

> *So, assemble [Congregare] like the locust.* Here we have the same word in the Hebrew as we had earlier at the very beginning of this chapter [v. 3]: 'severe destruction [*gravis ruinae*],' that is, a broad heaping up of the corpses of the slain [*multiplicata cadaveribus occisorum*], as I explained above, following an example of scripture from Genesis [Gen. 12:10]. So here we ought to translate: 'Become burdened, grow more forceful [*gravescere*] like the locust. Become burdened, grow more forceful [*gravescere*] like the grasshopper.' In fact, the Latin translator's translation with two words is an unnecessary waste, for in Hebrew it is just a single word.[23]

In contrast to the Vulgate, he translated both הִתְכַּבֵּד (*hiṯkabbēḏ*) and הִתְכַּבְּדִי (*hiṯkabbəḏî*) in the *Deutsche Bibel* as *Es wird dich vberfallen* ("it will assail you, attack you, ambush you").[24] Aside from his decision to translate the more negative connotation, compared to the Vulgate, his translation offered a profoundly more forceful reading. His reference to Nah 3:3, and thus also the implicit link to his translation there, *vnd grosse hauffen leichnam*, underscore the magnified potency that he sought to transmit in the German rendering of Nah. 3:15, under the direct influence of the semantic intensity that he perceived in the Hebrew text. In this case, his translation was based on the literal Hebrew.

Nahum 2:8

Luther argued for a forcefulness within the Hebrew phrase מְתֹפְפֹת עַל־לִבְבֵהֶן (*məṯōp̄əp̄ōṯ ʿal-liḇəḇēhen*, "drumming upon their breasts") in Nah. 2:8, which he did not believe the Vulgate adequately expressed with *murmurantes in cordibus suis* ("murmuring in their hearts"):

> *And her maidens play the timbrel over their own hearts* [*tympanizantes super cordibus suis*]. You see, this is the way we must translate this correctly, not as our Bible reads, 'moaning [*murmurantes*].' We have the same word also in the Psalm [Ps. 68:25], where it is correctly translated 'in the midst of those who *play the timbrel*, [*in medio tympanistriarum*] etc.' Therefore, he taunts her handmaidens in the same way that he taunted their queen. They weep and are overcome with grief as they bemoan their captivity. It is as

---

[23] "Congregare ergo ut bruchus. Eadem est hic vox in Hebraeo, quae est supra statim initio huius capitis: gravis ruinae, hoc est, aucta, multiplicata cadaveribus occisorum, sicut supra exposui secutus exemplum scripturae ex Genesi. Ita hic verti debuit: gravescere sicut bruchus, gravescere sicut locusta. Quod vero interpres latinus duobus verbis transtulit, intempestiva est copia, nam in hebraeo unum est tantum verbum." WA 13:392.14–19. LW 18:313.

[24] WA DB 11.2:294.15–WA DB 11.2:296.15. Cf. WA DB 4:257b.15–16.

if he were saying: 'What a beautiful dance they are presenting. Now that they are taken captive in this way, they are performing their drumming on their own breast [*ßie paucken itzund auff der brust*]. Surely this is a great dance'; that is, 'They are now beating their breasts [*iam tundunt pectora sua*], etc.' This is how the prophet compares their earlier delights and pleasant dances with their captivity.[25]

In contrast to the Vulgate, Luther translated this in the *Deutsche Bibel* as *vnd an jre brust schlahen* ("and beat on their breast").[26] His interpretation employed a literal adaptation of the Hebraism of playing timbrels on the breast, which he believed better expressed the extreme affective state of the maidens' mourning than the Vulgate's *murmurantes*. Moreover, he further enhanced the intensive reading in his Bible translation, where he interpreted מְתֹפְפֹת (*mətōpəpōt*) as beating, striking, or pounding the timbrels [*schlahen*], rather than simply playing them [*tympanizantes*].

Zephaniah 1:15

Luther argued that the Vulgate mistranslated יוֹם שֹׁאָה וּמְשׁוֹאָה (*yôm šō'â ûməšô'â*, "a day **of tempest/rushing over** and desolation/ruin") as *dies **calamitatis** et miseriae* ("a day **of calamity** and misery") in Zeph. 1:15:

> What we read as 'a day of ruin [*dies calamitatis*]' has been poorly translated from the Hebrew. It ought to have been translated in the same way as the evangelist Luke did in Ch. 21[:25]: 'At the roaring of the sea and the waves [*prae tumultu sonitus maris et fluctuum*]'; and as we have it in the Proverbs of Solomon [Prov. 3:25]: 'Do not be afraid of the sudden storm/uproar [*tumultu repentino*] of the wicked'; and in Ps. 65[:8]: 'Who confounds the depths of the sea [*profundum maris*], the sound of its waves [*sonum fluctuum eius*].' Therefore it should have been translated 'a day of tempest and attack [*dies tumultus et impetus*].' The prophet is showing that the Babylonians will come with a very great attack [*cum maximo impetu*]; they will roar [*tumultuaturos*] against the people of Judah as the sea is accustomed to thunder and roar [*sonare et tumultuari*] when strong winds stir it [*ventis agitatum valentibus*].[27]

---

[25] "Et ancillae tympanizantes super cordibus suis. Sic enim est proprie vertendum, non ut nostra biblia legunt: murmurantes. Idem enim vocabulum etiam est in psalmo, ubi recte versum est: in medio tympanistriarum etc. Sicut ergo reginae insultat, ita et ancillis, quae gemunt et moerore conficiuntur dolentes captivitatem suam q. d. Ich meyn, ßie tantzen nuhn auch fein, cum sic captivae abducuntur ßie paucken itzund auff der brust. Egregia scil. saltatio, hoc est, iam tundunt pectora sua etc. Sic comparat propheta delicias priores et choreas delicantes cum captivitate." WA 13:385.26–33. LW 18:303. This is according to the Altenburg recension. Cf. the Zwickau recension, which records Luther calling attention to "the force of the Hebrew word [*hebraei verbi vis*]." WA 13:358.31–33.

[26] WA DB 11.2:292.8. I am reading *schlagen* for Luther's *schlahen*, which does not appear in Grimm. The 1912 Luther Bible reads *schlagen* also.

[27] "Verum quod nos legimus 'dies calamitatis' male versum est ex hebraeo. Eodem autem modo verti debuisset, quo loquitur Lucas euangelista cap. 21: prae tumultu sonitus maris et fluctuum, et sicut est in Proverb. Salomonis: a tumultu repentino impiorum non metues, et psalm. 64: qui conturbas profundum maris sonum fluctuum eius. Ergo sic verti debuisset: dies tumultus et impetus. Significat autem propheta venturos Babylonios cum maximo impetu et tumultuaturos in Iudaeos non secus quam si mare ventis agitatum valentibus sonare et tumultuari

At first glance, his argument may seem trivial. *Calamitas* [*calamitatis*] certainly carries similar connotations as his suggested translation *tumultus*, and both fit the context of the verse. But his insistence that the Hebrew be interpreted with terminology that he found more intimately associated with storm is the key to understanding the role of Hebrew intensity in his translation here.

Luther translated יוֹם שֹׁאָה וּמְשׁוֹאָה (*yôm šō'â ûməšō'â*) in the *Deutsche Bibel* as *ein tag des wetters vnd vngestuems* ("a day of weather and storminess/violence/furiousness").[28] The root of the main term in his argument is שׁוא (*šw'*). The corresponding term in his reference to Prov. 3:25 is וּמִשֹּׁאַת (*ûmišō'at*, "or of **the tempest/rushing over [of]**"), which is derived from that same root. שׁוא (*šw'*) and its extensions have lexical meanings associated with storm: "to rush over," "a tempest," "storm," and "turbulence"; with further connotations such as "trouble" and "calamity."[29] שָׁאוֹן (*šə'ôn*, "rushing, tumult") in Ps. 65:8, however, comes from the root שׁאה (*š'h*), whose extensions have similar connotations associated with storm: "a din," "roar," and "crash [of waves, water]"; but additional meanings more explicitly congruent with *calamitas*: "destruction," "desolation," "misfortune," and "being extinguished."[30] Clearly both שׁוא (*šw'*) and שׁאה (*š'h*) are multifarious Hebrew terms, with strong connotations of destruction, but also linked to natural phenomena connected to extreme weather events.[31]

Luther's decision to focus his translation strictly on the storm motif ultimately was a choice that he believed had the highest emotional punch.[32] It mirrors many other decisions where he used the same methodology. When presented with the choice, he routinely selected the translation that would give the most intense reading. Moreover, Hebrew vocabulary associated with storm seems to have a particularly influential role throughout his Bible translation. He frequently exploited this type of figurative language, using storm motifs to emphasize especially affective readings of particular texts.[33] And while there is no

---

solet." WA 13:490.17–24. LW 18:334–5. I am making a very literal translation of שֹׁאָה (*šō'â*) as "tempest" or "rushing over," for the sake of clarity for the comparison.

[28] WA DB 11.2:314.15.

[29] BDB, 996. KB, 951.

[30] BDB, 980–1. KB, 935, and see 936 for further forms.

[31] BDB and KB indicate that שׁוא (*šw'*) is likely a parallel form of שׁאה (*š'h*). BDB, 996. KB, 935. See also TDOT 14:237, 447. Reuchlin's entry in the *Rudimenta* for שׁאה (*š'h*) includes: *Consternauit, deuastauit, desolatus,* and *calamitas* [p. 502]. The entry for שׁוא (*šw'*) [שׁוּ (*šû'*)] includes: *Clamor* and *fremitus* [p. 510]. Luther's Bible translation seems to deviate from Reuchlin's definitions. This and many similar examples in Luther's translations suggest that Raeder and others may overly credit the *Rudimenta* as the basis of Luther's Hebrew knowledge and translation decisions. Cf. Luther's translations of the Hebrew Bible passages that he cited for support in his lectures on Zephaniah: he rendered וּמִשֹּׁאַת (*ûmišō'at*) in Prov. 3:25 as *noch fur dem sturm* ("nor of the storm") [WA DB 10.2:18.25] and שָׁאוֹן (*šə'ôn*) in Ps. 65:8 as *das brausen* ("the roar") [WA DB 10.1:302.8 (1524)].

[32] Moreover, he perhaps could not find or settle on a similarly ambiguous German word that would fully convey the multifarious meaning of the Hebrew.

[33] See, for example, Luther's interpretation of Jon. 1:4. WA 13:245.15, 21–35. LW 19:10. This example appears in Ch. 5 of this study.

explicit reference to it in this case, he often further connected the motif of storm to his experiences of *Anfechtung*, which appears in many instances of his interpretation of the Minor Prophets.³⁴ The next section of this chapter examines this aspect of his translation – instances where he recognized some type of semantic intensity of the Hebrew text, where there was a further, demonstrable connection to his interpretation of *Anfechtung* in the verse.

Part II: Hebrew Semantic Intensity and Luther's Interpretation of *Anfechtung*

While Luther's attempt to replicate the semantic intensity of the Hebrew was a consistent feature of his Bible translation, it took on a special theological significance in a subset of examples that all relate to his conception of *Anfechtung*. The examples which follow examine the role of Hebrew semantic intensity in Luther's German translation in places where he made a direct connection between it and his interpretation of *Anfechtung* in the texts. Table 3.2 provides the full Hebrew Bible, Vulgate, and *Deutsche Bibel* verse for each example in this section.

Table 3.2: Hebrew semantic intensity and Luther's interpretation of *Anfechtung*: Jon. 2:3, Ps. 118:5, Zeph. 1:17, Obad. 1:9, Amos 5:5, and Hab. 3:2.

Verse	NASB	Hebrew Bible	Vulgate	*Deutsche Bibel*
Jon. 2:3	and he said, "I called out of my distress to the Lord, And He answered me. I cried for help from the depth of Sheol; You heard my voice.	וַיֹּאמֶר קָרָאתִי מִצָּרָה לִי אֶל־יְהוָה וַיַּעֲנֵנִי מִבֶּטֶן שְׁאוֹל שִׁוַּעְתִּי שָׁמַעְתָּ קוֹלִי	et dixit **clamavi de tribulatione mea ad Domi-num** et exaudivit me de ventre inferni clamavi et exaudisti vocem meam	vnd sprach. **Jch rieff zu dem HERRN jnn meiner angst**, vnd er antwortet mir, Jch schrey aus dem bauche der hellen, vnd du hoeretest meine stim. (1532) WA DB 11.2:264.3.

---

³⁴ See, for example, Luther's interpretation of Jon. 1:4–5, 2:4–6; Nah. 1:3 and the reference to it in the *Resolutiones disputationum de indulgentiarum virtute* (1518); and Is. 51:17. These are examined in Chs. 4 and 5 of this study. See also concerning Jon. 1:5: WA 13:228.27–31, WA 13:245.36–WA 13:246.3, WA 19:205.25–WA 19:211.19, LW 19:10–11, 53–59; and concerning Jon. 2:6: WA 13:233.19–24, WA 13:251.9–13, WA 19:228.23–31, LW 19:19, 78. See also Luther's lectures on Jon. 1:11 concerning the connection between *tentatio* and tempest. WA 13:247.33–248.13. Stolt cites this link between storm and emotion in Luther's writings; for example, in his preface to the Psalms. Stolt, *Rhetorik*, 52, citing Luther's text from WA DB 10.1:100.37–WA DB 10.1:102.1 [I provide the 1528 reference; Stolt cites the entire 1545 preface]. Storm references also played an integral role in Luther's exploitation of various facets of the mystical tradition. Ch. 5 of this study examines this assiduously.

Verse	NASB	Hebrew Bible	Vulgate	Deutsche Bibel
Ps. 118:5	From my distress I called upon the Lord; The Lord answered me and set me in a large place.	מִן־הַמֵּצַר קָרָאתִי יָּהּ עָנָנִי בַמֶּרְחָב יָהּ	**cum tribularer invocavi Dominum** et exaudivit me in latitudine Dominus.	**Ynn der angst rieff ich den HERRN an**, Vnd der HERR erhoeret mich ym weytem rawm. (1524) WA DB 10.1:492.5.
Zeph. 1:17	I will bring distress on men So that they will walk like the blind, Because they have sinned against the Lord; And their blood will be poured out like dust And their flesh like dung	וַהֲצֵרֹתִי לָאָדָם וְהָלְכוּ כַּעִוְרִים כִּי לַיהוָה חָטָאוּ וְשֻׁפַּךְ דָּמָם כֶּעָפָר וּלְחֻמָם כַּגְּלָלִים	**et tribulabo homines** et ambulabunt ut caeci quia Domino peccaverunt et effundetur sanguis eorum sicut humus et corpus eorum sicut stercora	**Jch wil den leuten bange machen**, das sie vmbher gehen sollen, wie die blinden, darumb, das sie wider den HERRN gesundigt haben, jr blut sol vergossen werden, als were es staub, vnd jr leib, als were es kot. (1532) WA DB 11.2:314.17.
Obad. 1:9	Then your mighty men will be dismayed, O Teman, So that everyone may be cut off from the mountain of Esau by slaughter.	וְחַתּוּ גִבּוֹרֶיךָ תֵּימָן לְמַעַן יִכָּרֶת־אִישׁ מֵהַר עֵשָׂו מִקָּטֶל	**et timebunt** fortes tui a meridie ut intereat vir de monte Esau	**Denn deine starcken zu Theman sollen zagen**, auff das sie alle auff dem gebirge Esau, durch den mord, ausgerottet werden (1532) WA DB 11.2:254.9.
Amos 5:5	But do not resort to Bethel And do not come to Gilgal, Nor cross over to Beersheba; For Gilgal will certainly go into captivity And Bethel will come to trouble.	וְאַל־תִּדְרְשׁוּ בֵּית־אֵל וְהַגִּלְגָּל לֹא תָבֹאוּ וּבְאֵר שֶׁבַע לֹא תַעֲבֹרוּ כִּי הַגִּלְגָּל גָּלֹה יִגְלֶה וּבֵית־אֵל יִהְיֶה לְאָוֶן	et nolite quaerere Bethel et in Galgala nolite intrare et in Bersabee non transibitis quia Galgala captiva ducetur **et Bethel erit inutilis**	Suchet nicht Bethel, vnd kompt nicht gen Gilgal, vnd gehet nicht gen Berseba, Denn Gilgal wird gefangen weg gefurt werden, **vnd Bethel wird jnn jamer komen**. (1532) WA DB 11.2:238.5. Suchet nicht Bethel, vnd kompt nicht gen Gilgal, vnd gehet nicht gen BerSeba, Denn Gilgal wird gefangen weggefuert werden, **vnd Bethel wird Beth-Auen werden**. (1545) WA DB 11.2:239.5.

Verse	NASB	Hebrew Bible	Vulgate	Deutsche Bibel
Hab. 3:2	Lord, I have heard the report about You and I fear. O Lord, revive Your work in the midst of the years, In the midst of the years make it known; In wrath remember mercy.	יְהוָה שָׁמַעְתִּי שִׁמְעֲךָ יָרֵאתִי יְהוָה פָּעָלְךָ בְּקֶרֶב שָׁנִים חַיֵּיהוּ **בְּקֶרֶב שָׁנִים** תּוֹדִיעַ **בְּרֹגֶז רַחֵם** תִּזְכּוֹר	Domine audivi auditionem tuam et timui Domine opus tuum in medio annorum vivifica illud **in medio annorum** notum facies **cum iratus** fueris misericordiae recordaberis	HERR, ich hab dein geruecht gehoeret, das ich mich entsetze, HERR, du machst dein werck lebendig **mitten jnn den jaren**, vnd lesst es kund werden mitten jnn den jaren, **Wenn truebsal da ist**, so denckstu der barmhertzigkeit. (1532) WA DB 11.2:306.2.

Jonah 2:3 and Psalm 118:5: צרר *(ṣrr) and Angst*

There are a limited number of Hebrew terms where a direct link to Luther's interpretation of *Anfechtung* can be shown. One of these is צָרָה (*ṣārâ*, "tightness, affliction, anguish, distress, tribulation"), which appears in Jon. 2:3 as well as in a related form in Ps. 118:5, which he cited for support in his translation of Jonah. It is this citation which illuminates the central role of Hebrew intensity in his interpretation relative to the Latin Vulgate.

Luther wrote in his commentary on Jonah, addressing Jon. 2:3:

> Do not cast your eyes down or take to your heels, but stand still, rise above this, and you will discover the truth of the verse [Ps. 118:5]: 'Out of my distress [*ynn meyner angst*] I called on the Lord; the Lord answered me.'[35]

Luther's focus was on מֵצַר (*mēṣar*) in Ps. 118:5. The root of that term is צרר (*ṣrr*), the same root from which Jon. 2:3's צָרָה (*ṣārâ*) is derived. He translated מִן־הַמֵּצַר קָרָאתִי יָּהּ (*min-hammēṣar qārāṯî yāh*, "Out of the **distress/pain/straits/tight place**, I called out to the Lord") in Ps. 118:5 as *Ynn der angst rieff ich den HERRN an* ("In [the] **Angst**, I called to the Lord").[36] Similarly, he translated קָרָאתִי מִצָּרָה לִּי אֶל־יְהוָה (*qārāṯî miṣṣārâ lî 'el-'ăḏōnāy*, "I called from my **tightness/anguish/sorrow/anxiety/tribulation/affliction** to the Lord") in Jon. 2:3 as *Jch rieff zu dem HERRN jnn meiner angst* ("I called out to the Lord in my *Angst*").[37] By contrast, the Vulgate rendered the text in Ps. 118:5 as *clamavi de tribulatione mea ad Dominum* ("I cried out from my **tribulation** to the Lord"); and the text in Jon. 2:3 as *cum tribularer invocavi Dominum* ("when I was **afflicted/in tribulation**, I called upon the Lord").

---

[35] "Schlahe nicht den kopff nydder odder fleuch, sondern stehe stille und far uber dich. So wirstu erfaren, das diser vers war sey: 'Ich rieff ynn meyner angst zum herrn und er antwortet myr'." WA 19:223.17–20. LW 19:72. Cf. the Zwickau text of Luther's lectures at WA 13:232.5–16, where he made the same reference.

[36] WA DB 10.1:492.5 (1524).

[37] WA DB 11.2:264.3.

Luther's translation choice of *Angst*, compared with the Vulgate's *tribulatio*, is important for understanding his attempt to reproduce the semantic intensity that he saw in the Hebrew text. Stolt, following the work of many linguistic scholars – notably Anna Wierzbicka – explains that there is a considerable gap between the present-day connotation of *Angst* and that of Luther's time.[38] Today many equate *Angst* with *Furcht* ("fear"); however, it is a mistake to apply this to Luther's perception of the word. Stolt cites numerous linguistic researchers, including Mario Wandruszka, Henning Bergenholtz, and Walter Schulz, concerning the shift in meaning that *Angst* has undergone. In *Frühneuhochdeutsch*, *Angst* carried the connotation of *tribulatio* – precisely what the Vulgate used to translate צרר (*ṣrr*) in Jonah and the Psalm. But *Angst* had a much broader meaning, also carrying connotations of *Bedrohung* ("threat"), *Bedrängnis* ("affliction, distress"), *Not* ("need, trouble, hardship"), *Gefahr* ("danger"), the inverse of *Geborgenheit* ("a feeling of security"), *pressura* ("pressure"), *angustia* ("narrowness, tightness"), and *tristitia* ("sadness").[39] This suggests that Luther's translation of צָרָה (*ṣārâ*) in Jon. 2:3 as *Angst* was a decidedly more variegated and emotionally-slanted reading than the Vulgate's *tribulatione*.

But there was a further, direct link to *Anfechtung* in Luther's translation of צרר (*ṣrr*). This appears in the *scholia* on Ps. 118:5, where he explicitly interpreted מֵצַר (*mēṣar*) as *Anfechtung*:

In Hebrew the word *Angst* means 'something narrow [*das Enge ist*].' I surmise that the German noun for *Angst* is also derived from an adjective meaning narrow [*enge*]. It implies fear [*bañge*] and pain [*wehe*], as in a process of clamping, squeezing, and pressing [*geklemmet, gedruckt vnd gepresset wird*]. *Anfechtungen* and misfortunes [*vngluck*] do squeeze and press, as is indicated by the proverb: 'The great wide world was too narrow for me.' In Hebrew 'in a large place' is used in contrast to 'the narrow [*die Enge*]' or *Angst* [*angst*], which mean affliction [*trubsal*] and distress [*not*]; 'a wide space' denotes consolation and help.[40]

The richness of his exegesis of מֵצַר (*mēṣar*) shows a profoundly intense and diverse reading, which he clearly was drawing from the multifariousness that

---

[38] Wierzbicka cites a shift in the meaning of *Angst* over time, from "affliction" to "fear" as part of an exhaustive investigation of *Angst* in German culture, its semantic history, and Luther's use of it. Anna Wierzbicka, *Emotions across Languages and Cultures: Diversity and Universals* (Cambridge: Cambridge University Press, 1999), 123–67, especially pp. 139–59.

[39] Wierzbicka, *Emotions*, 123–67, especially pp. 144–6, 159–63. Stolt, *Laßt uns fröhlich springen*, especially pp. 20–21, 53–90, also cautioning that even *Geborgenheit* does not have a proper equivalent in modern English. Stolt further contends that *Angst* cannot be understood as Luther did outside of its connection with "das Herzens." Stolt, *Laßt uns fröhlich springen*, 93.

[40] "Añgst ym Ebreischen laüt, als das Eñge ist, wie ich acht das ym deudschen auch Angst daher kome, das enge sey, dar inn einem bañge vnd wehe wird, vnd gleich geklemmet, gedruckt vnd gepresset wird, wie denn die anfechtungen vnd vngluck thun, nach dem sprich wort, Es war mir die weite wellt zu enge. Dagegen laut ym Ebreischen, das er hie sagt, ynn weitem raüm, das gleich, wie die Enge odder añgst heisst, trubsal vnd not, Also heisst, Weiter raüm trost vnd hulffe." WA 31.1:93.3–9 (*Scholien zum 118. Psalm. Das schöne Confitemini. 1529*). LW 14:59. Hovland also cites this in "An Examination," 227.

he saw as innate to the Hebrew – *bañge, wehe, Anfechtungen, vngluck, Enge, Angst, trubsal*, and *not*.⁴¹ It supports the contentions of Stolt, Wierzbicka, and other linguists concerning the broader *Frühneuhochdeutsch* understanding of *Angst*. Furthermore, it shows the clear role that Hebrew played in his German Bible rendering, and the further link between the Hebrew and his interpretation of *Anfechtung* in both Jon. 2:3 and Ps. 118:5.⁴²

Figure 3.1 below provides a visual depiction of the breadth of Luther's reading of צרר (*ṣrr*) in Jon. 2:3 and Ps. 118:5, as well as the links to *Anfechtung*. It lists the various Hebrew, German, and Latin words that he used in translating and commenting on these two verses. In addition, it shows the other verses in the Minor Prophets where he specifically addressed the same Hebrew root צרר (*ṣrr*), along with the German and Latin terms he used to explain it. The wide array of terminology which he used in his discussions of and allusions to *Anfechtung* as part of his Hebrew argumentation shows the profound complexity and multifarious quality of this facet of his theology.⁴³ To further illustrate the role of Hebrew in this interpretation, Figure 3.1 includes Job 9:23 and Is. 28:19, the only two places where Luther actually used the word *Anfechtung* in his translation of the Old Testament.⁴⁴

---

⁴¹ Cf. DWB 1:358–9, where Grimm includes *bange* in his definition for *Angst*.

⁴² The link between *Angst* and *Anfechtung* in Luther's thought has been emphasized by numerous scholars, most drawing upon Vogelsang's 1932 study. See Vogelsang, *Der angefochtene Christus*, especially pp. 6–79. Vogelsang delineates numerous types of *Angst* and *Anfechtung*. See also Beintker, *Die Überwindung*, 61, 66; McGrath, *Luther's Theology of the Cross*, 225; and Dietz, *Der Begriff*, 16, although the entire book addresses this. See also Birgit Stolt, who argues that "*Angst* is the strongest German '*affectus*-word' [that Luther uses] in the context of *Anfechtung* ['Angst' ist das stärkste deutsche affectus-Wort Luthers in Kontext der Anfechtung]." Stolt, *Laßt uns fröhlich springen*, 70.

⁴³ Concerning various terms associated with *Anfechtung* in Luther's thought, see: Gerhard Krause and Gerhard Müller, eds., *Theologische Realenzyklopädie*, vol. 2 (Berlin: Walter de Gruyter, 1978), 687–708; and Stolt, *Laßt uns fröhlich springen*, 58, 63–64, 66–70, 106, and 234–5. Stolt advises that the most common Latin term that Luther used in the *Tischreden* to describe the emotional side of *Anfechtung* was *tristitia*, which she says he rendered in his Bible translations as *Traurigkeit*; in Stolt, *Laßt uns fröhlich springen*, 69–70, and 234–5. For scholarly literature on Luther's use of *Anfechtung*, see Ch. 1 of this study.

⁴⁴ These are the only two locations that I am aware of where he used the word in his Hebrew Bible translation, outside of revision protocols, etc. and the apocrypha, which obviously should not be considered as the Hebrew Bible [see WA DB 3; WA DB 4; and WA DB 12]. Bornkamm discusses Luther's translation of Is. 28:19 in Bornkamm, *Luther und das Alte Testament*, 15, 186–7. Luther did not lecture on Job, thus only the Bible translation appears in this Figure. The terminology in this Figure is taken from: Is. 28:19: WA DB 11.1:90.19; WA DB 11.1:91.19; WA 31.2:167.10–21. Job 9:23: WA DB 10.1:26.23; WA DB 10.1:27.23. Ps. 118:5: WA DB 10.1:492.5; WA DB 10.1:493a.5; WA DB 10.1:493b.5; WA 4:15.27; WA 31.1:51a.8; WA 31.1:93a.3–9; WA 55.1:759–60; WA 55.2:889.45–WA 55.2:890.54. Obad. 1:12: WA DB 11.2:254.12; WA DB 11.2:255.12–WA DB 11.2:257.12. Jon. 2:3: WA DB 11.2:264.3; WA DB 11.2:265.3; WA 13:232.1–16; WA 13:249.20–35; WA 19:222.3–WA 19:224.7. Nah. 1:9: WA DB 11.2:290.9; WA DB 11.2:291.9; WA DB 4:253a.19–31; WA DB 4:253b.19–31; WA 13:351.22–WA 13:352.8; WA 13:377.24–WA 13:378.17.

Hebrew Semantic Intensity 117

זוּעַ: "tremble, quake, be in terror, shake violently"
זְוָעָה: "agitation, fear, vexation, a trembling, an object of trembling or terror"

vnfal (1528)
Anfechtung (1545)
Tentatio (1545 gloss)

זוּעַ
זְוָעָה
Is. 28:19

turbacione
tribulacione
adfliccione

vexare, uexacio, vexacione
Mouere de loco
wen man eynen hyn vnd wider pultert

נסה: "to test, try, prove, tempt, assay, put to the proof or test"
מַסָּה: "a testing, of men (judicial) or of God (querulous); temptation, trial; despair"

anfechtung (1524, 1545)

נסה
לְמַסַּת [מַסָּה]
Job 9:23

צרר: "to bind, be/make narrow, cause distress, besiege, be straitened, be bound; to show hostility toward, to vex"
צָרָה: "tightness; straits, distress, trouble; adversary, adversity, affliction, anguish, distress, tribulation"
מֵצַר: "distress, pain, straits; something tight; trouble"

anfechtungen
Angst, Aṅgst, angst, aṅgst
angustia
bange, baṅge
Enge, Eṅge, enge
geklemmt, gedruckt vnd gepresset wird
humiliasti
not
tribulatione, tribulatio
trubsal
vngluck
wehe

מֵצַר	צָרָה
Ps. 118:5	Obad. 1:12
	Jon. 2:3
	Nah. 1:9
	Zeph. 1:15
	Zeph. 1:17
	Zech. 10:11

adversitates
afflixistis, affligetis
affectus
Angst, angst
Angustiae, angustias, angustia, angustatur
bange machen
bombum
clangam
constringitur
conturbas profundum maris
cor et animum auferat
cum maximo impetu et tumultuaturos
enge, engen
fauces
feldgeschrey
fluctus tumultuantes, fluctuantes, fluctuum
impetus
jamers
nimium coarctatur
not
obstupefacti
pavorem
pavefactione illa cordium
quam si mare ventis agitatum valentibus sonare et tumultuari solet
resonantis maris
a folio arboris fugentur (i.e. the rustling leaf metaphor, an allusion to Lev. 26:36: וְרָדַף (אֹתָם קוֹל עָלֶה נִדָּף)
sonitum
sonitus maris et fluctuum, sonum fluctuum
tribulatio, cum tribularer, tribulatione, tribularer
tentatio, tentationes
Trübsal, truebsal
tumores maris
tumultus, tumultum, tumultu
Vnglueck, ungluck
verfolgung
wilchem engstlichem

Figure 3.1: Hebrew that Luther directly connected with *Anfechtung*, along with the German and Latin that he used to explain each in his exegesis: צרר (ṣrr), זוע (zwʿ), and נסה (nsh).

Zephaniah 1:17: צרר (ṣrr) and Bange Machen

The same term צרר (ṣrr) which Luther addressed in his translation of Jon. 2:3 appears in Zeph. 1:17. Here too, Luther's translation reflects his discernment of a heightened semantic intensity inherent in the word, which fed his interpretation of *Anfechtung* in the verse. He explained in the lectures,

> *And I will bring distress [et tribulabo] on men.* I do not understand that Hebrew word either. For it does not mean 'to bring distress [*tribulare*],' as our translator renders it. I say it this way: 'And I will resound [*et clangam*] among men. I will be heard from too [*Ich wil mich auch lassen horen*]. I will set up a hue and cry among you [*Ich wil eyn feldgeschrey unter euch anrichten*]. That is, I will strike terror [*pavorem*] in you that you may realize that I am waging war, that I am fighting against you.' You see, this is the way God wages war. He takes heart and courage away from those he intends to destroy, as I have mentioned several times earlier in other prophets. So it happens that they will very easily be put to flight without all the effort of the foe, yes, even by the leaf of a tree. Then they fight with absolutely no success. That sense he expresses when he adds: *So that they will walk like the blind.* It is as if he were saying: 'With that terror of their hearts [*pavefactione illa cordium*], I will cause them to be deprived of all their strategies. They will be unable to recover their senses. They will be awestruck [*obstupefacti*], and they will have no idea whether to flee, resist the enemy, or offer conditions for peace. They will be so confused [*Ita confusi*], so devoid of plans, that they will walk like blind men.'[45]

The Vulgate translated וַהֲצֵרֹתִי לָאָדָם (*wahăṣērōṭî lā'ādām*, "And I will make narrow for, cause distress to, afflict the man") in Zeph. 1:17 as *et **tribulabo** homines* ("and I will afflict the people"). While the Vulgate here echoed its rendering of צרר (ṣrr) in Jon. 2:3, Luther veered rather significantly from his translation there: *Jch wil den leuten **bange machen*** ("I will frighten, agitate, oppress the people").[46] Like *Angst* in Jon. 2:3, his translation of *bange machen* in this verse carried multiple layers of meaning and thus showed a more diverse and intensive reading of the Hebrew than the Vulgate's *tribulabo*.[47] In his lexical entry

---

Zeph. 1:15: WA DB 11.2:314.15; WA DB 11.2:315.15; WA 13:459.31–WA 13:460.10; WA 13:490.14–24. Zeph. 1:17: WA DB 11.2:314.17; WA DB 11.2:315.17; WA 13:460.12–18; WA 13:491.1–7. Zech. 10:11: WA DB 11.2:350.11; WA DB 11.2:351.11; WA 13:643.17–21; StL 14:1934.25.

[45] "Et tribulabo homines. Neque illam vocem hebraeam intelligo. Non enim significat tribulare, ut noster reddit interpres. Ego sic reddo: et clangam inter homines, Ich wil mich auch lassen horen. Ich wil eyn feldgeschrey unter euch anrichten, hoc est, incutiam vobis pavorem, ut sentiatis me gerere bellum, me contra vos pugnare. Sic enim solet deus bellum gerere, ut cor et animum auferat iis, quos est perditurus, sicut supra aliquoties in aliis prophetis admonui. Ita enim fit, ut facillime citra omnem hostis operam vel a folio arboris fugentur. Tum enim infelicissime pugnatur, et illam sententiam exprimit, quando subiicit: et ambulabunt ut caeci, q. d. pavefactione illa cordium efficiam, ut priventur omnibus consiliis, non poterunt ad se redire, obstupefacti ignorabunt prorsus, fugerene velint an hosti resistere aut conditiones pacis offerre. Ita confusi et expertes omnis consilii ambulabunt ut caeci." WA 13:490.38–WA 13:491.11. LW 18:335.

[46] WA DB 11.2:314.17.

[47] See Ch. 4 of this study, and Luther's use of *bange* in the context of Hab. 2:5 and 16, and parallels in Zech. 12:2 and 4, particularly concerning בַּשִּׁגָּעוֹן (*bašiggā'ôn*) in Zech. 12:4.

for *bange* [*bang*], Grimm lists *anxius / anxie* ("*anxious*"), *pavidus* ("trembling, fearful"), *pulsare* ("to agitate, push against"); and specifically for *Mittelhochdeutsch*, *enge* ("narrow, tight") and *angustus* ("narrow, strait, contracted").[48] Sanders adds *Bangigkeit* ("fear, anxiety, disquietude, restlessness"), *erregend* ("exciting, agitating"), and *beklemmend* ("oppressive, constricting, nightmarish"), and the particularly noteworthy *Angst*.[49]

Luther's vivid glosses for הַצֵרֹתִי (*hăṣērōṯî*) in the lectures – *clangam, feldgeschrey, pavefactione illa cordium,* and *obstupefacti* – underscore his intensified and more multidimensional interpretation, compared to what he saw in the Vulgate. And as with Jon. 2:3, he linked his interpretation of the Hebrew to *Anfechtung*. His choice of *bange* accomplished this in and of itself – it is one of the terms which he explicitly linked to *Anfechtung* in the *scholia* on Ps. 118:5 in his discussions of מֵצַר (*mēṣar*).[50] In addition, he evoked the metaphor of the rustling leaf from Lev. 26:36 and Job 13:25, something that he often used in his discussions of *Anfechtung*.[51]

Zeph. 1:17 is thus another example of an intentionally polysemous translation by Luther, a hermeneutical tool which produced a more intense German translation relative to the Vulgate, based on the Hebrew that he consulted. Moreover, it is further evidence of Luther's interpretation of Hebrew directly influencing his interpretation of *Anfechtung* in the Minor Prophets.

Obadiah 1:9: חָתַת (*ḥāṯaṯ*) and Zagen; and Hebrew Syntax

Luther argued for a more forceful reading of Obad. 1:9 than the Vulgate in two key places – one based on a lexical element of the Hebrew and the other syntactical. The first issue that he addressed was the Vulgate's translation of וְחַתּוּ

---

[48] DWB 1:1102. *Mittelhochdeutsch* is the period of the German language immediately preceding Luther's, and thus, an important consideration.

[49] WDS 1:77. See Wierzbicka concerning Luther's influence upon the dissemination of the German expression *angst und bange*; in Wierzbicka, *Emotions*, 141, 150. Also see R. E. Keller, *The German Language* (London: Faber and Faber, 1978), 449, cited by Wierzbicka in *Emotions*, 141. Cf. Luther's translation *kirren machen* in Amos 2:13, which seems to parallel *bange machen*; see Table A.2 in the Appendix.

[50] Stolt's research supports this conclusion. She also identifies *bange* with distress and anxiety, and argues for a further connection with Luther's multifarious understandings of *Angst* and *Anfechtung*. Stolt, *Laßt uns fröhlich springen*, 64–65, citing Wierzbicka, *Emotions*, 141, 150.

[51] This appears in many places in Luther's texts. He cites the rustling leaf in his exegesis of the Minor Prophets in: Jon. 1:7 [WA 19:211.26; LW 19:60]; Jon. 2:4 [WA 19:226.14–16; LW 19:75–76]; and Zech. 6:8 [StL 14:1876.15; LW 20:252]. Jon. 2:4 is further examined in Ch. 5 of this study. Many scholars cite his use of the metaphor elsewhere, including his exegesis of the Psalms and Genesis. See Hovland, "An Examination," 393–4; Hovland, "*Anfechtung* in Luther's Biblical Exegesis," in *Reformation Studies: Essays in Honor of Roland H. Bainton*, ed. Franklin H. Littell (Richmond, VA: John Knox Press, 1962), 48; and Bornkamm, *Luther und das Alte Testament*, 52–53.

(wəḥattû, "And [they] will be prostrated, broken down by violence or by confusion and fear, made afraid, terrified, amazed, discouraged") as *Et timebunt* ("And they will fear"):

And your mighty men shall be dismayed [Et timebunt], O Teman. More accurately this reads: 'Your mighty men will become fearful [*pavidi erunt*],' will become fleeting and sheepish [*fluchtig und schuchtern werden*]. You see, this properly means that fear [*pavorem*] which generally pervades an army that is about to be cut to pieces and sees no way of escape.[52]

Luther translated וְחַתּוּ (*wəḥattû*) in the *Deutsche Bibel* as *Denn ... sollen zagen* ("Then ... should fear/be in horror/tremble/hesitate").[53] *Zagen* is a rich term, carrying multiple layers of meaning, indicative of fear but also of the physical responses of trembling and hesitation. Luther's argument in the lectures that וְחַתּוּ (*wəḥattû*) should be translated as *pavidi erunt* rather than *timebunt* reinforces his Bible interpretation – *pavidi* conveys an intense meaning of fear, but also has connotations of physical trembling which *timebunt* lacks. Moreover, both *zagen* and *pavore* have numerous links to *Anfechtung* in his considerations of the Minor Prophets: *pavore* and *Anfechtung* in the lectures on Zeph. 1:17; *pavefacit* and *bange machen* [thus, an implicit link to *Anfechtung*] in his interpretation of Zech. 12:4; and *pavore, zagen,* and multiple links to the mystical tradition and *Anfechtung* in his interpretations of Ps. 31:23 and Jon. 2:5. Furthermore, Grimm and Sanders show numerous linguistic associations between *zagen, bange,* and *Angst,* as well as the connection to *pavor*.[54] Luther's translation of *zagen,* its association with *Anfechtung,* and the various other associations of terminology in his exegesis with *Anfechtung* demonstrate a much richer, more intensive understanding of חָתַת (*ḥātat*) than what he saw in the Vulgate's rendering.

His appraisal of the potency in the Hebrew Bible relative to the Vulgate in Obad. 1:9 is even more lucid in the second issue that he addressed concerning the Vulgate. Ultimately his concern was a matter of verse division and syntax. He argued concerning the latter segment of Obad. 1:9:

---

[52] "Et timebunt fortes tui Theman. Rectius: pavidi erunt fortes tui, fluchtig und schuchtern werden. Significat enim proprie pavorem illum, qui solet invadere exercitum aliquem in bello concidendum, quando scil. non vident, qua evadant." WA 13:219.10–13. LW 18:198.

[53] WA DB 11.2:254.9.

[54] Grimm explicitly links *zagen* to *pavere, timere,* and *bange* [DWB 31:27]; and also *furcht* and *scheu* [DWB 31:23]. Cf. Grimm [DWB 1:1104], where he provides *zagen* and *fürchten* as definitions for the term *bangen*; he also links *bang[e]* and *angst* in numerous places in his definition of *bang* [DWB 1:1102–3]. Sanders includes in his definitions for *Zagen*: *bang und scheu* [WDS 2.2:1691], and also provides as an example "in der Seele zagen, bangen"; thus, here, another link to *Anfechtung* through *bange* [WDS 2.2:1692]. Ch. 4 of this study examines the link between Hebrew and Luther's interpretation of *Anfechtung* in Zech. 12:4. Ch. 5 examines the link between Hebrew and Luther's interpretation of *Anfechtung* in Jon. 2:5 and Ps. 31:23.

So that every man from Mount Esau will perish. The Hebrew adds 'by slaughter [*prae mactatione*], etc.' 'Thus I will take care that everyone from Mount Esau will be wiped out, that not a single person will survive.' **Yet the Hebrew has far greater significance than can be rendered conveniently in another language**. It is as if he were saying: 'There will be a heap [of bodies] lying here and another heap there. They will be killed everywhere in the cities if any care to resist. Also in that terrible slaughter your wise men will be so greatly terrified [*conterrentur*] that they will become completely stupid, etc.'[55]

He translated **לְמַעַן יִכָּרֶת-אִישׁ מֵהַר עֵשָׂו מִקָּטֶל** (*ləmaʿan yikkāreṯ-ʾîš mēhar ʿēśāw miqqāṭel*, "so that man **might be cut off/cut down** from the mountain of Esau **by a violent death/slaughter**") as *auff das sie alle auff dem gebirge Esau, **durch den mord, ausgerottet werden*** ("that all of them upon the mountain of Esau **may be exterminated by murder**").[56] By contrast, the Vulgate translated the same phrase as *ut **intereat** vir de monte Esau* ("so that man **should perish** from the mountain of Esau"). Luther's main focus was מִקָּטֶל (*miqqāṭel*), which appears in the Hebrew Bible as part of v. 9. The Vulgate moved that term to the beginning of v. 10 and translated it there as *propter interfectionem* ("through [or, because of] murder [or, killing]").[57]

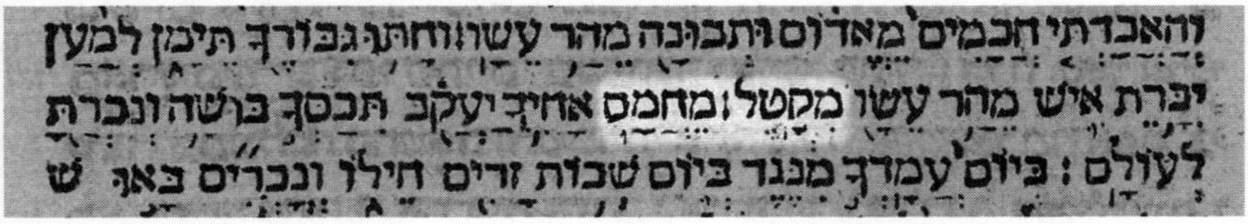
והאבדתי חכמים מאדום ותבונה מהר עשו: וחתו גבורך תימן למען
יכרת איש מהר עשו מקטל: מחמס אחיך יעקב תכסך בושה ונכרת
לעולם: ביום עמדך מנגד ביום שבות זרים חילו ונכרים באו ש

Figure 3.2: Obadiah 1:9–10, 1494 Brescia Hebrew Bible (*source:* Staatsbibliothek zu Berlin – Preußischer Kulturbesitz, 8° Inc 2840, fol. 422r [855]).[58]

Luther's decision to retain מִקָּטֶל (*miqqāṭel*) as part of v. 9 ensured that its force, as an adverbial prepositional phrase, on יִכָּרֶת-אִישׁ (*yikkāreṯ-ʾîš*) was preserved; in contrast to the Vulgate's rendering, which applied מִקָּטֶל (*miqqāṭel*) to v. 10, and thus lost that force in v. 9. Moreover, his translation retained the trope

55 "Ut intereat vir de monte Esau. In hebraeo: prae mactatione Fobad etc. Ita curabo, ut eradicetur vir de monte Esau, non remaneat aliquis superstes. Caeterum in hebraeo longe significantius est, quam ut possit commode in aliam linguam transfundi, q. d. es wirth hie eyn hauff liegen und dorth eyn hauff, occidentur passim in urbibus, si qui volent resistere et sic misera ista clade conterrentur tui sapientes, ut prorsus obbrutescant etc." WA 13:219.17–22. LW 18:198–9. Emphasis mine. Cf. similar comments he made concerning Nah. 3:3 [WA 13:362.15–23; WA 13:388.23–32; LW 18:307] and Nah. 3:15 [WA 13:368.11–20; WA 13:392.14–26; LW 18:313]. Also note the parallel with his exegesis of Joel 2:6 (this appears in Ch. 2 of this study).

56 WA DB 11.2:254.9.

57 The Vulgate, LXX, and Syriac all move their renderings of מִקָּטֶל (*miqqāṭel*) to the beginning of verse 10.

58 At Obad. 1:9–10, ":" indicates the verse division. Staatsbibliothek zu Berlin: https://digital.staatsbibliothek-berlin.de/werkansicht?PPN=PPN720865522&PHYSID=PHYS_0855&DMDID=.

of Hebrew repetition in יִכָּרֵת (*yikkāreṯ*) and מִקָּטֶל (*miqqāṭel*), which, as Ch. 2 showed, is a syntactical device in the Hebrew Bible which generates an intensified reading.[59]

The elevated Hebrew intensity further influenced Luther's interpretation of the verse in terms of *Anfechtung*. This appears in his lecture notes: "Extra tentationem [*Anfechtung*] sapientes sumus, in necessitate stulti sumus" – "Outside of *Anfechtung* [*tentationem*], we become wise. In necessity, we become fools."[60] That annotation, his other comments in the lectures, and his Bible translation all show the connection between slaughter, terror, and *Anfechtung* in his interpretation of the verse – another witness to the interaction between theology and philology in his Hebrew translation and exegesis. Obad. 1:9 is an excellent example of how Hebrew semantic intensity influenced Luther's translation in multiple ways, not always limited to vocabulary, but sometimes as part of the syntactical structure of the language.

Amos 5:5: אָוֶן *('āwen) and Jammer; and BethAuen*

Luther contended for a more intense and affective translation of וּבֵית־אֵל יִהְיֶה לְאָוֶן (*ûḇêṯ-'ēl yihyeh lə'āwen*, "and *Beth-el* will become **Aven** [nought, nothingness, vanity, trouble]") in Amos 5:5 than he saw in the Vulgate's *et Bethel erit* **inutilis** ("and *Bethel* will become **useless, injurious**"). The role of Hebrew semantic intensity in his translation is evident in two different German renderings that he made, one in the 1532 *Deutsche Bibel* and the other in the 1545 revision. His lecture comments help to elucidate both:

> *Bethel* shall come to nought [*inutilis*]. It will be in *Aphen*. Here we have the word *Aphen*, which I mentioned earlier. The prophet has used it here in its germane and native sense, as it is also used in Ps. 90[:10]: 'Their span is but toil [*labor*] and trouble [*dolor*].' So also here: '*Bethel* will be in *Aphen*,' that is, 'As you have performed your wicked righteousness at *Bethel* and as a result were unhappy and disturbed, so the Lord will bring the same thing to pass for you: *Bethel* into *Bethaphen*, this is: you will have heartbreak [*herczleid*] and misery [*jammer*] on account of it. This *Bethel* will become for you an occasion of great calamity [*maximi mali*].'[61]

His argument shows numerous manifestations of a more intense reading in the Hebrew Bible compared to the Vulgate. First, whereas the Vulgate translated

---

[59] See "The Hebrew Trope of Repetition" section in Ch. 2, pp. 76–81.

[60] WA 13:210 Note 29 H.

[61] "Bethel erit inutilis. Erit in Aphen. Hic est vocabulum Aphen, de quo supra dixi. Hic in sua germana et nativa significatione est usurpatum a propheta sicut et in psalmo 89: et amplius eorum labor et dolor. Ita hic: Bethel erit in Aphen hoc est: sicut vos impiam iustitiam fecistis in Bethel, unde taedium et molestiam habuistis, ita faciet vobis dominus idem: Bethel in Bethaphen, hoc est: yr werdt herczleid und jammer dar von haben. Hoc Bethel occasio vobis erit maximi mali." WA 13:181.22–28. LW 18:159. The Zwickau text adds "Aven, muhe, arbeit," a common translation argument that Luther makes elsewhere including in the Minor Prophets, the Major Prophets, and Ecclesiastes; WA 13:139.22–WA 13:140.3.

אָוֶן (*'āwen*) as *inutilis*, Luther put forward a far more visceral interpretation, both in the exegesis and in the German Bible. He translated וּבֵית־אֵל יִהְיֶה לְאָוֶן (*ûḇêṯ-'ēl yihyeh lǝ'āwen*) in 1532 as *vnd Bethel wird jnn jamer komen* ("and Bethel will come into **misery, calamity, affliction, distress**") – mirroring his argument concerning *jammer* in the lectures.[62] In those lectures, he additionally linked אָוֶן (*'āwen*) with *herczleid* ("heartbreak"); *labor* and *dolor* ("labor, toil, trouble" and "pain, suffering, anguish, distress, vexation"); and *muhe* and *arbeit* ("toil, trouble, pain" and "work").[63] Moreover, his argument concerning Amos 5:5 mirrored the interpretation that he proposed for אָוֶן (*'āwen*) in Amos 1:5 as *molestia cordium* ("vexation of the soul, of hearts").[64] These associations show a glaringly more multidimensional and intensely emotional understanding of אָוֶן (*'āwen*) than what he saw in the Vulgate's *inutilis*.

The 1545 *Deutsche Bibel* revision shows another way in which Hebrew semantic intensity played an integral role in his translation of Amos 5:5. There, Luther took a major liberty in his German translation, departing sharply from the letter of the Hebrew Bible. He translated וּבֵית־אֵל יִהְיֶה לְאָוֶן (*ûḇêṯ-'ēl yihyeh lǝ'āwen*) as *vnd Bethel wird **BethAuen** werden* ("and *Bethel* will become *Beth-Auen*") – that is, the house of God will become **the house of אָוֶן** (*'āwen*).[65] To make this change, he interposed בֵּית־ (*bêṯ-*, "house [of]") in front of אָוֶן (*'āwen*), despite the fact that it is not present in the Hebrew Bible.[66]

---

[62] WA DB 11.2:238.5. Grimm associates *Jammer* with *Not* ("affliction, distress"), *hochgradiges Elend* ("profound misery"), and *Leid* ("misfortune, hurt, pain"). DWB 10:2251.

[63] The modern German spellings are *Jammer, Herzeleid,* and *Mühe. Muhe* and *arbeit* appear in the Zwickau text of Luther's remarks on Amos 5:5. He commonly paired the two terms [*labor* and *dolor*; *Mühe* and *Arbeit*] in his discussions and translations of אָוֶן (*'āwen*), particularly where it appears in the Hebrew Bible as part of the phrase עָמָל וָאָוֶן (*'āmāl wā'āwen*, "toil/labor and nought/nothingness/vanity/trouble"). See, for example, his Bible translation of Ps. 90:10 in 1524 as *muehe vnd erbeyt* [WA DB 10.1:402.10]; in 1531 as *muehe vnd erbeit* [WA DB 10.1:403a.10]; and in 1545 as *Muehe vnd Erbeit* [WA DB 10.1:403b.10]. Cf. his lectures on Ecclesiastes, where he used the spelling *muhe und erbeyt* [WA 20:17a.12; WA 20:45a.8–9]. Raeder goes into extensive detail, in numerous places, concerning Luther's translation of the term and his consultation of Reuchlin's *Rudimenta*. See Raeder, *Grammatica Theologica*, 88, 101–8, 142, 147–8, 166–70, 180, 193–9, 206, 289; Raeder, *Das Hebräische*, 73, 162; and Raeder, *Die Benutzung*, 32–4, 62–66, 96.

[64] "Tractum est vocabulum a molestia cordium." WA 13:163.25. See LS, 468.

[65] WA DB 11.2:239.5. בֵּית- (*bêṯ–*) normally appears as בֵּית- (*bêṯ–*). It lacks the *dagesh* (the dot in the middle of the first letter) because of the preceding וּ (*û*, "and"). בֵּית אָוֶן (*bêṯ 'āwen*) literally means "house of pain, vexation," and בֵּית-אֵל (*bêṯ-'ēl*) means "house of God." Ch. 2 examines the inconsistency of Luther's transliteration methodology for אָוֶן (*'āwen*). Cf. Luther's criticism of Jerome's translation of בֵּית-אֵל (*bêṯ-'ēl*) as *domum dei* in Zech. 7:2; in those lectures, he explained his rule of thumb concerning the translation of בֵּית- (*bêṯ-*) in the Hebrew Bible. WA 13:612.32–37. LW 20:77. Cf. his comments in the *Operationes in Psalmos* concerning Ps. 5:6; WA Ar 2:238–9.

[66] The handwritten entries in his Old Testament record this already in 1538/39, as do the 1539–41 protocols. WA DB 4:236b.11–14 [1538/39]; WA DB 4:236a.11–17 [1539–41]. The 1538/39 handwritten entries in his Old Testament have a note that this was not from Luther's hand. The 1539–41 Protocols have the note: "*Beth Auen:* muehehause."

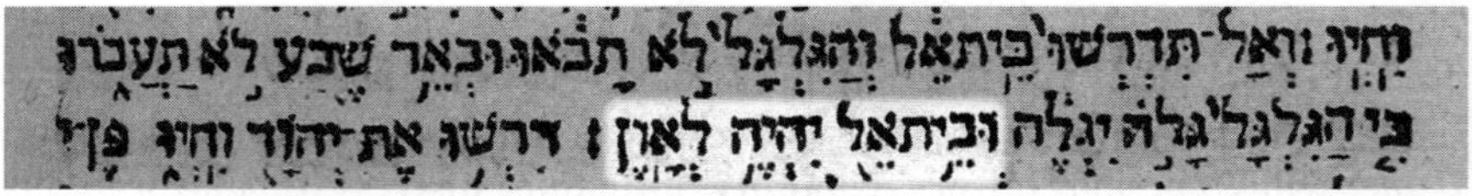

Figure 3.3: Amos 5:5, 1494 Brescia Hebrew Bible (*source:* Staatsbibliothek zu Berlin – Preußischer Kulturbesitz, 8° Inc 2840, fol. 419v [850]).[67]

In doing so, he made his metaphorical interpretation complete – the *house of God* would become a *house of pain*. Luther's translation adjustment was not altogether groundless. The construction בֵּית אָוֶן (*bêṯ 'āwen*) appears in numerous places in the Hebrew Bible, and his recollection of those places would surely have had some influence on his later rendering of Amos 5:5.[68] Nevertheless, it is an example of an intentional translation against the literal Hebrew; in this case, in an effort to convey the severity of what the Hebrew expressed.[69] Moreover, it shows an extreme deviation from the literal Hebrew with his addition of an extraneous word, a manipulation of the text which he made in order to complete the metaphor. Thus, while the 1532 translation of *jammer* showed an intensified reading relative to the Vulgate, the 1545 revision was even more so. Luther's construction of בֵּית אָוֶן (*bêṯ 'āwen*) moved from a descriptive narrative

---

[67] Staatsbibliothek zu Berlin: https://digital.staatsbibliothek-berlin.de/werkansicht?PPN=PPN720865522&PHYSID=PHYS_0850&DMDID=.

[68] For example, Luther lectured on Amos from December, 1524 until the end of January, 1525; see Hilton Oswald's general introduction at LW 18:xi. The Hosea lectures took place in July, 1524, therefore preceding the Amos lectures by several months. Luther's translation of בֵּית אָוֶן (*bêṯ 'āwen*) in Hosea thus offers insight into his familiarity with the appearance of the phrase in the Hebrew Bible, and the potential influence that this had on the translation and lectures on Amos which followed. Cf. Josh. 7:2 [*BethAuen*, 1524, WA DB 9.1:20.2; *BethAuen*, 1545, WA DB 9.1:21.2]; Josh. 18:12 [*BethAuen*, 1524, WA DB 9.1:58.12; *BethAauen*, 1545, WA DB 9.1:59.12]; 1 Sam. 13:5 [*Beth Auen*, 1524, WA DB 9.1:222.5; *BethAuen*, 1545, WA DB 9.1:223.5]; 1 Sam. 14:23 [*Beth Auen*, 1524, WA DB 9.1:228.23; *BethAuen*, 1545, WA DB 9.1:229.23]; Hos. 4:15 [*BethAuen*, 1532, WA DB 11.2:190.15; *BethAuen*, 1545, WA DB 11.2:191.15]; Hos. 5:8 [*BethAuen*, 1532, WA DB 11.2:192.8; *BethAuen*, 1545, WA DB 11.2:193.8]; and Hos. 10:5 [*BethAuen*, 1532, WA DB 11.2:202.5; *BethAuen*, 1545, WA DB 11.2:203.5].

[69] Luther was not averse to such deviations, particularly when they resulted in an exaggerated intensity of the reading. Cf. his addition of *nicht* in Jon. 2:5; addressed in Ch. 5 of this study. Cf. his ignoring both instances of לֹא- (*lō'-*, "no, not") in his rendering of בְּטֶרֶם לֹא-יָבוֹא (*baṭerem lō'-yāḇô'*, "before … comes") in Zeph. 2:2. WA DB 11.2:314.2. Most translators do the same for Zeph. 2:2, reading the negation as pleonastic; but not all agree. For more on this, see Wilhelm Gesenius, E. Kautzsch, and A. E. Cowley, *Gesenius' Hebrew Grammar*, 2nd rev. English ed. (Oxford: Clarendon Press, 1910), 483; Paul Joüon and T. Muraoka, *A Grammar of Biblical Hebrew* (Rome: Editrice Pontificio Istituto Biblico, 2006), 573; BDB, 382; DCH 4:521–2; and Aynat Rubinstein, Ivy Sichel, and Avigail Tsirkin-Sadan, "Superfluous Negation in Modern Hebrew and Its Origins," in *Language Contact and the Development of Modern Hebrew*, ed. Edit Doron (Leiden: Brill, 2016), 168. Thank you to Dr. Barak Dan, The Hebrew University of Jerusalem, for the insight on this – what we believe to be the only case in the Bible of a negation following the word בְּטֶרֶם (*baṭerem*).

reading – i. e. *Bethel* will "come into" something – to an entire transformation of the noun – i. e. *Bethel* will become *something*. The entire grammatical subject of the sentence metamorphosized, and it was a far more powerful reading.

Luther's interpretation of אָוֶן (*'āwen*) in Amos 5:5, though, evinces a further, tacit link with his theology of *Anfechtung*. While he did not expressly make that association in his remarks concerning Amos 5:5, he did elsewhere, inside and outside of the Minor Prophets. For example, in his commentary on Hab. 3:7, he linked *Angst* – and thus implicitly *Anfechtung* – to אָוֶן (*'āwen*).[70] In his lectures on Is. 6:5, he described the trial of conscience [*vexacio ... conscienciae*] as *tentacio* and *tentari* [that is, *Anfechtung*].[71] And as already noted, in his exegesis of Amos 1:5, he interpreted אָוֶן (*'āwen*) as *molestia cordium* ("vexation of the soul, of hearts"), also an allusion to *Anfechtung*.[72]

Luther's identification of אָוֶן (*'āwen*) with *Anfechtung* has gone all but unnoticed by most scholars, although Raeder did recognize the association.[73] He argued specifically that Luther's interpretation of כָּל־פֹּעֲלֵי־אָוֶן (*kol-pōʿălê-'āwen*, "all the workers of *Aven* [nought, nothingness, vanity, trouble]") in Ps. 14:4 should be read as the *Anfechtung* of the spirit [*Anfechtung des Geistes*] – the product of the works of אָוֶן (*'āwen*).[74] That judgment clearly parallels Luther's exegesis of אָוֶן (*'āwen*) in Amos 5:5 as *jammer* and *herczleid*. Moreover, it underscores a contention of Stolt's, that Luther's translations of *jammer* and *herzleid* in Genesis are important differentiators between his *Deutsche Bibel* and other German Bibles.[75] These various tacit connections to *Anfechtung* in his inter-

---

[70] WA 19:429.17–28.

[71] WA 31.2:49.30–WA 31.2:50.3, 7–9, 10–11. Is. 6:5 appears in Ch. 5 of this study.

[72] WA 13:163.25. See Ch. 5 of this study concerning the correlation between soul, heart, synteresis, and conscience in Jewish and Christian mystical traditions; "vexation of the heart" parallels "vexation of the conscience."

[73] Scholars, nevertheless, frequently associate Luther's *Anfechtung* with affliction. For example, see David P. Scaer, "The Concept of *Anfechtung* in Luther's Thought," 15 and Raeder, *Grammatica Theologica*, 206.

[74] Raeder, *Grammatica Theologica*, 206. Many translate *Aven* here as "iniquity." I keep it the same as in Amos 5:5 for the sake of consistency and for comparison. It is a complex and multifaceted, not to mention disputed, term.

[75] Stolt cites Luther's use of *Jammer* and *Herzleid* in his *Deutsche Bibel* as an important differentiator between it and modern revisions of it. As an example, she cites his translation of בְּיָגוֹן (*bəyāgōwn*, "in grief, sorrow, affliction") in Gen. 44:31 as *mit iamer* [cf. *Jammer* in Luther's lectures on Amos 5:5] in 1523 and *mit hertzenleide* [cf. *herczleid* in Luther's lectures on Amos 5:5] in the 1545 revision, in contrast to the *Einheitsübersetzung* [the modern German Bible update to Luther's translation] which renders בְּיָגוֹן (*bəyāgōwn*) as [*vor*] *Gram* ("from grief, aggrievement, ill will, hostile sentiment") or *Unglück* ("misfortune, mishap, disaster, calamity"). In Stolt, *Rhetorik*, 110–1; and in Stolt, "Luther's Translation of the Bible," 392–3. Luther made the same revision in his translation of יָגוֹן (*yāgōwn*) in Gen. 44:31 between 1523 and 1545 as he did with his translation of אָוֶן (*'āwen*) in Amos 5:5 between 1532 and 1545 – he changed his translation from *Jammer* to *Herzeleid*. It is also significant to note that in his 1529 Latin revision of the Vulgate, he translated בְּיָגוֹן (*bəyāgōwn*) in Gen. 44:31 as *cum dolore*

126   Chapter Three

pretation of Amos 5:5 are thus further evidence of the crucial role that Hebrew semantic intensity played in his reading of the verse.

Habakkuk 3:2: Gloss; and רֹגֶז (rōgez) and Truebsal[76]

Luther argued for the exceptional intensity of two Hebrew phrases in Hab. 3:2. He addressed the first, בְּקֶרֶב שָׁנִים (bəqereḇ šānîm, "in the midst of [the] years"), in his lectures:

> Thus he uses intensely burning words [Sic utitur valde verbis ardentibus], the sort of words used by those who are sorely afflicted [male affecti], who labor in the utmost peril [in summo periculo laborant]. When they think they are already done for, when everywhere there is despair and no hope of escape, then the Lord is present and helps them. In this way the Lord is present in the middle of the years, that is, he is the helper in the midst of tribulations [in tribulationibus mediis] and at the right times, as in the Psalm [Ps. 138:7]. Thus also Job says: 'When you think you are done for, etc. [cum te consumptum putabis etc.].'[77]

In the commentary, he continued his reflections:

> But he says 'in the midst of the years' and not 'in the midst of the days,' because he is speaking from the heart [er redet aus dem hertzen] of those in affliction [not]. For them a day is as long as a year; indeed, every period of time is long for them. He uses the phrase also because a year is the longest measure of time.[78]

Luther addressed the phrase yet again in the preface to his commentary on Habakkuk, which he also included in his preface to the book in the *Deutsche Bibel* (1532 and 1545):

> Because it is the work and manner of God that he would help when there is distress [Noth] and would come just at the right time. And as his song sings [Chapter 3:2]: 'He remembers mercy when tribulation [Trübsal] is present.' And as one says, 'Wenn der Strick am härtesten hält, so bricht er' ('When the rope holds tightest, it breaks').[79]

("when in pain, suffering, anguish, distress, vexation"), thus mirroring his interpretation of אָוֶן (ʾāwen) in the lectures on Amos 5:5. WA DB 5:66.37.

[76] Luther made numerous other references to Hebrew in his exegesis of this verse, which are not addressed in this study because of space and scope.

[77] "Sic utitur valde verbis ardentibus, sicut huiusmodi verbis solent uti male affecti, qui in summo periculo laborant et cum iam putant de se esse actum, cum ubique adest desperatio et nulla evadendi spes, tum adest dominus et iuvat eos. Atque sic adest in medio annorum dominus, hoc est, adiutor est in tribulationibus mediis et in opportunitatibus, [Ps. 138, 7.] ut est in psalmo. Sic etiam Iob ait: cum te consumptum putabis etc." WA 13:441.23–29. LW 19:136.

[78] "Er spricht aber 'unter den jaren', nicht 'unter den tagen'; das macht, er redet aus dem hertzen der ienigen, so ynn der not sind. Den selbigen ist ein tag ein jar lang, ja alle zeit ist yhn lang. Auch darumb, denn das jar ist das lengste mas der zeit." WA 19:426.22–25. LW 19:229.

[79] "Denn es sei GOttes Werk und Art also, daß er helfe, wenn es Roth thut, und komme mitten in der rechten Zeit, und wie sein Lied singt [Cap. 3, 2.]: 'Er gedenkt an Barmherzigkeit, wenn Trübsal da ist'; und wie man spricht: Wenn der Strick am härtesten hält, so bricht er." StL 14:1421.12-StL 14:1422.12. The orthography is slightly different in the *Deutsche Bibel*: WA DB 11.2:298.10–13; WA DB 11.2:299.10–14.

The force and emotion which he discerned in the Hebrew are clear: intensely using words that burn [*ardentibus*], in the uppermost danger [*in summo periculo*], badly afflicted [*male affecti*], in the midst of tribulations [*tribulationibus*], done for [*consumptum*], distress [*Roth*], speaking from the heart [*redet aus dem hertzen*], and the German saying *Wenn der Strick am härtesten hält, so bricht er* ("When the rope holds tightest, it breaks") make this unmistakable. Yet despite all this, he translated בְּקֶרֶב שָׁנִים (*bəqereḇ šānîm*) in the *Deutsche Bibel* as *mitten jnn den jaren* ("in the midst of the years"), just as the Vulgate did: *in medio annorum* ("in the midst of the years").[80] But he did not leave it at that. He added the gloss *mitten jnn der not* ("in the midst of the affliction"), which echoed his exegetical explanation and the intensified interpretation of the Hebrew.[81]

Luther also saw an extraordinary intensity in a second phrase in Hab. 3:2. He contended that בְּרֹגֶז (*bərōgez*, "in commotion, restlessness, anger, wrath") should be interpreted as *in perturbatione* ("in confusion, disorder, [mental] disturbance, distress, upheaval"), in contrast to the Vulgate's *cum iratus* ("when you are enraged"):

When you are enraged, may you remember mercy. I translate this way from the Hebrew: 'In trouble [*in perturbatione*] may you remember mercy.' He is not speaking about the trouble with which God was troubled but about the trouble with which we were troubled. Bernard treats this passage beautifully, but his opinion is not stated in this verse; it is not pertinent at this point. The Hebrew word, which in this place we translate 'trouble [*perturbationem*],' is also in Ps. 4[:4]: 'Be angry, but sin not.' This means, 'Do not be troubled, do not be so impatient that you sin, that you give place to wrath, etc.' And so this is the meaning of the prophet: 'Lord, remember mercy in our trouble or our agitation [*in perturbatione vel concussione nostra*], so that we will not be overcome by the trouble,' as that psalmist says in the Psalm [Ps. 85:8]: 'Let me hear what the Lord says to me, etc.,' lest the saints be turned to foolishness, that is, lest they, overcome by a long *Anfechtung* [*tentationis*], grumble at last against God. The Lord is present in his own place and at his own time, as the apostle says in Corinthians [1 Cor. 10:13]: 'God is faithful, and he will not let you be tested [*tentari*] beyond your strength, but with the *Anfechtung* [*tentatione*] will also provide the way of escape.'[82]

---

[80] WA DB 11.2:306.2. Cf. WA DB 4:259b.32–33.

[81] WA DB 11.2:306.2 (1532). The 1545 gloss reads *mitten in der Not*; WA DB 11.2:307.2.

[82] "Cum iratus fueris, misericordiae recordaberis. Ex hebraeo sic verto: in perturbatione recorderis misericordiae. Loquitur de perturbatione, non qua deus perturbatur sed qua nos perturbamur. Bernhardus egregie hunc locum tractat sed eius sententia non est in loco dicta, non servit huic instituto. Vocabulum autem hebraeum, quod hic vertimus perturbationem, est etiam in psalm. 4., ubi dicitur: irascimini et nolite peccare, hoc est, non perturbemini, non ita impatientes sitis, ut peccetis, ut detis locum irae etc. Est itaque sententia prophetae: domine recorderis misericordiae in perturbatione vel concussione nostra, ne vincamur perturbatione sicut ille dicit in [Ps. 85, 9.] psalmo: audiam, quid loquatur mihi dominus etc., ne sancti convertantur ad stultitiam, hoc est, ne murmurent tandem contra deum diuturnitate tentationis victi. Ita adest dominus suo loco et tempore sicut inquit apostolus in Corinthiis: fidelis deus, qui non sinit nos tentari ultra quam possumus et facit cum tentatione proventum." WA 13:441.37–WA 13:442.10. LW 19:136–7.

Later in the commentary, he further nuanced his interpretation:

In Hebrew the words 'in tribulation [*wenn truebsal da ist*]' read 'in confusion/disturbance [*in turbatione*],' that is, also in the midst of affliction [*not*], when the rope holds tightest [*wenn der strick am hertisten helt*], when trepidation and fear/horror/trembling [*das zittern und zagen*] are greatest; 'then,' he says, 'you remember mercy, then you help. Now, whoever wants to be saved must learn to know you thus.' This is comforting to believers, but unbearable for the ungodly.[83]

Luther translated בְּרֹגֶז (*bərōgez*) in the *Deutsche Bibel* in line with his commentary: *Wenn truebsal da ist* ("When there is tribulation").[84] That translation, together with his exegesis, shows a much richer, broader, and more intense understanding of בְּרֹגֶז (*bərōgez*) than what he saw in the Vulgate's *cum iratus*. His descriptions "in trouble or agitation [*in perturbatione vel concussione*]," "in confusion/disturbance [*in turbatione*]," and the same German idiom that he used to explain בְּקֶרֶב שָׁנִים (*bəqereḇ šānîm*) earlier in the verse, *wenn der strick am hertisten helt*, all make this clear.

Luther's remarks also show the distinct connection between his interpretation of the Hebrew semantic intensity and his interpretation of *Anfechtung* in the verse. *Tentationis, tentari,* and *tentatione* show the association indisputably.[85] His Bible rendering *Truebsal* further reinforces this; *Truebsal* has various links to his interpretation of *Anfechtung* elsewhere in the Minor Prophets, as well as in the *scholia* on Ps. 118:5 as part of his interpretation of צרר (*ṣrr*).[86] Furthermore, the biblical gloss *not* shows the association with *Anfechtung* – it too appears in his *scholia* on Ps. 118:5. And finally, his use of *zagen* in the commentary is an attestation to the link with *Anfechtung*, as demonstrated in the discussion of Obad. 1:9 earlier in this chapter. Hab. 3:2 is thus an excellent example of a text where Luther distinguished a heightened intensity that he believed was innate to the Hebrew, which he sought to replicate in his German rendering, and which furthermore bled over into his interpretation of *Anfechtung* in the text.

---

[83] "Und 'wenn truebsal da ist', das laut also ym Ebreischen: 'In turbatione', das ist, auch mitten ynn der not, wenn der strick am hertisten helt, das das zittern und zagen am grosten ist, 'als denn', spricht er, 'denckstu an barmhertzickeit', das du helffest. Wer nu wil selig werden, der mus dich so lernen kennen. Den gleubigen ists troestlich, aber den gottlosen untreglich." WA 19:427.3–8. LW 19:229. Some translate *Not* as "need" (i. e. the LW editor). While that is a plausible reading, I believe Luther was using it in the sense of "affliction." See DWB 13:905–22, especially p. 907.

[84] WA DB 11.2:306.2.

[85] Cf. Jerome's reflections on Hab. 3:2 in his commentary on Habakkuk, where he spoke of "quando temptationibus [a variation in spelling of *tentatio*, i. e. *Anfechtung*], quasi fluctibus operimur ('when [we are] in *Anfechtungen*, as though we are covered by waves')." This parallels Jon. 2:4, which is discussed in greater detail in Ch. 5 of this study. Jerome, *Commentarii in Prophetas Minores*, CCSL 76A:622.

[86] See Figure 3.1.

Summary and Conclusion

Luther's determination to reproduce the semantic intensity of the Hebrew language is one of the defining traits of his translation of the Minor Prophets. His heavy emphasis on "extreme" or extraordinary language, syntactical elements associated with semantic intensity, and multifarious terminology and expressions which exploit this intensity show that his interest was more than simply matching a German word to a Hebrew word, or modifying Vulgate renderings that he felt were incorrect or otherwise lacking, strictly based on lexical meanings. His interpretations show that he viewed emotive and intense readings of the Hebrew text as integral components of meaning, and thus an indispensable part of properly rendering Hebrew into German. Moreover, where he cited lexically-oriented information [i. e. the *intellectus*] to support his interpretation in the Minor Prophets, he nevertheless often still justified his translation choice on a particular option that represented the fullest expression of the semantic intensity [i. e. the *affectus*] that he saw in the Hebrew. This reinforces Stolt's argument that the *intellectus* and the *affectus* were integral, inseparable elements of Luther's translation. In light of this, Schleiermacher's notion of *Verfremdung* and *Entfremdung* is ultimately insufficient for explaining Luther's Hebrew translation. While the question of literal rendering versus dynamic equivalence is one that Luther constantly faced, it was never the sole consideration in his decisions.

Luther's translation of the Minor Prophets shows that his discernment of Hebrew semantic intensity in certain texts at times further influenced his theological interpretations of those texts. This was particularly so where he either identified Hebrew terms as synonyms of *Anfechtung*, or saw them as otherwise connected with it. Chief among these were צָרַר (*ṣrr*), זְוָעָה (*zəwāʿâ*), and מַסָּה (*massâ*). Furthermore, the Latin and German terminology that he linked to Hebrew in his theological interpretations of the texts – *Angst, bange machen, zagen, pavore*, etc. – show the great breadth of meaning which he saw in the Hebrew language.

This facet of Luther's translation has a strong parallel in the work of Buber and Rosenzweig. Even though it appeared centuries after Luther's, their Bible is particularly important as a point of comparison for many reasons. Their translation was profoundly focused on Luther's Bible. One of their main objectives was to render a revised German translation of the Hebrew Bible where they believed Luther's translation either fell short, or had become antiquated. Furthermore, they were German Jews.[87] This gave them a unique perspective. They were captivated by (and, in many ways, captive to) the German translation that was as much a part of the national identity as it was a religious text and *the* archetypal Bible – not only for German Lutherans, but also German Catho-

---

[87] Buber and Rosenzweig, *Die Schrift und ihre Verdeutschung*, 102.

lics and even German Jews.[88] Luther's influence in this regard was so strong, dominating even the German language itself, that Rosenzweig acknowledged it as a seemingly insurmountable obstacle, assessing the challenge of touching Luther's work as "the locked door of the impossible."[89] At the same time, Buber and Rosenzweig were Jews and believed that Luther's translation had a distinctly Christian bent that they wanted to clear away from the text.[90]

The Buber-Rosenzweig translation helps to place Luther's Bible in perspective. It shows that he could have gone further, and made an even bolder translation, as they did. It also shows that despite their criticism of Luther's translation as theologically biased and despite the fact that one of their major objectives was to eliminate this Christian bias through the update, their translation focused almost exclusively on the semantic intensity of the Hebrew text – just as his did. For all the criticisms that Jews and Christians directed at each other concerning tradition-biased translation – specifically in the case of Luther and in the case of Buber and Rosenzweig – when examining the changes that both made in the actual Bible translation, it was these types of elements which they frequently focused on. For Luther and Buber and Rosenzweig, it was the philology that oftentimes fueled the theological interpretation underlying their translations.

Finally, Luther's determination to reproduce Hebrew semantic intensity in his Bible, particularly in the Minor Prophets, is important for the history of the German language. It is of no small significance that many of the terms and expressions in Luther's Bible were predicated on his decisions on how to render more intense language in German. The emotional aspect of the Hebrew that Luther consulted was a crucial aspect of the lasting influence of those Hebrew texts on the German language today. The fact that one can trace a definitive influence of Hebrew in specific German choices that Luther made thus has momentous implications for the history of the German language. Luther's choice of regional linguistic variants, based on this influence, and the dissemination of those variants with the explosion of printing in his day illuminates the role of the Hebrew Bible in the history of the German language.

---

[88] Buber and Rosenzweig, *Die Schrift und ihre Verdeutschung*, 102.

[89] "Das verschlossene Tor eines Unmöglich." Buber and Rosenzweig, *Die Schrift und ihre Verdeutschung*, 95. Volker Leppin cautions against framing Luther as "creator" of the German language as we know it. Instead, he suggests that the most crucial achievement of Luther's Bible in relation to the German language was the transformation of the border between sacred and secular language. See Leppin, "'Biblia, das ist die ganze Heilige Schrift deutsch.' Luthers Bibelübersetzung zwischen Sakralität und Profanität," in *Protestantismus und deutsche Literatur*, ed. Jan Rohls and Gunther Wenz (Göttingen: V&R unipress, 2004), 13–26. He specifically states this argument on p. 14.

[90] On this point, see Benjamin, *Rosenzweig's Bible*, especially pp. 107–21.

Chapter Four

Inner-Biblical Interpretation in Luther's Hebrew Translation

Luther's use of biblical quotations and citations has been recognized for some time as one of the major aspects of his translation and exegesis still to be investigated. In his work *Luthers Exegese in der Frühzeit*, Meissinger identified Luther's use of biblical quotations as a key lacuna in Luther scholarship.[1] Bluhm likewise emphasized the need for further investigations into Luther's use of biblical quotations.[2] To date, however, this still remains a largely untapped area of research into his Hebrew, particularly so outside of the context of the Psalms. This is all the more surprising, because the quantity of biblical citations which appear in his discussion of Hebrew translation is stunning. Moreover, he frequently did not just rely on single quotations, but instead cited numerous different verses with Hebrew terms and phrases to support a particular translation.

Examining these quotations more closely can open new windows into Luther's Bible translation. For example, he frequently drew upon the ritual law code of the Old Testament, specifically the Priestly Code in the Pentateuch, for support of his translations in the Minor Prophets.[3] Yet often, when he did, he was more than simply identifying an equivalent Hebrew term in one location to support his translation in another. Through these quotations and citations, he

---

[1] Meissinger, *Luthers Exegese in der Frühzeit*, 23, 29–30, 84–85. Meissinger called for an analysis not only of Luther's use of biblical quotations, but the entire corpus of literature which Luther had at his disposal, through a reconstruction of "Luther's library." Meissinger's work was not focused on Luther's Hebrew, but rather his Bible translation in general.

[2] Bluhm, *Creative*, x, 3–36, with a note that Walther Köhler made the same observation. See also Bluhm, "An 'Unknown' Luther Translation of the Bible," *PMLA* 84 (1969): 1537–44.

[3] The "Priestly Code" (also commonly called the "Priestly Source," abbreviated as "P") refers to a tradition or body of material in the Pentateuch which addresses a number of laws and ceremonial practices of the ancient Israelites, especially those associated with sacrifice, offering, atonement, and purification. These laws play a prominent role in Leviticus and Numbers, although they appear in other books as well. Scholars have varying opinions concerning what should be classified as P, as opposed to other distinctions. For more on this, see Martin Noth, *A History of Pentateuchal Traditions*, trans. Bernhard W. Anderson (Englewood Cliffs, NJ: Prentice-Hall, 1972), 8–19, as well as many references throughout the book. See also Jacob Milgrom, "Priestly ('P') Source," in *The Anchor Bible Dictionary*, vol. 5, ed. David Noel Freedman (New York: Doubleday, 1992), 454–61. For a discussion of the sources of the Torah, including P, see also William K. Gilders, *Blood Ritual in the Hebrew Bible: Meaning and Power* (Baltimore, MD: Johns Hopkins University Press, 2004), 13–14 and Note 3.

was exploiting the ritual language of cultic purification, which he used to form multi-layered interpretations of the prophetic texts which he was translating.[4] His translation thus often reflected an interwoven interpretation of the Hebrew, incorporating numerous connotations and theological themes.

This chapter examines Luther's use of inner-biblical interpretation – the use of biblical texts to interpret or otherwise intentionally evoke other biblical texts.[5] It focuses specifically on examples where the ritual language of cultic purification plays a major role among the citations and allusions which he used to support his translation of Hebrew. There are many potential avenues in which an analysis of Luther's biblical citations could be done. The decision to restrict the scope to examples where this ritual language appears is based on one of the overriding objectives of this study – to elucidate the relationship between philology and theology in Luther's Hebrew translation. When Luther evoked this ritual language, many times he was doing so as part of an association of the texts with *Anfechtung*. This chapter will thus demonstrate how numerous voices within the biblical texts themselves fed Luther's German translation decisions in particular places.[6] Furthermore, it will show how, in certain instances, his interwoven interpretation reflected his theological readings of these texts, specifically in terms of *Anfechtung*.

---

[4] The "ritual language of cultic purification" is used in this study to refer to the language in the Priestly law code of the Hebrew Bible which addresses purification ritual – i. e. sacrifices, offerings, etc. The designation of "purification" is used, understanding that there is much debate among scholars concerning various Hebrew terminology associated with ritual sacrifice and offering, and to what extent each represents purification, atonement, ransom, cleansing, sanctification, etc. There is much overlap, and no term is without shortcomings. For more on this language, see Gary Anderson, "Sacrifice and Sacrificial Offerings. Old Testament," in *The Anchor Bible Dictionary*, vol. 5, ed. David Noel Freedman (New York: Doubleday, 1992), 870–86, especially pp. 873–5; Jonathan Klawans, *Impurity and Sin in Ancient Judaism* (New York: Oxford University Press, 2000), especially Ch. 1; Roy Gane, *Cult and Character: Purification Offerings, Day of Atonement, and Theodicy* (Winona Lake, IN: Eisenbrauns, 2005); Susan Haber, *"They Shall Purify Themselves": Essays on Purity in Early Judaism*, ed. Adele Reinhartz (Leiden: Brill, 2008), especially Section 1; and Jay Sklar, "Sin and Impurity: Atoned or Purified? Yes!" in *Perspectives on Purity and Purification in the Bible*, ed. Baruch J. Schwartz, et al. (New York: T & T Clark, 2008), 18–31. Many other scholars address this, including Jacob Milgrom, Jacob Neusner, and Baruch Schwartz.

[5] This "inner-biblical interpretation" definition is per G. Brooke Lester, "Inner-Biblical Interpretation," in *The Oxford Encyclopedia of Biblical Interpretation*, vol. 1, ed. Steven L. McKenzie (Oxford: Oxford University Press, 2013), 444–53.

[6] Commentaries and other extra-biblical sources which Luther consulted for his translations are generally excluded from consideration in this chapter, in order to highlight his use of scripture itself.

Intertextuality and Inner-Biblical Interpretation

A relatively recent method which modern scholars use to address this strain of biblical interpretation – i. e. the use of scriptural quotations – is *intertextuality*. Most scholars trace the coining of this term to Julia Kristeva's 1966 doctoral thesis *La Révolution du langage poétique*.[7] Intertextuality, roughly stated, seeks to take into account the many textual sources that inform any given text for the reader.[8] Scholars frequently identify Michael Fishbane's *Biblical Interpretation in Ancient Israel* as the seminal application of the approach in biblical criticism, though Fishbane never directly used the term there.[9] Instead, he adopted the phrase *inner-biblical exegesis*, which many scholars have subsequently dubbed *inner-biblical interpretation*.[10] Fishbane's work remains a milestone, as John Barton describes it, a "highly sophisticated discussion of cases of 'inner-biblical interpretation,' showing how later texts reflected a kind of proto-midrashic exegesis of earlier ones."[11]

Scholars typically distinguish two approaches to intertextuality: diachronic and synchronic. Diachronic intertextuality focuses on the historical (or "temporal," as John Barton suggests) relationship between texts, where associations between them are seen as reflecting an author of a later text drawing upon an earlier text, either intentionally or unintentionally.[12] Synchronic intertextuality, by contrast, focuses on the contemporaneous (or "spatial," as Barton suggests) relationship between texts. Here, associations between texts are seen as

---

[7] Kristeva's dissertation was published in 1974 in French as *La révolution du langage poétique* (Paris: Seuil, 1974). It was translated into English, in an abridged version, as: Kristeva, *Revolution in Poetic Language*, trans. Margaret Waller (New York: Columbia University Press, 1984). See also Julia Kristeva, *Desire in Language: A Semiotic Approach to Literature and Art*, ed. Leon S. Roudiez, trans. Thomas Gora, Alice Jardine, and Leon S. Roudiez (New York: Columbia University Press, 1980). Sources give conflicting dates on Kristeva's thesis, but 1966 seems to be correct. On this, see Julia Kristeva, *The Kristeva Reader*, ed. Toril Moi (Oxford: Basil Blackwell, 1986), 1; and John Barton, "Déjà Lu: Intertextuality, Method or Theory?" in *Reading Job Intertextually*, ed. Katharine Dell and Will Kynes (New York: Bloomsbury, 2013), 9.

[8] See Kristeva, *Desire in Language*, 65–66.

[9] Michael Fishbane, *Biblical Interpretation in Ancient Israel* (Oxford: Clarendon Press, 1985). This is per Katharine Dell and Will Kynes, eds., *Reading Job Intertextually* (New York: Bloomsbury, 2013), xvii. On the significance of Fishbane, see Barton, "Déjà lu," 4.

[10] On "inner-biblical interpretation," see Fishbane, *Biblical Interpretation*, abstract. On "inner-biblical exegesis," see Fishbane, *Biblical Interpretation*, 23, 24, 30, 42, 518. Fishbane took the phrase "inner-biblical exegesis" from his teacher and colleague, Professor Nahum M. Sarna of Brandeis University, who used the phrase in his own study of Psalm 89. Fishbane, *Biblical Interpretation*, vii–viii.

[11] Barton, "Déjà Lu," 4.

[12] Barton gives an excellent analysis of the differences in Barton, "Déjà lu." See also Will Kynes, *My Psalm Has Turned into Weeping: Job's Dialogue with the Psalms* (Berlin: De Gruyter, 2012), 18.

reflecting the perception of the reader, who makes connections between the texts, irrespective of whether the earlier text was intentionally cited or alluded to by the author of the later text, or even available to that author.[13] In reality, the lines between the two approaches are often blurred and they often overlap. Because of this, as Barton and Geoffrey Miller explain, the terminology can be confusing for non-specialists and specialists alike, so much so that many question its usefulness at all.[14] That said, the approach is so ubiquitous within biblical scholarship, for the time being anyway, that the language is unavoidable when breaching the subject – hence, the overview here. To keep things simple, this study does not adopt the method of intertextuality or associated language per se. Instead, it appropriates Fishbane's label *inner-biblical interpretation* (i. e. *inner-biblical exegesis*), with the general understanding that we are simply talking about Luther's use of biblical quotations and allusions as a tool of his Hebrew translation – Origen's *scriptura sui ipsius interpres* ("scripture is its own interpreter"). This study does, nevertheless, loosely follow the diachronic, historical approach of intertextuality, keeping in mind Luther's oft-stated understanding that the intentions of the authors of the biblical texts are critical for determining the proper meaning of Hebrew terms and concepts.[15] Furthermore, this study restricts its discussion to the Hebrew Bible, Vulgate, and *Deutsche Bibel*. Extra-biblical texts and commentaries, New Testament, Septuagint, Jewish Midrash, Greek literature, and extraneous medieval German literature are in general excluded, except to clarify specific points made concerning these three Bibles.

---

[13] Geoffrey D. Miller, "Intertextuality in Old Testament Research," *Currents in Biblical Research* 9 (2011): 284. Barton, "Déjà lu," 2. Kynes, *My Psalm Has Turned into Weeping*, 18. For more on these approaches, see Paul M. Joyce, "'Even if Noah, Daniel, and Job were in it ...' (Ezekiel 14:14): The Case of Job and Ezekiel," in *Reading Job Intertextually*, ed. Katharine Dell and Will Kynes (New York: Bloomsbury, 2013), 122–4; Kynes, *My Psalm Has Turned into Weeping*, 30, citing Richard B. Hays, *Echoes of Scripture in the Letters of Paul* (New Haven, CT: Yale University Press, 1989), 23; and Yair Hoffman, "The Technique of Quotation and Citation as an Interpretive Device," in *Creative Biblical Exegesis: Christian and Jewish Hermeneutics through the Centuries*, ed. Benjamin Uffenheimer and Henning Graf Reventlow (Sheffield: JSOT Press, 1988), 72. For a more thorough discussion of the differences and overlap between intertextual quotation, allusion, and echo, see Kynes, *My Psalm Has Turned into Weeping*, 30–33, especially pp. 30–31.

[14] Barton, "Déjà lu," 1–2. Miller, "Intertextuality," 283, 285–6.

[15] Luther made many references to the intentions of the prophet (i. e. the author of a particular text) when trying to discern the meaning of Hebrew terminology. See, for example: WA 13:386.30–WA 13:387.5; LW 18:304–5. Similar examples appear throughout his exegesis of the Minor Prophets.

Luther's Conception of *Anfechtung* as Sanctification by Terror

An important way in which Luther used inner-biblical interpretation to exploit the ritual language of cultic purification in his translation of the Minor Prophets was to merge illustrations of ritual sacrifice and purification with illustrations of his theological understanding of faith and justification. He often further linked this language with imagery of terror and the wrath of God. Given his immense body of work, it is challenging to definitively identify a single point of origin for his association of terror with purification. Nevertheless, in the 1513–15 *Dictata super Psalterium*, he already explicitly delineated an agency of sanctification by means of terror: *per terrorem enim sanctificat* ("for it makes holy by means of terror").[16] In the lectures on Psalm 111:9, he described an expiation of impurity where the key agency was contact with God's name:

> Holy and terrible [*Sanctum et terribile*] is his name. 'Holy,' because it is to be sanctified, as in the 'Lord's Prayer': 'Hallowed be your name.' And thus it is praise. 'Holy,' because it sanctifies; and again it is praise. But it is not holy [*sanctum*], unless it is at the same time 'terrible [*terribile*]': For by means of terror it sanctifies those who believe in it [*per terrorem enim sanctificat credentes in illud*].[17]

Luther made a similar exposition in the 1519–21 *Operationes in Psalmos*, with reference to this same verse. There, he made the explicit link to *tentatio* (*Anfechtung*).[18]

An underemphasized facet of Luther's conception of *Anfechtung* is how often, in his discussions of it and allusions to it, he drew upon ritual language of cultic purification in the law code of the Hebrew Bible.[19] The examples which follow examine Luther's Hebrew translation in the Minor Prophets through the lens of his biblical citations and allusions. They will show how numerous texts within the Hebrew Bible fed Luther's German translation decisions in particular places. They will further show how, through these quotations and citations, he frequently exploited the ritual language of cultic purification. Moreover, they will show how, in certain instances, he used this language to build his theological readings of these texts, specifically in terms of *Anfechtung*.

---

[16] WA 4:246.26.

[17] "Sanctum et terribile nomen eius. 'Sanctum', quia sanctificandum, ut in 'pater noster': 'Sanctificetur nomen tuum'. Et sic est laus. 'Sanctum', quia sanctificat: iterum est laus. Sed non sanctum, nisi simul sit 'terribile': per terrorem enim sanctificat credentes in illud." WA 4:246.23–26.

[18] WA 5:191.12–WA 5:194.16; the specific mention of *tentatio* is at WA 5:192.29. Cf. WA 19:323.25.

[19] Scholars have cited the general role of justification and the associated purification in Luther's *Anfechtung*. See Beintker, *Die Überwindung*, 9. Karl Holl goes into some detail about this in "Was verstand Luther unter Religion?" 67–80, especially p. 75.

Case Study #1:
Zechariah 2:13: מֵנִיף (*mēnîp*, "waving")

Tables 4.1 and 4.2 show the Hebrew, Latin, and German translations for Zech. 2:13, as well as for the biblical citations that Luther used to support his argument. The data in these tables drives the analysis which follows.

Table 4.1: Part One: Luther's translation of נוף (*nwp*, "wave"): Zech. 2:13, Lev. 7:30, Num. 8:11, Num. 8:21, and Ps. 68:10.

Verse	NASB	Hebrew Bible	Vulgate	*Deutsche Bibel*
Zech. 2:13	For behold, I will wave My hand over them so that they will be plunder for their slaves. Then you will know that the Lord of hosts has sent Me.	כִּי הִנְנִי מֵנִיף אֶת־יָדִי עֲלֵיהֶם וְהָיוּ שָׁלָל לְעַבְדֵיהֶם וִידַעְתֶּם כִּי־יְהוָה צְבָאוֹת שְׁלָחָנִי	quia ecce **ego levo manum meam super eos** et erunt praedae his qui serviebant sibi et cognoscetis quia Dominus exercituum misit me	Denn sihe, **Ich wil meine hand vber sie weben**, das sie sollen ein raub werden, denen, die jn gedienet haben, das jr solt erfaren, das mich der HERR Zebaoth gesand hat. (1532) WA DB 11.2:334.9–WA DB 11.2:336:9.
Lev. 7:30	His own hands are to bring offerings by fire to the Lord. He shall bring the fat with the breast that the breast may be presented as a wave offering before the Lord.	יָדָיו תְּבִיאֶינָה אֵת אִשֵּׁי יְהוָה אֶת־הַחֵלֶב עַל־הֶחָזֶה יְבִיאֶנּוּ אֵת הֶחָזֶה **לְהָנִיף** אֹתוֹ **תְּנוּפָה** לִפְנֵי יְהוָה	tenebit manibus adipem hostiae et pectusculum cumque ambo **oblata** Domino **consecrarit** tradet sacerdoti	Er sols aber mit seyner hand hertzu bringen zum opffer des HERRN, Nemlich das fett an der brust sol er bringen sampt der brust, **das sie eyn Webe werden** fur den HERRN. (1523) WA DB 8:350.30.
Num. 8:11	Aaron then shall present the Levites before the Lord as a wave offering from the sons of Israel, that they may qualify to perform the service of the Lord.	**וְהֵנִיף** אַהֲרֹן אֶת־הַלְוִיִּם **תְּנוּפָה** לִפְנֵי יְהוָה מֵאֵת בְּנֵי יִשְׂרָאֵל וְהָיוּ לַעֲבֹד אֶת־עֲבֹדַת יְהוָה	**et offeret** Aaron Levitas **munus** in conspectu Domini a filiis Israhel ut serviant in ministerio eius	**vnd** Aaron **sol** die Leuiten fur dem HERRN **Weben** von den kindern Jsrael, auff das sie dienen mugen an dem ampt des HERRN. (1523) WA DB 8:460.11.

Verse	NASB	Hebrew Bible	Vulgate	Deutsche Bibel
Num. 8:21	The Levites, too, purified themselves from sin and washed their clothes; and Aaron presented them as a wave offering before the Lord. Aaron also made atonement for them to cleanse them.	וַיִּתְחַטְּאוּ הַלְוִיִּם וַיְכַבְּסוּ בִּגְדֵיהֶם **וַיָּנֶף** אַהֲרֹן אֹתָם **תְּנוּפָה** לִפְנֵי יְהוָה וַיְכַפֵּר עֲלֵיהֶם אַהֲרֹן לְטַהֲרָם	purificatique sunt et laverunt vestimenta sua **elevavitque** eos Aaron in conspectu Domini et oravit pro eis	Vnd die Leuiten entsundigeten sich vnd wusschen yhre kleyder, **vnd** Aaron **Webet** sie fur dem HERRN vnd versunet sie, das sie reyn wurden. (1523) WA DB 8:460.21.
Ps. 68:10	You shed abroad a plentiful rain, O God; You confirmed Your inheritance when it was parched.	גֶּשֶׁם נְדָבוֹת **תָּנִיף** אֱלֹהִים נַחֲלָתְךָ וְנִלְאָה אַתָּה כוֹנַנְתָּהּ	pluviam voluntariam **elevasti** Deus hereditatem tuam laborantem tu confortasti	Gott deyn erbe ist durre, Du **woltest** eynen gnedigen regen **austeylen**, vnd lassen geraten. (1524) WA DB 10.1:310.10. Nu aber **gibstu** Gott einen gnedigen regen, Vnd dein erbe, das duerre ist, erquickestu. (1531) WA DB 10.1:311a.10.

Table 4.2: Part Two: Luther's translation of נשא (*nś'*, "lift up" or "raise"): Ps. 10:12 and Ps. 106:26.

Verse	NASB	Hebrew Bible	Vulgate	Deutsche Bibel
Ps. 10:12	Arise, O Lord; O God, lift up Your hand. Do not forget the afflicted.	קוּמָה יְהוָה אֵל **נְשָׂא** יָדֶךָ אַל-תִּשְׁכַּח עֲנָוִים	surge Domine Deus **leva manum** tuam noli oblivisci pauperum	Stehe auff HERR Gott, **erhebe deyne hand**, vergiss der elenden nicht. (1524) WA DB 10.1:130.12.
Ps. 106:26	Therefore He swore to them That He would cast them down in the wilderness	**וַיִּשָּׂא יָדוֹ לָהֶם** לְהַפִּיל אוֹתָם בַּמִּדְבָּר	**et levavit manum suam super eos** ut deiceret eos in deserto	**Vnd er hub auff seyne hand widder sie,** Das er sie nyderschluge ynn der wuesten. (1524) WA DB 10.1:456.26.

The book of Zechariah begins with God commanding Zechariah to urge the Israelites to turn from their evil ways and return to him. Ch. 2 continues with that same theme, outlining the prophecy of God's favor returning to Jerusalem.

In Zech. 2:13, the prophet communicates God's message that he is waving his hand (מֵנִיף, *mēnîp*, "[I] am waving") over the people.[20]

Luther took issue with the Vulgate's rendering of מֵנִיף אֶת־יָדִי עֲלֵיהֶם (*mēnîp 'eṯ-yāḏî 'ălêhem*, "I am waving my hand over them") in Zech. 2:13 as *ego levo manum meam super eos* ("I am lifting my hand over them") because he believed that its translation of the term מֵנִיף (*mēnîp*) was incorrect. By contrast, he translated מֵנִיף אֶת־יָדִי עֲלֵיהֶם (*mēnîp 'eṯ-yāḏî 'ălêhem*) into German as *Ich **wil** meine hand vber sie **weben*** ("I will wave my hand over them").[21] His interpretation was based on the lexical meaning, but also the contextual differentiation in the Bible between the waving hand [נוּף (*nwp*); *weben*] and the raised hand [נשא (*nś'*); *levo*]. He deployed numerous biblical citations to support his argument. In his commentary on Zechariah, he used two examples from the Psalms to justify his deviation from the Vulgate, and to reinforce his interpretation of the contrast between the raised hand and the waving hand:

> For the word 'wave [*weben*]' does not mean here 'to lift up [*aufheben*] the hand,' as he is in the habit of using it elsewhere and as we find it here and there in the Psalter [Ps. 106:26; Ps. 21:14; Ps. 10:12]: 'He lifted up his hands [*Er **hub** seine Hände **auf***], that he would make them fall'; likewise, 'Arise, Lord, lift up your right hand [*laß deine Rechte **sich erheben***],' etc.[22]

His translations of these Psalms were consistent with his argument concerning Zechariah; he translated וַיִּשָּׂא (*wayyiśśā'*, "and he lifted") in Ps. 106:26 as *Vnd er hub auff* ("and he lifted") and נְשָׂא (*nəśā'*, "lift") in Ps. 10:12 as *erhebe* ("elevate, raise, lift").[23] His lexical discrimination between מֵנִיף (*mēnîp*) in Zech. 2:13 and נשא (*nś'*) in Ps. 106:26 and Ps. 10:12 is thus clear.

But with a series of additional scriptural citations, Luther interwove further layers of meaning into his interpretation, broadening out from the basic lexical meaning of the Hebrew. He went on to quote Ps. 68:10, which he used to interpret מֵנִיף (*mēnîp*) as carrying a friendly and gracious connotation, in con-

---

[20] Translators frequently render מֵנִיף (*mēnîp*) in the future tense, in continuation from the previous narrative (ex. Zech. 2:9).

[21] WA DB 11.2:334.9–WA DB 11.2:336.9. *Weben* means to wave, but also to weave. See Grimm for the influence of Luther's Bible on this word in the German language: DWB 27:2621, 2636–7.

[22] "Dann das Wörtlein 'weben' heißt hier nicht, die Hand aufheben, wie er sonst pflegt zu reden, als im Psalter hin und wieder steht [Bs. 106, 26. Bs. 21, 14. Bs. 10, 12.]: 'Er hub seine Hände auf, daß er sie niederschlüge'; item, 'Erhebe dich, Herr, laß deine Rechte sich erheben' etc." StL 14:1817.45. LW 20:198. The LW renders *weben* as "shake." StL also records Ps. 21:14 in the quotation, which the LW omits. I translate according to StL. Furthermore, the WA and StL editors sometimes add verse references, in brackets, to clarify what Luther was quoting. Throughout this study, I leave these as they appear in the WA, as they help to ensure that his use of Bible quotations is not missed. Aside from these, Luther frequently explicitly specified the verse(s) that he was quoting or alluding to. These verses appear without brackets.

[23] Ps. 106:26: WA DB 10.1:456.26 (1524). Ps. 10:12: WA DB 10.1:130.12 (1524).

trast to נשא (*nś'*), which signaled the forthcoming wrath of God against his enemies:

> Not to overthrow [*stürzen*] them or cast them to the ground [*schmeißen zu Boden*] – for that is what is meant by raising [*erhoben*] or lifting [*erheben*] the hand over them ... [In contrast], this waving of the hand [*Handweben*] is a friendly and gracious waving [*gnädiges Weben*], as he also says in Ps. 68:10: 'He would have a merciful rain wave and hover [*gnädigen Regen lassen weben und schweben*] every now and then.' For it is the very same word that is here.[24]

This citation added a theological slant to his interpretation of מֵנִיף (*mēnîp*) in Zech. 2:13, framing it as an operation of grace and conversion. He explained this in the commentary:

> He now explains the work for which he has been sent and with which **he will effect this faith** and says, 'I will wave my hand over them' ... Instead, he desires to wave, and hover over, the Gentiles in all the world through his word and spirit; and in this way they are to be converted to him.[25]

Luther further developed his theological interpretation of מֵנִיף (*mēnîp*) in his lectures, where he argued that the term should be associated with the power of God:

---

[24] "Nicht sie zu stürzen oder zu schmeißen zu Boden; denn das heißt, die Hand über sie erhoben, oder erheben ... Denn dieses Handweben ist ein freundlich, gnädiges Weben. Auf welche Weise er auch Ps. 68, 10. spricht: er wolle einen gnädigen Regen lassen weben und schweben hin und wieder. Denn es ist eben dasselbige Wort, das hier steht." StL 14:1818.45. LW 20:198. Luther's German translation of the Hebrew in this Psalm did not match his translation of Ps. 10:12 and Ps. 106:26, which he also cited in his argument concerning Zech. 2:13. He translated תָּנִיף (*tānîp*) in Ps. 68:10 in 1524 as *austeylen* ("to distribute, mete out, deal out, dish out"), later revising it to *geben* [*gibstu*] ("to give") in the 1531 *Deutsche Bibel* revision. WA DB 10.1:310.10 (1524); WA DB 10.1:311a.10 (1531). Cf. WA DB 3:72.17–25. The modern German spelling of *austeylen* is *ausstseilen*. This translation is exceptional among all of the examples in Table 3.1, where he consistently translated נוף (*nwp*) as *weben*. While it does not pose a major difficulty here, this still underscores the examples in Ch. 2 of this study, which show how frequently his Bible translation did not match his exegesis. His lecture notes on Ps. 68 do not offer significant insight on this, as he did not address the issue directly there. See LW 10:325–6 and WA 55.1:478. Cf. Luther's argument that נֹשֵׂא (*nōśē'*, "am lifting/taking up") in Amos 5:1 represents the lifting of a burden over the individual – a signal of impending destruction by the wrath of God; he translated this as *machen*. WA 13:138.25–WA 13:139.2; WA 13:179.31–WA 13:180.10. LW 18:157; WA DB 11.2:238.1.

[25] "Erklärt er nun das Werk, dazu er gesandt wird, und damit er solchen Gehorsam zurichten soll, und spricht: 'Ich will meine Hand über sie weben' etc ... sondern durch sein Wort und Geist will er in aller Welt über den Heiden weben und schweben, dadurch sie bekehrt werden." StL 14:1817.44-StL 14:1818.45. LW 20:197–8. Emphasis mine. Cf. Luther's translation of תְּנוּפַת ... מֵנִיף (*tənûpat ... mēnîp*, "the waving of ... [which he] waves") in Is. 19:16 as *weben wird* ("will wave"); WA DB 11.1:70.16. In the lectures on Isaiah addressing that verse, he argued for a similar interpretation of the Hebrew as indicative of conversion, but with a starkly more strong link to fear of God's wrath. WA 31.2:115.21–23. LW 16:163–4.

For behold, I am raising [ego levo] my hand over them. This means: 'I am strong. I shall exercise my power against those who have despoiled you. In fact, I shall conquer them with your weakness.' ... *And you will know that the Lord.* He says in effect: 'When you are in **tribulation** [*ubi in tribulatione eritis*], when your foes will attack you, then your experience will have taught you, and you will know and understand that I have accomplished all this.'[26]

His use of the term *tribulatio* was, in this context, an implicit allusion to *Anfechtung*. Horst Beintker argued in his 1954 study that *tribulatio* is one of the most frequent terms which Luther used to speak of *Anfechtung* in the sense of aggression, assault, and the condition of affliction.[27] The work of numerous other scholars supports this, including Alister McGrath, Anita Gaide, Lorenz Diefenbach, and Charles Du Cange.[28] In addition, *tribulatio* is one of the terms that appears in Luther's interpretation of צָרָה (*ṣārâ*) – a Hebrew term with a direct link to his interpretation of *Anfechtung*, as addressed in Ch. 3 of this study.[29] This aspect of Luther's exegesis of Zech. 2:13 is all the more significant in light of his interpretation of מֵנִיף (*mēnîp*) as linked to the conversion and effecting of the faith of the Gentiles. This is precisely what Luther's theological understanding of *Anfechtung* was, and it parallels his conception of "sanctification by terror."

But the key piece of the puzzle for understanding Luther's synthesized interpretation of מֵנִיף (*mēnîp*) in Zech. 2:13, and the final link that tied the various scriptural quotations together, is his citation of three verses from Leviticus and Numbers. With these citations, he connected מֵנִיף (*mēnîp*) to the ritual language

---

[26] "Quia ecce ego levo manum meam super eos. Hoc est, potens sum, potestatem exercebo contra eos, qui vos spoliaverunt nempe vincam eos vestra infirmitate ... Et cognoscetis, quia dominus I. e. ubi in tribulatione eritis, ubi invademini ab inimicis, tum vel ipsa experientia docti cognoscetis et intelligetis me ista efficere omnia." WA 13:574.6–8, 20–22. LW 20:31–32. In the Latin lecture notes, the term Luther used (which the LW translates as "shake," and I render as "wave") was *levo*. This is a common phenomenon in the headings to Luther's lectures on the Minor Prophets. In the introductory lines of the verses that he addresses, the notes frequently list the verse as it appears in the Vulgate, followed by his argument, often against that rendering in the body of the text. Luther was almost certainly simply paraphrasing or reciting the verse from memory, and thus did not pay strict attention to the presence of *levo* as he quoted the verse. It could also be that he did this for the sake of clarity, since the students were familiar with the Vulgate.

[27] Beintker, *Die Überwindung*, 64–65.

[28] Beintker cited examples from Diefenbach and Du Cange to support the use of both terms by Luther – *tentatio* expressed the aggression or the assault, while *tribulatio* expressed the *condition* or *state* [*Zustand*] of *Anfechtung*. Beintker, *Die Überwindung*, 64–65. See also Lorenz Diefenbach, *Glossarium Latino-Germanicum mediae et infirmae aetatis* (Frankfurt am Main: Joseph Baer, 1857), 577. See also Charles Du Cange, *Glossarium ad scriptores mediae & infimae latinitatis* ... (Paris: printed by Gabrielis Martini, sold by Ludovicum Billaine, 1678), 1189 [this copy only lists *Contritio* and *amaritudo* for the entry, with the note "in Glossis antiquis MSS." Beintker must have been looking at a different copy, which he does not fully note in his bibliography or footnote]. See also McGrath, *Luther's Theology of the Cross*, 225 Note 61; and Anita Gaide, "Suffering and Hope in Martin Luther's Theology of the Cross and Latvian Lutheran Responses" (PhD diss., Toronto School of Theology, 2002), 178, 188.

[29] See Figure 3.1 in Ch. 3.

of cultic purification in the law code of the Hebrew Bible. He wrote in the commentary on Zechariah,

On the contrary, it [מֵנִיף (mēnîp)] means to move over [überher fahren] and hover [schweben], just as the priests waved [webeten] their offerings before the altar to the four corners of the world, for which reason the offerings are called 'wave offerings [Webeopfer]' (Num. 8:11, 21) or 'waving [Webe]' (Lev. 7:30).[30]

The Hebrew terms to which he was referring are וְהֵנִיף (wəhēnîp, "And will wave" [in the context of this verse, "And will offer"]) and תְּנוּפָה (tənûpâ, "[as] a wave offering") in Num. 8:11; וַיָּנֶף (wayyānep, "and waved" [in the context of this verse, "and offered"]) and תְּנוּפָה (tənûpâ, "[as] a wave offering") in Num. 8:21; and לְהָנִיף (ləhānîp, "to wave") and תְּנוּפָה (tənûpâ, "[as] a wave offering") in Lev. 7:30. While on the surface he was employing this terminology as part of his argument that the waving hand in Zechariah should be interpreted as a gracious sign, these citations also tacitly imported the additional underlying connotations of the Hebrew terms in their original contexts in those verses in the law code of the Hebrew Bible. The wave offering was made by the priests to consecrate offerings for the service of God, prior to burning certain sacrifices and offerings on the sacrificial altar, and prior to eating their consecrated portion of certain sacrifices and offerings.[31] It affirmed the consecration of the portion to God and its sanctity; as well as implicitly the sanctification of the priests, and thus their worthiness to eat the particular offering; and it also implicitly affirmed their cleanness, which was a requirement in order to present the offering.[32] Moreover, the wave offering was linked to atonement and/or remission of guilt in certain offerings and sacrifices.[33]

---

[30] "Sondern es heißt, überher fahren und schweben, gleichwie die Priester ihr Opfer webeten vor dem Altar in die vier Orte der Welt; daher es Webeopfer oder Webe heißt [4. Mos. 8, 11. 21. 3 Mos. 7, 30.]." StL 14:1817.45-StL 14:1818.45. LW 20:198.

[31] See Baruch J. Schwartz, "Wave Offering," in *The Oxford Dictionary of the Jewish Religion*, 2nd ed., ed. Adele Berlin (New York: Oxford University Press, 2011), 767–8. Schwartz describes the wave offering as "a ritual symbolizing the transfer of ownership from the offeror to the deity." Cf. Gary Anderson, who says that because the wave offering was not burned, it was not a "sacrifice." Anderson, "Sacrifice and Sacrificial Offerings," 873. Cf. Gary A. Anderson, *Sacrifices and Offerings in Ancient Israel: Studies in Their Social and Political Importance* (Atlanta: Scholars Press, 1987), 133–5, where he argues, nonetheless, for a link between the wave offering and sanctification and holiness. Cf. Milgrom, who links the wave offering to sacrifice, but argues against its existence in Israel and the ancient Near East. J. Milgrom, "The Alleged Wave-Offering in Israel and in the Ancient Near East," *Israel Exploration Journal* 22 (1972): 33–38. Cf. Num. 8:11, where the Levites themselves were presented before God as a wave offering, sanctifying them for service to God. See also TDOT 9:298–9.

[32] See Anderson, *Sacrifices and Offerings in Ancient Israel*, 133–5.

[33] See Louis Grossman, "Peace-Offering," in *The Jewish Encyclopedia*, vol. 9, ed. Isidore Singer (London: Funk and Wagnalls Company, 1905), 567. Grossman advises that this is attested to as early as Ezekiel, though not mentioned by "P." The "wave offering" is part of the "peace offering," one of a number of different types of offerings described in Leviticus. Cf. Gary Anderson, who cites the heavy weighting of P's sacrificial vocabulary toward "ritual of

Luther's choice of the biblical quotations in Leviticus and Numbers to support his reading of מֵנִיף (*mēnîp*) in Zech. 2:13 as an effecting of faith was intentional and methodical. He insisted on the German translation of *weben*, in contrast to *levo*, not only because it represented a more accurate reading of the literal Hebrew in מֵנִיף (*mēnîp*), but also because *weben* particularly evoked the ritual language of ancient Israelite cultic purification and "wave offerings" which were linked to sanctification. The sacrificial system would be a constant undertone for the German reader privy to the biblical texts, as it would have been for the ancient Israelite reader who was even more so familiar with the texts and terminology in Leviticus and Numbers. His use of these biblical quotations was thus in part a rhetorical tool, which created a multilayered interpretation of the wave: on the surface, a simple wave as distinct from a lifting of the hand; but underneath, carrying very specific meanings linked to sanctification in the service of God and cultic purification ritual.[34]

In sum, Luther's use of numerous scriptural citations to inform his translation of מֵנִיף (*mēnîp*) in Zech. 2:13 shows how the Hebrew in one place in scripture influenced his interpretation in another. It is a quintessential example of his use of inner-biblical interpretation for his Hebrew translation in the Minor Prophets. While his translation was predicated on a lexical issue, his solution to that issue had various ramifications for his related theological interpretation.

Case Study #2:
Zechariah 12:2 סַף־רַעַל (*sap-raʿal*, "cup of reeling")

Table 4.3 shows the parallel Hebrew, Latin, and German renderings for Zech. 12:2, as well as for the biblical citations that Luther used to elucidate the verse. The data in this table drives the analysis which follows.

---

atonement"; in Anderson, "Sacrifice and Sacrificial Offerings," 870–86, especially pp. 873–5. Also note the context of וַיָּנֶף (*wayyānep*, "and waved" [in the context of this verse, "and offered"]) and תְּנוּפָה (*tənûpâ*, "[as] a wave offering") in Num. 8:21, which appears along with וַיִּתְחַטָּאוּ (*wayyiṭḥaṭṭəʾû*, "And purified themselves") and וַיְכַפֵּר (*waykappēr*, "and made atonement").

[34] Cf. Luther's lecture remarks concerning another reference to the sacrificial system in Zech. 9:15: "Per euangelium sacrifico gentes efficioque, ut gentes sic sacrificatae fiant accepta oblatio domino." English translation: "Through the Gospel I make the Gentiles a sacrifice, in order that the Gentiles, thus sanctified [sacrificed], may become an acceptable offering to the Lord." WA 13:633.4–5; LW 20:101. Luther was loading the term *weben* to indicate (a) a friendly gesture, and (b) a wave offering, but also (c) a sanctification mark being applied to the Gentiles, and thus a theological event. Cf. his commentary on Zechariah, where he made a similar interpretation: StL 14:1920.35-StL 14:1922.40; LW 20:294–6. Zech. 9:15 also appears in Ch. 2 of this study.

Table 4.3: Luther's translation of סַף־רַעַל (*sap-raʿal*, "cup of reeling"):
Zech. 12:2, Ex. 12:22, Hab. 2:5, Hab. 2:16, Zech. 12:4, Ps. 60:5, and Is. 51:17.

Verse	NASB	Hebrew Bible	Vulgate	*Deutsche Bibel*
Zech. 12:2	"Behold, I am going to make Jerusalem a cup that causes reeling to all the peoples around; and when the siege is against Jerusalem, it will also be against Judah.	הִנֵּה אָנֹכִי שָׂם אֶת־יְרוּשָׁלַם **סַף־רַעַל** לְכָל־הָעַמִּים סָבִיב וְגַם עַל־יְהוּדָה יִהְיֶה בַמָּצוֹר עַל־יְרוּשָׁלָם	ecce ego ponam Hierusalem **superliminare crapulae** omnibus populis in circuitu sed et Iuda erit in obsidione contra Hierusalem	Sihe, ich wil Jerusalem zum **daumel becher** zu richten allen voelkern die vmbher sind, Denn es wird auch Juda gelten, wenn Jerusalem belegert wird. (1532) WA DB 11.2:354.2.
Ex. 12:22	You shall take a bunch of hyssop and dip it in the blood which is in the basin, and apply some of the blood that is in the basin to the lintel and the two doorposts; and none of you shall go outside the door of his house until morning.	וּלְקַחְתֶּם אֲגֻדַּת אֵזוֹב וּטְבַלְתֶּם בַּדָּם **אֲשֶׁר־בַּסַּף** וְהִגַּעְתֶּם אֶל־הַמַּשְׁקוֹף וְאֶל־שְׁתֵּי הַמְּזוּזֹת מִן־הַדָּם אֲשֶׁר **בַּסָּף** וְאַתֶּם לֹא תֵצְאוּ אִישׁ מִפֶּתַח־בֵּיתוֹ עַד־בֹּקֶר	fasciculumque hysopi tinguite sanguine **qui est in limine** et aspergite ex eo **superliminare** et utrumque postem nullus vestrum egrediatur ostium domus suae usque mane.	vnd nemet eyn puschel Jsopen vnd tunkket ynn das blut **ynn dem becken**, vnd beruret damit **die vber schwelle** vnd die zween pfosten, vnd gehe keyn mensch zu seyner haus thur eraus bis an den morgen. (1523) WA DB 8:236.22.
Hab. 2:5	"Furthermore, wine betrays the haughty man, So that he does not stay at home. He enlarges his appetite like Sheol, And he is like death, never satisfied. He also gathers to himself all nations And collects to himself all peoples.	וְאַף **כִּי־הַיַּיִן בּוֹגֵד גֶּבֶר יָהִיר** וְלֹא יִנְוֶה אֲשֶׁר הִרְחִיב כִּשְׁאוֹל נַפְשׁוֹ וְהוּא כַמָּוֶת וְלֹא יִשְׂבָּע וַיֶּאֱסֹף אֵלָיו כָּל־הַגּוֹיִם וַיִּקְבֹּץ אֵלָיו כָּל־הָעַמִּים	et quomodo **vinum potantem decipit** sic erit vir superbus et non decorabitur qui dilatavit quasi infernus animam suam et ipse quasi mors et non adimpletur et congregabit ad se omnes gentes et coacervabit ad se omnes populos	Aber **der wein betreugt** den stoltzen man, das er nicht bleiben kan, welcher seine seele auff sperret, wie die helle, vnd ist gerade, wie der tod, der nicht zu settigen ist, Sondern rafft zu sich alle Heiden, vnd samlet zu sich alle voelker. (1532) WA DB 11.2:304.5.

Verse	NASB	Hebrew Bible	Vulgate	Deutsche Bibel
Hab. 2:16	"You will be filled with disgrace rather than honor. Now you yourself drink and expose your own nakedness. The cup in the Lord's right hand will come around to you, And utter disgrace will come upon your glory.	שָׂבַעְתָּ קָלוֹן מִכָּבוֹד שְׁתֵה גַם-אַתָּה וְהֵעָרֵל תִּסּוֹב עָלֶיךָ **כּוֹס יְמִין** יְהוָה וְקִיקָלוֹן עַל-כְּבוֹדֶךָ	repletus est ignominia pro gloria bibe tu quoque **et consopire** circumdabit te **calix dexterae Domini** et vomitus ignominiae super gloriam tuam	Man wird dich auch settigen mit schande fur ehre, So sauffe du nu auch, **das du daumelst**. Denn dich wird vmbgeben **der kelch jnn der rechten des HERRN**, vnd must schendlich speien fur deine herrligkeit. (1532) WA DB 11.2:306.16.
Zech. 12:4	"In that day," declares the Lord, "I will strike every horse with bewilderment and his rider with madness. But I will watch over the house of Judah, while I strike every horse of the peoples with blindness.	בַּיּוֹם הַהוּא נְאֻם-יְהוָה אַכֶּה כָל-סוּס **בַּתִּמָּהוֹן** וְרֹכְבוֹ **בַּשִּׁגָּעוֹן** וְעַל-בֵּית יְהוּדָה אֶפְקַח אֶת-עֵינַי וְכֹל סוּס הָעַמִּים אַכֶּה בַּעִוָּרוֹן	in die illa dicit Dominus percutiam omnem equum **in stuporem** et ascensorem eius **in amentiam** et super domum Iuda aperiam oculos meos et omnem equum populorum percutiam in caecitate	Zu der zeit, spricht der HERR, wil ich alle rosse **schew**, vnd jren reutern **bange machen**, Aber vber Jerusalem wil ich meine augen offen haben, vnd alle rosse der voelcker mit blindheit plagen. (1532) WA DB 11.2:354.4.
Ps. 60:5	You have made Your people experience hardship; You have given us wine to drink that makes us stagger.	הִרְאִיתָ עַמְּךָ קָשָׁה הִשְׁקִיתָנוּ **יַיִן תַּרְעֵלָה**	ostendisti populo tuo duritiam potasti nos **vino consopiente**	Denn du liessest deyn volck eyn harttes sehen, Du trencktest vns mit **bitterm weyn**. (1524) WA DB 10.1:290.5.
				Denn du lessest deyn volck eyn harttes sehen, Du trenckest vns mit **daumel weyn**. (1528) WA DB 10.1:290.5.

Verse	NASB	Hebrew Bible	Vulgate	*Deutsche Bibel*
Is. 51:17	Rouse yourself! Rouse yourself! Arise, O Jerusalem, You who have drunk from the Lord's hand the cup of His anger; The chalice of reeling you have drained to the dregs.	הִתְעוֹרְרִי הִתְעוֹרְרִי קוּמִי יְרוּשָׁלִַם אֲשֶׁר שָׁתִית מִיַּד יְהוָה אֶת-כּוֹס חֲמָתוֹ אֶת-קֻבַּעַת כּוֹס הַתַּרְעֵלָה שָׁתִית מָצִית	elevare elevare consurge Hierusalem quae bibisti de manu Domini calicem irae eius usque ad fundum **calicis soporis** bibisti et epotasti usque ad feces	Wache auff, wache auff, stehe auff Jerusalem, die du von der hand des HERREN den kelch seines grymmes getrunken hast, die hefen **des daumel kelchs** hastu ausgetruncken, vnd die tropffen geleckt. (1528) WA DB 11.1:152.17.

Zech. 12 foretells the nations rising up against Jerusalem, but warns that God will make Jerusalem a stumbling block to those nations. Zech. 12:2 sets the stage for all of these events, describing Jerusalem as סַף־רַעַל (*sap-ra'al*, "a cup of reeling").

Luther contested the Vulgate's translation of סַף־רַעַל (*sap-ra'al*) in Zech. 12:2 as *superliminare crapulae* ("a lintel of reeling").[35] His issue was the rendering of סַף (*sap*) as *superliminare*, which he translated in the *Deutsche Bibel* as *becher* ("cup").[36] To make his case, he cited a number of biblical texts, the first of which was the account of the Passover in Exodus:

Behold I will make Jerusalem a lintel [superliminare] of reeling. Amazingly, most of the words here have been translated ineptly in our Bible. Jerome has followed the Septuagint and has translated 'lintel [*superliminare*],' but I do not like this. First, therefore, we will complete the grammatical account, for this is a very obscure passage. I translate and connect this passage as follows: 'Behold, I will make Jerusalem a cup of commotion [*ciphum commotionis*] for all the peoples round about, who also are against Judah in the siege against Jerusalem.' That is, in besieging Jerusalem they also want to lay siege to Judah. The fact that I translate 'cup [*ciphum*],' or 'saucer [*phialam*],' and not 'lintel [*superliminare*]' is based on the passage in Ex. 12[:22], even though in that very passage, Jerome has translated (but badly) the same word that is here as 'lintel [*limen*].' Actually, it should be read thus: 'Dip a small bundle of hyssop in the blood that is in the cup [*cipho*] and sprinkle the lintel [*superliminare*] with it.'[37]

---

[35] *Crapulae* could also be rendered as "of intoxication."

[36] WA DB 11.2:354.2. The modern German spelling of *daumel* is *Taumel*. *Daumel* could also be rendered as "staggering"; and *becher* as "goblet" or "mug."

[37] "Ecce ego ponam Hierusalem superliminare crapulae. Mirabiliter inepte sunt hic pleraque translata in nostris bibliis. Hieronymus secutus LXX interpretatus est superliminare sed mihi non placet. Primum ergo grammaticam rationem absolvemus, est enim hic locus perobscurus. Ego sic verto et connecto hunc locum: ecce ego ponam Hierusalem ciphum commotionis omnibus populis in circuitu, qui etiam contra Iudam sunt in obsidione contra Hierusalem i. e. in eo, quod obsident Hierusalem etiam Iudam volunt obsidere. Quod verto ciphum seu phialam et non superliminare, facit locus Exod. 12, quamvis et in illo ipso loco idem vo-

146   Chapter Four

The two phrases in Exodus which Luther was citing are אֲשֶׁר־בַּסַּף (*'ăšer-bassap*, "that is in the **cup**") and אֶל־הַמַּשְׁקוֹף (*'el-hammašqôp*, "the **lintel**"). The Vulgate translated these as *qui est in limine* ("that is in the lintel") and *superliminare* ("the lintel") – essentially the same term.[38] Luther, by contrast, differentiated between the two and rendered them as *ynn dem becken* ("in the basin") and *die vber schwelle* ("the upper threshold").[39] That distinction was the crux of his argument in Zech. 12:2 concerning Jerome's translation of סַף־רַעַל (*sap-ra'al*) as *superliminare crapulae*.[40]

While at first glance Luther's argument may appear to be primarily philological, this is hardly the case. His decision to support the translation of סַף (*sap*) as *becher* with a citation of the Passover in Exodus is especially important, because it made the connection to cultic purification ritual related to the commemoration of Passover.[41] The Passover ritual involved sacrifice, with the Levites passing the blood of the Passover offering to the priests, who would then purify the altar with it.[42] References to this purification ritual and Passover

---

cabulum, quod hic est, Hieronymus verterit: limen, sed male. Sic enim legendum est: fasciculumque hysopi tingite in sanguine, qui est in cipho, et aspergite ex eo superliminare etc." WA 13:654.18–29. LW 20:131–2. Cf. Luther's remarks in his commentary on Zechariah, where he also interpreted סַף (*sap*) as *Becher oder Löffel* ("cup or spoon"). StL 14:1950.2. LW 20:323–4. Cf. עַל־הַסַּף (*'al-hassap*, "upon the *threshold*") in Judg. 19:27, which Luther translated as *auff der schwelle* ("upon the *threshold*"); WA DB 9.1:158.27 (1524). Luther clearly took the context into account for his translation of Zech. 12:2, as the term סַף (*sap*) is ambiguous in meaning. See BDB, 706 and KB, 663–5. The Septuagint rendered this phrase in Zech. 12:2 as πρόθυρα σαλευόμενα ("trembling thresholds, doorsteps"). See LSJ, 1481 concerning πρόθυρα. For more on this, see W. H. Lowe, *The Hebrew Student's Commentary on Zechariah. Hebrew and LXX. With Excursus on Syllable-Dividing, Metheg, Initial Dagesh, and Siman Rapheh* (London: Macmillan, 1882), 107. See also Carol L. Meyers and Eric M. Meyers, *Zechariah 9–14: A New Translation with Introduction and Commentary*, AB 26C (New York: Doubleday, 1993), 313–4.

[38] *limen*: OXLAT 1:1134. *superlimen*: OXLAT 2:2069. Both mean "lintel" (threshold, doorway, etc.). See Nahum M. Sarna, *Exodus* שמות, JPS Torah Commentary (Philadelphia: Jewish Publication Society, 1991), 60 for a discussion on R. Akiba's understanding of סַף (*sap*) in Ex. 12:22 as "basin," in contrast R. Ishmael's understanding of it as "threshold" (in agreement with the LXX).

[39] WA DB 8:236.22. Luther eliminated the Hebrew repetition in his German translation by not including מִן־הַדָּם אֲשֶׁר בַּסַּף (*min-haddām 'ăšer bassap*, "from the blood that is in the cup"), which appears in the second part of the verse (by contrast, the Vulgate and LXX retained this repetition). See Ch. 2 of this study concerning Luther's handling of Hebrew repetition. The LXX renders these two phrases in Ex. 12:22 as: τοῦ παρὰ τὴν θύραν ("that is by the door, entrance") and τῆς φλιᾶς ("the door frame, lintel") [and later, the repeated παρὰ τὴν θύραν ("by the door, entrance")]. See LSJ, 811 concerning θύραν; LSJ, 1944 concerning φλιᾶς.

[40] Luther's German parallels the Latin suggestions that he made in his lectures on Zech. 12:2, *ciphum* and *phialam* (Luther appears to have spelled *siphum* as *ciphum*). Oxford defines *sipho* [*siphus*] as a tube that liquid is forced through; OXLAT 2:1953. Lewis and Short define it as a drinking-tube; LS, 1710. Lewis and Short define *phiala* as a broad, shallow drinking-vessel or a saucer; LS, 1369.

[41] פֶּסַח (*pesaḥ*) in Exodus is the same as the English "Passover."

[42] Gilders, *Blood Ritual*, 157.

appear in numerous places in the Hebrew Bible and in the New Testament (for example, John 11:55).⁴³ As was the case with his interpretation of Zech. 2:13, when Luther exploited this language in Ex. 12:22, he imported the underlying connotations and links which it had to this ritual language, not just the lexical meaning of סַף (sap).

Luther's choice of Ex. 12:22 for support was thus, in part, a play on the ambiguous figurative connotations of סַף (sap) – linked in the Hebrew Bible to protection, as in the Passover narrative, but also to destruction, as in the Zechariah narrative. In this interpretation, the cup that was an instrument of God's wrath in Zechariah operated as an antithetical allusion to the cup filled with blood that was a means of both purification and protection during the Passover. In this light, Luther's remarks in the lectures on Zech. 12:2 are much clearer: "That can be a two-sided victory – either in gentleness or in severity. That is, some of the enemies are devoured in wrath, some in mercy."⁴⁴ This antinomical view of God's wrath is the first of a number of allusions to his theology of *Anfechtung* in his interpretation of this verse.⁴⁵ Moreover, it was a clear invocation of ritual purification in the Hebrew Bible. Had Luther not wanted to make such an interpretation to support his translation argument in Zech. 12:2, he had numerous options aside from of the Passover citation to do so. This was thus a telling choice by Luther.

Luther's Quotations: Habakkuk 2:5, 2:16, and the associated Zechariah 12:4

In his consideration of Zech. 12:2, Luther went on to quote two verses from Habakkuk, which he used to further build his interpretation of סַף־רַעַל (sap-ra'al). With these quotations, he focused on the second part of the construction, רַעַל

---

⁴³ Gilders, *Blood Ritual*, 157. See also Michael Fishbane, *HAFTAROT הפטרות*, *The JPS Bible Commentary* (Philadelphia: Jewish Publication Society, 2002), 303–5. Raymond Brown cites Num. 9:10, which forbids unclean persons from participating in the regular Passover service. He (a) cites 2 Chron. 30:17–18 concerning purification and sanctification, (b) explains the need for those Israelites who lived in contact with Gentiles to purify themselves, and (c) cites Josephus making remarks concerning purification. Raymond E. Brown, S. S., *The Gospel According to John I–XII*, AB 29 (London: Yale University Press, 2006), 445. Josephus records Malichus asking Hyrcanus to entreat Herod not to bring foreigners among the Jewish people during their period of purification for a festival in Jerusalem. Josephus, *J. W.* 1.11.6 [§ 229]. See Flavius Josephus, *The Jewish War*. In *Loeb Classical Library. Josephus Vol. 2 [LCL 203]: Books 1–3*, ed. E. H. Warmington, trans. H. St. J. Thackeray (Cambridge, MA: Harvard University Press, 1967), 107. Brown notes this.

⁴⁴ "Bifariam potest illa victoria fieri vel in benignitate vel in austeritate, hoc est: aliqui inimicorum devorantur in ira, aliqui in misericordia." WA 13:655.5–7. LW 20:132.

⁴⁵ Luther's remarks concerning the reference to the sacrificial system in Zech. 9:15, noted earlier in connection with Case Study #1 (Zech. 2:13), parallel these remarks concerning Zech. 12:2. See WA 13:632.27–WA 13:633.10; LW 20:101. Cf. StL 14:1920.35-StL 14:1922.40; LW 20:294–6. Cf. his translation of כַּמִּזְרָק (kammizrāq, "like the *basin*") in Zech. 9:15, in which he used the same German term *becken* as he did for סַף (sap) in Ex. 12:22. WA DB 11.2:348.15.

(*ra'al*), and the multifarious quality that he saw in the term. It has various connotations associated with drunkenness; but also an associated theological significance as a metaphorical affliction from God. He explained in the lectures on Zechariah:

> Furthermore, what we have translated 'commotion' is a word filled with significance. It properly means 'staggering' or 'reeling,' as a drunken person generally does when neither his foot nor his mind performs its function satisfactorily. Hab. 2[:5]: 'As wine deceives the drinker, so will the proud man be, and he will not be honored, etc.'; [and v. 16:] 'Drink also and be stupefied,' i. e. 'Reel, as if [you are] drunk!'[46]

His remarks in his commentary on Habakkuk, where he specifically addressed Hab. 2:16, reinforce this interpretation. He did so with a flurry of additional scripture citations:

> But here in this and other passages, drinking or guzzling means as much as to suffer misfortune; and to pour out or to give to drink means as much as to punish, to torment, to torture [Ps. 116:13], and afflict in all sorts of ways. The common expression in the Psalter, 'the Lord's cup,' derives from that. Thus: 'Their cup is full of brimstone' [cf. Rev. 14:10]. Rev. 18[:6f.] also speaks of the red whore, saying: 'Pour out for her as she has poured out for you. And measure for her with the amount that she has measured for you.' Therefore the cup of the Lord is called the penalty that he pours out and distributes to everyone [Jer. 25:15f.]. Also read Jer. 25, where he bids all kings drink from the cup of the Lord, that they might become drunk, vomit, and fall, etc. In order to understand this fully and clearly, let us point out that a person who is drunk with wine in a physical sense typifies two other kinds of drunkenness excellently – first, to be drunk with great delight; second, to be drunk with great pain.[47]

These quotations illustrate a recurring phenomenon in his use of inner-biblical interpretation. To support his translation of a particular Hebrew word or phrase,

---

[46] "Deinde quod commotionem vertimus, plenae significationis vocabulum est, quod proprie significat nutare, vacillare ut ebrii solent, quando neque pes neque mens satis suum officium facit. Abacuc 2: quomodo vinum potantem decipit, sic erit vir superbus et non decorabitur etc. Bibe tu quoque et consopire i. e. vacilla tanquam ebrius." WA 13:654.29–33. LW 20:132. Cf. the lectures on Habakkuk; WA 13:438.8–11; LW 19:130.

[47] "Aber hie an diesem und der gleichen ort heisst trincken odder sauffen so viel als unglueck leyden, Und einschencken odder zu trincken geben so viel als straffen, peynigen, marteren [Ps. 116, 13] und allerley plage an thun. Da her kompt das gemeine wort ym Psalter: [Off. 14, 10] 'Der kilch des Herrn'. Item, 'yhrer kilch ist vol schwefel'. Also stehet auch [Off. 18, 6] Apoca. xviij. von der roten huren geschrieben: 'Schenckt yhr vol ein, wie sie euch eingeschenckt hat. Und messet yhr mit dem mass, da sie euch mit gemessen hat'. Also heist denn der kilch des Herrn die straffe, die er eim iglichen [Jer. 25, 15f.] einschenckt und zuteilet. Davon liese Jeremie .xxv., Da er heist alle koenige und leute trincken aus dem kilch des Herrn, das sie truncken werden, speyen und fallen etce. Und das wirs gantz und klerlich fassen: Wenn einer leiblich vom wein truncken ist, der ist ein gut furbilde zweyerley ander trunckenheit. Eine ist, wenn yemand fur grosser lust truncken wird; Die ander, wenn yemand fur grossem schmertzen truncken ist." WA 19:417.4–18. LW 19:219. These comments fall under Hab. 2:15 in Luther's commentary, but it is clear that he is referring to Hab. 2:16 in the portion quoted here.

he often cited a different Hebrew word or phrase. The parallels to סַף (sap) which he identified in his above remarks show this: כּוֹס (kôs, "cup") in Hab. 2:16, Ps. 116:13, and Jer. 25:15; and the parallels to רָעַל (ra'al) which he identified do the same: הַיַּיִן (hayyayin, "the wine") in Hab. 2:5; וְהֵעָרֵל (wəhē'ārēl, "and be uncovered/shut up [in horror/astonishment/stupification]") and יְמִין יְהוָה (yəmîn 'ǎdōnāy, "of the right hand of the Lord") in Hab. 2:16; and הַיַּיִן הַחֵמָה (hayyayin haḥēmâ, "of wine, [the one] of wrath, fury") in Jer. 25:15.[48] Moreover, his citations of Revelation (and Matthew which appears immediately prior to those remarks) were not even Hebrew! Such quotations of differing terminology to support his translation of Hebrew appear throughout his interpretation of the Minor Prophets.

The trope of drunkenness, though, was not the only tool which Luther used to build his interpretation of רָעַל (ra'al). He broadened that figurative interpretation of affliction from God yet further in his commentary on Habakkuk, where in his remarks on Hab. 2:5 he construed רָעַל (ra'al) as a loss of senses or bewilderment: "Bereft of all senses, speech, reason, and strength, he can neither speak nor work ... Thus also the Latin sages wrote that a drunkard is neither alive nor dead."[49] This understanding of רָעַל (ra'al) as disorientation is not an anomalous interpretation by Luther. A parallel appears in his lectures on Zech. 12:4, where he made explicit mention of his argument concerning רָעַל (ra'al) in Zech. 12:2. Moreover, he utilized the same citation of Hab. 2:16 which he used to support that translation of Zech. 12:2:

Their horses will be struck with astonishment [*stupor*]; they themselves, with madness [*amentia*]. And this is the explanation of the 'commotion [*commotionis*]' about which he

---

[48] Cf. Rashi's interpretation of Hab. 2:16: "'ערלה' כל לב. ותמהון בשממון האטם – הערל: כאן אף - 'ואיתערטל': תירגם ויונתן (מד,ט יח') בשר' 'ערל ,'לב 'ערל ;(ו,י 'ירי) אזנם' 'ערלה כמו הוא, אוטם לשון לשון' 'ערום ועריה' (יח' טז,ז). English translation: "Even here: הערל (*h'rl*) – become shut up in horror and bewilderment of heart. Every 'ערלה' (*'rlh*)' is an expression of that stoppage, like 'their ear is shut up [uncircumcised]' (Jer. 6:10); 'heart is shut up [uncircumcised],' 'flesh is shut up [uncircumcised]' (Ezek. 44:7). And Jonathan translated: 'And become naked [or uncircumcised/stopped up; ואיתערטל (*w'yt'rṭl*)'] – an expression of 'naked and nakedness [bare]' (Ezek. 16:7)." MG, *The Twelve Minor Prophets* [ספר תרי עשר], 230. Despite the similar spelling of הֶעָרֵל (*hē'ārēl*) and רָעַל (*ra'al*), the root of הֶעָרֵל (*hē'ārēl*) is ערל (*'rl*); thus, these are different Hebrew terms. Some sources read "astonishment" for שממון (*šimmwn*) [in Rashi's commentary]. I take "horror" from BDB, 1031; KB, 989. Thank you to Dr. Barak Dan, The Hebrew University of Jerusalem, for the insight on this.

[49] "Er kan widder reden noch schaffen, als der aller vernunfft, syn, sprachen, witz und krefft beraubt ist ... Also haben auch die Latinschen weisen geschrieben, das ein truncken mensch widder lebendig noch tod sey." WA 19:397.21–22, 25–27. LW 19:200. Luther specifically attributed this to בֹּגֵד (*bōgēd*) (and through the citation of Hab. 2:5 in his lectures on Zechariah, to רָעַל (*ra'al*)). This appears in the Habakkuk commentary: "'Boged' odder 'Woged': Wenn eyner so gar zu nicht odder veracht wird, das man gleich gewis ist, er sey und gelte nichts." English translation: "'Boged' or 'Woged' [בֹּגֵד (*bōgēd*)]. It describes a person who is completely ruined and despised, convincing us at once that he is nothing and is esteemed as nothing." WA 13:398.12–13. LW 19:201.

spoke a little earlier [i. e. Zech. 12:2]. That is, the Lord strikes terror [*pavefacit*] in the hearts of his enemies so that they cannot continue. They lose confidence in their side, as he says to the king of Babylon in Habakkuk [Hab. 2:16], 'And may you, too, be stupefied [*consopire*]' ... But God saves and cares for the godly, while the world believes that they are done for. The Lord looks on them with mercy and with favor. He does not allow a hair of their head to fall. In the midst of death and troubles, he is close to them.[50]

Luther was focusing on בַּתִּמָּהוֹן (*battimmāhôn*, "in astonishment") and בַּשִּׁגָּעוֹן (*baššiggāʿôn*, "in madness") in Zech. 12:4, which he framed as parallels to both רַעַל (*raʿal*) in Zech. 12:2 and וְהֵעָרֵל (*wəhēʿārēl*) in Hab. 2:16. He translated בַּתִּמָּהוֹן (*battimmāhôn*) in the *Deutsche Bibel* as shew ("[in] awe, timidity, dread"), and בַּשִּׁגָּעוֹן (*baššiggāʿôn*) as *bange machen* ("to frighten, agitate, oppress").[51] By contrast, the Vulgate translated בַּתִּמָּהוֹן (*battimmāhôn*) as *in stuporem* ("in astonishment") and בַּשִּׁגָּעוֹן (*baššiggāʿôn*) as *in amentiam* ("in madness, senselessness").

Luther's interweaving of madness, the fear of God, oppression, awe, and assault from God in his interpretation of סַף־רַעַל (*sap-raʿal*) in Zech. 12:2 were clear allusions to his theology of *Anfechtung*. His Bible translation of *bange machen* is one of the strongest among these, as Ch. 3 of this study shows.[52] Moreover, his interpretation of the Hebrew as *pavefacit* was another clear nod to *Anfechtung*, which is also discussed in greater detail in Ch. 3 [i. e. *pavore*].

In sum, with these quotations in Habakkuk, and in his explicit linking of Hab. 2:16, Zech. 12:2, and Zech. 12:4, Luther substantively enriched his interpretation of סַף־רַעַל (*sap-raʿal*) in Zech. 12:2, illustrating the rich meaning that he saw in רַעַל (*raʿal*) as *commotionis*.[53] The cup of the wrath of God, which may represent wrath or mercy – Luther was never certain when in the depths of *Anfechtung* – represented fear, anxiety, commotion, drunkenness, bewilderment, and being driven mad. He drew it all together in his translation of Zech. 12:2, looking back from his remarks in his commentary on Zechariah, addressing Zech. 12:4: "And this is the full interpretation of the cup of reeling and the

---

[50] "Illorum equi stupore percutiuntur, ipsi amentia. Atque haec est expositio commotionis, de qua dixit paulo superius, nempe cum dominus pavefacit corda hostium, ut non possint persistere, quin diffidant suae parti, sicut dicit ad regem Babylonis in Abacuc: consopire et tu ... Servantur autem pii et deo curae sunt, dum mundus putaret de ipsis actum esse, dominus aspicit eos misericordia et favore, non sinit capillum cadere de capite eorum, in media morte, in mediis malis est eis proximus." WA 13:656.2–6, 11–14. LW 20:134.

[51] WA DB 11.2:354.4. The modern German spelling for *schew* is *scheu*.

[52] See Figure 3.1 and the explicit association that Luther made between *bange* and *Anfechtung*, most prominently in the *scholia* on Ps. 118:5. Cf. also Luther's commentary interpretation of Hab. 2:16 as *unglueck leyden* with the data in Figure 3.1 in Ch. 3 of this study, the latter which shows that *Unglück* is one of the terms Luther used in his exegesis of Hebrew, which he linked to *Anfechtung*.

[53] He made this argument concerning רַעַל (*raʿal*) in the lectures on Zech. 12:2, and concerning שִׁגָּעוֹן (*šiggāʿôn*) in the lectures on 12:4.

heavy stone."⁵⁴ His use of inner-biblical interpretation enabled him to interweave various philological and theological elements to feed his translation and broaden his interpretation of סַף־רַעַל (sap-ra'al) in Zech. 12:2.

Luther's Quotation: Psalm 60:5

Luther went on to quote Ps. 60:5 in his lectures on Zechariah, and with it, added yet another layer of meaning into his interpretation of סַף־רַעַל (sap-ra'al), this one particularly affective. He drew upon the parallel between סַף־רַעַל (sap-ra'al) in Zech. 12:2 and יַיִן תַּרְעֵלָה (yayin tar'ēlâ, "wine of reeling, trembling, astonishment") in Ps. 60:5. Both רַעַל (ra'al) and תַּרְעֵלָה (tar'ēlâ) share the same root רעל (r'l), and a similar lexical meaning.⁵⁵ Luther was exploiting the context of the Psalm for his affective interpretation, the lamentation of being cast off by God: הִרְאִיתָ עַמְּךָ קָשָׁה הִשְׁקִיתָנוּ יַיִן תַּרְעֵלָה (hir'îtā 'amməkā qāšâ hišqîtānû yayin tar'ēlâ, "You caused your people to see a difficult [thing], you made us drink wine of reeling/trembling/astonishment").⁵⁶ He explained in the lectures on Zechariah:

There we have the same word [*consopiente* ('of stupefaction, astonishment, sleep')], which you will read more correctly as 'of commotion [*commotionis*].' Then, too, we have in Ps. 60:5: 'Wine of the sting of conscience [*vino compunctionis*], etc.'⁵⁷

He essentially interwove the two connotations into his interpretation of סַף־רַעַל (sap-ra'al), constructing a metaphorical interpretation of the Hebrew which took into account both the sense of agitation in *commotionis* and the sense of sting of conscience, remorse, or compunction in *compunctionis*. He thus fur-

---

⁵⁴ "Und dies ist fast die Auslegung des Taumelkelchs und Laststeins." StL 14:1951.7. LW 20:325.

⁵⁵ BDB, 947. KB, 900. According to Strong, רַעַל (ra'al) seems to be more associated with intoxication, and תַּרְעֵלָה (tar'ēlâ) with astonishment. See STR, 109 (Hebrew Dictionary section) [§H7478] and STR, 126 (Hebrew Dictionary section) [§H8653].

⁵⁶ Luther translated Ps. 60:5 in 1524 as *Denn du liessest deyn volck eyn harttes sehen, Du trencktest vns mit **bitterm** weyn* ("You let your people see a hard [thing], you gave us a bitter wine to drink"). WA DB 10.1:290.5. In 1528 he changed the translation to *Denn du lessest deyn volck eyn harttes sehen, Du trenckest vns mit **daumel** weyn* ("You let your people see a hard [thing], you gave us a reeling wine to drink"). WA DB 10.1:290.5. [Cf. WA DB 10.1:291a.5 (1531) and WA DB 10.1:291b.5 (1545), where his main modification concerning תַּרְעֵלָה (tar'ēlâ) was the appendage of *das wir daumelten*.] With the emendation, he mirrored his translation of סַף־רַעַל (sap-ra'al) in Zech. 12:2 as *daumel becher* ("reeling cup"), construing יַיִן תַּרְעֵלָה (yayin tar'ēlâ) in Ps. 60:5 as *daumel weyn* ("reeling wine").

⁵⁷ "Ubi idem est vocabulum, rectius [Ps. 59, 5.] leges: commotionis. Sic in psalmo: vino compunctionis etc." WA 13:654.34–35. LW 20:132. The bracketed Psalms reference in the WA margin clearly refers to "in psalmo" in the next sentence on that same line. I include the first sentence here, which addresses Is. 51:17, in order to show the link that Luther made between *commotionis* and *compunctionis*. The Hebrew term in focus is the same in both verses: תַּרְעֵלָה (tar'ēlâ). Lewis and Short define *commotio* as "a moving, motion" and "a rousing, exciting, agitation, commotion"; in contrast to *compunctio*, which they define as "a puncture" and "the sting of conscience, remorse." LS, 383, 395.

ther broadened his interpretation of רָעַל (ra'al) with this emotive component. This addition is especially significant, as it mirrors one of his key hermeneutical tools which was addressed in detail in Ch. 3 of this study: the exploitation of Hebrew semantic intensity. It is another of many witnesses to the influence of Hebrew intensity on Luther's Bible translation.

Luther's Quotation: Isaiah 51:17

A final, crucial verse that Luther quoted in his argument concerning Zech. 12:2 was Is. 51:17.[58] This quotation is particularly important for its explicit link to *Anfechtung*, thus serving as yet another indication of the influence of Hebrew on his interpretation of *Anfechtung* in the Prophets. In the lectures on Zechariah, he identified כּוֹס הַתַּרְעֵלָה (*kôs hattar'ēlâ*, "the cup of reeling, trembling, astonishment") in Is. 51:17 as a parallel to סַף־רַעַל (*sap-ra'al*) in Zech. 12:2: "So, too, we read in Is. 51:17: 'You have drunk the cup of sleep, stupefaction [*calicem soporis*] to the last drop,'" which he further argued would be read more accurately as "of commotion [*commotionis*]."[59] Luther's dispute with the Vulgate was its rendering of הַתַּרְעֵלָה (*hattar'ēlâ*) as *soporis*.[60] In contrast to the Vulgate,

---

[58] The WA reads Is. 29, not Is. 51:17. Luther's quotation, however, clearly matches Is. 51:17, hence the footnote in the LW, with their modification of this to Is. 51:17. Nevertheless, the Hebrew in Is. 29:9 which Luther addressed in his lectures is וְתִמְהוּ (*ûtəmāhû*, "and be amazed"), a different form of the same term that appears in Zech. 12:4: בַּתִּמָּהוֹן (*battimmāhôn*, "with astonishment"). Luther made extensive remarks on Is. 29:9 in his Isaiah lectures [WA 31.2:175.4–26; LW 16:242; see also WA 25:195.42–WA 25:196.6], which align quite well with his comments in the Zechariah lectures where he cited the verse. This may suggest that there was a lapse in the notetaking of his student, where perhaps Luther indeed addressed both Is. 29:9 and 51:17. Nevertheless, the link between the two in his exegesis seems likely, at least given the overlap of the Hebrew terminology and his commentary remarks connecting סַף־רַעַל (*sap-ra'al*) and stupefaction [וְתִמְהוּ (*ûtəmāhû*)].

[59] "Sic est Esa. 29: bibisti calicem soporis usque ad fundum." See WA 13:654.33–35. LW 20:132. See also the previous footnote concerning Is. 29 in the WA. As in Hab. 2:16, Luther's quotation of Is. 51:17 essentially positioned the term כּוֹס (*kôs*) as a synonym for סַף (*sap*) in Zech. 12:2. Both סַף (*sap*) and כּוֹס (*kôs*) describe some type of cup or chalice. Luther's argument, however, focused on the term that followed in both examples: רַעַל (*ra'al*). Concerning the date of his lectures on Is. 51, this was likely 1529; the lectures lasted from 1527–30, but were interrupted twice, so the precise date is not certain. See WA 31.2:viii; LW 16:ix–xi; LW 17:ix–x.

[60] *Consopiente* is a variant of *soporis*. Lewis and Short define *consopio* as: "to bring into an unconscious state, to put fast asleep, lull to sleep, to stupefy" and in the passive form, related to laws, "to become obsolete." LS, 434–5. Lefèvre's *Quincuplex Psalter*, and the 1506–08 Basel Vulgate for comparison, elucidate the broader dispute concerning this Hebrew term, as well as Luther's decision to cite both Is. 51:17 and Ps. 60:5 in his exegesis. The *Quincuplex Psalter* reads for תַּרְעֵלָה (*tar'ēlâ*) in Ps. 60:5: *Gallicum*: "compunctionis"; *Romanum*: "compunctionis"; *Hebraicum*: "consopiente"; *Vetus*: "stimulationis"; and *Cinciliatum*: "compunctionis." Lefèvre, *Qvincvplex Psalterium*, fols. 92v, 253r [Ps. 59:3]. The *Textus biblie* (Basel, 1506–08) reads *compunctionis*. *Textus biblie* (Basel, 1506–08), vol. 3, fol. 169r [Ps. 59:3]. By contrast, for הַתַּרְעֵלָה (*hattar'ēlâ*) in Is. 51:17, the *Textus biblie* (Basel, 1506–08) reads *soporis*. *Textus biblie* (Basel, 1506–08), vol. 4, fols. 87r–88v. The presence of both *consopiente* and

he translated כּוֹס הַתַּרְעֵלָה (*kôs hattar'ēlâ*) in Is. 51:17 as *des daumel kelchs* ("of the reeling goblet"), mirroring his translation of רַעַל (*ra'al*) in Zech. 12:2 as *daumel becher.*[61]

He made the explicit link to *Anfechtung* in his lectures on Is. 51:17:

You who have drunk at the hand of the Lord the cup of his wrath. The cup of God's wrath [*Calix irae dei*]! Who can grasp this, except faith alone, that the elect should drink from the cup of God's wrath [*calice irae dei*]? And yet the holy apostles and martyrs were exposed to the torments of this cup [*tormentis huius calicis*]. Princes and demons raged against them, though not more than they were permitted, and this cup was not inflicted [*infligitur*] on the elect by God but by the demon who never stops afflicting [*affligit*]. So great is the power of the storms [*moles procellarum*] that a certain measure of the cup is poured for each one, and he drinks it, that is, he suffers [*pacietur*]. The dregs of the cup of sleep, stupefaction [*Feces calicis soporis*], that is, 'All the way to the bottom, you drank the wine of the sting of conscience [*vinum compunccionis*]; reeling wine [*Tawmel weyn*] which makes you stagger [*nutare*] when you drink it.' Thus the church will be filled with that wrath of God [*ira dei*] to the point of staggering [*ad nutacionem*], and we will be so immersed in *Anfechtungen* [*ita tentacionibus immergi*] that there seems to be no help to enable us to look after our affairs. As the Psalm says [Ps. 107:27]: 'They were moved like drunken men [*Moti sunt sicut ebrii pedes* (*mei*)],' so that finally the number of examples will cause them to stagger to despair [*ad desperacionem vacillent*], until the morning star of grace rises in our darkness [cf. 2 Peter 1:19].[62]

In this passage, the allusions to *Anfechtung* are prolific: *infligitur* ("afflicted"), *affligit* ("afflicts"), *moles procellarum* ("the power of the storms"), *irae dei* ("of God's wrath"), and *ira dei* ("the wrath of God"); as are additional variants of

---

compunctionis in the *Quincuplex Psalter* columns for Ps. 60:5, a text which Luther undoubtedly consulted for his Psalms translations, helps to explain his choice of Is. 51:17 as an example for his translation argument here. In both verses, one finds not only the same Hebrew term, but the same Latin translation that Luther challenged. Interestingly, Luther was arguing against the Latin recension for Ps. 60:5 (i. e. in Lefèvre) which was based on the Hebrew Bible (*consopiente*), showing his readiness to challenge Jerome any time he believed that the Latin rendering of the Hebrew was in some way deficient.

[61] WA DB 11.1:152.17. Luther made this identical German translation relative to the Latin Vulgate in yet another location: Is. 51:22, which he cited in the commentary on Hab. 2:16. The Vulgate translated אֶת-כּוֹס הַתַּרְעֵלָה (*'et-kôs hattar'ēlâ*, "the cup of reeling/staggering") in Is. 51:22 as *calicem soporis* ("goblet of sleep"). Luther, by comparison, translated this into German as *den daumel kelch* ("the reeling goblet"). WA DB 11.1:154.22.

[62] "'Qui bibisti de manu domini calicem irae eius.' Calix irae dei. Quis illa apprehendit nisi sola fides, quod electi e calice irae dei biberent? At tamen apostoli sanctique martyres obiecti sunt tormentis huius calicis. Principes, demones insaniunt in illos, non tamen plus, quam illis permissum est, et calix ille a deo electis non infligitur, sed a demone, qui nunquam non affligit. Tanta est moles procellarum, ut eciam cuilibet certa mensura calicis infusa sit, quam bibet i. e. pacietur. 'Feces calicis soporis' i. e. ad fundum usque bibisti vinum compunccionis, Tawmel weyn, qui facit vos nutare, cum bibitis. Sic ista ira dei replebitur ecclesia usque ad nutacionem, et nos ita tentacionibus immergi, ut nullum consilium appareat, qua possimus rebus nostris consulere. [Ps. 107, 27] Sicut Psal ... 'Moti sunt sicut ebrii pedes mei' etc. adeo ut tandem ad [2. Petri 1, 19] desperacionem vacillent exemplis, donec Lucifer graciae exoriatur in tenebris nostris." WA 31.2:419.14–27. LW 17:203.

his interpretation of הַתַּרְעֵלָה (hattar‛ēlâ): *Moti sunt* ("moved, shaken, reeled"), *tormentis huius calicis* ("the torments of this cup"), and *ad desperacionem vacillent* ("that they might stagger to despair").[63] The allusion to storm is a particularly significant indicator of *Anfechtung*, as was explained in Ch. 3 of this study. The most important attestation to *Anfechtung* in Luther's lectures on Is. 51:17, however, is the interpretation of the experience as *tentatio* (Luther's frequently-used synonym for *Anfechtung*). Thus, with the words *et nos ita tentacionibus immergi* ("thus we are immersed in *Anfechtungen*"), this is unmistakable: Luther understood Jerusalem drinking from the cup of wrath, at the hand of God, as *Anfechtung*. In his translation and exegesis of Zech. 12:2, and the numerous instances of inner-biblical interpretation which he used to support that translation, one finds a very clear example of what he meant when he spoke of the *Anfechtung* of the prophets.[64]

Luther's many scriptural quotations, which he used to build his multi-layered interpretation of סַף־רַעַל (sap-ra‛al) in Zech. 12:2, show how significant his use of inner-biblical interpretation was for his Hebrew translation. They elucidate how he based his translation on a piece of text from the Passover narrative in the Pentateuch, but then broadened his interpretation. He did this by exploiting a diverse array of biblical quotations and allusions – some linked to purification and protection, and others to the wrath of God. He used this broadened interpretation to explain the theological meaning of the verse – which included numerous allusions to, and a specific reference to, his theology of *Anfechtung*. The end result was an interwoven, enriched, and theologically significant interpretation of the Hebrew.[65]

Case Study #3:
Nahum 1:3 וְנַקֵּה לֹא יְנַקֶּה (wənaqqēh lōʾ yənaqqeh, "and [he] will certainly not acquit")

Table 4.4 provides the parallel Hebrew, Latin, and German translations for Nah. 1:3, as well as for the Bible quotations that Luther used to support his interpretation of the verse.

---

[63] WA 13:250.18–24. Cf. Figure 3.1 in Ch. 3 of this study.
[64] "The *Anfechtung* of the prophets": as noted in the introduction to this study in Ch. 1.
[65] Luther's branching out for support is not unique. Cf. Rashi's comments concerning Zech. 12:2, where he cited בַּסַּף (bassap) in Ex. 12:22 (as did Luther); וְהָרְעָלוֹת (wəhārəʿālôt, "and the veils") in Is. 3:19 (i. e. the *shaking* of the woman's veil); and הָרְעָלוּ (hārəʿālû, "are made to shake") in Nah. 2:4 for his interpretation. MG, *The Twelve Minor Prophets* [ספר תרי עשר], 328. Reuchlin's *Rudimenta* entry for רָעַל (raʿal) includes references to Zech. 12, Ps. 60, Is. 3, and Nah. 2, as well as the definitions *tremor* ("tremor"), *tumultus* ("tumult"), and *fremitus* ("a rushing, resounding, murmuring"). *Rudimenta*, 495.

Table 4.4: Luther's translation of וְנַקֵּה לֹא יְנַקֶּה (wənaqqēh lōʾ yənaqqeh, "and [he] will certainly not acquit"): Nah. 1:3, Ps. 49:8, and Ex. 34:7.⁶⁶

Verse	NASB	Hebrew Bible	Vulgate	*Deutsche Bibel*
Nah. 1:3	The Lord is slow to anger and great in power, And the Lord will by no means leave the guilty unpunished. In whirlwind and storm is His way, And clouds are the dust beneath His feet.	יְהוָה אֶרֶךְ אַפַּיִם וּגְדוֹל־כֹּחַ וְנַקֵּה לֹא יְנַקֶּה יְהוָה בְּסוּפָה וּבִשְׂעָרָה דַּרְכּוֹ וְעָנָן אֲבַק רַגְלָיו	Dominus patiens et magnus fortitudine et **mundans non faciet innocentem** Dominus in tempestate et turbine viae eius et nebulae pulvis pedum eius	Der HERR ist gedueltig vnd von grosser krafft, **vnd lesst nichts vngestrafft**, Er ist der HERR, des wege jnn wetter vnd vngestueme sind, vnd vnter seinen fuessen dicke wolcken. (1532) WA DB 11.2:290.3. Der HERR ist Gedueltig vnd von grosser Krafft, **fur welchem niemand vnschuldig ist**, Er ist der HERR, des wege in Wetter vnd Sturm sind, vnd vnter seinen fuessen dikker staube. (1545) WA DB 11.2:291.3.
Ex. 34:7	Who keeps lovingkindness for thousands, who forgives iniquity, transgression and sin; yet He will by no means leave the guilty unpunished, visiting the iniquity of fathers on the children and on the grandchildren to the third and fourth generations.	נֹצֵר חֶסֶד לָאֲלָפִים נֹשֵׂא עָוֹן וָפֶשַׁע וְחַטָּאָה וְנַקֵּה לֹא יְנַקֶּה פֹּקֵד עֲוֹן אָבוֹת עַל־בָּנִים וְעַל־בְּנֵי בָנִים עַל־שִׁלֵּשִׁים וְעַל־רִבֵּעִים	qui custodis misericordiam in milia qui aufers iniquitatem et scelera atque peccata **nullusque apud te per se innocens est** qui reddis iniquitatem patrum in filiis ac nepotibus in tertiam et quartam progeniem	der du bewarist gnad ynn tausent gelid, vnd vergibst missethat, vbertrettung vnd sund, **vnd fur wilchem niemant vnschuldig ist**, der du die missethath der vetter heymsuchst auff kinder vnd kinds kinder, bis yns dritte vnd vierde gelid. (1523) WA DB 8:308.7.
Ps. 49:8	No man can by any means redeem his brother Or give to God a ransom for him.	אָח לֹא פָדֹה יִפְדֶּה אִישׁ לֹא־יִתֵּן לֵאלֹהִים כָּפְרוֹ	fratrem **redimens non redimet** vir nec dabit Deo propitiationem pro eo	**Kan doch** eyn bruder **niemand erloesen**, noch Gott iemand versunen. (1524) WA DB 10.1:256.8.

---

⁶⁶ Hebrew Bible versions differ on the spelling of וּגְדוֹל־כֹּחַ (*ûgədōl-kōaḥ*, "and great [in] power") in Nah. 1:3. I have rendered it as it appears in the 1494 Brescia Hebrew Bible, Staatsbibliothek Berlin, fol. 426v [864].

The Book of Nahum opens with numerous reflections on the greatness of God. However, the prophet also warns of God's wrath, and the fate of all who oppose God. It is this contrast that is the focus of Nah. 1:3.

In his lectures on Nahum, Luther argued against the Vulgate's addition of *mundans* ("cleansing") in Nah. 1:3, the equivalent of which does not appear in the Hebrew Bible in this verse.[67] He explained his decision in his lectures: "*And cleansing, the Lord will by no means make innocent* [*Et mundans non faciet innocentem*]. He speaks in the Hebrew fashion. We ought to translate this differently. For the participle *mundans* ('cleansing') should be omitted."[68] In his German rendering, Luther made two adjustments to correct the problem that he saw in the Latin. First, he eliminated the extraneous term that the Vulgate used in its translation of וְנַקֵּה לֹא יְנַקֶּה (*wənaqqēh lōʾ yənaqqeh*, "and [he] will certainly not acquit") as *et **mundans** non faciet innocentem* ("and **cleansing**, he will not make innocent").[69] Second, he more precisely accounted for the particular form in which the Hebrew term נקה (*nqh*) appears in this verse, in the *Piel binyan* (a particular Hebrew verb structure). In this construction, נקה (*nqh*) refers to a removal of guilt or exemption from punishment.[70] He thus translated the phrase in the 1532 *Deutsche Bibel* as *vnd lesst nichts vngestrafft* ("and leaves nothing unpunished"), with an emendation in 1545 to *fur welchem niemand vnschuldig ist* ("for which no one is innocent").[71] In this context, Luther's argument against the Vulgate's *mundans* is clear. But there was more behind that argument, which his biblical quotations reveal.

To support his translation, Luther cited two verses. The first was in Exodus, where the identical Hebrew phrase וְנַקֵּה לֹא יְנַקֶּה (*wənaqqēh lōʾ yənaqqeh*) appears. He explained, "The same thing that Moses said in Exod. 34[:7]: nothing with you is regarded innocent [*innocens est*] by him."[72] In this verse, in contrast to Nah. 1:3, the Vulgate omitted *mundans* in its rendering: *nullusque apud te per se innocens es* ("no one among you is [regarded] innocent by him"). Luther translated it as *vnd fur wilchem niemant vnschuldig ist* ("and for which no one is

---

[67] Nor does its equivalent appear in the LXX.

[68] "Et mundans non faciet innocentem. Hebraico more locutus est, nos aliter vertere debemus, nam participium mundans omittendum est." WA 13:374.23–24. LW 18:286.

[69] Lewis and Short also cite the "Levitical law of uncleanliness" in their definition of *mundo*. LS, 1175.

[70] In the *Qal binyan*, נקה (*nqh*) means "to empty" or "to be clean." BDB, 667. KB, 632. In his *Rudimenta* entry, Reuchlin included both nuances, "clean" and "judged innocent." *Rudimenta*, 334–5. See also Baruch A. Levine, *Numbers 1–20: A New Translation with Introduction and Commentary*, AB 4A (New Haven, CT: Yale University Press, 2008), 208. Gane quotes this in *Cult*, 342–3.

[71] WA DB 11.2:290.3 (1532); WA DB 11.2:291.3 (1545). Cf. WA DB 4:252a.15–23; WA DB 4:252b.15–25.

[72] "Idem est, quod Moses dixit Exod. 34: nullus apud te per se innocens est." WA 13:348.13 (this appears in the Zwickau text, thus is it not in the LW). The narrative of Ex. 34:7 describes God reiterating his justice as he gives Moses the new tablets of the ten commandments.

Inner-Biblical Interpretation in Luther's Hebrew Translation 157

innocent"), precisely as he translated it in the 1545 revision of Nah. 1:3.[73] This citation was straightforward. Luther's choice of Ex. 34:7 to support his rendering of Nah. 1:3 shows him finding the identical Hebrew phrase in another location, in a broadly similar context, and utilizing it to rationalize and confirm his translation decision.

But Luther cited a second verse, this one from the Psalms, in further support of his translation argument about Nahum. He explained in his lectures:

We have the same phrase in the Psalm [Ps. 49:8]: 'Redeeming, a brother will not redeem [*frater redimens non redimet*],' which we render in Latin as *frater non redimet* ('a brother will not redeem'). So here we translate it 'and he will not make innocent [*et non innocentabit*]' or 'he will make no one innocent [*neminem faciet innocentem*].'[74]

Yet despite his remarks, this phrase does not contain the same Hebrew term as appears in Nah. 1:3. Moreover, the meanings of the two terms are different. Luther's *Deutsche Bibel* translation reflects this, as does the Vulgate. He translated לֹא־פָדֹה יִפְדֶּה (*lōʾ-pādōh yipdeh*, "and [he] will certainly not ransom") in Ps. 49:8 as *Kan doch [eyn bruder] niemand erloesen* ("[A brother] can ransom no one"), which the Vulgate rendered similarly as *redimens non redimet* ("redeeming, he will not redeem").[75] Both make a distinction between פדה (*pdh*) in Ps. 49:8 as a ransom or payment (i. e. for the redemption of land or persons), and נקה (*nqh*) in Nah. 1:3 as an acquittal or a declaration of innocence. But the two terms do have some parallels. Both are used in discussions of ritual law in the Pentateuch.[76] And both appear, in their translations, in language and concepts which appear in theological formulas associated with justification – declared not guilty [i. e. נקה (*nqh*)] because of a price being payed for redemption [i. e. פדה (*pdh*)].[77] In this light, Luther's choice of לֹא־פָדֹה יִפְדֶּה (*lōʾ-pādōh yipdeh*) in

---

[73] See WA DB 8:308.7 (Ex. 34:7, 1523); WA DB 8:309.7 (Ex. 34:7, 1545). Cf. WA DB 3:268a.27–WA DB 3:269a.10; WA DB 3:269b.7–9. Luther's 1545 translation of Nah. 1:3 matches his translation of the same Hebrew in Ex. 34:7 exactly, *aside from orthographical differences and "vnd" not appearing in his rendering of Nah. 1:3*. His 1523 translation of Ex. 34:7 also matches his 1545 rendition of Ex. 34:7, aside from minor orthographical differences. Note also that his initial translation of Ex. 34:7 preceded the 1525 Nahum lectures by two years.

[74] "Eadem autem est phrasis in psalmo: frater redimens non redimet, quam orationem nos latine sic efferimus: frater non redimet. Ita hic: et non nocentabit sive neminem faciet innocentem." WA 13:374.25–27. LW 18:286. The footnote in the LW reads: "With the Zwickau manuscript, we have read *non innocentabit* for *non nocentabit*." I made the same adjustment, although I rendered the Latin "make innocent" instead of the LW's "clear the guilty."

[75] WA DB 10.1:256.8 (1524). "Release" is also a fair translation of *erlösen*.

[76] For more on the role of פדה (*pdh*) in the ritual law code of the Hebrew Bible, see TDOT 11:484–9. For more on נקה (*nqh*), see TDOT 9:553–63. Levine, Gane, etc. all address this also, as noted earlier.

[77] See the TDOT references in the previous footnote. Furthermore, while כָּפְרוֹ (*kāpərô*, "a ransom [for] him") appears in Ps. 49:8, Luther did not address it directly. כפר (*kpr*) is an extremely important, and disputed, term concerning atonement and purification in ancient Israelite ritual law. I do not address it here because Luther did not. For more on this term, see Jay Sklar, "Sin and Impurity" and Gane, *Cult*. The amount of scholarship on this issue is immense.

158   Chapter Four

Ps. 49:8 to support his translation of וְנַקֵּה לֹא יְנַקֶּה (wənaqqēh lōʾ yənaqqeh) in Nah. 1:3 seems to have a theological motivation behind it.

Luther's remarks concerning Nah. 1:3 in an earlier work, the *Resolutiones disputationum de indulgentiarum virtute* (1518), confirm this suspicion. His comments there reveal a clear association of נקה (*nqh*) with cultic purification and sacrifice, and, moreover, a theological motivation behind his argument in those later lectures. He wrote in the *Resolutiones*,

> David often experienced such consternation and trembling, as he confesses with groans in many different psalms. However, in this consternation is the beginning of salvation, for the 'fear of the Lord is the beginning of wisdom' [Ps. 111:10]. Nahum says that when the Lord cleanses [*mundans*], he makes no one innocent: 'His way is in whirlwind and storm, and the clouds are the dust of his feet' [Nah. 1:3 f.]. Here his lightnings flash, the earth sees it and is moved; here his arrows fly and stick fast, the voice of his thunder rolls, that is, rolls all around, the waters see and tremble; here, in short, God works a strange work in order that he may work his own work. This is true contrition of heart and humility of spirit, the sacrifice most pleasing to God. **Here is the sacrificial victim cut into pieces and the skin drawn and kindled for the burnt offering. And here (as they say) grace is infused.**[78]

Luther's graphic reference to sacrifice and cultic purification ritual evinces the unmistakable influence of the ritual law code of the Hebrew Bible on his interpretation of וְנַקֵּה לֹא יְנַקֶּה (wənaqqēh lōʾ yənaqqeh) in Nah. 1:3. His exegesis in the *Resolutiones* together with his lectures and translation of Nah. 1:3 shows that he did, in fact, view נקה (*nqh*) both in a ritual purification and a forensic context in the verse. Moreover, his remark in the *Resolutiones*, "Et hic infunditur ... gratia ('And here ... grace is infused')," reveals the theological impetus underlying his interpretation of the verse. With this statement, he clearly was identifying the text of Nah. 1:3 with justification, which he went on to make explicit later in the same tract:

> Actually man knows so little about his justification [*iustificationem*] that he believes he is very near condemnation, and he looks upon this, not as infusion of grace but as a dif-

---

[78] "Quam conturbationem et quassationem saepius expertus David multis eam in diversis psalmis confitetur gemitibus. In ista autem conturbatione [Ps. 111, 10.] incipit salus, Quia initium sapientiae timor domini. Hic dominus [Nah. 1, 3. f.] (ut ait Nahum i.) mundans neminem facit innocentem, et in tempestate et turbine viae eius, et nebulae pulvis pedum eius: hic allucent fulgura eius, videt et movetur terra: hic sagittae eius transeunt et infiguntur, et vox tonitrui eius volvitur, id est rotatur, vident aquae et timent: hic denique operatur opus alienum deus, ut operetur opus suum: haec est vera contricio cordis et humiliatio spiritus, gratissimum deo sacrificium: hic est mactata victima in membra conscissa et pelle detracta in holocaustum incensa. Et hic infunditur (ut vocant) gratia." WA 1:540:17–27. LW 31:99. Emphasis mine. When Luther cited Nah. 1:3 in the *Resolutiones*, he retained the term *mundans* which he argued against in the Nahum lectures. See the earlier remark in this chapter (in Case Study #1) concerning this phenomenon in the headings to Luther's lectures on the Minor Prophets. He was almost certainly simply paraphrasing or reciting the verse from memory, and thus did not pay strict attention to the presence of *mundans* as he quoted the verse.

fusion of the wrath of God upon him. Blessed is he, however, if he endures this *Anfechtung* [*tentationem*], for just when he thinks he has been consumed, he shall arise as the morning star.[79]

Luther's citation of Nah. 1:3 in the *Resolutiones* also shows how he construed God's wrath as part of the process of justification – that is, נקה (*nqh*) in Nah. 1:3. This is Luther's theology of *Anfechtung* [*tentatio*], which he made explicit in the *Resolutiones*. His remarks show how he saw Nah. 1:3 as a metaphorical representation of justification – and within the broader context of his quotation, of God making the individual holy by means of terror: *per terrorem enim sanctificat*.[80] Luther's graphic allusion to sacrificial ritual parallels similar extreme language that he frequently used to describe *Anfechtung* elsewhere in his texts.[81] Nah. 1:3 is distinctive as a particularly colorful example in his exegesis of the Minor Prophets. The picture that he painted of God's grace at work and of the operation of *Anfechtung* in the *Resolutiones* is one of the most lucid examples of such in his writings: whirlwind, storm, dust, clouds, earth moving, arrows, lightning, thunder, trembling, fear of God, wisdom, purification, a strange work, humbling, terror, wrath, hell, sacrificial victim cut into pieces, and *tentatio* (*Anfechtung*).[82] For Luther, this was "sanctification by terror."[83]

Thus while Luther's argument against the insertion of *mundans* in the Vulgate's translation of Nah. 1:3 had a clear basis as an issue of the literal accuracy of the Hebrew Bible, it also had a theological basis for his interpretation of the verse. It suggests that when he cited פדה (*pḏh*) in Ps. 49:8 to support his interpretation of נקה (*nqh*) in Nah. 1:3, it was at least in part this theological interpretation that he had in mind. Even though פדה (*pḏh*) and נקה (*nqh*) are distinct terms with distinct meanings (and surely Luther was aware of this), he still interpreted them as having some type of relative equivalence, by nature of both being inte-

---

[79] "Verum tunc adeo ignorat homo sui iustificationem, ut sese proximum putet damnationi, nec infusionem gratiae, sed effusionem irae dei super se hanc putet esse. Beatus tamen, si suffert hanc tentationem, quoniam cum se consumptum putaverit, orietur sicut Lucifer." WA 1:540:30–34. LW 31:100.

[80] *per terrorem enim sanctificat*: quoted earlier in this chapter from the 1513–15 *Dictata super Psalterium*. WA 4:246.23–26.

[81] He did so, for example, in his 1524 sermon that appears in the introduction to this study.

[82] These all come from the larger tract from which the above quotations are taken: WA 1:540.7–34.

[83] The question of how and whether to distinguish between sanctification and justification is beyond the present scope. For more on this subject, see Oswald Bayer, *Living By Faith: Justification and Sanctification* (Minneapolis: Fortress Press, 2017), especially p. 58. Here, Oswald advises: "Luther himself did not raise this question, since for him justification by faith alone meant that everything was said and done; living by faith is already the new life. When, nevertheless, Luther speaks about 'sanctification' he simply talks about justification. Justification and sanctification are not for him two separate acts that we can distinguish, as though sanctification follows after justification, and has to do so." This chapter follows Bayer's advice, given that its focus is solely on Luther's use of the terms in his texts.

gral pieces of the overall process of grace infusion which he interpreted וְנַקֵּה לֹא יְנַקֶּה (wənaqqēh lōʾ yənaqqeh) in Nah. 1:3 as describing.

Luther's interpretation of וְנַקֵּה לֹא יְנַקֶּה (wənaqqēh lōʾ yənaqqeh) in Nah. 1:3 and his use of biblical citations, both in his lectures on Nahum and in the *Resolutiones*, underscore the importance of inner-biblical interpretation for his translation of the Hebrew, and moreover the role of the ritual language of cultic purification in the Hebrew Bible in his translation of the verse. It shows how he situated both פדה (*pdh*) in Ps. 49:8 and נקה (*nqh*) in Nah. 1:3 (and ultimately Ex. 34:7) in the context of cultic purification ritual. Furthermore, it shows how he interwove nuances within each Hebrew term to inform both his German translation of Nah. 1:3, and his theological understanding of the process of justification. For him, it illustrated the encounter with God's wrath, the recognition of the ransom, and the acquittal – all as grace was infused.

Case Study #4:
Amos 8:1 כְּלוּב קָיִץ (kəlûḇ qāyiṣ, "basket of summer [fruit]") and Amos 8:2 בָּא הַקֵּץ (bāʾ haqqēṣ, "the end has come")

A final example of Luther's use of inner-biblical interpretation in his Hebrew translation can be found in Amos 8:1–2. Table 4.5 provides the parallel Hebrew, Latin, and German translations for Amos 8:1–2, as well as for a parallel reference in Jer. 5:27, which supports the analysis.

Table 4.5: Luther's translation of כְּלוּב קָיִץ (kəlûḇ qāyiṣ, "basket of summer [fruit]") and בָּא הַקֵּץ (bāʾ haqqēṣ, "the end has come"): Amos 8:1–2 and Jer. 5:27.

Verse	NASB	Hebrew Bible	Vulgate	*Deutsche Bibel*
Amos 8:1	Thus the Lord God showed me, and behold, there was a basket of summer fruit.	כֹּה הִרְאַנִי אֲדֹנָי יְהוִה וְהִנֵּה **כְּלוּב קָיִץ**	haec ostendit mihi Dominus Deus et ecce **uncinus pomorum**	Der HErr HERR zeigete mir ein gesichte, Vnd sihe, da stund **ein korb mit obs.** (1532) WA DB 11.2:244.1.
Amos 8:2	He said, "What do you see, Amos?" And I said, "A basket of summer fruit." Then the Lord said to me, "The end has come for My people Israel. I will spare them no longer.	וַיֹּאמֶר מָה־אַתָּה רֹאֶה עָמוֹס וָאֹמַר **כְּלוּב** קָיִץ וַיֹּאמֶר יְהוָה אֵלַי **בָּא הַקֵּץ** אֶל־עַמִּי יִשְׂרָאֵל לֹא־אוֹסִיף עוֹד עֲבוֹר לוֹ	et dixit quid tu vides Amos et dixi **uncinum pomorum** et dixit Dominus ad me **venit finis** super populum meum Israhel non adiciam ultra ut pertranseam eum	Vnd er sprach, Was sihestu Amos? Jch aber antwortet, **Ein korb mit obs**, Da sprach der HERR zu mir, **Das ende ist komen** vber mein volck, ich wil jm nicht mehr vbersehen. (1532) WA DB 11.2:244.2.

Verse	NASB	Hebrew Bible	Vulgate	*Deutsche Bibel*
Jer. 5:27	'Like a cage full of birds, So their houses are full of deceit; Therefore they have become great and rich.	כִּכְלוּב מָלֵא עוֹף כֵּן בָּתֵּיהֶם מְלֵאִים מִרְמָה עַל־כֵּן גָּדְלוּ וַיַּעֲשִׁירוּ	sicut decipula plena avibus sic domus eorum plenae dolo ideo magnificati sunt et ditati	Vnd jre heuser sind voller tuecke, **wie ein vogel baur voller lock vogel ist**, Daher werden sie gewaltig, reich vnd dick. (1532) WA DB 11.1:212.27.

Amos 8 relates a dark prophecy of destruction. It begins with a cryptic description of God showing Amos a basket of fruit, followed by God explaining the various terrors that he will inflict on Israel and the captivity that is to come. Amos 8:11 is perhaps the most poignant verse of the chapter, culminating in the removal of God's word from the people: "'Behold, days are coming,' declares the Lord God,/'When I will send a famine on the land,/Not a famine for bread or a thirst for water,/But rather for hearing the words of the Lord.'"[84]

In the lectures on Amos, Luther argued that כְּלוּב קָיִץ (*kəlûḇ qāyiṣ*, "a basket of summer [fruit]") in Amos 8:1 was a Hebrew pun that could not be properly translated into Latin or German. He discussed alternatives to the Vulgate's rendering of *uncinus pomorum* ("a hook of [i. e. for the purpose of obtaining] fruit"), which he translated in the German Bible as *ein korb mit obs* ("a basket with fruit").[85] He explained in the lectures on Amos:

A basket of summer fruit. Puns [*Allusiones*] in one language cannot be translated into another tongue. Here there is a pun [*allusio*] in Hebrew which we must circumscribe. The Hebrew word means a basket [*corbem*], a kind of cage [*caveam*], or a woven canister [*canistrum*], in which birds are kept and fattened. The interpretation is twofold. Some translate it as a basket of fruit [*canistrum fructuum*], others as a cage of birds [*caveam altilium*]. I like the latter translation, a place where birds are fattened for slaughter [*saginantur volucres, ut mactentur*]. The meaning, then, is this: the prophet seems to be saying: 'Because I say everything to this people in vain, destruction and death threaten it. Nothing else remains for it but a wretched death, because I see a cage filled with animals for slaughter [*caveam plenam animalibus mactandis*]. Whatever belongs to this people will be totally finished and devoured [*finietur et devorabitur totum*].' This we see clearly from what follows, where he explains that pun [*allusio*].[86]

---

[84] Amos 8:11 in the Hebrew Bible reads: הִנֵּה יָמִים בָּאִים נְאֻם אֲדֹנָי יְהוִה וְהִשְׁלַחְתִּי רָעָב בָּאָרֶץ לֹא־רָעָב לַלֶּחֶם וְלֹא־צָמָא לַמַּיִם כִּי אִם־לִשְׁמֹעַ אֵת דִּבְרֵי יְהוָה.

[85] WA DB 11.2:244.1.

[86] "Uncinus pomorum. Allusiones verborum in aliqua lingua non possunt in aliam linguam transfundi. Ita hic in hebraeo allusio quaedam vocum est, quam oportet nos circumloqui. Significat autem hebraeum vocabulum corbem vel caveam sive canistrum, in quo altilia retinentur et pascuntur. Bifariam autem interpretantur. Alii canistrum fructuum, alii caveam altilium vertunt, sed hoc posterius mihi placet, ubi scil. saginantur volucres, ut mactentur. Sententia ergo est q. sic d. propheta: Quia frustra omnia dicuntur huic populo, imminet ei devastatio et mactatio, nihil aliud eum manet quam miserabilis interitus, quia video caveam plenam animalibus mactandis: finietur et devorabitur totum quicquid est huius populi, sicut id patet clare ex

He went on to explain the second half of the Hebrew pun, which appears in Amos 8:2 as בָּא הַקֵּץ (bāʾ haqqēṣ, "the end has come"):

> *The end has come* [*Venit finis*] *upon My people Israel.* We have the same figure of speech in the Hebrew as if one were to say in German *Ich sehe ein Reis* and someone were to answer *Ich will dich recht reissen.* There is a big difference between *Reis* and *reissen*, yet there is a relation by paronomasia between the words. We have the same allusion [*allusio*] here, too, in the Hebrew, which we cannot render in the Latin language.[87]

The key to explaining the Hebrew pun – the assonance in the Hebrew קָיִץ (*qayiṣ* – pronounced "kāʾyēts") and קֵץ (*qēṣ* – pronounced "kāts") – was, in Luther's estimation, the motif of animal slaughter.[88] He saw the pun as a clear allusion to biblical sacrifice, which he exploited in his German translation through a literal rendering, to mimic the full expression of the Hebrew figure of speech.[89] That comprehensive meaning and the allusion in the pun would have been clearly obvious to the ancient Israelite reader; yet it was lacking in the Vulgate's translation of *uncinus* – i. e. "hook," instead of "basket" or "cage." Amos 8:1–2 differs from the previous case studies in that here, Luther made no explicit scriptural citation to support his association of the Hebrew term with ritual sacrifice in the Hebrew Bible. But that does not mean that there is no evidence of inner-biblical interpretation in his translation. This evidence appears in his translation of Jer. 5:27.

Parallel Reference: Jeremiah 5:27

The term כְּלוּב (*kəlûḇ*) appears in only three places in the Hebrew Bible: Amos 8:1, Amos 8:2, and Jer. 5:27. Because Luther did not explicitly cite Jer. 5:27 in

---

sequentibus, ubi allusio illa verborum exponitur." WA 13:196.26–WA 13:197.5. LW 18:179. Note the parallel to James 5:5 in the New Testament.

[87] "Venit finis super populum meum Israhel. Eadam forma verborum est in hebraeo ac si germanice dicas Ich ßehe eyn reis et respondeat aliquis Ich wil dich recht reissen. Longe aliud est frons seu ramus quam rapere et tamen agnominatio et affinitas vocum est. Eadem allusio hic quoque est in hebraeo, quae lingua latina non potest reddi." WA 13:197.6–10. LW 18:179–80.

[88] This is such an important type of vision in the Hebrew Bible that scholars have dubbed it an "assonance vision." In the entire Old Testament, it appears only in Amos 8:1–2 and Jer. 1:11–14. Christoph Levin, *Re-Reading the Scriptures: Essays on the Literary History of the Old Testament* (Tübingen: Mohr Siebeck, 2013), 227.

[89] On the requirement in the Torah that for any animal slaughtered, part of it needed to be given to God as a gift, see Lev. 17[:4]. There is great debate between R. Akiba and R. Ishmael on whether this represented a ban on nonsacrificial slaughter. Milgrom sides with Ishmael, taking the position that Lev. 17:3–4 is indeed such a ban. For more on this, see Jacob Milgrom, *Leviticus 17–22. A New Translation with Introduction and Commentary*, AB 3A (New York: Doubleday, 2000), 1452–63. In this light, the ancient Israelite reader would have made the connection between slaughter and ritual sacrifice in Jer. 5:27, and in the pun in Amos 8:1–2. In general, the mention of animal slaughter and sacrifice is extensive in the Torah, and it is beyond the present scope to note every occurrence.

his lectures on Amos, it is not possible to say with certainty whether he consulted it for his translation of Amos 8:1–2. But his comments in the lectures on Amos, which he used to support his translation there, were almost a verbatim quotation of Jer. 5:27: "a basket [*corbem*], a kind of cage [*caveam*], or a woven canister [*canistrum*], in which birds are kept and fattened." The text in Jeremiah reads: כִּכְלוּב מָלֵא עוֹף (*kiḵlûḇ mālēʾ ʿôp*, "as a cage full of bird[s]"). Moreover, it would be naive to hold a view of Luther translating each verse in isolation. The examples seen thus far show that this was never so. Furthermore, his consultation of Church Fathers, rabbinic sources, Hebrew lexicons, commentaries, and other translations is well-known and documented. It is thus difficult to believe that he was not aware of this text. Furthermore, it is difficult to believe that he did not have this parallel prophecy in mind as he made the allusion to animal slaughter and cultic purification ritual in support of his interpretation of the Hebrew pun in Amos.

Luther translated כִּכְלוּב מָלֵא עוֹף (*kiḵlûḇ mālēʾ ʿôp*) in Jer. 5:27 as *wie* **ein vogel baur** *voller lock vogel ist* ("as a birdcage is full of trapped birds"), in comparison to the Vulgate's rendering of *sicut* **decipula** *plena avibus* ("as a trap full of birds").[90] Both translations of כְּלוּב (*kəlûḇ*) are strikingly consistent with his exegesis of the same term in the lectures on Amos 8:1–2. Luther's interpretative liberty, in comparison to the restriction of the literal biblical text in Amos and Jeremiah, was in the identification of כְּלוּב (*kəlûḇ*) as a metaphor for animal sacrifice. That liberty, however, is not completely unique. Rashi, Kimhi, and the Targum all interpreted כְּלוּב (*kəlûḇ*) in Jer. 5:27 as a place where birds are fattened.[91] Luther's interpretation of כְּלוּב (*kəlûḇ*) was thus almost certainly influenced by the parallel scripture that he consulted, as well as quite likely secondary sources.

This example complements the others in this chapter by showing a different manner in which Luther exploited biblical quotations and citations to support his translation of a particular Hebrew text – not necessarily always through explicit mention of verses; but instead, either through allusion, or by employing the exact or almost exact same text as appears in another verse in the Bible. This is also a simpler example than the earlier case studies, where he often cited numerous scriptural passages to support his translation of the Hebrew, which

---

[90] WA DB 11.1:212.27. Cf. WA DB 4:90b.1–4.
[91] Jack R. Lundbom, *Jeremiah 1–20: A New Translation with Introduction and Commentary*, AB 21A (New York: Doubleday, 1999), 408. Lundbom disagrees, arguing that it indicates a net or a trap for birds. William McKane cites this interpretation of a birdcage and a place where birds are fattened [בית פטמא (*byt pṭmʾ*)], which appears in the Targum, Rashi, and Kimhi. McKane, *A Critical and Exegetical Commentary on Jeremiah*, ICC, vol. 1, rev. ed. (London: Bloomsbury, 2014), 133. Rashi's commentary reads: "כלוב – הוא מקום שמפטמין בו עופות; וכן תירגמו יונתן: 'כבית פיטמא'." English translation: "As a cage – It is a place where they fatten fowl; and thus Jonathan translated it: 'like a house of fattening.'" MG, *Jeremiah* [ספר ירמיהו], 40.

had many layers of meaning. Nevertheless, it mirrors these examples in that his translation was predicated on correcting a lexical issue with the Vulgate's rendering of a text in the Hebrew Bible. His allusion to, and exploitation of, Jer. 5:27 for his interpretation of Amos 8:1–2 moved his translation beyond that lexical issue, which ultimately enriched and filled out his interpretation of the Hebrew figure of speech and the link to ritual sacrifice.

Summary and Conclusion

Luther's use of biblical citations and quotations was an integral part of his method for translating the Minor Prophets from the Hebrew Bible. The manner in which he used these citations and quotations for his Hebrew translation was diverse. Many times, he used the same Hebrew term in one scriptural location to support a particular translation in another. At other times, he exploited a completely different Hebrew term to support his interpretation of another piece of Hebrew. That willingness to exploit and manipulate different Hebrew terminology than the source text which he was translating is an especially important hermeneutical tool that is not often mentioned by scholars, if at all. At still other times, he did not explicitly quote a passage, but instead made allusions to scriptural texts to support his translation. In addition, he often cited Bible verses in other tracts outside of his lectures and commentaries (for example, in the *Resolutiones*). These citations many times help to further illuminate his translation arguments concerning certain Hebrew terms and phrases.

Luther's translations also often reflect an interwoven, layered interpretation of Hebrew, incorporating numerous lexical elements and theological themes. He did not always rely on one citation in one place to justify a translation, but instead frequently quoted Hebrew terms in multiple texts for support. Moreover, while his arguments against the Vulgate were often based on questions of the lexical accuracy of its translations of the Hebrew Bible, his German translation and exegetical solutions many times went far beyond simply correcting the lexical problems. Instead, he used the Hebrew that he consulted to interweave much richer, multi-layered meanings into his German translation and his exegetical interpretations. Many of these quotations that made up the interwoven translation also influenced, and reflected – it is not always easy to tell the difference – his theological readings in many places of the Minor Prophets, particularly in terms of *Anfechtung*. In all, Luther's use of inner-biblical interpretation as part of his translation of the Minor Prophets show that his application of Origen's *scriptura sui ipsius interpres* maxim was much richer than may appear at first glance.

Chapter Five

Hebrew and Luther's Exploitation of the Mystical Tradition

For Luther, the Hebrew language had a spiritual dimension that could not be replicated by any other language, even by German. Like many in the humanist tradition of his time, he saw Hebrew as a mystical language. It was a unique medium both for the revelation of God and for direct interaction with God. A more robust understanding of the relationship between this mystical element of language and his translation work can provide new insights into a largely uncharted area of his Hebrew translation and exegesis, and further illuminate his theological thought in his academic mid-career. Moreover, it can offer greater insight into the history of sixteenth-century German Hebraic scholarship and the Jewish-Christian exegetical influences upon it.

Mysticism has further significance, though, because it was a key dimension of his theology of *Anfechtung*. In Luther's thought, *Anfechtung* was very much a strain of mysticism, albeit a distinctive breed in contrast to that of the more conventional medieval mystics. When discussing this mystical dimension of his *Anfechtung*, scholars often cite his reframing of the traditional tripartite rules *lectio, oratio,* and *contemplatio* as *oratio, meditatio,* and *tentatio [Anfechtung]*, viewing his key modification of that tradition as the replacement of *contemplatio* with *tentatio [Anfechtung]*.[1] Oswald Bayer, John Maxfield, and many others argue that with this substitution, Luther did not discard monastic contemplation, so much as he redefined it.[2] One of the major incarnations of this redefinition was his attribution of the wrath of God to spiritual contemplation. In Luther's consideration of the Minor Prophets, this ascription frequently occurred under the influence of the Hebrew which he consulted.

---

[1] Oswald Bayer, *Theology the Lutheran Way*, ed. and trans. Jeffrey G. Silcock and Mark C. Mattes (Minneapolis: Fortress Press, 2017), 22. See also Oswald Bayer, "Oratio, Meditatio, Tentatio: Eine Besinnung auf Luthers Theologieverständnis," *Lutherjahrbuch* 55 (1988): 7–59.

[2] Bayer, *Theology the Lutheran Way*, 22. John A. Maxfield, *Luther's Lectures on Genesis and the Formation of Evangelical Identity* (Kirksville, MO: Truman State University Press, 2008), 13–15, 73–75. Others make similar points. See Volker Leppin, "Luther's Roots in Monastic-Mystical Piety," in *The Oxford Handbook of Martin Luther's Theology*, ed. Robert Kolb, Irene Dingel, and L'ubomír Batka (Oxford: Oxford University Press, 2014), 49–61; and Volker Leppin, "Luther's Transformation of Medieval Thought: Continuity and Discontinuity," in *The Oxford Handbook of Martin Luther's Theology*, ed. Robert Kolb, Irene Dingel, and L'ubomír Batka (Oxford: Oxford University Press, 2014), 115–24.

While scholars have paid increasing attention to the role of the mystical tradition in Luther's theological thought in recent decades, little attention has been given to the relationship between Hebrew and mysticism in his theology and, more importantly, in his Bible translation. Aside from some cursory glances at his comments concerning the meaning of the Tetragrammaton, and part of the broader discussions of his Hebrew translation, it is an almost untouched subject, especially outside of the Psalms.[3] Luther's consideration of the Minor Prophets, however, shows that the Hebrew language did have an impact on his employment of the mystical tradition. This chapter will examine a number of these instances and elucidate this aspect of the role of Hebrew in his Bible translation and interpretation. It will demonstrate how a late medieval/early modern Christian Hebraist drew upon the mystical tradition in his Hebrew translation. While he did not utilize it in the same manner as some of the other mystics, such as Kabbalists or Dionysian mystical theologians, it still played an important role in his Bible translation and exegesis. The examples in this chapter will show that there was a distinct influence of the Hebrew language on Luther's exploitation of the mystical tradition in various places in the Minor Prophets. Moreover, this chapter will show that this influence consequentially permeated his interpretation of *Anfechtung* at various points. This insight concerning Luther's Hebrew contributes to the scholarly understanding of his diverse Bible translation methodology as well as the role of Hebrew in his translation and in his theological thought.

The Mystical Tradition in Context[4]

Luther's engagement with the mystical tradition had its roots in the Hebrew, Greek, and Latin scriptures, Greek philosophical thought, rabbinic Judaism, and early Christianity.[5] Greek philosophers such as Plato, Philo, Plotinus, Pro-

---

[3] Luther mentioned the Tetragrammaton in numerous places; for example, in the *Operationes in Psalmos*, addressing Ps. 5:12 [WA 5:184.4–WA 5:196.16; the main mentions of the Tetragrammaton end on p. 187]; in his lectures on Mic. 2:13 [WA 13:273.24–27]; and in *Vom Schem Hamphoras und vom Geschlecht Christi* (1543) [WA 53:573–649]. For more on this subject, see Robert J. Wilkinson, *Tetragrammaton: Western Christians and the Hebrew Name of God: From the Beginnings to the Seventeenth Century* (Leiden: Brill, 2015), 385–9; and Brooks Schramm, "On the *Schem Hamphoras* and on the Lineage of Christ, 1543," in *The Annotated Luther. Vol. 5: Christian Life in the World*, ed. Hans J. Hillerbrand (Minneapolis: Fortress Press, 2017), 609–66. Scholars obviously make the link between Luther and others such as Reuchlin who drew upon the mystical tradition. But little attention is given to Luther's actual translation work and Hebrew mysticism.

[4] "Mystical tradition" is used in this chapter as a general label to refer to all those traditions upon which Luther and his team explicitly and implicitly drew, rather than referring to a single tradition.

[5] Bernard McGinn, *The Presence of God: A History of Western Christian Mysticism.*

clus, and even Aristotle had integral roles in the evolution of Jewish and Christian mystisicm.[6] The influence of Greek philosophy on mystical discourse carried over to the rabbinic thinkers and Christian Church Fathers who influenced Luther and those in his translation circle. Christian mysticism's distinct footprint is found in Eastern Church Fathers and thinkers such as Origen, Evagrius, Pseudo-Dionysius (Dionysius the Areopagite), Gregory of Nyssa, Gregory Palamas, and Macarius.[7] Likewise, it influenced the thought and texts of those in the Western Church, including Augustine, Ambrose, Jerome, Bernard, and Cassian.[8] The influence of the Fathers on Luther's thought is unmistakable. They were the basis of much of his scholastic education, and he cited them regularly in his texts.

It would be easy to dismiss Jewish mysticism as irrelevant for Luther, but this would be a mistake. Not only did Luther mention Jewish mystical concepts and authors in his texts, he clearly drew on many other texts and authors who themselves drew on that tradition of Jewish mysticism.[9] This Jewish mystical tradition includes the Merkabah tradition and the Zoharic tradition (and thus the authors of the Sefer Yetsira, Pirkei Heikhalot, and the Zohar), the Hekhaloth Books, and individuals including Moses de León (Moshe ben Shem-Tov), Akiva, Saadia Gaon, Moses Nahmanides, and even Rashi.[10] A clear line of in-

---

Vol. 1: The Foundations of Mysticism (London: SCM Press, 1992), 3. Bernard McGinn, "Mysticism and the Reformation: A Brief Survey," *Acta Theologica* 35 (2015): 50–56. Volker Leppin examines this subject comprehensively in *Die fremde Reformation: Luthers mystische Wurzeln* (München: C. H. Beck, 2016).

[6] McGinn, *Foundations*, especially pp. 4–5, 23–61, 172, 198–200, 305.

[7] For more on these individuals, see: Kallistos Ware, *The Orthodox Way* (Crestwood, NY: St. Vladimir's Seminary Press, 1995); Brock Bingaman and Bradley Nassif, eds., *The Philokalia: A Classic Text of Orthodox Spirituality* (Oxford: Oxford University Press, 2012); John Anthony McGuckin, ed., *The Encyclopedia of Eastern Orthodox Christianity*, 2 vols. (Oxford: Wiley-Blackwell, 2011); Louise Nelstrop and Simon D. Podmore, eds., *Christian Mysticism and Incarnational Theology: Between Transcendence and Immanence* (Burlington, VT: Ashgate, 2013); and McGinn, *Foundations*, 108–30, 139–182.

[8] See McGinn, *Foundations*, 202–62; and Bernard McGinn, *The Presence of God: A History of Western Christian Mysticism. Vol. 2: The Growth of Mysticism* (New York: The Crossroad Publishing Company, 1999), 158–224.

[9] On Luther's mention of Jewish mystical authors, subjects, and texts, see for example his remarks on Kabbalah: WA 3:372.8–27; WA 40.1:452a.6; WA 2:491.7–9; and WA 55.2:854, 935. Cf. his remarks on Akiva (Akiba): WA 53:495.18–WA 53:496.15. See also Schramm, "On the *Schem Hamphoras*," 610–1, 616–9 on how Luther learned about the Jewish mystical tradition (specifically the text *Toledot Yeshu*, ca. 500 CE) through the fourteenth century monk Porchetus Salvaticus, and from the Jewish convert Antony Margaritha. Cf. WA 53:413; WA 53:569.13.

[10] See McGinn, *Foundations*, 9–22. On the Merkabah tradition and the Zoharic tradition, and the authors of the Sefer Yetsira, Pirkei Heikhalot, and the Zohar, see David R. Blumenthal, *Understanding Jewish Mysticism: A Source Reader. The Merkabah Tradition and the Zoharic Tradition* (New York: KTAV, 1978). On the Hekhaloth Books, see Gershom Scholem, *Jewish Gnosticism, Merkabah Mysticism, and Talmudic Tradition*, 2nd ed. (New York: Jewish Theological Seminary of America, 1965), especially p. 17 concerning Rashi following in the tra-

fluence can often be traced between Jewish and Christian mysticism, not to mention Christian Hebraists and humanists who drew on that mystical tradition. From Rashi to Lyra to Giovanni Pico della Mirandola to Reuchlin to Thomas Müntzer and Luther, this influence is unequivocal.[11] Lefèvre and Reuchlin are especially important for considering Luther's use of the mystical tradition, as he drew extensively on these two, and explicitly mentioned them in his reflections on Hebrew translations.[12] Moreover, as shown in Ch. 1 of this study, Luther's Hebrew translation team consulted the Bomberg Rabbinic Bibles that contain the Targum and Jewish commentaries which drew upon Jewish mysticism.

The contention that Jewish and Christian mysticism influenced each other should come as no surprise, as the themes and concepts which appear in the texts of Christian and Jewish mystics often overlap.[13] Moreover, Jews and Jewish-Christian converts who taught Christian Hebraists brought that Jewish mystical tradition with them, and the exchange of ideas between Jews and Christians, even if often polemical, inevitably led to a cross-pollination of their thought.[14]

Perhaps the most crucial contextual influence on Luther's mysticism was that of monastic mysticism. His experience living as a friar and thorough integration within a monastic-mystic environment, beginning in 1505, clearly played a critical role in his mystical bent.[15] McGinn argues that particularly in this monastic context, earlier mystical thought influenced the mystical thought of later periods in what he describes as a "layering effect."[16] He explains,

> It was through the institution of monasticism that the mystical theories found in Origen, and those of Augustine and other early Latin mystics, reached into the centuries to come. These spiritual systems, whether or not they were created specifically for a monastic context, soon became monastic.[17]

---

dition of the Merkabah mystics. Ch. 1 of this study discusses Rashi's influence upon Lyra and other Christian authors and Hebraists.

[11] See Hailperin, *Rashi and the Christian Scholars*.

[12] Reuchlin published several works that drew upon Jewish mysticism. See Posset, *Johann Reuchlin*, 625–712 (Ch. 13); and Price, *Johannes Reuchlin*, 81–94. On Luther's familiarity with Reuchlin's *De arte cabalistica* (Hagenau, 1517), see WA BR 1:149–51 [§ 61] (Luther's Feb. 22, 1518 letter to Spalatin). On Luther's familiarity with Reuchlin's *De verbo mirifico* (Basel, 1494), see WA 4:337.12 Note 1; WA 55.1:373 (notes); and WA 55.2:343 (notes). On Lefèvre and mysticism, see Vanderjagt, "*Ad fontes!*" 174–9.

[13] See McGinn, *Foundations*, 22, 131. See also Bernard McGinn, "Selective Affinities. Reflections on Jewish and Christian Mystical Exegesis," in *Creation and Re-Creation in Jewish Thought: Festschrift in Honor of Joseph Dan on the Occasion of his Seventieth Birthday*, ed. Rachel Elior and Peter Schäfer (Tübingen: Mohr Siebeck, 2005), 85–101.

[14] For more on this subject, see Eric Zimmer, "Jewish and Christian Hebraist Collaboration in Sixteenth-Century Germany," *Jewish Quarterly Review* 71 (1980): 69–88.

[15] Leppin, "Luther's Roots in Monastic-Mystical Piety," 50.

[16] McGinn, *Foundations*, 131.

[17] McGinn, *Foundations*, 131.

It was largely through this amalgamated framework that Luther encountered mystical authors and texts, and with which his Hebrew translation and exegetical activity eventually had to contend. His mediation and citation of the monastic mystics who preceded him are well-documented. He was significantly influenced by Jean Gerson, Bernard, Bonaventure, and Gabriel Biel.[18] His mentor and confessor Johann von Staupitz also played a significant role in his encounters with mystical authors within his monastic existence.[19]

Monastic mysticism especially influenced the specific breed of German mysticism which formed Luther's most immediate context, and with which scholarship most starkly associates him: the medieval German mystics of the "upper-Rhenish circle," attributed specifically to Meister Eckhart, Heinrich Seuse (Suso), and Johannes Tauler.[20] Of these, it would be difficult to argue that any had greater importance for him than the anonymous *Theologia Deutsch* and the sermons of Johannes Tauler (of Strasbourg).[21] This is, in part, clear from the

---

[18] Volker Leppin, "Mysticism in Martin Luther's Development and Thoughts," in *Oxford Research Encyclopedia of Religion* (Oxford: Oxford University Press, 2016), DOI: 10.1093/acrefore/9780199340378.013.260. Leppin, "Luther's Roots in Monastic-Mystical Piety." Erich Vogelsang, "Luther und die Mystik," *Luther-Jahrbuch* 19 (1937): 32–54, with a list of influences on pp. 32–33. Heiko A. Oberman, "Gabriel Biel and Late Medieval Mysticism," *Church History* 30 (1961): 259–87. Heiko A. Oberman, *The Harvest of Medieval Theology: Gabriel Biel and Late Medieval Nominalism* (Cambridge, MA: Harvard University Press, 1963). Theo Bell, *Divus Bernhardus: Bernhard von Clairvaux in Martin Luthers Schriften* (Mainz: Philipp von Zabern, 1993). Ronald K. Rittgers, *The Reformation of Suffering: Pastoral Theology and Lay Piety in Late Medieval and Early Modern Germany* (New York: Oxford University Press, 2012), 97.

[19] David C. Steinmetz, "Religious Ecstasy in Staupitz and the Young Luther," *The Sixteenth Century Journal* 11 (1980), 23–38. Leppin, *Die fremde Reformation*, 11–22. Volker Leppin, "Luther: A Mystic," *Dialog: A Journal of Theology* 56 (2017): 140–4. Volker Leppin, *Martin Luther: A Late Medieval Life*, trans. Rhys Bezzant and Karen Roe (Grand Rapids, MI: Baker Academic, 2017), 22–25. Volker Leppin, *Martin Luther* (Darmstadt: Wissenschaftliche Buchgesellschaft, 2006), 72–89. Ernst Wolf, "Johannes von Staupitz und die theologischen Anfänge Luthers," *Luther-Jahrbuch* 11 (1929): 43–86.

[20] Leppin, "Luther's Roots in Monastic-Mystical Piety." Vogelsang, "Luther und die Mystik," 32–54, especially pp. 41–43. Ozment cautions against focusing solely on the continuity, and ignoring the discontinuity, between Luther and German mysticism; Steven E. Ozment, *The Age of Reform 1250–1550: An Intellectual and Religious History of Late Medieval and Reformation Europe* (New Haven, CT: Yale University Press, 1980), 239–44. Cf. Steven E. Ozment, "Eckhart and Luther: German Mysticism and Protestantism," *The Thomist* 42 (1978): 259–80; see especially Bornkamm's list of differences between Eckhart's and Luther's theology, which Ozment includes on pp. 263–5. Cf. Leppin, "Luther's Transformation of Medieval Thought."

[21] Luther originally published an incomplete manuscript of the *Theologia Deutsch* in December, 1516, entitled *Eyn geystlich edles Buchleynn*. He subsequently published a complete copy on June 4, 1518, entitled *Ein deutsch Theologia*. A reprint was published later that year (September), entitled *Theologia Deutsch*, as it was known from then on. For the English translation, see *The Theologia Germanica of Martin Luther*, trans. Bengt Hoffman (London: SPCK, 1980). Hoffman's translation is based on Luther's 1518 edition. See WA 1:152–3 for the introduction and Luther's preface to the 1516 edition, and WA 1:375–9 [LW 31:73–74] for the introduction and Luther's preface to the 1518 edition. The current definitive critical edition,

preface to the 1518 edition of the *Theologia Deutsch*, where he wrote, "And that I might boast according to my old fool, after the Bible and St. Augustine, there has not appeared a book from which I have learned, and want to learn more, what God, Christ, man, and all things are."[22]

What was "Mysticism" for Luther?

Whether Luther was a "mystic," and moreover what role, if any, mysticism played in his theology and translation is a matter of dispute. He never fully defined it in his writings, and made varying statements concerning it – some positive, some negative.[23] Much of the debate is premised on how one understands the term mysticism, and more importantly how Luther understood it in his own late medieval, early modern context. There is no agreed definition for mysticism. The term itself invokes a myriad of connotations, often conflicting and anachronistic. Even oft-identified mystics dating back to Akiva, Origen, Dionysius the Areopagite, Evagrius Ponticus, and Saadia Gaon do not share a standard or agreed-upon delineation of mystical theology. Thus, one should not be surprised that this task is difficult in the case of Luther.[24]

---

based on numerous manuscripts in addition to Luther's 1516 and 1518 editions, is *Der Franckforter (Theologia Deutsch): Kritische Textausgabe*, trans. Wolfgang von Hinten (München: Artemis, 1982). An English translation, based on von Hinten, is *Theologia Deutsch-theologia Germanica. The Book of the Perfect Life*, trans. David Blamires (Walnut Creek, CA: AltaMira Press, 2003).

Concerning Tauler, Luther's copies of Tauler's sermons with Luther's marginal notes appear in the WA as *Luthers Randbemerkungen zu Taulers Predigten*, WA 9:95–104. For more on this subject, see Leppin, *Die fremde Reformation*, especially pp. 22–26; and Leppin, "Luther's Roots in Monastic-Mystical Piety." Steven E. Ozment compares Luther, Tauler, and Gerson in *Homo Spiritualis: A Comparative Study of the Anthropology of Johannes Tauler, Jean Gerson and Martin Luther (1509–16) in the Context of Their Theological Thought* (Leiden: Brill, 1969).

[22] "Und das ich nach meynem alten narren rueme, ist myr nehst der Biblien und S. Augustino nit vorkummen eyn buch, dar auß ich mehr erlernet hab und will, was got, Christus, mensch und alle ding seyn." WA 1:378.21–23.

[23] For example, see *De captivitate Babylonica ecclesiae praeludium* [*The Babylonian Captivity of the Church*] (1520), WA 6:484–573 [LW 36:3–127], especially WA 6:561.34–WA 6:562.14 [LW 36:109]. Cf. WA 3:372.8–27.

[24] Bengt Hägglund and Oberman suggest that the concept of *mysticism* can be useful when discussing Luther's thought, but one must accept that it can never be definitively or satisfactorily defined. Bengt Hägglund, "Luther und die Mystik," in *Kirche, Mystik, Heiligung und das Natürliche bei Luther. Vorträge des Dritten Internationalen Kongresses für Lutherforschung*, ed. Ivar Asheim (Göttingen: Vandenhoeck & Ruprecht, 1967), 87–88, referencing Oberman's "Hauptreferat" at the Third International Congress for Luther Research in Järvenpää (1956). This appears in the same volume, at: Heiko A. Oberman, "Simul gemitus et raptus: Luther und die Mystik," in *Kirche, Mystik, Heiligung und das Natürliche bei Luther. Vorträge des Dritten Internationalen Kongresses für Lutherforschung*, ed. Ivar Asheim (Göttingen: Vandenhoeck & Ruprecht, 1967), 40. Oberman's essay has been reprinted in multiple English books. See also Berndt Hamm, "Wie mystisch war der Glaube Luthers?" in *Gottes Nähe un-*

In an effort to formulate an accurate definition of mysticism, many discriminate between mysticism and mystical theology – mysticism indicating personal experience, and mystical theology representing the interpretation of those experiences. However, Bernard McGinn argues that stark distinctions between mysticism and mystical theology lead to a "misconception that has plagued the modern study of mysticism."[25] He argues that

the fact that the term 'mystical theology' antedated the coining of the term 'mysticism' by over a millennium points us in the right direction for appreciating the complex and unbreakable bonds between mysticism conceived of as a religious way of life and mystical theology.[26]

He offers two points of guidance for theological discourse concerning mysticism: first, that mysticism needs to be understood contextually; and second, that the *mystical text* and its place in the Christian [and Jewish] tradition, rather than *mystical experience*, should be the primary objects of study.[27] Volker Leppin offers similar guidance: "There, where authors are being read productively on the subject of transcendence breaking into the present, people are participating in mystical discourse."[28]

This chapter will follow McGinn's and Leppin's lead and will focus on Luther's explicit use of the mystical tradition and concepts in his Bible interpretation, rather than on his own accounts of mystical experience. It will operate under the understanding of *mysticism* and the tradition associated with it as the mystical texts, discourse, terminology, and conceptions from the ancient Greek, Jewish, and Christian traditions which Luther drew upon.[29] While Luther frequently argued for the importance and even the necessity of experience for a proper understanding of scripture, it is the terminology and concepts from the mystical tradition which provide the most cogent evidence of his drawing on that tradition for his Bible translation and exegesis.[30] Moreover,

---

mittelbar erfahren: Mystik im Mittelalter und bei Martin Luther, ed. Berndt Hamm and Volker Leppin (Tübingen: Mohr Siebeck, 2007), especially pp. 242–4.

[25] McGinn, *Foundations*, xiii–xiv.
[26] McGinn, *Foundations*, xiv.
[27] McGinn, *Foundations*, xv.
[28] Leppin, "Luther's Roots in Monastic-Mystical Piety," 49.
[29] "Mystical texts" refers to texts which address mysticism, mystical theology, and mystical discourse. It is beyond the scope of this study to further define every text which should be considered mystical, and what those parameters should be. Ultimately, even the identification of a mystical text is subjective, and thus it is unlikely that every reader will agree upon which texts should fall under the umbrella of the "mystical tradition." See also Johannes Altenstaig's *Vocabularius theologie* [Altenstaig, *Vocabularius theologie* (Hagenau: Henricus Gran for Ioannis Rynman, 1517)], a definitive late medieval theological dictionary, which includes mystical terminology. This work is cited by many scholars, including Oberman, "Simul gemitus et raptus," 45 [see the entire article for the broader subject of Luther and mysticism]; and Steinmetz, "Religious Ecstasy in Staupitz and the Young Luther," 25–26.
[30] Scholars see Luther's emphasis on experiential theology as a defining trait of his media-

Figure 5.1: Der Prophet Jona ausgelegt durch Martin Luther, Martin Luther [Erffurdt: Melchior Sachssen, 1526] (*source:* British and Foreign Bible Society (BFBS), Cambridge University Library, Classmark BSS.228.B26.2).

these provide the most unadulterated illustration of the influence of Hebrew on his manipulation of the mystical tradition in specific instances. This chapter will examine specific instances where Luther, as part of his translation of the Minor Prophets, (1) appropriated specific elements from the mystical tradition, and (2) modified that mystical tradition in his interpretation, linking it to the wrath of God, and many times even more specifically to *Anfechtung*. How he accomplished this was largely shaped by the Hebrew that he consulted.

Part I: Jonah as a Case Study

The book of Jonah is, among all of the Minor Prophets, the quintessential example of Luther's exploitation of the mystical tradition in his translation and exegesis. It was a particularly special book for him. He viewed the trials faced by Jonah as unique among all the figures in the Bible. Moreover, he identified with Jonah on a deep personal level. He said in his lectures concerning the assault from God on Jonah, "This was truly a strange and serious *Anfechtung* [*tentatio*], so much so that I can hardly imagine a stranger one. In fact, I would not easily believe such things if the Holy Spirit had not written them."[31] The first part of this chapter is therefore a case study of the influence of Hebrew on Luther's use of the mystical tradition in his interpretation of the Book of Jonah. Table 5.1 shows the parallel Hebrew, Latin, and German translations for Jon. 1:2, 1:4, 2:4, and 2:5, as well as the biblical citations that Luther adduced to support his interpretations.

Conscientia ("Conscience") and Ascent

One of the key attestations to the influence of Hebrew on Luther's employment of the mystical tradition in the Book of Jonah appears in his manipulation of *conscientia* ("conscience") as part of his interpretation of the text. *Conscientia* has a critical place in early and medieval Jewish and Christian mystical traditions, themselves influenced by Platonic and Aristotelian thought. While Platonic and Aristotelian texts form the basis for many of the medieval discussions of *conscientia*, Plato and Aristotle never used the term.[32] Much of the specific language that Luther drew upon seems to have first appeared in Jerome.[33]

---

tion of the mystical tradition, and moreover, of his theology of *Anfechtung*. See Hovland, "An Examination," 18, 30, 204, 259, 320–1; Beintker, *Die Überwindung*, 22–23; Bornkamm, *Luther und das Alte Testament*, 52–54; Robert Kolb, *Martin Luther: Confessor of the Faith*, (New York: Oxford University Press, 2009), 28; and Rittgers, *Reformation of Suffering*, 93, 97–8, 108.

[31] "Mira certe fuit haec tentatio et gravis, ut mihi vix aliqua videatur admirabilior et nisi spiritus sanctus scripsisset talia, non facile crederem." WA 13:248.34–36. LW 19:16.

[32] Per Douglas C. Langston, *From Bonaventure to MacIntyre. Conscience and other Virtues* (University Park, PA: Pennsylvania State University Press, 2001), 9.

[33] *Synteresis* is also spelled *synderesis*, among other variations. For more on this sub-

Table 5.1: Jonah case study: Jon. 1:2, 1:4, 2:4, 2:5; Ps. 31:23, 42:8, and 93:4.³⁴

Verse	NASB	Hebrew Bible	Vulgate	*Deutsche Bibel*
Jon. 1:2	"Arise, go to Nineveh the great city and cry against it, for their wickedness has come up before Me."	קוּם לֵךְ אֶל-נִינְוֵה הָעִיר הַגְּדוֹלָה וּקְרָא עָלֶיהָ **כִּי-עָלְתָה** רָעָתָם לְפָנָי	surge vade in Nineven civitatem grandem et praedica in ea **quia ascendit** malitia eius coram me	Mach dich auff, vnd gehe jnn die grosse stad Nineue, vnd predige drinnen, **Denn** jre bosheit **ist erauff komen** fur mich. (1532) WA DB 11.2:262.2.
Jon. 1:4	The Lord hurled a great wind on the sea and there was a great storm on the sea so that the ship was about to break up.	וַיהוָה **הֵטִיל** רוּחַ-גְּדוֹלָה **אֶל-הַיָּם וַיְהִי** סַעַר-גָּדוֹל בַּיָּם וְהָאֳנִיָּה חִשְּׁבָה לְהִשָּׁבֵר	Dominus autem **misit** ventum magnum **in mari et facta est** tempestas magna in mari et navis periclitabatur conteri	Da **lies** der HERR einen grossen wind **auffs** meer komen, vnd **hub sich** ein gros vngewitter auff dem meer, das man meinet, das schiff wuerde zubrechen. (1532) WA DB 11.2:262.4.
Jon. 2:4	"For You had cast me into the deep, Into the heart of the seas, And the current engulfed me. All Your breakers and billows passed over me.	וַתַּשְׁלִיכֵנִי מְצוּלָה בִּלְבַב יַמִּים וְנָהָר יְסֹבְבֵנִי **כָּל-מִשְׁבָּרֶיךָ וְגַלֶּיךָ** עָלַי עָבָרוּ	et proiecisti me in profundum in corde maris et flumen circumdedit me **omnes gurgites tui et fluctus tui** super me transierunt	Du warffest mich jnn die tieffe mitten im meer, das die flut mich vmbgaben, **Alle deine wogen vnd wellen** giengen vber mich. (1532) WA DB 11.2:264.4.
Jon. 2:5	"So I said, 'I have been expelled from Your sight. Nevertheless I will look again toward Your holy temple.'	**וַאֲנִי אָמַרְתִּי נִגְרַשְׁתִּי מִנֶּגֶד** עֵינֶיךָ אַךְ אוֹסִיף לְהַבִּיט אֶל-הֵיכַל קָדְשֶׁךָ	et ego dixi **abiectus sum a conspectu oculorum tuorum** verumtamen rursus videbo templum sanctum tuum	Das ich gedacht, ich were von deinen augen verstossen, Jch wuerde deinen heiligen tempel **nicht** mehr sehen. (1532) WA DB 11.2:264.5.

---

ject, see Ozment, *Homo Spiritualis*; and Michael G. Baylor, *Action and Person: Conscience in Late Scholasticism and the Young Luther* (Leiden: E. J. Brill, 1977). Many scholars believe that Jerome equated *conscientia* and *synteresis*, and that the distinction that many individuals made between conscience and soul, which they based on medieval manuscripts of Jerome's commentary, was actually based on a corruption of the Greek. For more on this subject, see Douglas Kries, "Origen, Plato, and Conscience (*Synderesis*) in Jerome's Ezekiel Commentary," *Traditio* 57 (2002): 67–83.

³⁴ Luther's later revisions of Ps. 42:8 have minor orthographical differences: WA DB 10.1:237a.8 (1531); WA DB 10.1:237b.8 (1545). Cf. WA DB 3:41.26–34; WA DB 3:540a.30–31. Luther's 1545 revision of Ps. 93:4 matches his 1531 rendering, aside from minor orthographical differences: WA DB 10.1:413b.4. Cf. WA DB 3:118.31–WA DB 3:119.8.

Verse	NASB	Hebrew Bible	Vulgate	Deutsche Bibel
Ps. 31:23	As for me, I said in my alarm, "I am cut off from before Your eyes"; Nevertheless You heard the voice of my supplications When I cried to You.	וַאֲנִי אָמַרְתִּי בְחָפְזִי נִגְרַזְתִּי מִנֶּגֶד עֵינֶיךָ אָכֵן שָׁמַעְתָּ קוֹל תַּחֲנוּנַי בְּשַׁוְּעִי אֵלֶיךָ	ego autem dixi **in excessu mentis meae** proiectus sum a facie oculorum tuorum ideo exaudisti vocem orationis meae dum clamarem ad te	Jch aber sprach **ynn meynem zagen**, ich byn von deynen augen verstossen, Darumb hastu meynes flehens stym gehoeret, da ich zu dyr schrey. (1524) WA DB 10.1:194.23.
Ps. 42:8	Deep calls to deep at the sound of Your waterfalls; All Your breakers and Your waves have rolled over me.	תְּהוֹם-אֶל-תְּהוֹם קוֹרֵא לְקוֹל צִנּוֹרֶיךָ כָּל-מִשְׁבָּרֶיךָ וְגַלֶּיךָ עָלַי עָבָרוּ	abyssus abyssum vocat in voce cataractarum tuarum **omnes gurgites tui et fluctus tui** super me transierunt	Eyn tieffe rufft der andern, vber dem brausen deyner flut, **alle deyne wasser woge vnd wellen** gehen vber mich. (1524) WA DB 10.1:236.8.
Ps. 93:4	More than the sounds of many waters, Than the mighty breakers of the sea, The Lord on high is mighty.	מִקֹּלוֹת מַיִם רַבִּים אַדִּירִים מִשְׁבְּרֵי-יָם אַדִּיר בַּמָּרוֹם יְהוָה	a vocibus aquarum multarum. Mirabiles **elationes maris**: mirabiles in altis dominus.	**Die wasser flut** sind mechtig von dem braussen grosser wasser, Der HERR ist mechtig ynn der hoehe. (1524) WA DB 10.1:412.4. **Die wasserwogen jm meer** sind gros, vnd brausen grewlich, Der HERR aber ist noch groesser jnn der hoehe. (1531) WA DB 10.1:413a.4.

Paul Strohm argues that, in fact, "The crucial event for the Christian appropriation of conscience was Jerome's choice of the Latin *conscientia* in his late 4th-century translation of the New Testament from Greek to Latin."[35] That language subsequently surfaced in the texts of Peter Lombard, Abelard, Bonaventure, and Biel; as well as the "upper-Rhenish circle" of German mysticism attributed specifically to Meister Eckhart, Seuse, and Tauler.[36] Similar language

---

[35] Paul Strohm, *Conscience: A Very Short Introduction* (New York: Oxford University Press, 2011), 8. Also see Kries, "Origen, Plato, and Conscience," 67–83.

[36] These authors obviously use similar term(s) to *conscientia* in their own languages, not always the term *conscientia*.

also appeared in early and medieval Jewish mystical texts, in both the Merkabah tradition and Zoharic tradition.[37]

In mystical discourse, *conscientia* is intimately related to and often discussed together with *synteresis*.[38] While Luther used both *conscientia* and *synteresis* in his early lectures on the Psalms, only *conscientia* appears in the lectures on the Minor Prophets. Nevertheless, the link between the two is important to recognize in the broader mystical tradition.

Scholars disagree about how Luther understood *conscientia*. Gerhard Ebeling argues that "Luther regarded the conscience simply as a symbol for the points 'where God and the world wrestle with one another.'"[39] Others, such as Bengt Hoffman, believe that his conception of conscience was more than symbolic.[40] Lohse argues that Luther understood *conscientia* as both "the innermost part of man," and, drawing on Hirsch, the "unmediated bearer of man's relationship to God."[41] That understanding of *conscientia* as the "bearer of man's relationship to God" parallels mystics such as Meister Eckhart, Tauler, and the author of the *Theologia Deutsch*, who saw *synteresis* as the meeting place between God and the human being.[42]

---

[37] See David S. Ariel, *The Mystic Quest: An Introduction to Jewish Mysticism* (Northvale, NJ: Jason Aronson, 1988), 195–6. On the role of the ascent of the soul in the *Zohar*, see Elliot R. Wolfson, "Forms of Visionary Ascent as Ecstatic Experience in the Zoharic Literature," in *Gershom Scholem's "Major trends in Jewish mysticism": 50 Years After. Proceedings of the Sixth International Conference on the History of Jewish Mysticism*, ed. Peter Schäfer and Joseph Dan (Tübingen: J. C. B. Mohr (Paul Siebeck), 1993). On the mystical ascent in Merkabah mysticism, the *Zohar*, and elsewhere, see Gershom G. Scholem, *Major Trends in Jewish Mysticism*, 3rd ed. (London: Thames and Hudson, 1955), especially Ch. 2 [lecture 2]; and Scholem, *Jewish Gnosticism*, especially Chs. 3 and 4. As with Christian authors, these authors obviously use term(s) similar to *conscientia* in their own languages, not always the term *conscientia*.

[38] See Cardinal Joseph Ratzinger's argument that *conscientia* would be better understood as *anamnesis* than *synteresis*. Ratzinger, "Conscience and Truth," in *On Conscience: Two Essays by Joseph Ratzinger*, ed. Edward J. Furton (Philadelphia: The National Catholic Bioethics Center; San Francisco: Ignatius Press, 2007), 30–38. [This was originally a keynote address of the Tenth Bishops' Workshop of the National Catholic Bioethics Center in February, 1991.]

[39] Bengt R. Hoffman, *Luther and the Mystics: A Re-examination of Luther's Spiritual Experience and His Relationship to the Mystics* (Minneapolis: Augsburg, 1976), 87. Inner quotation by Hoffman is Gerhard Ebeling, *Luther: Einführung in sein Denken* (Tübingen: J. C. B. Mohr (Paul Siebeck), 1964), 303: "Wo Gott und Welt ... miteinander ringen." Hoffman cautions that one should make a distinction between *synteresis* and *conscientia*; in Hoffman, *Luther and the Mystics*, 87 Note 52; cf. p. 142 Note 17.

[40] See Hoffman, *Luther and the Mystics*, 88.

[41] Bernhard Lohse, "Conscience and Authority in Luther," in *Luther and the Dawn of the Modern Era. Papers for the Fourth International Congress for Luther Research*, ed. Heiko A. Oberman (Leiden: E. J. Brill, 1974), 158–83; this citation is from p. 163. Emanuel Hirsch, *Lutherstudien*, vol. 1 (Gütersloh: C. Bertelsmann, 1954), 127.

[42] Per Hoffman, in the introduction to *The Theologia Germanica of Martin Luther*, trans. Bengt Hoffman (London: SPCK, 1980), 19. See also Hoffman, *Luther and the Mystics*, 88; and Ozment, *Mysticism and Dissent: Religious Ideology and Social Protest in the Sixteenth Century* (New Haven, CT: Yale University Press, 1973), especially pp. 5–8 on this concept in

Within mystical discourse, this intersection between God and the individual often occurs by means of the elevation or ascent of the *conscientia* and/or *synteresis*. It is an especially frequent motif, for example, in the texts of Pseudo-Dionysius and the Jewish mystics.[43] Many mystics link that ascent of the *conscientia* [or soul, person, mind] to spiritual contemplation, something which Luther flatly rejected. In his discussion of the Book of Jonah, he drew on that tradition, but modified it to serve his interpretation. In specific instances, Hebrew played a crucial role in the modifications he made.

Conscientia and Ascent in Luther's Translation of Jonah 1:2[44]

The Book of Jonah opens with God's word coming to the prophet Jonah, directing him to speak to the people of Nineveh. When Jonah flees, he too, like the people of Nineveh, becomes the target of God's wrath. In his reflections on Jon. 1:2, Luther linked the phrase כִּי־עָלְתָה רָעָתָם לְפָנָי (*kî-'ālətâ rā'ātām ləpānāy*, "for their evil has ascended before me") with the mystically-charged concepts of *conscientia* and ascent:

Their wickedness has come up before me. This is a Hebraism. God neither ascends nor descends, but scripture is accustomed to speak about God according to the feeling in our conscience [*conscientia*] that God is either well disposed toward us or angry with us. God is coming down to us when we feel him in our conscience [*conscientia*]. Our evil is arising before him when our conscience [*conscientia*] troubles us concerning sin, etc.[45]

However, rather than interpreting the Hebrew idiom as a contemplative *ascent* of the individual to God in the fashion of Dionysian or Kabbalistic theology, Luther altered the notion, framing it as a *descent* of God to the human *conscientia*.[46]

---

mystical theologians and also the relationship with "soul"; and p. 7 for Meister Eckhart's remarks on the *synteresis*. Many scholars argue for a development in Luther's understanding of these concepts. The objective here is simply to provide a basic picture of these concepts in his thought, as background to his use of them in his interpretation of the Minor Prophets, rather than make a comprehensive account of such development.

[43] *Variants* of the ascending conscience, person, intellect, etc. appear in these texts. Again, these authors obviously use similar term(s) and concepts in their own languages. See Dionysius, *Mystical Theology*, Chs. 1 and 5, where he describes this using negatives; in Pseudo-Dionysius Areopagite, *The Divine Names and Mystical Theology*, trans. John D. Jones (Milwaukee, WI: Marquette University Press, 1980), 211–4, 221–2. See also Ariel, *The Mystic Quest*, 195–6; and J. Abelson, *Jewish Mysticism* (London: G. Bell and Sons Ltd., 1913), 44, 47–9.

[44] Note that Luther also discussed the ascent of the conscience in his New Testament exegesis; for example, in his lectures addressing Gal. 2:14. WA 40.1:206a–210a. LW 26:116–7.

[45] "Ascendit malitia eius coram me. Hebraismus est, deus neque ascendit neque descendit sed ut in conscientia nostra sentimus vel propitium vel iratum deum, ita scriptura solet de deo loqui. Tum descendit ad nos, cum in conscientia eum sentimus, tum ascendit malitia nostra, cum tangit nos conscientia de peccato etc." WA 13:244.24–28. LW 19:8–9.

[46] For example, see Dionysius's description of Moses's "mystical" ascent of Mt. Sinai

This variation on the ascent of the *conscientia*, soul, person, or mind as the descent of God to the individual has a strong parallel in Tauler's *Sermons*. For example, Tauler said in a sermon on the parable of the five virgins in Matt. 25:

> Though it is true that by love man may rise so high that he can embrace God by union of will, yet it is true that God descends to the resigned and suffering man with all that He is; and there He is embraced by the loving soul, and He embraces it again and absorbs it into Himself. Thus the soul loses itself, and returns again to the Source from whence it came, and knows assuredly here, even in this life, as far as it possible, that hereafter it will enjoy Him for ever.[47]

He echoed these sentiments in other sermons. Alois Haas, for example, citing Tauler's *In omnibus requiem quesivi* (Sir. 24:7), argues that "This spirituality is

---

through an elimination of cognitive thought. Dionysius, *Mystical Theology*, Ch. 1; see especially 1000 C–D; in Pseudo-Dionysius Areopagite, *The Divine Names and Mystical Theology*, 211–4.

[47] "Wann wie wol es war ist/das man in der lieb hoch vff geen mag/daz man got vmbfengt vermittelst einheit der willen/dannocht ist es war/das got nider steigt in den gelassen leidsamen menschen/mitt allem daz er ist/Vnd do wirt er vmmfangen von der lieb habende sele/vnd vmbfengt sy wider/vnd verschlindet sy allzu(o)mal in sich. Vnd also wirt sy ir selbst verlorn/vnd also keret sy wider in iren vrsprung/do sy außgekommen ist/Vnd wirt hie in disem Leben versichert/so ferr als es hie müglich ist. vnd hie nachmals jn ewiglich zu(o) gebranchen [typographical error; this should be 'gebrauchen']." Johannes Tauler, *Predigten zu einen recht christlichen Leben* (Basel: Petri, 1521), fol. CCXXXIIIr. I would not change anything in this English translation, and thus have taken it from: Johannes Tauler, *The Inner Way: Being Thirty-Six Sermons for Festivals*, trans. Arthur Wollaston Hutton (London: Methuen, [1901]), 299–300. Whether Tauler authored this sermon is in dispute among modern scholars. It was printed for the first time in the 1521 Basel edition of Tauler's sermons. Many scholars now believe that certain sermons in this edition, some of which do not appear in the 1509 Augsburg edition in which Luther made his annotations (*Luthers Randbemerkungen zu Taulers Predigten*; see WA 9:95–104), were not Tauler's but should instead be attributed to others including Meister Eckhart, Seuse, and Ruysbroeck. Nevertheless, because the sermons appeared under Tauler's name in that edition, this shaped the subsequent reception history in which they were accepted as authentic sermons from him. I include this sermon here because (1) scholars believe that Luther obtained a copy of the Basel edition in 1521, and thus was almost certainly aware of the sermon as attributed to Tauler; and (2) regardless of whether the sermon was authored by Tauler or by another medieval mystical writer, this example still shows the parallel between Luther and the mystical tradition. For more on this subject, including the Dec. 26/27, 1521 letter from Melanchthon to Spalatin showing that Luther received a copy of a Tauler print at the Wartburg, likely the recently completed 1521 Basel edition, see: Philip Melanchthon, *Melanchthons Briefwechsel: kritische und kommentierte Gesamtausgabe*, vol. 1, ed. Heinz Scheible (Stuttgart-Bad Cannstatt: Frommann-Holzboog, 1977), 115 [§ 191]; Louise Gnädinger and Johannes G. Mayer, "Tauler, Johannes OP," in *Die deutsche Literatur des Mittelalters. Verfasserlexikon*, 2nd rev. ed., vol. 9, ed. Burghart Wachinger, et al. (Berlin: De Gruyter, 1995), 631–657, especially pp. 637, 649–51; Henrik Otto, *Vor- und frühreformatorische Tauler-Rezeption: Annotationen in Drucken des späten 15. und frühen 16. Jahrhunderts* (Gütersloh: Gütersloher Verlagshaus, 2003), 183 Note 49 (and on the broader subject of Luther's reception of Tauler, see pp. 183–214); Bernard McGinn, *The Mystical Thought of Meister Eckhart: The Man from Whom God Hid Nothing* (New York: Crossroad Publishing, 2001), 183 Note 3; and Hutton in the introduction to Tauler, *The Inner Way*, x–xi. Thank you to Dr. Andreas Zecherle, Universität Tübingen, for the thorough background on this.

characterized by a decisive paradox: it is a mysticism of ascent to the same degree it is a mysticism of descent."[48] Luther, however, modified the traditional mystical notion of the ascending *conscientia* much further than Tauler, framing the coming of God as not only a *descent* but also an *assault*. Luther's "adjustment" in Jon. 1:2 was the connection that he made between the mystical notion of *conscientia* and the encounter with that wrath. He identified עָלְתָה ... לְפָנָי (*'ālətâ ... ləpānāy*) as the meeting point between God and the individual at the point of *conscientia*, where the assault from God would take place. For him, the Hebrew in Jon. 1:2 carried a veiled, richer meaning buried within as a figure of speech, which was itself based on mystical conceptions concerning *conscientia*.

Luther's association of the wrath of God with *conscientia* parallels similar ideas found elsewhere in his interpretation of the Minor Prophets, which he likewise appropriated from the Hebrew. One of the most outstanding of these is in the lectures on Hosea, where he identified אָוֶן (*'āwen*) in Hos. 10:8 as the affliction of the mind, soul, or conscience [*afflictio mentis*]; which refers to the sin that vexes consciences [*iniquitatem, quae vexat conscientias*].[49] That identification of *afflictio mentis* and *vexatio conscientias* as אָוֶן (*'āwen*) meant *Anfechtung* (as Ch. 2 of this study demonstrates with numerous examples).[50]

In Jon. 1:2, the influence of Hebrew on Luther's interpretation of mysticism appears solely in the exegesis. He translated כִּי-עָלְתָה רָעָתָם לְפָנָי (*kî-'ālətâ rā'ātām ləpānāy*) literally in the *Deutsche Bibel* as *Denn jre bosheit ist erauff komen fur mich* ("For their wickedness has come up to me").[51] The Vulgate did the same, rendering it *quia ascendit malitia eius coram me* ("Because its wickedness has ascended before me"). But this was not so in other places in Jonah, where the Hebrew had a direct influence on Luther's German Bible translation.

Conscientia and Ascent in Luther's Translation of Jonah 1:4

Luther likewise exploited the mystical tradition behind the ascending *conscientia* in his interpretation of Jon. 1:4. He did so at two points. First, he focused on the term הֵטִיל (*hēṭîl*, "to hurl, throw, cast"). He translated וַיהוָה הֵטִיל רוּחַ-גְּדוֹלָה אֶל-הַיָּם (*wadōnāy hēṭîl rûaḥ-gədôlâ 'el-hayyām*, "And God cast a great wind into the sea") in Jon. 1:4 in the *Deutsche Bibel* as *Da lies der HERR einen grossen*

---

[48] Alois Haas, in the preface to Johannes Tauler, *Sermons*, trans. Maria Shrady (New York: Paulist Press, 1985), xv. This sermon appears in *Die Predigten Taulers: aus der Engelberger und der Freiburger Handschrift sowie aus Schmidts Abschriften der ehemaligen Strassburger Handschriften*, ed. Ferdinand Vetter (Berlin: Weidmann, 1910), 201–7 [fols. 54r–58v], with a specific reference to "206.4–5 [fol. 57v]."

[49] אָוֶן (*'āwen*) appears transliterated as *Aven* in those lecture notes: "Aven afflictio mentis est, inde refertur ad iniquitatem, quae vexat conscientias." WA 13:49 Note 22 H.

[50] *vexatio conscientias*: "vexation of the conscience." See Ch. 2 of this study. See also the Is. 6:5 example later in this current chapter.

[51] WA DB 11.2:262.2.

wind auffs meer komen ("Then God caused a great wind to arise, erupt upon the sea").[52] The Vulgate translated the same as *Dominus autem misit ventum magnum in mari* ("But God sent a great wind in the sea"). Luther argued that the Vulgate's translation of הֵטִיל (*hēṭîl*) as *misit* failed to convey the full meaning of the Hebrew. He distinguished within the term הֵטִיל (*hēṭîl*) an element of unexpectedness: the sudden onset of the storm which *misit* did not convey. He wrote in his 1526 commentary on Jonah,

> It must have been an unusual and unexpected storm that arose suddenly; for the text states that 'the Lord hurled a great wind upon the sea.' According to the Hebrew text, the Lord as it were hurled or slung this tempest upon the sea with a storm.[53]

The important thing to note at this point is his emphasis on elevation in his translation of [־אֶל] ... הֵטִיל (*hēṭîl* ... [*ʾel*-]) as *lies ... auff*[*s*] ... *komen*.

That interpretation of [־אֶל] ... הֵטִיל (*hēṭîl* ... [*ʾel*-]) further influenced his translation in the next segment of the verse, where he made a significant deviation from the literal Hebrew with his translation of וַיְהִי (*wayhî*, "and there was") as *vnd hub sich* ("and arose"), *hub sich* an archaic form of *heben* based on *hüben* which carries the connotation of rising or swelling as a storm, or being lifted up into the air.[54] The addition of *auff* ("upon") merely reinforced that nuance.[55]

Luther emphatically linked both parts of the verse with *conscientia* in the lectures. With that association, he both (1) made the link between the Hebrew and the mystical tradition, and (2) directly ascribed the experience to *Anfechtung*:

> *But the Lord hurled a great wind* ... In addition to being terrified by the wrath of the Lord in an external way, he felt the wrath of God in his conscience [*conscientia*] also. However, Jonah remained in the faith despite the fact that a much greater storm was raging in his heart and conscience [*conscientia*] than raged on the sea outside, etc. Because we are only spectators of tragedies of this sort, they do not appear so great and so terrible to us as they really are. But if we were experiencing them ourselves in our consciences [*conscientiis*], we would understand what it is to feel God's wrath against oneself and what that faith is, which, even in the middle of wrath, holds on to God as merciful and kind, etc. If this were happening to us, we would omit many useless questions with which we

---

[52] WA DB 11.2:262.4.

[53] "Es mus auch eyn sonderlich, unversehen wetter gewest seyn, das plotzlich daher komen ist, weyl der text sagt, Gott habe eynen grossen wind auffs meer geworffen. Denn also lautts ym Ebreyschen, das Gott den wind gleych habe so lassen komen, als wurffe odder stiesse er yhn auffs meer mit eym sturm." WA 19:205.17–21. LW 19:53.

[54] WA DB 11.2:262.4. Langenscheidt indicates that *hübe* is an obsolete form of *heben*. Otto Springer, ed., *Langenscheidts enzyklopädisches Wörterbuch der englischen und deutschen Sprache: "Der grosse Muret-Sanders,"* Pt. 2, Vol. 1, 5th ed. (Berlin: Langenscheidt, 1990), 818. The term is related to *erheben*, per OXDUD, 233; and per DDU, 482–3. Cf. *heben* in DWB 10:725. Luther's translation in Jon. 1:4 parallels his translation of Jon. 2:4, concerning the nuance of elevation which he saw in מִשְׁבָּרִים (*mišbārîm*), and translated as *wogen*. This example is evaluated in detail later in this chapter.

[55] See Table 5.1.

otherwise wretchedly torment ourselves in passages of this kind in scripture because we have not experienced such *Anfechtung* [*tentationem*]. This storm on the sea was surely greater than storms usually were. For even the sailors were terrified to such an extent that they related this storm to someone's sin. This caused Jonah, who was aware of his own guilt, to hide in the lowest part of the ship, but he was nowhere safe in his conscience [*conscientia*], since he had been touched by the wrath of God.[56]

The torrent of references to *conscientia* in his exegesis of this passage וַיהוָה הֵטִיל רוּחַ-גְּדוֹלָה אֶל-הַיָּם (*waḏōnāy hēṭîl rûaḥ-gəḏôlâ 'el-hayyām*) in Jon. 1:4 betrays the same implicit appropriation of the mystical tradition as in Jon. 1:2, thus demonstrating that the Hebrew idiom that influenced his interpretation of Jon. 1:2 carried over its influence to Jon. 1:4. Moreover, it shows him making the same modification of that mystically-based concept from an encounter with God grounded in contemplation to one associated with the wrath of God. Unlike Jon. 1:2, where he only implied the connection to *Anfechtung*, in Jon. 1:4, he explicitly identified it as *tentatio – Anfechtung*.[57]

Conscientia and Ascent in Luther's Translation of Jonah 2:4

When he addressed Jon. 2:4, Luther again drew upon the mystical tradition behind *conscientia* and ascent. This time he focused on מִשְׁבָּרִים (*mišbārîm*, "waves, waters, raging abysses").[58] He argued against the Vulgate's translation of כָּל-מִשְׁבָּרֶיךָ וְגַלֶּיךָ (*kol-mišbārêḵā wəgallêḵā*) as *omnes gurgites tui et fluctus tui* ("all your waves, raging abysses and your billows"), contending that מִשְׁבָּרִים (*mišbārîm*), which the Vulgate rendered as *gurgites* ("waves, raging abysses"),

---

[56] "Dominus autem misit ventum magnum ... praeterquam quod externe terrebatur ira domini, etiam in conscientia sensit iram dei. Attamen in fide permansit, quantumvis maiore existente tempestate in corde vel conscientia Ionae intrinsecus, quam in mari externe etc. Nos quia spectatores tantum sumus huiusmodi tragoediarum, non tantae et tam terribiles nobis apparent, quantae sunt. sed si ipsi experiremur in conscientiis nostris, tum intelligeremus, quid esset sentire iram dei erga se et quid sit fides, quae etiam in media ira deum misericordem apprehendit et clementem etc., quod si fieret, multas inutiles quaestiones omitteremus, quibus alioqui nos misere in huiusmodi locis scripturae torquemus extra tentationem constitui. Fuit omnino haec tempestas maior in mari, quam ut pro communi more fieri consueverat. Nam adeo etiam nautae territi sunt, ut alicuius peccato hanc referrent acceptam. Itaque Ionas huius mali sibi conscius abdit se intra infimam navis partem nullibi tutus in conscientia, timore irae dei tactus." WA 13:245.15, 21–35. LW 19:10. The Zwickau text includes the additional references: *magnum affectum, conscientia,* and *Conscientia gezcappelt.* WA 13:228.8–26.

[57] Thus, it reinforced the parallel with אָוֶן (*'āwen*) in Hos. 10:8. His emphasis on the role of experience for the proper interpretation of the verse also underscores the inherent link with the mystical tradition, such as in his 1515/16 note in the *Randbemerkungen zu Taulers Predigten*: "Unde totus iste sermo procedit ex theologia mystica, quae est sapientia experimentalis et non doctrinalis." WA 9:98.20–21. On Johannes Ficker's and A. V. Müller's dating of Luther's marginal notes on Tauler's *Sermons*, see Ozment, *Homo Spiritualis*, 1.

[58] מִשְׁבָּרִים (*mišbārîm*) appears in Jon. 2:4 with the prefix -כָּל (*kol-*, "all [of]") and the suffix -יךָ (*eyḵā-*, "your"). I refer to it throughout the chapter as מִשְׁבָּרִים (*mišbārîm*) in order to focus specifically on the term in question.

would be more correctly translated *elationes* ("elevations, high waves, acts of lifting"), citing the same word in Ps. 93:4 as support:

All your waves. This expression has been taken from a Psalm also. 'Waves [*gurgites*]' would be more correctly translated 'wave breaks [*fracturae*],' for it is the same word as in Ps. 93[:4]: 'Marvelous are the uprisings [*elationes*] of the sea,' where the ancient authors have translated 'heavings [*suspensurae*].' It actually designates what we Germans call *Bulgen*, or *Wellen* ('swelling surges, or waves'). And so this is the thought: 'Every storm and every movement of the sea covered me.' Aptly he says 'your' because he means, 'My conscience [*conscientia*] tells me that it is you who are bringing this punishment on me, this horror of death and of hell.' This is the punishment of consciences [*poena conscientiarum*], that in trouble we feel the wrath of God against us, that it is he who lays these misfortunes and very great afflictions on us.[59]

He translated כָּל־מִשְׁבָּרֶיךָ וְגַלֶּיךָ (*kol-mišbārêkā wǝgallêkā*) in Jon. 2:4 as *Alle deine wogen vnd wellen* ("All your surges and waves").[60] His initial argument was strictly based on the lexical definition of the Hebrew, which his translation of מִשְׁבָּרִים (*mišbārîm*) as *wogen* ("surges") reflects. *Wogen* particularly conveys the sense of elevation which he argued was more explicit in the Hebrew than the Latin *gurgites*.[61] His further identification of מִשְׁבָּרִים (*mišbārîm*) in the lectures as *Bulgen*, however, underscored that same more nuanced interpretation: *Bulgen* means *schwellende Woge, Welle* ("swelling surges, waves").[62]

---

[59] "Omnes gurgites tui. Et hoc petitum est ex psalmo. Caeterum quod nos legimus gurgites, rectius vertas 'fracturae'. Idem enim vocabulum est in psalmo 92: Mirabiles elationes maris, ubi antiqui scriptores verterunt: suspensurae. Significat autem proprie, quod Germani vocamus: Bulgen ader wellen. Est itaque sententia: Omnis tempestas et omnis impetus maris operuit me. Diserte autem dicit: tui, hoc est, conscientia mea mihi dictat te esse, qui intentet hanc poenam, hunc horrorem mortis et inferi. Et haec est poena conscientiarum in adversitate sentire iram dei contra nos, qui haec mala et has maximas adflictiones nobis intentet." WA 13:250.16–24. The footnote in the WA [concerning *Bulgen ader wellen*, in bold] calls attention to the Low German (*niederdeutschen*) forms. WA 13:250. LW 19:18. The modern Vulgate text for Ps. 93:4 differs from what Luther was reading (the modern edition reads *fluctus maris* rather than *elationes maris*), thus his reference to *elationes* in Ps. 93:4 is not entirely clear to the modern reader. To address this, the text for this verse in Table 5.1 comes from *Textus biblie* (Basel, 1506–08), vol. 3, fol. 228v [Ps. 92:4]. Cf. Luther's German translations of Ps. 93:4 in Table 5.1.

[60] WA DB 11.2:264.4. The same phrase כָּל־מִשְׁבָּרֶיךָ וְגַלֶּיךָ (*kol-mišbārêkā wǝgallêkā*) appears in Ps. 42:8, which also appears in the Zwickau text of the Jonah lectures as a citation from Luther [WA 13:232.22–23]. He translated it the same as in Jonah. See Table 5.1.

[61] Duden defines *Woge* as *hohe, starke Welle: schäumende*; with *Hohe* and *schäumende*; DDU, 1825. See Jerome's commentary, which addressed Jon. 2:4, where he refers to the LXX with *Omnes* elevationes *tuae et fluctus tui super me transierunt* ("All your elevations and your waves passed over me"). Jerome, *Commentarii in Prophetas Minores*, CCSL 76:397. This is additional implicit evidence of the Hebrew Bible's influence, in contrast to the Vulgate, through the LXX itself and Jerome's commentary. Jerome also interpreted this as *temptatio, temptatus*, and *temptationes* in his commentary on the verse. See Jerome, *Commentarii in Prophetas Minores*, CCSL 76:397, pointing to the Hebrew for his interpretation: *siue ut in Hebraico habetur* ("or more accurately, whereas it is furnished in Hebrew …").

[62] WDS 1:240.

Luther's subsequent argument that כָּל-מִשְׁבָּרֶיךָ וְגַלֶּיךָ (*kol-mišbārêkā wəgallêkā*) in Jon. 2:4 should be understood together with *conscientia* parallels his arguments in Jon. 1:2 and 1:4. And, as he did there, he modified the traditional mystical interpretation of *conscientia* and ascent, associated with spiritual contemplation, to one linked with spiritual assault – *poena conscientiarum*. That connection to the wrath of God also appeared in multiple further allusions to *Anfechtung* in his interpretation of מִשְׁבָּרִים (*mišbārîm*), not the least of which is his comment "what we Germans call *Bulgen*." Grimm cites the connection between *Bulgen* and *wogen*, but more importantly cites its link to *todesangst*, a term that Luther explicitly connected with *Anfechtung*.[63] Luther also made eight citations of the "rustling leaf" from Lev. 26:36 and Job 13:25 in the commentary remarks on Jon. 2:4 as part of his examination of מִשְׁבָּרִים (*mišbārîm*) and *conscientia* – unmistakable allusions to *Anfechtung*.[64]

One of the most striking facets of Luther's translation in Jon. 2:4 was the lasting linguistic impact of the German that he chose for his Bible. Grimm notes that *woge* first appeared in that form in the German language in Luther's Bible translation, the earlier form being *Wage*.[65] Grimm cites in his definitions for *woge*: *bewegtes wasser* ("moving, choppy water"), and *wogenschlag* ("pounding of waves").[66] This phonetic change, technically known as "rounding," was indicative of Luther's region of Germany, and thus no coincidence in terms of what became standard German. Such changes to the language were not innocuous – they aided in discriminating between homophones or near-homophones.[67] Sheila Watts explains that one of Luther's crucial significances for the German language was in the dissemination of such differing forms, which obviously the printing of his Bibles facilitated on a grand scale. The lasting value of such translations by Luther in his *Deutsche Bibel* was in rendering the German language more differentiated and nuanced. His use of this distinct form *woge*, which conveyed a unique nuance that he did not perceive in the preceding form of the word, is representative of the enormous influence that his Bible

---

[63] DWB 2:512. Concerning the link between *todesangst* and *Anfechtung*, see, for example, WA 30.2:583b.30 Note 1. Cf. WA 36:246b.12 Note 1. See also Beintker, *Die Überwindung*, 23.

[64] WA 19:226. LW 19:75–76. See also Bornkamm, *Luther und das Alte Testament*, 52–53; and Hovland, "An Examination," 393–4. Many other scholars note this connection in Luther between the "rustling leaf" and *Anfechtung*. Ch. 3 of this study discussed the great significance of that "rustling leaf" reference for his identification of *Anfechtung* in his texts. Cf. Jerome's commentary on Jonah, where, as part of his reflections on Jon. 2:4, he cites Job 7:1 and describes life of man on earth as *Temptatio* (a variation in spelling of *tentatio*, i. e. *Anfechtung*), which he further equates to *militia* ("warfare"). Jerome, *Commentarii in Prophetas Minores*, CCSL 76:397.

[65] DWB 30:977–92.

[66] DWB 30:977.

[67] Homophones are words that are pronounced the same, but have different meanings.

had on the German language.⁶⁸ Moreover, it shows the direct influence of the Hebrew on his German Bible translation, as he used the term to convey a connotation of elevation which he saw in the Hebrew but not in the Latin.

Gemitus ("Groan") in Luther's Translation of Jonah 2:4

The influence of מִשְׁבָּרִים (*mišbārîm*) on Luther's exploitation of the mystical tradition in Jon. 2:4 was not limited to the connection with ascent and *conscientia*. It also appears in the additional connection he made with *gemitus*, an integral concept in medieval German mysticism and one of the terms which Oberman argued is a crucial witness to mysticism in Luther's texts.⁶⁹ The appearance of *conscientia* and *gemitus* together in mystical discourse is commonplace, and many argue that the two concepts are intimately related. Hoffman explains that "In medieval scholasticism and mysticism the *gemitus* had its anthropological place in *synteresis*, the root of conscience."⁷⁰ Jerome went so far as to equate *gemitus* and *synteresis*.⁷¹ Thus, Luther's invocation of both *conscientia* and *gemitus* in his consideration of Jon. 2:4 has a firm precedent in the mystical tradition. He used *gemitus* in his interpretation of Jon. 2:4 to draw on this mystical tradition and further connect the experience of Jonah with the wrath of God. He did so under the influence of the phrase כָּל-מִשְׁבָּרֶיךָ (*kol-mišbārêḵā*).

The *Weimarer Ausgabe* records the following addition to the Zwickau text of Luther's lectures on Jonah:

Here, the spirit was demanding with unutterable groans [*gemitibus inenarrabilibus*]. All things are full of terror [*Terroris*] when faith wrestles in death [*fides luctatur in morte*]. Who would not be moved by this example?⁷²

---

⁶⁸ Thank you to Dr. Sheila Watts, University of Cambridge, for this insight.

⁶⁹ Hoffman, *Luther and the Mystics*, 141, 151. Oberman, "Simul gemitus et raptus," 55–59. See also Langston, *From Bonaventure to MacIntyre*, 74–75.

⁷⁰ Hoffman, *Luther and the Mystics*, 151. Oberman also cites Luther's marked interest in the *synderesis*, which Bonaventure understood to be "an affective power in man ... which intercedes with God with 'unutterable sighing' [*eine potentia affectiva im Menschen ... sie lege bei Gott mit unaussprechlichem Seufzen Fürsprache ein*]." Oberman, "Simul gemitus et raptus," 56. [The English translation is taken from: Heiko A. Oberman, "*Simul Gemitus et Raptus*: Luther and Mysticism," in *The Reformation in Medieval Perspective*, ed. Steven E. Ozment (Chicago: Quadrangle Books, 1971), 238. This is the original text, from Oberman's 1966 address to the Third International Congress for Luther Research. The German translations of Oberman's article which appear in other books are based on this English original.] See Bonaventure, *Commentaria in Quatuor Libros Sententiarum Magistri Petri Lombardi*, in *Opera omnia*, vol. 2, ed. PP. Collegii a S. Bonaventura (Ad Claras Aquas (Quaracchi): Collegii S. Bonaventurae, 1885), II *Sent.*, d. 39, a. 2, q. 1, ad 4. Cf. Bonaventure, II *Sent.*, d. 39, a. 2, q. 3, ad 5.

⁷¹ This is in Jerome's commentary on Ezek. 1:10: Jerome, *Commentariorum in Hiezechielem*, CCSL 75:12. See Oberman on this in "Simul gemitus et raptus," 56. See also Kries, "Origen, Plato, and Conscience," 67–83.

⁷² "Hic spiritus postulabat gemitibus inenarrabilibus. Terroris sunt omnia plena dum fides luctatur in morte. Quis isto exemplo non moveretur?" WA 13:231 Note 15 H. "H" refers to

That note appears at the line heading "Gurgites: fracturae tuae" – Luther was addressing כָּל־מִשְׁבָּרֶיךָ (kol-mišbārêkā). He said later in that same tract, "Such groans [gemitus] are at the moment of death unutterable [inenarrabiles]. Two deaths: to be submerged and to be devoured, to be digested in the fish."[73] As he did with *conscientia*, Luther modified the function of *gemitus* from its classical role in the Christian and Jewish mystical traditions upon which he drew. Rather than associating *gemitus* here with illumination and contemplation, he connected it to the wrath of God. His specific references to *terror* ("terror") and *fides luctatur in morte* ("faith wrestles in death") mirror analogous references that appear in his discussions of *Anfechtung* in other texts.[74]

Luther's "mystical shift" in Jon. 2:4 underscores Oberman's argument that Luther's usage of *gemitus* is very different from the usage of previous mystical authors. According to Oberman, Luther identified *gemitus* as *evidence of the mystical meeting with God*, in contrast to other mystics who framed *gemitus* as *part of the preparatory procedure for* that meeting. He explained that for Luther,

Gemitus is not another word for *facere quod in se est* or *humilitas* as some kind of condition for justification; rather it characterizes the life of the *sancti*, whose righteousness is hidden. It describes the state of complete identification with Christ. Whereas in the connection between *gemitus* and true penitence there is a basis for comparison with Abelard, Bernard and Gerson refer to *gemitus* as part of the preparatory stage in the third triad 'purgation – illumination – contemplation' or as initiation of the birth of God in the soul.[75]

There is a final, crucial point to be aware of in Luther's argument concerning מִשְׁבָּרִים (*mišbārîm*), which exposes another important influence of the Hebrew in his interpretation. Luther's exploitation of the mystical concept *gemitus ine-*

---

the *Hallenser Handschrift* s. § 8, from the Marienbibliothek zu Halle. See WA 13:iii–iv, vi. Luther's words are a clear allusion to *gemitibus inenarrabilibus* in Rom. 8:26 (Vulgate).

[73] "Tales gemitus sunt in articulo mortis inenarrabiles. duae mortes: submergi et consumi, digeri in pisce." WA 13:231.23–25.

[74] See, for example, WA 24:574. Hovland cites this in "An Examination," 259. See also Beintker, *Die Überwindung*, 19. Cf. Figure 3.1 in Ch. 3 of this study, and the similar parallel to *pavorem*.

[75] "'Gemitus' ist nicht ein anderes Wort für 'facere quod in se est' oder für 'humilitas' als Bedingung der Rechtfertigung, sondern kennzeichnet das Leben der Heiligen, deren Gerechtigkeit verborgen ist, und beschreibt den Zustand völliger Identität mit Christus. Während in der Verbindung von gemitus und wahrer Buße eine Vergleichsmöglichkeit mit Abaelard besteht, erwähnen Bernhard und Gerson den gemitus als Teil einer auf die Trias 'purgatio – illuminatio – contemplatio' vorbereitenden Stufe oder als den Beginn der Geburt Gottes in der Seele." Oberman, "Simul gemitus et raptus," 55–56. [The English translation is taken from: Heiko A. Oberman, "*Simul Gemitus et Raptus*: Luther and Mysticism," in *The Reformation in Medieval Perspective*, ed. Steven E. Ozment (Chicago: Quadrangle Books, 1971), 237–8. This is the original text, from Oberman's 1966 address to the Third International Congress for Luther Research. The German translations of Oberman's article which appear in other books are based on this English original.]

narrabilis accentuated his argument that מִשְׁבָּרִים (*mišbārîm*) be interpreted as *fracturae* ("wave breaks [breakers]"). The wave break is the height of the wave where the energy and force of the wave is the highest, immediately before it breaks apart.[76] His contention that מִשְׁבָּרִים (*mišbārîm*) should be interpreted as *fracturae* shows that it was not just the sense of elevation which he saw in the Hebrew, but also that of the wave break. His translation *wogen* reflects both senses of the Hebrew: (1) the elevation and rising motion, but also (2) the sense of breaking apart and the associated energy, in contrast to the Latin *gurgites*, which he did not see as conveying a fully equivalent meaning. One thus finds a clear, direct influence of the Hebrew both on his exegesis and on his German translation. His appreciation of a more nuanced meaning within the Hebrew כָּל־מִשְׁבָּרֶיךָ (*kol-mišbārêkā*), in contrast to the Latin *omnes gurgites tui*, is evident in the mystical connotations which he interwove with his exegesis and his German translation of *Alle deine wogen*.

Conscientia and *Gemitus* in Luther's Translation of Jonah 2:5

The impact of the Hebrew on Luther's interpretation of Jon. 1:2, 1:4, and 2:4 carried over into his exploitation of the mystical tradition for his translation of Jon. 2:5, where he anchored his interpretation of וַאֲנִי אָמַרְתִּי נִגְרַשְׁתִּי מִנֶּגֶד עֵינֶיךָ (*wa'ănî 'āmartî nigraštî minneged̲ 'ênêkā*) [*Das ich gedacht, ich were von deinen augen verstossen* ("That I thought, I was cast out from your eyes")] in Jon. 2:5 into כָּל־מִשְׁבָּרֶיךָ וְגַלֶּיךָ (*kol-mišbārêkā wəgallêkā*) [*Alle deine wogen vnd wellen* ("All your surges and waves")] in Jon. 2:4. Moreover, it shows another definitive link to *Anfechtung*. He wrote in the commentary:

> In one's conscience [*gewissen*] sin surely gives voice to such thoughts ... These thoughts of despair came to Jonah when he felt the wrath and the punishment of God physically and externally, as he was cast into the deep and as the waves and the billows passed over him [*mit wellen und wogen uberfallen ward*]. This he told us in v. 4 above and continues to tell us in what follows.[77]

The Vulgate translated וַאֲנִי אָמַרְתִּי נִגְרַשְׁתִּי מִנֶּגֶד עֵינֶיךָ (*wa'ănî 'āmartî nigraštî minneged̲ 'ênêkā*) in Jon. 2:5 as *et ego dixi abiectus sum a conspectu oculorum tuorum* ("And I said, 'I have been cast out from the view of your eyes'"). Luther translated this in the *Deutsche Bibel* as *Das ich gedacht, ich were von deinen*

---

[76] The figurative meaning of *fracturae*, from *frango*, may also have significance. Lewis and Short define this as: "[figuratively] to break down, subdue, overcome, crush, dishearten, weaken, diminish, violate, soften." LS, 775–6.

[77] "Und solchs bringt natuerlich die sunde ym gewissen mit sich ... Aber zu solchem gedancken und verzweyffeln ist Jona komen aus dem, das er den zorn und straffe gottes leyblich und eusserlich fulet, wie er yn die tieffe geworffen und mit den fluten umbgeben, mit wellen und wogen uberfallen ward, als er droben hat gesagt und noch weytter erzelet und spricht." WA 19:228.9, 18–22. LW 19:77–78.

augen verstossen ("That I thought, I was cast out from your eyes").⁷⁸ While his translation largely agreed with the Vulgate, his exegesis of the verse shows signs of a fuller mystical interpretation. The influence of Hebrew on that reading appears in his citation of כָּל־מִשְׁבָּרֶיךָ וְגַלֶּיךָ (*kol-mišbārêkā wəgallêkā*) from Jon. 2:4 – *mit wellen und wogen uberfallen ward* ("was assaulted with waves and surges"). That citation of מִשְׁבָּרִים (*mišbārîm*), which he explicitly associated with *conscientia* in his exegesis of v. 4, underscored his argument in v. 5 that וַאֲנִי אָמַרְתִּי (*wa'ănî 'āmartî*) be linked to *conscientia – ym gewissen* ("in the conscience"). Earlier, in his argument concerning Jon. 1:2, he had identified *conscientia* and its relationship to the feeling of ascending to and descending from God as a Hebraism. That Hebraism in Jon. 1:2 thus continued to influence his translation of v. 5.

Luther's citation of כָּל־מִשְׁבָּרֶיךָ וְגַלֶּיךָ (*kol-mišbārêkā wəgallêkā*) in Jon. 2:4, however, imported not only the mystical tradition behind *conscientia*, but also that behind *gemitus*. This was already clear in his argument concerning Jon. 2:4 that the Hebrew phrase should be linked to *gemitus*. It was made explicit in his comment on Jon. 2:5 where he contended for the link with *gemitibus inenarrabilibus*, and directly connected *gemitus* to *Anfechtung*: "This is one of the unutterable groans [*gemitibus inenarrabilibus*]. This is the ultimate sigh and the final death in *Anfechtung* [*tentatione*]."⁷⁹ His explicit citation of *Anfechtung* in v. 5, together with his direct linking of v. 4, underscores the earlier argument that connected מִשְׁבָּרִים (*mišbārîm*) directly to *Anfechtung*.⁸⁰ Thus, it is no exaggeration to assert that Luther was speaking of *Anfechtung* in v. 4, and that the influence of the Hebrew carried over to his interpretation of *Anfechtung* there also. His comments in v. 5 show this link indisputably. Therefore, there is further confirmation of the direct influence of the Hebrew language on both his exploitation of the mystical tradition and of *Anfechtung* in his Bible translation.

To summarize, Luther's use of *gemitus* in his interpretation of Jon. 2:5 is further evidence for the influence of מִשְׁבָּרִים (*mišbārîm*) on his exploitation of the mystical tradition in the verse. Moreover, it reinforces the previous points con-

---

⁷⁸ WA DB 11.2:264.5.

⁷⁹ This appears in Luther's lectures on Jonah: "Hoc unum est de gemitibus inenarrabilibus, hoc summum est suspirium et summa mors in tentatione." WA 13:250.28–29. LW 19:18. Note the same *gemitibus inenarrabilibus* appears in Luther's lectures addressing Mic. 4:9. WA 13:280; WA 13:322.3. See also WA 13:281.5.

⁸⁰ This study argued earlier that Luther's exegesis of *Bulgen* in Jon. 2:4 was linked to *Anfechtung*, because he used *Bulgen* in multiple places outside the lectures on Jonah within the specific context of *todesangst*, a term that he explicitly connected with *Anfechtung*. His use of *tods angst* in the commentary addressing Jon. 2:5 only reinforces this argument. See WA 19:228.18. As noted earlier in this chapter, his eight citations of the "rustling leaf" from Lev. 26:36 and Job 13:25 in the commentary addressing Jon. 2:4 as part of his examination of כָּל־מִשְׁבָּרֶיךָ (*kol-mišbārêkā*) and *conscientia* are furthermore undeniable allusions to *Anfechtung*. Cf. Luther's interpretation of Zeph. 1:17, where he cited the "rustling leaf" from Lev. 26:36 and Job 13:25 [addressed in Ch. 3 of this study].

cerning *conscientia* in Jon. 1:2, 1:4, and 2:4, demonstrating an analogous employment of the Hebrew in his interpretation of both mystical concepts. All four verses show how he modified these concepts from their more typical form in Christian and Jewish mystical literature, connecting them with the wrath of God, and thus either overtly or implicitly with his theology of *Anfechtung*. Luther's German translations of the Hebrew – כִּי-עָלְתָה (*kî-'ālətâ*) as *Denn ... ist erauff komen*; [אֶל-] ... הֵטִיל (*hēṭîl ... ['el-]*) as *lies ... auff[s] ... komen*; וַיְהִי (*wayhî*) as *vnd hub sich*; and מְשֻׁבָּרִים (*mišbārîm*) as *wogen* – are thus terms and phrases loaded with mystical intimation that is not readily evident on the surface.

Affectus ("Affection, Desire, The Innermost Part")
in Luther's Translation of Jonah 2:5

Affectus has a distinct role in Jewish mystical discourse, and it is frequently discussed within the context of Christian monastic mysticism.[81] Given Luther's use of authors steeped in Jewish mystical tradition, such as Reuchlin and Lefèvre, not to mention his profound relationship with and theological upbringing in the monastic context, it is no surprise to find the concept prevalent in his writings.[82] Many mystical theologians who influenced Luther saw *affectus* as closely related to other mystical concepts. They used it in analogous fashion as, for example, *conscientia*, to speak about the meeting place between God and the human being. Among those authors especially influential for Luther's understanding and use of *affectus*, scholars cite Gerson, Biel, Tauler, Bernard, and Bonaventure.[83]

The concept of *affectus* is especially important for understanding the influence of Hebrew on Luther's translation because he explicitly framed it as one of the pillars of his hermeneutic, especially in commenting on Jonah.[84]

---

[81] See Elliot R. Wolfson, *Through a Speculum that Shines: Vision and Imagination in Medieval Jewish Mysticism* (Princeton, NJ: Princeton University Press, 1994), especially p. 171. Wolfson discusses the "eye of the heart" in Jewish mysticism as linked to intellect, illumination, and a "vision of the heart."

[82] On Reuchlin and Lefèvre and mysticism, see the "The Mystical Tradition in Context" section of this chapter. Concerning the importance of Luther's time in the monastery, see: Leppin, "Luther's Roots in Monastic-Mystical Piety"; and John W. Kleinig, "Luther on the Practice of Piety," in *Lutheran Theological Journal* 48 (2014): 172–85. See also Wilhelm Maurer, *Der junge Melanchthon: zwischen Humanismus und Reformation*, vol. 2 (Göttingen: Vandenhoeck & Ruprecht, 1969), 251–2.

[83] Gordon Rudy, *Mystical Language of Sensation in the Later Middle Ages* (New York: Routledge, 2002), 103–9. Ozment, *Homo Spiritualis*, 117 Note 2, 187; although Ozment cautions that there still is a difference between Luther's specific use of *affectus* and Gerson's. Bell, *Divus Bernhardus*, 56–58. Maurer, *Der junge Melanchthon* 2:254–5. Karl-Heinz zur Mühlen, *Reformatorische Prägungen: Studien zur Theologie Martin Luthers und zur Reformationszeit* (Göttingen: Vandenhoeck & Ruprecht, 2011), 84–95. Heiko A. Oberman, *The Reformation: Roots and Ramifications*, trans. Andrew Colin Gow, rev. ed. (London: T & T Clark, 2004), 97–98.

[84] For example, Luther cited experience as essential for his interpretations of: Joel 2:14

Many scholars recognize the hermeneutical significance of *affectus* for him. Wilhelm Maurer, evoking Luther's *sine affectu et sine spiritu* ("without *affectus* and without the spirit"), argues that it is specifically the spiritual role of *affectus* which facilitated his understanding – and thus his translation and exegesis – of scripture: "Wie die geistlichen Affekte für die Gebetspraxis eine Rolle spielen, so erschließen sie für Luther auch das Verständnis der Heiligen Schrift."[85] Bell gives a similar assessment, arguing that Luther's emphasis on having the *animam Bernhardi* or *den Geist Bernhards* ("the spirit of Bernard") for interpreting scripture originated in the monastic *theologia affectiva*.[86] This pivotal role of *affectus* for his Bible translation, and the influence of Hebrew on it, come into full view in a critical translation decision that he made concerning Jon. 2:5.

Luther made a major change from both the Hebrew Bible and the Vulgate in his German translation of Jon. 2:5. He translated אַךְ אוֹסִיף לְהַבִּיט אֶל־הֵיכַל קָדְשֶׁךָ (*'ak 'ôsîp ləhabbîṭ 'el-hêkal qādəšekā*) as *Jch wuerde deinen heiligen tempel nicht mehr sehen* ("I would not see your holy temple again").[87] The Vulgate translated the same as *verumtamen rursus videbo templum sanctum tuum* ("Nevertheless, I will see your holy temple again"). The key difference in Luther's translation was his addition of *nicht*, not present in either the Hebrew or the Latin.[88] Moreover, he seemingly omitted the term אַךְ (*'ak*) in his German rendering. He explained the translation change in the lectures, saying,

Nevertheless I will again see your holy temple. I think this must be read and understood in a completely negative sense with this meaning: 'You don't think that I will ever see your holy temple, do you?'[89]

The Zwickau text of his lectures adds the following comment:

[WA 13:102.22–35; LW 18:99]; Jon. 1:4 [WA 13:245.15, 21–35; LW 19:10]; Jon. 2:5 [referenced by Luther in the *Tischreden*, WA TR 3:363.4–6 (§ 3503)]; and Zech. 1:8 [WA 13:555.27– WA 13:556.19; LW 20:14].

[85] Maurer, *Der junge Melanchthon* 2:252. English translation: "Just as the spiritual affections [*Affekte*] play a role in the practice of prayer, they also unlock the understanding of the Holy Scriptures for Luther." Luther's *sine affectu et sine spiritu* comes from the 1513 *Dictata super Psalterium*, addressing Ps. 69; WA 3:416.19. Bell also cites Luther's *sine affectu et sine spiritu* and Bernard's influence on his use of the phrase. Bell, *Divus Bernhardus*, 49. See also Raeder, *Das Hebräische*, 309.

[86] Bell, *Divus Bernhardus*, 56–57. See also WA 3:186.5.

[87] WA DB 11.2:264.5. I leave this Hebrew sentence untranslated in order not to predispose the reader concerning the Hebrew translation in question. See Table 5.1 for the English, German, and Latin translations of this sentence.

[88] This is not an isolated occurrence in Luther's Bible translation. See for example, Bluhm, *Creative*, 57–58, where he discusses Luther's addition of *new* [this is the correct spelling, according to Luther's use here] in Matt. 2:2, not present in either the Vulgate or the Greek NT, or Erasmus for that matter (i. e. *newgeborne*: WA DB 6:18.2 (1522); WA DB 6:19.2 (1546)).

[89] "Veruntamen rursus videbo templum sanctum tuum. Ego omnino negative puto intelligendum, et legendum esse puto, ut sit sententia: putas etiam, an unquam visurus sim templum sanctum tuum?" WA 13:251.1–3. LW 19:19.

[It is] not clear enough in this place with the Hebrews. In this manner I wish it to be accepted negatively, so that it might be a great disposition of wavering or doubt [*magnus affectus dubitantis*].[90]

There one finds the first cloaked evidence of mysticism in his translation argument: *affectus*. But that was just the beginning.

Luther's later revisions to his *Deutsche Bibel* help to illuminate his rationale in the initial 1532 edition, and in the 1525 lectures which preceded it. The 1538/39 handwritten entries in his copy of the Old Testament record the following thoughts, which he subsequently included as a gloss in the 1545 *Deutsche Bibel*:

No longer [*Nicht mehr*]. The Hebrew is a question. Whether, or if you will [*Nüm Vel an*], will I see the temple? This ought to be translated negatively. Do not trouble yourself over the Hebraists, who in the interpretation of scripture are followers of the rabbis, that is, an animal without discernment. They know nothing of the prophetic affections [*affectibus propheticis*] in such arduous matters, so that they cannot understand the words.[91]

That 1538/39 remark contains the second indication of mystical influence in his translation: *affectibus propheticis*. But despite his exegetical argument that the Hebrew should be interpreted as an interrogative, he translated it in the *Deutsche Bibel* as a statement. At least, so it appears at first glance.

One of the keys to unlocking Luther's translation of Jon. 2:5 is the term אַךְ (*'ak*), which he seems to have omitted in his *Deutsche Bibel* rendering. This question concerning אַךְ (*'ak*) is a philological enigma that persists to this day. Jack Sasson calls it "one of the most contested readings" in the entire Book of Jonah.[92] There are many opinions on the meaning of אַךְ (*'ak*) in Jon 2:5, which is translated a number of ways, most commonly "indeed," "nevertheless," or "however." One of the key witnesses here is the Septuagint (LXX), which rendered the sentence as an interrogative: ἆρα προσθήσω τοῦ ἐπιβλέψαι με πρὸς ναὸν τὸν ἅγιόν σου; ("Then indeed will I gaze again at your holy temple?").[93] Luther surely was aware of this, and Jerome explicitly mentioned it in his com-

---

[90] "Non satis in hoc constat Hebraeis. Negative ita vellem accipi, ut sit magnus affectus dubitantis." WA 13:233 Note 12 H. See the earlier footnote concerning "H" and the *Hallenser Handschrift* s. § 8. *Hebraeis* in this citation could be the Hebrews, Jews, or Hebrew scholars.

[91] "(Nicht mehr) Ebraice est quesitivum. Nüm Vel an videbo templum? hoc debet verti negative. Nec cures hic Ebraistas grammatistas, qui in sensu scripturae sunt Rabinistae, idest animal sine intellctü. Ipsi ⟨de⟩ [in] affectibus propheticis de rebus tam arduis nihil experti sunt, ideo nec verba intelligere possunt." See WA DB 4:244b.2–18 (the cited portion is WA DB 4:244b.7–18). The WA editor indicates that this note is from Luther's hand. The 1545 *Deutsche Bibel* gloss reads almost identically. WA DB 11.2:265.5. Later, in the 1539–41 protocols, a similar note [that he also included as a gloss in the 1545 *Deutsche Bibel*] appears: "Ach mocht ich i. e. numquid videbo templum. Alls quaesitive geredt." English translation: "I would like i. e. now I will see the temple. Spoken as a question." WA DB 4:244a.2–3.

[92] Jack M. Sasson, *Jonah: A New Translation with Introduction, Commentary, and Interpretation*, AB 24B (New York: Doubleday, 1990), 179.

[93] Note the Greek interrogative semicolon at the end of the sentence.

mentary on Jonah, which Luther undoubtedly read. Aside from the translation of אַךְ (*ʾak*) as an interrogative, which is ambiguous at best in the Hebrew, the LXX is a literal reading of the Masoretic Text for the remainder of the verse.[94]

Most ancient manuscript witnesses and commentators follow the Masoretic Text, but some contend that אַךְ (*ʾak*) is a corruption of the original Hebrew, and should be replaced with אֵיךְ (*ʾêk*, "how").[95] If אֵיךְ (*ʾêk*) and not אַךְ (*ʾak*) were the original Hebrew reading, and this was the grounds for Luther's exegetical argument that it be interpreted as an interrogative, it suggests that he either had a different text than we know today, with the accurate reading, or that he took on a scribal error.[96] Neither seems likely. Most scholars believe that the 1494 Brescia Hebrew Bible at the Staatsbibliothek Berlin contains notes from Luther's hand, and was his personal copy.[97] The text in Jon. 2:5 in the Brescia Bible clearly reads אַךְ (*ʾak*), not אֵיךְ (*ʾêk*). See Figure 5.2 below. The Brescia thus agrees with the Masoretic Text. Moreover, given the clarity of the script, it is doubtful that Luther mistook the pointing or letters.

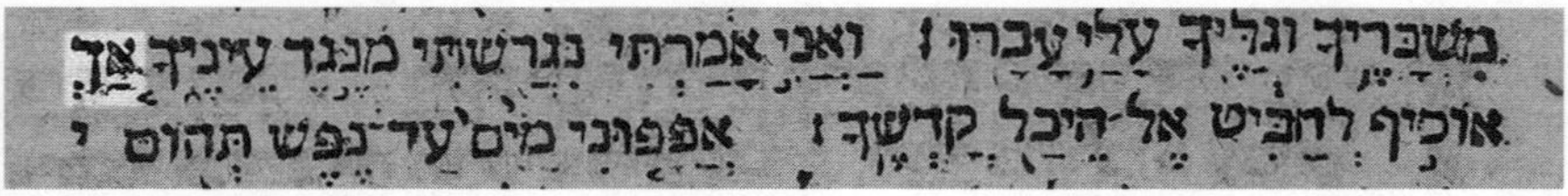
משבריך וגליך עלי עברו ׃ ואני אמרתי נגרשתי מנגד עיניך אך
אוסיף להביט אל־היכל קדשך ׃ אפפוני מים עד־נפש תהום

Figure 5.2: Jonah 2:5, 1494 Brescia Hebrew Bible (*source:* Staatsbibliothek zu Berlin – Preußischer Kulturbesitz, 8° Inc 2840, fol. 423r [857]).[98]

Luther's exegetical note *Nüm Vel an* in the 1538/39 handwritten entries in his copy of the Old Testament and in the 1545 gloss aids in unravelling the mystery concerning his translation. His argument for interpreting אַךְ (*ʾak*) as *num* is

---

94 By "Masoretic Text," I mean the Hebrew Bible as appears in BHS.

95 See Krause, *Studien*, 79 Note 4. See also W. Dennis Tucker, Jr., *Jonah: A Handbook on the Hebrew Text*, 54–55. Many scholars argue against the Masoretic Text reading. Leslie Allen summarizes the disparity of opinions as: Wellhausen, *BHK*, Bewer, Sellin, Wade, Weiser, Robinson, and Aalders read אֵיךְ (*ʾêk*); while Theodotion reads אַךְ (*ʾak*). Leslie Allen, *The Books of Joel, Obadiah, Jonah and Micah*. NICOT (Grand Rapids, MI: Eerdmans, 1976), 216 Note 17. It also seems unlikely that Luther based his judgment on Jewish exegesis, given his censure of Münster's interpretation, "Ego valde odio Iudaicas glossas." WA TR 3:363.6 [§ 3503]. Krause also cites this in *Studien*, 55 Note 8. Cf. Rashi, who interpreted Jon. 2:5 positively: "ידעתי כי אוסיף להביט אל היכל קדשך." English translation: "I *know* that I will again [more] gaze upon your holy temple" [emphasis mine]. MG, *The Twelve Minor Prophets* [ספר תרי עשר], 160. Cf. the 1527 edition of the *Wormser Propheten*, which also interpreted this positively. See Krause, *Studien*, 55–6.

96 Krause cites this possibility, as does Hayo Gerdes. See Krause, *Studien*, 79 Note 4; and Hayo Gerdes, "Überraschende Freiheiten in Luthers Bibelübersetzung," *Luther* 27 (1956): 78 [Krause cites this also].

97 See Burnett, "Luthers hebräische Bibel," 62–69, and Ch. 1 of this study.

98 Jon. 2:5 begins on fol. 423r. Staatsbibliothek zu Berlin: https://digital.staatsbibliothek-berlin.de/werkansicht?PPN=PPN720865522&PHYSID=PHYS_0857&DMDID=.

consistent with the LXX's ἄρα. Both are interrogative particles which in general expect a negative response.[99] Luther's interpretative liberty, which represented a monumental deviation from both the Hebrew Bible and the LXX, was the addition of *nicht*.[100] That insertion transformed the sentence from an interrogative to a declarative statement, thus interpreting the negative response from the particle אַךְ ((*'ak*) or ἄρα or *num*) for the German reader.

One can thus discern two major hermeneutical devices that fed Luther's decision: one grammatical/philological and one affective/mystically-informed. His interpretation of אַךְ (*'ak*) as an interrogative expecting a negative response was the first, philological tool.[101] This shows that he saw the LXX and Hebrew Bible as agreeing with one another.[102] The second hermeneutical tool was his reconstruction of the sentence as a declarative statement and his insertion of

---

[99] Herbert Weir Smyth indicates that ἄρα expects a yes or no response, but implies nothing as to which answer. SMY, 598 [§ 2650]. James Strong indicates that ἄρα expects a negative response. STR, 15 (Greek Dictionary section) [§G687]. Bernard A. Taylor suggests that ἄρα implies anxiety or impatience; in *Analytical Lexicon to the Septuagint. Expanded Edition* (Peabody, MA: Hendrickson, 2009), 71. LSJ also suggests that ἄρα implies anxiety or impatience, also suggesting that by itself, ἄρα "simply marks the question, the nature of which is determined by the context." LSJ, 233. On *num*, Lewis and Short suggest that *num* expects a negative response. LS, 1224. Oxford suggests concerning *num*: (a) it indicates "the possibility of a neg. answer is present in the speaker's mind through anxiety, caution, incredulity, etc."; and (b) it indicates a rhetorical question where a negative answer is demanded. OXLAT 2:1322. Cf. Hab. 3:8 where Luther translated the interrogative particle הֲ (*hă*) as a negative interrogative, with *nicht*. WA DB 11.2:308.8. The Vulgate translated this as *numquid*. Luther also argued in the lectures on Habakkuk that the Hebrew particle there indicated a question expecting a negative response. In those lectures he cited אִם (*'im*) in Ps. 95:11, making the same argument concerning that Hebrew term in the context of the verse. The Vulgate translated this as *ut non*. For more on the enigmatic ἄρα, see Kenneth Willis Clark, "The Meaning of αρα," in *Festschrift to Honor F. Wilbur Gingrich: Lexicographer, Scholar, Teacher, and Committed Christian Layman*, ed. Eugene Howard Barth and Ronald Edwin Cocroft (Leiden: Brill, 1972), 70–84. Clark emphasizes the tentative, uncertain, unresolved sense that the term has in the LXX; see especially pp. 72–73.

[100] Cf. Zeph. 2:2, where Luther omitted two instances of לֹא- (*lō'*-) in his rendering of the Hebrew, arguing that it was a Hebraism to express an affirmation through a negation. See WA DB 11.2:314.2, WA DB 11.2:315.2; WA 13:462.20–24, WA 13:493.9–12, LW 18:339. Zeph. 2:2 also appears in Ch. 3 of this study, in a footnote in the Amos 5:5 example.

[101] The argument here is not that Luther was correct or incorrect, but merely that this is how he read the Hebrew text. Cf. Cyril, who utilized a negation and a question mark, rendering the sentence: "Surely I shall never again gaze upon your holy temple?" Cyril of Alexandria, *Commentary on the Twelve Prophets*, vol. 2, The Fathers of the Church: A New Translation, vol. 116, trans. Robert C. Hill (Washington, D.C.: Catholic University of America Press, 2008), 164. And cf. Jerome, who rendered it affirmatively as *Verumtamen rursum videbo templum sanctum tuum* ("Nevertheless I will see your holy temple once again"). Jerome, *Commentarii in Prophetas Minores*, CCSL 76:398.

[102] Sasson argues that the lack of the interrogative particle in the Hebrew Bible's rendering is not an issue, advising, "I have couched [the Hebrew] ... as a rhetorical question expressing a wish. This solution is quite in conformity with the rules of Hebrew grammar, wherein a question can be posed without an interrogative particle and a wish can be expressed by means of the simple imperfect." Sasson, *Jonah*, 180, with a fuller explanation of the issue on pp. 179–81.

nicht. With this second device, he rendered the Hebrew with *affectibus propheticis*, which, he argued, is essential to its proper understanding. It straightforwardly conveyed the wavering, doubt, and depth of Jonah's despair, and his feeling that he was in the throes of death as he wrestled with God. Luther consequently transformed the entire disposition of the sentence from forward-looking to dejection – from hope to despair. Thus, contrary to how it may have appeared at first glance, Luther never ignored אַךְ (*'ak*) in his *Deutsche Bibel* rendering. In fact, it drove his interpretation of the verse.

This judgment helps to clarify and advance recent scholarship on Luther's translation of the Minor Prophets. Krause weighed the scholarly conversations concerning Luther's addition of *nicht*, concluding: "Aber sein 'negative vel quaesitive' (13.233 Anm.) stützt sich auf keine Textverbesserung, sondern auf den 'magnus affectus dubitantis', den er frei und richtig wiedergibt."[103] While he rightly discerned the significant role of *magnus affectus dubitantis* in Luther's translation, he failed to recognize, or at least to point out, that Luther's decision was not only driven by that affective, emotive hermeneutic, but was philologically grounded in his interpretation of אַךְ (*'ak*) as a particle expecting a negative response. Again, that interpretation was congruent with both the Greek ἄρα and the Latin *num*, which he included in the 1538/39 handwritten entries in his Old Testament copy to support his argument for the interpretation of the text as an interrogative. Moreover, Krause either overlooked or neglected to address the influence of the mystical tradition in Luther's translation and his manipulation of *affectus*.

To summarize, the Hebrew influenced Luther's translation of Jon. 2:5 both in terms of grammar and also in terms of provoking a mediation of the mystical tradition linked to *affectus*. The first was an impetus for the second. He used his twofold hermeneutical device to accomplish three things in the verse: (1) to correctly convey the Hebrew as he understood it, i.e. the specific function of אַךְ (*'ak*) in the context of the sentence as an interrogative expecting a negative response; (2) to convey more accurately the dire sense of wavering, doubt, and hopelessness – the *affectibus propheticis* – which he saw as integral to the correct interpretation of the verse; and (3) to intensify the sentence, which reinforced point (2). The third point is especially important, as it shows a clear effect of the Hebrew language on Luther's interpretation of mysticism by means of this aggravation of the intensity.

Luther's translation of אַךְ אוֹסִיף לְהַבִּיט אֶל־הֵיכַל קָדְשֶׁךָ (*'ak 'ôsîp ləhabbîṭ 'el-hêkal qāḏəšekā*) in Jon. 2:5 is an excellent example of his reluctance to translate on a merely literal basis. Had such a "literal" translation been his sole focus,

---

[103] Krause, *Studien*, 79 Note 4. English translation: "But his 'negative vel quaesitive [negative or interrogative]' (13.233) does not rely on any textual improvement but rather on the 'magnus affectus dubitantis [great affection (*affectus*) of wavering]', which he freely and correctly reproduces."

much in the Hebrew would have been lost. His translation also demonstrates his willingness to go against other Hebraists, specifically on this question of literalism. He argued vehemently against the teachers of Hebrew grammar, who, he asserted, were not experts in the *affectibus propheticis*. He opposed Jerome's translation of the verse, as well as his interpretation in his commentary on Jonah. He also hit back at his critics. When Sebastian Münster challenged him on his addition of *nicht* in Jon. 2:5, he fired back, as recorded in the *Tischreden*: "Yes, dear Muenster, you have not experienced such *Anfechtungen* [*tentationes*]. I have looked with Jonah into the whale when everything seemed hopeless."[104] That remark shows all the more that beyond any question, his mystically informed interpretation of Jon. 2:5 – at the explicit exploitation of *affectus* – was an identification of *Anfechtung*. Luther's translation of Jon. 2:5 is a quintessential example of how the Hebrew influenced his drawing upon and use of the mystical tradition in his German Bible translation, and moreover, how that influence carried over into his theological interpretation of *Anfechtung* in a particular text.

But the Hebrew influence on Luther's exploitation of the mystical tradition in Jon. 2:5 was not limited to *affectus*. This becomes clear when examining his interpretation of the rest of the verse.

Excessu[s] Mentis ("Excess of the Mind or Conscience") in Luther's Translation of Jonah 2:5

The Hebrew influence on Luther's exploitation of the mystical tradition appears clearly in his citation of Ps. 31:23 to support his translation and exegesis of Jon. 2:5. There, he focused on בְחָפְזִי (*bəḥāpəzî*, "in my alarm, fear, trembling, cowardice"): "The identical thought is in Ps. 31[:23], from which these words have been taken: 'I had said in my alarm [*in excessu mentis meae*], "I am driven far from your sight."'"[105] The Zwickau text shows a more thorough exposition of the Hebrew term: "From the Psalm [Ps. 31:23]: I said in my excess [*excessu*], i. e. my terror [*pavore*], and my haste [*festinatione*], 'cast off.'"[106] Luther, as many do, identified Ps. 31:23 as a parallel to Jon. 2:5, despite the fact that בְחָפְזִי (*bəḥāpəzî*) does not appear in Jon. 2:5.[107] He was drawing upon a con-

---

[104] "Ja, lieber Munster, tu non expertus es illas tentationes! Jch sahe mit Jona in den walfisch hinnein, ubi omnia videbantur desperata." WA TR 3:363.4–6 [§ 3503]. Reu also cites this in *Luther's German Bible*, 266.

[105] "Idem per omnia est in psalmo 30., unde haec sunt desumpta: Dixi, inquit, in excessu mentis meae: proiectus sum a facie oculorum tuorum." WA 13:250.38–40. LW 19:19. This is the Altenburg text.

[106] "Ex [Ps. 31, 23.] psalmo: dixi in excessu i. e. pavore et festinatione mea, abiectus." WA 13:233.6–7.

[107] See Table 5.1. The same phrase וַאֲנִי אָמַרְתִּי בְחָפְזִי (*wa'ănî 'āmartî bəḥāpəzî*), which appears in Ps. 31:23, appears in Ps. 116:11, with the exception of "and" at the beginning of the phrase. Both Luther and the Vulgate were consistent in their translations of this phrase in both

siderable assemblage of mystical tradition for the interpretation of Jonah: *proiectum esse me a te* ("I was cast out from before you"), *gemitibus inenarrabilibus* ("unutterable groans"), *conscientiam* ("conscience"), and *a facie oculorum tuorum* ("from your sight") in his exegesis of Jon. 2:5; not to mention in the *scholia* on Ps. 31:23: *Excessus iste mentis* ("This excess of the mind"), *extasi* ("amazement"), *humiliat coram deo* ("humbles himself before God"), *in extasi mentis* ("in the ecstasy of the mind"), and *in purissima illuminatione mentis* ("in the purest illumination of the mind").[108] These expressions have distinct places in mystical theology, particularly in the authors who shaped Luther's own mystical thought.[109] But he deviated from the manner in which they interpreted the text. Rather than frame Jon. 2:5, in parallel with Ps. 31:23, as either an experience of spiritual illumination, or some kind of allegorical account of an illuminatory journey of the soul, Luther saw these concepts in terms of the wrath of God.[110] He based that interpretation not only on the narrative of the story, but on specific elements that he saw in the Hebrew.

---

verses. Luther's interpretation of Ps. 116:11 provides many of the same proofs as that of Ps. 31:23, which further supports the argument for an influence of the Hebrew on his exploitation of the mystical tradition for his interpretation of Jon. 2:5. These include references to *in excessu meo*, *raptu mentis*, and *pavore passionis*. See WA 4:265.21–22 [Luther also included a chart, in which he delineated four meanings of the term *extasis*]. He also translated בְּחָפְזִי (*bəḥāpəzî*) in Ps. 116:11 as *zagen*, the same as he did in Ps. 31:23. See WA DB 10.1:488.11 (1524); WA DB 10.1:489a.11 (1531); and WA DB 10.1:489b.11 (1545).

[108] WA 13:250.25–40. LW 19:18–19. These *scholia* appear in the 1513 *Dictata super Psalterium*: WA 3:171.19–24. LW 10:144.

[109] Karl-Heinz zur Mühlen cites the prominent place of *extasis* and *excessus mentis* in Gerson's *De mystica theologia*. Zur Mühlen, *Nos extra nos: Luthers Theologie zwischen Mystik und Scholastik* (Tübingen: J. C. B. Mohr (Paul Siebeck), 1972), 52. See Jean Gerson, *De Mystica Theologia, Tractus primus speculativus, Pars 6, Consideratio 29, 4* [In: Jean Gerson, *Ioannis Carlerii de Gerson de mystica theologia*, ed. André Combes (Lucani: In Aedibus Thesauri Mundi, 1958), 74; the entire section (*Pars* 6) is on pp. 73–6.]. And see Jean Gerson, *De Mystica Theologia, Tractus primus speculativus, Pars 7, Consideratio 35, 3* [in: Gerson, *Ioannis Carlerii ...*, ed. André Combes, 94–95; the entire section (*Consideratio* 35) is on pp. 94–95]. Rudy cites Bonaventure's use of *excessus* and his connection of it to *affectus*. Rudy, *Mystical Language*, 108. See Bonaventure, *Intinerarium mentis in Deum*, in *Opera omnia*, vol. 5, ed. PP. Collegii a S. Bonaventura (Ad Claras Aquas (Quaracchi): Collegii S. Bonaventurae, 1891), *Itin.* 1.6; *Opera* 5.297b. Cf. Bonaventure, *Intinerarium mentis in Deum*, *Itin.* 7.4; *Opera* 5.312b. Note that there is a misprint in Rudy, *Mystical Language*, 108, for this second reference, indicating "*Opera* 5.12b," rather than the correct "*Opera* 5.312b." Ozment cites the role of *mentis* in Tauler's texts. Ozment, *Homo Spiritualis*, 18–19. See Johannes Tauler, *Renovamini spiritu mentis vestre*. [In *Die Predigten Taulers: aus der Engelberger und der Freiburger Handschrift sowie aus Schmidts Abschriften der ehemaligen Strassburger Handschriften*, ed. Ferdinand Vetter (Berlin: Weidmann, 1910), 259.1–5 [fol. 101r]]. The scholarship on *excessu mentis* is immense, and goes back to the Church Fathers and the monastics. It is impossible to cover all the views on it and its history within the space limitations of this study.

[110] Cf. Jewish mystical interpretations of the Book of Jonah. For example, Tanḥum b. Joseph Ha-Yerushalmi (thirteenth century) interpreted the story allegorically as a journey of the soul from the "angelic-intellectual realm" to the material world. See Raphael Dascalu, "Be-

The most obvious of these is the influence of the term חפז (ḥpz). The Vulgate translated וַאֲנִי אָמַרְתִּי בְחָפְזִי (wa'ănî 'āmartî bəḥāpəzî, "And I said in my haste/fear") in Ps. 31:23 as *ego autem dixi in excessu mentis meae* ("I said, however, in the excess of my mind"). Luther, by contrast, translated it in the *Deutsche Bibel* as *Jch aber sprach ynn meynem zagen* ("But I spoke in my horror/trembling/hesitation").[111] While the semantic range of the Hebrew term חפז (ḥpz) encompasses haste, flight, fear, and terror, the semantic range of the Latin *excessu* encompasses departure, demise, digression, and excess.[112] The German *Zage[n]* carries meanings of fear and terror which are intrinsic to the Hebrew, but which Luther saw as lacking in the Latin.[113] Reuchlin's *Rudimenta* entry for חפז (ḥpz) reinforces this; it includes in its definitions *pavore* ("terror"), one of the terms which Luther cited as support for his argument.[114]

The Latin Psalters which were translated from the Hebrew Bible, in contrast to the LXX, offer further evidence of a tacit influence of the Hebrew on Luther's translation. In Luther's day, there were two versions of the Vulgate Psalter in

---

tween Intellect and Intoxication: An Exploration of Tanḥum ha-Yerushalmi's Commentary to the Book of Jonah," *Jewish Quarterly Review* 105 (2015): 42–71, especially pp. 57–59. Concerning Jonah in the *Zohar*, see *Zohar*, in *Mystic Tales from the Zohar*, trans. with notes and commentary by Aryeh Wineman (Princeton, NJ: Princeton University Press, 1998), 99–117. Cf. Christian allegorical readings of Jonah, for example, in the *Glossa Ordinaria*, not to mention Jesus's words in Matt. 12:39–40. See Carolyn J. Sharp, ed., *The Oxford Handbook of the Prophets* (New York: Oxford University Press, 2016), 425.

[111] WA DB 10.1:194.23 (1524). Cf. the 1531 protocols on Ps. 31:23, where Luther identified *zagen* as *trepid [trepidare]* ("to hurry with alarm, be in confusion, waver, hesitate, tremble"). He also noted *ausgerott* ("exterminated, liquidated, killed off, wiped out") and *verworffen* ("discarded, cast away, rejected, destroyed") as part of the explanation for his translation choice of *verstossen* ("to cast out, to throw out"). WA DB 3:23.9–18. Cf. the notes in Luther's 1538/39 Old Testament: WA DB 3:532a.26–28.

For the sake of comparison, the 1466 Mentel Bible translated בְחָפְזִי (bəḥāpəzî) in Ps. 31:23 as *in der aufsteygung meines gemütz* ("in the elevation, ascent, soaring of my mind"); *Biblia Germanica* (Strasbourg: Johann Mentelin, 1466), fol. 181v. Similarly, the 1477 Zainer Bible reads *in der auffsteygung meins gemütes* ("in the elevation, ascent, soaring of my mind"); *Biblia Germanica* (Augsburg: Günther Zainer, 1477), fol. 289r [CCLxxxix]. The Mentel and Zainer Bibles are examples of a more rigid, word-for-word German translation of the Latin Vulgate. This further demonstrates how significantly Luther broke away from the Latin with his translation of *ynn meynem zagen*, under the influence of the Hebrew.

[112] KB, 320. BDB, 342. Cf. Luther's translation of וְחַתּוּ (wəḥattû) in Obad. 1:9 as *Denn ... sollen zagen* ("Then ... should fear, be in horror, hesitate"). WA DB 11.2:254.9. This appears in Ch. 2 of this study. Luther's exegesis of וְחַתּוּ (wəḥattû) there included *zagen* but also *pavidi erunt* and *pavorem*, which is quite significant given that Hilary of Poitier (whom Luther cited explicitly in his *scholia* on Ps. 31:23) translated חפז (ḥpz) in Ps. 31:23 as *pavor* rather than *excessus*. Luther himself explicitly identified *excessus* as *pavore* and *festinatione* in the Zwickau text on Ps. 31:23, hence the links are significant.

[113] Other connotations of *Zage[n]* include giving up hope, timidity, and cowardice. DWB 31:23, 27–28. WDS 2.2:1691–2. Also see Friedrich Kluge, *Etymologisches Wörterbuch der deutschen Sprache* (Straßburg: Karl J. Trübner, 1883), 380.

[114] See *Rudimenta*, 187. Raeder cites this in *Das Hebräische*, 154. See WA 13:233.6–7.

use.¹¹⁵ One was translated from the LXX, either contemporary to Jerome or perhaps pre-dating him. The other contained Jerome's Psalter – *iuxta Hebraicum* – which he based on the Hebrew Bible rather than the Greek LXX. These recensions do not agree in their reading of Ps. 31:23. The ones based on the Greek ἔκστασις read *excessus mentis*, where חפז (*ḥpz*) appears in the Hebrew Bible; while those based on the Hebrew read *stupore*. The Greek ἔκστασις, reflecting the Hebrew, has a broader meaning than the Latin *excessus*.¹¹⁶ ἔκστασις carries nuances of departure, demise, digression, and excess, all of which parallel the Latin *excessus*; but it also carries nuances of fear and dread, which *excessus* does not. *Stupor* parallels ἔκστασις, conveying the meaning of astonishment and amazement, but also fear and terror – additional nuances which *excessus* lacks. Luther most certainly consulted Lefèvre's *Quincuplex Psalter* (1509), which includes Jerome's *iuxta Hebraicum*, in his work on the Hebrew Bible.¹¹⁷ There was thus almost certainly an additional, implicit influence of the Hebrew on his translation through his consultation of these sources.¹¹⁸

Luther applied the meaning within the Hebrew text for his interpretation of Jon. 2:5, further demonstrating how he modified traditional interpretations of the mystical encounter with God associated with Jon. 2:5. He accomplished this, aside from various inferences to the wrath of God, through multiple links to *Anfechtung* – both tacit and explicit. His argument in the lectures on Jonah that חפז (*ḥpz*) should be interpreted as *pavore* is one example of these implicit connections. Ch. 2 of this study showed the connection between *pavore* and *Anfechtung* at multiple places in his translation and exegesis of the Minor Prophets.¹¹⁹ There was also a tacit connection to *Anfechtung* through the association in his writings between *zagen* and *entsetzen* ("to horrify"). In a 1522 sermon addressing Ps. 116:11, for example, he cited בְחָפְזִי (*bəḥāpəzî*) as *entsetzen* ("to horrify"), with a note in the text of that sermon adding *zagen*.¹²⁰ That reference

---

¹¹⁵ And others contain both variants. Thank you to Prof. Dr. Richard Rex, University of Cambridge, for this insight.

¹¹⁶ See Csaba Németh, "*Paulus Raptus* to *Raptus Pauli*: Paul's Rapture (2 Cor 12:2–4) in the Pre-Scholastic and Scholastic Theologies," in *A Companion to St. Paul in the Middle Ages*, ed. Steven R. Cartwright (Leiden: Brill, 2013), 357–8.

¹¹⁷ McGrath, *Luther's Theology of the Cross*, 65. Richard Rex, "Humanism," in *The Reformation World*, ed. Andrew Pettegree (London: Routledge, 2000), 60. Lefèvre's *Quincuplex Psalter* reads for בְחָפְזִי (*bəḥāpəzî*) in Ps. 31:23: *Gallicum*: "in excessu metis mee"; *Romanum*: "in pauore meo"; *Hebraicum*: "in stupore meo"; *Vetus*: "in extasi mea"; and *Cinciliatum*: "in excessu mentis meae." Lefèvre, *Qvincvplex Psalterium*, fols. 50v, 242r [Ps. 30:28].

¹¹⁸ The same could be said of the implicit influence of the Hebrew on Luther though the LXX. His citation of *extasi* in the *scholia* on Ps. 31:23 shows this. See also the previous footnote concerning Lefèvre's *Quincuplex Psalter*.

¹¹⁹ See Figure 3.1 in Ch. 3. Note especially Obad. 1:9, where Luther interpreted the term וַחַתּוּ (*wəhattû*) as both *zagen* [in the *Deutsche Bibel*] and *pavore* [in his lectures]. Moreover, he linked his interpretation to *tentationem* in his lectures. Ch. 3 examined Luther's translation of Obad. 1:9 in detail.

¹²⁰ See Luther's *Am dritten sontag des Advents Euangelium [Matth. 11, 2–10]* (1522): "An

is significant because *entsetzen* is a term that he explicitly linked to *Anfechtung* in other writings – for example, in *Von Abrahams Anfechtung und Trost*.[121] Finally, there is another important link between *zagen* and *Anfechtung*, which lexicographers make through the identification of *Zage[n]* with *bange*.[122] This connection is extremely significant, given Luther's equating of *bange machen* and *Anfechtung* at various places in his texts, as shown in Ch. 3 of this study (see Figure 3.1).

But the connection to *Anfechtung* was not simply implicit. Luther's remarks in the lectures on Jonah clearly show him interweaving the mystical tradition behind Jon. 2:5 and Ps. 31:23, his interpretation of *Anfechtung*, and his interpretation of the wrath of God: "Jonah thought he was done for both in body and soul"; "driving me to despair"; "Terrified by these signs of [your] wrath"; "I was done for"; "the final death in *Anfechtung* [*tentatione*]"; and "despair is so great in such *Anfechtungen* [*tentationibus*] and so powerful that even faith seems to go under."[123] With these illustrations, his interpretation of the mystical experience as an encounter with the wrath of God, and the connection to the *Anfechtung* is unmistakable. Scholarship on Luther's understanding of *excessus mentis* reinforces this judgment. Oberman, for example, cited the link between *excessus*, *tribulatio*, and *Anfechtung* in Luther's writings, and argued that he ultimately sourced this understanding from Augustine.[124] Zur Mühlen makes much the same observation.[125]

Luther's interweaving of various mystical elements with his own interpretation of Jon. 2:5 is another example of the ingenuity of his Bible translation. This is especially so when considering the additional etymological background of

---

dißem ort war David, da er sprach ps. 115⁵ [Ps. 116, 11]: Ich saget ynn meynem entsetzen: Alle menschen sind lugener." English translation: "David was in this place as he spoke [Ps. 116:11]: 'I said in my horror, "All men are liars."'" WA 10.1.2:157.21–22. The added note of *zagen* comes from the 1530 *Lu³* manuscript. See D. Brenner's explanation of the different manuscripts, the updates they represent, and Luther's supervision of them and his contributions to them in the preface to the *Adventspostille*: WA 10.1.2:ix–xi. The footnote in the *Weimarer Ausgabe* at 10.1.2:157.22 reads: "*Der Anfang lautet in der Vulgata:* ego dixi in excessu meo, *im hebr. Text:* אֲנִי אָמַרְתִּי בְחָפְזִי (*ănî 'āmartî bəḥāpəzî*), *bei Faber Stapulensis:* ego dixi in stupore meo." [There is no *shewa* underneath the פ (*p*) in בְחָפְזִי (*bəḥāpəzî*) in the WA; I have added this for the sake of clarity]. English translation: "The beginning is registered in the Vulgate: ego dixi in excessu meo; in the Hebrew text: אֲנִי אָמַרְתִּי בְחָפְזִי (*ănî 'āmartî bəḥāpəzî*); and by Faber Stapulensis: ego dixi in stupore meo."

[121] Concerning Luther's identification of *entsetzen* as *Anfechtung*, see, for example: Luther, *Von Abrahams Anfechtung und Trost*, in Martin Luther, *Dr. Martin Luthers Werke: In einer das Bedürfniss der Zeit berücksichtigenden Auswahl*, vol. 2 (Hamburg: Friedrich Perthes, 1826), 104.

[122] In Sanders, under *Zag*: WDS 2.2:1691. In Grimm, under *zagen*: DWB 31:27.

[123] WA 13:250.25–40. LW 19:18–19. Luther also interpreted Jonah's sleep as *tristitiae somnus* in his comments on Jon. 2:5. WA 13:245.36. Stolt links *tristitia* to *Anfechtung* in *Laßt uns fröhlich springen*, 68–70.

[124] Oberman, "Simul gemitus et raptus," 50–51.

[125] Zur Mühlen, *Nos extra nos*, 196.

the term *zagen*, which has roots in the mystical tradition through an association with *Seele* ("soul, mind, spirit"). Grimm explains that from the period of early *Neuhochdeutsch*, *zagen* came to denote a disposition of the soul.[126] It is significant that Luther did not choose a term such as *Furcht, Erschreckung*, etc. which would have easily conveyed the fear or terror that his exegesis of Jonah shows, but instead chose a term that itself was laden with mystical connotations and history. This is a further example, which underscores the many similar instances in this study, where Luther appears to have made a very deliberate translation choice of a term with multifarious, layered meaning for his German Bible.

Summary

If there were a single verse in the Minor Prophets to which one should look to see the profound influence of Hebrew on Luther's appropriation of the mystical tradition, it is Jon. 2:5. The number of discrete mystical concepts upon which he drew for his translation was exceptional among all his translations in the Minor Prophets. His translation of Jon. 2:5 also provides one of the clearest pictures in the Minor Prophets of the distinct influence of the Hebrew language on the experiential dimension of his translation methodology. As he said in the Jonah lectures, "These are not empty words, but the only people who can understand them are those who have at some time been in this kind of trouble."[127]

This examination of the influence of Hebrew on Luther's exploitation of the mystical tradition in his translation of the Minor Prophets now turns to the second and final section: silence and the "reduced to" idiom.

Case Studies Part II: Silence and the "Reduced to" Idiom: Zeph. 1:11, Obad. 1:5, and Hab. 2:20

Silence played a central role in the contemplative practices of medieval monasticism, as well as in the texts of medieval mystics. Luther, however, redefined this concept from how the mystics who shaped his thought understood it. For him, while silence was part of the experience of contemplative interaction with God, it also represented the threat of death and destruction within that encounter. Many scholars attribute Luther's engagement with the concept of mystical silence and negative theology to his *theologia crucis* ("theology of the

---

[126] DWB 31:27. Grimm lists various other meanings including *pavere* ("to be struck with fear"), *horrere* ("to shake or tremble with fear"), and *abjicio animum* ("to cast off the mind/soul"). Cf. WDS 2.2:1692, where Sanders provides as an example "in der Seele zagen, bangen." This is thus another link to *Anfechtung* through *bange*.

[127] "Non sunt haec vana verba neque intelligunt etiam ista nisi qui etiam aliquando hac parte laborarunt." WA 13:250.30–31. LW 19:18.

cross").¹²⁸ However, that interpretation is limiting. Apophatic theology had a much richer, multi-layered place in his theology and particularly in his Bible translation.

The theme of silence appears frequently in Luther's translation and exegesis of the Minor Prophets, and there are distinct signs of the influence of Hebrew on his interpretation of it. One such sign is seen in his recurring use of the "reduced to" idiom, which he argued was ultimately rooted in the Hebrew Bible. While he specifically linked that idiom to silence and thus articulated it as "reduced to silence" in some places, many variants of it appear in his lectures and commentaries on the Minor Prophets: "reduced to silence," "reduced to nothing," "reduced to a desert," "reduced to poverty," and many more. Although some scholars suggest that similar conceptions as this "reduced to" idiom were first used by Luther – for example, *resignatio ad infernum* – neither its ultimate origin nor its use within the context of mysticism were Luther's brainchild.¹²⁹ This expression appeared long before him, for instance in Jerome's commentary on Hosea as *redigatur ad nihilum*.¹³⁰ Moreover, the idiom itself seems an heirloom of mystical theological tradition. Zur Mühlen traces Luther's use of it to Tauler, citing "die explizite Einordnung des Taulerschen Gedankens der redactio in nihilum."¹³¹ Moreover, it has clear parallels in the *Theologia Deutsch*'s

---

¹²⁸ Many scholars do emphasize differences between Luther and Dionysian negative theology. See McGrath, *Luther's Theology of the Cross*, especially pp. 219–28; Rittgers, *Reformation of Suffering*, especially pp. 95–96; Zur Mühlen, *Nos extra nos*, 53–54; and Paul Rorem, *The Dionysian Mystical Theology* (Minneapolis: Fortress Press, 2015), 105–8. Cf. Bayer, *Theology the Lutheran Way*, 61; Leppin, "Luther's Roots in Monastic-Mystical Piety," 54–55; and Erwin Iserloh, "Luther und die Mystik," in *Kirche, Mystik, Heiligung und das Natürliche bei Luther. Vorträge des Dritten Internationalen Kongresses für Lutherforschung*, ed. Ivar Asheim (Göttingen: Vandenhoeck & Ruprecht, 1967), especially pp. 62–68.

¹²⁹ Kurt Ruh suggests that Luther was the first to name the formula *resignatio ad infernum*; Kurt Ruh, *Geschichte der abendländischen Mystik. Vol. 4: Die niederländische Mystik des 14. bis 16. Jahrhunderts* (München: C. H. Beck, 1999), 258; see also pp. 67, 112.

¹³⁰ Jerome was addressing Hos. 2:3. Jerome, *Commentarii in Prophetas Minores*, CCSL 76:19. On the general history of the *resignatio ad infernum* "tradition," see Clark R. West, "The Deconstruction of Hell: A History of the Resignatio ad Infernum" (PhD diss., Syracuse University, 2013). The phrase also appears in various places in the Vulgate. Concerning this concept in Staupitz, see Wolf, "Johannes von Staupitz," 57, 75–6. Ozment cites this in *Homo Spiritualis*, 214–5 Note 4.

¹³¹ Zur Mühlen, *Nos extra nos*, 197. English translation: "the explicit incorporation of the Tauleresque notion of *redactio in nihilum* [reduced to nothing]." It is also connected to Luther's "theology of the cross." See WA 1:363.28–29 [LW 31:55]: "ad nihilum redactus per crucem." Many scholars cite this, including Bayer, *Theology the Lutheran Way*, 24–5, and Note 53 (p. 25). Luther certainly used the idiom prior to his translation and exegesis of the Minor Prophets. See, for example, the *Dictata*: WA 3:23.35; WA 3:475.10; WA 3:487.7; and WA 4:511.22–23. See also the *Operationes*: WA 5:166.15; WA 5:167.27; WA 5:168.1; WA 5:168.13; WA 5:176.27; WA 5:284.19–20; WA 5:326.21; WA 5:445.29; and WA 5:632.14. There are many more examples.

Nichtigkeit, Meister Eckhart's *nichts*, and אַיִן (*'ayin*, "nothingness") in Jewish mysticism.[132]

The examples which follow examine the influence of Hebrew on Luther's exploitation of the mystical tradition behind silence, and, moreover, on his use and translation of the "reduced to" idiom. They specifically focus on two Hebrew terms: דמה (*dmh*) and הס (*hs*). Table 5.2 shows the Hebrew, Latin, and German translations for these examples.

Table 5.2: Silence and the "reduced to" idiom: Zeph. 1:11, Obad. 1:5, Is. 6:5, and Hab. 2:20.

Verse	NASB	Hebrew Bible	Vulgate	Deutsche Bibel
Zeph. 1:11	"Wail, O inhabitants of the Mortar, For all the people of Canaan will be silenced; All who weigh out silver will be cut off.	הֵילִילוּ יֹשְׁבֵי הַמַּכְתֵּשׁ כִּי נִדְמָה כָּל־עַם כְּנַעַן נִכְרְתוּ כָּל־נְטִילֵי כָסֶף	ululate **habitatores pilae conticuit** omnis populus Chanaan disperierunt omnes involuti argento	Heulet **die jr jnn der Muele wonet**, Denn das gantze kremer volck **ist dahin**, vnd alle die gelt samlen sind ausgerott. (1532) WA DB 11.2:312.11.
Obad. 1:5	"If thieves came to you, If robbers by night – O how you will be ruined! – Would they not steal only until they had enough? If grape gatherers came to you, Would they not leave some gleanings?	אִם־גַּנָּבִים בָּאוּ־לְךָ אִם־שׁוֹדְדֵי לַיְלָה אֵיךְ נִדְמֵיתָה הֲלוֹא יִגְנְבוּ דַיָּם אִם־בֹּצְרִים בָּאוּ לָךְ הֲלוֹא יַשְׁאִירוּ עֹלֵלוֹת	si fures introissent ad te si latrones per noctem **quomodo conticuisses** nonne furati essent sufficientia sibi si vindemiatores introissent ad te numquid saltim racemos reliquissent tibi	Wenn diebe oder verstoerer zu nacht vber dich komen werden, **wie soltu so stille werden**, Ja sie sollen gnug stelen, Vnd wenn die weinleser vber dich komen, so sollen sie dir kein nach lesen vberbleiben lassen, (1532) WA DB 11.2:254.5. Wenn Diebe oder Verstoerer zu nacht vber dich komen werden, **wie soltu so zu nicht werden**? Ja sie sollen gnug stelen, Vnd wenn die Weinleser vber dich komen, so sollen sie dir kein Nachlesen, vberbleiben lassen. (1545) WA DB 11.2:255.5.

---

[132] See Daniel C. Matt, "*Ayin*: The Concept of Nothingness in Jewish Mysticism," in *The Problem of Pure Consciousness: Mysticism and Philosophy*, ed. Robert K. C. Forman (New York: Oxford University Press, 1990), 121–59. See also Lydia Wegener, *Der 'Frankfurter'/'Theologia deutsch': Spielräume und Grenzen des Sagbaren* (Berlin: De Gruyter, 2016), 18.

Verse	NASB	Hebrew Bible	Vulgate	Deutsche Bibel
Is. 6:5	Then I said, "Woe is me, for I am ruined! Because I am a man of unclean lips, And I live among a people of unclean lips; For my eyes have seen the King, the Lord of hosts."	וָאֹמַר אוֹי-לִי כִּי-נִדְמֵיתִי כִּי אִישׁ טְמֵא-שְׂפָתַיִם אָנֹכִי וּבְתוֹךְ עַם-טְמֵא שְׂפָתַיִם אָנֹכִי יוֹשֵׁב כִּי אֶת-הַמֶּלֶךְ יְהוָה צְבָאוֹת רָאוּ עֵינָי	et dixi vae mihi **quia tacui** quia vir pollutus labiis ego sum et in medio populi polluta labia habentis ego habito et Regem Dominum exercituum vidi oculis meis	Da sprach ich, Wehe mir, **ich bin verderbet**, Denn ich bin vnreiner lippen, vnd wone vnter einem volck von vnreinen lippen, Denn ich habe den koenig den HERRN Zebaoth gesehen mit meinen augen. (1528) WA DB 11.1:40.5. DA sprach ich, Weh mir, **ich vergehe**, Denn ich bin vnreiner Lippen, vnd wone vnter einem Volck von vnreinen lippen, Denn ich habe den Koenig den HERRN Zebaoth gesehen mit meinen augen. (1545) WA DB 11.1:41.5.
Hab. 2:20	But the Lord is in His holy temple. Let all the earth be silent before Him.	וַיהוָה בְּהֵיכַל קָדְשׁוֹ **הַס** מִפָּנָיו כָּל-הָאָרֶץ	Dominus autem in templo sancto suo **sileat a facie eius** omnis terra	Aber der HERR ist jnn seinem heiligen tempel, **Es sey fur jm stille** alle welt. (1532) WA DB 11.2:306.20.

Zephaniah 1:11 נִדְמָה (nidmâ, "are silenced, undone")

Luther argued in his discussion of Zeph. 1:11 that silence is a special sign in the Minor Prophets, a cue that something more significant lies beneath the language. He explained in the lectures:

Since all the people of Canaan are silent [conticuit]. This expression is frequent in the Minor Prophets. Therefore we must take notice whenever they speak about silence [silentio] and keeping quiet [conticentia]. **To be silent [silere] means to be reduced to nothing [in nihilum redactum esse].** *In this way the prophets mark a silence [silentium] not so much of the mouth as of property – that there is no longer a use for property; that everything lies unused and in contempt. This is what we said above at the beginning of this prophet in the matter of the fish and birds being scraped up/together [corrasis].*[133]

---

[133] "Quoniam conticuit omnis populus Chanaan. Celebre est hoc verbum in minoribus prophetis, ideo observandum est, quandoquidem saepe de silentio, de conticentia loquuntur. Significat autem silere, in nihilum redactum esse. sicque non tam oris quam rerum silentium notant prophetae, nempe nullum amplius rerum usum esse, iacere et neglecta contemni omnia sicut supra de piscibus et volucribus corrasis diximus initio huius prophetae." WA 13:487.23–28. LW 18:330. Emphasis mine.

His focus was נִדְמָה (*nidmâ*), a rich, multivalent term, whose semantic range encompasses "to be dumb or silent"; "to fail or perish"; transitively "to destroy"; "to cease or to be cut down (off)"; "to be brought to silence"; and "to be undone."[134] The Vulgate translated נִדְמָה (*nidmâ*) as *conticuit* ("became silent").[135] Uncharacteristically for his Bible, where he most often avoided German idiomatic language in his Hebrew renderings, Luther rendered נִדְמָה (*nidmâ*) in the *Deutsche Bibel* into an idiomatic German phrase: *ist dahin*, literally meaning "to there," but used figuratively to mean "is gone," "lost or taken away," "dead," "destroyed," or "done for."[136] With this translation, he moved away from a literal to a figurative reading of the Hebrew, in line with mystical connotations of being lost or away, but also starkly indicative of ruin and destruction. That translation was the first evidence of his exploitation of the mystical tradition behind silence and interweaving it with his interpretation of the wrath of God. But there were additional evidences.

Another evidence of Luther drawing on and modifying the mystical tradition for that interpretation was his argument that "To be silent [*silere*] means to be reduced to nothing [*in nihilum redactum esse*]." He reiterated that argument in the same lectures with a torrent of additional variants of the "reduced to" idiom: *in pulverem rediguntur* ("reduced to dust"), *in nihilum redigemini* ("you will be reduced to nothing"), *in nihilum redactum esse* ("to be reduced to nothing"), *ist stil gemacht* ("was made silent/reduced to silence"), *redigetur in solitudinem* ("reduced to solitude"), *in nihilum redactus est* ("was reduced to nothing"), *redigetur in nihilum* ("reduced to nothing"), *redactus in nihilum* ("reduced to nothing"), and again, *in nihilum redactus est* ("was reduced to nothing").[137] The link to the Hebrew appears in his additional comments in the lectures, where he argued that, in fact, the source of that idiom was the prophet Zephaniah himself:

Wail, O inhabitants of the Mortar. From a purpose yet to come he gives them a name when he calls them 'inhabitants of the Mortar.' Here again we have some strange variations. Jerome thinks that Jerusalem is called the Mortar from the descent or from the valley of Siloah. Lyra also has a different idea. He thinks the name comes from Tiberias, which is located in a valley, etc. I disagree with them completely. First, we must warn that there is an ambiguity in our reading where we have 'inhabitants of the Mortar.' We have to show this lest we employ the ambiguity when we translate. This, we see, has been done here. *Pila* does not mean a ball which we use in play, but a mortar – ὅλμος, as Je-

---

[134] This is the same term that he equated with "silence," "reduced to nothing," and "reduced to a desert" in his interpretation of Hos. 10:7 and Obad. 1:5 (though slightly different forms). See Table A.5 in the Appendix.

[135] This comes from *conticesco*. LS, 448.

[136] WA DB 11.2:312.11. Cf. WA DB 4:261a.14–22; WA DB 4:261b.14–16. Luther's translation of נִדְמָה (*nidmâ*) as *ist dahin* parallels the exact same translation he made of נִדְמָה (*nidmeh*) in Hos. 10:7 [WA DB 11.2:202.7], as well as what appears in the 1539–41 Protocols for Obad. 1:5 [WA DB 4:242a.8]. See Ch. 2 of this study for more on Luther's use of idiomatic language in his Bible translation.

[137] See Table A.5 in the Appendix.

rome translates it. **Therefore the prophet has taken his metaphor from the function of a mortar.** The sense is this: 'So great a grinding disaster will come to pass in the city that they will be ground down and reduced to dust [*in pulverem rediguntur*] as we grind down herbs and other things which we mash in a mortar. So also Jerusalem will become like a mortar for you. In it you will be ground down and reduced to nothing [*in nihilum redigemini*].'[138]

Luther's focus was יֹשְׁבֵי הַמַּכְתֵּשׁ (*yōšəbê hammaḵtēš*), which the Vulgate translated as *habitatores pilae* ("the inhabitants of the mortar"). He translated יֹשְׁבֵי הַמַּכְתֵּשׁ (*yōšəbê hammaḵtēš*) in the *Deutsche Bibel* as *die jr jnn der Muele wonet* ("the ones who live in the mill"), largely the same as the Vulgate.[139] His exegetical device was to apply the metaphor associated with הַמַּכְתֵּשׁ (*hammaḵtēš*) [*pilae*; *Muele*] to נִדְמָה (*nidmâ*) [*conticuit*; *ist dahin*]. With this manipulation, he ultimately ascribed the metaphor that he saw in the Hebrew to *both* הַמַּכְתֵּשׁ (*hammaḵtēš*) and נִדְמָה (*nidmâ*), which resulted in his exegesis of נִדְמָה (*nidmâ*) as *in pulverem rediguntur, ist stil gemacht*, and the multitude of other variants of the "reduced to" idiom.[140] He clearly was drawing upon the mystical tradition with this idiom, in line with Tauler and Eckhart. But instead of interpreting it as associated with contemplation, mystical humility, or some other part of a process for reception of divine knowledge or wisdom, Luther focused on the aspect of destruction which he drew from the Hebrew נִדְמָה (*nidmâ*).[141]

---

[138] "Ululate habitatores pilae. A futuro effectu dat eis nomen, quando vocat habitatores pilae. Mire hic rursum variant. Hieronymus putat pilam vocari Hierusalem a descensu vel a valle Siloa. Lyra item aliter putat sic vocari a Tyberiade, quae est in valle sita. etc. Ego prorsus non cum eis sentio. Primum autem admonendum est amphiboliam esse in nostra lectione, quando legimus: habitatores pilae, praestandum autem est, ne amphibolia utamur in transferendo, id quod hic factum videmus. Significat autem pila non sphaeram, qua ludi solet sed mortarium ὅλμοςut Hieronymus transtulit. Itaque ab usu mortarii petita est haec prophetae metaphora. Estque sententia: tanta futura est calamitas et contritio in urbe, ut sicut in mortario contunduntur et in pulverem rediguntur herbae et alia quae tundimus, ita et tanquam mortarium fiet vobis Hierusalem, in qua contundemini vos et in nihilum redigemini." WA 13:487.4–16. LW 18:329–30. Emphasis mine. See Rashi's comment on this: "יושבי המכתש – נחלא דקדרון', שעמוק כמכתשת; זה תרגומו של יונתן." English translation: "The inhabitants of [the] Maktesh [ישבי המכתש (*yšby hmkṯš*)] – 'Kidron Valley,' which is as deep as mortar [Rashi has מכתשת (*mkṯšt*) here for 'mortar'; this also can mean a pothole; or also, a district in Jerusalem]. This is [according to] the Targum of Jonathan." And later in the same commentary, Rashi wrote: "יושבי המכתש – זו טבריא, שעמוקה מכל ארץ ישראל." English translation: "The inhabitants of [the] Maktesh [ישבי המכתש (*yšby hmkṯš*)] – This is Tiberias, which is deeper than all of the land of Israel." MG, *The Twelve Minor Prophets* [ספר תרי עשר], 246. On מַכְתֵּשׁ (*maḵtēš*), see KB, 523; HALOT 2:583.

[139] WA DB 11.2:312.11.

[140] Some of these appear in the Altenburg text and some in the Zwickau text. See Table A.5 in the Appendix.

[141] Long before Luther addressed דמה (*dmh*) in Zeph. 1:11, he remarked on דמה (*dmh*) in Ps. 65:2. He argued in the 1513 *Dictata super Psalterium* that דֻמִיָּה (*dumîyyâ*) in Ps. 65:2 should be interpreted as silence: "In Hebrew: 'To Thee, silence [*silentium*], praise'"; and he made numerous references to the mystical tradition associated with his interpretation of the term: *Nonne deo silebit anima mea* ("Will not my soul will silent before God?"); *vera Cab-*

A third attestation of Luther's manipulation of mystical thought for his interpretation of Zeph. 1:11 is his contention that נִדְמָה (*nidmâ*) should be further connected with *corrasis* ("being scraped up/together"). He was referring to his remarks earlier in the Zephaniah lectures, that אסף (*'sp*) in Zeph. 1:2 and 3 should be interpreted as *wegraffen* ("sweep away").[142] With this reference, he also was clearly drawing on the mystical tradition; *corrasis* is a synonym for *raptus*, an enormously important concept in mystical theology.[143] By linking *corrasis* to נִדְמָה (*nidmâ*) and the "reduced to" idiom, he modified the traditional mystical use of *raptus*, indicative not of a snatching away of the mind, spirit, or soul for a mystical, illuminatory encounter with God, but an encounter with God's wrath which resulted in death and destruction.[144]

Obadiah 1:5 אֵיךְ נִדְמֵיתָה *('êk nidmêtâ, "how you are silenced, undone")*

Luther addressed the same verb דמה (*dmh*) in Obad. 1:5, and again linked the term to the mystical tradition behind both silence and the "reduced to" idiom.[145] The manner in which he did so reveals additional evidence of the influence of the Hebrew term on his exploitation of the mystical tradition in his translation of the Minor Prophets. He argued concerning אֵיךְ נִדְמֵיתָה (*'êk nidmêtâ*) in Obad. 1:5:

How you would have become silent [Quomodo conticuisses]! This verb is used in various ways in scripture. Interpreters render it in different ways also. It occurs in Hos. 4[:5]: 'I had your mother silenced [*tacere feci*].' It also appears in Ps. 49[:13], where we read: 'Man, when he was in honor, could not understand; he is compared to beasts [that per-

---

ala ("true Kabbalah"); *extaticam et negativam theologiam* ("amazement and negative theology"); *stupore et admiration* ("amazement and wonder"); *theologia ... negative* ("negative theology"); *in summo mentis ocio* ("in the uppermost repose of the mind, soul"); *silentio* ("in silence"); *raptu* ("in rapture"); and *extasi* ("in amazement"). WA 3:372.8–27. On *ocio*, see *otium*; OXLAT 2:1406–7.

[142] WA 13:451.5–9. WA 13:481.15–17. LW 18:321.

[143] See LDH 1:1707, which defines *corrado* [based on the compound *con* (*com*) + *rado*] as *zusammenkratzen* or *zusammenscharren*, both words meaning "to scrape [something] together or up." Cf. OXLAT 1:493; LS, 473. This parallels Luther's argument that אסף (*'sp*) in Zeph. 3:18 should be interpreted as *corripiantur* ("may be snatched up/carried off"). See WA 13:477.15–WA 13:478.33; WA 13:507.36–WA 13:509.11; LW 18:361–3. On *corripio* [based on the compound *con* (*com*) + *rapio*], see OXLAT 1:493; LS, 473–4; and LDH 1:1710–12. Concerning the place of *raptus* in the mystical tradition, and in Luther, see: zur Mühlen, *Nos extra nos*, especially pp. 51–52, 198; Oberman, "Simul gemitus et raptus," 53–55; and Volker Leppin, "Mystik bei Luther," in *Gottes Nähe unmittelbar erfahren: Mystik im Mittelalter und bei Martin Luther*, ed. Berndt Hamm and Volker Leppin (Tübingen: Mohr Siebeck, 2007), 168–9. Zeph. 1:2 also appears in Ch. 2 of this study.

[144] Cf. Luther's argument that אסף (*'sp*) in Hos. 4:3 should be interpreted as *tollentur* ("taken up") or *auffrafen* ("taken away"), but also *finire* ("to end"). WA 13:16.19–21. LW 18:20. He was, perhaps, playing on the meaning within סוֹף (*sôp*, "end, finish, death").

[145] דמה (*dmh*) is the root. While the forms differ – נִדְמָה (*nidmâ*) in Zeph. 1:11, in contrast to אֵיךְ נִדְמֵיתָה (*'êk nidmêtâ*) in Obad. 1:5 – it is the same Hebrew term.

ish].' We also read in Ps. 4[:5]: 'Feel the sting of conscience upon your beds.' **This properly means to reduce something to silence and to nothing [*aliquid in silentium et in nihilum redigere*]**, to demolish some kingdom or people to such an extent that scarcely traces remain to be seen, so that they keep their silence and dare not utter a sound [*ut conticescant neque audeant mutire*], etc. This is just the way the Germans say about someone who has learned from his own evildoing, 'He has become so silent [*Er ist ßo feyn stil worden*].' Here the meaning is the same in every detail, as if he were saying: 'I will make you so small that you will be forced to be very quiet [*du ßolt recht stil werden*], for that calamity which is going to happen to you when I come against you with my army will be such that the attacks of thieves and robbers, no matter how great they might be, compared with this calamity are not to be considered attacks or depredation. You should have preferred to be oppressed and to be reduced to silence [*in silentium redigereris*] under the oppression of thieves. This, however, is not to be compared with the ruin that will occur when I come, etc. For I will leave you not a single bunch of grapes. I will take away everything you will have hidden, whether this be money or men whom you hoped you would save. So nothing will escape when I destroy [*vastante*].'[146]

His contention that נִדְמֵיתָה (*niḏmêṯâ*) be understood in terms of both silence and the "reduced to" idiom mirrored his argument in the lectures on Zephaniah, and as he did there, he identified a copious number of variants of the idiom as part of his argument (see Table A.5 in the Appendix).

Luther's translation of the term, however, changed between 1532 and 1545. In the 1532 *Deutsche Bibel*, he translated אֵיךְ נִדְמֵיתָה (*'êḵ niḏmêṯâ*) in Obad. 1:5 as *wie soltu* **so stille werden** ("how you should become so silent!").[147] But he amended that translation in the 1545 revision to *wie soltu* **so zu nicht werden?** ("how you should so become nothing/be so reduced to nothing/be so destroyed/be so undone?").[148] A Germanized rendering of the "reduced to" idiom, *zu nicht*

---

[146] "Quomodo conticuisses. Varius est usus huius verbi in scriptura, varie quoque interpretes reddiderunt. Est in 4. capito Ozeae: tacere feci matrem tuam. Et in psalmo 48, ubi nos legimus: homo cum esset in honore non intellexit, comparatus est iumentis. Item psalmo 4: cubilibus vestris compungite. Significat autem proprie: aliquid in silentium et in nihilum redigere, ita demoliri aliquod regnum aut populum aliquem, ut vix vestigia adpareant, ut conticescant neque audeant mutire etc. Sicut Germani dicunt de aliquo, qui suo malo doctus est: Er ist ßo feyn stil worden. Eadem per omnia hic est sententia q. d. ey ich wil dich feyn kleyn machen, du ßolt recht stil werden. Talis enim est futura ista tua calamitas veniente me cum exercitu meo contra te, ut insultus furum et latronum quantumvis magni ad hanc collati prorsus non iudicandi sint insultus aut depraedatio. optandum esset tibi, ut opprimereris et in silentium redigereris oppressus a furibus, sed non sunt ista conferenda cum excisione, quando ego veniam etc. Nam ego non relinquam tibi ullum racemum, omnia abscondita proferam. Haec sive pecunia fuerint sive homines, quos te servaturum sperabas. Adeo me vastante nihil evadet." WA 13:217.26–WA 13:218.10. LW 18:196–7. Emphasis mine. Medieval German sometimes renders *werden* with *wollen*; in these instances, *wil/will/wollen* is translated into English in the future tense. Accordingly, I have rendered *ich wil dich feyn kleyn machen* as "I will make you so small," in contrast to the LW's "I want to make you so small." I make similar adjustments in numerous places in this study.

[147] WA DB 11.2:254.5. The Vulgate translated this as *quomodo conticuisses* ("how you would have become silent"), largely the same as Luther's 1532 rendering.

[148] WA DB 11.2:255.5. Note also that in 1545, Luther changed this from a statement to a

werden has obvious links to the medieval German mystics of the "upper-Rhenish circle," echoing the *Nichts* and *Nichtigkeit* of Eckhart, Tauler, and the *Theologia Deutsch*. Notably, the 1539–41 Protocols show the following notation from his revision meetings: "*Nidma*, er ist da hin," mirroring his translation of נִדְמָה (*nidmâ*) in Zeph. 1:11 as *ist dahin*.[149] His Bible translation thus echoes his argument in the lectures concerning the dual meaning within דמה (*dmh*) – indicative of both silence [*conticuisses, tacere feci, silentium, stil worden*, and *stil werden*] which he took account of in his 1532 translation; and destruction and the wrath of God [*vastante* and *calamitas*] which he took account of in the 1545 revision and the 1539–41 Protocols. Moreover, his many scriptural citations to support that argument underscore his interwoven notions of silence and the wrath of God, which he saw in the multifarious Hebrew term נִדְמֵיתָה (*nidmêtâ*). Viewed together, Luther's *Deutsche Bibel* translations of דמה (*dmh*) in Zeph. 1:11, Obad. 1:5, and the scripture citations in his lectures on Obadiah demonstrate this breadth of meaning and the connection in his thought between silence and the wrath of God:

Table 5.3: Luther's *Deutsche Bibel* translations of דמה (*dmh*) in Zeph. 1:11, Obad. 1:5, and the scripture citations in his lectures on Obadiah.[150]

Hebrew	Luther's German	English Translation of Luther	Verse
וְדָמִיתִי (*wədāmîtî*)	Also wil ich ... hin richten	And I will put to death, execute	Hos. 4:5
נִדְמָה (*nidmâ*)	ist dahin	is gone, lost, dead, destroyed, done for	Zeph. 1:11
נִדְמֵיתָה (*nidmêtâ*)	so stille werden	to become so still	Obad. 1:5 (1532)
נִדְמֵיתָה (*nidmêtâ*)	zu nicht werden	to become nothing	Obad. 1:5 (1545)
נִדְמוּ (*nidmû*)	geschwigen ist	has become silent	Ps. 49:13 (1524)
נִדְמוּ (*nidmû*)	dahin ist	is gone, lost, dead, destroyed, done for	Ps. 49:13 (1528)
וְדֹמּוּ (*wədōmmû*)	vnd harret	and wait, remain	Ps. 4:5 (1524)

---

question, with the addition of the question mark. The 1538/39 handwritten entries in his Old Testament record *stille sein* and *zu nicht werden*, but not *ist dahin*. WA DB 4:242b.8–11 [the footnote at WA DB 4:242b.10 reads "schweigen und schweigen machen, vertilgen"].

[149] WA DB 4:242a.8 [the footnote at WA DB 4:242a.8 reads: "נִדְמֵיתָה (*nidmêtâ*)"].

[150] In Luther's 1531 and 1545 *Deutsche Bibel* translations of Ps. 49:13, neither *geschwigen ist* nor *dahin ist* appears. WA DB 10.1:257a.13; WA DB 10.1:257b.13. On *harret* in Ps. 4:5, Grimm advises that while *harren* has a connotation of "waiting" in the sense of hope and trust, in the "old language" it had a side connotation, which conveyed a threatening, ominous meaning, also suggesting a sense of doubt and uncertainty. DWB 10:494–6. Ps. 4:5: WA DB 10.1:112.5.

A final example of the influence of the Hebrew upon Luther's interpretation of mysticism in Obad. 1:5 is his linking of דמה (*dmh*) with *humilitas*. The Zwickau text records him arguing in the lectures that דמה (*dmh*) should be understood as the removal of *homut* ("arrogance, pride"), i. e. being made humble: "For it [they] will make you silent [*still*] and fainthearted, sheepish [*kleynlauttig*], etc., if they tear the pride [*homut*] away from you."[151] *Homut*, as the antithesis of *humilitas*, ultimately has strong ties to the mystical tradition. It is important to note that Luther's consideration of Obad. 1:5 was not an isolated place in his writings where he linked *humilitas* to *nichts*.[152] In his 1521 *Das Magnificat verdeutschet und ausgelegt*, for example, he remarked that he "Germanized" the Latin term *humilitas* with a translation of *nichtickeit* ("nothingness").[153] This link between *humilitas* and *Nichtigkeit* was not an innovation of Luther's, but rather was rooted in monastic mysticism; it appears particularly in the writings of Bernard.[154] His deviation from Bernard's understanding of that coupling was in his further interpretation of the mystical encounter with God through *humilitas* and *Nichtigkeit* as death (*ist dahin*) and destruction (*vastante*).[155] His argument that the removal of *homut* be understood as *nihilum* and *nichts* as part of his interpretation of דמה (*dmh*) is thus not only another example of how he drew on the mystical tradition for his Bible translation and exegesis, but also of how he modified that tradition to reflect the nuances that he saw in the Hebrew.

Parallel Reference: Isaiah 6:5: כִּי־נִדְמֵיתִי
(kî-nidmêtî, "For I am silenced, undone")

While the influence of the Hebrew on Luther's interweaving of mystical concepts with his interpretation of the wrath of God in Zeph. 1:11 and Obad. 1:5 is

---

[151] "Fures mochten dich still machen und kleynlauttig etc. wen sie dyr den homut weg rissen etc." WA 13:210.11–12. The modern German spelling is *Hochmut*.

[152] *Nichts* is the fuller rendering of *nicht* or *nichte*, which sometimes appear in Luther's writings.

[153] WA 7:560.35–36. Cf. Martin Luther, *Luther Deutsch. Die Werke Martin Luthers in neuer Auswahl für die Gegenwart. Vol. 5: Martin Luther. Die Schriftauslegung*, 2nd ed., ed. Kurt Aland (Stuttgart: Ehrenfried Klotz, 1963), 293. The modern German spelling is *Nichtigkeit*.

[154] Theo Bell and Walther Loewenich both discuss Luther's association of *humilitas* with *Nichtigkeit*, *Niedrigkeit*, and *Unterdrücktheit* within the context of Bernard, although they offer varying opinions concerning how far Luther diverged from Bernard, particularly concerning Bernard's understanding of *humilitas* as *Tugend* ("virtue"). Bell, *Divus Bernhardus*, 119–20. Von Loewenich, *Luthers Theologia Crucis*, 153–7. Von Loewenich further links *humilitas* to *tentatio* and *Anfechtung* in Luther's thought. Von Loewenich, *Luthers Theologia Crucis*, 157–64. See also Leppin, "Luther's Roots in Monastic-Mystical Piety," 53. Leppin goes into great detail concerning how Luther drew upon Bernard for his use of the concept of *humilitas*; but also how he transformed the concept from how Bernard used it.

[155] The meaning of "lost" in the idiom *ist dahin* seems to also play on the mystical interpretation.

clear, he made no specific reference to *Anfechtung* in either case. But that does not mean that he did not identify דמה (*dmh*) with *Anfechtung*. The explicit connection between דמה (*dmh*) and *Anfechtung* appears in his translation and exegesis of the term in Is. 6:5, where the "reduced to" idiom again appears. He cited the same Psalm [49] in his 1528–31 lectures on Isaiah as he did in his interpretation of Obad. 1:5, focusing on דמה (*dmh*):

And I said: 'Woe is me! For I was silent [tacui].' This passage conflicts with the one where God says that he cannot be seen, so that man may live (Ex. 33:20). But here, too, Isaiah grants that he is lost because of the vision (for in Hebrew 'I was silent [*Tacui*]' is used for 'I was lost [*perii*]'), so that nothing conflicts with that other passage, דָּמָה (*dāmâ*), that is, he is likened to, as in Ps. 49[:13]: 'Man, when he was in honor, etc. He is compared to beasts and has become like them.' This is an explanation with reference to beasts of burden that have perished and are nothing [*quae perierunt et nihil sunt*]. Thus the prophet says that he was completely reduced to nothing [*in nihil redactum*], or reduced to silence [*redactum in silencium*], of which let nothing more be said. For דָּמָה (*dāmâ*) means 'he was silent [*siluit*],' and דְּמָמָה (*dəmāmâ*) means 'silence [*silencium*],' as in Ps. 94[:17]: 'Almost it would have lived in hell.' In Hebrew: 'My soul in silence [*In silencio anima mea*].' ... This is the distress and trial of conscience [*vexacio tentacioque conscienciae* ('the vexation and *Anfechtung* of the conscience')] than which no other is more dreadful, namely, to be placed in *Anfechtung* [*Tentari*] concerning the Word and doctrine ... Isaiah feels this, and his conscience is tormented in final death [*et angitur consciencia eius in summa morte*].[156]

As was the case in Zeph. 1:11 and Obad. 1:5, there are numerous testimonies to the influence of דמה (*dmh*) on his interpretation of mysticism in this verse. One of these is his argument that while נִדְמֵיתִי (*nidmêṯî*, "I am silenced [many translate this 'I am undone']") literally means *Tacui* ("I was silent"), in this verse it is a surrogate for *perii* ("I was lost") – i. e. being lost in a spiritual vision.[157] But he also connected *perii* to the "reduced to" idiom, which he used in two particular iterations: *in nihil redactum* ("reduced to nothing") and *redactum in silencium* ("reduced to silence"). His reference to Ps. 49:13 and the

---

[156] "'Et dixi: Ve mihi, quia tacui.' Pugnat hic locus cum illo, ubi deus dicit se non posse videri, ut vivat homo. At concedit et hic Esaias se periisse (in hebreo enim 'Tacui' habetur pro 'perii') ex visione, ut nihil [Ps. 49, 13] pugnet cum isto loco. von דָּמָה i. e. assimilatus est, sic in Psal. 48. Homo cum in honore etc. comparatus est iumentis et similis factus est illis. Hoc exponitur de iumentis, quae perierunt et nihil sunt. Sic propheta se penitus in nihil redactum dicit vel redactum in silencium, de quo nihil dicatur amplius. [Ps. 94, 17] דָּמָה enim siluit et דְּמָמָה silencium significat Psal. 93. Paulominus habitasset in inferno. Hebraice: In silencio anima mea ... Haec est vexacio tentacioque conscienciae, qua non est horrendior alia, videlicet Tentari de verbo et doctrina ... Hoc sentit Esaias et angitur consciencia eius in summa morte." WA 31.2:49.30–WA 31.2:50.3, 7–9, 10–11. LW 16:71–72. I added the *lene dagesh* to the Hebrew terms.

[157] *Perii* (*pereo*) is a rich term, whose semantic range also encompasses: to pass away, to come to nothing, to vanish, to disappear, to be destroyed, to perish, to die, and to be undone. OXLAT 2:1471–2; LS, 1339. I omitted כִּי (*kî-*) and *quia*, which introduce the complete phrase in the Hebrew Bible and Vulgate, for the sake of clarity of the main term in focus.

"beasts that perish" parallels the connection with death and destruction in his use of the idiom in Zephaniah and Obadiah. That antinomical interpretation of דמה (*dmh*) as mystical silence and destruction was not limited to the lectures, but also appeared in his *Deutsche Bibel* translation. He translated כִּי-נִדְמֵיתִי (*kî-nidmêtî*, "For I am silenced") in 1528 as *ich bin verderbet* ("I have perished, gone wasted, decayed") with an emendation in 1545 to *ich vergehe* ("I have died, died away, decayed").[158] The Vulgate, by contrast, translated כִּי-נִדְמֵיתִי (*kî-nidmêtî*) as *quia tacui* ("because I was silent").

Another witness to the influence of the Hebrew on his interpretation of mysticism in Is. 6:5 is his argument that נִדְמֵיתִי (*nidmêtî*) be understood through the parallel in Ps. 94:17: כִּמְעַט שָׁכְנָה דוּמָה נַפְשִׁי (*kim'aṭ šāḵənâ ḏûmâ napšî*, "my soul almost dwelled in silence"), which he identified as *In silencio anima mea* ("My soul in silence") and further connected with *conscientia*. A critical part of Luther's framing of that link to *conscientia* was his argument that נִדְמֵיתִי (*nidmêtî*) be understood as the vexation of the conscience [*vexacio ... conscienciae*], which he more specifically delineated as *tentatio* – that is, *Anfechtung*.[159] This exploitation of *conscientia* with the link to his theology of *Anfechtung* is precisely the hermeneutical method which he employed in his interpretation of Jonah.[160] Here, he further linked *conscientia* to mystical silence, under the influence of the Hebrew term דמה (*dmh*).

The pairing of the "reduced to" idiom with *Anfechtung* to interpret the Hebrew is also significant. Numerous scholars remark on Luther's understanding of *Anfechtung* as *Nichtigkeit*. Zur Mühlen, for example, cites both Augustine's and Luther's interpretation of Ps. 116:11, arguing that *excessus* is understood both in terms of *Anfechtung* and *zu nichts geworden ist*.[161] Maurer argues for a similar link between *Vernichtigung* ("destruction, blotting out") and *Anfechtung* in Luther' thought.[162] Luther's exploitation of the ambiguity of the term דמה (*dmh*) in his interpretation of Is. 6:5 – potentially conveying a meaning associated with mystical silence and illumination, but also with destruction – parallels his method in Zeph. 1:11 and Obad. 1:5. Moreover, it shows the direct link between דמה (*dmh*) and *Anfechtung* in his thought. It is yet another example that helps to piece together a more complete picture of what Luther meant by the

---

[158] 1528: WA DB 11.1:40.5. 1545: WA DB 11.1:41.5. Cf. WA DB 4:45a.3. Cf. Nah. 1:12, where Luther translated ענה (*'nh*) as both *demuetigen* and *verderben*; thus also suggesting a link to *humilitas*, not to mention the dialectical interpretation of that term. WA DB 11.2:290.12; WA DB 11.2:291.12.

[159] This appears as *tentacio[que]* and *Tentari* in the Isaiah lectures, as noted in the main text above. Cf. Luther's reference to vexation of the conscience in his interpretation of Hos. 10:8, and his allusions to it in his interpretations of Jon. 1:2, 1:4, and 2:4. These all are discussed in Part 1 of this chapter.

[160] And, he did so in his interpretation of Hos. 10:8.

[161] Zur Mühlen, *Nos extra nos*, 196.

[162] Maurer, *Der junge Melanchthon* 2:254.

Anfechtung of the prophets: those persons who not only dispensed *Anfechtung* (recall Ch. 1), but experienced it themselves as part of their visions.

Habakkuk 2:20: הַס מִפָּנָיו *(has mippānāyw, "silence before him")*

In his consideration of Hab. 2:20, Luther identified a second Hebrew term with silence and the "reduced to" idiom: הס (*hs*). He argued that the phrase הַס מִפָּנָיו (*has mippānāyw*, "[Let there be] silence before him [God's face]") is a Hebraism:

> But soon he can set an example and show them that they will all perish [*vergehen ... werden*] and be reduced to nothing [*zu nichte werden*] and that they must keep silent before him [*also stille fur yhm sein*] when he comes. For in Hebrew the expression 'before him [*fur yhm*]' or 'before his countenance [*fur seim angesicht*]' means as much as when he comes or when he, coming to us, turns his face toward us ... Habakkuk wants to say: 'But when our God comes and visits/afflicts/haunts/bedevils/strikes [*heimsucht*], it will be silent [*stille*] in all the world' ... Thereby he sets things aright and effects silence [*still*] wherever he comes. No other god can do that.[163]

His contention that הס (*hs*) should be understood as both *stille* ("silence") and *zu nichte werden* ("reduced to nothing") mirrors his interpretation of דמה (*dmh*), exploiting the mystical tradition behind the "reduced to" idiom, *nichts*, and *Nichtigkeit*. And as he did with דמה (*dmh*), he argued that הס (*hs*) should be associated with both mystical silence and the destructive wrath of God. His exegesis of *stille* and *vergehen ... werden* reinforces this. But there were additional ways in which the Hebrew influenced his interpretation and manipulation of the mystical tradition in the verse.

One of these appears in his discussion in the lectures of מִפָּנָיו (*mippānāyw*, "before him" or "before his face"): "The expression 'the face of the Lord' in scripture indicates either the knowledge [*cognitionem*] or the coming of the Lord when he becomes known and is revealed [*revelatur*] to us."[164] His identification of *the face of God* as *revelation* is exactly what the mystics argued con-

---

[163] "Aber bald kan er sie lassen ein stuecklin sehen, das sie alzumal vergehen und zu nichte werden und muessen also stille fur yhm sein, wenn er kompt. Denn dis woertlin 'fur yhm' odder 'fur seim angesicht' lautet ym Ebreischen also viel, als: wenn er kompt odder das angesicht zu uns keret als der do kompt ... das Habacuc also wil sagen: Wenn aber unser Gott kompt und heimsucht, so wirds ynn aller welt stille ... damit macht ers schlecht und still, wo er hin kompt; das kan kein ander Gott thun." WA 19:423.15–19, 21–22, 24–25. LW 19:225. This is in the commentary on Habakkuk. Immediately following this, Luther explicitly identified Habakkuk's prophecies as *Anfechtung*. See WA 19:423.26–28; LW 19:225. [This is a general statement at the end of the chapter, and is not necessarily directed specifically at v. 20. Nevertheless, the overt citation of *Anfechtung* at this particular place is noteworthy and reinforces the overall link.]

[164] "Facies domini in scriptura significat cognitionem vel adventum domini, quando nobis innotescit et revelatur." WA 13:439.13–14. LW 19:132. Note the parallel with מִנֶּגֶד עֵינֶיךָ (*minneged 'ênêkā*) in Jon. 2:5 and Ps. 31:23. Both verses are discussed earlier in this chapter.

cerning *excessus* as the mystical ascent and cognitive illumination.¹⁶⁵ Luther did not necessarily dismiss the revelatory function of the experience, but rather reinterpreted its form – no longer a peaceful journey of the soul or intellect which left the individual in tears of ecstasy or joy, but an assault that carried the very real threat of death during the encounter. He effectively recast the experience as revelation by *Anfechtung*.

Luther made a further argument concerning מִפָּנָיו (*mippānāyw*), which shows a third evidence of the influence of Hebrew on his exploitation of mysticism in the verse. He contended that מִפָּנָיו (*mippānāyw*) be interpreted as *heimsucht*. *Heimsuchen* ("to visit") has a rich history in the mystical tradition, denoting earthly visitations from God, angelic figures, etc.¹⁶⁶ This argument, within the broader context and in relationship to his other remarks identifying הס (*hs*) as *zu nichte werden* and *vergehen ... werden*, reinforces the contention that he was drawing upon and modifying the mystical tradition as part of his translation of the verse. Moreover, it is another reflection of his dialectical interpretation of mystical silence.¹⁶⁷ It is also no accident that the term *heimsuchen* itself is ambiguous, while frequently used to indicate a friendly or gracious visitation from God, it also has connotations of "violent attack" and "invasion," according to Grimm.¹⁶⁸ Luther chose a very loaded term in *heimsucht*.

In sum, Luther's translation and exegesis of הַס מִפָּנָיו (*has mippānāyw*) in Hab. 2:20 shows the profound connection in his thought between mystical encounter with God, the reception of knowledge and revelation from God, and the wrath of God. It also gives further testimony to the important role of the concept of mystical silence in that connection. It is important to note that Luther made prolific use of the "reduced to" idiom in his engagement with the Minor Prophets, beyond the examples discussed here. Table A.5 in the Appendix provides an overview of its variants and occurrences. And while it appears in his translation and exegesis outside of these twelve books of the Hebrew Bible, his explicit attribution of its use to the prophet Zephaniah in the identification of the יֹשְׁבֵי הַמַּכְתֵּשׁ (*yōšəḇê hammaḵtēš*, "the inhabitants of the mortar") meta-

---

¹⁶⁵ See Oberman, "Simul gemitus et raptus," 45–51.

¹⁶⁶ For example, see Joachim Wach, *Types of Religious Experience, Christian and Non-Christian* (London: Routledge and Kegan Paul, 1951), 141. Grimm cites the association with the Feast of the Visitation of Mary ("das fest der heimsuchung der jungfrau Maria, da sie die Elisabeth besuchet"). DWB 10:883.

¹⁶⁷ Cf. Luther's interpretation of Amos 8:3, where he did the same. WA 13:197.24–25. LW 18:180. Luther's argument that הס (*hs*) should be interpreted as *vergehen ... werden* also parallels his 1545 *Deutsche Bibel* translation of דמה (*dmh*) in Is. 6:5 as *ich vergehe* ("I have died, died away, decayed"). See Table 5.2.

¹⁶⁸ DWB 10:883: "invasio violenta, irruptio in aedes alicujus cum armis," under *Heimsucht*. Cf. the same page, under *Heimsuchung*, where Grimm cites as examples: Is. 10:3; Jer. 23:12, 46:21, 50:31; and Ezek. 9:1. Langenscheidt also provides the definitions: "to afflict"; "to infest"; and "to haunt ... or be haunted (by ghosts)." Springer, *Langenscheidts enzyklopädisches Wörterbuch*, Pt. 2, Vol. 1, 761.

phor in Zeph. 1:11 suggest that it has an especially distinctive role in the Minor Prophets.

Summary and Conclusion

In many places in his translation of the Minor Prophets, Luther appropriated specific elements from the mystical tradition. When he did, he modified that mystical tradition in his interpretation, linking it to the wrath of God, many times explicitly as *Anfechtung*. These examples in the Minor Prophets show that mysticism played a role in his writings well into mid-career. This supports and augments the work of scholars who, in the past several decades, have argued for the important role of mysticism in Luther's writings and in his theology, especially Oberman, Hoffman, Lohse, zur Mühlen, and Leppin. The texts adduced in this chapter thus furnish a broadened frame of reference for understanding his engagement with the mystical tradition.

Moreover, these texts provide further evidence of the links between Luther's employment of certain terminology and the mystical tradition. In particular, his understanding of *conscientia* continues to be a topic of considerable discussion among scholars.[169] Some, including Ebeling, Bornkamm, and Ozment, draw too dark a line between Luther and the mystical tradition upon which he drew.[170] They either downplay the significance of the parallels between Luther's

---

[169] See Gerhard Ebeling, "Das Gewissen in Luthers Verständnis," in *Lutherstudien. Vol. 3: Begriffsuntersuchungen – Textinterpretationen – Wirkungsgeschichtliches* (Tübingen: J. C. B. Mohr (Paul Siebeck), 1985), 108–25; Hoffman, *Luther and the Mystics*, 87–88; Ozment, *Homo Spiritualis*, 99, 102, 117, 139–58, 173–4, 184–209, 214–6; Leppin, *Die fremde Reformation*, 138; Lohse, "Conscience and Authority in Luther"; Herbert Schlögel, "Das andere Gewissen (?) Einblicke in die gegenwärtige evangelische Ethik," *Catholica* 48 (1994): 175–90; Herbert Schlögel, "'Der Mensch ist Gewissen ...' Überlegungen zum Gewissensverständnis von Gerhard Ebeling," *Catholica* 43 (1989): 79–94; and Anders Schinkel, *Conscience and Conscientious Objections* (Amsterdam: Pallas Publications, 2007), especially pp. 171–94, and on Luther specifically, pp. 196–202. The entire vol. 1 of Hirsch's *Lutherstudien* focuses on Luther's doctrine of conscience; and Baylor devotes an entire chapter to the question of Luther's understanding of *synteresis*, though the book addresses the subject throughout; in Baylor, *Action and Person*, 157–208.

[170] See Bornkamm's contention that "nur Dilettanten der Geistesgeschichte können Luther zum Mystiker erklären ('only dilettantes of intellectual history [some translate this as spiritual history] can explain Luther as a mystic')"; in Heinrich Bornkamm, *Luthers geistige Welt* (Lüneburg: Heiland-Verlag, 1947), 264; which he revised in the second edition of his book to "Luther war kein Mystiker ('Luther was no mystic')"; in Heinrich Bornkamm, *Luthers geistige Welt*, 2nd ed. (Gütersloh: C. Bertelsmann, 1953), 315. Hoffman cites the first edition in *Luther and the Mystics*, 79. Cf. Ebeling's argument that *Gewissen* (*conscientia*) is a moral phenomenon both in scholasticism and mysticism; which he uses to further argue that one can differentiate Luther from both, since, in his view, Luther saw *Gewissen* as a theological phenomenon rather than a moral one. Ebeling, "Das Gewissen," 112–3 [§ 21 and § 22]. Ebeling is a particularly good example of a scholar who tries to systematize Luther's thought to explain away anything that would suggest that Luther truly was, in any fashion, a "mystic." The complexity of this attempt is glaring in "Das Gewissen," where he assembles a list of 83 observations con-

use of certain terms and concepts and their role in the mystical tradition; or, they attempt to reconcile (a) his use of these terms and concepts in places where it seems to align with mystical thought with (b) his use of these terms and concepts in other places in his writings where it does not seem to align with mystical thought. In order to accomplish this, these scholars erroneously "systematize" Luther, rather than acknowledge the parallels between his use of this terminology and mystical authors' use of it – even if these parallels appear only in certain instances.

For example, Luther's reflections on the Hebrew in the Minor Prophets suggest that he viewed conscience as a very real thing, where a very real spiritual battle took place, not, as Ebeling asserts, something merely symbolic.[171] Furthermore, in the examples examined in this chapter, Luther did not speak of *conscientia* as part of an ethical or moral decision-making process, in line with certain scholastic thought – for example, whereby *synteresis* is associated with an infallible ethical or moral principle, while *conscientia* is associated with a fallible ethical or moral choice that the individual makes, which may or may not be aligned with that principle.[172] By contrast, he often spoke of *conscientia* as a *locus* of *Anfechtung* – the assault from God. This supports the observations of scholars such as Leppin and Lohse who call attention to the parallels between Luther and the mystics who spoke of *conscientia* as the "place" where the "meeting" between God and man occurs.[173] Perhaps most important of all, the frequency with which mystical terminology appears in Luther's academic mid-career is profound. Hundreds of references to these terms appear in his reflections on the Minor Prophets: *conscientia, Gewissen, gemitus, affectus, excessus mentis, raptus,* and *Nichtigkeit*; as do the concepts of silence and apophatic theology, *Anfechtung*, and the "reduced to" idiom.[174] Furthermore, these terms and concepts do not appear independent of one another. When Luther discussed *conscientia*, for example, he also remarked on *gemitus, affectus, excessus mentis,* and *Anfechtung*.[175] Over and over again parallels with language that

---

cerning Luther's understanding of conscience, which, if nothing other than because of its mere size, lacks a unifying thread to substantiate his argument. Cf. Ozment's conclusion that there is "a chasm between his [Luther's] theological thought and that of Tauler and Gerson, which is quite incapable of being bridged"; in *Homo Spiritualis*, 214. Hoffman summarizes many of these scholarly arguments in *Luther and the Mystics*; see especially pp. 25–128.

[171] Ebeling, *Luther: Einführung in sein Denken*, 303; Hoffman, *Luther and the Mystics*, 87.

[172] See Ebeling, "Das Gewissen," 112 [§ 17]; and cf. the earlier footnote referencing [§ 21 and § 22] in Ebeling. Many other scholars cite and discuss this same issue concerning certain scholastic thought.

[173] See Leppin, *Die fremde Reformation*, 138; and Lohse, "Conscience and Authority in Luther," 163.

[174] *Conscientia* alone appears over 200 times in WA 13 and at least 13 times in WA 19; and *Gewissen* appears over 100 times in WA 19.

[175] See Luther's discussion of *conscientia, gemitus,* and *Anfechtung* in his reflections on

appears in Tauler, Eckhart, and other mystics appear in Luther's reflections. It becomes very difficult to construe all of this as coincidence. Luther's exploitation of the mystical tradition in his translation of the Minor Prophets, and the role of Hebrew in it, thus provide new insight into this unexplored facet of his Bible translation and interpretation.

This chapter also elucidates the relationship between Hebrew and *Anfechtung* in Luther's thought. While he would have certainly had the *Anfechtung* concept without Hebrew, it does show how certain elements in the Hebrew language impacted his translation of *Anfechtung* in particular instances where he also exploited the mystical tradition. Thus, it provides additional insight into the relationship between mysticism and *Anfechtung* in Luther's theology and in his Bible translation.

Finally, this chapter provides new philological insights into specific translations from Luther. It examines a number of his translations which have received little or no attention to date. It shows how Luther's engagement with the mystical tradition for his translation of the Minor Prophets left a lasting impact on certain elements of the German language, such as the *Neuhochdeutsch* term *wogen*. In all, it helps to supplement the previous chapters of this study and expand the field of vision concerning Luther's Hebrew.

Jon. 2:4. See Oberman's "Simul gemitus et raptus" also on the appearance of multiple mystical terms together in Luther's texts.

Chapter Six

Conclusion

In terms of language, Luther was, technically-speaking, a simple man. His German and Latin vocabulary and syntax were by and large straightforward. His language was not marked by lexical grandiloquence or complex constructions. He largely relied on his wit, sarcasm, and humor rather than using the erudite language that he most certainly would have been able to draw upon from his scholastic upbringing and academic life in the university. Perhaps this is one reason why he had such an affinity for Hebrew. He remarked of the language, "The Greeks express themselves with the best and most attractive words, but the Hebrew language shines with such simplicity and majesty that it cannot be imitated."[1] Nevertheless, much lies behind the simple letters of the Hebrew. The same can be said of Luther. There is much still to be discovered about Luther's theology, his thinking, and his history through his language.

This study has sought to make a fundamental contribution to scholarship on Martin Luther. Until now, investigation of Luther's interpretation and translation of Hebrew has focused almost exclusively on the Psalms. This study is the first comprehensive investigation to focus on any other part of the Hebrew Bible. It thus expands the frame of reference with which scholars can understand Luther's Hebrew. It provides detailed analysis of many examples of his Hebrew translation which have never before been discussed or examined in any detail, and it provides hundreds of examples of his methodological handling of Hebrew translation issues. And it includes one of the most exhaustive analyses to date of three key philological challenges that confronted him in translating the Bible: Hebrew figures of speech, the Hebrew trope of repetition, and Hebrew transliteration.

This research permits us to reach a number of conclusions about Luther's Hebrew translation in academic mid-career, roughly the mid-1520s to the early 1530s. First, by this period in his life, his struggles with the Hebrew language were not over. Despite having access to a range of Hebrew Bibles, a rich repository of literary resources, and a number of Hebraists and other philologists both inside and outside Wittenberg, he still had major issues with his translation of

---

[1] "Graeci optimis et suavissimis verbis locuti sunt. Hebrea autem lingua tali simplicitate et maiestate floret, ut imitari non possit." These are Luther's words in the *Tischreden* as recorded by Conrad Cordatus. WA TR 2:653.26–28 [§ 2779a]. Cordatus, *Tagebuch*, 254 [§ 992]. Cf. WA TR 1:524.10–30 [§ 1040].

the Minor Prophets. The difficulty and obscurity of the Hebrew language in the prophetic books of the Bible most certainly were partly to blame. Nevertheless, he faced many challenges in deciphering Hebrew vocabulary, grammar, and syntax, not to mention in making his way through the sea of contrasting opinions concerning translations for the most complicated language. He was just as perplexed, and probably more so, with how best to render Hebrew tropes and figures of speech into idiomatic German – something which his methodological vacillation shows strikingly. He never reached a point, even as he later revised his Bible, where he had a well-oiled methodology. Despite his reflections in *Sendbrief vom Dolmetschen* (1530) and *Summarien über die Psalmen und Ursachen des Dolmetschens* (1531–33), contradictions in his methodology abounded, and his vaunted rules of translation were not able to fully account for these.

These observations do not amount to a judgment on the correctness or incorrectness, or the quality, of his work. In fact, of the places in the Hebrew Bible where he conceded uncertainty, called attention to disagreement among translators and/or made a sharp protest himself, or about which his adversaries sharply challenged him, scholars disagree to this day concerning many of them: אַךְ (*'ak*) in Jon. 2:5; סַף־רַעַל (*sap-ra'al*) in Zech. 12:2; כְּלוּב (*kəlûḇ*) in Amos 8:1–2 [and Jer. 5:27]; נקה (*nqh*) in Nah. 1:3; בְּטֶרֶם לֹא־יָבוֹא (*bəṭerem lō'-yāḇô'*) in Zeph. 2:2; and there are many more. Across the various contradictions and issues of uncertainty which appear in this study, his main translation problems do not appear to be based on any overwhelming incompetence with the language. Quite the contrary. For an amateur translator – which for all intents and purposes he was – surrounded by, as Burnett notes, not necessarily the A-list of Hebraists of the day, some of the observations and insights which he was able to make are quite amazing.[2] It is clear, however, that despite his own increasing skills and the widening range of scholarly resources available to him, as he advanced to academic mid-career, the Hebrew text never stopped posing problems, and Luther never achieved complete consistency in responding to them. The contradictions in Luther's translation and exegesis of the Minor Prophets thus suggest that many scholars have been too ready to take Luther at his word concerning his principles of translation. Luther's persistent literal translations of Hebrew words and phrases show this all the more. His axiom concerning the idiomatic German of the "men in the market place" was often unreliable, even in light of other translation principles of his which scholars often cite to explain away the phenomenon.

This study also shows that Luther's ubiquitous attempts to reproduce the semantic intensity that he perceived in Hebrew were one of the definitive imprints of the language on his translation of the Minor Prophets, one with which he sought to differentiate his Bible from the Vulgate. The examples amassed

---

[2] See Burnett's comments on this in *Christian Hebraism in the Reformation Era*, 58.

in this study elucidate, to a greater extent than has been shown by scholars to date, the diversity of Luther's method in this regard. Sometimes he mimicked the Hebrew by employing especially forceful or emotionally evocative German translations. At other times, he translated the Hebrew with multifarious German terms, which simulated the layered, intensified meanings that he saw in the Hebrew text. In other instances, he reproduced what he saw as particularly intense Hebrew text by following verse divisions and word positioning in the Masoretic Text, as in Obad. 1:9. Still other times, he was willing to make extraordinary deviations from the literal Hebrew Bible: for example, his translation of וּבֵית־אֵל יִהְיֶה לְאָוֶן (*ûḇêṯ-'ēl yihyeh lə'āwen*) in Amos 5:5 as *vnd Bethel wird **BethAuen** werden* (1545), where he "inserted" text that was not present in the Hebrew Bible in order to complete his German rendition; his addition of *nicht* in his translation of Jon. 2:5; and his omission of ־ָם (*-ām*) in his rendering of Jon. 2:9 (1532).

These observations broaden the scholarly understanding of the role of emotion, semantic intensity, and culture-based language extremity in Luther's Bible, building upon the work of linguists such as Stolt and Wierzbicka concerning the importance of these elements in translation. Luther's Hebrew translation was not merely a matter of choosing between the hermeneutical methods expressed by Schleiermacher's notion of *Verfremdung* and *Entfremdung* [i. e. literal translation and dynamic equivalence]. It was far more nuanced. The integral role of the *affectus* as an inseparable part of the *intellectus*, the importance of duplicating indigenous Hebrew language "extremities," and the crucial place of culture-specific facets of the Hebrew language associated with emotion and intensity were all major factors in Luther's renderings of Hebrew into German.

The Buber-Rosenzweig translation helps to illuminate this facet of Luther's Bible. Their almost obsessive focus on features of the Hebrew language related to semantic intensity and auditory elements of the text mirrored Luther's, though they went much further than him. Nevertheless, their update to the *Deutsche Bibel* reinforces the indispensability of these elements in Hebrew to German translation. Though they were trying to improve upon Luther, the major focus of their translation was ultimately the same as his. Moreover, their criticisms of Luther, and the corresponding adjustments they made to render a more accurate German translation of Hebrew, were often not based on a question of how far to move between *Verfremdung* and *Entfremdung*. Rather, again and again, their translation focused on the most acoustic and emotionally powerful rendering of the Hebrew into the German – that is, to what extent they could translate the richest affective meaning of the Hebrew. Their efforts illuminate how the *Affektenlehre* of the Middle Ages and early modern period, which governed much of Luther's Bible translation, has lasting importance in Bible translation to this day.

This study also illuminates the massive role that inner-biblical interpretation – i. e. scriptural quotations and citations – played in Luther's translation of the Minor Prophets. It shows that he did not always simply cite one Hebrew term in one location to support his interpretation of that same term in another. Instead, he regularly cited multiple terms in multiple verses. More importantly, sometimes the Hebrew terms that he cited were different than the term in the Minor Prophets which he was translating. This exploitation of different Hebrew terminology than the source text which he was translating is a distinctive hermeneutical tool of his, which is largely overlooked by scholars.

These observations illuminate the great extent to which his German Bible translation reflected an interwoven, multi-layered interpretation of the Hebrew, incorporating numerous wider linguistic connotations and broader theological themes. He based these translations, informed by many other texts inside and outside the Minor Prophets, on what he perceived to be a much richer, multifarious meaning in the Hebrew. This study further shows how, through his heavy use of scriptural quotations, citations, and allusions, he often specifically exploited the ritual language of cultic purification in the law code of the Hebrew Bible in order to interweave theological readings into his interpretation and translation of the Minor Prophets. Most frequently this appeared as interpretations of the wrath of God as linked to purification, and, many times, included allusions to his theology of *Anfechtung*. These examples thus show that Luther's application of Origen's *scriptura sui ipsius interpres* maxim for his translation of the Minor Prophets was especially rich and diverse.

This study makes an important contribution to the scholarly understanding of Luther's implicit and explicit engagement with Jewish and Christian mystical traditions, elucidating the role it played in his academic mid-career Bible translation. Aside from Luther's discussions of the Tetragrammaton, scholars have generally not taken a serious look at the relationship between mysticism and Hebrew in his Bible translation. This study changes that. It uncovers many instances where Luther, as part of his translation of the Minor Prophets, appropriated specific elements from the mystical tradition, and modified that mystical tradition in his interpretation, linking it to the wrath of God and to *Anfechtung*. It demonstrates that how he accomplished this was often shaped by the Hebrew. One of the most illuminating examples of this is Luther's translation of Jonah, for which he drew extensively upon the mystical tradition. His many citations of the mystical tradition, and his modification of that tradition to link it with the wrath of God, were often predicated on nuances in the Hebrew terms and phrases which he argued carried different connotations than the rendering in the Vulgate. Luther's engagement with Hebrew shaped his exploitation of the mystical tradition not only in his translation of Jonah, but for his translation of the other books of the Minor Prophets as well.

This research builds upon the work of Oberman, Hoffman, Lohse, zur Mühlen, and Leppin. It identifies many Hebrew words and phrases which Luther connected with mysticism, thus broadening the frame of reference in which scholars can examine Luther's engagement with medieval mysticism, which has to date been mainly limited to his use of Greek, Latin, and German. This study also shows that despite many scholars' arguments that Luther largely dispensed with mysticism after his early years, this was not so. The mystical tradition played a prominent role in his thought in his academic mid-career. Moreover, his engagement with that tradition distinctly influenced the language that he chose for his German Bible. And that engagement was in many ways massive. Mystically influenced translation choices such as *zu nicht werden* in Obad. 1:5, *wogen* in Jon. 2:4, and *ist dahin* in Zeph. 1:11 remain in the German Bible to this day.[3] This research thus supports and augments the work of those scholars who argue for the great importance that mysticism played in Luther's theology.

Finally, this study shows that Luther's frequent association of various texts in the Minor Prophets with his theology of *Anfechtung* was many times shaped by the Hebrew that he consulted. This appears not just in those examples where he exploited the mystical tradition for his Bible translation, but across all of the categories examined in this study. When he discerned a semantic intensity in the Hebrew, for example, this often fed many of his theological interpretations of *Anfechtung* in the texts. Sometimes this appears as an explicit interpretation by Luther as *Anfechtung* or *tentatio*. At other times, it shows through his use of various terms that have distinct connections to *Anfechtung* in his other writings. The same phenomenon appears in his use of inner-biblical interpretation. When he exploited the ritual language of cultic purification, interweaving theological interpretations of purification with the wrath of God into his interpretations of the Minor Prophets, he often made allusions to *Anfechtung* through the terminology and imagery employed. In each, he linked the prophetic texts which described prophecies of calamity, judgment, God's coming wrath, and salvation with theological exegesis linked to purity, justification, and *Anfechtung*, based on this ritual language in the Hebrew Bible.

In addition to uncovering and elucidating many instances where Hebrew played a role in shaping his interpretation of *Anfechtung*, this study also identifies specific Hebrew words which he used as synonyms for *Anfechtung*, or otherwise linked to it. It also shows how Luther's collective translation decisions over a larger body of work had a common objective, and thus worked to build a "line" of interpretation in his German rendering of the Minor Prophets. The *Anfechtung* theme dominated his translation of the prophets.

Luther's translation of the Minor Prophets was one of the final pieces of his 1534 Bible translation. It was in many ways the definitive time for his Hebrew translation method. He was no longer a complete novice translator, as he had his New Testament translation under his belt, and now, much of the Old Testament.

---

[3] These often appear, of course, with minor orthographical modifications.

The final part of the Old Testament was in some ways the apex of his *Deutsche Bibel* work, where he was at the height of his skill as far as translating complete books of the Bible "from scratch." While his engagement with the Hebrew language would continue to the end of his life, as his Genesis lectures (his final lectures on the Hebrew Bible prior to his death in 1546) and subsequent Bible revisions especially show, it was at this time, in his academic mid-career, that he put the vast majority of his time into the translation and that the greatest development in his fundamental skills occurred.

Because all previous major studies of Luther's Hebrew have focused exclusively on his translation of the Psalms, scholars' knowledge of much of this period in his translation career is still relatively opaque. Even those studies which examine Luther's growth between his initial Psalms translations and his later revisions have a very narrow focus. Thus, many aspects of his Hebrew translation have remained unexplored. This study takes a step forward in changing this. It shows, in sum, that the Hebrew language defined Luther's German Bible much more than has been appreciated. The number of his German translation decisions which were governed or influenced by elements and features which he saw in the Hebrew was enormous. While each chapter of this study has examined one facet of the role of Hebrew in his German translation, this is by no means an exhaustive list of categories. Many more aspects of Luther's Hebrew await investigation. Moreover, many other books of the Hebrew Bible await this type of analysis. Thus, while this study makes inroads into the frontier in Luther scholarship concerning his use of language, it remains a frontier, imploring scholars to further exploration. It promises the scholarly world further insight into: sixteenth century Christian Hebraism, direct and indirect Jewish-Christian intellectual exchange, the work of many lesser known Hebraists of the time, the relationship between biblical languages and medieval mysticism, and Hebrew and German linguistics. Thus, as much as we know about Luther and about other Hebrew translators in the late medieval and early modern periods from their use of language, there is much more that can be discovered by examining the languages with which they engaged.

When Luther looked back on his German Bible, he said that there was more in his Bible translation than in all the commentaries [*mehr drinnen als in allen commentariis*].[4] His own words show his recognition that language could open a door into his world, into the world of the Bible, and into the world of the ancient Hebrews, in a way that not many other channels could. This is why he so fervently urged upon the two Swiss students at the Jena hotel the fundamental importance of languages to the correct understanding of scripture. And they would have their chance. On the Saturday following their encounter with the disguised knight at the Jena inn, the two Swiss students arrived in Wittenberg.

---

[4] WA TR 5:59.6–7 [§ 5324]. Krause cites this in *Studien*, 7.

They waited for their meeting with Jerome Schürpf, letters of introduction from their home university in hand. When they were called into the sitting room, there waiting was Martin Luther, dressed in the same knightly attire as he was wearing in Jena. With him were Philip Melanchthon, Justus Jonas, Nikolaus Amsdorf, and Augustine Schürpf, Jerome's brother. Luther greeted the two students, laughing, and pointing his finger at Melanchthon, whom he had told them about during their conversation at the Schwarzer Bär Inn.[5] Their journey in the biblical languages had just begun. In Wittenberg, they would have access to a wealth of intellectual and literary resources to help them along the way, much the same ones that Luther would as he was about to begin his translation of the Hebrew Bible.

---

[5] Kessler, *Sabbata*, 80.

Appendix

Pictured from left to right: Philip Melanchthon (1497–1560), Martin Luther (1483–1546), Johann Bugenhagen ("Pommeranus," 1485–1558), and Caspar Cruciger (1504–48) [Lithograph by Alphonse Léon Noël from a painting by Pierre-Antoine Labouchère, *Luther, Melanchthon, Pomeranus translate the Bible* (ca. 1846)] (*source*: Presbyterian Historical Society, Philadelphia, PA, MAPCASE 2:27).

Table A.1: General Interpretative Variances in Luther's Hebrew Translation in the Minor Prophets[1]

Part I: The Exegesis in Contrast to the *Deutsche Bibel*

Pro-Hebrew Exegetical Argument/Contra-Hebrew Deutsche Bibel Translation
Luther argued against the Vulgate in the exegesis, where the Vulgate and the Hebrew Bible do not agree; but translated the *Deutsche Bibel* the same as the Vulgate.

Verse	NASB English	Hebrew Bible	Vulgate	1532 *Deutsche Bibel*
Hos. 12:12	Iniquity	אָוֶן	idolum	abgoetterey
Hos. 13:2	Idols skillfully made	כִּתְבוּנָם עֲצַבִּים	quasi similitudinem idolorum	wie sie es erdencken koennen, nemlich, Goetzen
Joel 2:6	turn pale	קִבְּצוּ פָארוּר	redigentur in ollam	sind so bleich, wie die toepffen
Nah. 2:11	are grown pale	קִבְּצוּ פָארוּר	as sicut nigredo ollae	bleich sehen, wie ein toepffen
Hab. 1:4	Surround	מַכְתִּיר	praevalet adversus	vberforteilet

---

[1] The contradictions that appear in this table vary in extremity. Furthermore, some examples which appear in this table also appear in one or more of the other tables in the Appendix.

Table A.1: General Interpretative Variances 227

1545 *Deutsche Bibel*	Bible References	Exegetical References
Abgoetterey	WA DB 11.2:206.12; WA DB 11.2:207.12	WA 13:60.4; LW 18:67–68
wie sie es erdencken koennen, nemlich, Goetzen	WA DB 4:227b.1–3; WA DB 11.2:206.2; WA DB 11.2:207.2	WA 13:61.15–20; LW 18:69–70
sind so bleich, wie die toepffen	WA DB 4:229a.29–31; WA DB 11.2:218.6; WA DB 11.2:219.6	WA 13:73.27– WA 13:74.5; WA 13:97.20–38; LW 18:93
bleich sehen, wie ein toepffen	WA DB 11.2:292.11; WA DB 11.2:293.11	WA 13:359.29– WA 13:360.2; WA 13:386.30– WA 13:387.9; LW 18:304–5
vberforteilet	WA DB 4:258a.3–5; WA DB 4:258b.3–8; WA DB 11.2:302.4; WA DB 11.2:303.4	WA 13:397.21–30; WA 13:425.33– WA 13:426.7; WA 19:362.16– WA 19:363.7; LW 19:110; LW 19:164–5

Pro-Hebrew Exegetical Argument/Contra-Hebrew Deutsche Bibel Translation
Luther argued against the Vulgate in the exegesis, where the Vulgate and the Hebrew Bible disagree; but translated the *Deutsche Bibel* against both the Hebrew Bible and the Vulgate.

Verse	NASB English	Hebrew Bible	Vulgate	1532 *Deutsche Bibel*
Jon. 4:6	Plant	קִיקָיוֹן	hederam	Kuerbis
Mic. 1:10	Roll	הִתְפַּלָּשְׁתִּי	conspergite	vnd sitzt
Mic. 4:11	Let her be polluted	תֶּחֱנָף	lapidetur	Sie ist verbannet
Mic. 5:5	at its entrances	בִּפְתָחֶיהָ	in lanceis eius	mit jren blossen woffen
Mic. 6:9	Who has appointed its time	וּמִי יְעָדָהּ	et quis adprobabit illud	was gepredigt wird

Pro-Hebrew Exegetical Argument/Contra-Hebrew Deutsche Bibel Translation
Luther argued with the Vulgate in the exegesis, where the Vulgate and the Hebrew Bible agree; but translated the *Deutsche Bibel* against both the Hebrew Bible and the Vulgate.

Verse	NASB English	Hebrew Bible	Vulgate	1532 *Deutsche Bibel*
Joel 4:3	for a harlot	בַּזּוֹנָה	in prostibulum	vmb speise
Nah. 3:2	The noise of the whip, The noise of the rattling of the wheel, Galloping horses And bounding chariots!	קוֹל שׁוֹט וְקוֹל רַעַשׁ אוֹפָן וְסוּס דֹּהֵר וּמֶרְכָּבָה מְרַקֵּדָה	vox flagelli et vox impetus rotae et equi frementis et quadrigae ferventis equitis ascendentis	Denn da wird man hoeren die geisseln klappen, vnd die reder rasseln, die rosse schreien, vnd die wagen rollen

Table A.1: General Interpretative Variances

1545 *Deutsche Bibel*	Bible References	Exegetical References
Kuerbis	WA DB 4:245b.24–31; WA DB 11.2:266.6– WA DB 11.2:268.6; WA DB 11.2:267.6– WA DB 11.2:269.6	WA 13:239.8–23; WA 13:256.35– WA 13:257.7; WA 19:243.4–21; LW 19:29; LW 19:95
vnd sitzt	WA DB 11.2:272.10; WA DB 11.2:273.10	WA 13:264.20–33; WA 13:305.37–40; LW 18:217
Sie ist verbannet	WA DB 11.2:278.11; WA DB 11.2:279.11	WA 13:281.29– WA 13:282.2; WA 13:322.38– WA 13:323.5; LW 18:244–5
mit jren blossen woffen	WA DB 11.2:280.5; WA DB 11.2:281.5	WA 13:286.6–8; WA 13:327.10–18; LW 18:251
was gepredigt wird	WA DB 11.2:282.9; WA DB 11.2:283.9	WA 13:292.22–29; WA 13:335.4–11; LW 18:264

1545 *Deutsche Bibel*	Bible References	Exegetical References
vmb speise	WA DB 11.2:222.8; WA DB 11.2:223.8	WA 13:84.10–14; WA 13:116.16–27; LW 18:115
Denn da wird man hoeren die Geisseln klappen, vnd die Reder rasseln, die Rosse schreien, vnd die Wagen rollen.	WA DB 11.2:294.2; WA DB 11.2:295.2	WA 13:361.24– WA 13:362.23; WA 13:388.7–22; LW 18:306–7

Appendix

Contra-Hebrew Exegetical Argument/Pro-Hebrew Deutsche Bibel Translation
Luther argued against the Vulgate in the exegesis, where the Vulgate and the Hebrew Bible agree; but translated the *Deutsche Bibel* the same as both the Hebrew Bible and the Vulgate.

Verse	NASB English	Hebrew Bible	Vulgate	1532 *Deutsche Bibel*
Joel 3:3	Blood	דָּם	sanguinem	blut

Part II: The Lectures in Contrast to the Commentaries

Luther's argument in the lectures does not match that in the commentary, or he modified his argument in the commentary.

Verse	Lecture Argument	Commentary Argument	NASB English	Hebrew Bible	Vulgate
Hab. 1:8	lupi deserti	abends wolffe	than wolves in the evening	מִזְּאֵבֵי עֶרֶב	[velociores] lupis vespertinis
Zech. 4:2	die schalen	einen Reif	with its bowl on the top of it	וְגֻלָּה עַל־רֹאשָׁהּ	et lampas eius super caput ipsius
Zech. 11:7	Lust	sanft	Favor	נֹעַם	Decorem

Table A.1: General Interpretative Variances

1545 *Deutsche Bibel*	Bible References	Exegetical References
Blut	WA DB 11.2:222.3; WA DB 11.2:223.3	WA 13:81.22– WA 13:82.6; WA 13:112.20– WA 13:113.2; LW 18:110

1532 *Deutsche Bibel*	1545 *Deutsche Bibel*	Bible References	Exegetical References
denn die wolffe des abends	denn die Wolffe des abends	WA DB 4:258a.20–21; WA DB 11.2:302.8; WA DB 11.2:303.8	WA 13:399.14–25; WA 13:427.25–38; WA 19:368.22– WA 19:370.14; LW 19:112–3; LW 19:170–2
mit einer schalen oben drauff	mit einer Schalen oben drauff	WA DB 11.2:338.2; WA DB 11.2:339.2	WA 13:585.9–14; StL 14:1844.1– StL 14:1846.4; LW 20:43; LW 20:222–4
Sanfft	Sanfft	WA DB 11.2:352.7; WA DB 11.2:353.7	WA 13:647.7–25; StL 14:1941.16– StL 14:1943.19; LW 20:120–1; LW 20:315–6

Part III: The *Deutsche Bibel* Revisions

Translations where Luther cited the Hebrew in his exegetical argument, and the 1532 Deutsche Bibel translation differs from the 1545 Deutsche Bibel.

Verse	NASB English	Hebrew Bible	Vulgate	1532 *Deutsche Bibel*
Hos. 5:15[2]	they will earnestly seek Me	יְשַׁחֲרֻנְנִי	mane consurgunt ad me	so werden sie mich suchen muessen, vnd sagen
Joel 2:23	the early rain for your vindication	אֶת-הַמּוֹרֶה לִצְדָקָה	doctorem iustitiae	gnedigen regen
Joel 4:14	Multitudes, multitudes in the valley of decision	הֲמוֹנִים הֲמוֹנִים בְּעֵמֶק הֶחָרוּץ	populi populi in valle concisionis	Es werden hie vnd da hauffen volcks sein im Reisse tal
Jon. 2:9	their faithfulness	חַסְדָּם	misericordiam suam	**der** gnade
Mic. 1:11	The inhabitant of Zaanan	יוֹשֶׁבֶת צַאֲנָן	quae habitat in Exitu	Die stoltze
Mic. 2:6	'Do not speak out,' so they speak out. But if they do not speak out concerning these things	אַל-תַּטִּפוּ יַטִּפוּן לֹא-יַטִּפוּ לָאֵלֶּה	ne loquamini loquentes non stillabit super istos	Sie sagen, Man solle nicht predigen, Denn solche prediget trifft vns nicht
Nah. 2:3	For the Lord will restore the splendor of Jacob	כִּי שָׁב יְהוָה אֶת-גְּאוֹן יַעֲקֹב	quia reddidit Dominus superbiam Iacob	Denn der HERR wird Jacob den sieg geben

---

[2] The Vulgate places part of the verse in Hos. 5:15 and part in Hos. 6:1; the portion cited is 6:1 in the Vulgate.

Table A.1: General Interpretative Variances 233

1545 *Deutsche Bibel*	Bible References	Exegetical References
So werden sie mich **fruee** suchen muessen (vnd sagen)	WA DB 4:213b.4–7; WA DB 11.2:194.15; WA DB 11.2:195.15	WA 13:27.6–8; LW 18:31
Lerer zur gerechtigkeit	WA DB 4:231a.4–14; WA DB 4:231b.4–WA DB 4:232b.19; WA DB 11.2:220.23; WA DB 11.2:221.23	WA 13:78.19–28; WA 13:107.10–25; LW 18:104
ES werden hie vnd da hauffen Volcks sein im tal des Vrteils	WA DB 4:233a.8–23; WA DB 4:233b.8–21; WA DB 11.2:224.19; WA DB 11.2:225.19	WA 13:86.9–20; WA 13:120.14–27; LW 18:119–20
jre gnade	WA DB 4:244a.19–WA DB 4:245a.13; WA DB 4:244b.19–WA DB 4:245b.6; WA DB 11.2:264.9; WA DB 11.2:265.9	WA 13:234.6–25; WA 13:251.32–WA 13:252.6; WA 19:189.24–25; WA 19:230.21–WA 19:231.13; LW 19:20; LW 19:80–81
Die Einwonerin Zaenan	WA DB 4:246a.14–WA DB 4:247a.2; WA DB 4:246b.14–WA DB 4:247b.4; WA DB 11.2:272.11; WA DB 11.2:273.11	WA 13:265.1–32; WA 13:306.1–28; LW 18:217–8
Sje sagen, Man solle nicht treuffen, Denn solche Treuffe trifft vns nicht	WA DB 4:248a.16–19; WA DB 4:248b.16–24; WA DB 11.2:274.6; WA DB 11.2:275.6	WA 13:270.12–26; WA 13:310.23–38; LW 18:224–5
Denn der HERR wird die hoffart Jacob vergelten	WA DB 4:256b.7–21; WA DB 11.2:292.3; WA DB 11.2:293.3	WA 13:356.13–24; WA 13:382.35–WA 13:383.13; LW 18:299

Verse	NASB English	Hebrew Bible	Vulgate	1532 *Deutsche Bibel*
Nah. 2:3	Like the splendor of Israel	כִּגְאוֹן יִשְׂרָאֵל	sicut superbiam Israhel	wie er Jsrael den sieg gab

Table A.2: Luther's Translation of Hebrew Figures of Speech in the Minor Prophets[1]

Verse	Luther's Hermeneutic	Luther Calls It ...	NASB English	Hebrew Bible
Hos. 2:16	Interpretative[2]	Hebrew phrase (*phrasi hebraica*)	And speak kindly to her	וְדִבַּרְתִּי עַל-לִבָּהּ
Hos. 2:17	Literal	a proverb among the Hebrews (*apud Hebraeos in proverbium*)	And the valley of Achor	וְאֶת-עֵמֶק עָכוֹר
Hos. 2:24	Literal	allegory (*allegoriam*)	Jezreel	יִזְרְעֶאל
Hos. 4:3	Literal	metaphorical speech (*metaphorica locutio*)	Therefore the land mourns	עַל-כֵּן תֶּאֱבַל הָאָרֶץ
Hos. 4:7[3]	Literal	Hebrew expression (*Phrasis hebraica*)	The more they multiplied	כְּרֻבָּם

---

[1] If an additional manuscript note appears in the WA addressing the Hebraism, I do not add a separate line item, but simply cite the main line entry to which the note refers. Also, aside from egregious discrepancies with the Latin, I left the LW translation for the "Luther Calls It ..." column "as is." The English renderings in the LW are sometimes very inconsistent. Nevertheless, this will allow most readers who are familiar with or relying on the LW to more easily identify the text to which the Table refers for each entry. Finally, the figures of speech are often not addressed in every location, i.e. the LW, Zwickau text, Altenburg text, German commentary, but rather only in some or in one of these. Nevertheless, I include all relevant exegetical references throughout this table for the verses so that the reader has the full breadth of information for each translation, as the context many times still helps to illuminate the issue. This includes the WA DB 4 references.

1545 *Deutsche Bibel*	Bible References	Exegetical References
wie die hoffart Jsrael	WA DB 4:256b.7–21; WA DB 11.2:292.3; WA DB 11.2:293.3	WA 13:356.13–24; WA 13:382.35– WA 13:383.13; LW 18:299

Vulgate	1532 *Deutsche Bibel*	1545 *Deutsche Bibel*	Bible References	Exegetical References
et loquar ad cor eius	vnd freundlich mit jr reden	vnd freundlich mit jr reden	WA DB 11.2:186.14; WA DB 11.2:187.14	WA 13:9.17; LW 18:11
et vallem Achor	vnd das tal Achor	vnd das tal Achor	WA DB 4:208a.10–17; WA DB 4:208b.10–23; WA DB 11.2:186.15; WA DB 11.2:187.15	WA 13:9.19–22; LW 18:11
Hiezrahel	Jesreel	Jesreel	WA DB 11.2:188.22; WA DB 11.2:189.22	WA 13:12.21– WA 13:13.10; LW 18:14–15
propter hoc lugebit terra	Darumb wird das land jemerlich stehen	Darumb wird das Land jemerlich stehen	WA DB 11.2:188.3– WA DB 11.2:190.3; WA DB 11.2:189.3– WA DB 11.2:191.3	WA 13:16.14–15; LW 18:20
secundum multitudinem eorum	Jhe mehr jr wird	Je mehr jr wird	WA DB 4:210b.1–5; WA DB 11.2:190.7; WA DB 11.2:191.7	WA 13:17.18–20; LW 18:21

---

[2] Cf. the German greeting *sage mein freundlich hertz*, which E. Thiele und O. Brenner include, as reference, in *Luthers Sprichwörtersammlung* §412 [*sein Herz*]. WA 51:718–9, 728.

[3] Luther seems to have changed his mind from the time of the lectures, where he interpreted כְּרֻבָּם (*kərubbām*, "as they were increased") as a prefix, *noun*, and suffix. In his Bible translation, he rendered it as a prefix, *verb*, and suffix. Nevertheless, it was a literal Bible translation of the Hebrew. Wander lists *Je mehr, desto besser* as idiomatic; WAN 2:1008. Since Luther did not use the complete construction, I have not identified this example in Luther's translation as a German idiom.

Verse	Luther's Hermeneutic	Luther Calls It ...	NASB English	Hebrew Bible
Hos. 6:9	Literal	Hebrew expression (*hebraea vox*)	raiders	גְּדוּדִים
Hos. 7:10	Mixed[4]	Hebrew expression (*hebraea vox*)	Though the pride of Israel testifies against him	וְעָנָה גְאוֹן־יִשְׂרָאֵל בְּפָנָיו
Hos. 8:7[5]	Literal	figurative language (*Figurata est oratio*)	For they sow the wind / And they reap the whirlwind.	כִּי רוּחַ יִזְרָעוּ וְסוּפָתָה יִקְצֹרוּ
Hos. 8:7	Literal	Metaphor (*metaphora*); beautiful metaphor (*metaphora pulchra*)	The standing grain has no [heads]	קָמָה אֵין־לוֹ
Hos. 9:11	Literal	synecdoche (*Synecdochice*)	No birth, no pregnancy and no conception!	מִלֵּדָה וּמִבֶּטֶן וּמֵהֵרָיוֹן

---

[4] Cf. WA 29:584.24–25, where Luther used the idiomatic *ie demuetiger mensch, ie hoffertiger Geist*. Cornette cites this in *Proverbs*, 46. Cf. MERZ 1:33 concerning a fifteenth century handwritten note that reads: "Dorumb sullen wir alle demutig sein vnd sollen vns vor hoffart hüten leiplich vnd auch geistlich vnd sollen got vor augen haben so wirt vns das ewig leben." Cf. MERZ 1:38–39, 91–92, 389. And cf. MERZ 2:575, and notice the use of *vor augen*. Wander has many entries related to *Hoffart*, and several of these linked to Agricola. WAN 2:711–8. Wander also lists many examples for *Demuth/Demüthig/Demüthigen*. WAN 1:570–1. Grimm also lists various idiomatic uses of *Hoffart/hoffärtig* and *demütigen* (with various spellings); DWB 2:923; DWB 10:1667. Thus, there is evidence of multiple idiomatic influences of multiple parts of the phrase. Cf. Luther's translation of Hos. 5:5 as *Darumb sol die hoffart Jsrael fur jrem angesicht gedemuetigt werden*. WA DB 11.2:192.5. This is therefore a very challenging example to categorize. Because evidence exists of numerous German idioms, and Luther's general following of the Hebrew sentence structure and narrative (Israel, etc.), as well as his choice of *fur jren augen* instead of the more literal *fur jrem angesicht* which he used for Hos. 5:5, I have categorized this as "mixed."

Table A.2: Luther's Translation of Hebrew Figures of Speech

Vulgate	1532 Deutsche Bibel	1545 Deutsche Bibel	Bible References	Exegetical References
[fauces virorum] latronum	die stroeter	die Stroeter	WA DB 4:213a.27–WA DB 4:214a.3; WA DB 4:213b.27–WA DB 4:214b.4; WA DB 11.2:194.9; WA DB 11.2:195.9	WA 13:30.1–4; LW 18:34
et humiliabitur superbia Israhel in facie eius	Vnd die hoffart Jsrael wird fur jren augen gedemuetiget	Vnd die hoffart Jsrael wird fur jren augen gedemuetiget	WA DB 4:216a.7; WA DB 11.2:196.10; WA DB 11.2:197.10	WA 13:33.19–22; LW 18:38
quia ventum seminabunt et turbinem metent	Denn sie seen wind, vnd werden vngewitter einerndten	Denn sie seen Wind, vnd werden Vngewitter einerndten	WA DB 11.2:198.7; WA DB 11.2:199.7	WA 13:39.15–22; LW 18:44
culmus stans non est	Jr saat sol nicht auffkomen	Jr Saat sol nicht auffkomen	WA DB 11.2:198.7; WA DB 11.2:199.7	WA 13:39.23–26; LW 18:44
a partu et ab utero et a conceptu	das sie weder geberen, noch tragen, noch schwanger werden sollen	Das sie weder geberen, noch tragen, noch schwanger werden sollen	WA DB 11.2:200.11; WA DB 11.2:201.11	WA 13:45.16–26; LW 18:51

---

[5] Surely this German idiom is taken from biblical language; hence, the assignment as "literal." Nevertheless, many sources show idiomatic usage. See WAN 3:1825–9; WAN 1:845–6. See also DWB 3:167–8; DWB 14:1630–3. See also Cornette, *Proverbs*, 96. Cf. SING 2:190. Thank you to Prof. Dr. Lähnemann, University of Oxford, for your insight on this idiom.

Verse	Luther's Hermeneutic	Luther Calls It ...	NASB English	Hebrew Bible
Hos. 10:4	Literal[6]	pure metaphor (*Mera metaphora*); figure of speech (*figuram*)	And judgment sprouts like poisonous weeds in the furrows of the field.	וּפָרַח כָּרֹאשׁ מִשְׁפָּט עַל תַּלְמֵי שָׂדָי
Hos. 11:6	Literal[7]	custom of the Hebrew language (*Mos est hebraeae linguae*)	their gate bars	בַדָּיו
Hos. 12:1	Interpretative	a Hebrew phrase (*Phrasis hebraea*)	surrounds Me with lies	סְבָבֻנִי בְכַחַשׁ
Hos. 13:3	Literal[8]	beautiful simile (*pulchra similitudo*)	Like chaff	כְּמֹץ
Hos. 13:8	Literal[9]	synecdoche (*Synecdoche*)	their chests	סְגוֹר לִבָּם
Joel 1:3	Literal	Hebraism (*Hebraismus*)	about it	עָלֶיהָ
Joel 1:10	Literal	poetic figures of speech (*poeticas figuras*)	The land mourns	אָבְלָה אֲדָמָה
Joel 1:10	Mixed[10]	expression (*vox*); pure heroic figures of speech (*Merae heroicae figurae*)	The new wine dries up	הוֹבִישׁ תִּירוֹשׁ

---

[6] *Wie vnkraut* is from a German idiom equivalent to the English "to grow like weeds": *Wie Unkraut wuchern*. There is much evidence of sixteenth century idiomatic uses of *Unkraut*, and some evidence for idiomatic uses of *Galle*. See WAN 4:1462–4; Cornette, *Proverbs*, 143; SPAL 19:902–4; SPAL 53:2529; SING 1:183; SING 2:190; and SING 3:155. Nevertheless, this seems to be a quite literal translation reflecting weeds or poisonous weeds (hence Luther's change from *vnkraut* in 1532 to the more specific *Galle* in 1545). See DWB 4:1187.

[7] The modern German spelling is *Riegel*.

[8] Spalding shows idiomatic usage of *Spreu* dating to *Mittelhochdeutsch*, with explicit mention of Luther. SPAL 49:2315. Nevertheless, this is clearly a literal translation of the Hebrew here.

Table A.2: Luther's Translation of Hebrew Figures of Speech   239

Vulgate	1532 *Deutsche Bibel*	1545 *Deutsche Bibel*	Bible References	Exegetical References
et germinabit quasi amaritudo iudicium super sulcos agri	Vnd solcher rat gruenet auff allen furchen im felde, wie vnkraut	vnd solcher Rat gruenet auff allen furchen im felde, wie Galle	WA DB 4:221a.13; WA DB 4:221b.8–16; WA DB 11.2:202.4; WA DB 11.2:203.4	WA 13:48.20–22; LW 18:54
electos eius	jre rigel	jre Rigel	WA DB 11.2:204.6; WA DB 11.2:205.6	WA 13:53.15–16; LW 18:60
circumdedit me in negatione	ist allenthalben abgoetterey widder mich	ist allenthalben Luegen wider mich	WA DB 4:224a.24–26; WA DB 4:224b.24–WA DB 4:225b.3; WA DB 11.2:204.1; WA DB 11.2:205.1	WA 13:55.14–22; LW 18:63
sicut pulvis	Ja wie die sprew	Ja wie die Sprew	WA DB 4:227a.3–4; WA DB 11.2:206.3; WA DB 11.2:207.3	WA 13:62.7–8; LW 18:70
interiora iecoris eorum	jr verstocktes hertz	jr verstocktes Hertz	WA DB 11.2:208.8; WA DB 11.2:209.8	WA 13:62.25–27; LW 18:71
super hoc	dauon	dauon	WA DB 11.2:216.3; WA DB 11.2:217.3	WA 13:69.1–4; WA 13:89.19–22; LW 18:81
luxit humus	vnd der acker stehet jemerlich	vnd der Acker stehet jemerlich	WA DB 4:229b.21–26; WA DB 11.2:216.10; WA DB 11.2:217.10	WA 13:70.9–12; WA 13:92.3–14; LW 18:84
confusum est vinum	Der wein stehet jemerlich	der Wein stehet jemerlich	WA DB 4:229b.21–26; WA DB 11.2:216.10; WA DB 11.2:217.10	WA 13:70.9–12; WA 13:92.3–14; LW 18:84

---

[9] Luther's focus was on the synecdoche in "their," which he translated literally. His comments in the lectures make this clear.

[10] The term הוֹבִישׁ (*hôbîš*) is ambiguous, and carries a figurative meaning associated with "shame" and "confusion." But the more literal meaning is associated with "drying up." Therefore, I have assigned this half of the figure of speech as "interpretative," as Luther ensured that this figurative meaning was expressed to his German reader. The other half of the figure of speech is תִּירוֹשׁ (*tîrôš*), which Luther translated literally as *wein*. He thus still left the phrase rather obscure. Therefore, I classify this as a "mixed" translation.

Verse	Luther's Hermeneutic	Luther Calls It ...	NASB English	Hebrew Bible
Joel 1:14	Literal	Hebrew expression (*Phrasis hebraica*)	Consecrate a fast	קַדְּשׁוּ-צוֹם
Joel 1:19	Literal	metaphorically (*Metaphorice*)	For fire has devoured the pastures of the wilderness	כִּי אֵשׁ אָכְלָה נְאוֹת מִדְבָּר
Joel 1:19	Literal	metaphorically (*metaphorice*)	And the flame has burned up all the trees of the field	וְלֶהָבָה לִהֲטָה כָּל-עֲצֵי הַשָּׂדֶה
Joel 2:6	Mixed[11]	figure of speech (*figura loquendi*); metaphor (*metaphora*)	All faces turn pale	כָּל-פָּנִים קִבְּצוּ פָארוּר
Joel 2:7	Literal[12]	According to the Hebrew (*hebraica phrasi*)	And they each ... in line	וְאִישׁ בִּדְרָכָיו
Joel 2:12	Literal[13]	Hebraism (*Hebraismus*)	with all your heart	בְּכָל-לְבַבְכֶם
Joel 2:14	Interpretative[14]	Hebrew phraseology (*phrasis Hebraica*)	Who knows whether He will not turn and relent	מִי יוֹדֵעַ יָשׁוּב וְנִחָם

---

[11] This is German idiomatic language with *bleich*; and a literal translation with *toepffen*. Wander links *Er wirt so bleych wie ein asche, ascherfarb* to Agricola, among others. WAN 1:399, 598. Spalding cites the use of *bleich* associated with "fear" and also associated with "death" since *Mittelhochdeutsch*, with reference to Luther concerning the latter. SPAL 8:341. See the analysis in Ch. 2 of this study for additional information.

[12] *Jeglich* means "any." *Stracks* means "straightaway."

Table A.2: Luther's Translation of Hebrew Figures of Speech 241

Vulgate	1532 *Deutsche Bibel*	1545 *Deutsche Bibel*	Bible References	Exegetical References
sanctificate ieiunium	Heiliget eine Fasten	Heiliget eine Fasten	WA DB 11.2:216.14; WA DB 11.2:217.14	WA 13:70.20–21; WA 13:92.28; LW 18:85
quia ignis comedit speciosa deserti	denn das feur hat die awen jnn der wuesten verbrand	Denn das fewr hat die Awen in der wuesten verbrand	WA DB 11.2:218.19; WA DB 11.2:219.19	WA 13:71.10–15; WA 13:93.27–29; LW 18:86
et flamma succendit omnia ligna regionis	vnd die flamme hat alle beume auff dem acker angezuendet	vnd die flamme hat alle Beume auff dem acker angezuendet	WA DB 11.2:218.19; WA DB 11.2:219.19	WA 13:71.10–15; WA 13:93.30–32; LW 18:86
omnes vultus redigentur in ollam	Aller angesicht sind so bleich, wie die toepffen	Aller angesicht sind so bleich, wie die toepffen	WA DB 4:229a.29–31; WA DB 11.2:218.6; WA DB 11.2:219.6.	WA 13:73.27–WA 13:74.5; WA 13:97.20–38; LW 18:93
vir in viis suis	Ein jglicher ... stracks fur sich	Ein jglicher ... stracks fur sich	WA DB 11.2:218.7; WA DB 11.2:219.7	WA 13:74.6–11; WA 13:98.5–9; LW 18:93–94
in toto corde vestro	von gantzem hertzen	von gantzem hertzen	WA DB 11.2:218.12; WA DB 11.2:219.12	WA 13:75.3–21; WA 13:99.25–30; LW 18:95–96
quis scit si convertatur et ignoscat	Er wird sich ja noch widderumb erbarmen, vnd nach seiner straffe, gnade erzeigen	Wer weis, Es mag jn widerumb gerewen	WA DB 4:230a.13; WA DB 4:230b.13–26; WA DB 11.2:220.14; WA DB 11.2:221.14	WA 13:76.21–32; WA 13:102.16–21; LW 18:99

---

[13] Surely this German idiom is taken from biblical language; hence, the assignment as "literal." Nevertheless, see WA 51:718–19, 728 [§ 412]. Cf. WAN 2:618 [§ 444]; DWB 10:1213, 1216; and SPAL 20:910, with explicit mention of Luther.

[14] Luther explained in his analysis that the wavering doubt, but actually in an affirmative sense, is the Hebraism.

Verse	Luther's Hermeneutic	Luther Calls It …	NASB English	Hebrew Bible
Joel 2:22	German Idiom[15]	The Hebrew method of speaking (*Hebraicus modus loquendi*)	have yielded in full	נָתְנוּ חֵילָם
Joel 2:23	1532 Interpretative; 1545 Literal[16]	Hebrew expression (*Hebraica … vox*)	For He has given you the early rain for your vindication	כִּי-נָתַן לָכֶם אֶת-הַמּוֹרֶה לִצְדָקָה
Joel 2:26	Interpretative[17]	Hebrew expression (*Hebraica phrasis*)	You will have plenty to eat	וַאֲכַלְתֶּם אָכוֹל
Joel 3:4	Literal	metaphorically; (*metaphorice*); Hebrew expression (*vox hebraica, phrasi hebraica, Phrasis … hebraica*)	And the moon into blood	וְהַיָּרֵחַ לְדָם
Joel 4:1	Interpretative	Hebraism (*Hebraismus*)	in those days and at that time	בַּיָּמִים הָהֵמָּה וּבָעֵת הַהִיא
Joel 4:2	Literal	allegorically (*allegorice*), metaphorically (*metaphorice*)	[to the] valley of Jehoshaphat	[אֶל-]עֵמֶק יְהוֹשָׁפָט
Joel 4:8	Interpretative	Hebrew idiom (*Phrasis … hebraica*)	into the hand of	בְּיַד

---

[15] Spalding advises that *wohl* also has a history of idiomatic use in the sense of "well" or "to do good" since *Althochdeutsch*, and makes explicit mention of Luther. SPAL 56:2680. Cf. WAN 5:330–3; and DWB 30:1025–72, with mention of Agricola and Mathesius. This is really the focus of Luther's attention to the Hebraism in his lectures. Furthermore, Spalding advises, with specific reference to Luther, that *tragen* appears in the sense of "yield" or "produce" since early *Neuhochdeutsch*. SPAL 52:2471. There also are idiomatic uses in the sense of "bearing children" in the same period, with numerous mentions of Agricola, and one from Tauler. DWB 21:1080–6. And there are many other idiomatic uses of the word in other senses. See DWB 21:1048–1113; WAN 4:1281–2; WA 51:701, 730 [§ 267]; and SPAL 52:2470–2. Thus, on account of both terms, I have assigned this as a "German idiom."

Table A.2: *Luther's Translation of Hebrew Figures of Speech* 243

Vulgate	1532 *Deutsche Bibel*	1545 *Deutsche Bibel*	Bible References	Exegetical References
dederunt virtutem suam	sollen wol tragen	sollen wol tragen	WA DB 4:231a.1–3; WA DB 11.2:220.22; WA DB 11.2:221.22	WA 13:78.14–18; WA 13:107.3–8; LW 18:103–4
quia dedit vobis doctorem iustitiae	der euch gnedigen regen gibt	der euch Lerer zur gerechtigkeit gibt	WA DB 4:231a.4–14; WA DB 4:231b.4–; WA DB 4:232b.19; WA DB 11.2:220.23; WA DB 11.2:221.23	WA 13:78.19–28; WA 13:107.10–25; LW 18:104
et comedetis vescentes	das jr zu essen gnug haben sollet	Das jr zu essen gnug haben sollet	WA DB 11.2:220.26; WA DB 11.2:221.26	WA 13:79.3–5 WA 13:108.7–14; LW 18:105
et luna in sanguinem	vnd der mond jnn blut verwandelt werden	vnd der Mond in blut verwandelt werden	WA DB 11.2:222.4; WA DB 11.2:223.4	WA 13:81.22– WA 13:82.6; WA 13:113.3–7; LW 18:110
in diebus illis et in tempore illo	Jnn den tagen, vnd zur selbigen zeit	Jn den tagen, vnd zur selbigen zeit	WA DB 11.2:222.6; WA DB 11.2:223.6	WA 13:83.20; WA 13:115.1–20; LW 18:113
[in] valle Iosaphat	[jns] tal Josaphat	[ins] tal Josaphat	WA DB 11.2:222.7; WA DB 11.2:223.7	WA 13:83.23– WA 13:84.9; WA 13:115.21– WA 13:116.9; LW 18:113–4
in manibus	durch die	durch die	WA DB 11.2:222.13; WA DB 11.2:223.13	WA 13:84–31– WA 13:85.5; WA 13:117.19–25; LW 18:116

[16] See WAN 3:1576 [§ 26]: "Ein gnädiger Regen, ein reicher Segen." This comes from a 1605 source, so it is not certain that it was in use prior to Luther. Thus, I have categorized the 1532 translation as "interpretative."

[17] Luther's *gnug* refers to וְשָׂבוֹעַ (*wəśāḇôaʿ*). This verse also appears in Table A.3.

Appendix

Verse	Luther's Hermeneutic	Luther Calls It ...	NASB English	Hebrew Bible
Joel 4:8	Interpretative[18]	synecdoche (*synecdochen*)	to the Sabeans	לִשְׁבָאיִם
Joel 4:13	Literal	metaphorical exhortations (*Exhortationes metaphoricae*); metaphors (*metaphoricae*)	Put in the sickle, for the harvest is ripe	שִׁלְחוּ מַגָּל כִּי בָשַׁל קָצִיר
Joel 4:13	Literal	metaphorical exhortations (*Exhortationes metaphoricae*); metaphors (*metaphoricae*)	Come, tread, for the wine press is full; The vats overflow	בֹּאוּ רְדוּ כִּי-מָלְאָה גַּת הֵשִׁיקוּ הַיְקָבִים
Joel 4:14	1532 Literal; 1545 Interpretative[19]	Hebrew expression (*vox ... hebraeo*)	in the valley of decision	בְּעֵמֶק הֶחָרוּץ
Joel 4:18	Literal	pure metaphors (*meras metaphoras*)	The mountains will drip with sweet wine	יִטְּפוּ הֶהָרִים עָסִיס
Joel 4:18	Literal	figure (*figura*); synecdoche (συνεκδοχικῶς)	To water the valley of Shittim	וְהִשְׁקָה אֶת-נַחַל הַשִּׁטִּים
Amos 1:3	Literal	the figurative speech of scripture (*sententia tropum ... scripturae*)	For three ... and for four	עַל-שְׁלֹשָׁה ... וְעַל-אַרְבָּעָה
Amos 1:3	Literal	metaphorically (*methaphorice*)	Because they threshed Gilead with implements of sharp iron	עַל-דּוּשָׁם בַּחֲרֻצוֹת הַבַּרְזֶל אֶת-הַגִּלְעָד

---

[18] Instead of calling them Arabs, and thus mirroring the synecdoche for which he argued, Luther eliminated the synecdoche by means *of denen jnn/in* ("those in ...").

Table A.2: Luther's Translation of Hebrew Figures of Speech

Vulgate	1532 Deutsche Bibel	1545 Deutsche Bibel	Bible References	Exegetical References
Sabeis	denen jnn Reich Arabia	denen in Reicharabia	WA DB 11.2:222.13; WA DB 11.2:223.13	WA 13:84.31– WA 13:85.5; WA 13:117.26–35; LW 18:116–7
mittite falces quoniam maturavit messis	Schlahet die sicheln an, denn die ernd ist reiff	Schlahet die Sicheln an, denn die Ernd ist reiff	WA DB 11.2:222.18; WA DB 11.2:223.18	WA 13:86.3–8; WA 13:119.29– WA 13:120.13; LW 18:119
venite et descendite quia plenum est torcular exuberant torcularia	Kompt herab, denn die kelter ist vol, vnd die kelter leufft vber	Kompt herab, denn die Kelter ist vol, vnd die Kelter laufft vber	WA DB 11.2:222.18; WA DB 11.2:223.18	WA 13:86.3–8; WA 13:119.29– WA 13:120.13; LW 18:119
in valle concisionis	im Reisse tal	im tal des Vrteils	WA DB 4:233a.8–23; WA DB 4:233b.8–21; WA DB 11.2:224.19; WA DB 11.2:225.19	WA 13:86.9–20; WA 13:120.14–27; LW 18:119–20
stillabunt montes dulcedinem	werden die berge mit suuessem wein trieffen	werden die Berge mit suessem Wein trieffen	WA DB 4:233a.24–25; WA DB 11.2:224.23; WA DB 11.2:225.23	WA 13:87.4–14; WA 13:121.30–34; LW 18:122
et inrigabit torrentem Spinarum	der wird den strom Sittim wessern	der wird den strom Sittim wessern	WA DB 4:233a.24–25; WA DB 11.2:224.23; WA DB 11.2:225.23	WA 13:87.4–14; WA 13:122.5–14; LW 18:122
super tribus ... et super quattuor	Vmb drey vnd vier	Vmb drey vnd vier	WA DB 11.2:230.3; WA DB 11.2:231.3	WA 13:126.8–29; WA 13:162.1–8, 13– WA 13:163.4; LW 18:131
eo quod trituraverint in plaustris ferreis Galaad	darumb, das sie Gilead mit eisenen zakken gedroschen haben	Darumb, das sie Gilead mit eisenen Zacken gedrosschen haben	WA DB 11.2:230.3; WA DB 11.2:231.3	WA 13:126.30–33; WA 13:162.5–8; LW 18:131

---

[19] This is a multifarious Hebrew term. The rigidly literal meaning in this verse seems to be associated with "incision" or "a trench"; though it has various figurative meaning associated with "decision," "sharpness," and "diligence." See STR, 43 (Hebrew Dictionary section) [§H2742]; KB, 336; and BDB, 358.

Verse	Luther's Hermeneutic	Luther Calls It ...	NASB English	Hebrew Bible
Amos 1:5	Literal	figuratively (*figurate*); Metaphor (*Metaphora*)	the gate bar	בְּרִיחַ
Amos 1:6	Mixed[20]	Hebraism (*Hebraismus*)	Because they deported an entire population	עַל־הַגְלוֹתָם גָּלוּת שְׁלֵמָה
Amos 1:13	Literal[21]	metaphor (*metaphoram, metaphora*); metaphorically (*metaphorice*); figurative language (*figurarum*)	Because they ripped open the pregnant women of Gilead	עַל־בִּקְעָם הָרוֹת הַגִּלְעָד
Amos 2:13	Mixed[22]	Hebrew figure of speech (*Figura hebraica*)	Behold, I am weighted down beneath you	הִנֵּה אָנֹכִי מֵעִיק תַּחְתֵּיכֶם
Amos 2:14	Interpretative[23]	Hebraism (*Hebraica phrasis*)	Flight will perish from the swift	וְאָבַד מָנוֹס מִקָּל
Amos 3:3	Mixed[24]	Proverbs (*Proverbia*); proverbial (*proverbialis*); of the proverb (*proverbii*)	Do two men walk together unless they have made an appointment?	הֲיֵלְכוּ שְׁנַיִם יַחְדָּו בִּלְתִּי אִם־נוֹעָדוּ

---

[20] The Hebrew reads: "they have exiled an entire exile." Luther made a literal reading of the repetition, but added the interpretative *weiter* ("further"). Thus, I have categorized this as a "mixed" translation.

[21] The 1539–41 protocols provide insight into v. 13 also, though this information appears under v. 11 and v. 15. See WA DB 4:234a.3–13. Cf. the notes in Luther's 1538/39 Old Testament, which appear under v. 11, at WA DB 4:234b.3–9.

[22] This is a German idiom [*kirren machen*] blended with a Hebrew idiom [תַּחְתֵּיכֶם (*taḥtêkem*)], according to Luther's exegesis. On *kirren machen*, see DWB 11:839–43; and SPAL 31:1469.

Table A.2: Luther's Translation of Hebrew Figures of Speech

Vulgate	1532 Deutsche Bibel	1545 Deutsche Bibel	Bible References	Exegetical References
vectem	die rigel	die Rigel	WA DB 4:233b.30– WA DB 4:234b.2; WA DB 11.2:230.5; WA DB 11.2:231.5	WA 13:127.6–9; WA 13:163.14–17; LW 18:133
quod transtulerit captivitatem perfectam	Darumb, das sie die gefangenen, weiter gefangen	Darumb, das sie die Gefangenen, weiter gefangen	WA DB 11.2:230.6; WA DB 11.2:231.6	WA 13:128.1–11; WA 13:164.15–22; LW 18:134
quod dissecuerit praegnantes Galaad	Darumb, das sie die schwangere jnn Gilead zu rissen haben	Darumb, das sie die Schwangere in Gilead zu-rissen haben	WA DB 11.2:232.13; WA DB 11.2:233.13	WA 13:129.2–10; WA 13:165.26– WA 13:166.4; LW 18:136
ecce ego stridebo super vos	Sihe, ich wils vnter euch kirren machen	SJhe, Jch wils vnter euch kirren machen	WA DB 11.2:234.13; WA DB 11.2:235.13	WA 13:131.33– WA 13:132.3; WA 13:170.25–29; LW 18:143
et peribit fuga a veloce	Das der, so schnell ist, sol nicht entfliehen	Das der, so schnell ist, sol nicht entpfliehen	WA DB 11.2:234.14; WA DB 11.2:235.14	WA 13:132.4–5; WA 13:170.30– WA 13:171.3; LW 18:143
numquid ambulabunt duo pariter nisi convenerit eis	Muegen auch zween mit einander wandeln, sie seien denn eins vnternander?	MVgen auch zween mit einander wandeln, sie seien denn eins vnternander?	WA DB 11.2:234.3; WA DB 11.2:235.3	WA 13:132.26– WA 13:133.3; WA 13:172.1–14; LW 18:145

---

[23] Spalding indicates that the first idiomatic usage of *entfliehen* is *Frühneuhochdeutsch*, with specific reference to Luther. SPAL 14:646. I have categorized this as "interpretative," since there is nothing outside of this single entry which I have found, and thus the evidence is solely concerning Luther's own use of the term.

[24] The first portion of Luther's rendering is a literal translation (*MVgen auch zween mit einander wandeln*). The latter portion utilizes an existing German idiom: *eins sein* ("to be one"). See WAN 1:797. Cf. *Eins vmbs ander* in Cornette, *Proverbs*, 49. *Mûss ye eins sin* may also be an iteration of this; see MERZ 2:895.

Appendix

Verse	Luther's Hermeneutic	Luther Calls It ...	NASB English	Hebrew Bible
Amos 4:6	Literal[25]	a metaphor of the Hebrew language (*metaphora hebraeae linguae*)	But I gave you also cleanness of teeth	וְגַם-אֲנִי נָתַתִּי לָכֶם נִקְיוֹן שִׁנַּיִם
Amos 5:1	Literal	Hebraism (*Hebraismus*)	I take up for you	אָנֹכִי נֹשֵׂא עֲלֵיכֶם
Amos 5:1	Literal[26]	Hebraism (*phrasim hebraicam*)	as a dirge	קִינָה
Amos 5:4	Literal	Hebraism (*Hebraismus*)	that you may live	וִחְיוּ
Amos 5:5	1532 Interpretative; 1545 Literal[27]	beautiful allusion/play on words (*allusio pulcherrima*)	And Bethel will come to trouble	וּבֵית-אֵל יִהְיֶה לְאָוֶן
Amos 5:9	Mixed[28]	completely figuratively (*omnino figurative*); Hebrew expression (*vox hebraica*)	who flashes forth with destruction	הַמַּבְלִיג שֹׁד
Amos 5:26	Literal	Synecdoche (*Synecdoche*)	the star	כּוֹכַב

---

[25] Luther's translation of "idle teeth (*muessige zene*)," in contrast to the Hebrew "cleanness of teeth," seems at first glance to be an interpretative rendering. Luther said in the lectures, however, that he was translating it literally. Thus, I have assigned this as "literal." For reference, this German idiomatic usage appears in the eighteenth century, thus too late for consideration here; WAN 5:492 [§ 212].

[26] WAN 2:1361 has entries for this word, but the idiomatic usage seems to be biblically-based (see the Jeremiah reference). Cf. DWB 11:913–4. Nevertheless, Luther's rendering is clearly literal. Furthermore, because the Zwickau text includes *planctum* as part of the Hebraism, I have included this as a separate figure of speech from the previous entry in this table.

Table A.2: Luther's Translation of Hebrew Figures of Speech

Vulgate	1532 Deutsche Bibel	1545 Deutsche Bibel	Bible References	Exegetical References
unde et ego dedi vobis stuporem dentium	Darumb hab ich euch auch … muessige zene gegeben	DArumb hab ich euch auch … muuessige Zeene gegeben	WA DB 4:236a.6–8; WA DB 4:236b.6–9; WA DB 11.2:236.6; WA DB 11.2:237.6	WA 13:136.22–29; WA 13:177.12–29; LW 18:153
ego levo super vos	ich mus … vber euch machen	ich mus … vber euch machen	WA DB 11.2:238.1; WA DB 11.2:239.1	WA 13:138.25– WA 13:139.2; WA 13:179.31– WA 13:180.10; LW 18:157
planctum	dis klaglied	dis Klaglied	WA DB 11.2:238.1; WA DB 11.2:239.1	WA 13:138.25– WA 13:139.2; WA 13:179.31– WA 13:180.10; LW 18:157
et vivetis	so werdet jr leben	so werdet jr leben	WA DB 11.2:238.4; WA DB 11.2:239.4	WA 13:139.10–21; WA 13:181.4–8; LW 18:158–9
et Bethel erit inutilis	vnd Bethel wird jnn jamer komen	vnd Bethel wird BethAuen werden	WA DB 4:236a.11–17; WA DB 4:236b.11–14; WA DB 11.2:238.5; WA DB 11.2:239.5	WA 13:139.22– WA 13:140.3; WA 13:181.22–28; LW 18:159
qui subridet vastitatem	der … eine verstoerung anricht	Der … eine verstoerung anricht	WA DB 11.2:238.9; WA DB 11.2:239.9	WA 13:140.25–31; WA 13:182.13–18; LW 18:160–1
sidus	den stern	den Stern	WA DB 4:237a.21–28; WA DB 4:237b.21– WA DB 4:238b.23; WA DB 11.2:240.26; WA DB 11.2:241.26	WA 13:143.26– WA 13:144.14; WA 13:187.29; LW 18:167

---

[27] Cornette shows Luther's idiomatic use of *jammer*; though here in Amos 5:5 (1532), it seems pretty clearly interpretative when examining Luther's lecture remarks. See Cornette, *Proverbs*, 159. Cf. WAN 2:1003–4.

[28] *Anricht* has links to German idiomatic usage. The rest of the verse is a literal translation. Spalding indicates that *anrichten* has idiomatic roots in *Mittelhochdeutsch* associated with "preparing a meal," but then became associated with other "preparations," "installations," etc. in *Neuhochdeutsch*. SPAL 2:55. Clearly this aligns with Luther's explanatory comments in the lectures. See also DWB 1:427–8.

Verse	Luther's Hermeneutic	Luther Calls It ...	NASB English	Hebrew Bible
Amos 6:1	Literal	expression (*Verbum*)	And to those who feel secure	וְהַבֹּטְחִים
Amos 6:1	Literal	Hebrew phrase (*Hebraica phrasis*); Hebraism (*Hebraismus*); in the Hebrew idiom (*hebraica phrasi*)	To whom the house of Israel comes	וּבָאוּ לָהֶם בֵּית יִשְׂרָאֵל
Amos 6:3	Interpretative[29]	Hebraism (*Hebraismus*)	And would you bring near the seat of violence?	וַתַּגִּשׁוּן שֶׁבֶת חָמָס
Amos 6:8	Interpretative	Hebraism (*Hebraismus*); Through synecdoche (*Per synecdochen*)	and all it contains	וּמְלֹאָהּ
Amos 6:10	Literal	Hebrew phraseology (*phrasis ... hebraea, phrasis ... hebraica*)	For the name of the Lord is not to be mentioned	כִּי לֹא לְהַזְכִּיר בְּשֵׁם יְהוָה
Amos 6:12	Literal[30]	a rustic metaphor of the Tekoan rustic [Amos' hometown] (*rustica rustici Thecoensis metaphora*); rustic metaphor (*rustica metaphora*); of [the] metaphor (*metaphorae*)	Do horses run on rocks? Or does one plow them with oxen?	הַיְרֻצוּן בַּסֶּלַע סוּסִים אִם-יַחֲרוֹשׁ בַּבְּקָרִים

---

[29] Grimm shows numerous idiomatic uses of *trachten*, some including references to Agricola. But these are either near Luther's time, or later than Luther's time. Therefore, based on only this, it is difficult to substantiate Luther's use of an existing German idiom. See DWB 21:995–1004. Thus, I have assigned this as "interpretative." If earlier idiomatic usage could be substantiated, the argument could be made that the 1545 rendering should be "mixed," taking German idiomatic usage into account.

Table A.2: Luther's Translation of Hebrew Figures of Speech 251

Vulgate	1532 *Deutsche Bibel*	1545 *Deutsche Bibel*	Bible References	Exegetical References
et confiditis	vnd denen, die sich … verlassen	vnd denen die sich … verlassen	WA DB 4:238a.27–31; WA DB 4:238b.27–33; WA DB 11.2:240.1; WA DB 11.2:241.1	WA 13:144.21–29; WA 13:188.9–12; LW 18:168
ingredientes pompatice domum Israhel	im hause Jsrael	vnd gehen einher im hause Jsrael	WA DB 4:238a.27–31; WA DB 4:238b.27–33; WA DB 11.2:240.1; WA DB 11.2:241.1	WA 13:144.21–29; WA 13:188.13–20; LW 18:168–9
et adpropinquatis solio iniquitatis	Vnd jr regiert mit freuel	Vnd trachtet jmer nach freuel Regiment	WA DB 4:238a.34–; WA DB 4:239a.7; WA DB 4:238b.34–; WA DB 4:239b.9; WA DB 11.2:240.3; WA DB 11.2:241.3	WA 13:145.12–15; WA 13:189.11–14; LW 18:169
cum habitatoribus suis	mit allem das drinnen ist	mit allem das drinnen ist	WA DB 11.2:242.8; WA DB 11.2:243.8	WA 13:146.4–8; WA 13:190.20–22; LW 18:171
et non recorderis nominis Domini	Denn sie wolten nicht, das man des HERRN namens gedenkken solt	Denn sie wolten nicht, das man des HERRN Namens gedenkken solt	WA DB 11.2:242.10; WA DB 11.2:243.10	WA 13:146.14–24; WA 13:190.27–; WA 13:191.11; LW 18:171
numquid currere queunt in petris equi aut arari potest in bubalis	Wer kan mit rossen rennen, odder mit ochsen pfluegen auff felsen?	Wer kan mit Rossen rennen, oder mit Ochsen pfluegen auff Felsen?	WA DB 11.2:242.12; WA DB 11.2:243.12	WA 13:146.27–; WA 13:147.4; WA 13:191.15–24; LW 18:172

---

[30] Cf. WAN 3:1733–4 [§ 17, § 49]; though § 17 is clearly too late to be linked to Luther, and this is a literal rendering of the Hebrew regardless.

Verse	Luther's Hermeneutic	Luther Calls It ...	NASB English	Hebrew Bible
Amos 7:7	Interpretative[31]	Hebraism (*Hebraismus*)	the Lord was standing by a vertical wall	אֲדֹנָי נִצָּב עַל-חוֹמַת אֲנָךְ
Amos 8:1	Literal	pun in Hebrew (*hebraeo allusio*); puns (*Allusiones*); pun (*allusio*)	a basket of summer fruit	כְּלוּב קָיִץ
Amos 8:2	Literal[32]	Figure of speech in Hebrew (*verborum ... in hebraeo*); paronomasia (*agnominatio*); pun (*allusio*)	The end has come	בָּא הַקֵּץ
Amos 8:9	Literal[33]	Hebraisms (*Hebraica phrasi, hebraismi*); Hebraism (*Hebraismus*); metaphorically (*metaphorice*)	That I will make the sun go down at noon And make the earth dark in broad daylight.	וְהֵבֵאתִי הַשֶּׁמֶשׁ בַּצָּהֳרָיִם וְהַחֲשַׁכְתִּי לָאָרֶץ בְּיוֹם אוֹר
Amos 8:10	Literal[34]	Hebraism (*Hebraismus*)	And I will bring sackcloth on everyone's loins	וְהַעֲלֵיתִי עַל-כָּל-מָתְנַיִם שָׂק
Amos 9:9	Literal	Hebrew idiom (*phrasin hebraicam*)	But not a kernel will fall to the ground	וְלֹא-יִפּוֹל צְרוֹר אָרֶץ

---

[31] Luther explained the Hebrew figure of speech for the reader to some extent by adding *mit* ("with"). This is clearer in the lectures.

[32] Cf. WAN 1:817 [§ 68] and DWB 3:454; though this is clearly a literal rendering of the Hebrew.

[33] There are many German idioms linked to the sun going down, many later than Luther. For example, see WAN 4:624 [§ 314]. Nevertheless, clearly this is a literal rendering of the Hebrew by Luther.

Table A.2: Luther's Translation of Hebrew Figures of Speech

Vulgate	1532 Deutsche Bibel	1545 Deutsche Bibel	Bible References	Exegetical References
Dominus stans super murum litum	der HERR stund auff einer maure mit einer bleischnur gemessen	der HERR stund auff einer Maure mit einer Bleischnur gemessen	WA DB 4:240b.14–15; WA DB 11.2:244.7; WA DB 11.2:245.7	WA 13:148.22– WA 13:149.3; WA 13:193.23–27; LW 18:175
uncinus pomorum	ein korb mit obs	ein Korb mit obs	WA DB 11.2:244.1; WA DB 11.2:245.1	WA 13:150.26– WA 13:151.10; WA 13:196.26– WA 13:197.5; LW 18:179
venit finis	Das ende ist komen	Das ende ist komen	WA DB 4:240b.27–29; WA DB 11.2:244.2; WA DB 11.2:245.2	WA 13:150.26– WA 13:151.10; WA 13:197.6–10; LW 18:179–80
occidet sol meridie et tenebrescere faciam terram in die luminis	Wil ich die sonnen im mittage vntergehen lassen, vnd das land am hellen tage lassen finster werden	wil ich die Sonnen im mittage vntergehen lassen, vnd das Land am hellen tage lassen finster werde	WA DB 11.2:246.9; WA DB 11.2:247.9	WA 13:152.17–23; WA 13:198.26– WA 13:199.9; LW 18:182
et inducam super omne dorsum vestrum saccum	Jch wil vber alle lenden, den sack bringen	Jch wil vber alle Lenden, den Sack bringen	WA DB 11.2:246.10; WA DB 11.2:247.10	WA 13:152.24– WA 13:153.2; WA 13:199.10–15; LW 18:182
et non cadet lapillus super terram	vnd die koernlin sollen nicht auff die erden fallen	Vnd die Koernlin sollen nicht auff die erden fallen	WA DB 11.2:248.9; WA DB 11.2:249.9	WA 13:156.3–13; WA 13:204.13–25; LW 18:188

---

[34] This is an excellent example of how the German took on a biblical Hebraism into its language as an idiom, and moreover where Luther's translation helped to spread the use of that idiom. See DWB 14:1617 and WAN 3:1821 [§ 308] concerning the idiom *in Sack und Aschen sitzen*. Cf. SPAL 3:76. Nevertheless, Luther clearly made a literal rendering of the Hebrew here. Cf. Jon. 3:5–6.

Verse	Luther's Hermeneutic	Luther Calls It ...	NASB English	Hebrew Bible
Obad. 1:3	Literal	in the Hebrew fashion (*Hebraico more*)	You who live in the clefts of the rock	שֹׁכְנִי בְחַגְוֵי־סֶלַע
Jon. 1:2	Literal	Hebrew expression (*phrasis hebraea*); Hebraism (*Hebraismus*)	for their wickedness has come up before Me	כִּי־עָלְתָה רָעָתָם לְפָנָי
Jon. 1:9	Literal[35]	a way typical of the Hebrews (*Hebraico more*); expression (*phrasis*); Hebraism (*Hebraismus*); Hebraism / spoken in Hebrew (*auff Ebreisch geredt*)	and I fear the LORD God of heaven	וְאֶת־יְהוָה אֱלֹהֵי הַשָּׁמַיִם אֲנִי יָרֵא
Jon. 2:4	Interpretative	Hebraism (*Hebraismus*); Hebrew expression (*Hebraica phrasis*); expression (*phrasis*)	Into the heart of the seas	בִּלְבַב יַמִּים
Jon. 2:7	Literal	Pure metaphors (*Merae ... metaphorae*); elegant metaphors (*Metaphorae elegantes*)	The earth with its bars was around me forever	הָאָרֶץ בְּרִחֶיהָ בַעֲדִי לְעוֹלָם

---

[35] Surely this German idiom is taken from biblical language; hence, the assignment as "literal." Nevertheless, see WAN 2:109–10; DWB 8:1232–5; MERZ 1:185, 301; and MERZ 2:485, 503, 521–3, 526, 528–9.

Table A.2: Luther's Translation of Hebrew Figures of Speech

Vulgate	1532 Deutsche Bibel	1545 Deutsche Bibel	Bible References	Exegetical References
te habitantem in scissuris petrae	weil du jnn der felsen kluefften wonest	weil du in der Felsenklueff-ten wonest	WA DB 4:242b.4–7; WA DB 11.2:254.3; WA DB 11.2:255.3	WA 13:209.19–21; WA 13:216.31– WA 13:217.8; LW 18:195
quia ascendit malitia eius coram me	Denn jre bosheit ist erauff komen fur mich	Denn jre bosheit ist er auff komen fur mich	WA DB 11.2:262.2; WA DB 11.2:263.2	WA 13:227.10–20; WA 13:244.24–30; WA 19:193.22– WA 19:195.36; LW 19:8–9; LW 19:40–43
et Dominum Deum caeli ego timeo	vnd furchte den HERRN Gott von himel	vnd fuerchte den HERRN Gott von Himel	WA DB 11.2:262.9; WA DB 11.2:263.9	WA 13:230.9–18; WA 13:247.20–32; WA 19:214.16– WA 19:216.7; LW 19:13; LW 19:63–64
in corde maris	mitten im meer	mitten im Meer	WA DB 11.2:264.4; WA DB 11.2:265.4	WA 13:232.17– WA 13:233.3; WA 13:250.10–15; WA 19:226.6– WA 19:227.13; LW 19:18; LW 19:75–76
terrae vectes concluse-runt me in aeternum	Die erde hatte mich verriegelt ewiglich	Die Erde hatte mich verriegelt ewiglich	WA DB 11.2:264.7; WA DB 11.2:265.7	WA 13:233.25– WA 13:234.5; WA 13:251.16–20; WA 19:228.32– WA 19:229.16; LW 19:19–20; LW 19:78–79

Verse	Luther's Hermeneutic	Luther Calls It ...	NASB English	Hebrew Bible
Jon. 3:5	Literal[36]	Hebraism (*hebraismus*); Hebrew expression (*Phrasis ... hebraica, phrasin hebraicam, auff Ebreisch gered*); in the Hebrew manner (*Gleich wie auff Ebreische weyse*)	and put on sackcloth	וַיִּלְבְּשׁוּ שַׂקִּים
Jon. 3:6	Literal[37]	Hebraism (*Hebraismus*); Hebrew expression (*phrasis hebraica*)	and sat on the ashes	וַיֵּשֶׁב עַל-הָאֵפֶר
Jon. 4:11	Literal	an idiom of the Hebrew language (*phrasis ... hebraeae linguae*)	who do not know the difference between their right and left hand	אֲשֶׁר לֹא-יָדַע בֵּין-יְמִינוֹ לִשְׂמֹאלוֹ
Mic. 1:3	Literal[38]	The Hebrew expression (*Vox hebraea*)	[on] the high places [of]	עַל-[בָּמֳתֵי]
Mic. 1:10	Interpretative	Hebraism (*Hebraismus*)	At Beth-le-aphrah	בְּבֵית לְעַפְרָה
Mic. 1:11	Interpretative[39]	Hebraism (*Hebraismus*)	inhabitant of Shaphir	יוֹשֶׁבֶת שָׁפִיר

---

[36] Cf. Amos 8:10 and Jon. 3:6. The footnote remarks concerning Amos 8:10 in this table apply to this entry as well.

[37] Cf. Amos 8:10 and Jon. 3:5. The footnote remarks concerning Amos 8:10 in this table apply to this entry as well.

Table A.2: Luther's Translation of Hebrew Figures of Speech

Vulgate	1532 Deutsche Bibel	1545 Deutsche Bibel	Bible References	Exegetical References
et vestiti sunt saccis	Vnd zogen secke an	Vnd zogen Secke an	WA DB 11.2:266.5; WA DB 11.2:267.5	WA 13:236.3–25; WA 13:253.31–39; WA 19:234.27– WA 19:237.22; LW 19:24; LW 19:85–88
et sedit in cinere	vnd setzt sich jnn die asschen	vnd setzt sich in die Asschen	WA DB 11.2:266.6; WA DB 11.2:267.6	WA 13:236.3–25; WA 13:254.4–6; WA 19:237.9–22; LW 19:24; LW 19:88, 97
qui nesciunt quid sit inter dexteram et sinistram suam	die nicht wissen vnterscheid, was recht odder linck ist	die nicht wissen vnterscheid, was recht oder linck ist	WA DB 11.2:268.11; WA DB 11.2:269.11	WA 13:240.8–11; WA 13:257.32–39; WA 19:244.16–35; LW 19:30–31; LW 19:96–97
excelsa	die Hoehen	die Hoehen	WA DB 11.2:272.3; WA DB 11.2:273.3	WA 13:262.3–13; WA 13:302.21–29; LW 18:211–2
in domo Pulveris	[Sondern gehet] jnn die traurkamer	[Sondern gehet] in die Traurkamer	WA DB 11.2:272.10; WA DB 11.2:273.10	WA 13:264.20–33; WA 13:305.30–36; LW 18:216–7
habitatio Pulchra	Du schoene Stad	Du schoene Stad	WA DB 4:246a.14– WA DB 4:247a.2; WA DB 4:246b.14– WA DB 4:247b.4; WA DB 11.2:272.11; WA DB 11.2:273.11	WA 13:265.1–32; WA 13:306.1–28; LW 18:217–8

---

[38] There are many idiomatic uses of *Höhe* as representing power, authority, excellence, etc. See WAN 2:736–7. Nevertheless, this was a literal translation by Luther.

[39] Luther's focus concerning the Hebraism was יוֹשֶׁבֶת (*yôšebet*).

Verse	Luther's Hermeneutic	Luther Calls It …	NASB English	Hebrew Bible
Mic. 1:11	1532 Interpretative; 1545 Literal[40]	Hebraism (*Hebraismus*)	The inhabitant of Zaanan	יוֹשֶׁבֶת צַאֲנָן
Mic. 1:15	Literal[41]	Ironically (*ironice*); Pure allusion (*Mera … allusio*)	Moreover, I will bring on you The one who takes possession, O inhabitant of Mareshah.	עֹד הַיֹּרֵשׁ אָבִי לָךְ יוֹשֶׁבֶת מָרֵשָׁה
Mic. 2:1	Literal[42]	metaphor (*metaphora*); metaphorically (*metaphorice*)	iniquity	אָוֶן
Mic. 2:7	Interpretative	in the Hebrew fashion (*Hebraico more*)	Are these His doings?	אִם-אֵלֶּה מַעֲלָלָיו
Mic. 2:11	German Idiom[43]	Hebrew idiom (*phrasis hebraica*)	If a man walking after wind	לוּ-אִישׁ הֹלֵךְ רוּחַ
Mic. 3:10	Literal	Hebraism (*hebraismus*)	Who build Zion with bloodshed	בֹּנֶה צִיּוֹן בְּדָמִים
Mic. 3:11	Interpretative[44]	Hebraism (*hebraismus*)	pronounce judgment for a bribe	בְּשֹׁחַד יִשְׁפֹּטוּ

---

[40] The previous footnote applies here also.

[41] An argument could be made that Luther added a bit of flair and emphasis to the irony/allusion with his addition of *rechten*. But since he rendered the irony/allusion literally, I have assigned this simply as "literal."

[42] As a prime example of how complex the identification of Luther's use of existing idioms can be at times, Wander alone lists 231 idiomatic uses of *Schade*. WAN 4:42–52. Cf. Cornette, *Proverbs*, 98, 192; SING 2:190; DWB 14:1970, 1973–4; and WA 51:698–9, 730 [§ 245]. Nevertheless, Luther's lecture comments make it clear that he made a literal translation here.

Table A.2: Luther's Translation of Hebrew Figures of Speech

Vulgate	1532 Deutsche Bibel	1545 Deutsche Bibel	Bible References	Exegetical References
quae habitat in Exitu	Die stoltze	Die Einwonerin Zaenan	WA DB 4:246a.14– WA DB 4:247a.2; WA DB 4:246b.14– WA DB 4:247b.4; WA DB 11.2:272.11; WA DB 11.2:273.11	WA 13:265.1–32; WA 13:306.1–28; LW 18:217–8
adhuc heredem adducam tibi quae habitas in Maresa	Jch wil dir Maresa den rechten erben bringen	Jch wil dir Maresa den rechten Erben bringen	WA DB 4:247a.28– WA DB 4:248a.3; WA DB 4:247b.28– WA DB 4:248b.4; WA DB 11.2:274.15; WA DB 11.2:275.15	WA 13:267.15–24; WA 13:307.35– WA 13:308.9; LW 18:220
inutile	schaden	schaden	WA DB 4:248a.6–11; WA DB 4:248b.6–8; WA DB 11.2:274.1; WA DB 11.2:275.1	WA 13:268.5–14; WA 13:308.30– WA 13:309.3; LW 18:221–2
aut tales sunt cogitationes eius	Solte er solchs thun wollen?	Solte er solchs thun wollen?	WA DB 4:248a.25–26; WA DB 4:248b.25–26; WA DB 11.2:274.7; WA DB 11.2:275.7	WA 13:270.27– WA 13:271.8; WA 13:311.10–11; LW 18:225
utinam non essem vir habens spiritum	Were ich ein loser schwetzer	WEnn ich ein Jrregeist were	WA DB 4:249a.7–8; WA DB 4:249b.7–15; WA DB 11.2:274.11; WA DB 11.2:275.11	WA 13:271.33– WA 13:272.8; WA 13:312.10–14; LW 18:227
qui aedificatis Sion in sanguinibus	die jr Zion mit blut bawet	Die jr Zion mit blut bawet	WA DB 11.2:276.10; WA DB 11.2:277.10	WA 13:276.13–16; WA 13:316.1–5; LW 18:233
in muneribus iudicabant	richten vmb geschencke	richten vmb Geschencke	WA DB 11.2:276.11; WA DB 11.2:277.11	WA 13:276.17– WA 13:277.2; WA 13:316.6–20; LW 18:233

---

[43] Luther used two different German idioms. The first was *schwetzer* in 1532 (the modern German spelling is *schwätzer*, from the verb *schwatzen*). WAN 4:428–32. DWB 15:2349–59. The second was *Jrregeist* (the modern German spelling is *Irregeist*) in 1545. See SPAL 30:1400–2 concerning the *Mittelhochdeutsch* idiomatic roots of *irre*, associated with "losing one's way"; and the *Neuhochdeutsch* use of the term, applying it to other actions and feelings, with explicit mention of Luther.

[44] Luther's comments in the lectures focus on the prepositional use of בְּ (*bə*, "in") as the Hebraism, which he argues should be rendered in Latin as *propter* ("for [the sake of]") rather than *in* ("in"). His German rendering of *vmb* ("for"; the modern German spelling is *um*) adjusts for this, to make it clear for the German reader.

Verse	Luther's Hermeneutic	Luther Calls It ...	NASB English	Hebrew Bible
Mic. 3:12	Literal	prophetic figures of speech (*Figurae ... propheticae*); figures of speech (*figurae*)	Zion will be plowed as a field	צִיּוֹן שָׂדֶה תֵחָרֵשׁ
Mic. 3:12	Literal[45]	prophetic figures of speech (*Figurae ... propheticae*); figures of speech (*figurae*)	Jerusalem will become a heap of ruins	וִירוּשָׁלַ͏ִם עִיִּין תִּהְיֶה
Mic. 3:12	Literal[46]	prophetic figures of speech (*Figurae ... propheticae*); figures of speech (*figurae*)	And the mountain of the temple will become high places of a forest	וְהַר הַבַּיִת לְבָמוֹת יָעַר
Mic. 4:8	Literal[47]	metaphorically (*metaphorice*)	tower of the flock	מִגְדַּל־עֵדֶר
Mic. 4:11	German Idiom[48]	Hebrew expression (*Phrasis ... hebraica, hebraica phrasis*); Hebraism (*Hebraismus*)	And let our eyes gloat over Zion	וְתַחַז בְּצִיּוֹן עֵינֵינוּ
Mic. 4:13	Literal[49]	metaphorical expressions (*Metaphoricae ... locutiones*); poetic expressions (*Poeticae locutions*)	Arise and thresh, daughter of Zion	קוּמִי וָדוֹשִׁי בַת־צִיּוֹן
Mic. 4:13	Literal	metaphorical expressions (*Metaphoricae ... locutiones*); poetic expressions (*Poeticae locutions*)	For your horn I will make iron	כִּי־קַרְנֵךְ אָשִׂים בַּרְזֶל

---

[45] See KB, 699.

[46] *Wilden hoehe* ("wild heights") may appear to be idiomatic. However, none of the sources consulted show it as part of an idiom. Thus, I have shown it as "literal." I forgive Luther neglecting to make any translation of יָעַר (*yā'ar*, "forest") in his German rendering.

[47] *Thurm* ("tower") has some idiomatic usage. See WAN 4:1201–3. Nevertheless, Luther's translation is clearly a literal rendering here.

Table A.2: Luther's Translation of Hebrew Figures of Speech

Vulgate	1532 *Deutsche Bibel*	1545 *Deutsche Bibel*	Bible References	Exegetical References
Sion quasi ager arabitur	wird Zion ... wie ein feld zu pflueget	wird Zion ... wie ein Feld zupflueget	WA DB 11.2:276.12; WA DB 11.2:277.12	WA 13:277.3–10; WA 13:316.33– WA 13:317.7; LW 18:234–5
et Hierusalem quasi acervus lapidum erit	vnd Jerusalem zum stein hauffen	vnd Jerusalem zum Steinhauffen	WA DB 11.2:276.12; WA DB 11.2:277.12	WA 13:277.3–10; WA 13:316.33– WA 13:317.7; LW 18:234–5
et mons templi in excelsa silvarum	vnd der berg des tempels zu einer wilden hoehe werden	vnd der berg des Tempels zu einer wilden Hoehe werden	WA DB 11.2:276.12; WA DB 11.2:277.12	WA 13:277.3–10; WA 13:316.33– WA 13:317.7; LW 18:234–5
et tu turris Gregis [nebulosa]	thurm Eder	thurm Eder	WA DB 4:250a.11–13; WA DB 4:250b.11–14; WA DB 11.2:278.8; WA DB 11.2:279.8	WA 13:280.13–25; WA 13:321.8–24; LW 18:242
et aspiciat in Sion oculus noster	wir wollen vnser lust an Zion sehen	Wir wollen vnsere lust an Zion sehen	WA DB 11.2:278.11; WA DB 11.2:279.11	WA 13:282.3–11; WA 13:323.6–11; LW 18:245
surge et tritura filia Sion	Darumb mache dich auff vnd dressche du tochter Zion	Darumb mache dich auff vnd dressche du tochter Zion	WA DB 11.2:278.13– WA DB 11.2:280.13; WA DB 11.2:279.13– WA DB 11.2:281.13	WA 13:282.12–20; WA 13:323.22– WA 13:324.13; LW 18:245–6
quia cornu tuum ponam ferreum	denn ich wil dir eisern hoerner ... machen	Denn ich wil dir eisern Hoerner ... machen	WA DB 11.2:278.13– WA DB 11.2:280.13; WA DB 11.2:279.13– WA DB 11.2:281.13	WA 13:282.12–20; WA 13:323.22– WA 13:324.13; LW 18:245–6

---

[48] Luther explicitly identified *Ich sehe meine Lust dran* (literally, "I see my desire on it") as an equivalent German idiom in his lectures. I have thus assigned this as a "German idiom." See also DWB 12:1324.

[49] *Dreschen* ("to thresh") has many idiomatic usages. See WAN 1:696; DWB 2:1401–5; and SPAL 11:501–2. Nevertheless, Luther's translation is clearly a literal rendering here.

Verse	Luther's Hermeneutic	Luther Calls It …	NASB English	Hebrew Bible
Mic. 4:13	Literal	metaphorical expressions (*Metaphoricae … locutiones*); poetic expressions (*Poeticae locutions*)	And your hoofs I will make bronze	וּפַרְסֹתַיִךְ אָשִׂים נְחוּשָׁה
Mic. 4:13	Literal[50]	metaphorical expressions (*Metaphoricae … locutiones*); poetic expressions (*Poeticae locutions*)	That you may pulverize many peoples, That you may devote to the Lord their unjust gain And their wealth to the Lord of all the earth.	וַהֲדִקּוֹת עַמִּים רַבִּים וְהַחֲרַמְתִּי לַיהוָה בִּצְעָם וְחֵילָם לַאֲדוֹן כָּל־הָאָרֶץ
Mic. 5:1	Literal	Hebrew expression (*Phrasis hebraea, Phrasis … hebraica*)	among the clans of Judah	בְּאַלְפֵי יְהוּדָה
Mic. 5:4	Literal	Hebrew expression (*Phrasis … hebraea*)	Seven … and eight	שִׁבְעָה … וּשְׁמֹנָה
Mic. 7:12	Literal	Hebraisms (*Hebraismi*)	From Assyria and the cities of Egypt	לְמִנִּי אַשּׁוּר וְעָרֵי מָצוֹר
Mic. 7:12	Literal	Hebraisms (*Hebraismi*)	From Egypt even to the Euphrates	וּלְמִנִּי מָצוֹר וְעַד נָהָר

---

[50] See DWB 25:92, which helps to make clear that Luther made a literal translation with *verbannen* ("to ban"; but also used to mean declaring land, etc. holy and belonging to priests). Cf. SPAL 54:2546, which suggests this had a meaning of "to forbid" in the sixteenth century.

Table A.2: *Luther's Translation of Hebrew Figures of Speech*

Vulgate	1532 *Deutsche Bibel*	1545 *Deutsche Bibel*	Bible References	Exegetical References
et ungulas tuas ponam aereas	[ich wil dir ...] vnd eherne klawen machen	[ich wil dir ...] vnd eherne Klawen machen	WA DB 11.2:278.13–WA DB 11.2:280.13; WA DB 11.2:279.13–WA DB 11.2:281.13	WA 13:282.12–20; WA 13:323.22–WA 13:324.13; LW 18:245–6
et comminues populos multos et interficiam Domino rapinas eorum et fortitudinem eorum Domino universae terrae	vnd solt viel voelcker zurschmeissen, So wil ich jr gut dem HERRN verbannen, vnd jre habe dem Herrscher der gantzen welt	vnd solt viel Voelcker zurschmeissen, So wil ich jr Gut dem HERRN verbannen, vnd jre habe dem Herrscher der gantzen Welt	WA DB 11.2:278.13–WA DB 11.2:280.13; WA DB 11.2:279.13–WA DB 11.2:281.13	WA 13:282.12–20; WA 13:323.22–WA 13:324.13; LW 18:245–6
in milibus Iuda	gegen den tausenten jnn Juda	vnter den tausenten in Juda	WA DB 4:250b.26–WA DB 4:251b.2; WA DB 11.2:280.1; WA DB 11.2:281.1	WA 13:283.14–WA 13:284.2; WA 13:324.25–28; LW 18:247–8
septem ... et octo	sieben ... vnd acht	sieben ... vnd acht	WA DB 11.2:280.4; WA DB 11.2:281.4	WA 13:285.21–WA 13:286.5; WA 13:326.30–WA 13:327.7; LW 18:250–1
Assur et usque ad civitates munitas	von Assur vnd von festen stedten	von Assur vnd von festen stedten	WA DB 11.2:284.12; WA DB 11.2:285.12	WA 13:297.10–16; WA 13:341.1–9; LW 18:273–4
et a civitatibus munitis usque ad flumen	von den festen stedten bis an das Wasser	von den festen Stedten, bis an das Wasser	WA DB 11.2:284.12; WA DB 11.2:285.12	WA 13:297.10–16; WA 13:341.1–9; LW 18:273–4

Verse	Luther's Hermeneutic	Luther Calls It ...	NASB English	Hebrew Bible
Mic. 7:12	German Idiom[51]	Hebraisms (Hebraismi)	Even from sea to sea	וְיָם מִיָּם
Mic. 7:12	German Idiom[52]	Hebraisms (Hebraismi)	and mountain to mountain	וְהַר הָהָר
Nah. 1:1	Interpretative[53]	Hebrew expression (hebraica phrasis)	The oracle of Nineveh	מַשָּׂא נִינְוֵה
Nah. 1:3	Interpretative[54]	in the Hebrew fashion (Hebraico more); Hebraism (Hebraismus)	And ... will by no means leave the guilty unpunished.	וְנַקֵּה לֹא יְנַקֶּה
Nah. 1:8	Literal	Hebraism (Hebraismus)	But with an overflowing flood	וּבְשֶׁטֶף עֹבֵר
Nah. 1:11	Literal	Hebrew phrase (Hebraica phrasis); expression (phrasis)	From you has gone forth	מִמֵּךְ יָצָא
Nah. 1:12	Literal[55]	Hebrew manner (Hebraice)	Even so, they will be cut off	וְכֵן נָגוֹזּוּ
Nah. 1:14	Mixed[56]	Hebraism (Hebraismus)	Your name will no longer be perpetuated	לֹא־יִזָּרַע מִשִּׁמְךָ עוֹד

---

[51] Since Luther described this in the Latin lectures as *sicut nos dicimus* ("as we say") and then provided a German equivalent [*von eyner statt zu der andern* ("from one city to the next")], I have identified this as German idiomatic language. It is certainly not a German "proverb," but also seems to be quite clearly idiomatic in the German tongue, specifically where *zum andern/zu der andern* replaces the second item in the list in order to express distance.

[52] The previous footnote applies here also.

[53] Luther's focus was the Hebrew *construct state* (roughly equivalent to the English genitive case), which he argued was a Hebraism here. He rendered it as *vber* (the modern German spelling is *über*; "over"), thus explaining the Hebraism to the German reader.

[54] Luther identified this as a Hebraism in the lectures, thus I have included it both in Table A.2 and in Table A.3. This was a difficult example to categorize. The Hebrew (in the *Piel binyan*; see this example in Ch. 4 of this study) carries meanings of both (a) to leave unpun-

Table A.2: Luther's Translation of Hebrew Figures of Speech   265

Vulgate	1532 Deutsche Bibel	1545 Deutsche Bibel	Bible References	Exegetical References
et ad mare de mari	von einem meer zum andern	von einem Meer zum andern	WA DB 11.2:284.12; WA DB 11.2:285.12	WA 13:297.10–16; WA 13:341.1–9; LW 18:273–4
et ad montem de monte	von einem gebirge zum andern	von einem Gebirge zum andern	WA DB 11.2:284.12; WA DB 11.2:285.12	WA 13:297.10–16; WA 13:341.1–9; LW 18:273–4
Onus Nineve	Djs ist die Last vber Nineue	Djs ist die Last vber Nineue	WA DB 4:252b.8–12; WA DB 11.2:290.1; WA DB 11.2:291.1	WA 13:346.9–13; WA 13:372.18–27; LW 18:283
et mundans non faciet innocentem	vnd lesst nichts vngestrafft	fur welchem niemand vnschuldig ist	WA DB 4:252a.15–23; WA DB 4:252b.15–25; WA DB 11.2:290.3; WA DB 11.2:291.3	WA 13:348.8–20; WA 13:374.23–; WA 13:375.2; LW 18:286–7
et in diluvio praetereunte	Wenn die flut vber her leufft	Wenn die Flut vber her leufft	WA DB 11.2:290.8; WA DB 11.2:291.8	WA 13:350.31–; WA 13:351.11; WA 13:376.23–34; LW 18:289
ex te exivit	so von dir kompt	der von dir kompt	WA DB 4:254b.1–10; WA DB 11.2:290.11; WA DB 11.2:291.11	WA 13:353.1–8; WA 13:379.3–9; LW 18:292
et ... sic quoque adtondentur	so sollen sie doch vmbgehawen werden	Sollen sie doch vmbgehawen werden	WA DB 4:254a.11–15; WA DB 4:254b.11–33; WA DB 11.2:290.12; WA DB 11.2:291.12	WA 13:353.9–23; WA 13:379.21–29; LW 18:293
non seminabitur ex nomine tuo	das deines namens same keiner mehr sol bleiben	das deines namens same keiner mehr sol bleiben	WA DB 4:254b.34–; WA DB 4:255b.16; WA DB 11.2:290.14–; WA DB 11.2:292.14; WA DB 11.2:291.14–; WA DB 11.2:293.14	WA 13:354.1–21; WA 13:380.12–20; LW 18:294

---

ished and (b) to declare innocent. Because Luther used the all-encompassing *nichts* (1532) and *niemand* (1545) for emphasis, I assigned this as "interpretative."

⁵⁵ Grimm lists some idiomatic uses of *umhauen* from the sixteenth century. DWB 23:941–2. Nevertheless, surely the German idiomatic usage in this verse is taken from the literal biblical language; hence, the assignment as "literal."

⁵⁶ Most of Luther's translation here is a literal rendering; his use of *bleiben*, however, is interpretative. Thus, I have assigned this as "mixed." Also, there is some evidence of idiomatic usage associated with *das deines namens same*, though I am uncertain of the origin. For example, see WAN 3:871 [§ 5]. Cf. SPAL 43:2053; it is difficult not to link these to biblical usage, for which Spalding provides several examples. Nevertheless, Luther's translation of this portion is clearly taken from biblical language; hence, the assignment of this portion of his "mixed" translation as "literal."

Verse	Luther's Hermeneutic	Luther Calls It ...	NASB English	Hebrew Bible
Nah. 2:1	Literal	Hebrew mode (*hebraico more*); Hebraism (*hebraismu, hebraismo*)	on the mountains	עַל־הֶהָרִים
Nah. 2:1	1532 Interpretative;[57] 1545 Literal	Hebraism (*Hebraismus*)	Who announces peace!	מַשְׁמִיעַ שָׁלוֹם
Nah. 2:2	Mixed[58]	Allusion (*Alludit*); sarcastically (εἰρωνικῶς)	watch the road	צַפֵּה־דֶרֶךְ
Nah. 2:3	1532 Mixed; 1545 Interpretative[59]	prophetic metaphors (*Metaphorae ... propheticae*)	Even though devastators have devastated them	כִּי בְקָקוּם בֹּקְקִים
Nah. 2:3	Literal[60]	prophetic metaphors (*Metaphorae ... propheticae*)	And destroyed their vine branches	וּזְמֹרֵיהֶם שִׁחֵתוּ
Nah. 2:5	Interpretative[61]	Hebrew expressions (*hebraicae ... phrases*)	race madly in the streets	בַּחוּצוֹת יִתְהוֹלְלוּ

---

[57] See the explanation of this example in the main text of Ch. 2, particularly in the footnote there.

[58] Luther made an interpretative rendering of the "military" allusion, rather than translate it literally. Concerning the German idiomatic use of *wohl* (here, *wol*), see the entry in this table on Joel 2:22. Thus, I have assigned this as "mixed" (interpretative: *berenne*; German idiom: *wol*). That said, since the main emphasis of the idiom is really independent of *wol*, this could just as easily be categorized "interpretative." Aside from all of this, there are idiomatic uses of *berenne*, but they seem to be later than Luther. See DWB 1:1502–3.

[59] This example also appears in Table A.3. Luther read "emptiers" [in Hebrew] as "strippers" [in German], utilizing "vine branches" in the next part of the verse to establish the contextual meaning. This is the interpretative portion, which Luther used in both 1532 and

Table A.2: Luther's Translation of Hebrew Figures of Speech

Vulgate	1532 Deutsche Bibel	1545 Deutsche Bibel	Bible References	Exegetical References
super montes	auff den bergen	auff den Bergen	WA DB 4:255a.17–18; WA DB 4:255b.17–26; WA DB 11.2:292.1; WA DB 11.2:293.1	WA 13:354.22– WA 13:355.8; WA 13:380.35– WA 13:381.28; LW 18:295–6
et adnuntiantis pacem	der gute mehre bringet	der da Frieden predigt	WA DB 4:255a.17–18; WA DB 4:255b.17–26; WA DB 11.2:292.1; WA DB 11.2:293.1	WA 13:354.22– WA 13:355.8; WA 13:380.35– WA 13:381.28; LW 18:295–6
contemplare viam	Aber, Ja berenne die strassen wol	Aber, Ja berenne die strassen wol	WA DB 4:255a.28– WA DB 4:256a.4; WA DB 4:255b.28– WA DB 4:256b.6; WA DB 11.2:292.2; WA DB 11.2:293.2	WA 13:356.6–9; WA 13:382.27–32; LW 18:298–9
quia vastatores dissipaverunt eos	Man wird dich doch rein ablesen	Denn die Ableser werden sie ablesen	WA DB 4:256b.7–21; WA DB 11.2:292.3; WA DB 11.2:293.3	WA 13:356.25–31; WA 13:383.14–28; LW 18:299–300
et propagines eorum corruperunt	vnd deine feser verderben	vnd jre Feser verderben	WA DB 4:256b.7–21; WA DB 11.2:292.3; WA DB 11.2:293.3	WA 13:356.25–31; WA 13:383.14–28; LW 18:299–300
in itineribus conturbati sunt	rollen auff den gassen	rollen auff den gassen	WA DB 4:256b.28–30; WA DB 11.2:292.5; WA DB 11.2:293.5	WA 13:357.11–26; WA 13:384.10–20; LW 18:301

1545. In addition, in 1532, Luther utilized hyperbole with the German idiomatic *rein*. On the *Mittelhochdeutsch* history of *rein*, see SPAL 42:1978–80, with several references to Luther. Concerning בקק (*bqq*), see KLE, 81.

[60] On *Feser*, see DWB 3:1555.

[61] Luther's interpretation for the German reader explained the "rolling." But in doing so, he ignored the "rush madly" nuance of יִתְהוֹלְלוּ (*yithôləlû*), which the Vulgate conveys with the "confused, disordered" nuance in *conturbati sunt*. Many German idiomatic uses of *auf der Gasse(n)* and similar phrases appear in various sources, but it is difficult to attribute Luther's use of it in this translation to those idioms, as *Gasse* is a very common word. See: DWB 4:1443; WAN 1:1345–6; SPAL 20:917–8; and Cornette, *Proverbs*, 144. Cf. MERZ 1:144; and MERZ 2:434, 537, 557, 562.

Verse	Luther's Hermeneutic	Luther Calls It ...	NASB English	Hebrew Bible
Nah. 2:5	Interpretative[62]	Hebrew expressions (*hebraicae ... phrases*)	rush wildly in the squares	יִשְׁתַּקְשְׁקוּן בָּרְחֹבוֹת
Nah. 2:5	1532 Literal; 1545 Mixed[63]	Hebrew expressions (*hebraicae ... phrases*)	Their appearance is like torches	מַרְאֵיהֶן כַּלַּפִּידִם
Nah. 2:5	Mixed[64]	Hebrew expressions (*hebraicae ... phrases*)	They dash to and fro like lightning flashes	כַּבְּרָקִים יְרוֹצֵצוּ
Nah. 2:7	Mixed[65]	filled with ironies (*plenissima ... ironiis*)	The gates of the rivers are opened	שַׁעֲרֵי הַנְּהָרוֹת נִפְתָּחוּ
Nah. 2:7	Literal	filled with ironies (*plenissima ... ironiis*)	And the palace is dissolved	וְהַהֵיכָל נָמוֹג
Nah. 2:11	Mixed[66]	Hebrew figure of speech (*figura ... hebraica*)	And all their faces are grown pale	וּפְנֵי כֻלָּם קִבְּצוּ פָארוּר
Nah. 3:1	Interpretative	in the Hebrew custom (*hebraico more*)	to the bloody city	עִיר דָּמִים
Nah. 3:3	German Idiom[67]	Hebraism (*hebraismum*)	a mass of	[וְ]כֹבֶד

---

[62] Luther's interpretation for the German reader explained a facet of יִשְׁתַּקְשְׁקוּן (*yištaqšəqûn*). Nevertheless, as in the previous example, it was still an interpretative reading rather than a literal one.

[63] *Fackel(n)* appears in various places as part of German idioms, but it is difficult to attribute his use of it in this translation to those idioms. More importantly, Luther's translation is clearly a literal rendering of the Hebrew. See WAN 1:912–3. Cf. MERZ 1:292; and DWB 3:1227. The interpretative portion of Luther's 1545 translation is *Sie blicken*; the literal portion is *wie Fackeln*.

[64] See TDOT 13:421; KB, 882; and BDB, 930.

[65] Luther's translation was "literal;" but he made the addition of *doch*, which really points

Table A.2: Luther's Translation of Hebrew Figures of Speech

Vulgate	1532 Deutsche Bibel	1545 Deutsche Bibel	Bible References	Exegetical References
conlisae sunt in plateis	vnd rasseln auff den strassen	vnd rasseln auff den strassen	WA DB 4:256b.28–30; WA DB 11.2:292.5; WA DB 11.2:293.5	WA 13:357.11–26; WA 13:384.10–20; LW 18:301
aspectus eorum quasi lampades	Jr ansehen ist, wie fackeln	Sie blicken wie Fackeln	WA DB 4:256b.28–30; WA DB 11.2:292.5; WA DB 11.2:293.5	WA 13:357.11–26; WA 13:384.10–20; LW 18:301
quasi fulgura discurrentia	vnd faren vnter einander her, wie die blitze	vnd faren vnter einander her, wie die Blitzen	WA DB 4:256b.28–30; WA DB 11.2:292.5; WA DB 11.2:293.5	WA 13:357.11–26; WA 13:384.10–20; LW 18:301
portae fluviorum apertae sunt	Aber die thor an den wassern werden doch geoeffnet	Aber die Thor an den wassern werden doch geoeffenet	WA DB 4:256b.31–34; WA DB 11.2:292.7; WA DB 11.2:293.7	WA 13:358.9–18; WA 13:385.6–18; LW 18:302
et templum ad solum dirutum	vnd des Koenigs pallast wird vntergehe	vnd der Pallast wird vntergehen	WA DB 4:256b.31–34; WA DB 11.2:292.7; WA DB 11.2:293.7	WA 13:358.9–18; WA 13:385.6–18; LW 18:302
et facies omnium sicut nigredo ollae	vnd aller angesicht bleich sehen, wie ein toepffen	vnd aller Angesicht bleich sehen, wie ein toepffen	WA DB 11.2:292.11; WA DB 11.2:293.11	WA 13:359.29– WA 13:360.2; WA 13:386.30– WA 13:387.9; LW 18:304–5
civitas sanguinum	der moerdischen stad	der moerderischen Stad	WA DB 11.2:294.1; WA DB 11.2:295.1	WA 13:361.6–9; WA 13:387.23–30; LW 18:306
[et] gravis	[vnd] grosse hauffen	[vnd] grosse hauffen	WA DB 11.2:294.3; WA DB 11.2:295.3	WA 13:361.24– WA 13:362.23; WA 13:388.23–32; LW 18:307

to the irony, thus this is also "interpretative." Aside from this, *Wasser* and *Thor* appear together in German idiomatic usage; nevertheless, this portion of his translation is certainly a literal rendering of the Hebrew here. For more on this, see WAN 4:1822 [§ 536] and DWB 27:2295 (though these are slightly later than Luther's time).

⁶⁶ Luther utilized a German idiom with *bleich*; but his translation was literal with *toepffen*. Thus, this is a mixed translation. On *bleich*, see WAN 1 [§ 249] [this only appears in the online Wander edition, under "Gesicht" (http://woerterbuchnetz.de); the paper edition stops at § 222]; and SPAL 8:340, with mention of Luther.

⁶⁷ Many idiomatic uses of *grosse Haufen* appear prior to, during, and very shortly after Luther's time. See WAN 2:390–1 and SPAL 27:1252–4, both with direct mention of Luther. Cf. DWB 10:582–5.

Verse	Luther's Hermeneutic	Luther Calls It ...	NASB English	Hebrew Bible
Nah. 3:4	Interpretative	hebraism (*hebraismus*); in the Hebrew manner (*hebraico more*)	the mistress of sorceries	בַּעֲלַת כְּשָׁפִים
Nah. 3:4	Interpretative[68]	Hebraism (*Hebraismus*)	Who sells	הַמֹּכֶרֶת
Nah. 3:4	Literal	Figuratively and metaphorically (*Figurate et metaphorice*)	by her harlotries	בִּזְנוּנֶיהָ
Nah. 3:6	Literal[69]	an elegant expression in Hebrew (*Elegans ... in hebraeo verbum*); Hebrew expression (*phrasin hebraicam*)	And make you vile	וְנִבַּלְתִּיךְ
Nah. 3:13	Interpretative[70]	Hebrew fashion (*Hebraico more*)	are opened wide	פָּתוֹחַ נִפְתְּחוּ
Nah. 3:15	Literal[71]	Similes (*Similitudines*)	It will consume you as the locust does	תֹּאכְלֵךְ כַּיָּלֶק
Nah. 3:15	Mixed[72]	Similes (*Similitudines*)	Multiply yourself like the creeping locust	הִתְכַּבֵּד כַּיָּלֶק

---

[68] Instead of translating "sold," as the Hebrew reads, Luther focused on the receiving end of the action with "acquired"; thus, "who sells nations ..." became "who acquired nations." The figure of speech is the idea of betrayal or seduction. I have labeled this "interpretative," given Luther's adjustment. Thus far, I have found no firm evidence of an equivalent German idiom at or prior to Luther's time, though it seems to be idiomatic usage (cf. the English idiom "you've been taken" or "you've been had," which could certainly be put into the active voice as "to take someone").

[69] The modern German spelling is *schänden*. There are many German idiomatic uses of this word. For example, see WAN 4:99. Nevertheless, it is essentially a literal rendering of the Hebrew here. See TDOT 9:160–3; KB, 589; and BDB, 614.

Table A.2: Luther's Translation of Hebrew Figures of Speech

Vulgate	1532 Deutsche Bibel	1545 Deutsche Bibel	Bible References	Exegetical References
habentis maleficia	die mit zeuberey vmbgehet	die mit Zeuberey vmbgehet	WA DB 11.2:294.4; WA DB 11.2:295.4	WA 13:362.24– WA 13:363.16; WA 13:388.33–38; LW 18:307–8
quae vendidit	erworben hat	erworben hat	WA DB 11.2:294.4; WA DB 11.2:295.4	WA 13:362.24– WA 13:363.16; WA 13:389.1–15; LW 18:308
in fornicationibus suis	mit jrer hurerey	mit jrer Hurerey	WA DB 11.2:294.4; WA DB 11.2:295.4	WA 13:362.24– WA 13:363.16; WA 13:389.1–15; LW 18:308
et contumeliis te	vnd dich schenden	vnd dich schenden	WA DB 11.2:294.6; WA DB 11.2:295.6	WA 13:364.13–16; WA 13:389.36– WA 13:390.2; LW 18:309
adapertione pandentur	sollen ... geoeffent werden	sollen ... geoeffent werden	WA DB 11.2:294.13; WA DB 11.2:295.13	WA 13:366.23– WA 13:367.10; WA 13:391.15–18; LW 18:311
devorabit te ut bruchus	Es wird dich abfressen, wie die kefer	Es wird dich abfressen, wie die Kefer	WA DB 4:257b.15–16; WA DB 11.2:294.15– WA DB 11.2:296.15; WA DB 11.2:295.15– WA DB 11.2:297.15	WA 13:368.7–10; WA 13:391.35– WA 13:392.13; LW 18:312–3
congregare ut bruchus	Es wird dich vberfallen, wie kefer	Es wird dich vberfallen, wie Kefer	WA DB 4:257b.15–16; WA DB 11.2:294.15– WA DB 11.2:296.15; WA DB 11.2:295.15– WA DB 11.2:297.15	WA 13:368.11–20; WA 13:392.14–26; LW 18:312–3

---

[70] Cf. Nah. 2:7 in this table. This example also appears in Table A.3. Given Luther's elimination of the repetition, it is not a literal rendering; thus, I have assigned it as "interpretative."

[71] There are many German idiomatic uses of *fressen*. For example, see WA 51:710–1, 728 [§ 340]; Cornette, *Proverbs*, 141; DWB 4:135–7; WAN 1:1161–4; and SPAL 18:849–52, with specific mention of Luther. Cf. MERZ 1:176–7, 181, 200, 245; and MERZ 2:475, 485, 521, 588. Nevertheless, it is clearly a literal translation of the Hebrew here. Cf. Zech. 9:15 in this table.

[72] This was "interpretative" with *vberfallen*; and "literal" with *wie Kefer*. Modern German seems to have taken on the "locusts" figure of speech.

Verse	Luther's Hermeneutic	Luther Calls It ...	NASB English	Hebrew Bible
Nah. 3:15	Mixed[73]	Similes (*Similitudines*)	Multiply yourself like the swarming locust	הִתְכַּבְּדִי כָּאַרְבֶּה
Nah. 3:17	Literal	great irony (*magna ironia*); great and bitter irony (*magna et ... acerba ... ironia*)	Settling	הַחוֹנִים
Hab. 1:4	1532 Literal; 1545 Mixed[74]	Hebraism (*hebraismus*); in the Hebrew manner (*Hebraico more*)	And justice is never upheld	וְלֹא־יֵצֵא לָנֶצַח מִשְׁפָּט
Hab. 1:8	Literal	Hyperbole (*Hyperbole*)	swifter than leopards	וְקַלּוּ מִנְּמֵרִים
Hab. 1:8	Literal[75]	figures of speech (*gleichnissen*)	And keener than wolves in the evening	וְחַדּוּ מִזְּאֵבֵי עֶרֶב
Hab. 1:8	Mixed[76]	figures of speech (*gleichnissen*)	Their horsemen come galloping, Their horsemen come from afar;	וּפָשׁוּ פָּרָשָׁיו וּפָרָשָׁיו מֵרָחוֹק יָבֹאוּ

---

[73] This was "interpretative" with *vberfallen*; and "literal" with *wie Hewschrecken*. Modern German seems to have taken on the "locusts" figure of speech.

[74] *Sach gewinnen* has German idiomatic usage in the sixteenth century. See DWB 14:1594. Cf. WAN 3:1792 [§ 110]. The rest of the 1545 translation is literal. Thus, the 1545 rendering is a "mixed" translation.

[75] There are numerous idiomatic German usages which include *bissig* and *Wolf* (for

Table A.2: Luther's Translation of Hebrew Figures of Speech 273

Vulgate	1532 Deutsche Bibel	1545 Deutsche Bibel	Bible References	Exegetical References
multiplicare ut lucusta	Es wird dich vberfallen, wie hewschrecken	Es wird dich vberfallen wie Hewschrecken	WA DB 4:257b.15–16; WA DB 11.2:294.15–WA DB 11.2:296.15; WA DB 11.2:295.15–WA DB 11.2:297.15	WA 13:368.11–20; WA 13:392.14–26; LW 18:312–3
quae considunt	die sich ... lagern	die sich ... lagern	WA DB 4:257a.17–18; WA DB 4:257b.17–19; WA DB 11.296.17; WA DB 11.297.17	WA 13:369.15–WA 13:370.3; WA 13:393.10–17; LW 18:314
et non pervenit usque ad finem Iudicium	vnd kan kein recht zum ende komen	vnd kan kein rechte sach gewinnen	WA DB 4:258a.3–5; WA DB 4:258b.3–8; WA DB 11.2:302.4; WA DB 11.2:303.4	WA 13:397.5–20; WA 13:425.28–32; WA 19:361.27–WA 19:362.15; LW 19:109; LW 19:163–4
leviores pardis	sind schneller, denn die Parde	sind schneller, denn die Parde	WA DB 4:258a.20–21; WA DB 11.2:302.8; WA DB 11.2:303.8	WA 13:399.14–25; WA 13:427.25–38; WA 19:368.22–WA 19:370.14; LW 19:112–3; LW 19:170–2
et velociores lupis vespertinis	so sind sie auch beissiger, denn die wolffe des abends	So sind sie auch beissiger, denn die Wolffe des abends	WA DB 4:258a.20–21; WA DB 11.2:302.8; WA DB 11.2:303.8	WA 13:399.14–25; WA 13:427.25–38; WA 19:368.22–WA 19:370.14; LW 19:112–3; LW 19:170–2
et diffundentur equites eius equites namque eius de longe venient	Jre reuter zihen mit grossem hauffen von fernen daher	Jre Reuter ziehen mit grossem Hauffen von fernen da her	WA DB 4:258a.20–21; WA DB 11.2:302.8; WA DB 11.2:303.8	WA 13:399.14–25; WA 13:427.25–38; WA 19:368.22–WA 19:370.14; LW 19:112–3; LW 19:170–2

example, *wolfbeiszig* and *wölffbissig*), but these are difficult to firmly link to Luther's use. See DWB 30:1260; and WAN 5:349–80 [§ 178, § 257, § 278, § 553]. Nevertheless, it is clearly a literal rendering of the Hebrew here.

[76] See the entry in this table for Nah. 3:3 concerning the idiomatic uses of *grosse Haufen*. I have assigned this verse as "mixed," with the *grosse Haufen* portion identified as a "German idiom," and the rest as "literal," though Luther seems to have been really using it to make an interpretative reading.

Verse	Luther's Hermeneutic	Luther Calls It ...	NASB English	Hebrew Bible
Hab. 1:8	Literal	figures of speech (*gleichnissen*)	They fly like an eagle swooping down to devour	יָעֻפוּ כְּנֶשֶׁר חָשׁ לֶאֱכוֹל
Hab. 1:9	Literal[77]	the Hebrew manner (*der Ebreischen weyse*)	like sand	כָּחוֹל
Hab. 2:2	Literal	in the Hebrew tongue (*ynn der Ebreischen sprache*)	the vision	חָזוֹן
Hab. 2:5	Literal[78]	metaphor (*metaphoricam*)	So that he does not stay at home	וְלֹא יִנְוֶה
Hab. 2:5	Literal[79]	metaphorically (*metaphorice*)	He enlarges his appetite like Sheol	אֲשֶׁר הִרְחִיב כִּשְׁאוֹל נַפְשׁוֹ

---

[77] Surely this German idiom is taken from biblical language; hence, the assignment as "literal." Nevertheless, many sources show idiomatic usage. See DWB 14:1758–9; and SPAL 43:2055–6. Cf. WAN 3:1862 [§ 46] (though this is later than Luther).

Table A.2: Luther's Translation of Hebrew Figures of Speech

Vulgate	1532 *Deutsche Bibel*	1545 *Deutsche Bibel*	Bible References	Exegetical References
volabunt quasi aquila festinans ad comedendum	als floegen sie, wie die Adeler eilen zum ass	als floegen sie, wie die Adeler eilen zum ass	WA DB 4:258a.20–21; WA DB 11.2:302.8; WA DB 11.2:303.8	WA 13:399.14–25; WA 13:427.25–38; WA 19:368.22– WA 19:370.14; LW 19:112–3; LW 19:170–2
quasi harenam	wie sand	wie sand	WA DB 11.2:302.9; WA DB 11.2:303.9	WA 13:399.26– WA 13:400.6; WA 13:428.9–12; WA 19:371.14–23; LW 19:113; LW 19:173
visum	das gesicht	das Gesicht	WA DB 4:258b.26–29; WA DB 11.2:304.2; WA DB 11.2:305.2	WA 13:404.10– WA 13:405.4; WA 13:432.12–40; WA 19:389.28– WA 19:391.28; LW 19:120–1; LW 19:192–4
et non decorabitur	das er nicht bleiben kan	das er nicht bleiben kan	WA DB 4:259b.15–16; WA DB 11.2:304.5; WA DB 11.2:305.5	WA 13:406.15– WA 13:407.4; WA 13:434.37– WA 13:435.18; WA 19:396.16– WA 19:400.2; LW 19:124–5; LW 19:199–202
qui dilatavit quasi infernus animam suam	welcher seine seele auff sperret, wie die helle	Welcher seine Seele auffsperret, wie die Helle	WA DB 4:259b.15–16; WA DB 11.2:304.5; WA DB 11.2:305.5	WA 13:406.15– WA 13:407.4; WA 13:434.37– WA 13:435.18; WA 19:396.16– WA 19:400.2; LW 19:124–5; LW 19:199–202

---

[78] Luther interpreted this as a metaphorical expression of drunkenness (in his lectures).

[79] Luther also interpreted this as a metaphorical expression of drunkenness (in his lectures).

Verse	Luther's Hermeneutic	Luther Calls It …	NASB English	Hebrew Bible
Hab. 2:6	Interpretative[80]	proverb (*proverbium*); of the proverbs (*proverbiorum*)	Woe to him who increases what is not his	הוֹי הַמַּרְבֶּה לֹּא-לוֹ
Hab. 2:6	Literal[81]	proverb (*proverbium*); of the proverb (*proverbii*); an extraordinary proverb (*Egregium proverbium*); a saying of the Hebrews (*Dictio Hebraeorum*)	And makes himself rich with loans	וּמַכְבִּיד עָלָיו עַבְטִיט
Hab. 2:15	German Idiom[82]	Parable (*parabola*); figure of speech (*tropus*); the Hebrew manner of speech (*der Ebreischen weise zu reden*); figurative words (*verdreeten worten*); similes (*gleichnis*)	you who make … drink	מַשְׁקֵה
Hab. 2:15	Interpretative[83]	metaphor (*metaphora*)	So as to look on their nakedness	לְמַעַן הַבִּיט עַל-מְעוֹרֵיהֶם

---

[80] While this could have been categorized as "literal," Luther deviated in multiple places from the literal Hebrew. Thus, I have assigned this as "interpretative."

[81] עַבְטִיט (*'abṭîṭ*) is a *hapax legomenon*. Luther likely used the *Rudimenta* and/or commentaries for his rendering of *schlams* ("mud"), which modern lexicons suggest is based on the association with עֲבִי (*'ăḇî*, "denseness") or עֳבִי (*'ŏḇî*, "thickness"). See *Rudimenta*, 370 [Reuchlin's entry reads: "Vna dictio que tamen exponitur taquam due dictiones· scilicet densum lutum. Habacuk.ii. Aggrauat contra se densum lutu."]; HCLOT, 1006; and BDB, 716. Spalding suggests that the figurative use of *Schlamm* is rooted in *Mittelhochdeutsch*, and that it has been "brought

Table A.2: *Luther's Translation of Hebrew Figures of Speech*

Vulgate	1532 *Deutsche Bibel*	1545 *Deutsche Bibel*	Bible References	Exegetical References
vae ei qui multiplicat non sua	Weh dem, der sein gut mehret mit frembdem gut	WEh dem, der sein Gut mehret mit frembdem gut	WA DB 4:259b.17–18; WA DB 11.2:304.6; WA DB 11.2:305.6	WA 13:407.8; WA 13:435.25–27; WA 19:401.19– WA 19:402.24; LW 19:126; LW 19:204–5
et adgravat contra se densum lutum	vnd ladet nur viel schlams auff sich	vnd ladet nur viel schlams auff sich	WA DB 4:259b.17–18; WA DB 11.2:304.6; WA DB 11.2:305.6	WA 13:407.9–14; WA 13:435.28–36; WA 19:401.19– WA 19:402.24; LW 19:126; LW 19:204–5
qui potum dat	der du … einschenckest	der du … einschenckest	WA DB 11.2:306.15; WA DB 11.2:307.15	WA 13:410.10– WA 13:411.2; WA 13:437.29– WA 13:438.7; WA 19:416.10– WA 19:419.11; LW 19:129–30; LW 19:218–21
ut aspiciat nuditatem eius	das du seine schame sehest	das du seine schame sehest	WA DB 11.2:306.15; WA DB 11.2:307.15	WA 13:410.10– WA 13:411.2; WA 13:438.4–7; WA 19:416.10– WA 19:419.11; LW 19:130; LW 19:218–21

---

into general currency by Luther." SPAL 45:2126–7. Cf. DWB 15:430, though these examples are clearly too late to be linked to Luther. This is a literal rendering of the Hebrew, regardless.

[82] SPAL 13:591–2, with explicit mention of Luther. Cf. MERZ 2:891; DWB 3:267–8; and WAN 1:796.

[83] מְעוֹרֵיהֶם (*məʿôrêhem*) has a rigidly literal meaning of "their nakedness"; but also a figurative meaning of "their shame, disgrace." Thus, I have assigned this as "interpretative." See KB, 545; BDB, 735; and DCH 6:317. Luther also translated the possessive pronoun as "his" instead of "their"; though this is not essential to the main figure of speech rendering as interpretative. On German idiomatic uses, see DWB 14:2109, though these are a bit later than Luther.

Verse	Luther's Hermeneutic	Luther Calls It ...	NASB English	Hebrew Bible
Hab. 2:20	Interpretative[84]	expression (*woertlin*)	before Him	מִפָּנָיו
Hab. 3:4	Interpretative[85]	metaphorically (*metaphorice*)	He has rays flashing from His hand	קַרְנַיִם מִיָּדוֹ לוֹ
Hab. 3:6	Interpretative[86]	metaphors (*metaphoricos*); poetically (*poetice*); Metaphorically (*Metaphorice*)	the perpetual mountains	הַרְרֵי-עַד
Hab. 3:8	Interpretative[87]	Expression (*Phrasis*); Hebrew expression (*phrasis hebraica*); In accord with the Hebrew manner of speech (*nach Ebreischen zungen*)	N/A [no negation in the NASB]	הַבִּנְהָרִים [הֲ]
Hab. 3:10	Literal[88]	Personifications (*prosopopoeiae*); synecdoche (*synecdochen*)	The mountains	הָרִים

---

[84] The rigidly literal rendering of the Hebrew would be "from the face of him." Thus, even though it is universally understood as "in front of him," I have categorized this as "interpretative" since Luther ensured it was clearly understood by the German reader [also, Luther spelled it *fur* instead of the modern *vor* here]. Of course, he did not fully clarify the figure of speech for the German reader in the way he explains it in the lectures, but this is so for many of these examples, and one must ultimately decide on a category.

[85] The Hebrew word קַרְנַיִם (*qarnayim*) has a number of figurative meanings, among which is "rays." See BDB, 901–2; KB, 856; and DCH 7:327. Nevertheless, given that "horns" is the rigidly literal rendering, I have assigned this as "interpretative." Also, there are many German idiomatic uses of *Glanz* and *glänzen* (see DWB 7:7601 concerning Luther's spelling *glentzen*). See DWB 7:7601–24; WAN 1:1691–2; and SPAL 23:1059–62. Cf. MERZ 2:864. Given Grimm's advice that the biblical word gained an idiomatic character, and thus this is really biblically-grounded, I have not assigned this as a "German idiom."

Table A.2: Luther's Translation of Hebrew Figures of Speech

Vulgate	1532 Deutsche Bibel	1545 Deutsche Bibel	Bible References	Exegetical References
a facie eius	fur jm	fur jm	WA DB 11.2:306.20; WA DB 11.2:307.20	WA 13:412.5–13; WA 13:439.8–18; WA 19:423.6– WA 19:424.12; LW 19:131–2; LW 19:225–6
cornua in manibus eius	glentzen giengen von seinen henden	Glentzen giengen von seinen Henden	WA DB 4:260a.1–3; WA DB 4:260b.1–3; WA DB 11.2:306.4; WA DB 11.2:307.4	WA 13:414.22–24; WA 13:443.3–7; WA 19:428.12–25; LW 19:138; LW 19:231
montes saeculi	der welt berge	der Welt berge	WA DB 11.2:308.6; WA DB 11.2:309.6	WA 13:415.32– WA 13:416.4; WA 13:444.3–6; WA 19:429.2–13; LW 19:140; LW 19:231
numquid	nicht	nicht	WA DB 11.2:308.8; WA DB 11.2:309.8	WA 13:417.1–25; WA 13:444.35– WA 13:445.12; WA 19:430.2–18; LW 19:141–2; LW 19:232–3
Montes	Die berge	DJe Berge	WA DB 11.2:308.10; WA DB 11.2:309.10	WA 13:418.14–32; WA 13:445.34– WA 13:446.4; WA 19:431.1–17; LW 19:142–3; LW 19:233–4

[86] Here, Luther's interpretative reading utilized another metaphor, which his lecture and commentary remarks make clear. Since this is not a German idiom that I can find, I have assigned it as "interpretative."

[87] Luther's focus was on הֲ (hă), one of the ways in which Hebrew indicates an interrogative. He suggests this is a Hebraism. Nevertheless, he clearly seems to have been influenced by the Latin *numquid* concerning the expected negative response. Since there is nothing in the literal Hebrew to indicate the negation, I have assigned this as "interpretative."

[88] In the LW, this discussion appears under v. 9; in the WA, v. 10. I placed this under v. 10, given the reference to mountains. If one prefers "earth" in v. 9 as the focus, the same observation of a literal translation by Luther applies. See DWB 1:1505 concerning how biblical language sometimes assigns human sentiments to mountains.

Verse	Luther's Hermeneutic	Luther Calls It ...	NASB English	Hebrew Bible
Hab. 3:10	Interpretative	epiphonema (*epiphonema*, ἐπιφώνημα)[89]	The deep uttered forth its voice	נָתַן תְּהוֹם קוֹלוֹ
Hab. 3:13	Literal[90]	Harsh figure of speech (*Dura figura*); metaphor (*metaphora, metaphoram*); double metaphor (*Duplex metaphora, duplicem ... metaphoram*)	To lay him open from thigh to neck	עָרוֹת יְסוֹד עַד־צַוָּאר
Hab. 3:16	Literal	metaphor and expression unique to this prophet (*metaphora et phrasis huius prophetae singularis*); expression unique to this prophet (*phrasis propria huius prophetae*); Hebrew expressions (*Ebreische weise zu reden*)	Decay enters my bones	יָבוֹא רָקָב בַּעֲצָמַי
Zeph. 1:2	Mixed[91]	Synecdoche (*synecdochen*)	all things From the face of the earth	כֹּל מֵעַל פְּנֵי הָאֲדָמָה

---

[89] Epiphonema is a figure of speech which expresses an exclamation, or provides a particularly striking summary. See OLD 1:672. Furthermore, there seem to be German idiomatic uses of *hören lassen*, but these are difficult (a) to identify as such, and (b) to substantiate as influencing Luther here. See DWB 10:1809.

[90] Luther saw יְסוֹד (*yəsôd*, "foundation") as a reference to רֹאשׁ (*rōš*, "head"). With this in mind, his rendering of רֹאשׁ (*rōš*) as *heubt* ("head, as in 'principal'") [the modern German spelling is *Haupt*] in the exegesis clearer, as is his literal Bible rendering *grundfest*. *Grundfest[e]* and variations of it appear in German prior to Luther. See SPAL 25:1163; and DWB 9:800–7. Aside from this, the German language also makes idiomatic usage of *bis zum Hals / bis an den Hals* [not addressed explicitly by Luther]. Nevertheless, this is clearly a literal rendering of the Hebrew here, which suggests that the idiom was likely taken on from biblical language. See DWB 10:244, 249–50, 254; and WAN 2 [§ 130] [this only appears in the online Wander edition, under "Hals" (http://woerterbuchnetz.de); the paper edition stops at § 125].

Table A.2: Luther's Translation of Hebrew Figures of Speech 281

Vulgate	1532 *Deutsche Bibel*	1545 *Deutsche Bibel*	Bible References	Exegetical References
dedit abyssus vocem suam	die tieffe lies sich hoeren	Die Tieffe lies sich hoeren	WA DB 11.2:308.10; WA DB 11.2:309.10	WA 13:418.33–35; WA 13:446.5–6; WA 19:431.5–17; LW 19:143; LW 19:233–4
denudasti fundamentum usque ad collum	vnd entbloessest die grundfest bis an den hals	vnd entbloessest die Grundfest bis an den Hals	WA DB 11.2:308.13; WA DB 11.2:309.13	WA 13:420.10–24; WA 13:447.1–4; WA 19:432.15–27; LW 19:145; LW 19:235
ingrediatur putredo in ossibus meis	eiter gehet jnn meine gebeine	Eiter gehet in meine Gebeine	WA DB 4:260b.11; WA DB 11.2:308.16; WA DB 11.2:309.16	WA 13:421.29–33; WA 13:447.41– WA 13:448.2; WA 19:433.29–32; LW 19:146; LW 19:236
omnia a facie terrae	alles aus dem lande	alles aus dem Lande	WA DB 11.2:312.2; WA DB 11.2:313.2	WA 13:450.22; WA 13:481.5–17; LW 18:320–1

---

[91] Luther made a literal translation of the synecdoche in "all" [i. e. even though God says "all," some will remain on the face of the earth]. By contrast, he made an interpretative translation of "face of the earth," which he more specifically translated as a single country (*Land*; further defined in his exegesis as Judea).

Verse	Luther's Hermeneutic	Luther Calls It ...	NASB English	Hebrew Bible
Zeph. 1:4	Literal	Synecdoche (*synecdochen*)	against Judah And against all the inhabitants of Jerusalem	עַל־יְהוּדָה וְעַל כָּל־יוֹשְׁבֵי יְרוּשָׁלָ͏ִם
Zeph. 1:9	Literal[92]	expression (*vox*)	all who leap on the temple threshold	כָּל־הַדּוֹלֵג עַל־הַמִּפְתָּן
Zeph. 1:11	Interpretative[93]	metaphor (*metaphora*)	inhabitants of the Mortar	יֹשְׁבֵי הַמַּכְתֵּשׁ
Zeph. 1:11	German Idiom[94]	expression (*verbum*)	will be silenced	נִדְמָה
Zeph. 1:11	Interpretative	metaphor (*metaphora*)	Canaan	כְּנַעַן
Zeph. 1:17	German Idiom[95]	expression (*vocem*); Hebrew expression (*vocem hebraeam*)	I will bring distress on men	וַהֲצֵרֹתִי לָאָדָם
Zeph. 1:17	Literal	a Hebrew phrase (*hebraica ... phrasis*); Hebraism (*hebraismum*)	And their flesh like dung	וּלְחֻמָם כַּגְּלָלִים

---

[92] There are some German idiomatic uses of *Schwelle*. See DWB 15:2489–91; SPAL 47:2212; and Cornette, *Proverbs*, 101. Nevertheless, it is clearly a literal rendering of the Hebrew here.

[93] Because Luther rendered this "those who live in ..." rather than a rigidly literal "the inhabitants of ...," I have categorized this as "interpretative." See also Table A.4 in the Appendix; Luther was arguing here against Jerome and others that this is a common noun, rather than part of Jerusalem.

Table A.2: Luther's Translation of Hebrew Figures of Speech

Vulgate	1532 *Deutsche Bibel*	1545 *Deutsche Bibel*	Bible References	Exegetical References
super Iudam et super omnes habitantes Hierusalem	vber Juda vnd vber alle die zu Jerusalem wonen	vber Juda, vnd vber alle, die zu Jerusalem wonen	WA DB 4:260a.23; WA DB 4:260b.21–29; WA DB 11.2:312.4; WA DB 11.2:313.4	WA 13:451.16– WA 13:452.20; WA 13:481.30– WA 13:482.11; LW 18:321–2
omnem qui arroganter ingreditur super limen	die ... so vber die schwelle springen	die ... so vber die Schwelle springen	WA DB 4:261a.11–13; WA DB 11.2:312.9; WA DB 11.2:313.9	WA 13:455.17– WA 13:456.13; WA 13:485.35– WA 13:486.25; LW 18:327–9
habitatores pilae	die jr jnn der Muele wonet	die jr in der Muele wonet	WA DB 4:261a.14–22; WA DB 4:261b.14–16; WA DB 11.2:312.11; WA DB 11.2:313.11	WA 13:457.1–27; WA 13:487.4–22; LW 18:329–30
conticuit	ist dahin	ist dahin	WA DB 4:261a.14–22; WA DB 4:261b.14–16; WA DB 11.2:312.11; WA DB 11.2:313.11	WA 13:457.1–27; WA 13:487.23– WA 13:488.2; LW 18:330–1
Chanaan	kremer volck	Kremeruolck	WA DB 4:261a.14–22; WA DB 4:261b.14–16; WA DB 11.2:312.11; WA DB 11.2:313.11	WA 13:457.1–27; WA 13:487.23– WA 13:488.2; LW 18:330–1
et tribulabo homines	Jch wil den leuten bange machen	Jch wil den Leuten bange machen	WA DB 11.2:314.17; WA DB 11.2:315.17	WA 13:460.11–18; WA 13:490.38– WA 13:491.11; LW 18:335
et corpus eorum sicut stercora	vnd jr leib, als were es kot	vnd jr Leib, als were es Kot	WA DB 11.2:314.17; WA DB 11.2:315.17	WA 13:460.30– WA 13:461.20; WA 13:491.23–40; LW 18:336

---

[94] Many uses of *ist dahin* appear in Luther's time and going back to *Mittelhochdeutsch*. See DWB 2:685–92; and SPAL 10:444.

[95] There are many appearances of *bange*, some idiomatic, near to and prior to Luther's time; though some attribute its common use to Luther. See DWB 1:1101–4. On Luther's pairing of *bange* and *machen* (as well as *werden*, *tun*, etc.), see DWB 1:1102; and WAN 1:227.

Verse	Luther's Hermeneutic	Luther Calls It ...	NASB English	Hebrew Bible
Zeph. 2:2	Literal[96]	Hebraism (*Hebraismus*); custom of the Hebrew language (*mos ... hebraeae linguae*)	Before the burning anger of the Lord comes upon you	בְּטֶרֶם לֹא-יָבוֹא עֲלֵיכֶם חֲרוֹן אַף-יְהוָה
Zeph. 2:2	Literal[97]	Hebraism (*Hebraismus*); custom of the Hebrew language (*mos ... hebraeae linguae*)	Before the day of the Lord's anger comes upon you.	בְּטֶרֶם לֹא-יָבוֹא עֲלֵיכֶם יוֹם אַף-יְהוָה
Zeph. 2:4	Literal[98]	beautiful verbal allusion which is in the Hebrew (*In hebraeo est pulchra allusio verborum*); elegant verbal allusion, which is in the Hebrew (*elegantem verborum allusionem, quae est in hebraeo*)	Gaza	עַזָּה
Zeph. 2:4	Literal	allusion (*allusio*)	at noon	בַּצָּהֳרַיִם
Zeph. 2:4	Literal[99]	allusion in/alludes to (*alludit ad*)	And Ekron	וְעֶקְרוֹן
Zeph. 2:5	Interpretative	Hebraism (*hebraismus, Hebraismus*)	the inhabitants of the seacoast	יֹשְׁבֵי חֶבֶל הַיָּם
Zeph. 2:5	Interpretative[100]	Hebraism (*hebraismus*)	The nation of the Cherethites	גּוֹי כְּרֵתִים

---

[96] See the Amos 5:5 example in Ch. 3 of this study, where this issue is addressed in a footnote. In light of the argument for reading the negation as pleonastic, I have assigned this as "literal." One could very well dismiss that argument, and assign this as "interpretative." Because Luther translated this *ehe denn* instead of just *ehe*, there seems to be some emphatic nuance and/or a nuance of uncertainty (i. e. "if"; as addressed in that footnote) which he was reading into this.

Table A.2: Luther's Translation of Hebrew Figures of Speech

Vulgate	1532 Deutsche Bibel	1545 Deutsche Bibel	Bible References	Exegetical References
antequam veniat super vos ira furoris Domini	ehe denn des HERRN grimmiger zorn vber euch kome	Ehe denn des HERRN grimmiger zorn vber euch kome	WA DB 11.2:314.2; WA DB 11.2:315.2	WA 13:462.20–24; WA 13:493.9–12; LW 18:339
antequam veniat super vos dies furoris Domini	ehe der tag des HERRN zorn vber euch kome	Ehe der tag des HERRN zorns vber euch kome	WA DB 11.2:314.2; WA DB 11.2:315.2	WA 13:462.20–24; WA 13:493.9–12; LW 18:339
Gaza	Gasa	Gasa	WA DB 11.2:314.4; WA DB 11.2:315.4	WA 13:463.9–16; WA 13:493.36– WA 13:494.9; LW 18:340
in meridie	im mittage	im mittage	WA DB 11.2:314.4; WA DB 11.2:315.4	WA 13:463.17–20; WA 13:494.10–12; LW 18:340
et Accaron	vnd Accaron	vnd Accaron	WA DB 11.2:314.4; WA DB 11.2:315.4	WA 13:463.21; WA 13:494.13–15; LW 18:340
qui habitatis funiculum maris	denen, so am meer hinab wonen	denen, so am Meer hinab wonen	WA DB 4:261a.31–32; WA DB 4:261b.31–32; WA DB 11.2:314.5; WA DB 11.2:315.5	WA 13:463.22–28; WA 13:494.16–21; LW 18:340–1
gens perditorum	den kriegern	den Kriegern	WA DB 4:261a.31–32; WA DB 4:261b.31–32; WA DB 11.2:314.5; WA DB 11.2:315.5	WA 13:463.22–28; WA 13:494.22–23; LW 18:340–1

[97] The previous footnote applies here also.
[98] This also appears in Table A.4.
[99] This also appears in Table A.4.
[100] Luther did not fully explain the Hebraism in his translation as he did in the lectures. Nevertheless, it is an interpretative rendering of the Hebrew here, particularly as he ignored גּוֹי (gôy). Concerning the Krieger[n] ("warriors, soldiers") translation of כְּרֵתִים (kərēṯîm), which he addressed in the lectures, see BDB, 504; and KB, 458.

Verse	Luther's Hermeneutic	Luther Calls It …	NASB English	Hebrew Bible
Zeph. 3:6	Interpretative[101]	Hebrew expression (*phrasis hebraea*)	Their corner towers	פִּנּוֹתָם
Zeph. 3:6	Literal[102]	Metaphor (*Metaphora*)	I have made their streets desolate	הֶחֱרַבְתִּי חוּצוֹתָם
Zeph. 3:19	German Idiom[103]	a Mosaic word (*Mosaicum, Mosaicum … verbum*)	I am going to deal	עֹשֶׂה
Hag. 1:1	Interpretative	Hebraism (*hebraismus*)	by the prophet Haggai	בְּיַד-חַגַּי הַנָּבִיא
Hag. 1:5	German Idiom[104]	Hebraism (*hebraismus, Hebraismus*); a proverbial figure of speech (*proverbialis … est figura*)	Consider your ways	שִׂימוּ לְבַבְכֶם עַל-דַּרְכֵיכֶם
Hag. 1:9	Interpretative[105]	expression (*verbo*)	I blow it away	וְנָפַחְתִּי בוֹ
Zech. 1:2	Literal[106]	in the Hebrew fashion (*hebraico more*); Hebraism (*Hebraismus*)	was very angry	קָצַף … קֶצֶף

---

[101] The rigidly literal meaning is "their corners," though פָּנָה (*pānâ*) carries a figurative meaning of "corner *tower*." Thus, I have assigned it here as "interpretative." See BDB, 819; and KB, 767–8.

[102] There are some idiomatic uses of *leer* near Luther's time. Nevertheless, this is a literal rendering of the Hebrew here [I am forgiving Luther's emphasis with *so*]. See DWB 12:508; and WAN 2:1875–6. See also BDB, 351; and KB, 330. On the idiomatic use of *Gasse(n)*, see Nah. 2:5 in this table.

[103] German idiomatic uses of *Ausmachen* exist since at least *Mittelhochdeutsch*. See SPAL 4:141–2, with specific mention of Luther. Cf. DWB 1:913–6, also with mention of Luther; and WAN 1:194 (citing DWB).

Table A.2: Luther's Translation of Hebrew Figures of Speech

Vulgate	1532 Deutsche Bibel	1545 Deutsche Bibel	Bible References	Exegetical References
anguli earum	jre schloesser	jre Schloesser	WA DB 11.2:316.6; WA DB 11.2:317.6	WA 13:470.21–23; WA 13:501.38– WA 13:502.16; LW 18:353
desertas feci vias eorum	Darumb wil ich ... [vnd] jre gassen so leer machen	Darumb wil ich ... [vnd] jre Gassen so lere machen	WA DB 11.2:316.6; WA DB 11.2:317.6	WA 13:470.24–30; WA 13:502.17–19; LW 18:353
ego interficiam	ich wils ... aus machen	ich wils ... ausmachen	WA DB 11.2:318.19; WA DB 11.2:319.19	WA 13:478.34– WA 13:479.5; WA 13:509.12–18; LW 18:363–4
in manu Aggei prophetae	durch den Propheten Haggai	durch den Propheten Haggai	WA DB 11.2:322.1; WA DB 11.2:323.1	WA 13:513.22–24; WA 13:534.22; LW 18:371
ponite corda vestra super vias vestras	Schawet, wie es euch gehet	Schawet, wie es euch gehet	WA DB 11.2:322.5; WA DB 11.2:323.5	WA 13:514.34– WA 13:515.19; WA 13:535.30– WA 13:536.16; LW 18:373–4
et exsuflavi illud	so zersteube ichs doch	So zersteube ichs doch	WA DB 11.2:322.9; WA DB 11.2:323.9	WA 13:517.31– WA 13:518.6; WA 13:537.24–33; LW 18:376
iratus est ... iracundia	ist zornig gewest	ist zornig gewest	WA DB 11.2:332.2; WA DB 11.2:333.2	WA 13:548.20– WA 13:549.29; StL 14:1776.10; LW 20:6–8; LW 20:161

---

[104] Various idiomatic uses of *gehen* (i. e. *wie geht es*) exist since at least *Mittelhochdeutsch*. See SPAL 20:946, which also cites specific variations of *wie geht es* as appearing since Late *Mittelhochdeutsch*, with reference to Eckhart. This word also appears as part of numerous larger idioms. See DWB 5:2401, 2471–3; Cornette, *Proverbs*, 58, 145; WAN 5:1425 [§ 95, § 147–9, § 481 § 529–49]; and there are many more. The same can be said for *schauen*, in the sense of "consider" rather than "see" or "look." See SPAL 44:2085. Cf. DWB 14:2312.

[105] This example reinforces those which appear in Ch. 3 of this study, showing Luther's appreciation of the semantic intensity of the Hebrew. *Zersteuben* (the modern German spelling is *zerstäuben*) means "to turn to dust," "to pulverize," or "to atomize." The Hebrew נָפַח (*nāpaḥ*) literally means "to blow upon" or "to breathe upon." See BDB, 655–6; and KB, 624.

[106] Luther eliminated the Hebrew repetition. This example also appears in Table A.3 in the Appendix.

Verse	Luther's Hermeneutic	Luther Calls It ...	NASB English	Hebrew Bible
Zech. 1:5	Interpretative[107]	the Hebrew language in its own idiom (*lingua hebraea pro suo more*); Hebraism (*hebraismum*)	do they live forever?	הַלְעוֹלָם יִחְיוּ
Zech. 1:8	Literal[108]	in its idiom the Hebrew tongue (*hebraea lingua sua phrasi*)	and behold, a man was riding on a red horse	וְהִנֵּה־אִישׁ רֹכֵב עַל־סוּס אָדֹם
Zech. 2:11	Literal	altogether a Hebrew way of speaking (*gar eine hebräische Weise*)	with the daughter of Babylon	בַּת־בָּבֶל
Zech. 2:12	Interpretative[109]	the way of the Hebrew language (*der hebräischen Sprache Art*)	After glory	אַחַר כָּבוֹד
Zech. 3:9	Literal	allegory (*die Allegorie*)	the stone	הָאֶבֶן
Zech. 4:2	Interpretative	Hebraism (*hebraismus*)	on the top of it	עַל־רֹאשָׁהּ

---

[107] Luther's lecture remarks suggest that this was a theologically motivated interpretation concerning prophecy and the meaning of "forever."

[108] Luther made the argument in the lectures on Zech. 1:9, but he was citing the Hebrew from Zech. 1:8. I include the exegetical references for both verses. That said, Luther's lecture remarks are not completely clear concerning "riding," "sitting," or "ascending." See WA 13:557.1–4 and Note 2Z. Nevertheless, רָכַב (*rākab*) carries all three nuances. See BDB,

Table A.2: Luther's Translation of Hebrew Figures of Speech

Vulgate	1532 Deutsche Bibel	1545 Deutsche Bibel	Bible References	Exegetical References
numquid in sempiternum vivent	Leben sie auch noch?	Leben sie auch noch?	WA DB 11.2:332.5; WA DB 11.2:333.5	WA 13:552.26– WA 13:553.25; StL 14:1779.18– StL 14:1780.20; LW 20:11; LW 20:164–5
et ecce vir ascendens super equum rufum	Vnd sihe, Ein man sas auff eim roten pferde	vnd sihe, Ein Man sass auff eim roten Pferde	WA DB 4:265a.25–26; WA DB 11.2:332.8; WA DB 11.2:333.8	WA 13:555.27– WA 13:559.4; StL 14:1782.27– StL 14:1785.37; LW 20:13–17; LW 20:167–9
apud filiam Babylonis	bey der tochter Babel	bey der tochter Babel	WA DB 11.2:334.7; WA DB 11.2:335.7	WA 13:570.18– WA 13:571.12; StL 14:1808.23– StL 14:1810.27; LW 20:28; LW 20:189–91
post gloriam	jre macht hat ein ende	Jre macht hat ein ende	WA DB 11.2:334.8; WA DB 11.2:335.8	WA 13:571.13– WA 13:574.5; StL 14:1810.28– StL 14:1816.42; LW 20:28–31; LW 20:191–97
lapis	einen steine	einigen Stein	WA DB 11.2:336.9; WA DB 11.2:337.9	WA 13:582.24– WA 13:583.25; StL 14:1839.44– StL 14:1842.51; LW 20:40–41; LW 20:218–20
super caput ipsius	oben drauff	oben drauff	WA DB 11.2:338.2; WA DB 11.2:339.2	WA 13:585.9–14; StL 14:1844.1– StL 14:1846.4; LW 20:43; LW 20:222–4

938–9. Therefore, I have assigned this as a "literal" translation. One could certainly argue that this should be "interpretative," and that something like יָשַׁב (yāšaḇ, "sat") would be a more appropriate literal Hebrew equivalent for *sass* ("sat").

[109] Dr. Sheila Watts has suggested that this phrase seems to have become idiomatic after Luther used it. That said, in the sources I have consulted, so far I can find no evidence for its use prior to Luther. Thus, I have categorized it as "interpretative" here.

290   Appendix

Verse	Luther's Hermeneutic	Luther Calls It …	NASB English	Hebrew Bible
Zech. 4:7	Literal[110]	elliptic speech (*ecliptica oratio*)	you will become a plain	לְמִישֹׁר
Zech. 4:7	German Idiom[111]	Hebraism (*Hebraismus*); in the Hebrew fashion (*more hebraico, auf hebräische Weise*)	with shouts of "Grace, grace to it!"	תְּשֻׁאוֹת חֵן חֵן לָהּ
Zech. 4:10	Literal	allegory (*allegoriam*)	these are the eyes of the Lord	שִׁבְעָה-אֵלֶּה עֵינֵי יְהוָה
Zech. 4:14	Literal[112]	Hebraisms (*hebraismorum*); In Hebrew fashion (*auf hebräische Weise*)	anointed ones	בְנֵי-הַיִּצְהָר
Zech. 6:1	Interpretative[113]	Hebraism (*Hebraismus*)	and the mountains were bronze mountains	וְהֶהָרִים הָרֵי נְחֹשֶׁת
Zech. 6:1[114]	Literal	Allegory (*Allegoria*)	the two mountains	שְׁנֵי הֶהָרִים

---

[110] Given the preceding interrogative, Luther's reading of this as an interrogative is plausible in the context. Taking this into consideration, as well as his addition of *doch*, it still is so close to a literal reading of the Hebrew that I have categorized it as "literal."

[111] Many idiomatic uses and variations of *Glück zu* appear in Luther's time and prior. See DWB 8:226–75; WAN 1:1731–74; Cornette, *Proverbs*, 147; WA 51:684–5, 728 [§ 145]; and SPAL 23:1084–90.

[112] Although Luther translated בְנֵי (*bənê*) as "children" instead of "sons," the main weight of the Hebraism lies with "oil." Thus, I have assigned this as "literal."

Table A.2: Luther's Translation of Hebrew Figures of Speech

Vulgate	1532 Deutsche Bibel	1545 Deutsche Bibel	Bible References	Exegetical References
in planum	der doch ... eine ebene sein mus?	der doch ... eine ebene sein mus?	WA DB 4:266a.30–31; WA DB 11.2:338.7; WA DB 11.2:339.7	WA 13:588.10– WA 13:590.21; StL 14:1848.10– StL 14:1849.10; LW 20:45–47; LW 20:226
et exaequabit gratiam gratiae eius	das man rufen wird, glueck zu, glueck zu	das man rufen wird, Glueck zu, glueck zu	WA DB 4:266a.30–31; WA DB 11.2:338.7; WA DB 11.2:339.7	WA 13:588.10– WA 13:590.21; StL 14:1849.11– StL 14:1850.13; LW 20:46–47; LW 20:226–7
septem isti oculi Domini	[mit den] sieben, welche sind des HERRN augen	[mit den] sieben, welche sind des HERRN augen	WA DB 4:267b.1–3; WA DB 11.2:338.10; WA DB 11.2:339.10	WA 13:593.23– WA 13:594.7; StL 14:1851.18– StL 14:1852.19; LW 20:51; LW 20:229
filii olei	die ... oelekinder	die ... Olekinder	WA DB 11.2:338.14; WA DB 11.2:339.14	WA 13:594.25– WA 13:595.17; StL 14:1852.20– StL 14:1855.24; LW 20:52; LW 20:229–32
et montes montes aerei	Die selbigen berge aber waren eherne	die selbigen Berge aber waren Eherne	WA DB 11.2:340.1; WA DB 11.2:341.1	WA 13:604.18–19; StL 14:1870.1– StL 14:1871.3; LW 20:64; LW 20:247–8
duorum montium	zween bergen	zween Bergen	WA DB 11.2:340.1; WA DB 11.2:341.1	WA 13:605.29– WA 13:606.27; LW 20:65–67

[113] This example also appears in Table A.3. Luther explained the Hebrew figure of speech to the German reader as "the *same* mountains" rather than "the mountains were mountains ..." It is also important to differentiate between this entry in the table and the next two entries. In those two entries, Luther addressed Zech. 6:1 looking back from his lectures on Zech. 6:8, where he focused on a different figure of speech (i. e. allegory).

[114] Luther addressed this in the lectures on Zech. 6:8. This is an exception in this table, insofar as for this entry on Zech. 6:1, I only include the LW and WA for the lectures on Zech. 6:8. Furthermore, Luther did not address v. 1–3 in his commentary on v. 8. Finally, recall the earlier guidance concerning Luther's misuse of linguistic terminology.

Verse	Luther's Hermeneutic	Luther Calls It ...	NASB English	Hebrew Bible
Zech. 6:1[115]	Literal	Allegory (*Allegoria*)	bronze	נְחֹשֶׁת
Zech. 6:2[116]	Literal	Allegory (*Allegoria*)	red horses	סוּסִים אֲדֻמִּים
Zech. 6:2[117]	Literal	Allegory (*Allegoria*)	black horses	סוּסִים שְׁחֹרִים
Zech. 6:3[118]	Literal	Allegory (*Allegoria*)	white horses	סוּסִים לְבָנִים
Zech. 6:3[119]	Literal	Allegory (*Allegoria*)	strong dappled horses	סוּסִים בְּרֻדִּים אֲמֻצִּים
Zech. 6:8	Literal	In Hebrew ... an expression (*In hebraeo ... verbum*)	Then He cried out to me	וַיַּזְעֵק אֹתִי
Zech. 8:12	Literal	Hebraism (*hebraismus*); beautiful metaphor (*pulchrae metaphorae*)	For there will be peace for the seed	כִּי־זֶרַע הַשָּׁלוֹם
Zech. 9:6	Interpretative	in Hebrew fashion (*auf hebräisch geredet*)	And a mongrel race will dwell in Ashdod	וְיָשַׁב מַמְזֵר בְּאַשְׁדּוֹד
Zech. 9:12	Interpretative[120]	Hebraism (*hebraismus*)	prisoners who have the hope	אֲסִירֵי הַתִּקְוָה

---

[115] The previous footnote applies here also.
[116] The previous footnote applies here also.
[117] The previous footnote applies here also.
[118] The previous footnote applies here also.
[119] The previous footnote applies here also.

Table A.2: Luther's Translation of Hebrew Figures of Speech

Vulgate	1532 Deutsche Bibel	1545 Deutsche Bibel	Bible References	Exegetical References
aerei	eherne	Eherne	WA DB 11.2:340.1; WA DB 11.2:341.1	WA 13:605.29– WA 13:606.27; LW 20:65–67
equi rufi	rote rosse	rote Rosse	WA DB 11.2:340.2; WA DB 11.2:341.2	WA 13:605.29– WA 13:606.27; LW 20:65–67
equi nigri	schwartze rosse	schwartze Rosse	WA DB 11.2:340.2; WA DB 11.2:341.2	WA 13:605.29– WA 13:606.27; LW 20:65–67
equi albi	weisse rosse	weisse Rosse	WA DB 11.2:340.3; WA DB 11.2:341.3	WA 13:605.29– WA 13:606.27; LW 20:65–67
equi varii fortes	scheckicht starcke rosse	scheckichte starcke Rosse	WA DB 11.2:340.3; WA DB 11.2:341.3	WA 13:605.29– WA 13:606.27; LW 20:65–67
et vocavit me	Vnd er rieff mir	Vnd er rieff mir	WA DB 4:268a.28; WA DB 11.2:342.8; WA DB 11.2:343.8	WA 13:605.11–28; StL 14:1875.13– StL 1876.15; LW 20:65; LW 20:252
sed semen pacis erit	Sondern sie sollen samen des friedes sein	Sondern sie sollen samen des Friedes sein	WA DB 11.2:346.12; WA DB 11.2:347.12	WA 13:618.23– WA 13:619.2; StL 14:1899.16–17; LW 20:84–85; LW 20:274–5
et sedebit separator in Azoto	Zu Asdod werden frembde wonen	Zu Asdod werden Frembde wonen	WA DB 4:270a.12–14; WA DB 4:270b.12–16; WA DB 11.2:348.6; WA DB 11.2:349.6	WA 13:624.27–33; StL 14:1910.11; LW 20:92; LW 20:285–6
vincti spei	jr die jr auff hoffnunge gefangen ligt	jr, die jr auff hoffnung gefangen ligt	WA DB 11.2:348.12; WA DB 11.2:349.12	WA 13:629.22– WA 13:630.6; StL 14:1916.24– StL 14:1917.27; LW 20:98; LW 20:291–2

---

[120] Because Luther rendered this as "those who are imprisoned by hope" rather than a rigidly literal "the prisoners of hope …," I have categorized this as "interpretative." One could certainly argue that this should be "literal." Also, there is a similar German idiom that appears shortly after Luther's time; but his rendering is so close to the Hebrew, that it is difficult to link his translation to this idiom, if it did exist prior to this. See WAN 2:724 [§ 62]. Spalding also cites numerous idiomatic uses of *hoffen* and *Hoffnung*. SPAL 29:1356–8. The word *Hoffnung* itself, nevertheless, is clearly a literal rendering of תִּקְוָה (*tiqwâ*).

Appendix

Verse	Luther's Hermeneutic	Luther Calls It ...	NASB English	Hebrew Bible
Zech. 9:15[121]	Literal	of metaphors and in figurative language (*metaphorarum et figuratis sermonibus*); beautiful metaphors (*pulchrae metaphorae*)	And they will devour	וְאָכְלוּ
Zech. 9:15[122]	Literal	of metaphors and in figurative language (*metaphorarum et figuratis sermonibus*); beautiful metaphors (*pulchrae metaphorae*)	And they will drink and be boisterous as with wine	וְשָׁתוּ הָמוּ כְּמוֹ-יָיִן
Zech. 9:15[123]	Literal	of metaphors and in figurative language (*metaphorarum et figuratis sermonibus*); beautiful metaphors (*pulchrae metaphorae*); metaphor (*metaphora*)	And they will be filled like a sacrificial basin, Drenched like the corners of the altar.	וּמָלְאוּ כַּמִּזְרָק כְּזָוִיּוֹת מִזְבֵּחַ
Zech. 9:16	Interpretative[124]	metaphors (*metaphoris, metaphoras, metaphorae*); alludes (*alludit*); allegory (*allegorium*); allegorically (ἀλληγορικῶς); obscure metaphors and figures of speech (*obscuris metaphoris et figuris*)	For they are as the stones of a crown	כִּי אַבְנֵי-נֵזֶר

---

[121] Luther also addressed this in the lectures on the next verse, Zech. 9:16. There are numerous German idiomatic uses of *fressen*. Cf. and see Nah. 3:15 in this table for the scholarly references on *fressen*. Nevertheless, this is clearly a literal rendering of the Hebrew here.

[122] Luther also addressed this in the lectures on the next verse, Zech. 9:16. Spalding attributes the idiomatic use of *rumoren* in the German language to Luther. SPAL 43:2028. Nevertheless, this is clearly a literal rendering of the Hebrew here.

[123] Luther also addressed this in the lectures on the next verse, Zech. 9:16.

Table A.2: Luther's Translation of Hebrew Figures of Speech

Vulgate	1532 Deutsche Bibel	1545 Deutsche Bibel	Bible References	Exegetical References
et devorabunt	das sie fressen	Das sie fressen	WA DB 11.2:348.15; WA DB 11.2:349.15	WA 13:632.10–WA 13:634.35; StL 14:1920.35–StL 14:1923.43; LW 20:100–3; LW 20:294–7
et bibentes inebriabuntur quasi vino	das sie trinken vnd rumorn als vom wein	das sie trinken vnd rumorn als vom Wein	WA DB 11.2:348.15; WA DB 11.2:349.15	WA 13:632.10–WA 13:634.35; StL 14:1920.35–StL 14:1923.43; LW 20:100–3; LW 20:294–7
et replebuntur ut fialae et quasi cornua altaris	vnd vol werden als das becken, vnd wie die ecken des altars	vnd vol werden als das Becken, vnd wie die Ecken des Altars	WA DB 11.2:348.15; WA DB 11.2:349.15	WA 13:632.10–WA 13:634.35; StL 14:1920.35–StL 14:1923.43; LW 20:100–3; LW 20:294–7
quia lapides sancti	Denn ... geweihete steine	Denn ... heilige Steine	WA DB 4:271b.9–11; WA DB 11.2:348.16–WA DB 11.2:350.16; WA DB 11.2:349.16–WA DB 11.2:351.16	WA 13:633.11–WA 13:634.35; StL 14:1922.41–StL 14:1923–43; LW 20:101–3; LW 20:296–7

---

[124] Luther interpreted this within the context of Num. 6, which his exegesis makes clear. Furthermore, נֵזֶר (*nēzer*) / נֶזֶר (*nezer*) [both spellings are valid] is an ambiguous term. Both "crown" and "consecration" are legitimate renderings, though "crown" is the more rigidly literal one. Thus, I have assigned this as "interpretative." Given the Hebrew ambiguity, one could certainly argue that this should be assigned as "literal." See BDB, 634; and KB, 605. There are also various idiomatic uses of these terms. Concerning *geweiht*, see MERZ 1:376. Concerning *heilig*, see WA 51:677, 728 [§ 97]; WAN 2:461–2; and SPAL 27:1273–5, with specific mention of Luther. Because this is so close to the literal Hebrew, and thus ultimately biblically based, I found it difficult to assign this as Luther somehow utilizing a German idiom.

Verse	Luther's Hermeneutic	Luther Calls It ...	NASB English	Hebrew Bible
Zech. 9:16	Literal	metaphors (*metaphoris, metaphoras, metaphorae*); alludes (*alludit*); allegory (*allegorium*); allegorically (ἀλληγορικῶς); obscure metaphors and figures of speech (*obscuris metaphoris et figuris*)	Sparkling in His land	מִתְנוֹסְסוֹת עַל־אַדְמָתוֹ
Zech. 10:1	Interpretative[125]	figurative language (*figuris*)	rain ... at the time of the spring rain	מָטָר בְּעֵת מַלְקוֹשׁ
Zech. 10:1	Literal[126]	figurative language (*figuris*)	storm clouds	חֲזִיזִים
Zech. 10:2	Literal[127]	figurative language (*figuris*)	the teraphim	הַתְּרָפִים
Zech. 10:2	Literal[128]	figurative language (*figuris*)	And the diviners	וְהַקּוֹסְמִים

---

[125] See BDB, 545; and KB, 486. This is an interpretative rendering, given Luther's choice not to include מָטָר בְּעֵת (*māṭār bəʿēṯ*) as part of his translation. This example does not appear in Table A.3 because I could not identify Luther as explicitly recognizing the repetition (technically, repetition of subject matter, since the terms are different) of מָטָר (*māṭār*) and מַלְקוֹשׁ (*malqôš*), which he essentially eliminated.

[126] See HALOT 1:302.

[127] There are many German idiomatic uses of *Götzen* prior to and during Luther's time. See DWB 8:1430–48, especially pp. 1431, 1444–6; Grimm cites Bahder's opinion that Luther was the first to use the word in the sense of *Abgott* ("idol"); whereas before him it had the sense

Table A.2: Luther's Translation of Hebrew Figures of Speech

Vulgate	1532 Deutsche Bibel	1545 Deutsche Bibel	Bible References	Exegetical References
elevantur super terram eius	es werden jnn seinem lande ... auffgericht werden	es werden in seinem Lande ... auffgericht werden	WA DB 4:271b.9–11; WA DB 11.2:348.16–WA DB 11.2:350.16; WA DB 11.2:349.16–WA DB 11.2:351.16	WA 13:633.11–WA 13:634.35; StL 14:1922.41–StL 14:1923–43; LW 20:101–3; LW 20:296–7
pluviam in tempore serotino	spat regen	Spatregen	WA DB 11.2:350.1; WA DB 11.2:351.1	WA 13:636.5–18; StL 14:1924.1–StL 14:1926.2; LW 20:105; LW 20:299
nives	gewolcken	gewolcken	WA DB 11.2:350.1; WA DB 11.2:351.1	WA 13:636.19–WA 13:637.2; StL 14:1924.1–StL 14:1926.2; LW 20:105–6; LW 20:299
simulacra	die Goetzen	die Goetzen	WA DB 4:271a.13–26; WA DB 4:271b.13–15; WA DB 11.2:350.2; WA DB 11.2:351.2	WA 13:637.3–5; StL 14:1926.3–4; LW 20:106; LW 20:299–300
et divini	die Warsager	die Warsager	WA DB 4:271a.13–26; WA DB 4:271b.13–15; WA DB 11.2:350.2; WA DB 11.2:351.2	WA 13:637.6–12; StL 14:1926.5–StL 14:1927.5; LW 20:106; LW 20:300–1

---

of *dummkopf* ("fool") and *bildwerk* ("work of art"); DWB 8:1430. Spalding suggests that Luther used it more narrowly to indicate false gods in contrast to the true God; SPAL 24:1115–7. Also see WAN 2:116; and Cornette, *Proverbs*, 147. Based on Grimm's advice, and that it is such a literal rendering of the Hebrew, I have assigned this as "literal."

[128] There are many German idiomatic uses of *Wahrsager* shortly after Luther's time [as well as an equivalent from Cicero, which Wander provides]. See DWB 27:973–5; and WAN 4:1765–6. Cf. MERZ 1:338; MERZ 2:445; and SPAL 55:2618. Nevertheless, clearly this is a literal rendering of the Hebrew here.

Verse	Luther's Hermeneutic	Luther Calls It …	NASB English	Hebrew Bible
Zech. 10:2	Interpretative[129]	figurative language (*figuris*)	lying visions	שֶׁקֶר
Zech. 10:2	Literal	figurative language (*figuris*)	And … dreams	וַחֲלֹמוֹת
Zech. 10:2	Literal[130]	figures of speech (*figuris verborum*); in obscure terms and with figurative language (*occulte et figuratis verbis*)	They comfort in vain	הֶבֶל יְנַחֵמוּן
Zech. 10:2	Interpretative[131]	figures of speech (*figuris verborum*); in obscure terms and with figurative language (*occulte et figuratis verbis*)	Therefore the people wander like sheep, They are afflicted, because there is no shepherd.	עַל־כֵּן נָסְעוּ כְמוֹ־צֹאן יַעֲנוּ כִּי־אֵין רֹעֶה
Zech. 10:3	Literal[132]	metaphor (*metaphora*); Spoken figuratively (*Loquitur … figurative*)	And will make them like His majestic horse in battle	וְשָׂם אוֹתָם כְּסוּס הוֹדוֹ בַּמִּלְחָמָה

---

[129] Luther's addition of *eitel* accentuates the "lies" as "vain lies." This is not a greatly interpretative reading of the figure of speech, but a diversion from the strict literal Hebrew nonetheless. Cf. MERZ 1:39; and MERZ 2:910 – both use *eitel* [i. e. *eitel* and *lär*] as a translation of Gen. 1:2's תֹהוּ וָבֹהוּ (*tōhû wābōhû*, "[the earth was] formless and void").

[130] Luther seems to have been reading the two Hebrew terms as nouns in apposition (with an inferred "is"); thus I have categorized this as "literal." One could certainly argue that if he recognized יְנַחֵמוּן (*yənaḥēmûn*) as a verb, this should be "interpretative," as he diverged slightly from the literal Hebrew.

Table A.2: Luther's Translation of Hebrew Figures of Speech

Vulgate	1532 *Deutsche Bibel*	1545 *Deutsche Bibel*	Bible References	Exegetical References
mendacium	eitel luegen	eitel Luegen	WA DB 4:271a.13–26; WA DB 4:271b.13–15; WA DB 11.2:350.2; WA DB 11.2:351.2	WA 13:637.6–12; StL 14:1926.5– StL 14:1927.5; LW 20:106; LW 20:300–1
et somniatores	vnd ... trewme	vnd ... Trewme	WA DB 4:271a.13–26; WA DB 4:271b.13–15; WA DB 11.2:350.2; WA DB 11.2:351.2	WA 13:637.6–12; StL 14:1926.5– StL 14:1927.5; LW 20:106; LW 20:300–1
vane consolabantur	vnd jr troesten ist nichts	Vnd jr troesten ist nichts	WA DB 4:271a.13–26; WA DB 4:271b.13–15; WA DB 11.2:350.2; WA DB 11.2:351.2	WA 13:637.13–31; StL 14:1927.6; LW 20:106–7; LW 20:301
idcirco abducti sunt quasi grex adfligentur quia non est eis pastor	Darumb gehen sie jnn der jrre, wie eine herd, vnd sind verschmacht, weil kein Hirte da ist.	Darumb gehen sie in der jrre, wie ein Herd, vnd sind verschmacht, weil kein Hirte da ist.	WA DB 4:271a.13–26; WA DB 4:271b.13–15; WA DB 11.2:350.2; WA DB 11.2:351.2	WA 13:637.13–31; StL 14:1927.7; LW 20:106–7; LW 20:301
et posuit eos quasi equum gloriae suae in bello	vnd wird sie zu richten, wie ein geschmueckt ros zum streit	Vnd wird sie zurichten, wie ein geschmueckt Ross zum streit	WA DB 11.2:350.3; WA DB 11.2:351.3	WA 13:638.12– WA 13:639.8; StL 14:1928.9; LW 20:107–8; LW 20:302

---

[131] *Jnn der jrre* is a departure from the literal Hebrew (which simply reads "travel"). Thus, I have assigned this as "interpretative." Spalding suggests that since early *Neuhochdeutsch*, *verschmachen* meant "to languish, pine away," and links it to *schmachen*. More importantly, he links this to Luther. See SPAL 45:2148. That said, the word appears before Luther; see MERZ 1:139, 290, 302, 309, 312, 323–4, 379, 393, 398, 415; and MERZ 2:494, 497, 504–6, 511, 526, 535, 539, 554, 557, 560, 587. I found this still difficult at this point to link to German idiomatic use, aside from its appearance in MERZ. Ultimately this was not enough evidence for me to change this assignment to include a "German idiom."

[132] One could argue that either (a) Luther's change from "his" horse to "a" horse, or (b) his translation of *geschmueckt* could be grounds for categorizing this as "interpretative." Luther's translation is so close that I have categorized this as "literal." Cf. MERZ 1:42.

Verse	Luther's Hermeneutic	Luther Calls It ...	NASB English	Hebrew Bible
Zech. 10:4	Literal	obscurely and figuratively (*obscure et figurative*); Hebrew expression (*phrasis hebraea*)	the cornerstone	פִּנָּה
Zech. 10:4	Literal[133]	obscurely and figuratively (*obscure et figurative*); Hebrew expression (*phrasis hebraea*)	the tent peg	יָתֵד
Zech. 10:8	Interpretative[134]	lovely phrase or idiom of the Hebrew tongue (*Elegans ... phrasis vel idiotismus hebraeae linguae*); in the Hebrew manner (*hebräisch geredet*)	I will whistle for them	אֶשְׁרְקָה לָהֶם
Zech. 11:1	Literal	Metonymy (μετονυμίαν); Figure of speech (*Figura ... loquendi*); metaphor (*metaphora*); synecdoche (*synecdochen*)	O Lebanon	לְבָנוֹן
Zech. 11:3	Interpretative[135]	Hebraism (*Hebraismus*)	There is a sound of the shepherds' wail	קוֹל יִלְלַת הָרֹעִים

---

[133] German idiomatic uses of *Nagel* appear during Luther's time. See WAN 3:864 [§ 92], [§ 119 – this only appears in the online Wander edition, under "Nagel" (http://woerterbuchnetz.de); the paper edition stops at § 114]; and Cornette, *Proverbs*, 88, 178. Cf. DWB 13:257–63; MERZ 1:275; and MERZ 2:478, 555, 617, 813. Nevertheless, this is a literal rendering of the Hebrew here.

[134] There are many German idiomatic appearances of *blasen* ("to blow") in and prior to Luther's time. See WAN 1:392–3; SING 1:179; MERZ 2:585; and DWB 2:68–70. But this seems clearly to be a theologically influenced choice by Luther. See his lecture comments,

Table A.2: Luther's Translation of Hebrew Figures of Speech

Vulgate	1532 *Deutsche Bibel*	1545 *Deutsche Bibel*	Bible References	Exegetical References
Angulus	Die Ecken	Die Ecken	WA DB 11.2:350.4; WA DB 11.2:351.4	WA 13:639.9–26; StL 14:1928.10; LW 20:108–9; LW 20:302
Paxillus	Die … Negel	Die … Negel	WA DB 11.2:350.4; WA DB 11.2:351.4	WA 13:639.9–26; StL 14:1928.10; LW 20:108–9; LW 20:302
sibilabo eis	Jch wil zu jn blasen	Jch wil zu jnen blasen	WA DB 11.2:350.8; WA DB 11.2:351.8	WA 13:642.3–12; StL 14:1931.19– StL 14:1932.19; LW 20:112; LW 20:305
Libane	Libanon	Libanon	WA DB 11.2:352.1; WA DB 11.2:353.1	WA 13:644.17–28; StL 14:1936.1–2; LW 20:116–7; LW 20:310
vox ululatus pastorum	Man hoeret die Hirten heulen	Man hoeret die Hirten heulen	WA DB 11.2:352.3; WA DB 11.2:353.3	WA 13:645.4–8; StL 14:1937.5–7; LW 20:117; LW 20:311

which show this. Furthermore, he used *blasen* (*blies*) for his translation of Gen. 2:7 (God breathing into Adam's nostrils); WA DB 8:40.7. Thus, I have assigned this as "interpretative." It is close to the literal Hebrew, but not a true literal rendering of אֶשְׁרְקָה (*'ešrəqâ*, "to whistle, hiss, signal"). See BDB, 1056; and KB, 1011.

[135] Luther clearly departed from the literal Hebrew a bit, thus I have assigned this as "interpretative." *Heulen* also shows idiomatic usage. See Cornette, *Proverbs*, 154; WA 51:718, 730 [§ 409]; and SPAL 28:1319. Nevertheless, Luther translated *Heulen* literally from the Hebrew.

Verse	Luther's Hermeneutic	Luther Calls It ...	NASB English	Hebrew Bible
Zech. 11:3	Literal[136]	Among the Hebrew-speaking (*Hebraeis*)	the young lions'	כְּפִירִים
Zech. 11:3	Literal	metaphors (*metaphorae*)	of the Jordan	הַיַּרְדֵּן
Zech. 11:8	Interpretative[137]	Hebraism (*Hebraismus*)	for my soul was impatient with them	וַתִּקְצַר נַפְשִׁי בָּהֶם
Zech. 11:12	German Idiom[138]	Hebraism (*hebraismus*)	If it is good in your sight	אִם-טוֹב בְּעֵינֵיכֶם
Zech. 13:5	Interpretative[139]	Hebrew manner of speaking (*hebraicus modus loquendi*)	a man sold me	אָדָם הִקְנַנִי
Mal. 3:8	Mixed[140]	Hebraism (*Hebraismus*)	Will a man rob God?	הֲיִקְבַּע אָדָם אֱלֹהִים
Mal. 3:10	Literal[141]	Hebrew phrase (*Phrasis hebraea*); simile (*similitudo*); metaphor (*metaphora*)	open ... heaven	אֶפְתַּח ... הַשָּׁמַיִם

---

[136] There are some idiomatic uses of *Löwe*. See Cornette, *Proverbs*, 172; WA 51:684, 728 [§ 144]; SPAL 35:1634–6, with mention of Luther; and WAN 3:238–44, also with mention of Luther [for example, § 58]. Cf. DWB 12:15–17 (with mention of Mathesius in 12:1217 [§ 4]); MERZ 1:323, 344, 385, 410–1, 416–7; and MERZ 2:475–7, 483–5, 617–8, 837. Nevertheless, it is clearly a literal rendering of the Hebrew here.

[137] There are many German idiomatic uses of *mögen*, but it seems a stretch to try to apply any here, given that "I don't like you" is such a direct statement. Furthermore, Luther did not use the comparable idiom that he mentioned in his lectures [*Er ist kurtz angebunden*; WA 13:648.3]. For reference on such idiomatic uses, though, see WAN 3:690–1; and Cornette, *Proverbs*, 86, 177.

[138] There are many idiomatic uses of *gefallen* [in the sense of "to like, please"] near to and prior to Luther's time. See Cornette, *Proverbs*, 57; WAN 1:1413–15 (including numerous entries from Agricola); and DWB 4:2103–15. Cf. MERZ 2:557, 560; and SPAL 11:476 concerning the early *Neuhochdeutsch* connection between pleasure (*gefallen*) and service (*dienen*), with references to Luther and to the Mentel Bible.

[139] There are some idiomatic uses of *Dienen/Dienst*, but this is such a common word, often

Table A.2: Luther's Translation of Hebrew Figures of Speech

Vulgate	1532 Deutsche Bibel	1545 Deutsche Bibel	Bible References	Exegetical References
Leonum	die jungen lewen	die jungen Lewen	WA DB 11.2:352.3; WA DB 11.2:353.3	WA 13:645.9–11; StL 14:1937.5–7; LW 20:117; LW 20:311
Iordanis	des Jordans	des Jordans	WA DB 11.2:352.3; WA DB 11.2:353.3	WA 13:645.12–22; StL 14:1937.7; LW 20:117–8; LW 20:311
et contracta est anima mea in eis	Denn ich mocht jr nicht	Denn ich mocht jr nicht	WA DB 11.2:352.8; WA DB 11.2:353.8	WA 13:648.1–7; StL 14:1943.21; LW 20:121; LW 20:317
si bonum est in oculis vestris	Gefellets euch	Gefellets euch	WA DB 11.2:352.12; WA DB 11.2:353.12	WA 13:649.17–35; StL 14:1945.25; LW 20:123–4; LW 20:318
Adam exemplum meum	ich habe gedienet	ich habe Menschen gedienet	WA DB 4:273a.27–29; WA DB 4:273b.27–; WA DB 4:274b.5; WA DB 11.2:356.5; WA DB 11.2:357.5	WA 13:665.22–31; StL 14:1961.10; LW 20:147; LW 20:334
si adfiget homo Deum	Jsts recht, das ein mensch Gott teusscht	Jsts recht, das ein Mensch Gott teusscht	WA DB 11.2:372.8; WA DB 11.2:373.8	WA 13:697.20–; WA 13:698.10; LW 18:413–14
Aperuero ... caeli	des himels ... auffthun werde	des Himels ... auffthun werde	WA DB 4:278b.8–11; WA DB 11.2:372.10; WA DB 11.2:373.10	WA 13:698.20–; WA 13:699.2; LW 18:414

with clear roots in biblical language, that it is difficult to categorize it as idiomatic German. Thus, I have assigned this as "interpretative." Concerning the biblical roots of this word, see SPAL 11:475. For broader reference, see Cornette, *Proverbs*, 47; SING 2:188; SING 3:153; DWB 2:1108, 1111; and SPAL 11:475–7.

140 The modern German spelling of *teusschen* is *täuschen*. This term seems to have idiomatic usage in and prior to Luther's time. See DWB 21:210–12, with mention of Luther; Cornette, *Proverbs*, 106, 229; and MERZ 1:89. On the difficulty of the Hebrew term הֲיִקְבַּע (*hăyiqbaʻ*) in Mal. 3:8, see BDB, 867; KB, 820; and HALOT 3:1062. Based on this information, I have categorized Luther's translation of this term as showing evidence of drawing upon German idiomatic usage; and his translation of the Hebrew interrogative הֲ (*hă*) as *Jsts recht, das* ("Is it right, that …?") as "interpretative." In sum, Luther used a mixed method here.

141 There are various idiomatic uses of *Himmel*. See Cornette, *Proverbs*, 70, 154; WA 51:679, 728 [§ 115]; WA 51:666, 728 [§ 16]; SPAL 28:1322–6; WAN 2:645–57 (including numerous entries by Agricola, Luther, and Mathesius); MERZ 1:44, 290, 413; and MERZ 2:520, 549, 664–6, 795, 868. Cf. DWB 10:1332–41. Nevertheless, clearly this is a literal rendering of the Hebrew here.

Table A.3: Luther's Translation of the Hebrew Trope of Repetition in the Minor Prophets[1]

Verse	Luther's Hermeneutic	Form of the Repetition	NASB English	Hebrew Bible
Hos. 2:21–22	Interpretative Retain	General Apposition of Terminology	And I will betroth you to Me ... Yes, I will betroth you to Me ... And I will betroth you to Me	וְאֵרַשְׂתִּיךְ לִי ... וְאֵרַשְׂתִּיךְ לִי ... וְאֵרַשְׂתִּיךְ לִי
Hos. 5:14	Literal Retain	General Apposition of Terminology	I, even I	אֲנִי אֲנִי
Joel 1:6	Eliminate	General Apposition of Terminology	Its teeth are the teeth	שִׁנָּיו שִׁנֵּי
Joel 1:7	Eliminate[2]	Paronomastic Infinitive	It has stripped them bare	חָשֹׂף חֲשָׂפָה
Joel 2:26	Eliminate[3]	Paronomastic Infinitive	You will have plenty to eat	וַאֲכַלְתֶּם אָכוֹל
Amos 1:3	Literal Retain[4]	Distributive	For three ... and for four	עַל-שְׁלֹשָׁה ... וְעַל-אַרְבָּעָה
Amos 1:6	Interpretative Retain	Cognate Accusative	Because they deported an entire population	עַל-הַגְלוֹתָם גָּלוּת שְׁלֵמָה

---

[1] If an additional manuscript note appears in the WA addressing the repetition, I do not add a separate line item, but simply refer to the main line entry to which the note refers. Also, the repetition is often not addressed in every location, i.e. the LW, Zwickau text, Altenburg text, German commentary, but rather only in some or in one of these. Nevertheless, I try to include all relevant exegetical references throughout this table for the verses so that the reader has the full breadth of information for each translation.

[2] I disregard the repeated sentiment of לְקִצָפָה (*liqṣāpâ*), which precedes the phrase חָשֹׂף חֲשָׂפָה (*ḥāśōp ḥăśāpāh*), and which Luther retained in his translation. He very well may have

Table A.3: Luther's Translation of the Hebrew Trope of Repetition

Vulgate	1532 *Deutsche Bibel*	1545 *Deutsche Bibel*	Bible References	Exegetical References
et sponsabo te mihi ... et sponsabo te mihi ... et sponsabo te mihi	Ja ... wil ich mich mit dir verloben	Ja ... wil ich mich mit dir verloben	WA DB 11.2:188.19–20; WA DB 11.2:189.19–20	WA 13:11.4–WA 13:12.20; LW 18:13–14
ego ego	Jch, Jch	Jch, Jch	WA DB 11.2:192.14–WA DB 11.2:194.14; WA DB 11.2:193.14	WA 13:26.19; LW 18:30
dentes eius ut dentes	das hat zene	Das hat Zeene	WA DB 11.2:216.6; WA DB 11.2:217.6	WA 13:69.17–22; WA 13:90.28–WA 13:91.5; LW 18:82–83
nudans spoliavit eam	schelet jn	schelet jn	WA DB 11.2:216.7; WA DB 11.2:217.7	WA 13:69.23–27; WA 13:91.6–22; LW 18:83
et comedetis vescentes	das jr zu essen [gnug] haben sollet	Das jr zu essen [gnug] haben sollet	WA DB 11.2:220.26; WA DB 11.2:221.26	WA 13:79.3–5 WA 13:108.7–14; LW 18:105
super tribus ... et super quattuor	Vmb drey vnd vier	Vmb drey vnd vier	WA DB 11.2:230.3; WA DB 11.2:231.3	WA 13:126.8–29; WA 13:162.1–8, 13–WA 13:163.10; LW 18:131–3
quod transtulerit captivitatem perfectam	Darumb, das sie die gefangenen, weiter gefangen	Darumb, das sie die Gefangenen, weiter gefangen	WA DB 11.2:230.6; WA DB 11.2:231.6	WA 13:128.1–11; WA 13:164.15–22; LW 18:134

---

been addressing that, rather than the paronomastic infinitive. This is ultimately unclear. But given that he led off his comments with *Nudans spoliavit eam*, I believe he was addressing the paronomastic infinitive. Also, the Brescia Bible reads in this place: חָשֹׁף חֲשָׂפָה (*ḥāśōp ḥăśāpâ*). 1494 Brescia Hebrew Bible, Staatsbibliothek Berlin, fol. 416r [843]. In the Brescia Bible, the ink makes some of the pointing here uncertain, though not שׁ (*š*) in contrast to שׂ (*ś*).

[3] Luther's *gnug* refers to וְשָׂבוֹעַ (*wəśāḇôaʿ*). This verse also appears in Table A.2.

[4] I forgive Luther's omission of the second עַל (*ʿal*) here, since he still replicated the distributive repetition.

Verse	Luther's Hermeneutic	Form of the Repetition	NASB English	Hebrew Bible
Amos 4:6, 8–11[5]	Literal Retain	General Apposition of Terminology	"Yet you have not returned to Me," declares the Lord.	וְלֹא־שַׁבְתֶּם עָדַי נְאֻם־יְהוָה
Amos 8:9	Literal Retain	General Apposition of Subject Matter	That I will make the sun go down **at noon** And make the earth dark **in broad daylight**	וְהֵבֵאתִי הַשֶּׁמֶשׁ **בַּצָּהֳרִים וְהַחֲשַׁכְתִּי לָאָרֶץ בְּיוֹם אוֹר**
Obad. 1:9	Literal Retain	General Apposition of Subject Matter	So that everyone may be cut off from the mountain of Esau by slaughter.	לְמַעַן **יִכָּרֶת־אִישׁ** מֵהַר עֵשָׂו **מִקָּטֶל**
Jon. 4:1	Interpretative Retain	Cognate Accusative	But it greatly displeased Jonah	וַיֵּרַע אֶל־יוֹנָה רָעָה גְדוֹלָה
Mic. 2:4	Eliminate	Cognate Accusative	And utter a bitter lamentation	וְנָהָה נְהִי

---

[5] Luther addressed the repeated phrase in the lectures on v. 12, but he was clearing referring to vv. 6, 8–11.

Table A.3: *Luther's Translation of the Hebrew Trope of Repetition* 307

Vulgate	1532 *Deutsche Bibel*	1545 *Deutsche Bibel*	Bible References	Exegetical References
et non estis reversi ad me dicit Dominus (4:6) et non redistis ad me dicit Dominus (4:8–11)	noch bekeret jr euch nicht zu mir, spricht der HERR. (4:6, 8–10) Noch keret jr euch nicht zu mir, spricht der HERR (4:11)	Noch bekeret jr euch nicht zu mir spricht der HERR (4:6, 9–11) Noch bekeret jr euch nicht zu mir, spricht der HERR (4:8)	WA DB 4:236a.6–8; WA DB 4:236b.6–9; WA DB 11.2:236.6, 8–11; WA DB 11.2:237.6, 8–11	WA 13:136.22–29; WA 13:137.3– WA 13:138.3; WA 13:177.12–29; WA 13:177.32– WA 13:178.34; LW 18:153–5
occidet sol meridie et tenebrescere faciam terram in die luminis	Wil ich die sonnen **im mittage** vntergehen lassen, vnd das land **am hellen tage** lassen finster werden	wil ich die Sonnen **im mittage** vntergehen lassen, vnd das Land **am hellen tage** lassen finster werden	WA DB 11.2:246.9; WA DB 11.2:247.9	WA 13:152.17–23; WA 13:198.26– WA 13:199.9; LW 18:182
ut **intereat** vir de monte Esau	auff das sie alle auff dem gebirge Esau, **durch den mord, ausgerottet werden**	auff das sie alle auff dem gebirge Esau, **durch den mord ausgerottet werden**	WA DB 4:242a.25–28; WA DB 11.2:254.9; WA DB 11.2:255.9	WA 13:211.7–10; WA 13:219.17–22; LW 18:198–9
et adflictus est Iona **adflictione** magna	Das **verdros** Jona fast seer	Das **verdros** Jona fast seer	WA DB 11.2:266.1; WA DB 11.2:267.1	WA 13:238.1–16; WA 13:254.35– WA 13:255.40; WA 19:239.20– WA 19:244.35; LW 19:26–7; LW 19:91–7
et … cum suavitate	vnd klagen	vnd klagen	WA DB 4:248a.12–13; WA DB 4:248b.12–15; WA DB 11.2:274.4; WA DB 11.2:275.4	WA 13:269.15–19; WA 13:309.36–39; LW 18:223

Verse	Luther's Hermeneutic	Form of the Repetition	NASB English	Hebrew Bible
Mic. 2:6	Eliminate	Cognate Accusative[6]	'Do not speak out,' so they speak out. But if they do not speak out concerning these things	אַל־תַּטִּפוּ יַטִּיפוּן לֹא־יַטִּפוּ[7]
Mic. 7:12	Interpretative Retain	Distributive	Even from sea to sea	וְיָם מִיָּם
Mic. 7:12	Interpretative Retain	Distributive	and mountain to mountain	וְהַר הָהָר
Nah. 1:3	Eliminate	Paronomastic Infinitive	And … will by no means leave the guilty unpunished	וְנַקֵּה לֹא יְנַקֶּה
Nah. 2:3	Literal Retain	General Apposition of Terminology	the **splendor** of Jacob Like the **splendor** of Israel	אֶת־**גְּאוֹן** יַעֲקֹב כִּ**גְאוֹן** יִשְׂרָאֵל
Nah. 2:3	1532 Interpretative Retain; 1545 Literal Retain	General Apposition of Terminology	Even though devastators have devastated them	כִּי בְקָקוּם בֹּקְקִים
Nah. 3:13	Eliminate	Paronomastic Infinitive	are opened wide	פָּתוֹחַ נִפְתְּחוּ

---

[6] Luther's lecture comments *ne stilletis stillam* ("do not drip a drop") make it clear that he interpreted this as a cognate accusative. Nevertheless, the phrase in particular and the verse in general are ultimately still mysterious. Francis I. Anderson and David Noel Freedman's advice is poignant: "Micah is playing a tune on this word that we can no longer hear." See Anderson and Freedman, *Micah: A New Translation with Introduction and Commentary*, AB 24E (New York: Doubleday, 2000), 302–7; the quotation is from p. 303.

Table A.3: Luther's Translation of the Hebrew Trope of Repetition

Vulgate	1532 *Deutsche Bibel*	1545 *Deutsche Bibel*	Bible References	Exegetical References
ne loquamini loquentes non stillabit	Sie sagen, Man solle nicht **predigen**, Denn solche prediget trifft vns nicht	Sje sagen, Man solle nicht **treuffen**, Denn solche Treuffe trifft vns nicht	WA DB 4:248a.16–19; WA DB 4:248b.16–24; WA DB 11.2:274.6; WA DB 11.2:275.6	WA 13:270.12–26; WA 13:310.23–38; LW 18:224–5
et ad mare de mari	von einem meer zum andern	von einem Meer zum andern	WA DB 11.2:284.12; WA DB 11.2:285.12	WA 13:297.10–16; WA 13:341.1–9; LW 18:273–4
et ad montem de monte	von einem gebirge zum andern	von einem Gebirge zum andern	WA DB 11.2:284.12; WA DB 11.2:285.12	WA 13:297.10–16; WA 13:341.1–9; LW 18:273–4
et mundans non faciet innocentem	vnd lesst nichts vngestrafft	fur welchem niemand vnschuldig ist	WA DB 4:252a.15–23; WA DB 4:252b.15–25; WA DB 11.2:290.3; WA DB 11.2:291.3	WA 13:348.8–20; WA 13:374.23–; WA 13:375.2; LW 18:286–7
superbiam Iacob sicut **superbiam** Israhel	Jacob den **sieg** [geben], wie [er] Jsrael den **sieg** [gab]	die **hoffart** Jacob [vergelten], wie die **hoffart** Jsrael	WA DB 4:256b.7–21; WA DB 11.2:292.3; WA DB 11.2:293.3	WA 13:356.13–24; WA 13:382.35–; WA 13:383.13; LW 18:299
quia vastatores dissipaverunt eos	Man wird dich doch rein ablesen	Denn die Ableser werden sie ablesen	WA DB 4:256b.7–21; WA DB 11.2:292.3; WA DB 11.2:293.3	WA 13:356.25–31; WA 13:383.14–28; LW 18:299–300
adapertione pandentur	sollen ... geoeffent werden	sollen ... geoeffent werden	WA DB 11.2:294.13; WA DB 11.2:295.13	WA 13:366.23–; WA 13:367.10; WA 13:391.15–18; LW 18:311

---

[7] In his lectures, Luther specifically addressed the cognate accusative repetition. Thus, the reader should beware of being distracted by the superfluous appearance of the term [יִטְּפוּ (*yaṭṭipû*)], outside of this construction. This advice applies for the Hebrew Bible, Vulgate, and Luther's *Deutsche Bibel* translations.

Verse	Luther's Hermeneutic	Form of the Repetition	NASB English	Hebrew Bible
Nah. 3:15	Literal Retain	Distributive[8]	There fire will consume you, The sword will cut you down; It will consume you as the locust does	תֹּאכְלֵךְ אֵשׁ תַּכְרִיתֵךְ חֶרֶב תֹּאכְלֵךְ כַּיָּלֶק
Nah. 3:15	Literal Retain	General Apposition of Terminology	Multiply yourself like the creeping locust, Multiply yourself like the swarming locust.	הִתְכַּבֵּד כַּיֶּלֶק הִתְכַּבְּדִי כָּאַרְבֶּה
Hab. 1:5	Eliminate	General Apposition of Terminology[9]	Be astonished! Wonder!	וְהִתַּמְּהוּ תְּמָהוּ
Hab. 1:8	Interpretative Retain[10]	Distributive	Their horsemen come galloping, Their horsemen come from afar	וּפָשׁוּ פָּרָשָׁיו וּפָרָשָׁיו מֵרָחוֹק יָבֹאוּ
Hab. 2:3	Interpretative Retain	Paronomastic Infinitive	For it will certainly come	כִּי־בֹא יָבֹא

---

[8] Because Luther said *et occidet vos omnes* ("and they will kill *all of you*") in the lectures, he was identifying the repetition as distributive here. See WA 13:391.38-WA 13:392.1; LW 18:312.

[9] This is a *Hitpael* imperative followed by *Qal* imperative (Hebrew grammatical constructions). The Hebrew Bible also reads, later in the verse, כִּי־פֹעַל פֹּעֵל *(kî-pōʿal pōʿēl)* – a cognate

Table A.3: *Luther's Translation of the Hebrew Trope of Repetition* 311

Vulgate	1532 *Deutsche Bibel*	1545 *Deutsche Bibel*	Bible References	Exegetical References
ibi **comedet te** ignis peribis gladio devorabit te ut bruchus	Aber das feur wird dich **fressen**, vnd das schwerd toedten, **Es wird dich abfressen**, wie die kefer	Aber das fewr **wird dich fressen**, vnd das Schwert toedten, **Es wird dich abfressen**, wie die Kefer	WA DB 4:257b.15–16; WA DB 11.2:294.15– WA DB 11.2:296.15; WA DB 11.2:295.15– WA DB 11.2:297.15	WA 13:368.3–10; WA 13:391.35– WA 13:392.13; LW 18:312
congregare ut bruchus **multiplicare** ut lucusta	**Es wird dich vberfallen,** wie kefer, **Es wird dich vberfallen,** wie hewschrecken	**Es wird dich vberfallen,** wie Kefer, **Es wird dich vberfallen** wie Hewschrecken	WA DB 4:257b.15–16; WA DB 11.2:294.15– WA DB 11.2:296.15; WA DB 11.2:295.15– WA DB 11.2:297.15	WA 13:368.11–20; WA 13:391.35– WA 13:392.14–26; LW 18:313
et admiramini et obstupescite	vnd verwundert euch	vnd verwundert euch	WA DB 4:258b.9–14; WA DB 11.2:302.5; WA DB 11.2:303.5	WA 13:397.31– WA 13:398.7; WA 13:426.8–22; WA 19:363.8– WA 19:365.11; LW 19:110–1; LW 19: 165–7
et diffundentur **equites eius equites** namque eius de longe venient	**Jre reuter** zihen **mit grossem hauffen** von fernen daher	**Jre Reuter** ziehen **mit grossem Hauffen** von fernen da her	WA DB 4:258a.20–21; WA DB 11.2:302.8; WA DB 11.2:303.8.	WA 13:399.14–25; WA 13:427.36–38; WA 19:369.14– WA 19:370.14 LW 19:113; LW 19:171
quia veniens veniet	sie wird gewislich komen	Sie wird gewislich komen	WA DB 4:258a.30–31; WA DB 4:258b.30–37; WA DB 11.2:304.3; WA DB 11.2:305.3	WA 13:405.10–19; WA 13:433.12–24; WA 19:393.7–27; LW 19:122; LW 19:195–6

accusative, which Luther eliminated in his rendering *Denn ich wil etwas thun*. He did not, however, address that specifically, so I have not included it in the chart.

[10] Luther combined וּפָשׁוּ (*ûpāšû*) and יָבֹאוּ (*yāḇō'û*) into one verb in his German translation.

Verse	Luther's Hermeneutic	Form of the Repetition	NASB English	Hebrew Bible
Hab. 3:5	Literal Retain[11]	General Apposition of Subject Matter	Before Him goes pestilence, And plague comes after Him.	לְפָנָיו יֵלֶךְ דָּבֶר וְיֵצֵא רֶשֶׁף לְרַגְלָיו
Zeph. 1:2	Eliminate	Paronomastic Infinitive	I will completely remove	אָסֹף אָסֵף
Hag. 1:5, 7[12]	Interpretative Retain	General Apposition of Terminology	Consider your ways! (1:5) Consider your ways! (1:7)	שִׂימוּ לְבַבְכֶם עַל־דַּרְכֵיכֶם (1:5) שִׂימוּ לְבַבְכֶם עַל־דַּרְכֵיכֶם (1:7)
Hag. 2:15, 18[13]	Interpretative Retain	General Apposition of Terminology	do consider from this day onward (2:15) Do consider from this day onward (2:18)	שִׂימוּ־נָא לְבַבְכֶם מִן־הַיּוֹם הַזֶּה וָמָעְלָה (2:15) שִׂימוּ־נָא לְבַבְכֶם מִן־הַיּוֹם הַזֶּה וָמָעְלָה (2:18)
Zech. 1:2	Eliminate	Cognate Accusative	The Lord was very angry with your fathers	קָצַף יְהוָה עַל־אֲבוֹתֵיכֶם קָצֶף

---

[11] There are various opinions concerning the meaning of רֶשֶׁף (rešep). See BDB, 958; KB, 911; and TDOT 14:10–16.

[12] Luther mentioned this repetition, looking back from his exegesis of Hag. 2:15 also. See WA 13:543.27–29; LW 18:385. This example was difficult to classify. One could argue that

Table A.3: Luther's Translation of the Hebrew Trope of Repetition

Vulgate	1532 Deutsche Bibel	1545 Deutsche Bibel	Bible References	Exegetical References
ante faciem eius ibit **mors** et egredietur **diabolus** ante pedes eius	Fur jm her gieng **pestilentz**, Vnd **plage** gieng aus, wo er hin tratt.	FVr jm her gieng **Pestilentz**, Vnd **Plage** gieng aus, wo er hin trat.	WA DB 11.2:308.5; WA DB 11.2:309.5	WA 13:415.1–17; WA 13:443.12–26; WA 19:428.27–32; LW 19:139; LW 19:231
congregans congregabo	Jch wil ... weg nemen	JCh wil ... wegnemen	WA DB 11.2:312.2; WA DB 11.2:313.2	WA 13:450.22; WA 13:481.5–17; LW 18:320–1
ponite corda vestra super vias vestras (1:5) ponite corda vestra super vias vestras (1:7)	Schawet, wie es euch gehet (1:5) Schawet, wie es euch gehet (1:7)	Schawet, wie es euch gehet (1:5) Schawet, wie es euch gehet (1:7)	WA DB 11.2:322.5, 7; WA DB 11.2:323.5, 7	WA 13:514.34–; WA 13:515.19; WA 13:516.1–5; WA 13:535.30–; WA 13:536.20; LW 18:373–4
et nunc ponite corda vestra a die hac et supra (2:15) ponite corda vestra ex die ista et in futurum (2:18)	Vnd nu schawet, wie es euch gangen ist, von diesem tage an vnd zuuor (2:15) So schawet nu drauff von diesem tage an vnd zuuor (2:18)	VND nu schawet, wie es euch gegangen ist, von diesem tage an vnd zuuor (2:15) SO schawet nu drauff, von diesem tag an vnd zuuor (2:18)	WA DB 11.2:326.16, 19; WA DB 11.2:327.16, 19	WA 13:528.24–; WA 13:529.19; WA 13:529.30–; WA 13:530.5; WA 13:543.27–; WA 13:544.7; LW 18:385–6
iratus est Dominus super patres vestros **iracundia**	Der HERR **ist zornig gewest** vber ewre Veter	Der HERR **ist zornig gewest** vber ewer Veter	WA DB 11.2:332.2; WA DB 11.2:333.2	WA 13:548.20–; WA 13:549.29; StL 14:1776.10; LW 20:6–8; LW 20:161

it should be "Literal Retain," focusing specifically on the repetition. But it was a not a literal rendering, thus I have assigned this as "Interpretative Retain."

[13] The previous footnote concerning the assignment as "Interpretative Retain" applies here also.

Verse	Luther's Hermeneutic	Form of the Repetition	NASB English	Hebrew Bible
Zech. 1:3	Literal Retain	General Apposition of Terminology	the Lord of hosts ... the Lord of hosts ... the Lord of hosts	יְהוָה צְבָאוֹת ... יְהוָה צְבָאוֹת ... יְהוָה צְבָאוֹת
Zech. 4:7	Interpretative Retain	Distributive[14]	Grace, grace to it!	חֵן חֵן לָהּ
Zech. 6:1[15]	Interpretative Retain	General Apposition of Terminology	and the mountains were bronze mountains	וְהֶהָרִים הָרֵי נְחֹשֶׁת
Zech. 12:12	Interpretative Retain	Distributive[16]	every family by itself	מִשְׁפָּחוֹת מִשְׁפָּחוֹת לְבָד
Mal. 3:1	Literal Retain	General Apposition of Terminology	And will suddenly come ... behold, is coming	וּפִתְאֹם יָבוֹא ... הִנֵּה-בָא

---

[14] Luther explicitly identified this as distributive repetition both in the lectures and in the German commentary.

[15] This example also appears in Table A.2.

[16] Luther explicitly identified this as distributive repetition in the lectures.

Table A.3: *Luther's Translation of the Hebrew Trope of Repetition*   315

Vulgate	1532 *Deutsche Bibel*	1545 *Deutsche Bibel*	Bible References	Exegetical References
Dominus exercituum ... Dominus exercituum ... Dominus exercituum	der HERR Zebaoth ... der HERR Zebaoth ... der HERR Zebaoth	der HERR Zebaoth ... der HERR Zebaoth ... der HERR Zebaoth	WA DB 4:265b.18–22; WA DB 11.2:332.3; WA DB 11.2:333.3	WA 13:549.30– WA 13:551.27; StL 14:1776.11– StL 14:1779.16; LW 20:8–9; LW 20:161–3
gratiam gratiae eius	glueck zu, glueck zu	Glueck zu, glueck zu	WA DB 4:266a.30–31; WA DB 11.2:338.7; WA DB 11.2:339.7	WA 13:589.8– WA 13:590.21; StL 14:1849.11– StL 14:1850.13 LW 20:46–47; LW 20:226–7
et montes montes aerei	Die selbigen berge aber waren eherne	die selbigen Berge aber waren Eherne	WA DB 11.2:340.1; WA DB 11.2:341.1	WA 13:604.18–19; WA 13:605.29– WA 13:606.27; StL 14:1870.1– StL 14:1871.3; LW 20:64–67 LW 20:247–8
familiae et familiae seorsum	ein jglich geschlechte besonders	ein jglich Geschlechte besonders	WA DB 11.2:354.12; WA DB 11.2:355.12	WA 13:661.11– WA 13:662.12; StL 14:1957.21; LW 20:141–2; LW 20:330
et statim veniet ... ecce venit	Vnd bald wird komen ... Sihe, Er kompt	Vnd bald wird komen ... Sihe, Er kompt	WA DB 4:277a.9–19; WA DB 11.2:370.1; WA DB 11.2:371.1	WA 13:693.19–30; LW 18:409

Table A.4: Luther's Use of Hebrew Transliteration in the Minor Prophets[1]

Verse	Luther's Hermeneutic	Category	NASB English	Hebrew Bible
Hos. 1:6	Transliterated	Geographical Regions or Peoples	Lo-ruhamah	לֹא רֻחָמָה
Hos. 2:2	Transliterated	Geographical Regions or Peoples	Jezreel	יִזְרְעֶאל
Hos. 2:17	Transliterated	Geographical Regions or Peoples	And the valley of Achor	וְאֶת-עֵמֶק עָכוֹר
Hos. 2:18	Mixed	Cultural- and/or Ethno-Specific Customs, Practices, and Rituals	Baali	בַּעְלִי
Hos. 3:2	Transliterated	Cultural- and/or Ethno-Specific Customs, Practices, and Rituals	and a homer	וְחֹמֶר
Hos. 3:4	Interpretative	Cultural- and/or Ethno-Specific Customs, Practices, and Rituals	ephod	אֵפוֹד
Hos. 3:4	Interpretative	Cultural- and/or Ethno-Specific Customs, Practices, and Rituals	or household idols	וּתְרָפִים
Hos. 4:15	Transliterated	Geographical Regions or Peoples	Beth-aven	בֵּית אָוֶן

---

[1] If an additional manuscript note appears in the WA addressing the transliteration, I do not add a separate line item, but simply refer to the main line entry to which the note refers. Also, the transliteration is often not addressed in every location, i. e. the LW, Zwickau text, Altenburg text, German commentary, but rather only in some or in one of these. Nevertheless, I try to include all relevant exegetical references throughout this table for the verses so that the reader has the full breadth of information for each translation.

Table A.4: Luther's Use of Hebrew Transliteration

Vulgate	1532 *Deutsche Bibel*	1545 *Deutsche Bibel*	Bible References	Exegetical References
absque misericordia	Loryhamo	LoRyhamo	WA DB 4:207b.22–24; WA DB 11.2:184.6; WA DB 11.2:185.6	WA 13:5.1–9; LW 18:5
Hiezrahel	Jezreel	Jezreel	WA DB 11.2:184.11– WA DB 11.2:186.11; WA DB 11.2:185.11– WA DB 11.2:187.11	WA 13:6.13–20; LW 18:7
et vallem Achor	vnd das tal Achor	vnd das tal Achor	WA DB 4:208a.10–17; WA DB 4:208b.10–23; WA DB 11.2:186.15; WA DB 11.2:187.15	WA 13:9.19–22; LW 18:11
Baali	Mein Baal	mein Baal	WA DB 11.2:186.16; WA DB 11.2:187.16	WA 13:10.5–9; LW 18:12
et ... choro	Vnd ... Homer	Vnd ... Homer	WA DB 11.2:188.2; WA DB 11.2:189.2	WA 13:14.11–12; LW 18:17
ephod	Leibroeck	Leibrock	WA DB 4:209a.3–6; WA DB 4:209b.3–6; WA DB 11.2:188.4; WA DB 11.2:189.4	WA 13:14.15– WA 13:15.3; LW 18:17
et ... therafin	vnd ... Gottesdienst	vnd ... Heiligthum	WA DB 4:209a.3–6; WA DB 4:209b.3–6; WA DB 11.2:188.4; WA DB 11.2:189.4	WA 13:14.15– WA 13:15.3; LW 18:17
Bethaven	BethAuen	BethAuen	WA DB 4:210a.25–26; WA DB 11.2:190.15; WA DB 11.2:191.15	WA 13:20.15–20; LW 18:24

Verse	Luther's Hermeneutic	Category	NASB English	Hebrew Bible
Hos. 5:1	Transliterated	Geographical Regions or Peoples	at Mizpah	לְמִצְפָּה
Hos. 6:8[2]	Transliterated	Geographical Regions or Peoples	Gilead	גִּלְעָד
Hos. 12:8	Interpretative	Geographical Regions or Peoples	merchant	כְּנַעַן
Hos. 13:14	Interpretative	Geographical Regions or Peoples[3]	of Sheol	שְׁאוֹל
Joel 4:2	Transliterated	Geographical Regions or Peoples	to the valley of Jehoshaphat	אֶל-עֵמֶק יְהוֹשָׁפָט
Amos 1:5	Transliterated	Geographical Regions or Peoples	from the valley of Aven	מִבִּקְעַת-אָוֶן
Amos 1:12	Transliterated	Geographical Regions or Peoples	upon Teman	בְּתֵימָן
Amos 1:15	Interpretative	Names of Individuals[4]	Their king	מַלְכָּם
Amos 2:2	Transliterated	Geographical Regions or Peoples	Kerioth	הַקְּרִיּוֹת

---

[2] Luther referenced this in his lectures on Joel 4:2 for his transliteration argument concerning Jehoshaphat. WA 13:116.5–9; LW 18:114. Luther argued there that the prophet himself [Joel] was in err, "misusing the proper noun and ... making it a common noun!"

[3] One could argue that this should be understood differently than "Geographical Regions or Peoples," but given the four potential categories that I have chosen, this seemed the most fitting.

Table A.4: Luther's Use of Hebrew Transliteration

Vulgate	1532 *Deutsche Bibel*	1545 *Deutsche Bibel*	Bible References	Exegetical References
speculationi	zu Mizpa	zu Mizpa	WA DB 4:211a.5–6; WA DB 4:211b.5–6; WA DB 11.2:192.1; WA DB 11.2:193.1	WA 13:22.13– WA 13:23.7; LW 18:26
Galaad	Gilead	Gilead	WA DB 11.2:194.8; WA DB 11.2:195.8	WA 13:29.4–12; LW 18:33
Chanaan	der Kauffman	der Kauffman	WA DB 4:225a.21–23; WA DB 11.2:206.8; WA DB 11.2:207.8	WA 13:58.22– WA 13:59.7; LW 18:66–67
inferni	der Helle	der Helle	WA DB 4:227a.13–18; WA DB 4:227b.13–17; WA DB 11.2:208.14; WA DB 11.2:209.14	WA 13:63.16– WA 13:64.9; LW 18:71–72
in valle Iosaphat	jns tal Josaphat	ins tal Josaphat	WA DB 11.2:222.7; WA DB 11.2:223.7	WA 13:83.23– WA 13:84.9; WA 13:115.21– WA 13:116.9; LW 18:113–4
de campo Idoli	auff dem felde Auen	auff dem felde Auen	WA DB 4:233b.30– WA DB 4:234b.2; WA DB 11.2:230.5; WA DB 11.2:231.5	WA 13:127.10–12; WA 13:163.19–27; LW 18:133
in Theman	gen Theman	gen Theman	WA DB 11.2:230.12; WA DB 11.2:231.12	WA 13:128.31–34; WA 13:165.18–24; LW 18:135–6
Melchom	jr Koenig	jr Koenig	WA DB 4:234a.11–13; WA DB 11.2:232.15; WA DB 11.2:233.15	WA 13:129.16–18; WA 13:166.11–16; LW 18:137
Carioth	Kirioth	Kirioth	WA DB 11.2:232.2; WA DB 11.2:233.2	WA 13:129.21–29; WA 13:166.34; LW 18:138

---

[4] I have assigned this to the "Geographical Regions or Peoples" category, given Luther's argument that the transliterated version is the name of a god.

Verse	Luther's Hermeneutic	Category	NASB English	Hebrew Bible
Amos 5:5	1532 Interpretative; 1545 Transliterated	Geographical Regions or Peoples[5]	And Bethel will come to trouble	וּבֵית-אֵל יִהְיֶה לְאָוֶן
Amos 5:26	1532 Interpretative; 1545 Transliterated	Names of Individuals[6]	Sikkuth	אֵת סִכּוּת
Amos 5:26	1532 Transliterated; 1545 Interpretative	Names of Individuals[7]	your king	מַלְכְּכֶם
Amos 5:26	1532 Interpretative; 1545 Transliterated	Names of Individuals[8]	and Kiyyun	וְאֵת כִּיּוּן
Obad. 1:3	Interpretative	Geographical Regions or Peoples	in the clefts of the rock	בְּחַגְוֵי-סֶלַע
Obad. 1:9	Transliterated	Geographical Regions or Peoples	Teman	תֵּימָן
Obad. 1:19	Interpretative	Geographical Regions or Peoples	of the Negev	הַנֶּגֶב
Obad. 1:20	Interpretative	Geographical Regions or Peoples	of the Negev	הַנֶּגֶב
Jon. 1:1	Transliterated	Names of Individuals	the son of Amittai	בֶן-אֲמִתַּי

---

[5] The focus of the transliteration fluctuation is *Aven*. But I included the whole phrase, since it is addressed in the exegesis. Luther was playing on the dual meaning of the word as (a) a city name and (b) the meaning behind that name.

[6] The exegesis makes it clear that the transliteration question centers on an individual's name.

Table A.4: Luther's Use of Hebrew Transliteration 321

Vulgate	1532 *Deutsche Bibel*	1545 *Deutsche Bibel*	Bible References	Exegetical References
et Bethel erit inutilis	vnd Bethel wird jnn jamer komen	vnd Bethel wird BethAuen werden	WA DB 4:236a.11–17; WA DB 4:236b.11–14; WA DB 11.2:238.5; WA DB 11.2:239.5	WA 13:139.22– WA 13:140.3; WA 13:181.22–28; LW 18:159
tabernaculum	die huetten	den Sicchuth	WA DB 4:237a.21–28; WA DB 4:237b.21– WA DB 4:238b.23; WA DB 11.2:240.26; WA DB 11.2:241.26	WA 13:143.26– WA 13:144.14; WA 13:187.29; LW 18:167
Moloch vestro	ewrs Molochs	ewrn Koenig	WA DB 4:237a.21–28; WA DB 4:237b.21– WA DB 4:238b.23; WA DB 11.2:240.26; WA DB 11.2:241.26	WA 13:143.26– WA 13:144.14; WA 13:187.29; LW 18:167
et … idolorum	vnd die goetzen	vnd Chiun	WA DB 4:237a.21–28; WA DB 4:237b.21– WA DB 4:238b.23; WA DB 11.2:240.26; WA DB 11.2:241.26	WA 13:143.26– WA 13:144.14; WA 13:187.29; LW 18:167
in scissuris petrae	jnn der felsen kluefften	in der Felsenkluefften	WA DB 4:242b.4–7; WA DB 11.2:254.3; WA DB 11.2:255.3	WA 13:209.19–21; WA 13:216.31– WA 13:217.8; LW 18:195
a meridie	Theman	Theman	WA DB 4:242a.25–28; WA DB 11.2:254.9; WA DB 11.2:255.9	WA 13:210.29–31; WA 13:219.10–16; LW 18:198
ad austrum	gegen mittage	gegen Mittage	WA DB 4:243b.14–18; WA DB 11.2:256.19; WA DB 11.2:257.19	WA 13:213.6–17; WA 13:222.5–14; LW 18:202
austri	gegen mittage	gegen Mittage	WA DB 11.2:256.20; WA DB 11.2:257.20	WA 13:213.22–29; WA 13:222.26–31; LW 18:203
filium Amathi	dem son Amithai	dem son Amithai	WA DB 11.2:262.1; WA DB 11.2:263.1	WA 13:225.2–13; WA 13:241.2–23; WA 19:191.10–24; LW 19:3; LW 19:38

---

[7] The exegesis makes it clear that the transliteration question centers on an individual's name.

[8] The exegesis makes it clear that the transliteration question centers on an individual's name.

Verse	Luther's Hermeneutic	Category	NASB English	Hebrew Bible
Jon. 1:3	Interpretative	Geographical Regions or Peoples	to Tarshish	תַּרְשִׁישָׁה
Jon. 1:3	Transliterated	Geographical Regions or Peoples	to Joppa	יָפוֹ
Jon. 4[9]	Transliterated	Names of Individuals	Jonah	יוֹנָה
Jon. 4[10]	Transliterated	Geographical Regions or Peoples	Nineveh	נִינְוֵה
Jon. 4[11]	Transliterated	Geographical Regions or Peoples	Joppa	יָפוֹ
Mic. 1:10	Interpretative	Cultural- and/or Ethno-Specific Customs, Practices, and Rituals	At Beth-le-aphrah	בְּבֵית לְעַפְרָה
Mic. 1:11	Interpretative	Geographical Regions or Peoples	inhabitant of Shaphir	יוֹשֶׁבֶת שָׁפִיר

---

[9] This appears in the prologue to Luther's German commentary. There, he made "general" reference to the term, rather than focusing on its appearance in a particular verse. I include the common NASB, Vulgate, and *Deutsche Bibel* translations of יוֹנָה (*yônâ*) in the Book of Jonah for the sake of clarity in the chart.

[10] This appears in the prologue to Luther's German commentary. There, he made "general" reference to the term, rather than focusing on its appearance in a particular verse. I include the common NASB, Vulgate, and *Deutsche Bibel* translations of נִינְוֵה (*nînəwēh*) in the Book

Table A.4: Luther's Use of Hebrew Transliteration

Vulgate	1532 Deutsche Bibel	1545 Deutsche Bibel	Bible References	Exegetical References
in Tharsis	[vnd wolt] auffs meer	[vnd wolt] auffs Meer	WA DB 11.2:262.3; WA DB 11.2:263.3	WA 13:227.21– WA 13:228.5; WA 13:244.31– WA 13:245.14; WA 19:196.1– WA 19:197.6; LW 19:9–10; LW 19:43–44
Ioppen	gen Japho	gen Japho	WA DB 11.2:262.3; WA DB 11.2:263.3	WA 13:228.5; WA 13:245.10–14; WA 19:197.7–32; LW 19:9–10; LW 19:44–45
Iona	Jona	Jona	N/A	WA 19:245.2–23; LW 19:97
Nineve	Nineue	Nineue	N/A	WA 19:245.2–23; LW 19:97
Ioppen	Japho	Japho	N/A	WA 19:246.28– WA 19:247.15; LW 19:99
in domo Pulveris	jnn die traurkamer	in die Traurkamer	WA DB 11.2:272.10; WA DB 11.2:273.10	WA 13:264.20–33; WA 13:305.30–36; LW 18:216–7
habitatio Pulchra	Du schoene stad	Du schoene Stad	WA DB 4:246a.14– WA DB 4:247a.2; WA DB 4:246b.14– WA DB 4:247b.4; WA DB 11.2:272.11; WA DB 11.2:273.11	WA 13:265.1–32; WA 13:306.1–15; LW 18:217

---

of Jonah for the sake of clarity in the chart. The Vulgate translates this as both *speciosam* and *Nineve* in different places.

[11] This appears in the prologue to Luther's German commentary. There, he made "general" reference to the term, rather than focusing on its appearance in a particular verse. I include the common NASB, Vulgate, and *Deutsche Bibel* translations of יָפוֹ (*yāpô*) in the Book of Jonah for the sake of clarity in the chart.

Verse	Luther's Hermeneutic	Category	NASB English	Hebrew Bible
Mic. 1:11	1532 Interpretative; 1545 Transliterated	Geographical Regions or Peoples	inhabitant of Zaanan	יוֹשֶׁבֶת צַאֲנָן
Mic. 1:14	Transliterated	Geographical Regions or Peoples	The houses of Achzib	בָּתֵּי אַכְזִיב
Mic. 1:15	Transliterated	Geographical Regions or Peoples	inhabitant of Mareshah	יוֹשֶׁבֶת מָרֵשָׁה
Mic. 2:1	Interpretative	Cultural- and/or Ethno-Specific Customs, Practices, and Rituals	Iniquity	חֹשְׁבֵי־אָוֶן
Mic. 4:8	Transliterated	Geographical Regions or Peoples	tower of the flock	מִגְדַּל־עֵדֶר
Mic. 6:10[12]	1532 Interpretative; 1545 Transliterated	Cultural- and/or Ethno-Specific Customs, Practices, and Rituals	And a ... Measure	וְאֵיפַת
Nahum[13]	Transliterated	Names of Individuals	Nahum	נַחוּם
Nah. 1:1	Transliterated	Geographical Regions or Peoples	Nineveh	נִינְוֵה

---

[12] The protocols show "v. 17" here, as well as "10." Clearly it is v. 10 that is being addressed.

Table A.4: Luther's Use of Hebrew Transliteration

Vulgate	1532 *Deutsche Bibel*	1545 *Deutsche Bibel*	Bible References	Exegetical References
quae habitat in Exitu	Die stoltze	Die Einwonerin Zaenan	WA DB 4:246a.14– WA DB 4:247a.2; WA DB 4:246b.14– WA DB 4:247b.4; WA DB 11.2:272.11; WA DB 11.2:273.11	WA 13:265.1–32; WA 13:306.16–28; LW 18:217–8
domus Mendacii	Der stad Achsib	Der stad Achsib	WA DB 4:247a.20–22, 24–28; WA DB 4:247b.20–26; WA DB 11.2:274.14; WA DB 11.2:273.14– WA DB 11.2:275.14	WA 13:267.6–8; WA 13:307.27–34; LW 18:219–20
quae habitas in Maresa	Maresa	Maresa	WA DB 4:247a.28– WA DB 4:248a.3; WA DB 4:247b.28– WA DB 4:248b.4; WA DB 11.2:274.15; WA DB 11.2:275.15	WA 13:267.15–24; WA 13:307.35– WA 13:308.9; LW 18:220
qui cogitatis inutile	denen, die schaden zu thun trachten	denen, die schaden zu thun trachten	WA DB 4:248a.6–11; WA DB 4:248b.6–8; WA DB 11.2:274.1; WA DB 11.2:275.1	WA 13:268.5–14; WA 13:308.30– WA 13:309.3; LW 18:221–2
turris Gregis	thurm Eder	thurm Eder	WA DB 4:250a.11–13; WA DB 4:250b.11–14; WA DB 11.2:278.8; WA DB 11.2:279.8	WA 13:280.13–25; WA 13:321.8–24; LW 18:242
et mensura	vnd ... das mas	vnd der ... Epha	WA DB 4:251a.12–13; WA DB 4:251b.12–19; WA DB 11.2:282.10; WA DB 11.2:283.10	WA 13:292.30– WA 13:293.2; WA 13:335.12–34; LW 18:264–5
Naum	Nahum	Nahum	N/A	WA 13:345.3–20; WA 13:371.2– WA 13:372.8; LW 18:281–2
Nineve	Nineue	Nineue	WA DB 4:252b.8–12; WA DB 11.2:290.1; WA DB 11.2:291.1	WA 13:346.9–13; WA 13:372.18–27; LW 18:283

---

[13] This appears in Luther's lectures at the introduction to the Book. There, he made "general" reference to the term, rather than focusing on its appearance in a particular verse. I include the common NASB, Vulgate, and *Deutsche Bibel* translations of נָחוּם (*naḥûm*) in the Book of Nahum for the sake of clarity in the chart.

Verse	Luther's Hermeneutic	Category	NASB English	Hebrew Bible
Nah. 1:4[14]	Transliterated	Geographical Regions or Peoples	Bashan	בָּשָׁן
Nah. 3:8	1532 Transliterated; 1545 Mixed[15]	Geographical Regions or Peoples	than No-amon	מִנֹּא אָמוֹן
Hab. 2:13	Mixed	Names of Individuals	the Lord of hosts	יְהוָה צְבָאוֹת
Hab. 3:3	Interpretative	Geographical Regions or Peoples	from Teman	מִתֵּימָן
Hab. 3:3	Interpretative	Names of Individuals	And the Holy One	וְקָדוֹשׁ
Hab. 3:3	Transliterated	Technical Biblical Language	Selah	סֶלָה
Hab. 3:9	Transliterated	Technical Biblical Language	Selah	סֶלָה

---

[14] Cf. Zech. 11:2.

[15] In 1532 Luther transliterated the city name נֹא (*nō'*), and ignored אָמוֹן (*'āmôn*), which he addressed in the lectures [i. e. the full phrase נֹא אָמוֹן (*nō' 'āmôn*)]. There, he contended that אָמוֹן (*'āmôn*) refers to the inhabitants, who were some type of artisans. One could argue that

Table A.4: Luther's Use of Hebrew Transliteration

Vulgate	1532 Deutsche Bibel	1545 Deutsche Bibel	Bible References	Exegetical References
Basan	Basan	Basan	WA DB 4:252b.26–WA DB 4:253b.6; WA DB 11.2:290.4; WA DB 11.2:291.4	WA 13:349.18–22; WA 13:375.22–28; LW 18:287–8
ab Alexandria populorum	denn die grosse stad No	denn die stad No der Regenten	WA DB 4:257a.11–15; WA DB 4:257b.11–14; WA DB 11.2:294.8; WA DB 11.2:295.8	WA 13:365.3–WA 13:366.4; WA 13:390.5–18; LW 18:309–10
Domino ... exercituum	HERRN Zebaoth	HERRN Zebaoth	WA DB 11.2:306.13; WA DB 11.2:307.13	WA 13:409.11–12; WA 13:437.10–16; WA 19:414.5–29; LW 19:128; LW 19:216–7
ab austro	von mittage	vom Mittage	WA DB 4:259a.34; WA DB 4:259b.34; WA DB 11.2:306.3; WA DB 11.2:307.3	WA 13:414.9–18; WA 13:442.11–37; WA 19:427.10–WA 19:428.10; LW 19:137–8; LW 19:229–30
et Sanctus	vnd der Heilige	Vnd der Heilige	WA DB 4:259a.34; WA DB 4:259b.34; WA DB 11.2:306.3; WA DB 11.2:307.3	WA 13:414.9–18; WA 13:442.11–37; WA 19:427.10–WA 19:428.10; LW 19:137–8; LW 19:229–30
SEMPER	Sela	Sela	WA DB 4:259a.34; WA DB 4:259b.34; WA DB 11.2:306.3; WA DB 11.2:307.3	WA 13:414.9–18; WA 13:442.11–37; WA 19:427.10–WA 19:428.10; LW 19:137–8; LW 19:229–30
SEMPER	Sela	Sela	WA DB 4:260b.4–5; WA DB 11.2:308.9; WA DB 11.2:309.9	WA 13:418.8–13; WA 13:445.26–33; WA 19:430.19–29; LW 19:142–3; LW 19:233

the only transliteration issue here is נֹא (nōʾ), but I believe that the entire construction נֹא אָמוֹן (nōʾ ʾāmôn) is ultimately at issue because Luther was trying to identify the city. Cf. the NASB and see WA DB 4:257a.11–15 and WA DB 4:257b.11–14. Consequently, I have categorized the 1545 translation, where he transliterated נֹא (nōʾ) and interpreted אָמוֹן (ʾāmôn), as "mixed."

Verse	Luther's Hermeneutic	Category	NASB English	Hebrew Bible
Zeph. 1:4	1532 Interpretative; 1545 Transliterated	Cultural- and/or Ethno-Specific Customs, Practices, and Rituals	of the idolatrous priests	הַכְּמָרִים
Zeph. 1:5	Transliterated	Names of Individuals [18]	by Milcom	בְּמַלְכָּם
Zeph. 1:11	Interpretative	Geographical Regions or Peoples	O inhabitants of the Mortar	יֹשְׁבֵי הַמַּכְתֵּשׁ
Zeph. 1:11	Interpretative	Geographical Regions or Peoples	of Canaan	כְּנַעַן
Zeph. 2:4	Transliterated[19]	Geographical Regions or Peoples	Gaza	עַזָּה
Zeph. 2:4	Transliterated[20]	Geographical Regions or Peoples	And Ekron	וְעֶקְרוֹן
Zeph. 2:5	Interpretative	Geographical Regions or Peoples	of the Cherethites	כְּרֵתִים
Zeph. 2:6	Interpretative	Cultural- and/or Ethno-Specific Customs, Practices, and Rituals	**pastures, With caves** for shepherds	נְוֹת כְּרֹת רֹעִים
Zeph. 2:13	Transliterated	Geographical Regions or Peoples	Nineveh	אֶת־נִינְוֵה

---

[16] "(Mueche) Camarim" and an explanation appear in the gloss.

[17] "(Camarim)" and an explanation appear in the gloss.

[18] I have assigned this to the "Names of Individuals" category, given Luther's argument that the transliterated version may be the name of an idol.

Table A.4: Luther's Use of Hebrew Transliteration 329

Vulgate	1532 *Deutsche Bibel*	1545 *Deutsche Bibel*	Bible References	Exegetical References
aedituorum	der Muenche[16]	der Camarim[17]	WA DB 4:260a.23; WA DB 4:260b.21–29; WA DB 11.2:312.4; WA DB 11.2:313.4	WA 13:452.5–20; WA 13:482.12–30; LW 18:322–3
in Melchom	bey Malchom	bey Malchom	WA DB 4:260b.30–31; WA DB 11.2:312.5; WA DB 11.2:313.5	WA 13:453.1–20; WA 13:483.6– WA 13:484.4; LW 18:323–5
habitatores pilae	die jr jnn der Muele wonet	die jr in der Muele wonet	WA DB 4:261a.14–22; WA DB 4:261b.14–16; WA DB 11.2:312.11; WA DB 11.2:313.11	WA 13:457.1–16; WA 13:487.4–22; LW 18:329–30
Chanaan	kremer [volck]	Kremeruolck	WA DB 4:261a.14–22; WA DB 4:261b.14–16; WA DB 11.2:312.11; WA DB 11.2:313.11	WA 13:457.17–24; WA 13:487.23– WA 13:488.2; LW 18:330–1
Gaza	Gasa	Gasa	WA DB 11.2:314.4; WA DB 11.2:315.4	WA 13:463.9–16; WA 13:493.36– WA 13:494.9; LW 18:340
et Accaron	vnd Accaron	vnd Accaron	WA DB 11.2:314.4; WA DB 11.2:315.4	WA 13:463.21; WA 13:494.13–15; LW 18:340
perditorum	den kriegern	den Kriegern	WA DB 4:261a.31–32; WA DB 4:261b.31–32; WA DB 11.2:314.5; WA DB 11.2:315.5	WA 13:463.22–28; WA 13:494.22–23; LW 18:341
requies pastorum	**eitel** Hirten**heuser**	eitel Hirtenheuser	WA DB 11.2:314.6; WA DB 11.2:315.6	WA 13:463.31– WA 13:464.10; WA 13:494.27–35; LW 18:341
speciosam	Nineue	Nineue	WA DB 4:262a.10–11; WA DB 11.2:316.13; WA DB 11.2:317.13	WA 13:466.12–20; WA 13:497.7–16; LW 18:345

---

[19] This also appears in Table A.2.
[20] This also appears in Table A.2.

Verse	Luther's Hermeneutic	Category	NASB English	Hebrew Bible
Zeph. 2:14	Interpretative	Cultural- and/or Ethno-Specific Customs, Practices, and Rituals[21]	Both the pelican	גַּם-קָאַת
Zeph. 2:14	Interpretative	Cultural- and/or ethno-specific customs, practices, and rituals[22]	Birds will sing	קוֹל יְשׁוֹרֵר
Hag. 1:1[23]	Transliterated	Names of Individuals	in the hand of Haggai	בְּיַד-חַגַּי
Zech. 1:3	Mixed	Names of Individuals	the Lord of hosts	יְהוָה צְבָאוֹת
Zech. 3:1	Transliterated	Names of Individuals	and Satan	וְהַשָּׂטָן
Zech. 3:8	Transliterated	Names of Individuals	the Branch	צֶמַח
Zech. 6:12	Transliterated	Names of Individuals	Branch	צֶמַח

---

[21] One could argue that this should be understood differently than "Cultural- and/or Ethno-Specific Customs, Practices, and Rituals," but given the four potential categories that I have chosen, this seemed the most fitting.

Table A.4: Luther's Use of Hebrew Transliteration

Vulgate	1532 Deutsche Bibel	1545 Deutsche Bibel	Bible References	Exegetical References
et onocrotalus	Auch rhordomel	Auch Rhordomel	WA DB 4:262a.12–18; WA DB 4:262b.12–15; WA DB 11.2:316.14; WA DB 11.2:317.14	WA 13:466.21–29; WA 13:497.22–28; LW 18:345–6
vox cantantis	vnd werden … singen	vnd werden … singen	WA DB 4:262a.12–18; WA DB 4:262b.12–15; WA DB 11.2:316.14; WA DB 11.2:317.14	WA 13:466.30–36; WA 13:497.29– WA 13:498.5; LW 18:346
in manu Aggei	durch den Propheten Haggai	durch den Propheten Haggai	WA DB 11.2:322.1; WA DB 11.2:323.1	WA 13:513.22–24; WA 13:534.22; LW 18:371
Dominus exercituum	der HERR Zebaoth	der HERR Zebaoth	WA DB 4:265b.18–22; WA DB 11.2:332.3; WA DB 11.2:333.3	WA 13:549.30– WA 13:551.27; StL 14:1776.11– StL 14:1779.16; LW 20:8.8; LW 20:161–3
et Satan	Vnd der Satan	Vnd der Satan	WA DB 11.2:336.1; WA DB 11.2:337.1	WA 13:578.20– WA 13:579.2; StL 14:1824.1– StL 14:18.1830.17; LW 20:36–37; LW 20:204–9
orientem	Zemah	Zemah	WA DB 4:266a.28; WA DB 11.2:336.8; WA DB 11.2:337.8	WA 13:582.10–23; StL 14:1837.36– StL 14:1839.43; LW 20:40; LW 20:215–7
Oriens	Zemah	Zemah	WA DB 4:268a.30; WA DB 11.2:342.12; WA DB 11.2:343.12	WA 13:607.33– WA 13:608.14; StL 14:1878.20– StL 14:1880.25; LW 20:69; LW 20:254–6

---

[22] The previous footnote applies here also.
[23] See WA 13:513.23–34 for Luther's discussion of Haggai's name and the Hebrew word for festival [חַג (ḥag)].

Verse	Luther's Hermeneutic	Category	NASB English	Hebrew Bible
Zech. 7:2	Transliterated	Geographical Regions or Peoples	the town of Bethel	בֵּית-אֵל
Zech. 9:1	Transliterated	Geographical Regions or Peoples	against the land of Hadrach	בְּאֶרֶץ חַדְרָךְ
Zech. 9:16[24]	Interpretative	Cultural- and/or Ethno-Specific Customs, Practices, and Rituals	the stones of a crown	אַבְנֵי-נֵזֶר
Zech. 10:2	Interpretative	Cultural- and/or Ethno-Specific Customs, Practices, and Rituals	the teraphim	הַתְּרָפִים
Zech. 10:10	Transliterated	Geographical Regions or Peoples	of Gilead and Lebanon	גִּלְעָד וּלְבָנוֹן
Zech. 11:1	Transliterated[25]	Geographical Regions or Peoples	O Lebanon	לְבָנוֹן
Zech. 11:2[26]	Transliterated	Geographical Regions or Peoples	of Bashan	בָּשָׁן

---

[24] See Luther's lectures on Zech. 10:3, where he addressed this also. WA 13:638.1–5; LW 20:107. Cf. his remark in the preface to Zech. 10 in the lectures also. WA 13:635.24-WA 13:636.4; LW 20:105.

[25] In both the 1532 and 1545 *Deutsche Bibel*, however, Luther included a gloss explaining that Jerusalem was built from [the cedars of] Lebanon.

Table A.4: Luther's Use of Hebrew Transliteration

Vulgate	1532 *Deutsche Bibel*	1545 *Deutsche Bibel*	Bible References	Exegetical References
ad domum Dei	gen Bethel	gen Bethel	WA DB 11.2:342.2; WA DB 11.2:343.2	WA 13:612.32– WA 13:613.4; StL 14:1883.2– StL 14:1884.3; LW 20:77; LW 20:259–60
in terra Adrach	vber das land Hadrach	vber das land Hadrach	WA DB 4:270a.2–4; WA DB 4:270b.2–6; WA DB 11.2:346.1– WA DB 11.2:348.1; WA DB 11.2:347.1– WA DB 11.2:349.1	WA 13:623.13–24; StL 14:1907.3– StL 14:1908.4; LW 20:90; LW 20:283
lapides sancti	geweihete steine	heilige Steine	WA DB 4:271b.9–11; WA DB 11.2:348.16– WA DB 11.2:350.16; WA DB 11.2:349.16– WA DB 11.2:351.16	WA 13:633.27– WA 13:634.35; StL 14:1922.42– StL 14:1923–43; LW 20:102–3; LW 20:296–7
simulacra	die Goetzen	die Goetzen	WA DB 4:271a.13–26; WA DB 4:271b.13–15; WA DB 11.2:350.2; WA DB 11.2:351.2	WA 13:637.3–5; StL 14:1926.3–4; LW 20:106; LW 20:299–300
Galaad et Libani	Gilead vnd Libanon	Gilead vnd Libanon	WA DB 4:271b.26–30; WA DB 11.2:350.10; WA DB 11.2:351.10	WA 13:643.1–12; StL 14:1933.22– 23; LW 20:113–4; LW 20:306–7
Libane	Libanon	Libanon	WA DB 11.2:352.1; WA DB 11.2:353.1	WA 13:644.17–28; StL 14:1936.1–2; LW 20:116–7; LW 20:310
Basan	Basan	Basan	WA DB 4:272a.2–3; WA DB 11.2:352.2; WA DB 11.2:353.2	WA 13:644.36–40; StL 14:1937.4; LW 20:117; LW 20:311

---

[26] See Luther's lectures on Nah. 1:4, where he explained the meaning behind the transliterated word. WA 13:349.18–22; WA 13:375.22–28; LW 18:287–8.

Verse	Luther's Hermeneutic	Category	NASB English	Hebrew Bible
Zech. 11:7	Interpretative	Cultural- and/or Ethno-Specific Customs, Practices, and Rituals[27]	Favor	נֹעַם
Zech. 11:7	Interpretative	Cultural- and/or Ethno-Specific Customs, Practices, and Rituals[28]	Union	חֹבְלִים
Zech. 14:5[29]	1532 Interpretative; 1545 Mixed	Geographical Regions or Peoples	to Azal	אֶל־אָצַל
Mal. 3:1	Interpretative	Names of Individuals	My messenger	מַלְאָכִי

---

[27] One could argue that this should be understood differently than "Cultural- and/or Ethno-Specific Customs, Practices, and Rituals," but given the four potential categories that I have chosen, this seemed the most fitting.

[28] The previous footnote applies here also.

[29] Luther's Zechariah *lectures* end at Ch. 13. Thus, there is no exegetical reference for the lectures for this verse. Luther's Zechariah *commentary*, by contrast, covers the entire book including Ch. 14.

Table A.4: Luther's Use of Hebrew Transliteration   335

Vulgate	1532 *Deutsche Bibel*	1545 *Deutsche Bibel*	Bible References	Exegetical References
Decorem	Sanfft	Sanfft	WA DB 11.2:352.7; WA DB 11.2:353.7	WA 13:647.7–25; StL 14:1941.16– StL 14:1943.19; LW 20:120–1; LW 20:315–6
Funiculos	Wehe	Weh	WA DB 11.2:352.7; WA DB 11.2:353.7	WA 13:647.7–25; StL 14:1941.16– StL 14:1943.19; LW 20:120–1; LW 20:315–6
ad proximum	nahe hinan	nahe hinan … an Azal	WA DB 4:274b.28–33; WA DB 11.2:358.5; WA DB 11.2:359.5	StL 14:1966.7– StL 14:1967.7; LW 20:339
angelum meum	meinen Engel	meinen Engel	WA DB 4:277a.9–19; WA DB 11.2:370.1; WA DB 11.2:371.1	WA 13:692.10– WA 13:693.2; LW 18:408

Table A.5: Luther's Use of the "Reduced To" Idiom in his Interpretation of the Minor Prophets[1]

Verse	Luther's Latin/German	English Translation	Exegetical References	Bible References
Hos. 4:3	redigetur in magnam penuriam	will be reduced to great poverty	WA 13:16.14–15	
Hos. 4:5[2]	Redigere in nihilum	To be reduced to nothing	WA 13:17.10	
Hos. 8:6	redigetur in nihilum	will be reduced to nothing	WA 13:39.14	
	soll ... .zu pueluert werden	will be pulverized	N/A	WA DB 11.2:198.6[3]
Hos. 9:11	redigetur in solitudinem	will be reduced to solitude	WA 13:45.21; LW 18:51	
Hos. 10:7	redigentur in vastitatem	will be reduced to a desert	WA 13:49.15	
	redactis in nihilum	reduced to nothing	WA 13:49.16	
	redactus est in nihilum	was reduced to nothing	WA 13:49.17–18	
	ad nihilum redactus est	was reduced to nothing	WA 13:49 Note 15 H	
Joel 2:6	redigentur in ollam	will be reduced in a pot	WA 13:73.27	

---

[1] The examples in this table come from both the Altenburg and the Zwickau texts, as well as from the StL and WA DB where relevant, for comparison. This table shows only those occurrences in verses where (1) Luther explicitly cited the Hebrew in his argument, and (2) he cited the "reduced to" idiom to support the interpretation of that same verse. Additionally, this table includes those occurrences in verses which (3) Luther referenced in support of those verses with the explicit Hebrew citations. There are numerous additional appearances of the idiom in the Minor Prophets outside of these criteria. Also, LW references are not included in this table, given that they can sometimes be misleading with the English. Manuscript notations in the WA are included in this table where relevant, since the entries show only the specific "reduced to" idiom text. Furthermore, not every example includes a Latin or German equivalent to "reduced to." Nevertheless, Luther's comments in the exegesis make the parallels clear, and he often uses one instance of the "reduced to" idiom along with similar phrases to further drive his argument. Finally, I intentionally make rigidly literal translations in this table for the sake of comparison and to ensure clarity of Luther's use of the biblical idiom.

[2] Luther did not explicitly cite the Hebrew in this verse. He did, however, reference it in the lectures on Obad. 1:5, where he cited the Hebrew.

[3] The 1545 revision reads identically, except for the spelling adjustment: *zupuluert werden*. WA DB 11.2:199.6.

Table A.5: Luther's Use of the "Reduced To" Idiom

Verse	Luther's Latin/German	English Translation	Exegetical References	Bible References
Joel 2:6 (cont.)	redigentur in ollam	will be reduced in a pot	WA 13:97.20	
	Redigentur	will be reduced	WA 13:97.35	
Amos 1:3	contrivit et convertit prorsus in nihilum	was utterly ground down and turned into nothing	WA 13:126.31	
	in pulverem redegit	was reduced to dust	WA 13:163.2	
Obad. 1:3	Non solum non eris nihil munita sed et nihil eris	Not only will you not be defended with nothing but you will be nothing	WA 13:209.25–26	
	prorsus redigeris in nihilum	you will be utterly reduced to nothing	WA 13:217.13–14	
Obad. 1:5	redacta fuisses in nihilum, ut sileres[4]	you would have been reduced to nothing, that you would be silent	WA 13:209 Note 22 H	
	redigere in nihilum	to be reduced to nothing	WA 13:210.9–10	
	Ich wil dich stil machen	I will make you silent	WA 13:210.10	
	ich wil dich klein machen	I will make you small	WA 13:210.10	
	Fures mochten dich still machen und kleynlauttig[5]	For it would make you silent and fainthearted/sheepish	WA 13:210.11–12	
	tacere feci matrem tuam[6]	I had your mother silenced	WA 13:217.27–28	
	in silentium et in nihilum redigere	to be reduced to silence and to nothing	WA 13:217.30–31	
	Er ist ßo feyn stil worden	he has become so very silent	WA 13:218.1	

---

[4] This appears under Obad. 1:3, but Luther was clearly addressing Obad. 1:5; *Quomodo conticuisses* precedes the explanation.

[5] Grimm indicates that *kleinlaut* is usually a designation of *kleinmut*. DWB 11:1115.

[6] Luther was also citing Hos. 4:5 here, as his lecture notes show.

Verse	Luther's Latin/German	English Translation	Exegetical References	Bible References
Obad. 1:5 *(cont.)*	ey ich wil dich feyn kleyn mach-en, du ßolt recht stil werden	in any case, I will make you very small, that you [should] become silent	WA 13:218.2–3	
	in silentium redig-ereris	might be reduced to silence	WA 13:218.6	
	Er ist still worden	he has been si-lenced	WA 13:218 Note 1 D	
	wie soltu so stille werden	how you should be-come so still		WA DB 11.2:254.5 (1532)
	wie soltu so zu nicht werden	how you should so become nothing		WA DB 11.2:255.5 (1545)
	wie soltu so ⟨stille sein⟩	how you should be-come so still		WA DB 4:242b.9 (1538/39 hand-written entries in Luther's Old Testament)
	wie soltu so zu nicht werden	how you should so become nothing		WA DB 4:242b.10 (1538/39 hand-written entries in Luther's Old Testament)
	schweigen machen	to make silent		WA DB 4:242b.10 Note 3 (1538/39 hand-written entries in Luther's Old Testament)
Jon. 1:3	ist ... zu nichte worden	became nothing	WA 19:200.1	
	mus ... zu nicht werden	must become noth-ing	WA 19:200.17	
	mus ... zu nicht werden	must become noth-ing	WA 19:200.19	
	zu nichte	[to] nothing	WA 19:200.29	

Table A.5: Luther's Use of the "Reduced To" Idiom

Verse	Luther's Latin/German	English Translation	Exegetical References	Bible References
Jon. 1:5	zu nichte machen	to make nothing	WA 19:211.10	
Jon. 4:1–2	zu nichte	[to] nothing	WA 19:242.12	
Mic. 1:3	in nihilum prorsus redacturus est	will utterly reduce to nothing	WA 13:302.27–28	
Mic. 1:8	sint redigenda in nihilum	may be reduced to nothing	WA 13:263.17	
	redigenda esse in nihilum	to be reduced to nothing	WA 13:304.24	
Mic. 2:10	zu bettler machen	to make a beggar	WA 13:271.27	
Mic. 3:11	ad nihilum redigetur	will be reduced to nothing	WA 13:276 Note 26 H	
Mic. 3:12	redactus in nihilum	reduced to nothing	WA 13:277.5	
	in nihilum redigetur	will be reduced to nothing	WA 13:316.35	
Mic. 4:11	redigent te	will reduce you	WA 13:281.31	
	redigentur in vanitatem	will be reduced to vanity	WA 13:282.1	
	tu rediges eos in nihilum	you will reduce them to nothing	WA 13:323.4	
Mic. 4:13[7]	in nihilum rediges	you will reduce to nothing	WA 13:282.14	
Nah. 1:1	in nihilum redigentur	will be reduced to nothing	WA 13:346.13	
Nah. 1:4–6	redigere in nihilum	to be reduced to nothing	WA 13:349 Note 23 zm	
	in nihilum redigere	to be reduced to nothing	WA 13:375.27	
Nah. 1:10	in nihilum redigetur	will be reduced to nothing	WA 13:352.17	
Nah. 1:12	zu nicht worden	became nothing		WA DB 4:254a.14 (1539–41 Protocols)

---

[7] Luther cited Is. 33:1 here.

Verse	Luther's Latin/German	English Translation	Exegetical References	Bible References
Nah. 1:14	zu nicht	[to] nothing		WA DB 4:255b.8 (1538/39 hand-written entries in Luther's Old Testament)
	zu nicht worden	became nothing		WA DB 4:255b.16 (1538/39 hand-written entries in Luther's Old Testament)
Nah. 2:11	redigentur in ollam	will be reduced in a pot	WA 13:386.31	
Hab. 1:3	zu bettler macht	makes him a beggar [reduces (him) to beggary]	WA 19:358.19–20	
Hab. 1:11	zu nicht	[to] nothing	WA 19:373.5	
Hab. 2:5	zu nicht wird	will become nothing	WA 19:398.5	
	zu nichte werden	to become nothing	WA 19:398.9	
	zu nicht odder veracht wird	will become nothing or despised	WA 19:398.12	
Hab. 2:10	yhre narung yhn kurtz und geringe gemacht	decreased and reduced their sustenance	WA 19:410.1	
	den wird auch yhre narunge verkurtzt	For their sustenance will also be reduced	WA 19:410.4	
Hab. 2:16	zu nicht und zu schanden werde	may become nothing and a disgrace	WA 19:419.15	
Hab. 2:20	zu nichte werden [und muessen also stille fur yhm sein]	to become nothing (to be reduced to nothing) [and must also be silent before him]	WA 19:423.16	

Table A.5: Luther's Use of the "Reduced To" Idiom

Verse	Luther's Latin/German	English Translation	Exegetical References	Bible References
Hab. 2:20 *(cont.)*	Es sey fur jm stille alle welt	Let all the world be silent before him		WA DB 11.2:306.20[8]
Zeph. 1:11	ist stil gemacht	was made silent, reduced to silence	WA 13:457.13–14	
	redigetur in solitudinem	will be reduced to solitude	WA 13:457.14	
	in nihilum redactus est	was reduced to nothing	WA 13:457.15–16	
	redigetur in nihilum	will be reduced to nothing	WA 13:457.24	
	redactus in nihilum	reduced to nothing	WA 13:457.25	
	in nihilum redactus est	was reduced to nothing	WA 13:457 Note 13 H	
	in pulverem rediguntur	reduced to dust	WA 13:487.14	
	in nihilum redigemini	you will be reduced to nothing	WA 13:487.16	
	in nihilum redactum esse	to be reduced to nothing	WA 13:487.25–26	
Zeph. 2:13	illas redigam in desertum	I will reduce it to a desert	WA 13:466.19	
	redigam in nihilum	I will reduce to nothing	WA 13:497.16	
Zeph. 2:14	redigentur omnia in solitudinem	everything will be reduced to solitude	WA 13:497.21	
Zeph. 2:15	redacta in solitudinem	was reduced to solitude	WA 13:498.24	
Hag. 1:9	in nihilum redigere	to be reduced to nothing	WA 13:537.28	
Zech. 1:5	redactae in paupertatem	were reduced to poverty	WA 13:552 Note 26 Z	
Zech. 2:9	qui prorsus in nihilum redigit	which utterly reduces to nothing	WA 13:569.17	

---

[8] The 1545 revision reads identically, except for the capital "W" in *Welt*. WA DB 11.2:307.20.

342   Appendix

Verse	Luther's Latin/German	English Translation	Exegetical References	Bible References
Zech. 2:9 (cont.)	in nihilum redigit non aliter atque pulverem	reduces to nothing, just as dust	WA 13:569.21–22	
Zech. 2:12	redacta est ... in paupertatem	was reduced to poverty	WA 13:571 Note 13 Z	
Zech. 2:13	in nihilum redigat	may [it] be reduced it to nothing	WA 13:574.11	
	daß sie sollen ein Raub werden	that they shall become a plunder	StL 14:1816.42 (V. 9)	
Zech. 4:7	redigaris a domino in planum	may you be reduced by the Lord to level ground	WA 13:589.1	
	immo redacto te in planum	indeed, when you have been reduced to a reduced to a plain	WA 13:589.3–4	
	rediget te	will reduce you	WA 13:589 Note 3 Z	
	redigetur in planum	will be reduced to a plain	WA 13:589 Note 8 Z	
	redigetur in planitiem	will be reduced to a plain	WA 13:590.5	
Zech. 7:13–14	Ist das edle Land zur Wüstung gemacht	the precious land was made a deserted site	StL 14:1892.23– StL 14:1893.23	
	so wird er zerspringen und zermalmt werden in eitel Stücke, ja, in eitel Staub	so will he be shattered and crushed into nothing but pieces, yes, into nothing but dust	StL 14:1893.23	
	ist das Edele land zur wuestunge gemacht	the precious land was made a deserted site		WA DB 11.2:344.14[9]

---

[9] The 1545 revision reads identically, except for a minor orthographical modification: *ist das Edle land zur wuestunge gemacht.* WA DB 11.2:345.14.

Table A.5: Luther's Use of the "Reduced To" Idiom

Verse	Luther's Latin/German	English Translation	Exegetical References	Bible References
Zech. 7:14	redacta sunt in solitudinem	were reduced to solitude	WA 13:615.19	
	redacta in desertum	was reduced to a desert		WA DB 4:269a.12–13 (1539–41 Protocols)
Zech. 14:10	wird alles schlecht Feld sein[10]	everything will be a flat field	StL 14:1969.17	
	Es soll alles gleich und eben, einig und schlecht werden	Eveything will become equal and even, will become united and flat	StL 14:1969.17	
	sollen geniedriget werden	will become lowered, humbled	StL 14:1969.17	
	Was krumm ist, soll recht, und was uneben ist, soll schlecht werden	What is warped will become straight, and what is uneven will become flat	StL 14:1969.17	
	wie auff eim gefilde	like upon a field		WA DB 11.2:358.10[11]
Mal. 3:24	redigam prorsus in nihilum	I will utterly reduce to nothing	WA 13:703.8	

---

[10] Per Grimm, *schlecht* also has a meaning as the opposite of *krumm*. Thus, I have translated this as "flat," and not "bad." DWB 15:519.

[11] The 1545 revision reads identically, except for minor orthographical modifications: *Wie auff einem Gefilde*. WA DB 11.2:359.10.

Bibliography

I. Works of Martin Luther

Archiv zur Weimarer Ausgabe der Werke Martin Luthers. Texte und Untersuchungen. 10 vols. Weimar: Böhlau, 1981–2017.
Biblia, das ist die gantze heilige Schrifft: Deudsch auffs new zugericht, Wittenberg 1545. 3 vols. Edited by Hans Volz. München: Deutsche Taschenbuch, 1974.
Dr. Martin Luthers Sämmtliche Schriften. 23 vols. Edited by Johann Georg Walch. St. Louis: Concordia Publishing House, 1880–1910.
Dr. Martin Luthers Werke: In einer das Bedürfniss der Zeit berücksichtigenden Auswahl. 10 vols. Hamburg: Friedrich Perthes, 1826.
D. Martin Luthers Werke. Kritische Gesamtausgabe. 73 vols. Weimar: Böhlau, 1883–2009.
D. Martin Luthers Werke. Kritische Gesamtausgabe. Briefwechsel. 18 vols. Weimar: Böhlau, 1930–85.
D. Martin Luthers Werke. Kritische Gesamtausgabe. Die Deutsche Bibel. 12 vols. Weimar: Böhlau, 1906–61.
D. Martin Luthers Werke. Kritische Gesamtausgabe. Tischreden. 6 vols. Weimar: Böhlau, 1912–21.
In Oseam prophetam annotationes. Basel: Thomas Wolffius, 1526.
Luther Deutsch. Die Werke Martin Luthers in neuer Auswahl für die Gegenwart. 10 vols. Edited by Kurt Aland. Stuttgart: Ehrenfried Klotz, 1959–69. [Vol. 1: 1969; Vol. 2: 1962; Vol. 3: 1961, 3rd ed.; Vol. 4: 1964, 2nd ed.; Vol. 5: 1963, 2nd ed.; Vol. 6: 1966, 2nd ed.; Vol. 7: 1967, 2nd ed.; Vol. 8: 1965, 2nd ed.; Vol. 9: 1960, 3rd ed.; Vol. 10: 1959], with a supplementary lexicon [1973, 3rd ed.] and register [1974].
Luther's Works. 75 vols. Edited by Jaroslav Pelikan, Helmut T. Lehmann, and Christopher Boyd Brown. Philadelphia: Fortress Press; St. Louis: Concordia Publishing House, 1955-.
Martin Luther. Edited by E. G. Rupp and Benjamin Drewery. London: Edward Arnold, 1970. [English translation of selected works of Luther.]

II. Other Primary Sources (Pre-1800)

Bibles and Bible Manuscripts

Ben Ḥayyim ibn Adonijah, Jacob. *Jacob Ben Chajim Ibn Adonijah's Introduction to the Rabbinic Bible, Hebrew and English; with Explanatory Notes by Christian D. Ginsburg.* 2nd ed. Edited and translated by Christian D. Ginsburg. London: Longmans, Green, Reader, and Dyer, 1867.

Biblia Germanica. Strasbourg: Johann Mentelin, 1466.
Biblia Germanica. Augsburg: Günther Zainer, 1477.
Biblia Hebraica [*Torah, Neviim, Ketuvim*]. Brescia: Gershom Soncino, 1494.
Biblia Hebraica [חֲמִשָּׁה חוּמְשֵׁי תּוֹרָה]. Venice: Daniel Bomberg, 1528.
Lefèvre d'Étaples, Jacques. *Qvincvplex Psalterium: Gallicum. Romanum. Hebraicum. Vetus. Conciliatu*[*m*]. Paris: Henri Estienne, 1509.
Merzdorf, J. F. L. Theodor. *Die deutschen Historienbibeln des Mittelalters. Nach vierzig Handschriften*. 2 vols. Tübingen: L. F. Fues, 1870 [for Stuttgart: Litterarischer Verein].
The Monsee Fragments. Newly Collated Text with Introduction, Notes, Grammatical Treatise, and Exhaustive Glossary and a Photo-Lithographic Fac-Simile. Edited by George Allison Hench. Strassburg: Karl. J. Trübner, 1890.
Textus biblie cu[m] Glosa ordinaria Nicolai de Lyra postilla, Mortalitatibus eiusdem, Pauli Burgensis Additio[n]ibus, Matthie Thoring Replicis Prima [-Sexta] pars. 6 vols. Basel: Johann Froben, Johann Petri für Johann Amerbach, 1506–08. [The volumes in this edition are numbered 1, 3, 4, 5, 6, and 7.]

Other

Altenstaig, Johannes. *Vocabularius theologie*. Hagenau: Henricus Gran for Ioannis Rynman, 1517.
Bonaventure. *Commentaria in Quatuor Libros Sententiarum Magistri Petri Lombardi*. In *Opera omnia*, vol. 2. Edited by PP. Collegii a S. Bonaventura. Ad Claras Aquas (Quaracchi): Collegii S. Bonaventurae, 1885.
–. *Intinerarium mentis in Deum*. In *Opera omnia*, vol. 5. Edited by PP. Collegii a S. Bonaventura. Ad Claras Aquas (Quaracchi): Collegii S. Bonaventurae, 1891.
Cordatus, Conrad. *Tagebuch über Dr. Martin Luther. Geführt von Dr. Conrad Cordatus 1537*. Edited by H. Wrampelmeyer. Halle: Max Niemeyer, 1885.
Cyril of Alexandria. *Commentary on the Twelve Prophets*, vol. 2. The Fathers of the Church: A New Translation, vol. 116. Translated by Robert C. Hill. Washington, D. C.: Catholic University of America Press, 2008.
Dionysius [Pseudo-Dionysius Areopagite]. *The Divine Names and Mystical Theology*. Translated by John D. Jones. Milwaukee, WI: Marquette University Press, 1980.
Du Cange, Charles. *Glossarium ad scriptores mediae & infimae latinitatis ...* Paris: printed by Gabrielis Martini, sold by Ludovicum Billaine, 1678.
Gerson, Jean. *Ioannis Carlerii de Gerson de mystica theologia*. Edited by André Combes. Lucani: In Aedibus Thesauri Mundi, 1958.
Jerome. *S. Hieronymi Presbyteri opera*. Pars I: *Opera exegetica*, 4. *Commentariorum in Hiezechielem libri XIV*. Corpus Christianorum: Series Latina, vol. 75. Edited by Francisco Glorie. Turnhout: Brepols, 1964.
–. *S. Hieronymi Presbyteri opera*. Pars I: *Opera exegetica*, 6. *Commentarii in Prophetas Minores. Commentariorum in Ionam Prophetam*. In *Corpus Christianorum: Series Latina*, vol. 76. Edited by M. Adriaen. Turnhout: Brepols, 1969.
–. *S. Hieronymi Presbyteri opera*. Pars I: *Opera exegetica*, 6. *Commentarii in Prophetas Minores. Commentariorum in Osee Prophetam libri III*. In *Corpus Christianorum: Series Latina*, vol. 76. Edited by M. Adriaen. Turnhout: Brepols, 1969.
–. *Ancient Christian Texts: Commentaries on the Twelve Prophets. Vol. 1: Jerome*. Edited by Thomas P. Scheck. Downer's Grove, IL: IVP Academic, 2016.

Josephus, Flavius. *The Jewish War.* In *Loeb Classical Library. Josephus Vol. 2 [LCL 203]: Books 1–3*. Edited by E. H. Warmington. Translated by H. St. J. Thackeray. Cambridge, MA: Harvard University Press, 1967.
Kessler, Johannes. *Johannes Kesslers Sabbata mit kleineren Schriften und Briefen. Unter Mitwirkung von Prof. Dr. Emil Egli und Prof. Dr. Rudolf Schoch in Zürich* [1519–39]. Edited by Historischer Verein des Kantons St. Gallen. St. Gallen: Fehr, 1902.
Mathesius, Johannes. *Historien, Von des Ehrwirdigen in Gott seligen theuren Manns Gottes, D. Martin Luthers, Anfang, Lere, Leben, Standhafft bekentnuß seines Glaubens, unnd Sterben, Ordenlich der Jarzal nach, wie sich solches alles habe zugetragen, Beschriben Durch Herrn M. Johann Mathesium den Eltern.* Nürnberg: Katharinam Gerlachin, und Johanns vom Berg Erben, 1580. [Originally published in 1566, Nürnberg.]
Melanchthon, Philip. *Melanchthons Briefwechsel: kritische und kommentierte Gesamtausgabe.* Vol. 1. Edited by Heinz Scheible. Stuttgart-Bad Cannstatt: Frommann-Holzboog, 1977.
Reuchlin, Johannes. *De rudimentis Hebraicis.* Pforzheim: Thomas Anselm, 1506.
Tauler, Johannes. *The Inner Way: Being Thirty-Six Sermons for Festivals.* Translated by Arthur Wollaston Hutton. London: Methuen, [1901].
–. *Die Predigten Taulers: aus der Engelberger und der Freiburger Handschrift sowie aus Schmidts Abschriften der ehemaligen Strassburger Handschriften.* Edited by Ferdinand Vetter. Berlin: Weidmann, 1910.
–. *Predigten zu einen recht christlichen Leben.* Basel: Petri, 1521.
–. *Sermons.* Translated by Maria Shrady. New York: Paulist Press, 1985.
Theologia Deutsch. The Theologia Germanica of Martin Luther. Translated by Bengt Hoffman. London: SPCK, 1980. [Based on Luther's 1518 edition.]
Theologia Deutsch. Der Franckforter (Theologia Deutsch): Kritische Textausgabe. Translated by Wolfgang von Hinten. München: Artemis, 1982. [Based on numerous manuscripts in addition to Luther's 1516 and 1518 editions.]
Theologia Deutsch. Theologia Deutsch-theologia Germanica. The Book of the Perfect Life. Translated by David Blamires. Walnut Creek, CA: AltaMira Press, 2003. [Based on von Hinten's critical edition.]
Wakefield, Robert. *Oratio de laudibus & utilitate trium linguarum Arabicae Chaldaicae & Hebraicae, atque idiomatibus hebraicis quae in utroque testamento inveniuntur.* London: Winandum de Vorde, [1524]. [Published in English as Wakefield, Robert. *On the Three Languages [1524].* Edited and translated by G. Lloyd Jones. Binghamton, NY: Medieval & Renaissance Texts & Studies in conjunction with the Renaissance Society of America, 1989.]
Zohar. In *Mystic Tales from the Zohar.* Translated with notes and commentary by Aryeh Wineman. Princeton, NJ: Princeton University Press, 1998.

III. Secondary Sources

Bibles

Biblia Hebraica Stuttgartensia [תורה נביאים וכתובים]. 5th ed. Edited by Karl Elliger and Wilhelm Rudolph. Stuttgart: Deutsche Bibelgesellschaft, 1997.

Biblia Sacra Vulgata. Editio quinta. Edited by Robert Weber and Roger Gryson. Stuttgart: Deutsche Bibelgesellschaft, 2007.

Mikraot Gedolot Haketer [*Miḳra'ot gedolot ha-Keter*] [מקראות גדולות הכתר]. *A Revised and Augmented Scientific Edition of "Mikra'ot Gedolot." Based on the Aleppo Codex and Early Medieval MSS.* 13 vols. Edited by Menachem Cohen. Ramat-Gan: Bar-Ilan University, 1992-.

New American Standard Bible. Edited by the Lockman Foundation. Carol Stream, IL: Creation House, 1971.

Septuaginta (LXX). Editio altera. Edited by Alfred Rahlfs and Robert Hanhart. Stuttgart: Deutsche Bibelgesellschaft, 2006.

Other

Abelson, J. *Jewish Mysticism.* London: G. Bell and Sons Ltd., 1913.

Aland, Kurt, Ernst Otto Reichert, and Gerhard Jordan. *Hilfsbuch zum Lutherstudium.* 3rd rev. ed. Witten: Luther-Verlag, 1970.

Allen, Leslie. *The Books of Joel, Obadiah, Jonah and Micah.* NICOT. Grand Rapids, MI: Eerdmans, 1976.

Anderson, Francis I. and David Noel Freedman. *Micah: A New Translation with Introduction and Commentary.* AB 24E. New York: Doubleday, 2000.

Anderson, Gary A. *Sacrifices and Offerings in Ancient Israel: Studies in Their Social and Political Importance.* Atlanta: Scholars Press, 1987.

–. "Sacrifice and Sacrificial Offerings. Old Testament." In *The Anchor Bible Dictionary*, vol. 5, edited by David Noel Freedman, 870–86. New York: Doubleday, 1992.

Ariel, David S. *The Mystic Quest: An Introduction to Jewish Mysticism.* Northvale, NJ: Jason Aronson, 1988.

Bainton, Roland H. *Here I Stand: A Life of Martin Luther.* London: Hodder and Stoughton, 1951.

Baring, G. "Die 'Wormser Propheten', eine vorlutherische evangelische Prophetenübersetzung aus dem Jahre 1527." *Archiv für Reformationsgeschichte* 31 (1934): 23–41.

Barthélemy, Dominique. *Studies in the Text of the Old Testament: An Introduction to the Hebrew Old Testament Text Project. Textual Criticism and the Translator.* Vol. 3. Translated by Sarah Lind. Winona Lake, IN: Eisenbrauns, 2012.

Barton, John. "Déjà lu: Intertextuality, Method or Theory." In *Reading Job Intertextually*, edited by Katharine Dell and Will Kynes, 1–16. New York: Bloomsbury, 2013.

Bauch, Gustav. "Die Einführung des Hebräischen in Wittenberg. Mit Berücksichtigung der Vorgeschichte des Studiums der Sprache in Deutschland." *Monatsschrift für Geschichte und Wissenschaft des Judentums* 48 (1904): 22–32; 77–86; 145–60; 214–23; 283–99; 328–40; 461–90.

Bayer, Oswald. *Living By Faith: Justification and Sanctification.* Minneapolis: Fortress Press, 2017.

–. "Oratio, Meditatio, Tentatio: Eine Besinnung auf Luthers Theologieverständnis." *Lutherjahrbuch* 55 (1988): 7–59.

–. *Theology the Lutheran Way.* Edited and translated by Jeffrey G. Silcock and Mark C. Mattes. Minneapolis: Fortress Press, 2017.

Baylor, Michael G. *Action and Person: Conscience in Late Scholasticism and the Young Luther.* Leiden: E. J. Brill, 1977.

Beintker, Horst. *Die Überwindung der Anfechtung bei Luther. Eine Studie zu seiner Theologie nach den Operationes in Psalmos 1519–21*. Berlin: Evangelische Verlagsanstalt, 1954.
Bell, Theo. *Divus Bernhardus: Bernhard von Clairvaux in Martin Luthers Schriften*. Mainz: Philipp von Zabern, 1993.
Benjamin, Mara H. *Rosenzweig's Bible: Reinventing Scripture for Jewish Modernity*. Cambridge: Cambridge University Press, 2009.
Benzing, Josef, and Helmut Claus. *Lutherbibliographie. Verzeichnis der gedruckten Schriften Martin Luthers bis zu dessen Tod*. 2 vols. Baden-Baden: Librairie Heitz, 1966 (vol. 1). Baden-Baden: Valentin Koerner, 1994 (vol. 2).
Beutel, Albrecht. "Erfahrene Bibel: Verständnis und Gebrauch des verbum dei scriptum bei Luther." *Zeitschrift für Theologie und Kirche* 89 (1992): 302–39.
—. *In dem Anfang war das Wort: Studien zu Luthers Sprachverständnis*. Tübingen: J. C. B. Mohr (Paul Siebeck), 1991.
Bindseil, Heinrich Ernst, and Hermann Agathon Niemeyer. *Dr. Martin Luthers Bibelübersetzung nach der letzten Original-Ausgabe*. 7 vols. Halle: Druck und Verlag der Canstein'schen Bibel-Anstalt, 1848–55.
Bingaman, Brock and Bradley Nassif, eds. *The Philokalia: A Classic Text of Orthodox Spirituality*. Oxford: Oxford University Press, 2012.
Bluhm, Heinz. "An 'Unknown' Luther Translation of the Bible." *PMLA* 84 (1969): 1537–44.
—. *Luther Translator of Paul: Studies in Romans and Galatians*. New York: Peter Lang, 1984.
—. *Martin Luther: Creative Translator*. St. Louis: Concordia Publishing House, 1965.
—. *Studies in Luther – Luther Studien*. Bern: Peter Lang, 1987.
Blumenthal, David R. *Understanding Jewish Mysticism: A Source Reader. The Merkabah Tradition and the Zoharic Tradition*. New York: KTAV, 1978.
Bornkamm, Heinrich. *Luther in Mid-Career 1521–1530*. Edited by Karin Bornkamm. Translated by E. Theodore Bachmann. London: Darton, Longman & Todd, 1983.
—. *Luther und das Alte Testament*. Tübingen: J. C. B. Mohr (Paul Siebeck), 1948.
—. *Luthers geistige Welt*. Lüneburg: Heiland-Verlag, 1947. [This was published in a second edition as: Bornkamm, Heinrich. *Luthers geistige Welt*. 2nd ed. Gütersloh: C. Bertelsmann, 1953.]
Botterweck, G. Johannes, Helmer Ringgren, eds. *Theological Dictionary of the Old Testament*. Translated by John T. Willis. 15 vols. Vols.1 and 2: rev. ed., 1977. Vols. 4–7: translated by David E. Green. Vol. 8: translated by Douglas W. Stott. Vols. 7, 8, and 14: edited by Heinz-Josef Fabry. Grand Rapids, MI: Eerdmans, 1974–2006. [Originally published in German as Botterweck, G., Helmer Ringgren, and Heinz-Josef Fabry, eds. *Theologisches Wörterbuch zum Alten Testament*. 8 vols. Stuttgart: W. Kohlhammer, 1970–2000.]
Bowers, John Waite. "Language Intensity, Social Introversion, and Attitude Change." *Speech Monographs* 30 (1963): 345–52.
Bradac, James J., John Waite Bowers, and John A. Courtright. "Three Language Variables in Communication Research: Intensity, Immediacy, and Diversity." *Human Communication Research* 5 (1979): 257–69.
Brecht, Martin. *Martin Luther: Shaping and Defining the Reformation 1521–1532*. Translated by James L. Schaaf. Minneapolis: Fortress Press, 1990.

Brisman, Shimeon. *History and Guide to Judaic Dictionaries and Concordances. Vol. 3, Pt. 1 of Jewish Research Literature.* Hoboken, NJ: KTAV, 2000.
Brown, Francis, S. R. Driver, and Charles A. Briggs, eds. *A Hebrew and English Lexicon of the Old Testament: With an Appendix Containing the Biblical Aramaic. Based on the Lexicon of William Gesenius as Translated by Edward Robinson.* Rev. ed. Oxford: Clarendon Press, [1959].
Brown, Raymond E., S. S. *The Gospel According to John I–XII.* AB 29. London: Yale University Press, 2006.
Brug, John F. *Textual Criticism of the Old Testament: Principles and Practice.* 2nd printing. Mequon, WI: Chesed VeEmet Publishing, 2014.
Buber, Martin. *The Letters of Martin Buber: A Life of Dialogue.* Edited by Nahum N. Glatzer and Paul Mendes-Flohr. Translated by Richard and Clara Winston and Harry Zohn. New York: Schocken Books, 1991. [Originally published in German as Buber, Martin. *Briefwechsel aus sieben Jahrzehnten.* 3 vols. Edited by Grete Schaeder. Heidelberg: Lambert Schneider, 1972–75.]
Buber, Martin, and Franz Rosenzweig. *Die Schrift und ihre Verdeutschung.* Berlin: Schocken, 1936. [Subsequently published in English as Buber, Martin, and Franz Rosenzweig. *Scripture and Translation.* Translated by Lawrence Rosenwald with Everett Fox. Bloomington, IN: Indiana University Press, 1994.]
Bühler, Paul. *Die Anfechtung bei Martin Luther.* Zürich: Zwingli-Verlag, 1942.
Burnett, Stephen G. "Christian Aramaism in Reformation-Era Europe." In *Seeking Out the Wisdom of the Ancients: Essays Offered to Michael V. Fox on the Occasion of His Sixty-Fifth Birthday*, edited by Ronald L. Troxel, Kelvin G. Friebel, and Dennis R. Magary, 421–36. Winona Lake, IN: Eisenbrauns, 2005.
–. *Christian Hebraism in the Reformation Era (1500–1660). Authors, Books, and the Transmission of Jewish Learning.* Leiden: Brill, 2012.
–. "Christian Hebrew Printing in the Sixteenth Century: Printers, Humanism and the Impact of the Reformation." *Helmantica: Revista de Filología Clásica y Hebrea* 51 (2000): 13–42.
–. "Jüdische Vermittler des Hebräischen und ihre christlichen Schüler im Spätmittelalter." In W*echselseitige Wahrnehmung der Religionen im Spätmittelalter und in der Frühen Neuzeit. Vol. 1: Konzeptionelle Grundfragen und Fallstudien (Heiden, Barbaren, Juden)*, edited by Ludger Grenzmann, Thomas Haye, Nikolaus Henkel, and Thomas Kaufmann, 173–88. Berlin: Walter de Gruyter, 2009.
–. "Luthers hebräische Bibel (Brescia, 1494) – Ihre Bedeutung für die Reformation." In *Meilensteine der Reformation: Schlüsseldokumente der frühen Wirksamkeit Martin Luthers*, edited by Irene Dingel and Henning P. Jürgens, 62–69. Gütersloh: Gütersloher Verlaghaus, 2014.
–. "Martin Luther and Christian Hebraism." In *Oxford Research Encyclopedia of Religion.* Oxford: Oxford University Press, 2016. DOI: 10.1093/acrefore/9780199340378.013.274.
–. "Philosemitism and Christian Hebraism in the Reformation Era (1500–1620)." In *Geliebter Feind – gehasster Freund: Antisemitismus und Philosemitismus in Geschichte und Gegenwart*, edited by Irene A. Diekmann and Elke-Vera Kotowski, 135–46. Berlin: Verlag für Berlin-Brandenburg, 2009.
–. "Reassessing the 'Basel-Wittenberg Conflict': Dimensions of the Reformation-Era Discussion of Hebrew Scholarship." In *Hebraica Veritas? Christian Hebraists and*

the Study of Judaism in Early Modern Europe, edited by Allison P. Coudert and Jeffrey S. Shoulson, 181–201. Philadelphia: University of Pennsylvania Press, 2004.

—. "'Spokesmen for Judaism': Medieval Jewish Polemicists and their Christian Readers in the Reformation Era." In *Reuchlin und seine Erben: Forscher, Denker, Ideologen und Spinner*, edited by Peter Schäfer and Irina Wandrey, 41–51. Ostfildern: Jan Thorbecke, 2005.

—. "The Strange Career of the *Biblia Rabbinica* among Christian Hebraists, 1517–1620." In *Shaping the Bible in the Reformation: Books, Scholars and Their Readers in the Sixteenth Century*, edited by Bruce Gordon and Matthew McLean, 63–84. Leiden: Brill, 2012.

—. "The Targum in Christian Scholarship to 1800." In *A Jewish Targum in a Christian World*, edited by Alberdina Houtman, Eveline van Staalduine-Sulman, and Hans-Martin Kirn, 250–65. Leiden: Brill, 2014.

Chinchilla, Rosa Helena. "The Complutensian Polyglot Bible (1520) and the Political Ramifications of Biblical Translation." In *La traducción en España: ss. XIV–XVI*, edited by Roxana Recio, 169–90. León: Universidad de León, 1995.

Clark, Kenneth Willis. "The Meaning of ἀρα." In *Festschrift to Honor F. Wilbur Gingrich: Lexicographer, Scholar, Teacher, and Committed Christian Layman*, edited by Eugene Howard Barth and Ronald Edwin Cocroft, 70–84. Leiden: Brill, 1972.

Clines, David J. A., ed. *The Dictionary of Classical Hebrew*. 9 vols. Vols. 1–5: Sheffield: Sheffield Academic Press, 1993–2001. Vols. 6–9: Sheffield: Phoenix Press, 2007–16.

Cornette, James C., Jr. *Proverbs and Proverbial Expressions in the German Works of Martin Luther*. Edited by Wolfgang Mieder and Dorothee Racette. Bern: Peter Lang, 1997.

Darlow, T. H., and H. F. Moule. *Historical Catalogue of the Printed Editions of Holy Scripture in the Library of the British and Foreign Bible Society. Vol. 2: Polyglots and Languages other than English*. London: Bible House, 1911.

Dascalu, Raphael. "Between Intellect and Intoxication: An Exploration of Tanḥum ha-Yerushalmi's Commentary to the Book of Jonah." *Jewish Quarterly Review* 105 (2015): 42–71.

Daxelmüller, Christoph. "Zwischen Kabbala und Martin Luther – Elijah Levita Bachur, eine Jude zwischen den Religionen." In W*echselseitige Wahrnehmung der Religionen im Spätmittelalter und in der Frühen Neuzeit. Vol. 1: Konzeptionelle Grundfragen und Fallstudien (Heiden, Barbaren, Juden)*, edited by Ludger Grenzmann, Thomas Haye, Nikolaus Henkel, and Thomas Kaufmann, 231–50. Berlin: Walter de Gruyter, 2009.

Dell, Katharine, and Will Kynes, eds. *Reading Job Intertextually*. New York: Bloomsbury, 2013.

Diefenbach, Lorenz. *Glossarium Latino-Germanicum mediae et infirmae aetatis*. Frankfurt am Main: Joseph Baer, 1857.

Dietz, Thorsten. *Der Begriff der Furcht bei Luther*. Tübingen: Mohr Siebeck, 2009.

Dudenredaktion. *Duden Deutsches Universalwörterbuch*. 5th ed. Mannheim: Dudenverlag, 2003.

Dudenredaktion and the German Section of the Oxford University Press Dictionary Department, eds. *Oxford Duden German Dictionary*. 3rd ed. Oxford: Oxford University Press, 2005.

Dunkelgrün, Theodor. "The Hebrew Library of a Renaissance Humanist. Andreas Masius and the Bibliography to his *Iosuae Imperatoris Historia* (1574) with a Latin Edition and an Annotated English Translation." *Studia Rosenthaliana* 42–43 (2010–11): 197–252.

Ebeling, Gerhard. "Die Anfänge von Luthers Hermeneutik." *Die Zeitschrift für Theologie und Kirche* 48 (1951): 172–230. [Published in English as Ebeling, Gerhard. "The Beginnings of Luther's Hermeneutics." *Lutheran Quarterly* 7 (1993): 129–58, 315–38, 451–68 (Published in three parts, in vol. 7 issues 2, 3, and 4).]

—. "Das Gewissen in Luthers Verständnis." In *Lutherstudien. Vol. 3: Begriffsuntersuchungen – Textinterpretationen – Wirkungsgeschichtliches*, 108–25. Tübingen: J. C. B. Mohr (Paul Siebeck), 1985.

—. *Luther: Einführung in sein Denken.* Tübingen: J. C. B. Mohr (Paul Siebeck), 1964.

—. *Luthers Seelsorge: Theologie in der Vielfalt der Lebenssituationen an seinen Briefen dargestellt.* Tübingen: J. C. B. Mohr (Paul Siebeck), 1997.

Ellington, John. "Schleiermacher Was Wrong: The False Dilemma of Foreignization and Domestication." *Technical Papers for the Bible Translator* 54 (2003): 301–17.

Farrar, Frederic W. *History of Interpretation: Eight Lectures Preached before the University of Oxford in the Year MDCCCLXXXV. On the Foundation of the Late Rev. John Bampton.* London: Macmillan, 1886.

Ficker, Johannes. *Hebräische Handpsalter Luthers.* Heidelberg: Carl Winters Universitätsbuchhandlung, 1919.

Fishbane, Michael. *Biblical Interpretation in Ancient Israel.* Oxford: Clarendon Press, 1985.

—. *HAFTAROT הפטרות. The JPS Bible Commentary.* Philadelphia: Jewish Publication Society, 2002.

Freier, Moritz. *Luthers Busspsalmen und Psalter: Kritische Untersuchung nach jüdischen und lateinischen Quellen.* Leipzig: J. C. Hinrichs, 1918.

Friedman, Jerome. *Most Ancient Testimony: Sixteenth-Century Christian-Hebraica in the Age of Renaissance Nostalgia.* Athens, OH: Ohio University Press, 1983.

Froude, James Anthony. *Luther: A Short Biography.* London: Longmans, Green, and Co., 1883. [Reprinted from the Contemporary Review.]

Fuerst, Julius. *A Hebrew & Chaldee Lexicon to the Old Testament. With an Introduction Giving a Short History of Hebrew Lexicography.* Translated by Samuel Davidson. 3rd ed. Leipzig: Bernhard Tauchnitz; London: Williams & Norgate, 1867.

Füssel, Stephan. *The Book of Books: The Luther Bible of 1534. A Cultural-Historical Introduction.* Köln: Taschen, 2003.

Gaide, Anita. "Suffering and Hope in Martin Luther's Theology of the Cross and Latvian Lutheran Responses." PhD diss., Toronto School of Theology, 2002.

Galli, Barbara Ellen. *Franz Rosenzweig and Jehuda Halevi: Translating, Translations and Translators.* Montreal: McGill-Queen's University Press, 1995.

Gane, Roy. *Cult and Character: Purification Offerings, Day of Atonement, and Theodicy.* Winona Lake, IN: Eisenbrauns, 2005.

Garner, Kathleen. "Rewriting Scripture for the Twentieth Century: The Buber-Rosenzweig Bible Translation and the National Politics of Language." Thesis, University of Michigan, 2014.

Geiger, Ludwig. *Das Studium der hebräischen Sprache in Deutschland vom Ende des XV. bis zur Mitte des XVI. Jahrhunderts.* Breslau: Schletter, 1870.

Georges, Karl Ernst. *Ausführliches lateinisch-deutsches Handwörterbuch.* 2 vols. 8th rev. ed. by Heinrich Georges. Hannover: Hahn, 1913–18.

Gerdes, Hayo. "Überraschende Freiheiten in Luthers Bibelübersetzung." *Luther* 27 (1956): 71–80.
Gesenius, Wilhelm, E. Kautzsch, and A. E. Cowley. *Gesenius' Hebrew Grammar.* 2nd rev. English ed. Oxford: Clarendon Press, 1910.
Gilders, William K. *Blood Ritual in the Hebrew Bible: Meaning and Power.* Baltimore, MD: Johns Hopkins University Press, 2004.
Ginsburg, Christian D. *Coheleth: Commonly Called the Book of Ecclesiastes. Translated from the Original Hebrew, with a Commentary, Historical and Critical.* London: Longman, Green, Longman, and Roberts, 1861.
–. *Introduction to the Massoretico-Critical Edition of the Hebrew Bible.* London: Trinitarian Bible Society, 1897.
Glare, P. G. W. *Oxford Latin Dictionary.* 2 vols. 2nd ed. Oxford: Oxford University Press, 2012.
Gnädinger, Louise and Johannes G. Mayer. "Tauler, Johannes OP." In *Die deutsche Literatur des Mittelalters. Verfasserlexikon,* 2nd rev. ed., vol. 9, edited by Burghart Wachinger, Gundolf Keil, Kurt Ruh, Werner Schröder, and Franz Josef Worstbrock, 631–57. Berlin: De Gruyter, 1995.
Gordon, Bruce. *The Swiss Reformation.* Manchester: Manchester University Press, 2002.
Gow, Andrew C. "The Contested History of a Book: The German Bible of the Later Middle Ages and Reformation in Legend, Ideology, and Scholarship." *Journal of Hebrew Scriptures* 9 (2009): 1–37.
Grimm, Jacob, and Wilhelm Grimm. *Deutsches Wörterbuch von Jacob und Wilhelm Grimm.* 16 vols. Leipzig: S. Hirzel, 1854–1961.
Grislis, Egil. "Luther's Understanding of the Wrath of God." *The Journal of Religion* 41 (1961): 277–92.
–. "The Experience of the *Anfechtungen* and the Formulation of Pure Doctrine in Martin Luther's *Commentary on Genesis.*" *Consensus* 8 (1982): 19–31.
Gross, Daniel M. "Introduction: Being-Moved: The Pathos of Heidegger's Rhetorical Ontology." In *Heidegger and Rhetoric,* edited by Daniel M. Gross and Ansgar Kemmann, 1–46. Albany, NY: State University of New York Press, 2005.
Grossman, Avraham. "The School of Literal Jewish Exegesis in Northern France." In *Hebrew Bible/Old Testament: The History of Its Interpretation. Vol. 1: From the Beginnings to the Middle Ages (Until 1300). Pt. 2: The Middle Ages,* edited by Magne Sæbo, 321–71. Göttingen: Vandenhoeck & Ruprecht, 2000.
Grossman, Louis. "Peace-Offering." In *The Jewish Encyclopedia,* vol. 9, edited by Isidore Singer, 566–8. London: Funk and Wagnalls Company, 1905.
Haber, Susan. *"They Shall Purify Themselves": Essays on Purity in Early Judaism.* Edited by Adele Reinhartz. Leiden: Brill, 2008.
Haemig, Mary Jane. "Martin Luther on Hosea." *Word & World* 28 (2008): 169–76.
Hagen, Kenneth. *A Theology of Testament in the Young Luther: The Lectures on Hebrews.* Leiden: E. J. Brill, 1974.
Hägglund, Bengt. "Luther und die Mystik." In *Kirche, Mystik, Heiligung und das Natürliche bei Luther. Vorträge des Dritten Internationalen Kongresses für Lutherforschung,* edited by Ivar Asheim, 84–94. Göttingen: Vandenhoeck & Ruprecht, 1967.
Hailperin, Herman. "Nicolas de Lyra and Rashi: The Minor Prophets." In *Rashi Anniversary Volume,* edited by H. L. Ginsberg, 115–47. New York: Jewish Publication Society, 1941.
–. *Rashi and the Christian Scholars.* Pittsburgh: University of Pittsburgh Press, 1963.

Hamm, Berndt. "Wie mystisch war der Glaube Luthers?" In *Gottes Nähe unmittelbar erfahren: Mystik im Mittelalter und bei Martin Luther*, edited by Berndt Hamm and Volker Leppin, 237–87. Tübingen: Mohr Siebeck, 2007.

Harnack, Theod. *Luthers Theologie mit besonderer Beziehung auf seine Versöhnungs- und Erlösungslehre*. 2 vols. Erlangen: Theodor Blaesing, 1862 (vol. 1). Erlangen: Andreas Deichert, 1886 (vol. 2).

Hays, Richard B. *Echoes of Scripture in the Letters of Paul*. New Haven, CT: Yale University Press, 1989.

Herrmann, Erik. "Luther's Absorption of Medieval Biblical Interpretation and His Use of the Church Fathers." In *The Oxford Handbook of Martin Luther's Theology*, edited by Robert Kolb, Irene Dingel, and L'ubomír Batka, 71–90. Oxford: Oxford University Press, 2014.

Hirsch, Emanuel. *Luthers deutsche Bibel. Ein Beitrag zur Frage ihrer Durchsicht*. München: Kaiser, 1928.

—. *Lutherstudien*. 2 vols. Gütersloh: C. Bertelsmann, 1954.

Hobbs, R. Gerald. "Pluriformity of Early Reformation Scriptural Interpretation." In *Hebrew Bible/Old Testament: The History of Its Interpretation. Vol. 2: From the Renaissance to the Enlightenment*, edited by Magne Sæbø, 452–511. Göttingen: Vandenhoeck & Ruprecht, 2008.

Hoffman, Bengt R. *Luther and the Mystics: A Re-examination of Luther's Spiritual Experience and His Relationship to the Mystics*. Minneapolis: Augsburg, 1976.

Hoffman, Yair. "The Technique of Quotation and Citation as an Interpretive Device." In *Creative Biblical Exegesis: Christian and Jewish Hermeneutics through the Centuries*, edited by Benjamin Uffenheimer and Henning Graf Reventlow, 71–79. Sheffield: JSOT Press, 1988.

Holl, Karl. "Luthers Bedeutung für den Fortschritt der Auslegungskunst." In *Gesammelte Aufsätze zur Kirchengeschichte. Vol. 1: Luther*. 6th rev. ed. [compiled volume by Holl], 544–82. Tübingen: J. C. B. Mohr (Paul Siebeck), 1932.

—. "Was verstand Luther unter Religion?" In *Gesammelte Aufsätze zur Kirchengeschichte. Vol 1: Luther*. 6th rev. ed. [compiled volume by Holl], 1–110. Tübingen: J. C. B. Mohr (Paul Siebeck), 1932.

Hovland, Clarence Warren. "An Examination of Luther's Treatment of *Anfechtung* in his Biblical Exegesis from the Time of the Evangelical Experience to 1545." PhD diss., Yale University, 1950.

—. "*Anfechtung* in Luther's Biblical Exegesis." In *Reformation Studies: Essays in Honor of Roland H. Bainton*, edited by Franklin H. Littell, 46–60. Richmond, VA: John Knox Press, 1962.

Iserloh, Erwin. "Luther und die Mystik." In *Kirche, Mystik, Heiligung und das Natürliche bei Luther. Vorträge des Dritten Internationalen Kongresses für Lutherforschung*, edited by Ivar Asheim, 60–83. Göttingen: Vandenhoeck & Ruprecht, 1967.

Jay, Martin. "Politics of Translation: Siegfried Kracauer and Walter Benjamin on the Buber-Rosenzweig Bible." *The Leo Baeck Institute Year Book* 21 (1976): 3–24.

Jones, G. Lloyd. *The Discovery of Hebrew in Tudor England: A Third Language*. Manchester: Manchester University Press, 1983.

Joüon, Paul, and T. Muraoka. *A Grammar of Biblical Hebrew*. Rome: Editrice Pontificio Istituto Biblico, 2006.

Joyce, Paul M. "'Even if Noah, Daniel, and Job were in it ...' (Ezekiel 14:14): The Case of Job and Ezekiel." In *Reading Job Intertextually*, edited by Katharine Dell and Will Kynes, 118–28. New York: Bloomsbury, 2013.
Junghans, Helmar. *Der junge Luther und die Humanisten*. Weimar: Böhlau, 1984.
—. *Martin Luther und die Rhetorik*. Stuttgart/Leipzig: Verlag der Sächsischen Akademie der Wissenschaften zu Leipzig: In Kommission bei S. Hirzel, 1998.
Kaufmann, Thomas. *Luthers Juden*. Stuttgart: Reclam, 2014. [Published in English as Kaufmann, Thomas. *Luther's Jews*. Translated by Lesley Sharpe and Jeremy Noakes. Oxford: Oxford University Press, 2017.]
Keller, R. E. *The German Language*. London: Faber and Faber, 1978.
Kim, Joo-Kyung, Marie-Catherine de Marneffe, and Eric Fosler-Lussier. "Adjusting Word Embeddings with Semantic Intensity Orders." In *Proceedings of the 1st Workshop on Representation Learning for NLP*, 62–69. Berlin: Association for Computational Linguistics, 2016.
Kirn, Hans-Martin. "Traces of Targum Reception in the Work of Martin Luther." In *A Jewish Targum in a Christian World*, edited by Alberdina Houtman, Eveline van Staalduine-Sulman, and Hans-Martin Kirn, 266–88. Leiden: Brill, 2014.
Klawans, Jonathan. *Impurity and Sin in Ancient Judaism*. New York: Oxford University Press, 2000.
Klein, Ernest. *A Comprehensive Etymological Dictionary of the Hebrew Language for Readers of English*. Jerusalem: Carta Jerusalem; Haifa: University of Haifa, 1987.
Kleinig, John W. "Luther on the Practice of Piety." *Lutheran Theological Journal* 48 (2014): 172–85.
Klepper, Deeana Copeland. *The Insight of Unbelievers: Nicholas of Lyra and Christian Reading of Jewish Text in the Later Middle Ages*. Philadelphia: University of Pennsylvania Press, 2007.
Kluge, Friedrich. *Etymologisches Wörterbuch der deutschen Sprache*. Straßburg: Karl J. Trübner, 1883.
Koehler, Ludwig, and Walter Baumgartner, eds. *The Hebrew and Aramaic Lexicon of the Old Testament*. 5 vols. Subsequently revised by Walter Baumgartner and Johann Jakob Stamm, with assistance from Benedikt Hartmann, Ze'ev Ben-Hayyim, Eduard Yechezkel Kutscher, and Philippe Reymond. Translated and edited under the supervision of M. E. J. Richardson. Leiden: E. J. Brill, 1994–2000.
—. *Lexicon in Veteris Testamenti Libros*. Leiden: Brill, 1953.
Koenig, Walter H. "Luther as a Student of Hebrew." *Concordia Theological Monthly* 24 (1953): 845–53.
Kolb, Robert. *Martin Luther and the Enduring Word of God: The Wittenberg School and Its Scripture-Centered Proclamation*. Grand Rapids, MI: Baker Academic, 2016.
—. *Martin Luther: Confessor of the Faith*. New York: Oxford University Press, 2009.
Köstlin, Julius, and D. Gustav Kawerau. *Martin Luther: Sein Leben und seine Schriften*. 2 vols. 5th rev. ed. Berlin: Alexander Duncker, 1903.
Krause, Gerhard. *Studien zu Luthers Auslegung der Kleinen Propheten*. Tübingen: J. C. B. Mohr (Paul Siebeck), 1962.
Krause, Gerhard, and Gerhard Müller, eds. *Theologische Realenzyklopädie*. 36 vols. Berlin: Walter de Gruyter, 1977–2004.
Kries, Douglas. "Origen, Plato, and Conscience (*Synderesis*) in Jerome's Ezekiel Commentary." *Traditio* 57 (2002): 67–83.

Kristeva, Julia. *Desire in Language: A Semiotic Approach to Literature and Art.* Edited by Leon S. Roudiez. Translated by Thomas Gora, Alice Jardine, and Leon S. Roudiez. New York: Columbia University Press, 1980.
—. *The Kristeva Reader.* Edited by Toril Moi. Oxford: Basil Blackwell, 1986.
—. *Revolution in Poetic Language.* Translated by Margaret Waller. New York: Columbia University Press, 1984. [Originally published in French as Kristeva, Julia. *La révolution du langage poétique.* Paris: Seuil, 1974.]
Kusukawa, Sachiko. *A Wittenberg University Library Catalogue of 1536.* Cambridge: LP Publications, 1995.
Kynes, Will. *My Psalm Has Turned into Weeping: Job's Dialogue with the Psalms.* Berlin: De Gruyter, 2012.
Langston, Douglas C. *From Bonaventure to MacIntyre. Conscience and other Virtues.* University Park, PA: Pennsylvania State University Press, 2001.
Leppin, Volker. "'Biblia, das ist die ganze Heilige Schrift deutsch.' Luthers Bibelübersetzung zwischen Sakralität und Profanität." In *Protestantismus und deutsche Literatur*, edited by Jan Rohls and Gunther Wenz, 13–26. Göttingen: V&R unipress, 2004.
—. *Die fremde Reformation: Luthers mystische Wurzeln.* München: C. H. Beck, 2016.
—. "Luther: A Mystic." *Dialog: A Journal of Theology* 56 (2017): 140–4.
—. "Luther's Roots in Monastic-Mystical Piety." In *The Oxford Handbook of Martin Luther's Theology*, edited by Robert Kolb, Irene Dingel, and L'ubomír Batka, 49–61. Oxford: Oxford University Press, 2014.
—. "Luther's Transformation of Medieval Thought: Continuity and Discontinuity." In *The Oxford Handbook of Martin Luther's Theology*, edited by Robert Kolb, Irene Dingel, and L'ubomír Batka, 115–24. Oxford: Oxford University Press, 2014.
—. *Martin Luther.* Darmstadt: Wissenschaftliche Buchgesellschaft, 2006.
—. *Martin Luther: A Late Medieval Life.* Translated by Rhys Bezzant and Karen Roe. Grand Rapids, MI: Baker Academic, 2017. [Originally published in German as Leppin, Volker. *Martin Luther: Vom Mönch zum Feind des Papstes.* Darmstadt: Lambert Schneider, 2013.]
—. "Mysticism in Martin Luther's Development and Thoughts." In *Oxford Research Encyclopedia of Religion.* Oxford: Oxford University Press, 2016. DOI: 10.1093/acrefore/9780199340378.013.260.
—. "Mystik bei Luther." In *Gottes Nähe unmittelbar erfahren: Mystik im Mittelalter und bei Martin Luther*, edited by Berndt Hamm and Volker Leppin, 165–85. Tübingen: Mohr Siebeck, 2007.
Lester, G. Brooke. "Inner-Biblical Interpretation." In *The Oxford Encyclopedia of Biblical Interpretation*, vol. 1, edited by Steven L. McKenzie, 444–53. Oxford: Oxford University Press, 2013.
Levin, Christoph. *Re-Reading the Scriptures: Essays on the Literary History of the Old Testament.* Tübingen: Mohr Siebeck, 2013.
Levine, Baruch A. *Numbers 1–20: A New Translation with Introduction and Commentary.* AB 4A. New Haven, CT: Yale University Press, 2008.
Lewin, Reinhold. *Luthers Stellung zu den Juden. Ein Beitrag zur Geschichte der Juden in Deutschland während des Reformationszeitalters.* Berlin: Trowitzch & Sohn, 1911.
Lewis, Charlton T., and Charles Short. *A Latin Dictionary founded on Andrews' Edition of Freund's Latin Dictionary. Revised, Enlarged, and in Great Part Rewritten by Charlton T. Lewis.* Oxford: Clarendon Press, 1987.

Liddell, Henry George, Robert Scott, and Henry Stuart Jones, eds. *A Greek-English Lexicon*. 9th ed. with rev. supplement. Oxford: Clarendon Press, 1996.
Lindsay, Thomas M. *Luther and the German Reformation*. Edinburgh: T. & T. Clark, 1900.
Lohse, Bernhard. "Conscience and Authority in Luther." In *Luther and the Dawn of the Modern Era. Papers for the Fourth International Congress for Luther Research*, edited by Heiko A. Oberman, 158–83. Leiden: E. J. Brill, 1974.
Lowe, W. H. *The Hebrew Student's Commentary on Zechariah. Hebrew and LXX. With Excursus on Syllable-Dividing, Metheg, Initial Dagesh, and Siman Rapheh*. London: Macmillan, 1882.
Lundbom, Jack R. *Jeremiah 1–20: A New Translation with Introduction and Commentary*. AB 21A. New York: Doubleday, 1999.
Mackert, Christoph. "Luthers Handexemplar der hebräischen Bibelausgabe von 1494 – Objektbezogene und besitzgeschichtliche Aspekte." In *Meilensteine der Reformation: Schlüsseldokumente der frühen Wirksamkeit Martin Luthers*, edited by Irene Dingel and Henning P. Jürgens, 70–78. Gütersloh: Gütersloher Verlaghaus, 2014.
Matt, Daniel C. "*Ayin*: The Concept of Nothingness in Jewish Mysticism." In *The Problem of Pure Consciousness: Mysticism and Philosophy*, edited by Robert K. C. Forman, 121–59. New York: Oxford University Press, 1990.
Mattox, Mickey Leland. *"Defender of the Most Holy Matriarchs": Martin Luther's Interpretation of the Women in Genesis in the Enarrationes in Genesin, 1535–1545*. Leiden: Brill, 2003.
Maurer, Wilhelm. *Der junge Melanchthon: zwischen Humanismus und Reformation*. 2 vols. Göttingen: Vandenhoeck & Ruprecht, 1967–69.
Maxfield, John A. *Luther's Lectures on Genesis and the Formation of Evangelical Identity*. Kirksville, MO: Truman State University Press, 2008.
McGinn, Bernard. *The Mystical Thought of Meister Eckhart: The Man from Whom God Hid Nothing*. New York: Crossroad Publishing, 2001.
–. "Mysticism and the Reformation: A Brief Survey." *Acta Theologica* 35 (2015): 50-65.
–. *The Presence of God: A History of Western Christian Mysticism. Vol. 1: The Foundations of Mysticism*. London: SCM Press, 1992.
–. *The Presence of God: A History of Western Christian Mysticism. Vol. 2: The Growth of Mysticism*. New York: The Crossroad Publishing Company, 1999.
–. "Selective Affinities. Reflections on Jewish and Christian Mystical Exegesis." In *Creation and Re-Creation in Jewish Thought: Festschrift in Honor of Joseph Dan on the Occasion of his Seventieth Birthday*, edited by Rachel Elior and Peter Schäfer, 85–101. Tübingen: Mohr Siebeck, 2005.
McGrath, Alister E. *The Intellectual Origins of the European Reformation*. 2nd ed. Oxford: Blackwell Publishing, 2004.
–. *Luther's Theology of the Cross: Martin Luther's Theological Breakthrough*. 2nd ed. Oxford: Wiley-Blackwell, 2011.
McGuckin, John Anthony, ed. *The Encyclopedia of Eastern Orthodox Christianity*. 2 vols. Oxford: Wiley-Blackwell, 2011.
McKane, William. *A Critical and Exegetical Commentary on Jeremiah*. ICC. 2 vols. Rev. ed. London: Bloomsbury, 2014.
–. *Selected Christian Hebraists*. Cambridge: Cambridge University Press, 1989.
Meissinger, Karl August. *Luthers Exegese in der Frühzeit*. Leipzig: M. Heinsius Nachfolger, 1911.

Mesguich, Sophie Kessler. "Early Christian Hebraists." In *Hebrew Bible/Old Testament: The History of Its Interpretation: II: From the Renaissance to the Enlightenment*, edited by Magne Sæbo, 254–75. Göttingen: Vandenhoeck & Ruprecht, 2008.

Meyers, Carol L. and Eric M. Meyers. *Zechariah 9–14: A New Translation with Introduction and Commentary*. AB 26C. New York: Doubleday, 1993.

Michel, Stefan. *Die Kanonisierung der Werke Martin Luthers im 16. Jahrhundert*. Tübingen: Mohr Siebeck, 2016.

Michelet, M. *The Life of Luther. Written by Himself.* Translated by William Hazlitt. London: David Bogue, 1846.

Miletto, Gianfranco, and Giuseppe Veltri. "Hebrew Studies in Wittenberg (1502–1813): From Lingua Sacra to Semitic Studies." *European Journal of Jewish Studies* 6 (2012): 1–22.

Milgrom, Jacob. "The Alleged Wave-Offering in Israel and in the Ancient Near East." *Israel Exploration Journal* 22 (1972): 33–38.

–. *Leviticus 17–22. A New Translation with Introduction and Commentary*. AB 3A. New York: Doubleday, 2000.

–. "Priestly ('P') Source." In *The Anchor Bible Dictionary*, vol. 5, edited by David Noel Freedman, 454–61. New York: Doubleday, 1992.

Miller, Geoffrey D. "Intertextuality in Old Testament Research." *Currents in Biblical Research* 9 (2011): 283–309.

Nelstrop, Louise and Simon D. Podmore, eds. *Christian Mysticism and Incarnational Theology: Between Transcendence and Immanence*. Burlington, VT: Ashgate, 2013.

Németh, Csaba. "*Paulus Raptus* to *Raptus Pauli*: Paul's Rapture (2 Cor 12:2–4) in the Pre-Scholastic and Scholastic Theologies." In *A Companion to St. Paul in the Middle Ages*, edited by Steven R. Cartwright, 349–92. Leiden: Brill, 2013.

Noth, Martin. *A History of Pentateuchal Traditions*. Translated by Bernhard W. Anderson. Englewood Cliffs, NJ: Prentice-Hall, 1972.

Oberman, Heiko A. "Gabriel Biel and Late Medieval Mysticism." *Church History* 30 (1961): 259–87.

–. *The Harvest of Medieval Theology: Gabriel Biel and Late Medieval Nominalism*. Cambridge, MA: Harvard University Press, 1963.

–. *Luther: Mensch zwischen Gott und Teufel*. Berlin: Severin und Siedler, 1982.

–. *The Reformation: Roots and Ramifications*. Translated by Andrew Colin Gow. Rev. ed. London: T & T Clark, 2004.

–. "Simul gemitus et raptus: Luther und die Mystik." In *Kirche, Mystik, Heiligung und das Natürliche bei Luther. Vorträge des Dritten Internationalen Kongresses für Lutherforschung*, edited by Ivar Asheim, 20–59. Göttingen: Vandenhoeck & Ruprecht, 1967. [Published in English as Oberman, Heiko A. "*Simul Gemitus et Raptus*: Luther and Mysticism." In *The Reformation in Medieval Perspective*, edited by Steven E. Ozment, 219–51. Chicago: Quadrangle Books, 1971.]

Opitz, Peter. "The Exegetical and Hermeneutical Work of John Oecolampadius, Huldrych Zwingli and John Calvin." In *Hebrew Bible/Old Testament: The History of Its Interpretation. Vol 2: From the Renaissance to the Enlightenment*, ed. Magne Sæbo, 407–51. Göttingen: Vandenhoeck & Ruprecht, 2008.

Otto, Henrik. *Vor- und frühreformatorische Tauler-Rezeption: Annotationen in Drucken des späten 15. und frühen 16. Jahrhunderts*. Gütersloh: Gütersloher Verlagshaus, 2003.

Ozment, Steven E. *The Age of Reform 1250–1550: An Intellectual and Religious History of Late Medieval and Reformation Europe.* New Haven, CT: Yale University Press, 1980.
—. "Eckhart and Luther: German Mysticism and Protestantism." *The Thomist* 42 (1978): 259–80.
—. *Homo Spiritualis: A Comparative Study of the Anthropology of Johannes Tauler, Jean Gerson and Martin Luther (1509–16) in the Context of Their Theological Thought.* Leiden: E. J. Brill, 1969.
—. *Mysticism and Dissent: Religious Ideology and Social Protest in the Sixteenth Century.* New Haven, CT: Yale University Press, 1973.
Pahl, Theodor. *Quellenstudien zu Luthers Psalmenübersetzung.* Weimar: Böhlau, 1931.
Pelikan, Jaroslav. *Luther the Expositor: Introduction to the Reformer's Exegetical Writings.* St. Louis: Concordia Publishing House, 1959. [Included as a companion volume to LW.]
Penkower, Jordan S. "A 14th Century Ashkenazi Hebrew Bible Codex with Later Inscriptions in Latin and Hebrew by Luther, Melanchthon, Jonas and Ziegler." *Codices Manuscripti* 82/83 (2012): 43–60.
Platzhoff, Hermann. *Luthers erste Psalmenübersetzung sprachwissenschaftlich untersucht.* PhD diss., Universität Halle, 1887.
Podmore, Simon D. *Struggling with God: Kierkegaard and the Temptation of Spiritual Trial.* Cambridge: James Clarke, 2013.
Posset, Franz. *Johann Reuchlin (1455–1522): A Theological Biography.* Berlin: De Gruyter, 2015.
—. *Renaissance Monks: Monastic Humanism in Six Biographical Sketches.* Leiden: Brill, 2005.
Price, David H. *Johannes Reuchlin and the Campaign to Destroy Jewish Books.* Oxford: Oxford University Press, 2011.
Raeder, Siegfried. *Die Benutzung des masoretischen Textes bei Luther in der Zeit zwischen der ersten und zweiten Psalmenvorlesung (1515–1518).* Tübingen: J. C. B. Mohr (Paul Siebeck), 1967.
—. "The Exegetical and Hermeneutical Work of Martin Luther." In *Hebrew Bible/Old Testament: The History of Its Interpretation. Vol. 2: From the Renaissance to the Enlightenment,* edited by Magne Sæbo, 363–406. Göttingen: Vandenhoeck & Ruprecht, 2008.
—. *Grammatica Theologica: Studien zu Luthers Operationes in Psalmos.* Tübingen: J. C. B. Mohr (Paul Siebeck), 1977.
—. *Das Hebräische bei Luther: untersucht bis zum Ende der ersten Psalmenvorlesung.* Tübingen: J. C. B. Mohr (Paul Siebeck), 1961.
—. "Luther als Ausleger und Übersetzer der Heiligen Schrift." In *Leben und Werk Martin Luthers von 1526 bis 1546. Festgabe zu seinem 500. Geburtstag,* vol. 1, edited by Helmar Junghans, 253–78. Göttingen: Vandenhoeck & Ruprecht, 1983.
—. "Voraussetzungen und Methode von Luthers Bibelübersetzung." In *Geist und Geschichte der Reformation. Festgabe Hanns Rückert zum 65. Geburtstag. Dargebracht von Freunden, Kollegen und Schülern,* edited by Heinz Liebing and Klaus Scholder, 152–78. Berlin: Walter de Gruyter, 1966.
Ratzinger, Cardinal Joseph [now Pope Benedict XVI]. "Conscience and Truth." In *On Conscience: Two Essays by Joseph Ratzinger,* edited by Edward J. Furton, 11–41. Philadelphia: The National Catholic Bioethics Center; San Francisco: Ignatius Press,

2007. [This was originally a keynote address of the Tenth Bishops' Workshop of the National Catholic Bioethics Center in February, 1991.]
Reichert, Otto. *D. Martin Luthers Deutsche Bibel.* Tübingen: J. C. B. Mohr (Paul Siebeck), 1910.
—. *Die Wittenberger Bibelrevisionskommissionen von 1531–1541 und ihr Ertrag fuer die deutsche Lutherbibel.* Leignitz: Sehffarth, 1905.
Reu, M. *Luther's German Bible: An Historical Presentation, Together with a Collection of Sources.* St. Louis: Concordia Publishing House, 1984. [Concordia Heritage Series. Reprint of Columbus, OH: The Lutheran Book of Concern, 1934.]
Rex, Richard. "Humanism." In *The Reformation World*, edited by Andrew Pettegree, 51–70. London: Routledge, 2000.
—. "Humanism and Reformation in England and Scotland." In *Hebrew Bible/Old Testament: The History of Its Interpretation. Vol. 2: From the Renaissance to the Enlightenment*, edited by Magne Sæbo, 512–35. Göttingen: Vandenhoeck & Ruprecht, 2008.
—. *The Theology of John Fisher.* Cambridge: Cambridge University Press, 1991.
Rhodes, Erroll F. "Medieval Versions." In *The Oxford Companion to the Bible*, edited by Bruce M. Metzger and Michael D. Coogan, 755–8. New York: Oxford University Press, 1993.
Risch, Adolf. "Luthers Bibelverdeutschung." *Schriften des Vereins für Reformationsgeschichte* 40 (1922):1–82.
Rittgers, Ronald K. *The Reformation of Suffering: Pastoral Theology and Lay Piety in Late Medieval and Early Modern Germany.* New York: Oxford University Press, 2012.
Rorem, Paul. *The Dionysian Mystical Theology.* Minneapolis: Fortress Press, 2015.
Rosenthal, Erwin I. J. "Sebastian Münster's Knowledge and Use of Jewish Exegesis." In *Studia Semitica Vol 1: Jewish Themes* [compiled volume by Rosenthal], 127–45. Cambridge: Cambridge University Press, 1971.
Rubinstein, Aynat, Ivy Sichel, and Avigail Tsirkin-Sadan, "Superfluous Negation in Modern Hebrew and Its Origins." In *Language Contact and the Development of Modern Hebrew*, edited by Edit Doron, 161–79. Leiden: Brill, 2016.
Rudy, Gordon. *Mystical Language of Sensation in the Later Middle Ages.* New York: Routledge, 2002.
Ruh, Kurt. *Geschichte der abendländischen Mystik.* 4 vols. München: C. H. Beck, 1990–99.
Sanders, Daniel. *Wörterbuch der deutschen Sprache.* 2 vols. Leipzig: Otto Wigand, 1860–65.
Sarna, Nahum M. *Exodus* שמות. JPS Torah Commentary. Philadelphia: Jewish Publication Society, 1991.
Sasson, Jack M. *Jonah: A New Translation with Introduction, Commentary, and Interpretation.* AB 24B. New York: Doubleday, 1990.
Scaer, David P. "The Concept of *Anfechtung* in Luther's Thought." *Concordia Theological Quarterly* 47 (1983): 15–30.
Schaff, Philip. *History of the Christian Church. Modern Christianity: The German Reformation A. D. 1517–1530*, Pt. 2. Edinburgh: T. & T. Clark, 1888.
Schenker, Adrian. "From the First Printed Hebrew, Greek and Latin Bibles to the First Polyglot Bible, the Complutensian Polyglot: 1477–1517." In *Hebrew Bible/Old Testament: The History of Its Interpretation. Vol. 2: From the Renaissance to the Enlightenment*, edited by Magne Sæbo, 276–91. Göttingen: Vandenhoeck & Ruprecht, 2008.

Schinkel, Anders. *Conscience and Conscientious Objections.* Amsterdam: Pallas Publications, 2007.
Schjoldager, Anne. *Understanding Translation.* Aarhus: Academica, 2014.
Schleiermacher, Friedrich. "Über die verschiedenen Methoden des Übersetzens." In *Kritische Gesamtausgabe. Part 1: Schriften und Entwürfe. Vol. 11: Akademievorträge*, edited by Martin Rößler and Lars Emersleben, 65–94. Berlin: Walter de Gruyter, 2002. [This was a lecture given by Schleiermacher at the June 24, 1813 meeting of the Königlich-Preußischen Akademie der Wissenschaften in Berlin.]
Schlögel, Herbert. "Das andere Gewissen (?) Einblicke in die gegenwärtige evangelische Ethik." *Catholica* 48 (1994): 175–90.
–. "'Der Mensch ist Gewissen …' Überlegungen zum Gewissensverständnis von Gerhard Ebeling." *Catholica* 43 (1989): 79–94.
Schmidt, Hans. "Luthers Übersetzung des 46. Psalms." *Luther-Jahrbuch* 8 (1926): 98–119.
Scholem, Gershom G. *Jewish Gnosticism, Merkabah Mysticism, and Talmudic Tradition.* 2nd ed. New York: Jewish Theological Seminary of America, 1965.
–. *Major Trends in Jewish Mysticism.* 3rd ed. London: Thames and Hudson, 1955.
Schramm, Brooks. "On the *Schem Hamphoras* and on the Lineage of Christ, 1543." In *The Annotated Luther. Vol. 5: Christian Life in the World*, edited by Hans J. Hillerbrand, 609–66. Minneapolis: Fortress Press, 2017.
Schwartz, Baruch J. "Wave Offering." In *The Oxford Dictionary of the Jewish Religion*, 2nd ed., edited by Adele Berlin, 767–8. New York: Oxford University Press, 2011.
Schwarz, W. *Principles and Problems of Biblical Translation. Some Reformation Controversies and their Background.* Cambridge: Cambridge University Press, 1955.
Sharp, Carolyn J. ed. *The Oxford Handbook of the Prophets.* New York: Oxford University Press, 2016.
Shivade, Chaitanya, Marie-Catherine de Marneffe, Eric Fosler-Lussier, and Albert M. Lai. "Corpus-Based Discovery of Semantic Intensity Scales." In *Proceedings of the North American Association of Computational Linguistics Annual Meeting (NAACL)*, 483–83. Denver: Association for Computational Linguistics, 2015.
Siegfried, [Carl]. "Raschi's Einfluss auf Nicolaus von Lira und Luther in der Auslegung der Genesis." *Archiv für wissenschaftliche Erforschung des Alten Testamentes* (1869): 428–56.
Siever, Holger. "Schleiermacher über Methoden, Zweck und Divination." In *Friedrich Schleiermacher and the Question of Translation*, edited by Larisa Cercel and Adriana Şerban, 153–72. Berlin: De Gruyter, 2015.
Singer, Samuel. *Sprichwörter des Mittelalters.* 3 vols. Bern: Herbert Lang, 1944–47.
Sklar, Jay. "Sin and Impurity: Atoned or Purified? Yes!" In *Perspectives on Purity and Purification in the Bible*, edited by Baruch J. Schwartz, David P. Wright, Jeffrey Stackert, and Naphtali S. Meshel, 18–31. New York: T & T Clark, 2008.
Smith, Preserved. *The Life and Letters of Martin Luther.* Edited by Robert Backhouse. London: Hodder & Stoughton, 1993. [First published by John Murray (London, 1911).]
Smyth, Herbert Weir. *Greek Grammar.* Rev. ed. Cambridge, MA: Harvard University Press, 1956.
Sorning, Karl. "Some Remarks on Linguistic Strategies of Persuasion." In *Language, Power and Ideology: Studies in Political Discourse*, edited by Ruth Wodak, 95–113. Philadelphia: John Benjamins, 1989.

Spalding, Keith. *An Historical Dictionary of German Figurative Usage.* 60 Fascicles. Oxford: Basil Blackwell, 1959–2000. [Fascicles 1–40 with the assistance of Kenneth Brooke; Fascicles 51–60 with the assistance of Gerhard Müller-Schwefe.]
Spitz, Lewis W. *Luther and German Humanism.* Aldershot: Variorum, 1996.
Springer, Otto, ed. *Langenscheidts enzyklopädisches Wörterbuch der englischen und deutschen Sprache: "Der grosse Muret-Sanders."* 4 vols. Deutsch-Englisch, 5th ed. Englisch-Deutsch, 9th ed. Berlin: Langenscheidt, 1989–90.
Steinmetz, David C. "Religious Ecstasy in Staupitz and the Young Luther." *The Sixteenth Century Journal* 11 (1980): 23–38.
Stern, David. *The Jewish Bible: A Material History.* Seattle: University of Washington Press, 2017.
Stolt, Birgit. *"Laßt uns fröhlich springen!" Gefühlswelt und Gefühlsnavigierung in Luthers Reformationsarbeit. Eine kognitive Emotionalitätsanalyse auf philologischer Basis.* Berlin: Weidler, 2012.
–. "Luther's Faith of 'the Heart': Experience, Emotion, and Reason." In *The Global Luther: A Theologian for Modern Times,* edited by Christine Helmer, 131–50. Minneapolis: Fortress Press, 2009.
–. "Luther's Translation of the Bible." *Lutheran Quarterly* 28 (2014): 373–400.
–. *Martin Luthers Rhetorik des Herzens.* Tübingen: Mohr Siebeck, 2000.
Strohm, Paul. *Conscience: A Very Short Introduction.* New York: Oxford University Press, 2011.
Strong, James. *The Exhaustive Concordance of the Bible.* London: Hodder and Stoughton, 1894.
Taylor, Bernard A. *Analytical Lexicon to the Septuagint. Expanded Edition.* Peabody, MA: Hendrickson, 2009.
Thyen, Dietrich. "Luthers Jesajavorlesung." PhD diss., Universität Heidelberg, 1964.
Tillmans, Walter G. *The World and Men around Luther.* Minneapolis: Augsburg, 1959.
Tregelles, Samuel Prideaux. *An Account of the Printed Text of the Greek New Testament: With Remarks on its Revision upon Critical Principles.* London: Samuel Bagster and Sons, 1854.
Tucker, W. Dennis, Jr. *Jonah: A Handbook on the Hebrew Text.* Waco, TX: Baylor University Press, 2006.
Vanderjagt, Arjo. "*Ad fontes!* The Early Humanist Concern for the Hebraica veritas." In *Hebrew Bible/Old Testament: The History of Its Interpretation. Vol. 2: From the Renaissance to the Enlightenment,* edited by Magne Sæbo, 154–89. Göttingen: Vandenhoeck & Ruprecht, 2008.
Vogelsang, Erich. *Die Anfänge von Luthers Christologie.* Berlin: Walter de Gruyter, 1929.
–. *Der angefochtene Christus bei Luther.* Berlin: Walter de Gruyter, 1932.
–. "Luther und die Mystik." *Luther-Jahrbuch* 19 (1937): 32–54.
Volz, Hans. "German Versions." In *The Cambridge History of the Bible. Vol. 3: The West from the Reformation to the Present Day,* edited by S. L. Greenslade, 94–109. Cambridge: Cambridge University Press, 1963.
–. *Martin Luthers deutsche Bibel: Entstehung und Geschichte der Lutherbibel.* Edited by Henning Wendland. Hamburg: Friedrich Wittig, 1978.
–. "Melanchthons Anteil an der Lutherbibel." *Archiv für Reformationsgeschichte* 45 (1954): 196–233.

Von Abel, Wolfgang, and Reimund Leicht. *Verzeichnis der Hebraica in der Bibliothek Johannes Reuchlins.* Ostfildern: Jan Thorbecke, 2005.
Von Loewenich, Walther. *Luthers Theologia Crucis.* Witten: Luther-Verlag, 1967.
Wach, Joachim. *Types of Religious Experience: Christian and Non-Christian.* London: Routledge and Kegan Paul, 1951.
Walther, Wilhelm. *Luthers Deutsche Bibel: Festschrift zur Jahrhundertfeier der Reformation.* Berlin: Ernst Siegfried Mittler und Sohn, 1918.
Waltke, Bruce K., and M. O'Connor. *An Introduction to Biblical Hebrew Syntax.* Winona Lake, IN: Eisenbrauns, 1990.
Wander, Karl Friedrich Wilhelm, ed. *Deutsches Sprichwörter-Lexikon: Ein Hausschatz für das deutsche Volk.* 5 vols. Leipzig: Brockhaus, 1867–80.
Ware, Kallistos. *The Orthodox Way.* Crestwood, NY: St. Vladimir's Seminary Press, 1995.
Watanabe, Morimichi. "Martin Luther's Relations with Italian Humanists. With Special Reference to Ioannes Baptista Mantuanus." *Lutherjahrbuch* 54 (1987): 23–47.
Wegener, Lydia. *Der 'Frankfurter'/'Theologia deutsch': Spielräume und Grenzen des Sagbaren.* Berlin: De Gruyter, 2016.
West, Clark R. "The Deconstruction of Hell: A History of the Resignatio ad Infernum." PhD diss., Syracuse University, 2013.
Wierzbicka, Anna. *Emotions across Languages and Cultures: Diversity and Universals.* Cambridge: Cambridge University Press, 1999.
Wilkinson, Robert J. *Tetragrammaton: Western Christians and the Hebrew Name of God: From the Beginnings to the Seventeenth Century.* Leiden: Brill, 2015.
Williams, Benjamin. "*Glossa Ordinaria* and *Glossa Hebraica*. Midrash in Rashi and the *Gloss*." *Traditio* 71 (2016): 179–201.
Wolf, Ernst. "Johannes von Staupitz und die theologischen Anfänge Luthers." *Luther-Jahrbuch* 11 (1929): 43–86.
Wolfson, Elliot R. "Forms of Visionary Ascent as Ecstatic Experience in the Zoharic Literature." In *Gershom Scholem's "Major trends in Jewish mysticism": 50 Years After. Proceedings of the Sixth International Conference on the History of Jewish Mysticism*, edited by Peter Schäfer and Joseph Dan, 209–35. Tübingen: J. C. B. Mohr (Paul Siebeck), 1993.
–. *Through a Speculum that Shines: Vision and Imagination in Medieval Jewish Mysticism.* Princeton, NJ: Princeton University Press, 1994.
Wolgast, Eike. *Die Wittenberger Luther-Ausgabe. Zur Überlieferungsgeschichte der Werke Luthers im 16. Jahrhundert.* Niewkoop: De Graaf, 1971.
Wood, A. Skevington. *Captive to the Word. Martin Luther: Doctor of Sacred Scripture.* Exeter: Paternoster Press, 1969.
Zahl, Simeon. "The Bondage of the Affections: Willing, Feeling, and Desiring in Luther's Theology, 1513–1525." In *The Spirit, the Affections, and the Christian Tradition*, edited by Dale M. Coulter and Amos Yong, 181–205. Notre Dame, IN: University of Notre Dame Press, 2016.
Zimmer, Eric. "Jewish and Christian Hebraist Collaboration in Sixteenth-Century Germany." *Jewish Quarterly Review* 71 (1980): 69–88.
Zobel, Hans-Jürgen. "Die Hebraisten an der Universität zu Wittenberg (1502–1817)." In *Altes Testament – Literatursammlung und Heilige Schrift. Gesammelte Aufsätze zur Entstehung, Geschichte und Auslegung des Alten Testaments*, edited by Julia Männchen and Ernst-Joachim Waschke, 201–28. Berlin: Walter de Gruyter, 1993.

Zur Mühlen, Karl-Heinz. "Die Affektenlehre im Spätmittelalter und in der Reformationszeit." *Archiv für Begriffsgeschichte* 35 (1992): 93–114.
—. *Nos extra nos: Luthers Theologie zwischen Mystik und Scholastik*. Tübingen: J. C. B. Mohr (Paul Siebeck), 1972.
—. *Reformatorische Prägungen: Studien zur Theologie Martin Luthers und zur Reformationszeit*. Göttingen: Vandenhoeck & Ruprecht, 2011.

Index of Scriptural, Ancient, and Medieval Sources[1]

Hebrew Bible

Genesis
1:2   298 n. 129
2:7   301 n. 134
12:10   108–9, 108 n. 21, 109 n. 23
13:2   108, 108 n. 21
44:31   125–6 n. 75
49:11   54–5, 55 n. 21

Exodus
12:22   143, 145–7, 145 n. 37, 146 n. 38, 147 n. 45, 154 n. 65
33:19   36 n. 162
33:20   209
34:7   155–7, 156 n. 72, 157 n. 73

Leviticus
7:30   136, 141, 141 n. 30
17:3–4   162
17:4   162
26:36   117, 119, 183, 187 n. 80

Numbers
6   295 n. 124
8:11   136, 141, 141 n. 30–31
8:21   136–7, 141, 141 n. 30, 142 n. 33
9:10   147 n. 43

Deuteronomy
32:14   55, 55 n. 21

Joshua
*   4

7:2   124 n. 68
18:12   124 n. 68

Judges
19:27   146 n. 37

[1] Samuel
13:5   124 n. 68
14:23   124 n. 68

Isaiah
3   154 n. 65
3:19   154 n. 65
6:5   125, 125 n. 71, 179 n. 50, 201–2, 208–11, 212 n. 167
10:3   212 n. 168
19:16   139 n. 25
28:19   116–7, 116 n. 44
29:9   152 n. 58–59
33:1   339 n. 7
51   152 n. 59
51:17   112 n. 34, 143, 145, 151 n. 57, 152–4, 152–3 n. 58–60
51:22   153 n. 61
52:7   36 n. 162

Jeremiah
1:11–14   162 n. 88
5:27   160–4, 162 n. 89, 218
6:10   149 n. 48
20:17   108 n. 20
23:12   212 n. 168

---

[1] As in the main text, all Bible citations in this index are provided according to the Hebrew Bible numbering, unless otherwise noted. For more on this, see p. 47 n. 1.

25:15[f]	148–9, 148 n. 47	12:1	238–9
46:21	212 n. 168	12:8	87, 318–9
49:1	84 n. 113	12:12	87–88, 88 n. 133, 226–7
49:3	84 n. 113	13	5, 25, 40 n. 179
50:31	212 n. 168	13:2	226–7
		13:3	238–9

Ezekiel

1:10	184 n. 71
9:1	212 n. 168
16:7	149 n. 48
44:7	149 n. 48

13:8	238–9
13:14	318–9

Joel

*	21 n. 80
1:3	81 n. 103, 95 n. 169, 238–9
1:6	304–5

Hosea

1:6	316–7
2:2	316–7
2:3	200 n. 130
2:16	234–5
2:17	95 n. 169, 234–5, 316–7
2:18	88–89, 316–7
2:21–22	79, 304–5
2:24	234–5
3:2	85, 316–7
3:4	85, 85 n. 116, 86–87 n. 126, 316–7
3:14	86–87 n. 126
4:3	205 n. 144, 234–5, 336
4:5	205, 206 n. 146, 207, 336, 337 n. 6
4:7	95 n. 169, 234–5
4:15	87, 87 n. 132, 124 n. 68, 316–7
5:1	318–9
5:5	236 n. 4
5:8	124 n. 68
5:14	78, 79 n. 91, 304–5
5:15	232–3, 232 n. 2
6:1	232 n. 2
6:8	82, 83 n. 108, 318–9
6:9	95 n. 169, 236–7
7:10	66 n. 48, 72 n. 74, 236–7
8:6	336
8:7	236–7
9:11	61 n. 34, 236–7, 336
10:1	81 n. 103
10:4	238–9
10:5	87, 87–88 n. 132, 124 n. 68
10:7	203 n. 134 and 136, 336
10:8	179, 181 n. 57, 210 n. 159–60
11:6	238–9

1:7	304–5
1:10	72 n. 74, 238–9
1:13	76 n. 86
1:14	69, 95 n. 169, 240–1
1:19	240–1
2:6	49–52, 51 n. 9, 52 n. 12, 66 n. 48, 72 n. 74, 121 n. 55, 226–7, 240–1, 336–7
2:7	240–1
2:12	240–1
2:14	188–9 n. 84, 240–1
2:22	242–3, 266 n. 58
2:23	73, 95 n. 169, 232–3, 242–3
2:26	95 n. 169, 304–5
3:3	49–50, 54–55, 230–1
3:4	95 n. 169, 242–3
4:1	242–3
4:2	242–3, 318–9, 318 n. 2
4:3	228–9
4:8	242–5
4:13	244–5
4:14	73 n. 81, 95 n. 169, 232–3
4:18	244–5

Amos

1:3	95 n. 169, 244–5, 304–5, 337
1:5	86–87 n. 126, 87, 87 n. 132, 123, 125, 246–7, 318–9
1:6	72 n. 74, 80, 246–7, 304–5
1:11	105, 107–8, 246 n. 21
1:12	87, 87 n. 131, 318–9
1:13	246–7, 246 n. 21
1:15	84, 88 n. 133, 89 n. 141, 246 n. 21, 318–9
2:2	86, 318–9

2:13	66 n. 48, 72 n. 74, 119 n. 49, 246–7	1:2	173–4, 177–81, 183, 186–8, 210 n. 159, 254–5
2:14	71, 95	1:3	322–3, 338
3:3	66 n. 48, 72 n. 74, 246–7	1:4	111 n. 33, 112 n. 34, 173–4, 179–81, 180 n. 54, 183, 186–8, 188–9 n. 84, 210 n. 159
4:6	248–9, 306–7		
4:8–11	306–7, 306 n. 5		
4:12	306 n. 5	1:4–5	112 n. 34
5:1	95 n. 169, 139 n. 24, 248–9	1:5	112 n. 34, 339
5:4	95 n. 169, 248–9	1:7	119 n. 51
5:5	73 n. 81, 87, 87 n. 132, 90 n. 145, 95 n. 169, 112–3, 122–6, 123 n. 63, 125–6 n. 74–75, 192 n. 100, 219, 248–9, 249 n. 27, 284 n. 96, 320–1	1:9	95 n. 169, 254–5
		1:11	112 n. 34
		2:3	112–9, 116 n. 44
		2:4	119 n. 51, 128 n. 85, 173–4, 180 n. 54, 181–8, 181 n. 58, 182 n. 61, 183 n. 64, 187 n. 80, 210 n. 159, 214–5 n. 175, 221
5:9	66 n. 48, 72 n. 74, 248–9		
5:26	84 n. 113, 89, 95 n. 169, 248–9, 320–1		
		2:4–6	112 n. 34
6:1	95 n. 169, 250–1	2:5	120, 120 n. 54, 124 n. 69, 173–4, 186–199, 187 n. 80, 188–9 n. 84, 191 n. 95 and 98, 194–5 n. 107, 198 n. 123, 211 n. 164, 218–9
6:3	250–1		
6:8	250–1		
6:10	89 n. 138, 95 n. 169, 250–1		
6:12	250–1	2:6	112 n. 34
7:7	89 n. 138, 252–3	2:7	254–5
8	161	2:9	60–62, 61 n. 33 and 35, 62 n. 38, 219, 232–3
8:1–2	160–4, 162 n. 88–89, 218		
8:3	212 n. 167	3:5	67, 69, 95 n. 169, 256–7, 256 n. 37
8:9	95 n. 169, 252–3, 306–7		
8:10	67, 69, 95 n. 169, 252–3, 256 n. 36–37	3:5–6	253 n. 34
		3:6	67, 67 n. 55, 69, 256–7, 256 n. 36
8:11	161, 161 n. 84		
9:9	95 n. 169, 252–3	4	322–3
		4:1	79, 306–7
Obadiah		4:1–2	339
1:3	85 n. 118, 254–5, 320–1, 337, 337 n. 4	4:6	228–9
		4:11	74, 256–7
1:5	199, 201, 203 n. 134 and 136, 205–10, 205 n. 145, 221, 336 n. 2, 337–8, 337 n. 4		
		Micah	
		1:3	256–7, 339
1:9–10	87, 87 n. 131, 112–3, 119–22, 121 n. 58, 128, 196 n. 112, 197 n. 119, 219, 306–7, 320–1	1:8	64 n. 42, 339
		1:10	67, 70, 70 n. 60, 85, 85 n. 116, 228–9, 256–7, 322–3
1:12	116 n. 44, 117	1:11	73 n. 81, 86, 90 n. 145, 232–3, 256–9, 322–5
1:19	83, 320–1		
1:20	83, 87, 87 n. 129, 320–1	1:14	324–5
		1:15	258–9, 324–5
Jonah		2:1	87–88, 88 n. 133, 95 n. 169, 258–9, 324–5
*	21 n. 80		
1:1	84, 84 n. 110, 320–1	2:4	79–80, 80 n. 96, 306–7

2:6	232–3, 308–9	3:2	49–50, 53–54, 228–9
2:7	258–9	3:3	75, 105–6, 108–9, 109 n. 23, 121 n. 55, 268–9, 273 n. 76
2:10	339		
2:11	75, 258–9	3:4	270–1
2:13	89 n. 138, 105, 107, 166 n. 3	3:6	270–1
3:3	52	3:8	96 n. 173, 326–7
3:10	71, 71 n. 63, 95, 258–9	3:13	79–80, 80 n. 96, 270–1, 308–9
3:11	258–9, 339	3:15	72, 95 n. 169, 105–6, 109, 121 n. 55, 270–3, 294 n. 121, 310–1
3:12	260–1, 339		
4:8	260–1, 324–5		
4:9	187 n. 79	3:17	272–3
4:11	75, 228–9, 260–1, 339		
4:13	95 n. 169, 260–3, 339	*Habakkuk*	
5:1	40 n. 178	1:3	87–88, 88 n. 133, 340
5:2	95 n. 169	1:4	66 n. 48, 73, 226–7, 272–3
5:4	262–3	1:5	77–78 n. 90, 80
5:5	228–9	1:8	55–57, 57 n. 25 and 28, 66 n. 48, 72 n. 74, 79, 95 n. 169, 230–1, 272–5, 310–1
6:9	49–50, 52–54, 228–9		
6:10	89–90, 324–5, 324 n. 12		
6:17	324 n. 12	1:9	95 n. 169, 274–5
7:12	79, 262–5, 308–9	1:11	340
		2:2	95 n. 169, 274–5
Nahum		2:3	80, 310–1
1:1	95 n. 169, 264–5, 324–5, 339	2:5	75, 118 n. 47, 143, 147–149, 149 n. 49, 274–5, 340
1:3	76 n. 86, 112 n. 34, 154–60, 155 n. 66, 157 n. 73, 158 n. 78, 218, 264–5, 308–9		
		2:6	276–7
		2:10	340
1:4	326–7, 333 n. 26	2:13	86–87 n. 126, 88–89, 88 n. 133, 89 n. 138, 326–7
1:4–6	339		
1:8	75, 95 n. 169, 264–5	2:15	86–87 n. 126, 95 n. 169, 148 n. 47, 276–7
1:9	116 n. 44, 117		
1:10	339	2:16	118 n. 47, 143–4, 147–51, 148 n. 47, 149 n. 48, 150 n. 52, 152 n. 59, 153 n. 61, 340
1:11	95 n. 169, 264–5		
1:12	210 n. 158, 264–5, 339		
1:14	72 n. 74, 264–5, 340	2:20	199, 201–2, 211–3, 278–9, 340–1
2	51, 52 n. 11, 154 n. 65		
2:1	69, 73, 95 n. 169, 266–7	3:2	47 n. 1, 112–4, 126–8, 128 n. 85
2:2	66 n. 48, 72 n. 74, 266–7	3:3	85, 85 n. 118, 87, 89 n. 138, 326–7
2:3	66 n. 48–49, 73 n. 81, 81, 95 n. 169, 232–5, 266–7, 308–9	3:4	95 n. 169, 278–9
		3:5	312–3
2:4	154 n. 65	3:6	278–9
2:5	66 n. 49, 71 n. 67, 71–72, 73 n. 81, 266–9, 286 n. 102	3:7	87–88, 88 n. 133, 125
		3:8	192 n. 99, 278–9
2:7	72 n. 74, 268–9, 271 n. 70	3:9	85, 85 n. 118, 279 n. 88, 326–7
2:8	105–6, 109–10	3:10	95 n. 169, 278–81, 279 n. 88
2:11	49–52, 52 n. 12, 66 n. 48, 72 n. 74, 226–7, 268–9, 340	3:13	80 n. 96, 95 n. 169, 280–1
		3:16	75, 280–1
3:1	71, 71 n. 63, 95, 268–9		

Zephaniah

*	21 n. 80
1:2	72 n. 74, 80, 95 n. 169, 205, 205 n. 143, 280–1
1:3	86–87 n. 126, 205
1:4	90, 95 n. 169, 282–3, 328–9
1:5	84 n. 113, 88 n. 133, 89 n. 141, 96 n. 173, 328–9
1:9	95 n. 169, 282–3
1:11	75, 83, 83–84 n. 109, 86–87 n. 126 and 128, 87, 96 n. 173, 199, 201–13, 204–5 n. 141, 205 n. 145, 221, 282–3, 328–9, 341
1:15	105–6, 110–2, 117, 118 n. 44
1:17	95 n. 169, 112–3, 117–20, 118 n. 44, 187 n. 80, 282–3
2:2	124 n. 69, 192 n. 100, 218, 284–5
2:4	82–83, 83 n. 108, 284–5, 328–9
2:5	70, 70 n. 60, 83, 83–84 n. 109, 87, 87 n. 129, 284–5, 328–9
2:6	328–9
2:13	84 n. 114, 328–9, 341
2:14	96 n. 173, 330–1, 341
2:15	341
3:3	57 n. 28
3:6	286–7
3:18	205 n. 143
3:19	68, 70, 70 n. 60, 286–7

Haggai

*	21 n. 80
1:1	84, 84 n. 110, 286–7, 330–1
1:5	76 n. 86, 286–7, 312–3
1:7	76 n. 86, 312–3
1:9	95 n. 169, 286–7, 341
1:13	84 n. 112
2:15	76 n. 86, 312–3, 312 n. 12
2:18	76 n. 86, 312–3

Zechariah

1:2	76 n. 86, 79–80, 80 n. 96, 286–7, 312–3
1:3	78–79, 79 n. 91, 86–87 n. 126, 88–89, 88 n. 133, 89 n. 138–9, 314–5, 330–1
1:5	288–9, 341
1:8	188–9 n. 84, 288–9, 288–9 n. 108
1:9	288–9 n. 108
2:9	138 n. 20, 341–2
2:11	69, 95 n. 169
2:12	288–9, 342
2:13	136–42, 139 n. 24, 147, 147 n. 45, 342
3:1	84, 84 n. 110, 330–1
3:8	89 n. 138, 330–1
3:9	288–9
4:2	230–1, 288–9
4:7	75, 290–1, 314–5, 342
4:10	95 n. 169, 290–1
4:14	69, 95 n. 169, 290–1
5:10–11	25 n. 103
6:1	290–3, 291 n. 113–4, 314–5
6:2	292–3
6:3	292–3
6:1–3	95 n. 169, 291 n. 114
6:8	95 n. 169, 119 n. 51, 291 n. 113–4, 292–3
6:12	89 n. 138, 330–1
6:13	99 n. 1
7:2	123 n. 65, 332–3
7:13–14	342
7:14	343
8:12	292–3
9:1	94 n. 168, 96 n. 173, 332–3
9:6	292–3
9:9	40 n. 178
9:12	95 n. 169, 292–3
9:15	67, 69–70, 95 n. 169, 142 n. 34, 147 n. 45, 271 n. 71, 294–5
9:16	95 n. 169, 294–7, 294 n. 121–3, 332–3
10	332 n. 24
10:1	95 n. 169, 296–7
10:2	95 n. 169, 296–9, 332–3
10:3	95 n. 169, 298–9, 332 n. 24
10:4	95 n. 169, 300–1
10:8	95 n. 169, 300–1
10:10	82–83, 83 n. 108, 332–3
10:11	117, 118 n. 44
11:1	74, 300–1, 332–3
11:2	326 n. 14, 332–3
11:3	70, 95 n. 169, 300–3

11:7	55–56, 58–9, 230–1, 334–5		196 n. 111–2, 197 n. 117–8, 211 n. 164
11:8	75, 302–3		
11:10	58	32	33 n. 142
11:12	302–3	38	33 n. 142
12	145, 154 n. 65	42:8	174–5, 174 n. 34, 182 n. 60
12:2	118 n. 47, 142–54, 146 n. 37 and 40, 147 n. 45, 150 n. 53, 151 n. 56, 152 n. 59, 154 n. 65, 218	46	33–4
		49	209
		49:8	155, 157–60, 157 n. 77
		49:13	205–10, 206 n. 146, 207 n. 150, 209 n. 156
12:4	118 n. 47, 120, 120 n. 54, 143–4, 149–51, 152 n. 58	51	33 n. 142
		60	154 n. 65
12:12	314–5	60:5	143–4, 151–2, 151 n. 56–57, 152–3 n. 60
13	334 n. 29		
13:5	302–3	65:2	204–5 n. 141
14	334 n. 29	65:8	110–1, 110 n. 27, 111 n. 31
14:5	88, 90 n. 145, 96 n. 173, 334–5	68	139 n. 24
14:10	343	68:10	136–9, 139 n. 24
14:21	87, 87 n. 129	68:19	104 n. 16
Malachi		68:25	109, 110 n. 25
		69	189 n. 85
*	21 n. 80	85:8	127, 127 n. 82
3:1	40 n. 178, 79 n. 91, 84, 84 n. 112, 314–5, 334–5	90:10	122, 122 n. 61, 123 n. 63
		93:4	174–5, 174 n. 34, 181–2, 182 n. 59
3:8	66 n. 48, 72 n. 74, 302–3, 303 n. 140		
		94:17	209–10, 209 n. 156
3:10	302–3	95:11	192 n. 99
3:24	343	102	33 n. 142
Psalms		106:26	137–8, 138 n. 22–23, 139 n. 24
*	4	107:27	153, 153 n. 62
1	37 n. 168	110	36
1–22	37 n. 169	110:6	108
1–150	37 n. 169	111:9	135
1:2	37	111:10	158, 158 n. 78
4	37	116:11	194–5 n. 107, 197–8, 197–8 n. 120, 210
4:4	127, 127 n. 82		
4:5	206–7, 206 n. 146, 207 n. 150	116:13	148–9, 148 n. 47
5:6	123 n. 65	118:5	112–7, 116 n. 44, 119, 128, 150 n. 52
5:12	166 n. 3		
6	33 n. 142	130	33 n. 142
10:12	137–8, 138 n. 22–3, 139 n. 24	138:7	126, 126 n. 77
14	37	142:5	71, 95
14:4	125	143	33 n. 142
16:1	85	*Proverbs*	
17	37		
21:14	138, 138 n. 22	*	4
31:23	9 n. 31, 120, 120 n. 54, 174–5, 194–9, 194–5 n. 105–7,	3:25	110–1, 111 n. 31

Job
*   4
7:1   183 n. 64
9:23   116–7, 116 n. 44
13:25   119, 183, 187 n. 80

Song of Songs
*   21 n. 80

Ruth
*   21 n. 80

Lamentations
*   21 n. 80

Ecclesiastes
*   4, 21 n. 80, 122 n. 61, 123 n. 63

Esther
*   4, 21 n. 80

Ezra
*   21 n. 80

Nehemiah
*   21 n. 80

[2] Chronicles
30:17–18   147 n. 43

Deuterocanonical Books

Wisdom of Solomon
*   7 n. 25

Ecclesiasticus / Sirach
*   7 n. 25

[Sir.] 24:7   178–9

Maccabees
*   7 n. 25

New Testament

Matthew
2:2   189 n. 88
12:39–40   195–6 n. 110
25   178

Luke
1:28   93, 104 n. 16,
21:25   110, 110 n. 27

John
11:55   146–7

Romans
3:28   62
8:26   184–5 n. 72
9:15   36 n. 162
10:15   36 n. 162

1 Corinthians
10:13   127, 127 n. 82

Galatians
2:14   177 n. 44

James
5:5   161–2 n. 86

2 Peter
1:19   153, 153 n. 62

Revelation
*   149
14:10   148, 148 n. 47
18:6f   148, 148 n. 47

Other Ancient and Medieval Texts

Jewish

Ḥayyim Jacob b.

Jacob Ben Chajim Ibn Adonijah's Introduction to the Rabbinic Bible 21 n. 84

Ibn Ezra, R. Abraham

Commentaries on the Prophets (Former and Latter) 25
Commentaries on the Psalms and other books 21, 24, 33, 35

Jonathan / R. Yonatan ben Uziel / Jonathan ben Uzziel / Pseudo Jonathan

Babylonian Targum on the prophets / Targum of Jonathan 25, 25 n. 103, 27
Jerusalem Targum / Targum Pseudo-Jonathan 25 n. 103
Targum remarks cited by Rashi
 - MG, *Jeremiah* [ספר ירמיהו], 40 [Jer. 5:27] 163, 163 n. 91
 - MG, *The Twelve Minor Prophets* [ספר תרי עשר], 230 [Hab. 2:16] 149 n. 48
 - MG, *The Twelve Minor Prophets* [ספר תרי עשר], 230 [Zeph. 1:11] 204 n. 138

Josephus, Flavius

The Jewish War
 - *J. W.* 1.11.6 [§ 229] 147 n. 43

Kimhi, R. David / RaDaK

מכלול *(Mikhlol)* 25, 25 n. 107, 27 n. 108, 28
ספר השורשים *(Sefer ha-Shorashim)* 27 n. 108
Commentaries on the Prophets (Former and Latter) 25, 27, 27 n. 112, 31 n. 134, 163, 163 n. 91
Commentaries on the Psalms and other books 21, 24, 24 n. 100, 33, 35

Kimhi, R. Moses

מהלך שבילי הדעת *(Mahalakh Shevilei ha-Da'at)* 25–27

Levita, Elijah / Elijah b. Asher ha-Levi

Masoret ha-Masoret (Venice, 1538) 28

Pirqei Eliyahu (Pesaro, 1520) 28
Sefer ha-Baḥur (Rome, 1517; Basel, 1525) 28
Sefer ha-Harkava (Basel, 1525) 28

Naḥmanides / R. Moses b. Naḥman / RaMBaN

Commentary on the Pentateuch 22

Onkelos

Targum Onkelos 21, 21 n. 83, 25

Rashi / R. Solomon b. Isaac / Shlomo Yitzhaki

Commentaries on the Prophets (Former and Latter)
 - * 25, 25 n. 104
 - MG, *Jeremiah* [ספר ירמיהו], 40 [Jer. 5:27] 163, 163 n. 91
 - MG, *The Twelve Minor Prophets* [ספר תרי עשר], 160 [Jon. 2:5] 191 n. 95
 - MG, *The Twelve Minor Prophets* [ספר תרי עשר], 230 [Hab. 2:16] 149 n. 48
 - MG, *The Twelve Minor Prophets* [ספר תרי עשר], 246 [Zeph. 1:11] 204 n. 138
 - MG, *The Twelve Minor Prophets* [ספר תרי עשר], 328 [Zech. 12:2] 154 n. 65
Commentaries on the Talmud, Psalms, and other books 21, 24, 24 n. 98, 33, 35

Saba, R. Abraham

Zeror ha-Mor (Venice, 1523) 22

Tanḥum b. Joseph Ha-Yerushalmi

Commentary on the Book of Jonah 195–6 n. 110

Various Authors and Contributors / Author Unknown

Hekhaloth Books 167–8, 167–8 n. 10
Pirkei Heikhalo 167–8, 167–8 n. 10
Sefer Yetsira 167–8, 167–8 n. 10
Toledot Yeshu 167 n. 9
Zohar 167–8, 167–8 n. 10, 175–6, 176 n. 37, 195–6 n. 110

Christian

Adrianus, Matthäus
Hebrew grammar and other Hebrew books 27, 27 n. 113 and 116

Altenstaig, Johannes
Vocabularius theologie (Hagenau, 1517) 171 n. 29

Aurogallus, Matthäus / Matthäus Goldhahn
Compendium Hebreae Grammatices (Wittenberg, 1523) 27, 27 n. 113
Hebrew grammars, one of which was published 14 n. 52

Bodenstein, Andreas / Andreas Karlstadt
Distinctiones Thomistarum (1507) 12 n. 40

Bonaventure
Commentaria in Quatuor Libros Sententiarum Magistri Petri Lombardi
- II Sent., d. 39, a. 2, q. 1, ad 4   184 n. 70
- II Sent., d. 39, a. 2, q. 3, ad 5   184 n. 70

Intinerarium mentis in Deum, in *Opera omnia*
- Itin. 1.6; Opera 5.297b   195 n. 109
- Itin. 7.4; Opera 5.312b   195 n. 109

Böschenstein, Johannes
Twelve Hebrew books between 1514 and 1524, including Hebraicae grammaticae institutiones (Wittenberg, 1518) 27, 27 n. 113

Burgos, Paul von / Burgensis / Solomon ha-Levi / Paul de Santa María
Additiones 1–1100 ad postillam Nicolae de Lyra, Gen.-Apoc. (Lyon, 1490) (*see also* Jerome, *Textus biblie* ...) 23–24, 23–24 n. 96–97
Translations of portions of the Psalms 23

Capito, Wolfgang F.
Hebraicarum Institutionum Libri Duo (Basel, 1518; Strasbourg, 1525) 28, 31 n. 134

Institutiuncula in Hebraeam Linguam (Basel, 1516) 28

Cassiodorus
Commentary on the Psalms 33 n. 142

Cordatus, Conrad
Tagebuch (1537)
- 250 [§ 976]   64 n. 44
- 250 [§ 978]   64 n. 44
- 250 [§ 979]   64 n. 44
- 254 [§ 992]   217 n. 1

Cyril of Alexandria
Commentary on the Twelve Prophets 192 n. 101

Denck, Hans and Ludwig Hätzer
Alle Propheten nach Hebräischer Sprach verteutscht / Wormser Propheten (Worms, 1527) 3–5, 5 n. 20, 23, 23 n. 95, 191 n. 95

Dionysius the Areopagite / Pseudo-Dionysius
Mystical Theology
- Chs. 1 and 5   177 n. 43
- Ch. 1, 1000 C-D   177–8 n. 46

Erasmus / Desiderius Erasmus Roterodamus / Erasmus of Rotterdam
Instrumentum: Novum instrumentum omne, diligenter ab Erasmo Roterdamo recognitum ... una cum Annotationibus (Basel, 1516) 17, 17 n. 60, 28, 28 n. 117, 36, 36 n. 162, 189 n. 88

Gerson, Jean
De mystica theologia
- *Tractus primus speculativus*, Pars 6, Consideratio 29, 4   195 n. 109
- *Tractus primus speculativus*, Pars 7, Consideratio 35, 3   195 n. 109

Giustiniani, Agostino
Polyglot Psalter (Genoa, 1516) 28–29

Jerome / Hieronymus

Commentarii in Prophetas Minores
- * 24, 24 n. 101, 25 n. 104, 30 n. 130
- CCSL 76:19 [Hos. 2:3] 200 n. 130
- CCSL 76:397 [Jon. 2:4] 182 n. 61, 183 n. 64
- CCSL 76:398 [Jon. 2:5] 192 n. 101
- CCSL 76A:622 [Hab. 3:2] 128 n. 85

Commentariorum in Hiezechielem
- CCSL 75:12 [Ezek. 1:10] 184 n. 71

iuxta Hebraicum 23, 196–7

Late fourth century translation of the New Testament from Greek to Latin 175

Vulgate 13 n. 46, 19 n. 71, 30, 33–34, 33 n. 148, 42, 47–215, 218, 220, 226–335

Kessler, Johannes

Sabbata 1–2, 1 n. 1–3, 222–3, 223 n. 5

Lascaris, Constantine

De octo partibus orationis liber primus (Venice, 1500) 11–12 n. 39

Lefèvre d'Étaples, Jacques / Jacobus Faber Stapulensis

Qvincvplex Psalterium: Gallicum. Romanum. Hebraicum. Vetus. Conciliatu[m] (Paris, 1509)
- * 23, 49–50 n. 8
- Fols. 50v, 242r [Ps. 30:28 / 31:23] 197, 197 n. 117–8
- Fols. 92v, 253r [Ps. 59:3 / 60:5] 152–3 n. 60
- [Ps. 115:5 / 116:11] 197–8 n. 120

Lombard, Peter

Libri Quattuor Sententiarum 12–13, 13 n. 46, 184 n. 70

Luther, Martin

BIBLES AND RELATED TEXTS

Das Alte Testament deutsch (1523) 4
Das Ander teyl des alten Testaments (1524) 4

Brescia Bible (Brescia, 1494) [Luther's personal Hebrew Bible]
- * 19–21, 19–20 n. 75, 21 n. 77–81, 22 n. 86, 33, 36–37
- Fol. 416r [843] [Joel 1:7] 304–5 n. 2
- Fol. 419v [850] [Amos 5:5] 124
- Fol. 422r [855] [Jon. 1:9–10] 121
- Fol. 423r [857] [2:9] 61, 191
- Fol. 426v [864] [Nah. 1:3] 155 n. 66
- [1181] 20
- [1192] 20

Deutsche Bibel
- history of translation, compilation, and editions 4–7, 7 n. 25, 39–40, 39 n. 175, 40 n. 176
- text citations and references 47–343

Das Dritte teyl des alten Testaments (1524) 4

Handexemplar des Alten Testaments (1538/39) / Handschriftliche Einträge ins Alte Testament 1538/39
- background 7, 7 n. 26, 40, 40 n. 177
- text citations and references 47–215, 226–343

Preface to the Old Testament 90
Die Propheten alle Deudsch (1532) 5–6
Revisionsprotokolle (revision commissions and records)
- background 7, 7 n. 26, 13–16, 14 n. 54, 33, 40–41, 40 n. 176–7, 41 n. 182
- text citations and references 47–215, 226–343

Septembertestament (New Testament translation) 93 n. 161
Vulgata-Revision 1529 125–6 n. 75
Vulgate, Luther's personal copy 13 n. 46, 23–24 n. 96, 30, 30 n. 129, 34

LECTURES AND COMMENTARIES

Additio in locum Hoseae cap. 13 (1545) 4–5 n. 17, 25 n. 103, 40 n. 179
Galations (1516–17) 36, 177 n. 44
Genesis (1535–45) 119 n. 51, 222
Hebrews (1517–18) 32 n. 137, 36
In Oseam prophetam annotationes (Basel, 1526) 4, 4–5 n. 17
Isaiah (1528–30) 17 n. 60, 65 n. 46, 139 n. 25, 152 n. 58, 208–10, 210 n. 159

Jonah, Habakkuk, and Zechariah, commentaries (1526–27)
- history, compilation, and editions 4–5, 5 n. 18, 7, 24–25, 25 n. 103, 40–41, 40 n. 178, 41 n. 180–2
- text citations and references 47–215, 226–343

Minor Prophets, lectures (1524–26)
- history, compilation, and editions 4–7, 4–5 n. 17–18, 7 n. 27, 40–41, 40 n. 178–9, 41 n. 180–2
- text citations and references 47–215, 226–343

Psalms
- * 31–39, 119 n. 51
- *Dictata super Psalterium (1513–15)* 13, 35–38, 37 n. 169, 101 n. 10, 116 n. 44, 117, 135, 135 n. 16–17, 159 n. 80, 167 n. 9, 168 n. 12, 170 n. 23, 189 n. 85–86, 194–9, 194–5 n. 107, 195 n. 108, 196 n. 112, 197 n. 118, 200 n. 131, 204–5 n. 141
- *Operationes in Psalmos (1519–21)* 13, 35–38, 37 n. 169, 85, 123 n. 65, 135, 166 n. 3, 200 n. 131
- *Scholien zum 118. Psalm. Das schöne Confitemini 1529* 115, 115 n. 40, 117, 119, 128, 150 n. 52

Romans (1515–16) 36

BRIEFWECHSEL (LETTERS)
* 90
Feb. 22, 1518 letter to Spalatin [§ 61] 168 n. 12
May 22, 1519 letter to Spalatin [§ 179] 10–11 n. 37
June 1, 1521 letter to Francis Von Sickingen 2 n. 5
June 10, 1521 letter to Spalatin [§ 417] 2 n. 5
Jan 13, 1522 letter to Amsdorf [§ 449] 14 n. 54
Mar. 5, 1522 letter to Frederick the Wise [§ 455] 1–2 n. 4
May 29, 1522 letter to Johann Lang [§ 501] 13 n. 46
Nov. 3, 1522 letter to Spalatin [§ 546] 4 n. 11

Dec. 11, 1522 letter to Spalatin [§ 553] 16 n. 57
Dec. 12, 1522 letter to Spalatin [§ 556] 16, 16 n. 57
Feb. 23, 1524 letter to Spalatin [§ 714] 4, 4 n. 15
May 4, 1527 letter to Spalatin [§ 1099] 23 n. 95
May 4, 1527 letter to Linck [§ 1100] 23 n. 95
June 14, 1528 letter to Linck [§ 1285] 16, 16 n. 57, 97, 97 n. 175
Oct. 10, 1531 letter to Spalatin [§ 1872] 5, 5 n. 22

SERMONS
Am dritten sontag des Advents Euangelium [Matth. 11, 2 –10] (1522) / Adventspostille 197–8, 197–8 n. 120
Predigt am Palmsonntag, nachmittags / Die palmarum Vesperi (1540) 40 n. 178
SERMO in die Purificationis Mariae (1517) 40 n. 178
Ein Sermon auff das Ewangelium [Joh. 8, 46.]. Quis ex vobis arguet me de peccato. Johannis. viij.(1523) 93 n. 161
Über das erste Buch Mose, Predigten sampt einer Unterricht, wie Moses zu leren ist (1523/24) 9, 9 n. 32, 159, 159 n. 81
Was Christus fur ein konig und wie es umb sein konigreich gethan sey, aus dem propheten Michea am funfften Capittel geprediget (1532) 40 n. 178

TISCHREDEN ("TABLE TALK")
* 90
[§ 1040] 10, 10 n. 35, 27, 27 n. 110, 217 n. 1
[§ 2771a] 64, 64 n. 44, 68
[§ 2779a] 217, 217 n. 1
[§ 3503] 188–9 n. 84, 191 n. 95, 194, 194 n. 104
[§ 4777] 9–10, 10 n. 34
[§ 5026] 18–19 n. 70
[§ 5324] 222, 222 n. 4

OTHER WRITINGS

Betbüchlein (1522) 93 n. 161
De captivitate Babylonica ecclesiae praeludium (1520) 170 n. 23
Das Magnificat verdeutschet und ausgelegt (1521) 208
Randbemerkungen zu Taulers Predigten 169–70 n. 21, 178 n. 47, 181 n. 57
Rationis Latomianae confutation (1521) 2 n. 5
Resolutiones disputationum de indulgentiarum virtute (1518) 9 n. 31, 112 n. 34, 157–60, 158 n. 78, 164
Sendbrief vom Dolmetschen (1530) 8, 23 n. 95, 41–42, 62, 90–97, 218
Sprichwörtersammlung
 – * 65–66 n. 48
 – [§ 16] 303 n. 141
 – [§ 97] 295 n. 124
 – [§ 115] 303 n. 141
 – [§ 144] 302 n. 136
 – [§ 145] 290 n. 111
 – [§ 245] 258 n. 42
 – [§ 267] 242 n. 15
 – [§ 340] 271 n. 71
 – [§ 409] 301 n. 135
 – [§ 412] 235 n. 2, 241 n. 13
 – [§ 444] 241 n. 13
Summarien über die Psalmen und Ursachen des Dolmetschens (1531–33) 8, 41–42, 90–97, 218
Theologia Deutsch, Preface (1516 and 1518) (see Author Unknown, in this Index)
Vom Schem Hamphoras und vom Geschlecht Christi (1543) 166 n. 3, 167 n. 9
Von Abrahams Anfechtung und Trost 197–8, 198 n. 121
Von den letzten Worten Davids (1543) 90
Zu den Sentenzen des Petrus Lombardus. 1510/11 12–13, 13 n. 46

Lyra, Nicholas von

Postilla on the Minor Prophets 25, 25 n. 104
Postillae perpetuae in vetus et novum testamentum (see also Jerome, *Textus biblie* ...) 23–24, 23–24 n. 96–97
Translations of portions of the Psalms 23

Manutius, Aldus

Introductio perbrevis ad hebraicum linguam (Venice, 1500) 25 n. 106

Marschalk, Nikolaus

Introductio ad litteras hebraicas utilissima (1501) 11–12 n. 39
Introductio perbrevis ad hebraicam linguam (ca. 1502) 11–12 n. 39

Mathesius, Johannes

Historien, Von des Ehrwirdigen in Gott seligen theuren Manns Gottes, D. Martin Luthers, Anfang, Lere, Leben, Standhafft bekentnuß seines Glaubens, unnd Sterben, Ordenlich der Jarzal nach, wie sich solches alles habe zugetragen, Beschriben Durch Herrn M. Johann Mathesium den Eltern 13–15, 13–14 n. 50, 15 n. 55

Melanchthon, Philip

May 21, 1519 letter to Spalatin [§ 179] 10–11 n. 37
Dec. 26/27, 1521 letter to Spalatin [§ 191] 178 n. 47

Münster, Sebastian

'Arukh ha-Shorashim, Dictionarium hebraicum (Basel, 1523) 28
Chaldaica grammatica antehac a nemine attentata ... (Basel, 1527) 28, 31 n. 134
Dictionarium chaldaicum (Basel, 1527) 28, 31 n. 134
Dictionarium hebraicum (1539) 31 n. 134
Hebraica Biblia [Latina] (1534–35; 1546) 22, 22 n. 86 and 88–90, 31 n. 134
Reprint of Levita's Masoret ha-Masoret (Basel, 1539) 28

Oecolampadius, Johannes

1528 Isaiah commentary (a printing of his lectures) 17 n. 60

Pagninus, Santes

Enchiridion expositionis vocabulorum Haruch (Rome, 1523) 28
Thesaurus linguae sanctae lexicon Hebraicum (Lyons, 1529) 28, 31 n. 134

Translation of David Kimhi's מכלול
(Mikhlol) (Lyons, 1526) 25 n. 107, 28

Pellikan, Konrad

De modo legendi et intelligendi Hebraeum (Strasbourg, 1504) 25 n. 106, 28, 28 n. 117, 36, 36 n. 162

Hebraicum Psalterium (Basel, 1516) 23

Reuchlin, Johannes

Codex Reuchlinianus 3 (manuscript of the prophets from 1105) 27, 27 n. 112

De accentibus et orthographia linguae Hebraicae (Hagenau, 1518) 27, 31 n. 134

De arte cabalistica (Hagenau, 1517) 168, 168 n. 12

De rudimentis Hebraicis / Rudimenta / Rudimenta Hebraica (Pforzheim, 1506)
- * 12, 12 n. 42, 13 n. 46, 24–25 n. 102, 25–29, 25 n. 106, 36, 36 n. 162, 123 n. 63
- *Rudimenta*, 42 26
- *Rudimenta*, 187 196, 196 n. 114
- *Rudimenta*, 334–5 156 n. 70
- *Rudimenta*, 370 276–7 n. 81
- *Rudimenta*, 406–7 57 n. 28
- *Rudimenta*, 495 154 n. 65
- *Rudimenta*, 502 111 n. 31
- *Rudimenta*, 510 111 n. 31

De verbo mirifico (Basel, 1494) 168, 168 n. 12

In septem psalmos poenitentiales hebraicos interpretatio / Septem Psalmi poenitentiales Hebraici cum grammatica Latina (Tübingen, 1512) 23, 27, 36, 36 n. 162

Spengler, Lazarus

1520 letter to Pirkheimer 22 n. 86

Tauler, Johannes

Sermons
- * 169, 169–70 n. 21
- *1509 Augsburg edition* 178 n. 47
- *1521 Basel edition* 178 n. 47

- *In omnibus requiem quesivi [Sir. 24:7]* 178–9
  - Fols. 54r–58v [201–7] 178–9, 179 n. 48
  - Fol. 57v [206.4–5] 178–9, 179 n. 48
- *Predigten zu einen recht christlichen Leben [25] (Basel, 1521)*
  - Fol. CCXXXIIIr 178, 178 n. 47
- *Renovamini spiritu mentis vestre*
  - Fol. 101r [259.1–5] 195 n. 109

Wakefield, Robert

Oratio de laudibus & utilitate trium linguarum Arabicae Chaldaicae & Hebraicae, atque idiomatibus hebraicis quae in utroque testamento inveniuntur (London, 1524) 17, 17 n. 61

Zamora, Alphonso of

Vocabularium hebraicum totius veteris testamenti cum aliis dictionibus chaldaicis ibi contentis (1520) 28–29, 29 n. 123

Various Authors and Contributors

Glossa Ordinaria 23, 23–24 n. 96, 30 n. 129, 195–6 n. 110

Textus biblie cu[m] Glosa ordinaria Nicolai de Lyra postilla, Mortalitatibus eiusdem, Pauli Burgensis Additio[n]ibus, Matthie Thoring Replicis Prima [-Sexta] (Basel,1506–08)
- * 23–24 n. 96, 30, 30 n. 129, 49–50 n. 8
- Vol. 3, fol. 169r [Ps. 59:3] 152–3 n. 60
- Vol. 3, fol. 228v [Ps. 92:4] 182 n. 59
- Vol. 4, fols. 87r–88v [Is. 51:17] 152–3 n. 60

Author Unknown [with introduction by Luther]

Theologia Deutsch [Der 'Frankfurter' / Eyn geystlich edles Buchleynn / Ein deutsch Theologia] 169–70, 169–70 n. 21, 170 n. 22, 176, 176–7 n. 42, 200–1, 206–7

Index of Hebrew, German, Latin, and Greek Terms[1]

Hebrew Terms

[אבד] וְאָבַד 71, 95, 246–7
אֲבוֹתֵיכֶם 79–80, 155, 312–3
[אבל] אָבְלָה 234–5, 238–9
הָאֶבֶן 288–9, 294–5, 332–3
אָדֹם 288–9, 292–3
אֲדֹנָי 89 n. 138, 160, 161 n. 84, 252–3, 262–3
אָדָם 113, 118, 282–3, 302–3
אֲדָמָה 238–9, 280–1, 296–7
אָוֶן (see also בֵּית אָוֶן) 87–88, 87–88 n. 132, 113, 122–6, 123 n. 63 and 65, 125–6 n. 75, 179, 179 n. 49, 181 n. 57, 219, 226–7, 248–9, 258–9, 318–21, 324–5
אוֹפָן 50, 53–54, 228–9
אוֹר 252–3, 306–7
אַחַר 288–9
אֵיךְ 191, 191 n. 95, 201, 205–6, 205 n. 145
אֵין (particle) 106, 236–7, 298–9
אַיִן (noun) 200–1
וְאֵיפֹת 89–90, 324–5

אִישׁ 75, 113, 121, 143, 155, 202, 240–1, 258–9, 288–9, 306–7
אַךְ 174, 189–94, 191 n. 95, 218
אָכוֹל 242–3, 304–5
אַכְזִיב 324–5
[אכל] וְאָכְלוּ 56, 68–69, 72, 106, 240–3, 270–1, 274–5, 294–5, 304–5, 310–1
אֶל (preposition) 79, 88, 112, 114, 143, 146, 160, 174–5, 179–81, 188–9, 191 n. 95, 193, 242–3, 306–7, 318–9, 334–5
אֵל (see also בֵּית-אֵל) 137, 160
אַל (particle) 113, 137, 232–3, 308–9
אֱלֹהִים 137, 155, 254–5, 302–3
בְּאַלְפֵי 155, 262–3
אִם 161 n. 84, 192 n. 99, 201, 246–7, 250–1, 258–9, 302–3
אָמוֹן 326–7, 326–7 n. 15
אַמִּצִים 292–3
[אמר] אָמַרְתִּי 105, 112, 160, 174–5, 186–7, 194–5 n. 107, 196, 197–8 n. 120, 202
אֲמִתַּי 84, 320–1

---

[1] Hebrew terms and phrases are listed alphabetically by main term or root. I normally retain noun prefixes and suffixes "as is" in the Hebrew Bible, though I eliminate hyphenated prefixes. In those instances, the pointing is retained "as is" (as with terms pulled from construct state). In order to aid the reader, Hebrew nouns appear in bold where it may be otherwise confusing to identify the indexed term. Verbs generally appear alphabetically by root, with that root in brackets. Different binyans generally appear as separate line items. Participles appear with or without roots, depending on the context.

For all terms, generally only one conjugation appears on any given line item. Likewise, I only include one orthographical variation for each term (minor orthographical differences exist throughout medieval Bible editions, literature, and colloquial language). Where different parts of speech share very similar forms (i. e. Latin nouns and verbs), entries are often consolidated. Nevertheless, page numbers for occurrences of all conjugations and orthographical variations are provided.

Finally, transliterations appear "as is" in the references; these are not true German and Latin forms.

אָנָה 252–3
אֲסִירֵי 292–3
אָסֵף[אסף] 80, 143, 205, 205 n. 143–4, 312–3
אַף־יְהוָה 284–5
אֵפוֹד 85, 316–7
הָאֵפֶר 67, 67 n. 55, 69, 256–7
אֵצֶל 88, 88 n. 137, 334–5
כָּאַרְבֶּה 72, 106, 272–3, 310–1
אַרְבֶּעָה 105, 244–5, 304–5
אֶרֶץ 50, 161 n. 84, 202, 204 n. 138, 234–5, 252–5, 262–3, 306–7, 332–3
וַאֲרַשְׂתִּיךְ[ארש] 79, 304–5
אֵשׁ 50, 106, 136, 240–1, 310–1
בְּאַשְׁדּוֹד 292–3
אַשּׁוּר 262–3

בָּבֶל 69, 288–9
בֶּגֶד[בגד] 75, 149 n. 49
בַּדָּיו 238–9
בָּא[בוא] 56, 75, 78–80, 113, 124 n. 69, 160, 161 n. 84, 162, 201, 218, 244–5, 250–3, 272–3, 280–1, 284–5, 310–1, 311 n. 10, 314–5
וַהֲבֵאתִי[בוא] 252–3, 258–9, 306–7
וְהַבֹּטְחִים 250–1
וּמִבְטָן 236–7
בְּטֶרֶם 124 n. 69, 218, 284–5
בְּיַד 84, 242–3, 286–7, 330–1
בֵּין 74, 256–7
בַּיִת- (see also וְהַר הַבַּיִת) 123, 123 n. 65, 143–4, 161, 163 n. 91, 324–5
בֵּית אָוֶן (see also אָוֶן) 87, 123 n. 65, 124–5, 124 n. 68, 316–7
בֵּית־אֵל 113, 122–3, 123 n. 65, 219, 248–9, 320–1, 332–3
בֵּית יְהוּדָה 144
בֵּית יִשְׂרָאֵל 250–1
בְּבֵית לְעַפְרָה 67, 70, 85, 256–7, 322–3
[בלג] הַמַּבְלִיג 248–9
בִּלְתִּי 246–7
בָּמֹתֵי 256–7, 260–1
בֵּן 69, 84, 136, 155, 290–1, 290 n. 112, 320–1
בָּנָה[בנה] 71, 258–9
בַּעֲדִי 254–5
בַּעְלִי 89, 270–1, 316–7
בְּפָנָיו 236–7

בְּצֶעָם 262–3
[בקע] בִּקְעָם 246–7
מִבְקַעַת 318–9
בְּקָקִים [בקק] / בָּקְקוּם 81, 81 n. 103, 266–7
בְּקֶרֶב שָׁנִים 114, 126–8
בַּבְּקָרִים 250–1
בְּרֻדִּים 292–3
בַּרְזֶל 244–5, 260–1
בְּרִיחַ 246–7, 254–5
כַּבְּרָקִים 71–72, 268–9
[בשל] בָּשֵׁל 244–5
בָּשָׁן 326–7, 332–3
בַּת 69, 260–1, 288–9

גָּאוֹן 232–7, 308–9
גּוֹי 143, 284–5, 285 n. 100
וְגָלָה 230–1
נָגוֹזּוּ[גזז] 264–5
גָּלוּת/הַגְלוֹתָם[גלה] 80, 246–7, 304–5
וְגָלִיךְ 174–5, 181–3, 182 n. 60, 186–7
כַּגְּלִילִים 113, 282–3
גִּלְעָד 82–83, 244–7, 318–9, 332–3
נְגֵרַשְׁתִּי[גרש] 174, 186–7
גַּת 244–5

דָּבָר 312–3
[דבר]וְדִבַּרְתִּי 234–5
[דהר]דֹּהֵר 50, 53–54, 228–9
[דוש]דּוּשָׁם 244–5, 260–1
הַדּוֹלֵג 282–3
דָּם 50–51, 54–55, 71, 95, 143, 146 n. 39, 230–1, 242–3, 258–9, 268–9
[דמה]נִדְמָה 75, 201–11, 203 n. 136, 205 n. 145, 207 n. 149, 282–3
[דקק]וַהֲדִקּוֹת 262–3
דֶּרֶךְ 155, 240–1, 266–7, 286–7, 312–3

ה (interrogative) 192 n. 99, 246–7, 250–1, 278–9, 279 n. 87, 288–9, 302–3, 303 n. 140
הֶבֶל 60, 298–9
הוֹדוֹ 298–9
הוֹי 276–7
[היה]וַיְהִי 113, 122–3, 143, 174, 180–1, 188, 219, 248–9, 260–1, 320–1
וְהַהֵיכָל 174, 189–94, 191 n. 95, 202, 268–9
[הלך]הֹלֵךְ 75, 246–7, 258–9, 312–3

Hebrew Terms

יִתְהוֹלָלוּ [הלל] 266–7, 267 n. 61
הָמוּ [המה] 67–68, 70, 294–5
הֲמוֹנִים 232–3
הִנֵּה 78–79, 143, 160, 161 n. 84, 246–7, 288–9, 314–5
הַס 201–2, 211–2, 212 n. 167
הַר 69, 244–5, 266–7, 278–9, 290–1, 314–5
וְהַר הַבַּיִת 260–1
וְהַר הָהָר 79, 264–5, 308–9
מֵהַר עֵשָׂו 113, 121, 306–7
הָרוֹת 246–7
וּמֵהַרְיוֹן 236–7

מִזְאָבֵי 56–57, 57 n. 28, 230–1, 272–3
כְּזָוִיֹּת מִזְבֵּחַ 67–68, 70, 294–5
בַּזּוֹנָה 228–9
זוֹעָה 117, 129
[זכר] לְהַזְכִּיר 250–1
וּזְמֹרֵיהֶם 266–7
בִּזְנוּנֶיהָ 270–1
[זעק] וַיִּזְעַק 292–3
[זרע] יִזְרַע 264–5
[זרע] יִזְרְעוּ 236–7
זֶרַע (noun) 292–3

חֹבְלִים/חֶבֶל 56, 58–59, 58 n. 29, 70, 284–5, 334–5
בְחָגְוֵי 254–5, 320–1
חַגַּי 84, 286–7, 330–1, 331 n. 23
[חדד] וְחַדּוּ 56, 272–3
חַדְרָךְ 94 n. 168, 332–3
כָּחוֹל 274–5
וְחֹמֶר 85, 316–7
חוֹמַת 252–3
חוּצוֹתָם 266–7, 286–7
[חוש] חָשׁ 56, 274–5
חֹשְׁבֵי 324–5
[חזה] וְתַחַז 75, 260–1
חָזוֹן 274–5
חֲזִיזִים 296–7
[חיה] וְחָיוּ 248–9, 288–9
חֵילָם 242–3, 262–3
וַחֲלֹמוֹת 298–9
הַחַמָּה 149
חָמָס 250–1
חֵן 75, 290–1, 314–5
[חנה] הַחוֹנִים 272–3

[חנף] תֶּחֱנָף 228–9
חַסְדָּם 60–62, 61 n. 35, 62 n. 38, 232–3
בְחָפְזִי 175, 194–99, 194–5 n. 107, 196 n. 111–2, 197 n. 117, 197–8 n. 120
[חרב] הֶחֱרַבְתִּי 286–7
חֶרֶב 105–6, 310–1
חָרוֹן 284–5
הֶחָרוּץ 232–3, 244–5
[חרם] וְהַחֲרַמְתִּי 262–3
[חרש] יַחֲרוֹשׁ 250–1
[חרש] תֶּחֱרַשׁ 260–1
[חשך] וְהַחְשַׁכְתִּי 252–3, 306–7
[חשף] חָשֹׂף 304–5, 304–5 n. 2
[חתת] וְחַתּוּ 113, 119–20, 196 n. 112, 197 n. 119

טוֹב 302–3
הֵטִיל ... [אֶל־]/[טול] הֵטִיל 174, 179–81, 188

[יבש] הוֹבִישׁ 238–9, 239 n. 10
יָגוֹן 125 n. 75
יָדִי (see also בְּיַד) 136–138, 145, 278–9
יָדַע [ידע] 74, 136, 191 n. 95, 240–1, 256–7
יְהוּדָה 143–4, 262–3, 282–3
יָמִין and יְהוָה, אַף-יְהוָה צְבָאוֹת (see also יְהוָה)
50, 79–80, 89 n. 138, 105, 112–4, 136–7, 144–5, 155, 160, 161 n. 84, 174–5, 179–81, 202, 232–3, 250–1, 254–5, 262–3, 290–1, 306–7, 312–3
יְהוָה צְבָאוֹת 78–79, 88–89, 89 n. 138, 136, 202, 314–5, 326–7, 330–1
יְהוֹשָׁפָט 242–3, 318–9
יוֹם 106, 110–1, 144, 161 n. 84, 242–3, 252–3, 284–5, 306–7, 312–3
יוֹנָה 79, 84, 306–7, 322–3, 322 n. 9
הַיֶּרֶשׁ 258–9
יוֹשֶׁבֶת 70, 82–83, 86, 201–4, 204 n. 138, 212–3, 232–3, 256–9, 257 n. 39, 282–5, 322–5, 328–9
יִזְרְעֶאל 234–5, 316–7
יַחְדָּו 246–7
יַיִן 67–68, 70, 75, 143–4, 148–51, 151 n. 56, 294–5
יְלָלַת 300–1

Index of Hebrew, German, Latin, and Greek Terms

חֵלֶק 72, 72 n. 71 and 73, 106, 270–1, 310–1
הַיָּם 70, 79, 174–5, 179–81, 254–5, 264–5, 284–5, 308–9
יְמִין יְהוָה 144, 149
יְמִינוֹ (see also יְמִין יְהוָה) 74, 256–7
יְסוֹד 280–1, 280 n. 90
[יעד]יְעָדָהּ 50, 52–53, 228–9
[יעד]נוֹעֲדוּ 246–7
יַעֲקֹב 232–3, 308–9
יַעַר 260–1, 260 n. 46
יָפוֹ 322–3, 323 n. 11
[יצא]יָצָא 73, 105, 264–5, 272–3, 312–3
הַיִּצְהָר 69, 290–1
הַיְקָבִים 244–5
[ירא]יְרֵא 50, 114, 254–5
[ירד]רְדוּ 244–5
הַיַּרְדֵּן 70, 302–3
יְרוּשָׁלַ͏ִם 143, 145, 260–1, 282–3
וְהַיָּרֵחַ 242–3
[ישב]וְיָשַׁב 67, 67 n. 55, 69, 256–7, 288–9 n. 108, 292–3
יִשְׂרָאֵל 136, 160, 204 n. 138, 234–7, 250–1, 308–9
יַחַד 300–1

[כבד]וּמַכְבִּיד 276–7
[כבד]הִתְכַּבֵּד 72, 72 n. 73, 106, 109, 270–3, 310–1
כָּבוֹד 144, 288–9
וְכָבֵד 75, 106, 108–9, 268–9
כּוֹכָב 248–9
כּוֹס 145, 149, 152–3, 152 n. 59, 153 n. 61
כּוֹס יְמִין יְהוָה 144
בְּכַחַשׁ 238–9
כִּיּוּן 89, 320–1
כָּלוּב 160–4, 163 n. 91, 218, 252–3
הַכְּמָרִים 89–90, 328–9
כְּנַעַן 87, 87 n. 128, 201, 282–3, 318–9, 328–9
כְּנַעֲנִים 87
כְּפִירִים 302–3
כָּרֹת 328–9
[כרת]יְכָרֵת 113, 121–2, 201, 306–7
[כרת]תִּכְרִיתָךְ 106, 310–1
כְּרֻתִים 82–83, 83–84 n. 109, 284–5, 285 n. 100, 328–9

כְּשָׁפִים 270–1
[כתר]מַכְתִּיר 226–7

לֹא 74, 105, 113, 124 n. 69, 143, 154–61, 161 n. 84, 192 n. 100, 218, 232–3, 250–3, 256–7, 264–5, 274–7, 284–5, 306–9
וְלֹא ... לָנֶצַח 73, 272–3
לֹא רֻחָמָה 316–7
לָהֶם (see also שִׂימוּ לְבַבְכֶם) 106, 109–10, 174, 234–5, 238–41, 254–5
לְבַד 314–5
לְבָנוֹן 74, 82–83, 300–1, 332–3
לְבָנִים 292–3
[לבש]וַיִּלְבְּשׁוּ 67, 69, 256–7
מִלָּדָה 236–7
וְלֶהָבָה 240–1
[להט]לְהָטָה 240–1
לוֹ (particle) 75, 258–9
וּלְחָמָם 113, 282–3
לְעוֹלָם 254–5, 288–9
כַּלַּפִּידִים 71 n. 67, 268–9
לִפְנֵי 105, 107, 136–7, 174, 177–9, 254–5, 312–3

חַסְדָּם (see םָ-)
מִגְדָּל 260–1, 324–5
מַגָּל 244–5
מִדְבָּר 137, 240–1
[מוג]נָמוֹג 268–9
הַמֹּכֶרֶת 270–1
כְּמֹץ 238–9
הַמּוֹרָה 73, 232–3, 242–3
כַּמִּזְרָק 67–68, 70, 147 n. 45, 294–5
מָטָר בְּעֵת מַלְקוֹשׁ 296–7, 296 n. 125
לְמִישֹׁר 290–1
מִכְתָּם 85, 85 n. 119
מִכְתָּם לְדָוִד 85
הַמַּכְתֵּשׁ 82–83, 83–84 n. 109, 201–4, 204 n. 138, 212–3, 282–3, 328–9
[מלא]וּמְלָאוּ 67–68, 70, 161, 163, 244–5, 294–5
מַלְאָכִי/מַלְאָךְ 84, 84 n. 112, 334–5
וּמְלֵאָה 250–1
בַּמִּלְחָמָה 298–9
מַלְכָּם 84, 84 n. 113, 89, 105, 318–21, 328–9
מַמְזֵר 292–3

Hebrew Terms

מִנֶּגֶד עֵינֶיךָ 174–5, 186, 211 n. 164
מָנוֹס 71, 95, 246–7
מַסָּה/לְמַסֵּת 117, 129
מְעוֹרֵיהֶם 276–7, 277 n. 83
וְמַעֲלָה 312–3
מַעֲלָלָיו 258–9
מִפָּנָיו 50, 202, 211–3, 278–9
הַמִּפְתָּן 282–3
מָצוֹר 143, 262–3
לְמִצְפָּה 318–9
הַמֵּצַר 113–9, 128–9
מַרְאֵיהֶן 71 n. 67, 268–9
וּמֶרְכָּבָה 50, 53–54, 228–9
מָרֵשָׁה 258–9, 324–5
מִשְׁבָּרֶיךָ 174–5, 180 n. 54, 181–8, 181 n. 58, 182 n. 60, 187 n. 80
וּמְשׁוֹאָה 106, 110–2, 111 n. 31
מִשְׁפָּחוֹת 314–5
מִשְׁפָּט 73, 238–9, 272–3
הַמַּשְׁקוֹף 143, 145–6
מַשָּׂא 264–5
מָתְנַיִם 50, 67, 69, 252–3

נָא 312–3
נָאוֹת 240–1
[נאם] נְאֻם 144, 161 n. 84, 306–7
[נבט] הַבִּיט 174, 189–94, 191 n. 95, 276–7
הַנָּבִיא 286–7
[נבל] וְנִבַּלְתִּי 270–1
הַנֶּגֶב 82–83, 83–84 n. 109, 320–1
[נגשׁ] וַתִּגַּשׁוּן 250–1
נָהִי/[נהה] וְנָהָה 79, 306–7
נָהָר 174, 262–3, 268–9, 278–9
מִנּוֹא 326–7, 326–7 n. 15
[נוה] יָנְוֶה 143, 274–5
נֹעַם 56, 58–59 n. 31, 230–1, 334–5
[נוף] מֵנִיף 136–42, 138 n. 20, 139 n. 24–25, 141–2 n. 33
נְוֹת 328–9
נֵזֶר 294–5, 295 n. 124, 332–3
נַחוּם 84, 324–5, 325 n. 13
נְחוּשָׁה 262–3
נְחֹשֶׁת 290–3, 314–5
נַחַל 204 n. 138, 244–5
[נחם] וְנִחָם 240–1
[נחם] יְנַחֲמוּן 298–9, 298 n. 30
[נטף] יִטְּפוּ 232–3, 244–5, 308–9, 309 n. 7

נִינְוֵה 174, 264–5, 322–5, 322–3 n. 10, 328–9
מִנְּמֵרִים 56, 272–3
[נסס] מִתְנוֹסְסוֹת 296–7
[נסע] נָסְעוּ 298–9
[נפח] וְנָפַחְתִּי 286–7, 287 n. 105
[נפל] יִפּוֹל 252–3
נַפְשׁוֹ 75, 143, 210, 274–5, 302–3
[נצב] נִצָּב 252–3
[נקה] וְנַקֵּה 154–60, 156 n. 70, 157 n. 76, 218, 264–5, 308–9
נִקָּיוֹן 248–9
[נשׂא] נָשָׂא 136–42, 139 n. 24, 155, 248–9
כַּנֶּשֶׁר 56, 274–5
[נתן] נָתַן 50, 73, 242–3, 248–9, 280–1

[סבב] סְבָבֻנִי 238–9
[סבב] יְסֹבְבֻנִי 174
סָגוֹר 238–9
סוּס 50, 53–54, 56, 144, 228–9, 250–1, 288–9, 292–3, 298–9
וְסוּפָתָה 236–7
סְכּוֹת 89, 320–1
סֶלָה 85, 326–7
סֶלַע 85 n. 118, 250–1, 254–5, 320–1
סַף 142–54, 145–6 n. 37–39, 147 n. 45, 151 n. 56, 152 n. 58–59, 154 n. 65, 218

עַבְטִיט 276–7, 276–7 n. 81
[עבר] עָבַר 75, 105, 113, 174–5, 264–5
עַד (noun) 278–9
עַד-צַוָּאר 280–1
עֵדֶר 260–1, 324–5
[עוף] יְעֹפֵף 56, 274–5
עוֹף 161, 163
[עוק] מֵעִיק 246–7
עַזָּה 82–3, 284–5, 328–9
עַיִן 260–1
עֵינֵי (see also מִנֶּגֶד עֵינֶיךָ) 75, 144, 202, 260–1, 290–1, 302–3
עִיר 50, 71, 95, 174, 262–3, 268–9
עָכוֹר 234–5, 316–7
עַל-רֹאשָׁהּ 230–1, 288–9
[עלה] עָלָה 105, 107, 174, 177–9, 187–8, 254–5
[עלה] וְהַעֲלֵיתִי 67, 69, 106, 252–3
עַם 87, 201–2

עָמָל וָאָוֶן 123 n. 63
עֵמֶק 232–5, 242–5, 316–9
[ענה] וְעָנָה 236–7, 298–9
[ענה] וְעִנְּתֽךָ 210 n. 158
עָסִיס 244–5
עָפָר (see also בְּבֵית לְעַפְרָה) 67 n. 55, 113
עֲצַבִּים 226–7
עֲצִי 240–1
בַּעֲצָמִי 75, 280–1
וְעִקָּרוֹן 284–5, 328–9
עֶרֶב 56–57, 57 n. 28, 230–1, 272–3
[ערה] עָרוֹת 280–1
[ערל] וְהָעָרֵל 144, 147–51, 149 n. 48
[עשה] עֹשֶׂה 68, 70, 286–7
וּבְעֵת (see also מָטָר בְּעֵת מַלְקוֹשׁ) 242–3

פָּארוּר 50–52, 52 n. 12, 226–7, 240–1, 268–9
פֶּגֶר 106, 108
[פדה] פָּדֹה 154–60, 157 n. 76
הַפָּרֵץ 105, 107
[פוש] וּפָשׁוּ 56, 79, 272–3, 310–1, 311 n. 10
[פלש] הִתְפַּלָּשְׁתִּי 67 n. 55, 228–9
פִּנָּה 286, 286 n. 101, 300–1
(מִפָּנָיו) לְפָנָי, בְּפָנָי, and פָּנִים (see also) 50, 240–1, 268–9, 280–1
[פעל] / פֹּעַל 114, 125, 310–1 n. 9
[פרח] וּפָרַח 238–9
וּפַרְסֹתַיִךְ 262–3
פָּרָשָׁיו 56, 79, 106, 272–3, 310–1
וּפִתְאֹם 78–79, 314–5
[פתח] פָּתוֹחַ 79–80, 270–1, 302–3, 308–9
[פתח] נִפְתְּחוּ 79–80, 268–71, 308–9
בִּפְתָחֶיהָ 228–9

צָאנָן 86, 232–3, 258–9, 324–5
לִצְדָקָה 73, 232–3, 242–3
בַּצָּהֳרַיִם 252–3, 284–5, 306–7
צֹאן 56, 298–9
צוֹם 69, 240–1
צִיּוֹן 71, 75, 258–61
צֶמַח 89 n. 138, 330–1
[צפה] צַפֵּה 266–7
צָרָה 106, 112–9, 128–9, 140
צָרוֹר 252–3
[צרר] וַהֲצֵרֹתִי 113, 118–9, 282–3

קָאַת 330–1
[קבע] הֲיִקְבַּע and interrogative] 302–3, 303 n. 140
[קבץ] קִבְצוּ 50–52, 52 n. 12, 226–7, 240–1, 268–9
[קדש] קַדְּשׁוּ 69, 240–1
קָדְשֽׁךָ (adjective) 174, 189, 191, 191 n. 95, 193, 202
וְקָדוֹשׁ (noun) 89 n. 138, 326–7
קוֹל 50, 53–54, 106, 112, 117, 175, 228–9, 280–1, 300–1, 330–1
[קום] קוּמִי 137, 145, 174, 260–1
וְהַקּוֹסְמִים 296–7
מִקְטָל 113, 121–2, 121 n. 57, 306–7
קִינָה 248–9
קַיִץ 160–4, 252–3
קִיקָיוֹן 228–9
מַקֵּל 71, 95, 246–7
[קלל] וְקַלּוּ 56, 272–3
קָמָה 236–7
[קנה] הַקְנַנִי 302–3
הַקֵּץ 160–4, 252–3
קָצִיר 244–5
קֶצֶף / [קצף] קָצַף 79–80, 286–7, 312–3
[קצר] יִקְצֹרוּ 75, 236–7, 302–3
[קרא] קְרָאתִי 50, 56, 112–4, 174
הַקְּרִיּוֹת 86, 86 n. 121, 318–9
קַרְנַיִם 260–1, 278–9, 278 n. 85

כָּרֹאשׁ (multiple meanings) 105, 230–1, 238–9, 280 n. 90, 288–9
[רבב] [כַּ]רְבָם 234–5, 235 n. 3
[רבה] [הֲ]מַרְבֶּה 276–7
לְרַגְלָיו 155, 312–3
בְּרֹגֶז 126–8
רוּחַ 75, 174, 179–81, 236–7, 258–9
רֹעֶה 298–301, 328–9
[רוץ] הֲיָרֻצוּן and interrogative] 250–1
[רוץ] יְרוֹצֵצוּ 71–72, 268–9
[רחב] הָרְחִיב 143, 274–5
בָּרְחֹבוֹת 268–9
מֵרָחוֹק 56, 79, 272–3, 310–1
רַחֲמָיו (see also לֹא רֻחָמָה) 105, 107–8
[רכב] רֹכֵב 144, 288–9, 288–9 n. 108
רָעָה 79, 79 n. 93, 174, 177–9, 254–5, 306–7
רַעַל 142–54, 149 n. 48–49, 150 n. 53, 151 n. 55–56, 152 n. 58–59, 154 n. 65, 218

German Terms   385

וַיֵּרַע[רעע] 79, 79 n. 93, 306–7
רַעַשׁ 50, 53–54, 228–9
רָקָב 75, 280–1
מְרַקֵּדָה[רקד] 50, 53–54, 228–9
רֶשֶׁף 312–3, 312 n. 11

שְׁאוֹל 112, 143, 274–5, 318–9
שָׁאוֹן 111, 111 n. 31
לִשְׁבָאִים 244–5
שְׁבִי/[שבה]שְׁבִיתָ 104 n. 16
שִׁבְעָה 262–3, 290–1
שַׁבָּת 250–1
בַּשִּׁגָּעוֹן 118 n. 47, 144, 149–50, 150 n. 53
שָׁאָה 106, 110–2, 110–1 n. 27 and 31
וּמְשֹׁאַת 111, 111 n. 31
שָׁב[שוב] 240–1, 232–3, 306–7
שֹׁד 248–9
בְּשַׁחַד 258–9
שׁוֹט 50, 53–54, 228–9
הַשִּׁיקוּ[שוק] 244–5
שְׁחֹרִים 292–3
יְשַׁחֲרֻנְנִי[שחר] 232–3
שִׁחֲתוּ[שחת] 105, 107–8, 266–7
הַשִּׁטִּים 244–5
וּבְשֶׁטֶף 75, 264–5
יְשׁוֹרֵר[שיר] 330–1
שֹׁכְנֵי[שכן] 210, 254–5
שָׁלוֹם 73, 266–7, 292–3
שְׁלִישָׁה 105, 155, 244–5, 304–5
שָׁלְחוּ[שלח] 136, 244–5
שְׁלֹמֹה 80, 246–7, 304–5
בְּשֵׁם 50, 250–1, 264–5
וּשְׁמֹנָה 262–3
הַשָּׁמַיִם 50, 254–5, 302–3
מַשְׁמִיעַ[שמע] 73, 266–7
הַשֶּׁמֶשׁ 252–3, 306–7
שְׁנֵי 56, 246–7, 290–1

שָׁנַיִם 248–9, 304–5
שַׁעֲרֵי 268–9
יִשְׁפְּטוּ[שפט] 258–9
שָׁפִיר 256–7, 322–3
וְהִשְׁקָה[שקה] 244–5, 276–7
יִשְׁתַּקְשְׁקוּן[שקק] 268–9, 268 n. 62
שֶׁקֶר 298–9
אֶשְׁרְקָה[שרק] 300–1, 300–1 n. 134
וְשָׁתוּ[שתה] 67–68, 70, 144, 147–51,
  294–5

וְשָׁבוֹעַ[שבע] 143–4, 243 n. 17, 305 n. 3
שָׂדֶה 238–41, 260–1
וְהַשָּׂטָן 84, 330–1
וְשָׂם[שים] 143, 260–3, 298–9
שִׂימוּ לְבַבְכֶם 286–7, 312–3
לִשְׂמֹאלוֹ 74, 256–7
שַׂק 67, 69, 252–3, 256–7

כִּתְבוּנָם 226–7
תְּהוֹם 175, 280–1
תַּחְתֵּיכֶם 246–7, 246 n. 22
תֵּימָן 87, 113, 318–21, 326–7
תִּירוֹשׁ 238–9, 239 n. 10
תַּלְמֵי 238–9
תְּמָהוּ[תמה] 80, 152 n. 58, 310–1
וְהִתַּמְּהוּ[תמה] 80, 310–1
בַּתִּמָּהוֹן 144, 149–51, 149 n. 48, 152 n. 58
תְּנוּפָה 136–42, 139 n. 25, 141–2 n. 33
מָתְפָּת[תפף] 106, 109–10
הַתִּקְוָה 292–3, 293 n. 20
תַּרְעֵלָה 144–5, 151–4, 151 n. 55–57,
  152–3 n. 60, 153 n. 61
הַתְּרָפִים 85, 296–7, 316–7, 332–3
תַּרְשִׁישָׁה 322–3
תְּשֻׁאוֹת 75, 290–1

German Terms

abends 56–7, 57 n. 25 and 28, 230–1,
  272–3
abfressen 72, 106, 270–1, 310–1
abgoetterey 87–88, 226–7, 238–9
ablesen / Ableser 81, 81 n. 102, 266–7,
  308–9
Accaron 284–5, 328–9

Achor 234–5, 316–7
Achsib 324–5
acht 262–3
acker 238–41
Adeler 56, 274–5
allenthalben 238–9
am ... hinab 70, 284–5

Amithai 84, 320–1
Anfechtung (*see* Index of Subjects; *see also* tentatio / tentari in this Index)
angesicht 50, 211, 211 n. 163, 236 n. 4, 240–1, 268–9
angezuendet 240–1
Angst (*see also* todesangst) 106, 112–20, 114 n. 35, 115 n. 38–40, 116 n. 41–42, 119 n. 49–50, 120 n. 54, 125, 129
anricht 118, 118 n. 45, 248–9, 249 n. 28
ansehen 268–9
Asdod 292–3
asschen 67, 67 n. 55, 69, 240 n. 11, 253 n. 34, 256–7
Assur 262–3
auch noch 288–9
Auen / Aven / Aphen (*see also* BethAuen / Bethaven / Bethaphen) 87–88, 87–88 n. 132, 122–6, 122 n. 61, 125 n. 74, 179 n. 49, 318–9, 320 n. 5
auff sperret 143, 274–5
auffgericht 296–7
auffkomen 236–7
auffthun 302–3
augen (*see also* von deinen augen) 144, 202, 236–7, 236 n. 4, 290–1
aus machen 68, 68 n. 59, 70, 286–7, 286 n. 103
ausgerottet 113, 121–2, 306–7
austeylen 137, 139 n. 24
awen 240–1
Azal 88, 88 n. 135, 334–5

Baal 88–89, 316–7
Babel 69, 288–9
bald 78–79, 314–5
bange machen / bange 113–20, 115 n. 40, 116 n. 41, 118 n. 47, 119 n. 49–50, 120 n. 54, 129, 144, 149–51, 197–8, 199 n. 126, 282–3, 283 n. 95
Basan 326–7, 332–3
bawet 71, 258–9
becher 142–54, 145–6 n. 36–37, 151 n. 56
becken 67–68, 70, 142–54, 147–8 n. 45, 294–5
beissiger 56, 272–3
bekeret 306–7
berenne 266–7, 266 n. 58

berg (*see also* gebirge) 69, 244–5, 260–1, 266–7, 278–9, 290–1, 314–5
berg des tempels 260–1
besonders 314–5
BethAuen / Bethaven / Bethaphen 87–88, 87–88 n. 132, 113, 122–6, 122 n. 61, 123 n. 66, 124 n. 68, 219, 248–9, 316–7, 320–1
Bethel 113, 122–6, 122 n. 61, 219, 248–9, 320–1, 332–3
betreugt 143
bettler 339–40
beume 240–1
bis an den hals 280–1, 280 n. 90
bitterm 144, 151 n. 56
blasen 300–1, 300–1 n. 134
bleiben 143, 264–5, 265 n. 56, 274–5
bleich 50–52, 52 n. 11, 226–7, 240–1, 240 n. 11, 268–9, 269 n. 66
bleischnur 252–3
blicken 268–9, 268 n. 63
blitze 71–72, 106, 268–9
blossen woffen 228–9
blut 50, 54–55, 71, 113, 143, 230–1, 242–3, 258–9
bosheit 174, 179, 254–5
brausen 111 n. 31, 175
bringen 67, 69, 73, 136, 252–3, 258–9, 267–8
brust 106, 109–10, 110 n. 25, 136

Camarim 89–90, 90 n. 144, 328–9, 328 n. 16–17,
Canaan / Chananitern 87
Chiun 89, 320–1

daumel / Taumel 142–54, 145 n. 36, 151 n. 54 and 56, 153 n. 61
dauon 238–9
demuetigen 210 n. 158, 236–7, 236 n. 4
doch 81, 81 n. 102, 155, 157, 264–9, 268 n. 65, 286–7, 290–1, 290 n. 110, 308–9
dressche 260–1
drey 105, 244–5, 304–5
drinnen 174, 250–1
durch 84, 113, 121, 242–3, 286–7, 306–7, 330–1

Durchbrecher / durch brechen 105, 107

ebene / eben 290–1, 343
Ecken 300–1
ecken des altars 67–68, 70, 294–5
Edele 342, 342 n. 9
Eder 260–1, 324–5
ehe / ehe denn 284–5, 284 n. 96
eherne 262–3, 290–3, 314–5
eilen 56, 274–5
einerndten 236–7
einschenckest 148 n. 47, 276–7
Einwonerin 86, 232–3, 258–9, 324–5
eisern 244–5, 260–1
eitel 298–9, 298 n. 129, 328–9, 342
eiter 280–1
Elend 56, 123 n. 62, 137
ende / zum ende 73, 73 n. 80, 160–4, 252–3, 272–3, 288–9
Enge 115–9, 115 n. 40
Engel 84, 334–5
entbloessest 280–1
entfliehen 71, 246–7, 247 n. 23
entsetzen 50, 114, 197–8, 197–8 n. 120–1
Epha 89–90, 89 n. 142, 324–5
erauff komen 174, 179, 186–8, 254–5
erbarmen 240–1
erben 258–9
erde 50, 252–5
erdencken 226–7
erhebe 136–42, 138 n. 22, 139 n. 24, 180 n. 54
erloesen 155, 157–8
ernd 244–5
erworben 270–1
erzeigen 240–1
essen 56, 57 n. 25, 242–3, 274–5, 304–5
etwas 310–1 n. 9
ewiglich 254–5

fackeln 268–9, 268 n. 63
fallen 106, 148 n. 47, 252–3
faren 61 n. 33 and 35, 71–72, 268–9
fast seer 79, 306–7
Fasten 69, 240–1
feld 238–9, 260–1, 318–9, 343
feldgeschrey 117–9, 118 n. 45
felsen 250–1

felsen kluefften 254–5, 320–1
feser 266–7, 267 n. 60
festen 262–3
feur 50, 106, 240–1, 310–1
finster / Finsternis 47 n. 1 and 2, 106, 252–3, 306–7
flamme 240–1
fliehen / fluchtig 56, 71, 120, 120 n. 52, 246–7, 274–5
flut 174–5, 186 n. 77, 264–5
frembde 276–7, 292–3
fressen 67–69, 106, 271 n. 71, 294–5, 294 n. 121, 310–1
freuel 250–1
freundlich 139 n. 24, 234–5, 235 n. 2
Frieden 73, 266–7, 292–3
fruee 232–3
fur jm 50, 105, 107, 174, 177–9, 202, 236–7, 236 n. 4, 254–5, 278–9, 312–3, 341
furchen 238–9
Furcht (*see also* Angst) 50, 115, 120 n. 54, 198–9
furchte 254–5, 120 n. 54

Galle 238–9, 238 n. 6
Gasa 82–83, 284–5, 328–9
gassen 266–7, 267 n. 61, 286–7, 286 n. 102
gebeine 280–1
geben 50, 73, 73 n. 77, 137–9, 139 n. 24, 232–5, 242–3, 248–9, 308–9
geberen 236–7
gebirge (*see also* berg) 79, 264–5, 308–9
gebirge Esau 113, 121, 306–7
gedacht 174, 186–8
gedencken 250–1
gedienet 136, 302–3
gedrosschen 244–5
gedruckt 115, 115 n. 40, 117
gefangen / gefangenen 80, 104 n. 16, 106, 113, 246–7, 292–3, 304–5
Gefellets 302–3, 302 n. 138
gefilde 343, 343 n. 11
gehen 67, 113, 143, 174–5, 256–7, 278–81, 298–9
gehen einher 250–1
geisseln 50, 53–54, 54 n. 18, 228–9

geklemmt 115, 115 n. 40, 117
gemessen 252–3
geniedriget / Niedrigkeit 208 n. 154, 343
geoeffnet 268–9
gepresset 115, 115 n. 40, 117
gerechtigkeit 73, 73 n. 77
gerewen 240–1
geringe 340
geschencke 258–9
geschlechte 314–5
geschmueckt 298–9, 299 n. 132
geschwigen 206–7 n. 148, 207, 207 n. 150, 338
gesicht 160, 274–5
geweihete 294–5, 295 n. 124, 332–3
gewislich 80, 310–1
Gewissen 186–7, 186 n. 77, 213–4 n. 170, 214–5, 214 n. 174
gewolcken 296–7
gieng aus 312–3
Gilead 82–83, 244–7, 318–9, 332–3
gleich 343
glentzen / glentzenden 106, 278–9, 278 n. 85
glueck zu 75, 290–1, 314–5
gnade 59 n. 31, 60–62, 61 n. 34–35, 62 n. 38, 93, 93 n. 161, 94 n. 168, 155, 232–3, 240–1
gnedigen 73, 73 n. 77, 137–39, 139 n. 24, 232–3, 242–3, 243 n. 16
gnug 201, 242–3, 243 n. 17, 304–5, 305 n. 3
goetzen 89, 226–7, 296–7, 320–1, 332–3
Gott 61 n. 34 and 37, 126 n. 79, 137, 155, 180 n. 53, 186 n. 77, 211 n. 163, 254–5, 302–3
Gottes dienst 61 n. 37, 85, 316–7
grimmiger 284–5
gross 56, 75, 78–79, 106, 108–9, 155, 174–5, 179–81, 180 n. 53, 268–9, 269 n. 67, 272–3, 273 n. 76, 310–1, 326–7
gruenet 238–9
grundfest 280–1, 280 n. 90
gulden kleynod 85
gut 262–3, 276–7
gute mehre 73, 73 n. 78, 266–7

habe (noun) 262–3
Hadrach 94 n. 168, 332–3
Haggai 84, 286–7, 330–1, 331 n. 23
hand 136–42, 138 n. 22, 139 n. 24–25, 145, 278–9
harret 207, 207 n. 150
hauffen 56, 72 n. 69, 75, 78–79, 106, 108–9, 232–3, 260–1, 268–9, 269 n. 67, 272–3, 273 n. 76, 310–1
hause Jsrael 250–1
heilige (adjective) 174, 189, 202, 294–5, 295 n. 124, 332–3
Heilige (noun) 89 n. 138, 326–7
Heiliget (verb) 69, 240–1
Heiligthum 85, 316–7
heimsucht 155, 211–2, 211 n. 163, 212 n. 166 and 168
helle (noun) 112, 143, 274–5, 318–9
hellen (adjective) 252–3, 306–7
Helt (noun) 105, 107
her auff faren 105, 107
her durch brechen 105, 107
her gehen 105, 312–3
herd 298–9
HERR (*see also* rechten des HERRN) 50, 79–80, 89 n. 138, 105, 112–4, 114 n. 35, 136–7, 138 n. 22, 144–5, 148 n. 47, 155, 160, 174–5, 179–80, 202, 232–3, 250–5, 262–3, 290–1, 306–7, 312–3
HERR Zebaoth 78–79, 88–89, 136, 202, 314–5, 326–7, 330–1
[des] HERRN zorn 186 n. 77, 284–5
Herrscher 262–3
hertz 50, 126–8, 126 n. 78, 234 n. 2, 238–41
hertzenleide 122–6, 122 n. 61, 123 n. 63, 125–6 n. 75
heulen 201, 300–1, 301 n. 135
hewschrecken 71–72, 106, 272–3, 272 n. 73, 310–1
hie vnd da 232–3
himel 50, 254–5, 302–3, 303 n. 141
hin richten 207
hin tratt / hin trat 312–3
Hirte 298–301
Hirten heuser 328–9
hoehe 175, 256–7, 260–1, 260 n. 46

German Terms 389

hoere 50, 53–4, 112, 114, 175, 228–9, 280–1, 300–1
hoerner 260–1
hoffart 232–7, 236 n. 4, 308–9
hoffnunge 292–3, 293 n. 120
Homer 83, 316–7
homut 208, 208 n. 151
hub auff 137–42
hub sich [auff] 174, 179–81, 187–8
huetten 89, 320–1
hurerey 270–1
hyn und wider pultert 117

ist dahin 75, 201–8, 203 n. 136, 206–7 n. 148, 207 n. 150, 208 n. 155, 220–1, 282–3, 283 n. 94

Ja 79, 126 n. 78, 194 n. 104, 201, 238–41, 266–7, 304–5, 342
Jacob 232–3, 308–9
Jammer / jemerlich 87–88 n. 132, 113, 117, 122–6, 122 n. 61, 123 n. 62–63, 125–6 n. 75, 234–5, 238–9, 248–9, 249 n. 27, 320–1
Japho 322–3
Jerusalem 73–74, 74 n. 84, 83–84 n. 109, 88 n. 137, 137–8, 143–5, 147 n. 43, 153–4, 203–4, 204 n. 138, 260–1, 282–3, 282 n. 93, 332 n. 25
Jesreel 234–5, 316–7
jglich / jglicher 240–1, 314–5
Jhe mehr 234–5, 235 n. 3
[jnn der] jrre 298–9, 299 n. 131
Jona 84, 306–7, 322–3
Jordans 70, 302–3
Josaphat 242–3, 318–9
Jrregeist 75, 258–9, 259 n. 43
Jsrael (*see also* hause Jsrael) 136, 234–7, 236 n. 4, 308–9
Juda 143, 262–3, 282–3
jungen lewen 302–3
jungfrau 106, 212 n. 66

Kauffman 87, 318–9
kefer 71–72, 72 n. 71 and 74, 106, 270–1, 271 n. 72, 310–1
kelch 144–5, 151 n. 54, 152–3, 153 n. 61
kelter 244–5

keret 178 n. 47, 211 n. 63, 306–7
kinder (*see also* oele kinder) 105, 107–8, 136, 155
Kirioth 85–86, 318–9
kirren machen 119 n. 49, 246–7, 246 n. 22
klagen 78–79, 306–7
klaglied 248–9
klappen 50, 53–54, 228–9
klawen 262–3
kleinmut 337 n. 5
kleyn 206 n. 146, 337–8
kleynlauttig 208, 208 n. 151, 337, 337 n. 5
[ewrn / jr] Koenig / Koenigin 84, 89, 105–6, 148 n. 47, 202, 268–9, 318–21
koernlin 252–3
kome 73, 73 n. 80, 78–80, 113, 115 n. 40, 122–3, 160, 201, 211 n. 163, 248–9, 252–3, 264–5, 272–3, 284–5, 310–1, · 314–5, 320–1
Kompt herab 244–5
korb 160–4, 252–3
kot 113, 282–3
kremer 87, 201, 282–3, 328–9
kriegern 82–83, 284–5, 285 n. 100, 328–9
krumm 343, 343 n. 10
Kuerbis 228–9
kurtz 75, 302 n. 137, 340

ladet 276–7
lagern 272–3
land 234–5, 252–3, 280–1, 281 n. 91, 296–7, 306–7, 332–3, 342, 342 n. 9
Last 264–5
leben 248–9, 288–9
leer 286–7, 286 n. 102
leib 113, 282–3
Leibroeck 85, 316–7
leichnam 106, 108–9
lenden 50, 67, 69, 252–3
Lerer 73, 73 n. 77, 232–3, 242–3
leufft ... vber 244–5, 264–5
leuten 113, 118–9, 148 n. 47, 282–3
Libanon 73–74, 74 n. 83, 82–83, 300–1, 332–3
lies ... auff[s] ... komen 179–81, 180 n. 53, 187–8

linck 256–7
lock 161, 163
Loryhamo 316–7
loser schwetzer 75, 258–9
luegen 238–9, 298–9
lust / lustig 58, 58 n. 29, 59, 59 n. 31, 75, 148 n. 47, 230–1, 260–1, 261 n. 48

mache … auff 260–1
macht (noun) 288–9
Malchom 84 n. 113, 328–9
Maresa 258–9, 324–5
mas 89–90, 324–5
maure 252–3
meer 70, 79, 174–5, 179–80, 180 n. 53, 254–5, 264–5, 284–5, 308–9, 322–3
mehret 276–7
Mensch 59 n. 31, 61 n. 33, 143, 149 n. 49, 170 n. 22, 178 n. 47, 198–9 n. 120, 236 n. 4, 302–3
MICHTHAM 85
mit einander 246–7, 247 n. 24
mittage 82–83, 87, 252–3, 284–5, 306–7, 320–1, 326–7
mitten jnn den jaren 114, 126–8, 126 n. 78–9
Mizpa 318–9
mocht 190 n. 91, 208 n. 151, 302–3, 302 n. 137, 337
moerdischen 57 n. 25, 71, 268–9
Molochs 89, 320–1
mond 242–3
mord 113, 121–2, 306–7
muehe / muehe vnd erbeit 87–88, 123 n. 63 and 66
Muele 82–83, 201–5, 282–3, 328–9
Muenche 89–90, 90 n. 144, 328–9, 328 n. 16
muessige 248–9, 248 n. 25

nahe hinan [… an] 88, 88 n. 135, 334–5
Nahum 84, 324–5, 325 n. 13
namen 50, 74 n. 83, 88 n. 135, 250–1, 264–5, 265 n. 56
narung 340
Negel 300–1
nicht (verb) 62, 71, 74, 124 n. 69, 156, 174, 188–94, 190 n. 91, 192 n. 99, 219, 232–3, 236–7, 246–7, 250–3, 256–7, 274–5, 278–9, 302–3, 306–9
nichts / Nichtigen / Nichtigkeit 60, 149 n. 49, 155–6, 199–215, 206–7 n. 148, 208 n. 152–4, 211 n. 163, 221, 264–5, 264–5 n. 54, 298–9, 308–9, 338–40
niemand 72 n. 69, 155–7, 264–5, 264–5 n. 54, 308–9
Nineue 174, 264–5, 322–5, 322–3 n. 10, 328–9
No (noun) 326–7, 326–7 n. 15
Not (noun) 115–7, 115 n. 140, 123 n. 62, 126–8, 126 n. 78, 127 n. 81, 128 n. 83
nu 312–3

oben drauff 230–1, 288–9
obs 160–4, 252–3
ochsen 250–1
oele kinder 69, 290–1

Pallast 268–9
Parde 56, 272–3
pestilentz 312–3
pferde 288–9
pfluegen / zu pflueget 250–1, 260–1
plage 312–3
poena conscientiarum 182–3, 182 n. 59
predigen (verb) 50, 52–53, 73, 174, 228–9, 266–7
prediget (noun) 59 n. 31, 232–3, 308–9
Propheten 84, 286–7, 330–1

rasseln 50, 53–54, 228–9, 268–9
rat 238–9
Raub / raubisch / beraubt 57, 57 n. 25, 136, 149, 149 n. 49, 342
recht (various) 73, 126 n. 79, 138, 138 n. 22, 162, 162 n. 87, 206, 206 n. 146, 256–9, 258–9 n. 41, 272–3, 302–3, 303 n. 140, 338, 343
rechten des HERRN 144
reden 126–7, 126 n. 78, 138 n. 22, 149 n. 49, 234–5
reder 50, 53–54, 54 n. 18, 228–9
regen (*see also* spat regen) 73, 73 n. 77, 137, 139, 139 n. 24, 232–3, 242–3, 243 n. 16

German Terms 391

Regenten 326–7
regiert 250–1
Regiment 250–1
Reich Arabia 244–5
reiff 244–5
rein / vnreinen 50, 81, 202, 266–7, 266–7 n. 59, 308–9
Reisse 232–3, 244–5
reissen / zureissen 56–57, 57 n. 24, 105, 161–2, 162 n. 87, 246–7
rennen 250–1
reuter 56, 79, 106, 144, 272–3, 310–1
rhordomel 330–1
richten / zurichten 139 n. 25, 143, 258–9, 298–9
rieff [... an] 50, 75, 112–4, 114 n. 35, 175, 290–3
rigel 238–9, 238 n. 7, 246–7
rollen 50, 53–54, 228–9, 266–7
ros 50, 53–54, 56, 144, 228–9, 250–1, 292–3, 298–9
rote 148 n. 47, 288–9, 292–3
Roth 126–7, 126 n. 79
rumorn 67–68, 70, 294–5

saat 236–7
sach gewinnen 73, 272–3, 272 n. 74
sack 67, 69, 252–3, 253 n. 34, 256–7
sagen 197–8 n. 120, 211 n. 163, 232–3, 235 n. 2, 308–9
samen 264–5, 265 n. 56, 292–3
sand 274–5
Sanfft 56, 58–59, 59 n. 31, 230–1, 334–5
Satan 84, 330–1
schaden 87–88, 258–9, 258 n. 42, 324–5
schalen 230–1
schame 276–7
schawet 286–7, 287 n. 104, 312–3
scheckicht 292–3
schelet 304–5
schenden / schanden / schande 144, 270–1, 270 n. 69, 340
schew 120 n. 54, 144, 149–50, 150 n. 51
schlahen 106, 109–10, 110 n. 26
Schlahet ... an 244–5
schlams 276–7, 276–7 n. 81
schlecht 61 n. 33, 211 n. 163, 343, 343 n. 10

schloesser 286–7
schnell 56, 71, 246–7, 272–3
schoene 256–7, 322–3
schreien 50, 53–54, 228–9 (*see also* feldgeschrey)
schuchtern 120, 120 n. 52
schwanger 105, 107–8, 236–7, 246–7
schwartze 52 n. 11, 74, 292–3
schweigen 206–7 n. 148, 338
schwelle 143, 145–7, 145–6 n. 37, 181–2, 282–3, 282 n. 92
schwerd / Schwert 105–6, 310–1
seele 102 n. 13, 120 n. 54, 143, 185 n. 75, 198–9, 199 n. 126, 274–5
seen 236–7
sehen 50–51, 75, 144, 151 n. 56, 160, 162, 174, 189, 202, 211 n. 163, 226–7, 260–1, 261 n. 48, 268–9, 276–7
seien ... eins vnternander 246–7, 247 n. 24
Sela 85, 85 n. 118, 326–7
selbigen 106, 242–3, 290–1, 314–5
setzt / sitzt 61 n. 33, 67, 67 n. 55, 69, 228–9, 253 n. 34, 256–7, 288–9, 288–9 n. 108
Sicchuth 89, 320–1
sicheln 244–5
sieben 262–3, 290–1
sieg 232–5, 308–9
Sihe (interjection) 78–79, 136, 143, 160, 246–7, 288–9, 314–5
singen 97 n. 175, 126 n. 79, 330–1
Sittim 244–5
son 84, 320–1
sonnen 252–3, 306–7
spat regen 296–7
speise 228–9
sprew 238–9, 238 n. 8
spricht 105, 112, 144, 160, 175, 196, 202, 306–7
springen 282–3
stad 50, 71, 88 n. 135, 174, 256–7, 262–3, 268–9, 322–7
starcke 113, 292–3
Staub 113, 155, 342
steine 260–1, 288–9, 294–5, 332–3
stern 248–9

stille 114 n. 35, 201–11, 206 n. 146,
    206–7 n. 148, 208 n. 151, 211 n. 163,
    337–8, 340–1
stoltze 85–86, 143, 232–3, 258–9, 324–5
stracks 240–1, 240 n. 12
straffe (*see also* vngestrafft) 148 n. 47,
    186 n. 77, 240–1
strassen 266–9
streit 298–9
stroeter 236–7
strom 244–5
Stücke 342
sturm 111 n. 31, 155, 180 n. 53
suchen 113, 232–3

tag 57 n. 25, 106, 110–2, 126 n. 78, 242–
    3, 252–3, 284–5, 306–7, 312–3
tal 232–5, 242–5, 316–9
tausenten 155, 262–3
teusscht 302–3, 303 n. 140
Theman 87, 113, 119–20, 318–21
thor 105, 268–9, 268–9 n. 65
thun 115 n. 40, 148 n. 47, 211 n. 163,
    258–9, 283 n. 95, 310–1 n. 9,
    324–5
thurm 260–1, 260 n. 47, 324–5
tieffe 174–5, 186 n. 77, 280–1
tochter 69, 260–1, 288–9
todesangst (*see also* Angst) 183,
    183 n. 63, 187 n. 80
toedten 106, 310–1
toepffen 50–52, 226–7, 240–1, 240 n. 11,
    268–9, 269 n. 66
trachten 250–1, 250 n. 29, 324–5
tragen 236–7, 242–3, 242 n. 15
Traurigkeit 116 n. 43
traurkamer 67, 70, 85, 256–7, 322–3
trewme 298–9
trieffen / treuffen / Treuffe 232–3, 244–5,
    308–9
trifft 232–3, 308–9
trincken 67–68, 70, 74 n. 83, 148 n. 47,
    294–5
troesten / trost 115 n. 40, 298–9
Trübsal 106, 114–7, 115 n. 40, 126–8,
    126 n. 79, 128 n. 83

vber her leufft 264–5

vberfallen 71–72, 106, 109, 186–7,
    186 n. 77, 270–3, 271 n. 72, 272 n. 73,
    310–1
vberforteilet 226–7
verbannen 228–9, 262–3, 262 n. 50
verbrand 240–1
verderben 202, 209–10, 210 n. 158,
    266–7
verdros 78–79, 306–7
verfolgung / verfolget 105, 117
vergehe 202, 208–12, 211 n. 163,
    212 n. 167
vergelten 232–3, 308–9
verkurtzt 340
verlassen (various) 60, 61 n. 33 and 35
    and 37, 97 n. 175, 250–1
verloben 78–79, 304–5
verlorn 71
verriegelt 254–5
verschmacht 9 n. 32, 298–9, 299 n. 131
verstocktes 239–40
verstoerung / verstoerer 201, 248–9
verstossen 174–5, 186–7, 196 n. 111
vertrawen 78–79
verwandelt 242–3
verwundert 80, 310–1
Veter 79–80, 312–3
vier 105, 141 n. 30, 155, 244–5,
    304–5
vmb 105, 228–9, 244–5, 258–9,
    259 n. 44, 304–5
vmb bracht 105, 107–8
vmbgehawen 264–5
vmbgehet 270–1
vmbher gehen 113
vnfal 117
vngestrafft 155–6, 264–5, 308–9
vngestuems 106, 110–2, 155
vngewitter 174, 236–7
vngluck 115–7, 115 n. 40, 125–6 n. 75,
    148, 148 n. 47, 150 n. 52
vnkraut 238–9, 238 n. 6
vnschuldig 155–60, 264–5, 308–9
vnter einander her 71–72, 268–9
vnter euch 118–9, 118 n. 45, 246–7
vntergehen 252–3, 268–9, 306–7
vnterscheid 256–7
vogel 161, 163

vogel baur 161, 163
vol 67–68, 70, 93, 93 n. 161, 94 n. 168,
    148 n. 47, 161, 163, 244–5, 294–5
volck 87, 144, 151 n. 56, 160, 201–2,
    232–3, 282–3, 328–9
von deinen augen 174–5, 186–7
von einem … zum andern 78–79, 264–5,
    264 n. 51, 308–9
von fernen daher 56, 78–79, 272–3,
    310–1
Vrteils 232–3, 244–5

wagen 50, 53–54, 228–9
wandeln 246–7, 247 n. 24
Warsager 296–7, 297 n. 128
wasser 175, 183, 262–3, 268–9,
    268–9 n. 65
wasser flut (*see also flut*) 175
wasser woge (*see also wogen*) 175
weben / Webe 136–42, 138 n. 21–22,
    139 n. 24–25, 141 n. 30, 142 n. 34
weg nehmen 80, 312–3
Weh 56, 58–59, 59 n. 31, 114–7,
    115 n. 40, 202, 276–7, 334–5
wein 67–68, 70, 74 n. 83, 143–4,
    148 n. 47, 151 n. 56, 153, 153 n. 62,
    238–9, 239 n. 10, 244–5, 294–5
weisse 292–3
weiter 80, 246–7, 246 n. 20, 304–5
wellen 174–5, 181–8, 182 n. 59 and 61,
    186 n. 77
welt 139 n. 25, 141 n. 30, 202, 211 n. 163,
    262–3, 278–9, 341, 341 n. 8
wessern 244–5
wetter 106, 110–2, 155, 180 n. 53
widder 113, 137, 238–9
widderumb 240–1
wie es … gehet 286–7, 287 n. 104, 312–3

wind 174, 179–81, 180 n. 53, 236–7
wissen 74, 240–1, 256–7
wogen / Wage 174–5, 180 n. 54, 181–8,
    182 n. 61, 186 n. 77, 215, 221
wol 44 n. 64, 59 n. 31, 242–3, 242 n. 15,
    266–7, 266 n. 58
wolffe 56–57, 57 n. 24–25 and 28, 230–1,
    272–3, 272–3 n. 75
wonen 70, 82–83, 201–4, 254–5, 282–5,
    292–3, 328–9
wuesten 56–57, 57 n. 25, 137, 240–1
wuestunge 342, 342 n. 9

zacken 244–5
Zaenan 85–86, 86 n. 125, 232–3, 258–9,
    324–5
Zagen / Zage 113, 119–22, 120 n. 54,
    128–9, 128 n. 83, 175, 194–9,
    194–5 n. 107, 196 n. 111–3, 197 n. 119,
    197–8 n. 120, 198 n. 122, 199 n. 126
zeit 126 n. 78–79, 144, 242–3
Zemah 89 n. 138, 330–1
zene 248–9, 248 n. 25, 304–5
zermalmt 342
zerspringen 342
zersteube 286–7, 287 n. 105
zeuberey 270–1
zihen 56, 78–79, 105, 272–3, 310–1
Zion 71, 75, 258–61
zogen … an 67, 69, 256–7
zorn / zornig (*see also* [des] HERRN
    zorn) 79–80, 105, 286–7, 312–3
zu pueluert 336, 336 n. 3
zurschmeissen 262–3
zuuor 312–3
zween 56, 143, 246–7, 247 n. 24,
    290–1

Latin Terms

a conspectu 174, 186–7
a facie 50, 175, 194–5, 194 n. 105, 202,
    278–9, 280–1
abducti 106, 298–9
abiectus 174, 186–7, 194 n. 106

absque 316–7
abyssus 175, 280–1
Accaron 284–5, 328–9
acervus 260–1
Achor 234–5, 316–7

Index of Hebrew, German, Latin, and Greek Terms

ad ... de 264–5, 308–9
[ad] proximum 88, 334–5
Adam 302–3
adapertione 270–1, 308–9
adducam 258–9
adfiget 302–3
adflictus / adflictione 117, 182 n. 59, 298–9, 306–7
adgravat 276–7
admiramini 310–1
adnuntiantis 266–7
adprobabit 50, 52–53, 228–9
adpropinquatis 250–1
Adrach 332–3
adtondentur 264–5
adversitates 117, 182, 182 n. 59
aedificatis 258–9
aedituorum 328–9
aereas 262–3, 290–3, 314–5
affectus 43, 101, 101 n. 10, 103, 116 n. 42, 117, 129, 181 n. 56, 188–94, 195 n. 109, 214–5, 219
ager 238–9, 260–1
Aggei 286–7, 330–1
agitatum 110, 110–1 n. 27, 117
albi 292–3
Alexandria 326–7
amaritudo 140 n. 28, 238–9
Amathi 320–1
ambulabunt 113, 118 n. 45, 246–7
amentiam 144, 149–50, 150 n. 50
anamnesis (*see also* synteresis / synderesis) 176 n. 38
angelum meum 334–5
Angulus 286–7, 300–1
angustia 106, 115, 117–9
anima 117, 143, 189, 204–5 n. 141, 209–10, 209 n. 156, 274–5, 302–3
ante / antequam 105, 107 n. 17, 284–5, 312–3
apertae 144, 268–9, 302–3
aquila 56, 274–5
arari 250–1, 260–1
ascendens 50, 53–54, 105, 107 n. 17, 174, 177 n. 45, 179, 228–9, 254–5, 288–9, 288–9 n. 108
aspectus 150 n. 50, 260–1, 268–9, 276–7
Assur 262–3

auferat 117, 118 n. 45
austrum 320–1, 326–7
avibus 161, 163
Azoto 292–3

Baali 316–7
Babylonis / Babylonios 110–1 n. 27, 150 n. 50, 288–9
Basan 326–7, 332–3
bello 120 n. 52, 298–9
BethAuen / Bethaven / Bethaphen 316–7
Bethel 113, 122–6, 122 n. 61, 248–9, 320–1
bibentes 54–55, 55 n. 21, 67–68 n. 56, 145, 152 n. 59, 153 n. 62, 294–5
bombum 117
bonum 302–3
bruchus 106, 109 n. 23, 270–1, 310–1
bubalis 250–1

cadet 150 n. 50, 252–3
caeli 50, 254–5, 302–3
calamitatis 106, 110–2, 110–1 n. 27, 111 n. 31, 204 n. 138, 206–7, 206 n. 146
calicem 142–54, 152 n. 59, 153 n. 61–62
calix dexterae Domini 144
campo 318–9
cantantis 330–1
captivitatem 110 n. 25, 246–7, 304–5
Carioth 318–9
Chanaan 201, 202 n. 133, 282–3, 318–9, 328–9
choro 316–7
cinere 256–7
circumdedit 144, 174, 238–9
civitas 50, 85–86, 174, 262–3, 268–9
clamavi 50, 112, 114, 175
clangam 117–9, 118 n. 45
cogitationes / cogitatis 58 n. 29, 59 n. 30, 258–9, 324–5
comedet 56, 106, 240–3, 274–5, 304–5, 310–1
comminues 262–3
compunctionis 151–4, 151 n. 57, 152–3 n. 60, 153 n. 62
conceptu 236–7

Latin Terms

concisionis 52 n. 11, 120 n. 52, 232–3, 244–5
concluserunt 254–5
confiditis 250–1
confusum 238–9
congregare 51–52, 51 n. 9, 52 n. 11, 58 n. 29, 72 n. 73, 106, 109, 109 n. 23, 143, 270–1, 310–3
conlisae 268–9
conscientia (*see also* synteresis / synderesis) 43, 173–88, 194–5, 210, 213–5, 213–4 n. 170 and 174–5
consecrarit 136
considunt 272–3
consolabantur 298–9
consopire / soporis 144–54, 148 n. 46, 150 n. 50, 152–3 n. 59–62
conspergite 228–9
constringitur 117
consurgunt / surge 137, 145, 174, 232–3, 260–1
contemplare 266–7
conterrentur 120–1, 121 n. 55
conticuit 201–7, 202 n. 133, 203 n. 135, 206 n. 146–7, 282–3, 337 n. 4
contracta 302–3
contrivit 203–4, 204 n. 138, 337
contumeliis 270–1
conturbas profundum maris 110–1, 110–1 n. 27, 117
conturbati 110 n. 27, 117, 158 n. 78, 266–7, 267 n. 61
convenerit 246–7
convertatur 105, 127 n. 82, 240–1, 337
cor 50, 106, 109–10, 110 n. 25, 117–9, 118 n. 45, 123, 123 n. 64, 125, 150 n. 50, 158 n. 78, 174, 181 n. 56, 234–5, 240–1, 254–5, 286–7, 312–3
coram 105, 107 n. 17, 174, 177–9, 177 n. 45, 195, 254–5
corbem 161, 161 n. 86, 163
cornu 260–1, 278–9
cornua altaris 294–5
corpus 106, 108, 108 n. 21, 113, 282–3
corrasis 202–5, 202 n. 133, 205 n. 143
corruperunt 266–7
crapulae 142–54, 145 n. 35 and 37

culmus 236–7
currere 250–1

dat 204 n. 138, 242–3, 248–9, 276–7, 280–1
de longe 56, 272–3, 310–1
decipula 161, 163
decorabitur (verb) 143, 148 n. 46, 274–5
Decorem (noun) 56, 230–1, 334–5
dentes 248–9, 304–5
denudasti (*see also* nudans / nuditatem) 280–1
descendite 177 n. 45, 244–5
deserti 56–57, 57 n. 24, 230–1, 240–1, 286–7, 341, 343
Deus 118 n. 45, 127 n. 82, 137, 158 n. 78, 160, 177 n. 45, 209 n. 156, 254–5, 302–3
devorabit 67–68 n. 56, 106, 147 n. 44, 161, 161–2 n. 86, 270–1, 294–5, 310–1
dexteram (*see also* calix dexterae Domini) 256–7
diabolus 312–3
dicit 57 n. 24, 64 n. 44, 105, 112, 122 n. 61, 127 n. 82, 144, 150 n. 50, 156 n. 72, 160, 174–5, 182 n. 59, 186–7, 194 n. 105–6, 196, 197–8 n. 120, 202, 202 n. 133, 209 n. 156, 306–7
dies 106, 110–1, 110–1 n. 27, 144, 242–3, 252–3, 284–5, 306–7, 312–3
diffundentur 56, 272–3, 310–1
dilatavit 143, 274–5
diluvio 264–5
dirutum 268–9
discurrentia 268–9
dissecuerit 246–7
dissipaverunt 50, 266–7, 308–9
divini 296–7
doctorem 232–3, 242–3
dolor (*see also* labor et dolor) 125–6 n. 75
Dominus 50, 89 n. 138, 105, 112–4, 122 n. 61, 126 n. 77, 127 n. 82, 136–7, 140 n. 26, 142 n. 34, 144–5, 150 n. 50, 153 n. 62, 155, 158 n. 78, 160, 174–5, 179–80, 181 n. 56, 202, 211 n. 164, 250–5, 262–3, 290–1, 306–7, 312–3, 342

396 Index of Hebrew, German, Latin, and Greek Terms

Dominus exercituum 89 n. 138, 136, 202, 314–5, 326–7, 330–1
domo Pulveris 256–7, 322–3
domum Dei 123 n. 65, 332–3
domum Israhel 250–1
domum Iuda 144
domus 143, 161, 324–5
dorsum 252–3
dulcedinem 244–5
duo pariter 246–7
duorum 56, 59 n. 30, 290–1

ecce 136, 140 n. 26, 143, 145 n. 37, 160, 246–7, 288–9, 314–5
egredietur 105, 143, 312–3
elationes maris 175, 181–4, 182 n. 59
Electos 238–9
elevasti / elevationes 137, 145, 182 n. 61, 296–7
ephod 316–7
equites 50, 53–54, 54 n. 17, 56, 228–9, 272–3, 310–1
equum 50, 53–54, 54 n. 17, 56, 144, 150 n. 50, 228–9, 250–1, 288–9, 292–3, 298–9
exaequabit 290–1
excelsa 256–7, 260–1
excessu[s] mentis 43, 175, 194–99, 194 n. 105, 195 n. 109, 197 n. 117, 214–5
exemplum 109 n. 23, 153 n. 62, 184–5 n. 72, 302–3
Exitu / exivit 86, 86 n. 123, 232–3, 258–9, 264–5, 324–5
exsuflavi 286–7
extasi 194–9, 194–5 n. 107 and 109, 197 n. 117–8, 204–5 n. 141
exuberant 244–5

faciam 154–60, 156 n. 68, 157 n. 74, 158 n. 78, 174, 205–7, 206 n. 146, 252–3, 264–5, 286–7, 306–9, 337
facies (*see also* a facie) 50–52, 51 n. 9, 52 n. 11, 211 n. 164, 236–7, 268–9, 312–3
falces 244–5
familiae 314–5
fauces 117, 236–7

ferreum 244–5, 260–1
ferventis 50, 53–54, 228–9
festinans / festinatione 56, 194, 194 n. 106, 196 n. 112, 274–5
fialae 294–5
filia 260–1, 288–9
filium 136, 155, 290–1, 320–1
finis 106, 160–4, 162 n. 87, 252–3
flagelli 50, 53–54, 54 n. 18, 58–59, 58 n. 29, 228–9
flamma 54 n. 17, 240–1
fluctus / fluctus maris 117, 174–5, 181–4, 182 n. 59 and 61
fluctus tumultuantes 117
flumen 174, 262–3
fluviorum 268–9
fornicationibus 270–1
fortes 113, 120 n. 52, 292–3
fortitudinem 155, 262–3
frementis / fremitus 50, 53–54, 111 n. 31, 154 n. 65, 228–9
fuga 117, 118 n. 45, 246–7
fulgura / fulgurantis 54 n. 17, 106, 158 n. 78, 268–9
fundamentum 280–1
Funiculos 56, 58–59, 58 n. 29, 284–5, 334–5
furoris Domini 284–5
futurum 312–3

Galaad 244–7, 318–9, 332–3
Gaza 284–5, 328–9
gemitus / gemitus inenarrabilibus 43, 158 n. 78, 184–8, 184–5 n. 72 and 75, 187 n. 79, 194–5, 214–5, 214–5 n. 175
gens 284–5
germinabit 238–9
gladio 54 n. 17, 105–6, 310–1
gloriae 144, 288–9, 298–9
gratia 93, 158, 158 n. 78, 159 n. 79, 290–1, 314–5
gravis / gravis ruinae 106, 108–9, 108 n. 21, 109 n. 23, 173 n. 31, 268–9
grex / Gregis 56, 260–1, 298–9, 324–5
gurgites 174–5, 181–6, 182 n. 59

habitat / habitatores / habitatio 86, 86 n. 123, 201, 203–4, 204 n. 138,

Latin Terms

209 n. 156, 232–3, 250–1, 254–9, 270–1, 282–5, 322–5, 328–9
harenam 274–5
hederam 228–9
heredem 258–9
Hierusalem 143, 145, 145–6 n. 37, 204 n. 138, 260–1, 282–3
Hiezrahel 234–5, 316–7
homo 52 n. 11, 107 n. 19, 113, 118–9, 118 n. 45, 159 n. 79, 206 n. 146, 209 n. 156, 282–3, 302–3
humilitas / humiliatio / humiliabitur 43, 117, 158 n. 78, 185, 185 n. 75, 195, 208, 208 n. 154, 210 n. 158, 236–7
humus 113, 238–9

Iacob 232–3, 308–9
ibit 312–3
idolum 226–7, 318–21
iecoris 238–9
ieiunium 240–1
ignis 106, 240–1, 310–1
ignoscat 240–1
impetus 50, 53–54, 54 n. 17, 110, 110–1 n. 27, 117, 182, 182 n. 59, 228–9
in aeternum 254–5
in manu 242–3, 278–9, 286–7, 330–1
in medio annorum 114, 126 n. 77, 127
inducam 252–3
inebriabuntur 294–5
infernus (*see also resignatio ad infernum* in the Index of Subjects) 112, 143, 209 n. 156, 274–5, 318–9
ingredientes 250–1, 280–3
iniquitatis 155, 179, 179 n. 49, 250–1
innocens 155–60, 156 n. 68 and 72, 157 n. 74, 158 n. 78, 264–5, 308–9
inrigabit 244–5
intereat 113, 121, 121 n. 55, 161 n. 86, 306–7
interfectionem / interficiam 106, 121, 262–3, 286–7
interiora 238–9
inutilis 113, 122–6, 122 n. 61, 181 n. 56, 248–9, 258–9, 320–1, 324–5
invocavi 113–4
Iona 181 n. 56, 306–7, 322–3
Ioppen 322–3

Iordanis 302–3
Iosaphat 242–3, 318–9
ira / iratus 106, 114, 126–8, 127 n. 82, 145, 147 n. 44, 177 n. 45, 286–7, 312–3
ira ... Domini / ira dei (*see also* ira / iratus) 142–54, 153 n. 62, 159 n. 79, 181 n. 56, 182 n. 59, 284–5
iracundia 286–7, 312–3
Israhel 136, 160, 162 n. 87, 234–7, 250–1, 308–9
itineribus 266–7
Iuda / Iudaeos 110–1 n. 27, 143–4, 145–6 n. 37, 262–3, 282–3
Iudicium / iudicabant 108 n. 21, 238–9, 258–9, 272–3
iustitiae 122 n. 61, 232–3, 242–3

labor et dolor 122–3, 122 n. 61, 123 n. 63
lampas 230–1, 268–9
lanceis 228–9
lapidetur 228–9
lapillus 252–3
lapis 260–1, 288–9, 294–5, 332–3
latronum 201, 206 n. 146, 236–7
Leonum 302–3
leviores 56, 272–3
levo 136–42, 140 n. 26, 248–9
Libane 74 n. 83, 300–1, 332–3
ligna 240–1
limen 142–54, 145–6 n. 37–38, 282–3
litum 252–3
loquentes 232–5, 308–9
lucusta 106, 272–3, 310–1
lugebit 51 n. 9, 52 n. 11, 234–5, 238–9
luminis 252–3, 306–7
luna 242–3
lupis 56–57, 57 n. 24, 230–1, 272–3
lutum 276–7, 276 n. 81

magna 54 n. 17, 108, 108 n. 21, 155, 174, 179–80, 181 n. 56, 189–90, 190 n. 90, 193, 193 n. 103, 306–7, 336
maleficia 270–1
malitia 174, 177 n. 45, 179, 254–5
mane 232–3
manu (*see also* in manu) 136–42, 140 n. 26, 145, 153 n. 62

mare 110–2, 110–1 n. 27, 117, 174–5, 179–80, 181 n. 56, 182 n. 59, 254–5, 264–5, 284–5, 308–9
Maresa 258–9, 324–5
maturavit 244–5
Melchom 318–9, 328–9
mendacium / Mendacii 298–9, 324–5
mensura 153 n. 62, 324–5
meridie 113, 252–3, 284–5, 306–7, 320–1
messis 244–5
metent 236–7
milibus 155, 262–3
miseriae 106, 110–1
misericordia 60, 62 n. 38, 105, 107–8, 107–8 n. 19, 114, 127 n. 82, 147 n. 44, 150 n. 50, 155, 181 n. 56, 232–3, 316–7
misit 53 n. 14, 136, 174, 179–81, 181 n. 56, 244–5
molestia cordium 122–3, 123 n. 64, 125, 125 n. 72
Moloch 320–1
mons templi 260–1
monte Esau 113, 121, 121 n. 55, 306–7
montes 244–5, 264–7, 278–9, 290–1, 308–9, 314–5
mors 143, 182 n. 59, 185 n. 73, 187 n. 79, 312–3
Mouere de loco 117
multiplicare 72 n. 73, 106, 109, 109 n. 23, 272–3, 276–7, 310–1
multitudinem 106, 108, 108 n. 21, 234–5
mundans 154–60, 156 n. 68–69, 158 n. 78, 264–5, 308–9
munitas 262–3, 337
munus 136, 258–9
murmurantes 106, 109–10, 110 n. 25, 127 n. 82
murum 252–3

Naum 52 n. 11, 324–5
ne 232–3, 308–9
negatione 238–9
nesciunt 256–7
nigredo 50–52, 51 n. 9, 52 n. 11, 226–7, 268–9, 292–3
nihilum 43, 200–8, 200 n. 131, 202 n. 133, 204 n. 138, 206 n. 146, 336–43

nimium coarctatur 117
Nineve 84–85 n. 114, 174, 264–5, 322–5, 322–3 n. 10, 328–9
nives 296–7
nomine / nominat 50, 58 n. 29, 86 n. 123, 135 n. 17, 204 n. 138, 250–1, 264–5
non (*see also* ut non) 105, 113, 143, 154–60, 156 n. 68, 157 n. 74, 232–3, 236–7, 250–3, 258–9, 264–5, 272–7, 298–9, 306–9, 337, 342
nudans / nuditatem (*see also* denudasti) 276–7, 304–5, 304–5 n. 2
nullusque 154–60
num / numquid 188–94, 190 n. 91, 192 n. 99, 201, 246–7, 250–1, 278–9, 279 n. 87, 288–9

obstupefacti 117–9, 118 n. 45
obstupescite 310–1
occidet 67–68, 121 n. 55, 252–3, 306–7, 310 n. 8
octo 262–3
oculus 54 n. 17, 144, 174–5, 186–8, 194–5, 194 n. 105, 202, 260–1, 290–1, 302–3
offeret / oblate 67–68, 136, 142 n. 34
olei 290–1
ollam 50–52, 51 n. 9, 52 n. 11–12, 226–7, 240–1, 268–9, 336–7, 340
onocrotalus 330–1
Onus 264–5
Oriens 330–1
ossibus 280–1

pacem 266–7, 292–3
pandens 105, 107, 107 n. 17, 270–1, 308–9
pardis 56, 272–3
partu 236–7
pastor 298–301, 328–9
patres 135 n. 17, 155, 312–3
paupertatem / pauperum 56, 137, 341–2
pavore / pavere / pavidus / pavefacit / pavefactione 51 n. 9, 117–20, 118 n. 145, 120 n. 52 and 54, 129, 149–50, 150 n. 50, 185 n. 74, 194–9, 194–5 n. 106–7, 196 n. 112, 197 n. 117 and 119, 199 n. 126

Paxillus 300–1
pedes 153, 153 n. 62, 155, 158 n. 78, 312–3
penuriam 336
perditorum 284–5, 328–9
perfectam 246–7, 304–5
peribit / perii 106, 208–11, 209 n. 156–7, 246–7, 310–1
perturbatione 127–8, 127 n. 82
pervenit 272–3
petrae 250–1, 254–5, 320–1
pilae 201, 203–4, 204 n. 138, 282–3, 328–9
planctum 248–9, 248 n. 26
planitiem 342
planum 290–1, 342
plateis 268–9
plaustris 244–5
plena 93, 160–4, 161–2 n. 86, 244–5
pluviam in tempore serotino 296–7
pomorum 160–4, 161–2 n. 86, 253–4
pompatice 250–1
ponite 143, 145–6 n. 37, 260–3, 286–7, 298–9, 312–3
populi 50, 67–68 n. 56, 143–4, 145–6 n. 37, 160, 161–2 n. 86–87, 201–2, 202 n. 133, 206 n. 146, 232–3, 246–7, 262–3, 304–5, 326–7
portae 268–9
post 288–9
potum 143–4, 148 n. 46, 276–7
praegnantes 246–7
praetereunte 264–5
praevalet adversus 226–7
propagines 266–7
prophetae 51 n. 9, 52 n. 11, 64 n. 42, 67–68 n. 56, 110–2 n. 25 and 27, 122 n. 61, 127 n. 82, 161–2 n. 86, 202 n. 133, 204 n. 138, 209 n. 156, 286–7
propter 56, 121, 234–5, 259 n. 44
prostibulum 228–9
Pulchra 256–7, 322–3
pulvis 155, 158 n. 78, 203–4, 204 n. 138, 238–9, 256–7, 322–3, 337, 341–2
putredo 280–1

quadrigae 50, 53–54, 228–9

quattuor 105, 244–5, 304–5

rapinas 262–3
raptus / rapio 205, 205 n. 143, 214
recorderis 114, 127 n. 82, 250–1
reddidit 107–8 n. 19, 118 n. 45, 155, 162 n. 87, 206 n. 146, 232–3
redigentur 43, 50–52, 51 n. 9, 52 n. 11–12, 199–213, 200 n. 130–1, 202 n. 133, 206 n. 146, 209 n. 156, 226–7, 240–1, 336–43
redimens 154–60, 157 n. 73–74
redistis 306–7
regionis 240–1
replebuntur 144, 153 n. 62, 294–5
requies 328–9
resonantis maris 117
reversi 306–7
rotae 50, 53–54, 54 n. 17, 228–9
rufi 288–9, 292–3

Sabeis 244–5
saccum 252–3, 256–7
sanctificate / Sanctus 135, 135 n. 17, 159, 159 n. 80, 173–4, 189, 189 n. 89, 192 n. 101, 240–1, 294–5, 326–7, 332–3
sanguinem 50, 54–55, 55 n. 21, 113, 143, 145–6 n. 37, 230–1, 242–3, 258–9, 268–9
Satan 330–1
scissuris 50, 254–5, 320–1
scit 240–1
secundum 234–5
sedit 54 n. 17, 256–7, 292–3
semen / seminabitur 236–7, 264–5, 292–3
SEMPER 326–7
[in] sempiternum 288–9
seorsum 314–5
separator 292–3
septem 262–3, 290–1
si 240–1, 302–3
sibilabo 300–1
sidus 248–9
sileat /silentium 202–11, 202 n. 133, 204–5 n. 141, 206 n. 146, 209 n. 156, 337–8
silvarum 260–1

similitudinem 226–7
simulacra 296–7, 332–3
sinistram 256–7
Sion 258–61
sol 252–3, 306–7
solio 250–1
solitudinem 203, 336, 341, 343
somniatores 298–9
sonare / sonum / sonitus 110, 110–1 n. 27, 117
speciosa 240–1, 322–3 n. 10, 328–9
speculationi 318–9
spei 292–3
Spinarum 244–5
spiritum 158 n. 78, 173 n. 31, 184 n. 72, 189, 189 n. 85, 258–9
spoliavit 140 n. 26, 304–5, 304–5 n. 2
sponsabo 304–5
stans 236–7, 252–3
statim 314–5
stercora 113, 282–3
stillabit 232–3, 244–5, 308–9, 308 n. 6
stimulationis 152–3 n. 60
stridebo 246–7
stupore 144, 149–150, 150 n. 50, 194–9, 197–8 n. 117 and 120, 204–5 n. 141, 248–9
suavitate 306–7
subridet 248–9
succendit 240–1
sulcos 238–9
super caput 230–1, 288–9
super vos 246–9, 284–5
superbia 232–7, 308–9
superliminare (*see* limen)
supra 312–3
synteresis / synderesis (*see also* conscientia) 125 n. 72, 173–7, 173–4 n. 33, 176 n. 38–39, 176–7 n. 42, 184, 213–5, 213 n. 169

tabernaculum 320–1
tacui 202, 205–11, 206 n. 146, 209 n. 156, 337
tempestas 155, 158 n. 78, 174, 181 n. 56, 182 n. 59
templum (*see also* mons templi) 174, 189–90, 189 n. 89, 190 n. 91, 192 n. 101, 202, 268–9
tempore (*see also* pluviam in tempore serotino) 127 n. 82, 242–3
tenebrescere 252–3, 306–7
tentatio / tentari 9, 9 n. 30, 61 n. 33, 112 n. 34, 117, 122, 125–8, 127 n. 82, 128 n. 85, 135, 135 n. 18, 140 n. 28, 153–4, 153 n. 62, 158–9, 159 n. 79, 165, 173, 173 n. 31, 180–1, 181 n. 56, 182 n. 61, 183 n. 64, 187, 187 n. 79, 193–4, 194 n. 104, 197 n. 119, 198, 208 n. 154, 209–10, 209 n. 156, 210 n. 159, 221
terra 50, 55 n. 21, 108 n. 21, 158 n. 78, 202, 234–5, 252–5, 262–3, 280–1, 296–7, 306–7, 332–3
Tharsis 322–3
Theman 120 n. 52, 318–9
therafin 316–7
timeo / timor 50, 113–4, 119–20, 120 n. 52 and 54, 158 n. 78, 181 n. 56, 254–5
torcular 244–5
torrentem 244–5
transtulerit 246–7, 304–5
tribulabo / tribulatione 106, 112–9, 118 n. 45, 126–8, 126 n. 77, 140, 140 n. 26 and 28, 198, 282–3
tribus 105, 245–6, 304–5
tristitia 52 n. 11, 115, 116 n. 43, 198 n. 123
tritura 244–5, 260–1
tumores maris 117
tumultus 110–1, 110–1 n. 27, 117, 154 n. 65
turbatione 117, 128, 128 n. 83
turbinem 106, 155, 158 n. 78, 236–7
turris 260–1, 324–5

ululatus / ululate 201, 204 n. 138, 300–1
uncinus 160–4, 161–2 n. 86, 253–4
ungulas 262–3
[usque] ad collum 280–1
[usque] ad finem 272–3
ut non 192 n. 99
utero 236–7

utinam 258–9

vae 202, 276–7
valentibus 110, 110–1 n. 27, 117
valle 204 n. 138, 232–5, 242–5, 316–9
vane / vanitates 60, 199 n. 127, 298–9, 339
varii 292–3
vastante / vastatores 206–8, 206 n. 146, 266–7, 308–9
vastitatem 248–9, 336
vectes 246–7, 254–5
veloce 56, 230–1, 246–7, 272–3
vendidit 270–1
veniens 56, 160, 162, 162 n. 87, 206 n. 146, 244–5, 252–3, 272–3, 284–5, 310–1, 314–5
ventum 110, 110–1 n. 27, 117, 174, 179–80, 181 n. 56, 236–7
verumtamen 174, 188–94, 192 n. 101
vescentes 242–3, 304–5
vespertinis 56–57, 57 n. 24, 230–1, 272–3
vestiti / vestimenta 256–7

vexacio ... conscienciae / vexatio conscientias / vexacio tentacioque conscientiae 179, 179 n. 50, 209, 209 n. 156, 210, 210 n. 159
vexare / uexacio / vexacione 117
viam 155, 158 n. 78, 240–1, 266–7, 286–7, 312–3
vincti 292–3
vinum 143–4, 148 n. 46, 151, 151 n. 57, 153, 153 n. 62, 238–9, 294–5
violaverit 105, 107–8, 107–8 n. 19
vir 113, 121, 121 n. 55, 143, 148 n. 46, 155, 202, 236–7, 240–1, 258–9, 288–9, 306–7
virtutem 242–3
visum 274–5
vivent 288–9, 248–9
vocavit / vox 50, 54, 54 n. 17, 55 n. 21, 56, 57 n. 24, 58 n. 29, 109 n. 23, 112, 118 n. 45, 158 n. 78, 161 n. 86, 162 n. 87, 175, 182 n. 59, 204 n. 138, 228–9, 280–1, 292–3, 300–1, 330–1
volabunt 56, 274–5
vultus 50–52, 52 n. 11, 240–1

Greek Terms

ἆρα 188–94, 192 n. 99
ἔκστασις 194–9
θύραν 142–54, 146 n. 39

πρόθυρα 142–54, 145–6 n. 37
φλιᾶς 142–54, 146 n. 39

Index of Subjects

"קְרֵי and כְּתִיב" (*see also* Hebrew Bibles: Masoretic Text and diachritics) 47
אָיִן (*see* Index of Hebrew, German, Latin, and Greek Terms)

Abelard, Peter 173–5
Adam, Michael 17–18
Adrianus, Matthäus 10–12, 10–11 n. 37, 15–16, 18, 18–19 n. 68 and 70, 27, 27 n. 113 and 116
affectibus propheticis 190, 190 n. 91, 192–4
affectus (*see* "*intellectus* and *affectus*"; and Index of Hebrew, German, Latin, and Greek Terms)
"*Affekt* and *Intellekt*" (*see* "*intellectus* and *affectus*")
Affektenlehre 101, 103, 219
Agricola, Johannes 21–22
Akiba, R. / Akiva R. / Akiba ben Yosef 146 n. 38, 162 n. 89, 167, 167 n. 9, 170
Alemanno, Yohanan 17–18
"alienation effect" (*see* "distancing effect")
Altenstaig, Johannes 171 n. 29
Ambrose 167
Amsdorf, Nikolaus / Nikolaus von Amsdorf 14 n. 54, 15–16, 16 n. 57, 223
anamnesis (and *synteresis*) 176 n. 38
ancient Israelites
– cultural and/or ethno-specific customs, practices, and rituals 67–70, 82–83, 85, 316–35
– ritual language of cultic purification 42–43, 131–64, 220–1

Anfechtung (*see also tentatio / tentari* in Index of Hebrew, German, Latin, and Greek Terms)
– "*Anfechtung* of the prophets" 9, 39, 154, 154 n. 64, 210–1, 211 n. 163
– background and scholarship 8–10, 8–9 Notes 29–30, 10 n. 34
– Luther's Hebrew translation and interpretation, and V, 3 n. 10, 39–45, 61 n. 33, 104, 111–29, 115 n. 40, 116 n. 42–43, 119 n. 50–51, 120 n. 54, 125 n. 73, 128 n. 85, 132, 139–40, 140 n. 28, 147–54, 150 n. 52, 157–60, 164–6, 173, 171–3 n. 30, 179–88, 183 n. 63–64, 187 n. 80, 194, 197–9, 198 n. 121 and 123, 199 n. 126, 208–15, 208 n. 154, 214–5 n. 175, 220–1
– as mystical theology 165
– as "sanctification by terror" (*per terrorem enim sanctificat*) 135, 135 n. 17, 140, 159, 159 n. 80
Angst (*see* Index of Hebrew, German, Latin, and Greek Terms)
animam Bernhardi / den Geist Bernhards 189
apophatic theology (*see* mysticism, medieval: concepts and terminology, Christian)
Aquinas, Thomas 100–1
Arabic language 17 n. 61
Aramaic language (*see also* Hebrew Bibles)
– dictionaries and grammar guides 28
– skills of Christian Hebraists 17 n. 61, 24–25 n. 102
– Targums 13, 21, 27
Aristotle 166–7, 173
"assonance vision" 162, 162 n. 88

Index of Subjects

Augustine 84–85 n. 114, 100–1, 167–70, 170 n. 22, 198, 210
Aurogallus, Matthäus / Matthäus Goldhahn 10–14, 11 n. 38, 14 n. 52–54, 22 n. 88, 27, 27 n. 113, 35 n. 154
Ave Maria 93, 94 n. 168, 104 n. 16

beer, German 74, 74 n. 83
Bernard / Bernhard von Clairvaux 127, 127 n. 82, 167–9, 185, 185 n. 75, 188–9, 189 n. 85, 208, 208 n. 154
Biel, Gabriel 168–9, 173–5, 188
Bodenstein, Andreas / Andreas Karlstadt 11–12, 12 n. 40, 16
Bonaventure 100–1, 168–9, 173–5, 184 n. 70, 188, 195 n. 109
Bora, Katharina von 4
Böschenstein, Johannes 10–12, 10–11 n. 37, 17–18, 27, 27 n. 113
Buber, Martin (*see* German Bibles: Buber-Rosenzweig Bible)
Bucer, Martin 21–22
Bugenhagen, Johannes / "Dr. Pommer" / "Pommeranus" 13–14, 14 n. 53, 225
Burgos, Paul von / Burgensis / Solomon ha-Levi / Paul de Santa María 18 n. 69, 23–24, 23–24 n. 96–97, 24–25 n. 102, 30 n. 129

"Calman" 17–18
Campensis, Johannes / Johannes Campanus 15–16
Capito, Wolfgang F. 15–16, 28, 31 n. 134
Cassian 167
Cassiodorus 33 n. 142, 84–85 n. 114
Christian Hebraism, medieval and early modern
– individuals at the University of Wittenberg 10–15, 24
– individuals outside of the University of Wittenberg 15–17
– Jewish teachers for Christians 17–18
– literary resources 19–31
Christology 55, 55 n. 23, 90, 95, 95 n. 170
Church Fathers 10 n. 36, 163, 166–7, 195 n. 109

Cicero 297 n. 128
Coburg Fortress or Castle / Veste Coburg 5
Conradi, Tilman / Thiloninus Philymnus Syasticanus 10–12, 12 n. 41, 15–16, 16 n. 57
conscientia (*see* Index of Hebrew, German, Latin, and Greek Terms)
Cordatus, Conrad 64 n. 44, 217 n. 1
Cruciger, Caspar 13–14, 13 n. 50, 14 n. 53, 21–22, 22 n. 88, 225
Cyril of Alexandria 192 n. 101

De León, Moses / Moshe ben Shem-Tov 167
Del Medigo, Elia 17–18
Denck, Hans 5, 23
Diet of Augsburg 4
Dietrich, Veit 4–5 n. 17, 15–16, 16 n. 57
Dionysius the Areopagite / Pseudo-Dionysius 166–7, 170, 177, 177 n. 43, 177–8 n. 46, 200 n. 128
"distancing effect" (*see also* "*intellectus* and *affectus*"; and "*Verfremdung* and *Entfremdung*") 100
Drach, Johannes / Draconites 16 n. 57

Eck, Johannes 17–18
Eckhart, Meister / Eckhart von Hochheim 43, 168–9, 169 n. 20, 173–5, 176–7 n. 42, 178 n. 47, 200–1, 204, 206–7, 214–5, 287 n. 104
Einbürgerung (*see also* "*Verfremdung* and *Entfremdung*") 100 n. 5
Einhorn, Werner 18 n. 68
emotion, in language (*see also* "distancing effect"; German language: semantic intensity; Hebrew language: semantic intensity; "*intellectus* and *affectus*"; and "*Verfremdung* and *Entfremdung*") 42, 54, 99–104, 99 n. 2, 108, 111, 112 n. 34, 115, 116 n. 43, 122–30, 151–2, 193, 218–9
Erasmus / Desiderius Erasmus Roterodamus / Erasmus of Rotterdam 4, 16–17, 17 n. 60, 28, 28 n. 117, 36, 36 n. 162, 189 n. 88

"estrangement effect" (*see* "distancing effect")
Evagrius / Evagrius Ponticus 167, 170
excessu[s] mentis (*see* Index of Hebrew, German, Latin, and Greek Terms)

Fagius, Paulus / Paul Büchelin 17–18, 18 n. 67
"faith alone" / *sola fide* / *alleyn durch den glawben*, in Luther's Bible exegesis and translation
– πίστει in Rom. 3:28 62
– parallel חַסְדָּם (*ḥasdām*) in Jon. 2:9 60–62
"fanatics" / *Schwärmer* 4
Fishbane, Michael 133–4, 133 n. 9–10
Flacius Illyricus, Matthias 15–16, 16 n. 57
Förster, Johann 13–15, 15 n. 55
Friedrich III, Elector of Saxony / Frederick the Wise 1–2 n. 4, 4, 10, 18
"*Frömmigkeit* and *Weisheit*" (*see* "*Verfremdung* and *Entfremdung*")
Furcht (*see* Index of Hebrew, German, Latin, and Greek Terms)

Gaon, Saadia 167, 170
gemitus (*see* Index of Hebrew, German, Latin, and Greek Terms)
George, Duke of Saxony 1–2 n. 4, 2
German Bibles
– Buber-Rosenzweig Bible 42, 93 n. 163, 100 n. 5, 101–3, 102 n. 11–13, 103 n. 14, 129–30, 129 n. 87, 130 n. 88–89, 219
– *Deutsche Bibel* (*see* Index of Scriptural, Ancient, and Medieval Sources: Luther, Martin)
– *Einheitsübersetzung* 125–6 n. 75
– fourth century Gothic Bible, fragments 29 n. 125
– Mentel Bible (Strasbourg, 1466) 23 n. 95, 29, 29 n. 127, 33–34, 196 n. 111, 302 n. 138
– Merzdorf *Historienbibeln* 65–66 n. 48, 236 n. 4, 247 n. 24, 254 n. 35, 267 n. 61, 268 n. 63, 271 n. 71, 277 n. 82, 278 n. 85, 295 n. 124, 297 n. 128, 298 n. 129, 299 n. 131–2, 300–1 n. 133–4, 302 n. 136 and 138, 303 n. 140–1
– Monsee Fragments 29 n. 125
– *Prophetenbibel* / *Wormser Bibel* / Zürich translation (1529) 5, 5 n. 20
– Roberger Bible (1483) 33
– *Septembertestament* (*see* Index of Scriptural, Ancient, and Medieval Sources: Luther, Martin)
– *Wormser Propheten* (*see* Index of Scriptural, Ancient, and Medieval Sources: Denck, Hans and Ludwig Hätzer)
– Zainer Bible (Augsburg, 1477) 23 n. 95, 29, 196 n. 111
– *Zürcher Bibel* (1531) 5 n. 20
German language
– cultural context and 63, 100, 115 n. 38, 219
– eras 29 n. 125–7, 115–6, 118–9, 119 n. 48, 182 n. 59, 198–9, 215, 238 n. 8, 240 n. 11, 242 n. 15, 247 n. 23, 249 n. 28, 259 n. 43, 266–7 n. 59, 276–7 n. 81, 283 n. 94, 286 n. 103, 287 n. 104, 299 n. 131, 302 n. 138
– figures of speech / idioms / proverbs (*see also* mysticism, medieval: silence and the "reduced to" idiom) 56–57, 57 n. 24, 65–66, 65–66 n. 48, 68, 68 n. 59, 70, 70 n. 60, 73–75, 73 n. 80, 79, 90–97, 115, 115 n. 40, 128, 162, 162 n. 87, 203, 203 n. 136, 208 n. 155, 217–8, 234–303
– influence of the Hebrew language and Luther's translation on (*see also* German Bibles: Buber-Rosenzweig Bible) 41–45, 90–97, 129–30, 130 n. 89, 138 n. 21, 164, 183–4, 213–5, 217–23
– regional linguistic variants 2, 130, 183–4
– "sacred style" / technical biblical language, and (*see* Hebrew language: "sacred style" / technical biblical language)
– semantic intensity (*see* Hebrew language: semantic intensity)

- technical linguistic considerations 102–3, 126 n. 79, 157 n. 73, 174 n. 34, 183–4, 183 n. 67, 221 n. 3, 342 n. 9, 343 n. 11
- vernacular / colloquial / "Germanizing" 34, 59, 59 n. 31, 64–65, 64 n. 44, 65 n. 45, 85 n. 115, 88, 90–97, 206–8, 218

Gerson, Jean 168–9, 169–70 n. 21, 185, 185 n. 75, 188, 188 n. 83, 195 n. 109, 213–4 n. 170

Gewissen (*see* Index of Hebrew, German, Latin, and Greek Terms)

Giustiniani, Agostino 28–29

Glossa Ordinaria (*see* Index of Scriptural, Ancient, and Medieval Sources: Various Authors and Contributors)

Greek Bibles (*see also* Polygot Bibles)
- general references and relevance for Luther's Hebrew 13, 13 n. 50, 19 n. 72, 29–30, 30 n. 130, 104 n. 16, 166, 173–5, 173–4 n. 33, 189 n. 88, 196–7
- Aldine (Venice, 1518) 30, 30 n. 131
- Erasmus's *Instrumentum* (Basel, 1516) (*see* Index of Scriptural, Ancient, and Medieval Sources: Erasmus)

Greek language, literature, and philosophy 3, 3 n. 7, 10, 10 n. 35, 14 n. 51, 16, 47, 92, 101 n. 9, 134, 166–7, 171, 190 n. 93, 217, 217 n. 1, 220–1

Gregory of Nyssa 167

Gregory Palamas 167

Hätzer, Ludwig 5, 23

Ḥayyim, Jacob b. 18 n. 69, 21, 21 n. 84

Hebrew Bibles (*see also* Polygot Bibles)
- Bomberg's Rabbinic Bible 21–22, 21 n. 82–83, 22 n. 86, 24–25, 24 n. 100, 31 n. 134, 168
- Brescia Bible (Brescia, 1494), Luther's copy (*see* Index of Scriptural, Ancient, and Medieval Sources: Luther, Martin)
- commentaries (*see also* Index of Scriptural, Ancient, and Medieval Sources) 10 n. 36, 14 n. 52, 21–25, 21 n. 83, 22 n. 86, 24–25 n. 98 and 100 and 102, 31 n. 134, 33, 35, 35 n. 154, 134, 149 n. 48, 163, 163 n. 91, 166–8, 204 n. 138
- dictionaries and grammar guides 12, 12 n. 42, 14 n. 52, 16, 23, 25–28, 31 n. 134, 163
- fourteenth century Ashkenazi Hebrew Bible codex that Luther and members of his team consulted 19 n. 74
- Masoretic Text and diachritics 21, 35–37, 37 n. 166, 47, 57, 57 n. 28, 88, 89 n. 138, 103, 103 n. 14–15, 121, 121 n. 58, 123 n. 65, 197–8 n. 120, 191, 191 n. 94–95, 209 n. 156, 219, 304–5 n. 2
- Münster's *Hebraica Biblia [Latina]* (1534–35; 1546) (*see* Index of Scriptural, Ancient, and Medieval Sources: Münster, Sebastian)
- Targums / Chaldaean Bible 13, 13 n. 50, 21, 21 n. 83, 25, 25 n. 103, 27, 33, 35, 163, 163 n. 91, 168, 204 n. 138

Hebrew language
- cultural context and (*see also* ancient Israelites: cultural and/or ethno-specific customs, practices, and rituals) 63, 100, 161, 161 n. 86, 219
- figures of speech / idioms / proverbs V, 8, 16 n. 57, 42, 47–75, 93, 95–97, 100, 109–10, 160–4, 177, 177 n. 45, 179, 181, 187, 192 n. 100, 203–4, 204 n. 138, 211, 217–8, 234–303
- *hapax legomena* 47, 94–95, 94 n. 168, 276–7 n. 81
- Hebrew repetition, trope of V, 8, 48, 63, 76–81, 88, 121–2, 146 n. 39, 217, 246 n. 20, 271 n. 70, 287 n. 106, 296 n. 125, 304–15
- Hebrew transliteration V, 13 n. 46, 47–48 n. 3, 48, 63, 67 n. 55, 81–90, 94 n. 168, 96–97, 123 n. 65, 179 n. 49, 217, 282 n. 93, 316–35
- "literal sense" / spiritual sense of 53 n. 16
- medieval and early modern scholarship (*see* Christian Hebraism, medieval and early modern)

Index of Subjects

- obscurity of / *Ebreische finsternis* V, 41–42, 47–97, 145, 145–6 n. 37, 217–8
- purity of 10, 10 n. 35
- "sacred style" / technical biblical language 74 n. 82, 82–83, 85, 85 n. 117, 100, 130 n. 89, 316–35
- semantic intensity V, 8, 42–43, 53–54, 54 n. 19, 76, 79–80, 99–130, 151–2, 193, 218–9, 221, 287 n. 105
- simplicity of 217
- technical linguistic considerations 57, 76, 76 n. 86, 79 n. 93, 102–3, 119–22, 156, 156 n. 70, 264–5 n. 53–54, 298 n. 130, 310–1 n. 9

Hilary of Poitier 196 n. 112
homut (*see* Index of Hebrew, German, Latin, and Greek Terms)
Humanism, medieval and early modern 10–31, 11–12 n. 39, 17 n. 62, 100–1, 101 n. 7, 165, 167–8
humilitas (*see* Index of Hebrew, German, Latin, and Greek Terms)
Hyrcanus [Johanan] 147 n. 43

Ibn Ezra, R. Abraham 21, 24–5, 33, 35
inner-biblical interpretation / inner-biblical exegesis (*see also* intertextuality) V, 23 n. 94, 42–43, 131–64, 219–21
"*intellectus* and *affectus*" (*see also* "distancing effect"; and "*Verfremdung* and *Entfremdung*") 101, 101 n. 10, 103, 129, 219
intertextuality 133–4, 133 n. 7, 134 n. 13
Ishmael, R. / Yishmael ben Elisha 146 n. 38, 162 n. 89

"Jacob" 18–19 n. 70
Jerome / Hieronymus 23–24, 24 n. 101, 25 n. 104, 30 n. 130, 33–34, 43, 52, 53 n. 14, 56–58, 57 n. 24, 58 n. 29, 83–84 n. 109, 84–85 n. 114, 86, 86 n. 123, 107, 107–8 n. 19, 123 n. 65, 128 n. 85, 145–6, 145–6 n. 37, 152–3 n. 60, 167, 173–5, 173–4 n. 33, 182 n. 61, 183 n. 64, 184, 184 n. 71, 190–1, 192 n. 101, 193–4, 196–7,

200, 200 n. 130, 203–4, 204 n. 138, 282 n. 93
Jewish-Christian intellectual exchange (*see also* Christian Hebraism, medieval and early modern)
- converts to Christianity 18, 18 n. 68–69, 18–19 n. 70, 167 n. 9, 168, 168 n. 14
- Hebrew Bibles and commentaries (*see* Hebrew Bibles)
- Luther's speculated personal interactions with 18, 18–19 n. 70
- mysticism 167–8, 167–8 n. 9–14
- teachers of Christians (*see* Christian Hebraism, medieval and early modern: Jewish teachers for Christians)

Jonas, Justus / Jodocus Koch 13–14, 14 n. 53, 19 n. 74, 223
Jonathan / R. Yonatan ben Uziel / Jonathan ben Uzziel 25, 25 n. 103, 27, 149 n. 48, 163 n. 91, 204 n. 138
Josephus, Flavius 147 n. 43

Kabbalah / Cabbala (*see* mysticism, medieval: concepts and terminology, Jewish)
Keller, John 10–11 n. 37
Kessler, Johannes (Swiss student in Kessler's *Sabbata*) 1–2, 1 n. 1–3, 222–3, 223 n. 5
Kimhi, R. David / RaDaK 21, 24–28, 24 n. 100, 25 n. 107, 27 n. 108, 31 n. 134, 33, 35, 163, 163 n. 91
Kimhi, R. Moses 25–27
Kolomotrie 101–3, 102 n. 13
Kristeva, Julia (*see* intertextuality)

Lang, Johannes 16
Lascaris, Constantine 11–12 n. 39
Latin Bibles (*see also* Polygot Bibles)
- commentaries 17 n. 60, 23–24, 23–24 n. 96–98 and 101, 134 (*see also* Index of Scriptural, Ancient, and Medieval Sources)
- Psalters based on the LXX in contrast to those based on Jerome's *iuxta Hebraicum* 196–7

408 Index of Subjects

- *Textus biblie* (Basel, 1506–08) (*see* Index of Scriptural, Ancient, and Medieval Sources: Various Authors and Contributors)
- *Vulgata-Revision 1529* (*see* Index of Scriptural, Ancient, and Medieval Sources: Luther, Martin)
- Vulgate (*see* Index of Scriptural, Ancient, and Medieval Sources: Jerome)
- Vulgate, Luther's personal copy (*see* Index of Scriptural, Ancient, and Medieval Sources: Luther, Martin)

Latin language 10, 10 n. 35, 91, 91 n. 149, 162, 162 n. 87

"*lectio, oratio,* and *contemplatio*" / "*oratio, meditatio,* and *tentatio*" 165

Lefèvre d'Étaples, Jacques / Jacobus Faber Stapulensis 23–24, 23 n. 92, 24 n. 98, 49–50 n. 8, 53 n. 16, 84–85 n. 114, 152–3 n. 60, 168, 168 n. 12, 188, 188 n. 82, 196–7, 197 n. 117–8, 197–8 n. 120

Leitworte 101–3, 102 n. 13

Leo X, Pope 19 n. 72

Leonard [David] 18 n. 68

Leucorea (*see* Wittenberg University, and other medieval European)

Levita, Elijah / Elijah b. Asher ha-Levi 17–18, 18 n. 67, 28

Linck, Wenzeslaus 15–16, 16 n. 57, 23 n. 95, 97, 97 n. 175

liturgy, and Hebrew Bible 103

Loans, Jacob b. Yehiel 17–18

Lombard, Peter 12–13, 13 n. 46, 173–5, 184 n. 70

Luther, Martin
- arguments that the prophets themselves erred in their use of Hebrew 318 n. 2
- biographical info 1–4, 10, 15, 44–45, 217, 222–3
- citations of different Hebrew terminology than the source text which he was translating 147–9, 164, 220
- citations of non-Hebrew terms to interpret Hebrew terms 149 (*see also* the New Testament references in the Index of Scriptural, Ancient, and Medieval Sources)
- *Deutsche Bibel*: history of translation, compilation, and editions; and text citations and references (*see* Index of Scriptural, Ancient, and Medieval Sources: Luther, Martin)
- "insertion" of terms not present in the Hebrew Bible 122–6, 188–94, 189 n. 88, 219
- lectures and commentaries: history, compilation, and editions; and text citations and references (*see* Index of Scriptural, Ancient, and Medieval Sources: Luther, Martin)
- literal translation compared to interpretative (dynamic / functional equivalence) 234–303
- mixed / hybrid translation method 65–66, 71–72, 81–83, 88–89, 234–303
- multilayered / interwoven translations 131–64, 220
- "removal" of terms that appear in the Hebrew Bible 60–62
- revision commissions and records: background; and text citations and references (*see* Index of Scriptural, Ancient, and Medieval Sources: Luther, Martin)
- "rules" of translation 42, 55, 55 n. 23, 63, 81–87 n. 126, 90–97, 123 n. 65, 217–8
- significance of translation for German Catholics, Lutherans, and Jews 129–30, 130 n. 89
- significance of translation for German national identity 129–30, 130 n. 89
- spiritual assault (*see Anfechtung*)
- state of scholarship on Luther's Hebrew 3, 31–39, 90–97, 217
- statistical data about Luther's Minor Prophets translation 65–66, 77–78, 81–83
- translation team / Sanhedrin 13–16
- variableness / inconsistency of his Hebrew translation V, 41–42, 47–97, 123 n. 65, 139 n. 24, 140 n. 26, 158 n. 78, 217–8, 226–335

Lyra, Nicholas von 23–25, 23–24 n. 96–98, 24–25 n. 102 and 104, 30 n. 129,

33, 84–85 n. 114, 167–8, 167–8 n. 10, 203–4, 204 n. 138

Macarius 167
Malichus 147 n. 43
Mantuanus, Baptisma 16–17
Manutius, Aldus 25 n. 106
Margaritha, Antonius / Antony Margaritha / Anton Margaritha 17–18, 18 n. 68, 167 n. 9
Marschalk, Nikolaus 10–12, 11–12 n. 39
Masoretic Text (*see* Hebrew Bibles)
Mathesius, Johannes 13–15, 13–14 n. 50, 15 n. 55, 31
Maximilian I 10
Melanchthon, Philip 3 n. 7, 10–14, 10–11 n. 37, 14 n. 51 and 53–54, 19 n. 74, 21–22, 22 n. 86 and 88, 35 n. 154, 65 n. 46, 178 n. 47, 223, 225
Merkabah tradition (*see* mysticism, medieval: concepts and terminology, Jewish)
Mithridates, Flavius 17–18
Moellin, R. Moshe, of Weissenburg 17–18
monasticism (*see* mysticism, medieval: monasticism / monastic mysticism)
Moses (Bible) 64, 64 n. 44, 68, 68 n. 58, 93, 156, 156 n. 72, 177–8 n. 46, 286–7
Münster, Sebastian 15–16, 21–22, 22 n. 88 and 90, 28, 31 n. 134, 191 n. 195, 194, 194 n. 104
Müntzer, Thomas 167–8
mysticism, medieval
– *Anfechtung*, and 43, 120, 125, 125 n. 72, 165–215, 220–1
– concepts and terminology, Christian (*see also* in Index of Hebrew, German, Latin, and Greek Terms: *affectus*; *conscientia*; *excessu[s] mentis*; *gemitus*; *Gewissen*; *humilitas*; *nichts / Nichtigkeit*; *raptus*; and *synteresis / synderesis*) 43, 125 n. 72, 171–215, 220–1
– concepts and terminology, Jewish (*see also* in Index of Hebrew, German, Latin, and Greek Terms: אין) 43, 125 n. 72, 166–8, 167–8 n. 9–10, 168 n. 12, 175–7, 176 n. 37, 177 n. 43,

185, 188, 188 n. 81, 195–6 n. 110, 200–1, 204–5 n. 141
– definitions 170–3
– German mysticism / "upper-Rhenish circle" (*see also* Tauler, Johannes; Eckhart, Meister; Seuse, Heinrich; and *Theologia Deutsch*) 169–70, 169 n. 20, 173–5, 184, 206–7
– Greek roots 166–7, 173
– Luther's Hebrew translation and interpretation, and V, 43, 112 n. 34, 120, 165–215, 220–2, 336–43
– monasticism / monastic mysticism 10 n. 36, 165, 168–9, 185, 185 n. 75, 188–9, 188 n. 82, 195 n. 109, 199, 208, 208 n. 154
– scholarly arguments concerning Luther, and 165–6, 166 n. 3, 169–70, 169 n. 20, 170 n. 24, 171–3 n. 30, 176, 176–7 n. 42, 178 n. 47, 183 n. 64, 184, 188–9, 188 n. 83, 189 n. 85, 193, 193 n. 103, 198–200, 200 n. 128–9 and 131, 210, 213–5, 220–1
– silence and the "reduced to" idiom 43, 51–52, 52 n. 11–12, 75, 199–215, 226–7, 240–1, 282–3, 336–43
– spiritual contemplation 165, 177, 181, 183, 185, 185 n. 75, 199, 204

Naḥmanides / R. Moses b. Naḥman / RaMBaN 22, 167–8
negative theology (*see* mysticism, medieval: concepts and terminology, Christian)
nichts / Nichtigkeit (*see* Index of Hebrew, German, Latin, and Greek Terms)

Oecolampadius, Johannes 16–17, 17 n. 60
offerings, ritual (*see* ancient Israelites)
Onkelos 21, 21 n. 83, 25
Origen 133–4, 164, 167–70, 220
Osiander, Andreas 15–16, 16 n. 57

"P" source / Priestly Source / Priestly Code 131–2, 131 n. 3, 132 n. 4, 141–2 n. 33
Pagninus, Santes 25 n. 107, 28, 31 n. 134, 33

Passover 145–7, 146 n. 41, 147 n. 43, 154
Peasants Revolt (1524–25) 4
Pellikan, Konrad 15–18, 19–20 n. 75, 21–23, 25 n. 106, 28, 28 n. 117, 36, 36 n. 162
Philo 166–7
Pico della Mirandola, Giovanni 16–18, 167–8
Plato 166–7, 173
Plotinus 166–7
Polygot Bibles
– general references and relevance for Luther's Hebrew 28–30, 28 n. 121
– Complutensian (Alcalá de Henares, 1514–17) 28–30, 28 n. 122, 29 n. 123
– Giustiniani's Psalter (*see* Index of Scriptural, Ancient, and Medieval Sources: Giustiniani, Agostino)
Porchetus / Porchetus Salvaticus 167 n. 9
Praetensis, Felix 18 n. 69, 19 n. 72, 21
printing, medieval and early modern 5, 5 n. 20, 12 n. 40, 17 n. 60, 18 n. 69, 19–31, 19 n. 72, 25 n. 106–7, 28 n. 121, 29 n. 126–7, 31 n. 134, 39 n. 175, 40 n. 176, 48–49, 130, 169–70 n. 21, 178 n. 47, 183–4
Proclus 166–7
protocols, of Georg Rörer / *Revisionsprotokolle* (*see* Index of Scriptural, Ancient, and Medieval Sources: Luther, Martin)
purification, ritual (*see* ancient Israelites: ritual language of cultic purification)

raptus (*see* Index of Hebrew, German, Latin, and Greek Terms)
Rashi / R. Solomon b. Isaac / Shlomo Yitzhaki 21, 23–25, 24 n. 98, 25 n. 104, 33, 35, 149 n. 48, 154 n. 65, 163, 163 n. 91, 167–8, 167–8 n. 10, 191 n. 95, 204 n. 138
Ratzinger, Cardinal Joseph 176 n. 38
redigatur ad nihilum 43, 200, 200 n. 130
resignatio ad infernum 200, 200 n. 129–30
Reuchlin, Johannes 12–18, 12 n. 42, 13 n. 46, 17 n. 60, 21–29, 24–25 n. 102–3 and 106, 27 n. 112,
28 n. 117, 31 n. 134, 33, 36, 36 n. 162, 84–85 n. 114, 111 n. 31, 123 n. 63, 154 n. 65, 156 n. 70, 166 n. 3, 167–8, 168 n. 12, 188, 188 n. 82, 196, 276–7 n. 81
Rörer, Georg (*see also* Luther, Martin: revision commissions and records) 7, 7 n. 26, 13–14, 14 n. 53–54, 31, 40
Rosenzweig, Franz (*see* German Bibles: Buber-Rosenzweig Bible)
rustling leaf, Lev. 26:36 and Job 13:25 (*see also Anfechtung*) 117–9, 118 n. 45, 119 n. 51, 183, 183 n. 64, 187 n. 80
Ruysbroeck, Johannes / Jan van Ruysbroeck 178 n. 47

Saba, R. Abraham 22
Sacrament of the Altar controversy 4
sacrifices, ritual (*see* ancient Israelites)
"Sanhedrin," Luther's (*see* Luther, Martin: translation team / Sanhedrin)
Schleiermacher, Friedrich (*see also* "*Verfremdung* and *Entfremdung*") 42, 99–101, 100 n. 5, 129, 219
scholasticism, medieval (*see also* Wittenberg University, and other medieval European) 166–7, 184, 213–4, 213–4 n. 170 and 172, 217
Scholem, Gershom 101–3, 103 n. 14
Schürpf, Augustine 222–3
Schürpf, Jerome 222–3
Schwarzer Bär Inn (Jena, Germany) 1–2, 222–3
scriptura sui ipsius interpres (*see also* Origen) 134, 164, 220
Septuagint / LXX (*see* Greek Bibles)
Sforno, Obadiah 17–18
Spalatin, Georg 2 n. 5, 4–5, 10–11 n. 37, 15–16, 16 n. 57, 22 n. 86, 23 n. 95, 168 n. 12, 178 n. 47
Spengler, Lazarus 22 n. 86
Spengler, Wolfgang (Swiss student in Kessler's *Sabbata*) 1–2, 222–3
Staupitz, Johann von 168–9, 200 n. 130
Seuse (Suso), Heinrich 168–9, 173–5, 178 n. 47

synteresis / synderesis (*see* Index of Hebrew, German, Latin, and Greek Terms)
Syriac Bible 121 n. 57

Tanḥum b. Joseph Ha-Yerushalmi 195–6 n. 110
Tauler, Johannes 43, 168–9, 169–70 n. 21, 173–9, 178 n. 47, 179 n. 48, 181 n. 57, 188, 195 n. 109, 200, 200 n. 131, 204, 206–7, 213–4 n. 170, 214–5
tentatio (*see* Index of Hebrew, German, Latin, and Greek Terms; and *Anfechtung* in this Index)
Tetragrammaton 89 n. 138, 166, 166 n. 3, 220
theodicy (*see Anfechtung*)
Theodotion 191 n. 95
theologia crucis / Theology of the Cross 199–200, 200 n. 128 and 131
Theologia Deutsch (*see* Index of Scriptural, Ancient, and Medieval Sources: Author Unknown [with introduction by Luther])

Valla, Lorenzo 16–17
"*Verfremdung* and *Entfremdung*" (*see also* "distancing effect"; and "*intellectus* and *affectus*") 42, 100–1, 129, 219
Visitations, Church 4
Viterbo, Cardinal Egidio da / Giles of Viterbo / Giles Antonini 17–18
Vulgate (*see* Latin Bibles)

Wakefield, Robert 16–17, 17 n. 61–62
Wartburg Castle / Tower 1–2, 14 n. 54, 178 n. 47
wine, German 74, 74 n. 83
Wittenberg University, and other medieval European 1–2, 4–5, 10–31, 217, 222–3
Wittenberg University Library 30–31, 31 n. 133–4

Zamora, Alphonso of 28–29, 29 n. 123
Ziegler, Bernhard 13–15, 15 n. 55, 17–18, 19 n. 74
Zoharic tradition (*see* mysticism, medieval: concepts and terminology, Jewish)

Spätmittelalter, Humanismus, Reformation

Studies in the Late Middle Ages, Humanism and the Reformation

edited by Volker Leppin (Tübingen)

in association with

Amy Nelson Burnett (Lincoln, NE), Johannes Helmrath (Berlin)
Matthias Pohlig (Berlin), Eva Schlotheuber (Düsseldorf)

The series *Studies in the Late Middle Ages, Humanism and the Reformation* (SMHR) focuses on the period between the late 13th century and the 17th century, including both epochs of the late Middle Ages and the early modern age. Particular attention is paid to the religious incentives which emerged in the church reform movements and the Reformation. In addition, it will deal with the entire range of cultural forces as represented by Renaissance humanism, which covers several epochs. The editor-in-chief of the series is Volker Leppin (Professor for Church History at the Eberhard Karls Universität Tübingen), he is supported by Amy Nelson Burnett (Professor for Renaissance, Reformation and Early Modern History at the University of Nebraska-Lincoln, USA), Johannes Helmrath (Professor for Medieval History II at the Humboldt-Universität zu Berlin), Matthias Pohlig (Juniorprofessor for Early Modern History at the Westfälischen Wilhelms-Universität Münster) and Eva Schlotheuber (Professor for Medieval History II at the Heinrich-Heine-Universität Düsseldorf).

ISSN: 1865-2840
Suggested citation: SMHR

All available volumes can be found at *www.mohrsiebeck.com/smhr*

Mohr Siebeck
www.mohrsiebeck.com